The Handbook of
SOCIAL POLICY

The Handbook of
SOCIAL POLICY

Edited by

James Midgley
Martin B. Tracy
Michelle Livermore

Sage Publications, Inc.
International Educational and Professional Publisher
Thousand Oaks ▪ London ▪ New Delhi

For information:

Sage Publications, Inc.
2455 Teller Road
Thousand Oaks, California 91320
E-mail: order@sagepub.com

Sage Publications Ltd.
6 Bonhill Street
London EC2A 4PU
United Kingdom

Sage Publications India Pvt. Ltd.
M-32 Market
Greater Kailash I
New Delhi 110 048 India

Printed in the United States of America

Library of Congress Cataloging-in-Publication Data

Main entry under title:
The handbook of social policy / edited by James Midgley,
    Martin B. Tracy and Michelle Livermore.
        p. cm.
    Includes bibliographical references and index.
    ISBN 0-7619-1561-3 (cloth: alk. paper)
    1. United States—Social policy. 2. Social service—United States.
    3. Public welfare—United States. I. Midgley, James.
    II. Tracy, Martin. III. Livermore, Michelle.
    HN65 .H345 1999
    361.6'1'0973—dc21   99-6716

00   01   02   03   10   9   8   7   6   5   4   3   2

Acquiring Editor:	Jim Nageotte
Editorial Assistant:	Heidi Van Middlesworth
Production Editor:	Diana E. Axelsen
Editorial Assistant:	Cindy Bear
Typesetter/Designer:	Marion Warren
Indexer:	Mary Mortensen
Cover Designer:	Candice Harman

Contents

Preface

The idea for this book came from Jim Nageotte of Sage Publications, who believed that the format of Sage's successful series of handbooks would be well-suited to social policy and social work. Although Sage has published a number of handbooks covering a wide range of topics, none has previously dealt with the issues facing social workers and social administrators. It was at the 1997 Annual Program Meeting of the Council on Social Work Education in Chicago that Jim first raised the prospect of launching a series of handbooks in social policy and social work. Various potential editors and authors were consulted, and within the year, the *Handbook of Social Policy* had been commissioned.

It has been an exciting although daunting venture. To commission, collect, and edit no less than 33 separate chapters covering such a wide range of subject matter by a variety of authors is a formidable task. That it has been accomplished in a timely way and without much difficulty owes a great deal to the cooperation and enthusiasm of the chapter authors, whose understanding and helpfulness made the task possible. We are in their debt for their willingness to participate. Special thanks for Jim Nageotte and his staff at Sage, who were consistently helpful and understanding. Jacqueline Tasch coped extremely well with the heavy demands of the copyediting, and we are grateful to her for her commitment to the project. Many thanks also to Diana Axelsen, who saw the book through production. Thanks to Michèle Lingre for her efforts to ensure that the book has been properly marketed.

We have enjoyed working on this project. As was noted earlier, the task of putting together a comprehensive volume dealing with many diverse aspects of social policy has been exciting. We hope the book will be a helpful resource to those who wish to have a broad overview of the subject. We also hope that it will stimulate and foster further, more detailed reading of this important field.

JAMES MIDGLEY
University of California at Berkeley

MARTIN B. TRACY
Southern Illinois University at Carbondale

MICHELLE LIVERMORE
Louisiana State University

Introduction

Social Policy and Social Welfare

JAMES MIDGLEY

MARTIN B. TRACY

MICHELLE LIVERMORE

Social welfare may be defined as a condition or state of human well-being. This condition occurs when human beings are secure and contented, knowing that their basic needs for nutrition, health, shelter, and income have been met and that they are reasonably protected against major life risks. A condition of social well-being is also characterized by a sense that problems are being managed and that goals are being accomplished.

This definition transcends the conventional view of social welfare as a range of services provided by charities and social services agencies to the poor, needy, and vulnerable. Although the term is most frequently associated with charitable organizations and public welfare departments, this was not its original meaning. Indeed, the term *social welfare* is derived from the greeting *farewell,* which means to travel, to go and be well. It is a pity that the term *social welfare* is now so narrowly defined and that it has even acquired a pejorative connotation. In an attempt to revitalize its original meaning, this book will use the broader, more inclusive meaning of the term. It is the more encompassing notion of social welfare as human well-being that is the primary concern of this book.

A condition of social well-being is usually associated with individuals, but it also pertains to families, groups, organizations, neighborhoods, communities, and even whole societies. The ability to meet needs, manage problems, and achieve goals is as much a feature of organizations, communities, and societies as it is of individuals.

It is difficult to measure the extent to which people, organizations, and communities have attained a condition of social well-being. Nevertheless, research in the field has become increasingly sophisticated, and social scientists now use a variety of statistical techniques to operationalize the concept. Among the most useful of these techniques are social indicators, which measure social welfare at both the national and international level. These indicators show that some countries have far higher levels of welfare than others. Although some countries have high incomes, good standards of health, education, and housing, and low rates of crime and other social problems, many others are characterized by poverty, low standards of living, and high rates of violence. As this research reveals, the notion of social welfare is not some abstract or academic idea but a fundamental, tangible characteristic of the human condition.

The promotion and maintenance of social well-being has historically been regarded as a private matter. It has long been accepted that the enjoyment of social well-being is a function of individual effort and the supports provided by families. In the United States, the involvement of external agents such as neighbors, churches, philanthropic agencies, and government social service departments has traditionally been viewed as a "safety net" function that comes into operation when individuals and their families are unable to cope with the challenges they face.

However, it has been recognized that people's welfare is affected by many complex events that are beyond individual control. For example, economic growth, which depends on business enterprise, has a direct bearing on employment opportunities and incomes and thus on the welfare of individuals and families. When the economy expands, employment opportunities increase, with positive implications for income and social well-being. On the other hand, when the economy experiences a recession, employment opportunities decline, with the result that many people lose their jobs and experience a decline in income. These developments have grave consequences for social welfare. Similarly, conflict between cultural groups can have a devastating effect on social welfare, not only through the direct experience of violence but also as a result of economic disruption. As recent events in Africa reveal, falling agricultural production caused by civil wars and tribal violence has resulted in serious food shortages and contributed to the deaths of millions of innocent people.

The recognition that human well-being is the result not only of individual effort but of wider economic, social, and other forces has fostered the belief that governments should seek to address those forces that create conditions of "illfare." It also legitimates the claim that governments can intervene positively to promote the welfare of their citizens. Although this is not a new idea, it is only during this century that it has gained widespread acceptance. Attempts by governments to promote economic growth, to provide education to all citizens, and to regulate commercial activities are all concerned with improving people's welfare. In addition, the provision of a wide range of social services that transcend the traditional safety-net approach, as well as the use of legal regulation, the tax system, and the judicial process to promote human well-being, has a tangible impact on social welfare.

Governments seek to enhance the welfare of their citizens through social policies. As is shown in Chapter 1 of this book, policies are statements that prescribe and routinize the courses of action of organizations. Governments make extensive use of policies to carry out their many complex functions. Throughout the world, governments have formulated and implemented policies to maintain law and order, ensure national defense, promote economic development, and discharge their many other obligations.

Although governments may formulate social policies to enhance the welfare of their citizens, it should be recognized that they can also formulate and implement social policies that are designed to cause harm or that unintentionally cause harm. There are many examples of how governments have made decisions that have a negative affect on people's welfare. However, the study of social policy has focused primarily on those actions of governments that are intended to promote or maintain people's welfare. As is shown in later chapters of this book, the claim that government intervention enhances human well-being remains controversial.

Social scientists have been studying the social policies of government systematically only for the last 50 years or so, but a good deal of information is now available about the way social policies are formulated and how these policies are implemented through the social services, legal regulations, the tax system, and the courts. Social scientists have also traced the history of social policy, studied the ideologies that influence social policy making, and assessed the impact of social policy. The result is an evolving body of knowledge that will continue to illuminate the many complex ways the state can promote and maintain the well-being of citizens.

THE SCOPE OF THIS BOOK

The Handbook of Social Policy is an attempt to document the now substantial body of knowledge about government social policies that has been accumulated since the 1950s, when the study of social policy first emerged as an organized field of academic endeavor. The *Handbook* has been compiled specifically for American readers, and it is, therefore, exclusively concerned with social policy in the United States. However, many of its authors make references to other countries, and in the final section, a chapter by two distinguished scholars seeks to examine American social policy in an international context. This chapter seeks to link social policy in the United States to events in other nations.

The *Handbook* hopes to provide a "state-of-the-art" account of American social policy at the end of the 20th century. It is divided into five parts. Part I, which is introductory in nature, seeks to define social policy and to examine the wider social, economic, political, and cultural context in which social policies are formulated. It is also concerned with two technical aspects of social policy, namely, policy analysis and policy practice. Finally, attention is given to the impact of social policy.

Part II examines the history of social policy in the United States from colonial times to the present. This part covers more than 300 years of social policy development and shows how changing social, political, and economic realities have contributed to a continuously evolving system of government social welfare, which at some times has sought to expand the role of the state in social welfare and at others to retrench it. This part of the book seeks to offer an introductory historical overview that will acquaint readers with the most critical events in the history of American social policy development and show how its evolution has been affected by wider social, economic, political, and cultural forces.

Part III of the book covers the social services. Research into the social services is the best developed part of the field of social policy, and, today, many different aspects of social service provision in the United States have been documented. Scholars have gathered a great deal of information about the legislative basis for social service provision, the administrative aspects of social service delivery, the costs of the social services, and their impact on different client groups and the population at large. The 12 chapters in this part of the book seek to document these different aspects and also to highlight issues arising out of the study of different social service provisions. The section covers the most familiar social services, such as child welfare, social security, and mental health, but it also includes chapters on urban development and employment services.

Part IV is concerned with the political economy of social policy. Although the process of social policy making is a technical activity, in which research, policy analysis, and other objective factors play an important role, it is also influenced by ideological beliefs. Indeed, many social policy writers claim that these beliefs play a critically important role in social policy. They contend that most social policy decisions are shaped by values and beliefs. Because of its importance, a variety of competing political economies of social policy are discussed. After describing the institutional approach, which has long dominated social policy thinking, attention is given to the conservative approach, critical social policy, welfare pluralism, feminist and multicul-tural approaches, the developmental perspective, and finally the ecological approach.

The final part of the book contains two chapters. As mentioned earlier, one of these seeks to examine American social policy in an international context. The last chapter, which is written jointly by the editors, speculates on the future of social policy. Al-though it is extremely difficult to predict the future, the authors seek to identify those factors that will shape social policy and to discern the way social policy may evolve.

As noted previously, *The Handbook of Social Policy* is an attempt to provide a state-of-the-art overview of the field at the end of the 20th century. Given the com-plexity of the subject and the now substantial body of knowledge that has been accu-mulated, this is a formidable task, which has not been facilitated by length constraints. The editors are painfully aware that many of the chapters are able to provide only an overview of very complex issues and that some topics may not have received the in-depth analysis they deserve. It is also the case that some topics, which are only referred to in chapters, would have benefitted from separate, more detailed treatment. For ex-ample, the impact of the tax system on social welfare has been mentioned in several chapters, but it could, conceivably, have merited a chapter of its own. This is also true of the way social policy interacts with the nonprofit sector and the wider civil society. Nevertheless, the book's wide coverage should meet the needs of readers who wish to familiarize themselves with the field. It should also serve as a pointer for further read-ing. The authors of the individual chapters have sought not only to provide helpful summaries of their topics but to provide bibliographies that will satiate even the most voracious readers. We hope that the *Handbook* will satisfy the need for a comprehen-sive yet accessible introduction to a vast field of human endeavor, which has, over the years, made a difference to the lives and well-being of millions of people.

PART ONE

The Nature of Social Policy

Part I provides a framework for the rest of the book. The first chapter offers a definition of social policy. It shows that the term *social policy* is a complex one that has been defined differently by different scholars. It offers a broad interpretation of the field that will accommodate diverse perspectives and interpretations.

In Chapter 2, the abstract, definitional issues in the first chapter are applied to a more practical discussion of how social policy is formulated and implemented in the United States. Chapter 2 also considers the many different forces that impinge on social policy makers and influence the way social policies evolve. Finally, it provides an important overview of the many complex factors that impinge on social policy.

Chapter 3 examines the economic context in which social policy functions. It shows that social policies are formulated and implemented not only within a fiscal framework but also within a wider economic environment in which growth, employment, and other economic realities are vital determinants of social welfare.

The next two chapters are concerned with issues of policy analysis and policy practice. As will be seen, these fields are closely related. Chapter 4 focuses on the steps that characterize the policy-making process and foster decision making. Chapter 5 deals with the implementation of social policy and with the role of the professional policy practitioner in ensuring the effective implementation of policy decisions.

The last chapter in Part I discusses the impact of social policy. Although it is often assumed that social policies and programs are carefully evaluated to ensure that they meet their goals, this is not always the case. Chapter 6 shows how the impact of social policies can be assessed and how their wider effects can be measured.

CHAPTER ONE

The Definition of Social Policy

JAMES MIDGLEY

The increasing complexity of social life has necessitated the more frequent routinization of human activities. Today, most people find that their lives are increasingly subjected to routines. Routinization is particularly noticeable in formal organizations, and it is essential to their functioning. Commercial firms, government agencies, hospitals, universities, and many other organizations can operate effectively only if most of their activities are routinized.

Routinization is achieved through the formulation and implementation of policies. Policies are statements that prescribe courses of action in organizations. They govern the internal functioning of organizations, their external relations, and the way they attain their goals. They are codified in documentary form and facilitate standardized decision making. The implementation of policies is known as administration. Management is the direction of policy implementation.

The effective implementation of the activities of governments requires the formulation of a myriad of policies that deal with all aspects of the way the state operates. Perhaps of greatest interest are policies that shape the way it seeks to discharge its obligations to maintain law and order, ensure national defense, engage in international relations, promote economic development, and ensure the well-being of the population. The documentation, analysis, and interpretation of these policies has become a major preoccupation of legal scholars, organizational experts, and social scientists. They have acquired extensive knowledge of the policies governing international relations, national security, economic development, and other fields. The academic study of these policies is now well established at universities, specialized research institutes or think tanks, and government agencies concerned with policy analysis. The study of public policy is well developed, and most research universities now have academic departments or schools devoted to this task.

Public policies that affect the welfare of citizens are known as social policies. Although governments have formulated social policies for many centuries, it is only since World War II that these policies have been subjected to systematic academic inquiry. This inquiry takes place within schools of public policy, academic departments of economics, political science, and sociology, and also at schools of social work. Although social policy is a relatively new field of academic inquiry, it has grown rapidly in recent years.

The term *social policy* involves two aspects: First, it refers to the actual policies and programs of governments that affect people's welfare. Second, it connotes an academic field of inquiry concerned with the description, explanation, and evaluation of these policies. In seeking to define social policy, this chapter deals with these two aspects separately.

SOCIAL POLICY AS AN ACTIVITY OF GOVERNMENT

Governments affect the welfare of people through social policies in many different ways. First, they formulate policies that are specifically intended to enhance people's welfare. For example, governments may seek to improve social conditions by introducing new social service programs. Second, governments may affect social welfare indirectly through economic, environmental, or other policies that, nevertheless, have an impact on social conditions. For example, an economic policy that enhances trade with another country may create new employment opportunities and thus raise the incomes and welfare of those who are involved in increased commerce. Third, government social policies may affect people's welfare in unforeseen and unintended ways. A policy focused on one group may in fact bring unintended benefits to another group.

Unfortunately, social policies introduced with the best intentions may have the opposite effect. Richard Titmuss (1974) pointed out that social policy does not always enhance welfare but may in fact cause *illfare*. For example, social policy writers of quite different ideological persuasions have argued that public assistance or "welfare" does not in fact have a benevolent impact on the standards of living of poor families but rather it stigmatizes them, controls them, or traps them in a cycle of dependency (Abramovitz, 1988; Murray 1984). Although harm is usually unintended, social policies may be introduced with the deliberate intention of causing harm to some groups of people. An example is the adoption of racist or discriminatory policies. The exclusion of immigrants from receiving social welfare benefits is another example of the use of social policy to diminish the welfare of a particular group of people.

Of the different ways of influencing human welfare through social policy, the direct method is the most common. Social policy scholars have identified three direct mechanisms by which governments seek to promote social welfare. The first of these are policies that result in the creation of *social service programs.* Most governments have adopted policies that introduce social services, govern the way they operate, and define their goals. Conventionally, these services operate in the fields of health, education, housing, income security, and family and community welfare. The last two fields are often classified under the heading of "social welfare policy." Some social policy writers contend that the study of social policy should not be limited to these social services, but that government transportation policies, cultural and recreational policies, urban planning policies, and immigration policies should also be included. On the other hand, as the study of social policy has become more specialized, there has been a tendency to separate health, education, and housing from the mainstream of social policy research. Nevertheless, as is shown in Part III of this book, the definition of social policy used here is fairly broadly based.

A second way of affecting social well-being through social policy is the use of *statutory regulation.* Governments regularly enact legislation that mandates employers, homeowners, educational institutions, commercial firms, and many others to adopt measures that have a direct impact on social welfare. Although the use of legal regulations has not been adequately researched by social policy scholars, it is clear that activities in many areas of welfare, such as housing, health, incomes, employment, and education, are shaped by government regulation. The minimum wage, rent control, affirmative action, and a host of other statutory prescriptions and proscriptions all affect peoples' welfare.

A third way in which governments influence welfare is through the *tax system.* The use of the tax system in this way is known as fiscal welfare. As Christopher Howard (1997) has shown, governments can have a direct impact on social welfare by using the tax code to create incentives or disincentives. For example, tax incentives to save for retirement, to create educational accounts for children, or to obtain a mortgage to finance the purchase of a home are widely used by ordinary citizens and clearly affect their welfare. Of particular interest to social policy scholars is the way the fiscal system encourages employers to provide occupational benefits for their workers. The commercial tax code contains numerous incentives of this kind. Titmuss (1958) described these provisions as occupational welfare, which, together with fiscal welfare, plays a major role in improving the well-being of many middle-class people—but not the poor—because they are in regular employment or participating fully in the tax system.

In addition to the direct actions of governments, the courts play a major role in social policy. The courts have not only interpreted government legislation but taken constitutional issues into account when deciding cases that affect the welfare of individuals or groups of people. These decisions influence many aspects of social welfare, ranging from access to the social services to wider social issues such as civil rights, immigration, and abortion.

As may be seen from this discussion, government social policies operate in intricate ways to affect social welfare. Because of the complexity of social policy, it is perhaps not surprising that academic study in the field is still relatively underdeveloped. Social policy's subject matter is so complex that it defies simple interpretation. Nevertheless, significant progress has been made in understanding the way social policies contribute to people's well-being.

SOCIAL POLICY AS AN ACADEMIC FIELD

Although the academic study of social policy has only been formalized in recent times, scholars have historically taken an interest in the subject. Many commentaries on the way the actions of the state affect the welfare of human beings have been produced over the centuries. These commentaries have often been prescriptive, making recommendations for improving social conditions, and often, they were formulated as blueprints setting out a vision for an ideal society. Although utopian writings of this kind are frequently dismissed as the ramblings of idealistic dreamers, they inspired social reformers to campaign for progressive social change and influenced the emergence of social policy.

Utopianism continues to exert a powerful influence on social policy thinking today. Indeed, because of the subject's normative commitments, this is not surprising. Even detached writings that purport to provide a factual account of government policies are often infused with normative preferences. It is for this reason that most social policy scholars recognize the critical role of values and ideologies in the field and stress the need to explicate them. Although the role of ideology was not given much attention in social policy research until British scholars such as Titmuss (1971, 1974) and Vic George and Paul Wilding (1976) stressed their importance during the 1970s, ideological preferences have long shaped the way social policy writers interpret government welfare activities. The importance of ideology is revealed in the different ways social policy writers use statistical evidence to support their views.

Although social policy is permeated by values, there has been a tendency to avoid ideology and stress the scientific nature of the enterprise. Early pioneers of the study of social policy believed that scientific methods could be applied, not only to explain natural phenomena but to understand and improve social conditions. The 19th-century French mathematician, Auguste Comte, was an enthusiastic advocate of scientific social planning. Although Comte is widely regarded as one of the founders of sociology, his ideas had direct relevance for the emergence of social policy as an applied field.

The use of scientific methods in social welfare was fostered by the introduction of the census in the early 19th century. The census permitted the collection of a large amount of statistical data on social conditions and provided information on which proposals for social reform could be based. The availability of census data was complemented by the findings of early ethnographic studies of workers and poor people. This research fostered the emergence of the social survey at the end of the 19th century. The survey was a powerful tool that activists used to expose social injustice and campaign for social reform.

The surveys of poverty and its associated social ills by Charles Booth, Paul Kellogg, and Seebohm Rowntree exposed many middle-class citizens to the harsh conditions under which poor people lived, engendering a degree of sympathy for their plight. The findings of these surveys were also used by trade union leaders, middle-class reformers, progressive politicians, and intellectuals to pressure governments to take ameliorative action. Leading reformers, such as Beatrice and Sidney Webb in England and Jane Addams and her followers in the United States, made extensive and effective use of these data to campaign for progressive social change.

By the 1930s, social science information was frequently used in social policy making. Statistical data about the extent of unemployment and poverty in the Great Depression played a significant role in the development of New Deal social policies. Also relevant were the results of earlier social experiments that sought to address these problems. Campaigns for the introduction of social insurance resulted in the enactment of the nation's first unemployment insurance statute in Wisconsin in 1932 and helped persuade the Roosevelt Administration that social security could significantly reduce the incidence of poverty among the unemployed, elderly, and other needy groups (Leuchtenburgh, 1963; Skocpol & Ikenbery, 1995).

The rapid expansion of government involvement in social welfare, which followed the New Deal in the United States and the publication of the Beveridge Report in Britain, played a major role in the creation of social policy as an academic subject. Although social welfare had previously been studied at universities, often at schools of social work, the emergence of the welfare state facilitated a much more systematic examination of the social policies of governments and their effects on people's well-being.

The appointment of Richard Titmuss to the first professorial position in social policy at the London School of Economics in 1950 gave added impetus to the development of social policy as an academic subject. Although Titmuss was not a university graduate, he had written several books on social issues and was appointed on the recommendation of T. H. Marshall, the head of the London School of Economics's sociology department. Titmuss was appointed head of the Department of Social Science and Administration and recruited new faculty whose academic work soon enhanced the subject's reputation. Their research also influenced the social policies of the British Labor Party. When the party won the 1964 election, Titmuss and his colleagues played a major role in shaping the government's social policy agenda (Reisman, 1977).

Titmuss's work influenced the development of the study of social policy in Britain and many other countries. His department at the London School of Economics served as a model for the adoption of social policy as an academic subject in many British universities where interdisciplinary departments of social policy or social administration, as they are also known, were established. British social policy writers are widely respected for the sophistication of their analyses of social policies.

Despite some exceptions, academic departments of social policy have not emerged in the United States. Here, the study of social policy is pursued in other academic settings, including schools of public policy and social work and academic departments of sociology, political science, and economics. Although social policy is not established as a distinctive academic field to the same extent that it is in Britain and other Anglophone nations, a great deal of knowledge about government social policies has been generated in the United States.

Features of Social Policy Inquiry

Although the academic knowledge that has been accumulated about government social policies is now sizable and complex, it is possible to summarize the salient features of the field in terms of the purposes of social policy inquiry. Four primary purposes of this research may be identified.

First, academic inquiry into social policy has been concerned with understanding *the policy-making process and the way policies are implemented*. This research draws extensively on organization and management theory as well as quantitative techniques, and a substantial literature on the subject now exists. Studies of the policy-making process are particularly concerned with the way the process is influenced by rational decision making. Known as administration, or increasingly as policy practice, the field is also concerned with the implementation of policy. Academic studies have clarified the steps, skills, and procedures involved in implementing social policies. The challenges facing managers seeking to direct the implementation of social policies have also been exposed.

Second, social policy inquiry has sought to *describe social conditions and the social policies that respond to them*. The bulk of social policy writing has been concerned with description, and the descriptive literature is now extensive. Primarily concerned with documentation, it seeks to present narrative accounts of social conditions and social programs. Much of the literature is concerned with the social services, describing their history, statutory basis, and programmatic features. As shown in Part III of this book, this activity is now well developed. Descriptive endeavor has also given rise to the construction of conceptual representations of social policies. Typologies of social policy that seek to classify particular social policy approaches, or even the features of the social policies of nation states as a whole, are now commonplace.

Third, social policy inquiry has sought to *explain social conditions and the way social policies emerge and function to affect these conditions.* Although still relatively underdeveloped, social policy inquiry has made a good deal of progress in formulating theoretical explanations. Research in the field has been largely concerned with explaining the reasons for the introduction of social service programs and the social functions they serve in society. Social policy scholars, particularly in Britain, have also sought to incorporate the insights of sociological theory into these analyses.

Finally, social policy inquiry has sought to *evaluate the effectiveness of social policy and to determine its outcomes.* Given the subject's normative nature, evaluative research is central to the field. Much social policy research is concerned, either directly or indirectly, with assessing the effectiveness of government social policy interventions. Nevertheless, many social policy writers would concede that evaluative research, although technically sophisticated, is still inadequately applied in the real world of policy implementation. Although evaluation forms a central component of service delivery, social programs are regularly implemented without adequate thought to evaluating their outcomes. This is not only the case with the social services but with far more complicated areas of social policy investigation, such as the effects of fiscal and regulatory policies on welfare. Despite its importance, evaluation remains a neglected topic in social policy.

THE FUTURE OF SOCIAL POLICY

For much of the post-war period, social policy has been dominated by the assumption that people's welfare can best be enhanced through government intervention. However, since the 1980s, this assumption has been challenged by academic writers who believe that government involvement in social welfare is inefficient, unnecessary, and even harmful (Friedman, 1962; Gilder, 1981; Murray, 1984). Their ideas have inspired conservative political leaders. With the electoral successes of right-wing governments, social policies have changed significantly over the last two decades to incorporate greater privatization, decentralization, and the increased participation of nongovernmental agencies in service delivery. Budgetary allocations for the social services have also been reduced, and the seemingly inexorable expansion of state welfare since World War II has been halted. These developments have created a new social and political climate in which social policy thinking must operate, posing new challenges for those working in the field. Some of these challenges are examined in more depth in the final chapter of this book.

REFERENCES

Abramovitz, M. (1988). *Regulating the lives of women: Social welfare policy from colonial times to the present*. Boston: South End Press.

Friedman, M. (1962). *Capitalism and freedom*. Chicago: University of Chicago Press.

George, V., & Wilding, P. (1976). *Ideology and social welfare*. London: Routledge & Kegan Paul.

Gilder, G. (1981). *Wealth and poverty*. London: Buchan & Enright.

Howard, C. (1997). *The hidden welfare state: Tax expenditure and social policy in the United States*. Princeton, NJ: Princeton University Press.

Leuchtenburgh, W. E. (1963). *Franklin Roosevelt and the New Deal*. New York: Harper.

Murray, C. (1984). *Losing ground: American social policy 1950-1980*. New York: Basic Books.

Reisman, D. A. (1977). *Richard Titmuss: Welfare and society*. London: Heinemann.

Skocpol, T., & Ikenbery, G. R. (1995). The road to social security. In T. Skocpol (Ed.), *Social policy in the United States* (pp. 136-166). Princeton, NJ: Princeton University Press.

Titmuss, R. M. (1958). The social divisions of welfare: Some reflections on the search for equity. In R. M. Titmuss (Ed.). *Essays on the welfare state* (pp. 34-55). London: Allen & Unwin.

Titmuss, R. M. (1971). *The gift relationship*. London: Allen & Unwin.

Titmuss, R. M. (1974). *Social policy: An introduction*. London: Allen & Unwin.

CHAPTER TWO

An Overview of American Social Policy

DIANA M. DINITTO

This overview of social policy is necessarily broad because various aspects of social policy affect every individual from cradle to grave. Social policy functions, even narrowly defined, consume most of the federal budget and a growing percentage of state and local budgetary allocations (Bureau of the Census, 1997; Committee on Ways and Means, 1996). The stakes involved are also ideological, because Americans have divergent views of social policy.

THE MANY CONTEXTS OF SOCIAL POLICY

Many facets of American life affect social policy, and social policy has reciprocal influences on the lives of Americans. No other social welfare unit is more important in this regard than the family. Families are expected to provide food, shelter, and other necessities for their members and to direct their young to conform to the norms and laws of society. Social policy helps families or surrogate families carry out these many social functions, for example, by providing a public school education and by establishing health care facilities.

There is, however, no overarching family policy in the United States (DiNitto & Gustavsson, 1998). Social policy can interfere with the family's ability to carry out its functions as much as it helps them do so. For instance, families might disagree with mandates about the limits of discipline as defined in the states' child abuse statutes. In other situations, social policies, or the absence of them, may leave families without a means to fulfill their functions. For example, families may be unable to obtain health care for their child through private or public means. Many of the other gaps between what a family is supposed to do and the policies available to assist them have to do with families' financial constraints. Others involve ideological differences. For example, parents may oppose state laws that allow minors to obtain an abortion without their consent.

Many other developed countries have family policies that are much broader than in the United States, which has long operated under the premise that social policy should be used to intervene in family affairs only as a last resort. Libertarians support this laissez-faire or reactive posture. Others prefer more proactive policies, such as the public provision of health care and child care. Both the family and governments are intimately involved in social welfare functions, and often, there is considerable tension between these social institutions as families carry out their socially prescribed mandates.

Religion has long been a motivator for doing charitable works. Even with the vast expansion of government aid, churches continue to supplement public and private responses to those in need. Church-related organizations generally support social legislation such as public assistance and minimum wage laws. Most churches, however, demur from overt involvement in the political arena, preferring to go about their work in other ways. An exception is the fundamentalist religious Right, which has attempted to influence social policy through direct political involvement, especially on the issue of abortion.

Religious involvement in social welfare has been supported by writers who have gained notoriety for their position that social policy has spawned a series of misguided social programs (Olasky, 1992, 1996). They see public relief as an impersonal and ineffective system of entitlements that should be replaced by a more personal relationship with the givers. Those of the evangelical persuasion feel that they can provide the spiritual guidance as well as other services that may be necessary for the downtrodden to help lift themselves out of poverty or degradation. In 1996, Congress passed a major revision of the Aid to Families with Dependent Children (AFDC) and other public assistance programs under the Personal Responsibility and Work Opportunity Reconciliation Act. The act allows monies to be channeled to religious groups for programs to assist public assistance recipients, signaling what might be a new role for religion in social welfare.

The country's economic situation also plays a major role in social welfare programs. In their well-known book, *Regulating the Poor*, Piven and Cloward (1971) took the position that "the key to understanding relief-giving is in the functions it

serves for the larger economic and political order, for relief is a secondary and supportive institution" (p. xii). They saw a direct relationship between the number of people
needed in the workforce and the expansion and contraction of social welfare programs to fit the situation. Corporate enterprises, from small businesses to multinational conglomerates, have a vested interest in social legislation that affects workers
(minimum wage legislation, health care legislation, and tax policy, e.g., Social Security taxes). The labor movement is equally concerned about these issues. Corporations pour a lot of money into promoting legislation and supporting candidates that
are "pro business." Labor unions and professional organizations do the same to protect their interests.

The country's economic (budgetary and monetary) policies also affect social welfare. There are different views about the economic policies that promote the well-
being of the greatest number of people. According to Keynesian economics, when unemployment is high, prices are expected to drop to accommodate the reduction in
workers' incomes, and when unemployment is low, prices are expected to rise as
workers earn more and demand more goods and services. However, during the
1970s, both unemployment and inflation remained high, causing President Reagan to
adopt a policy of "supply side" economics. It included attempts to cut taxes and the
growth rate of government expenditures so people would save and invest more, thus
boosting the economy. Benefits were supposed to accrue to everyone, even trickling
down to those in the lower income brackets. But the greatest benefits seemed to go to
the wealthy, who gained substantially from the tax cuts. Poverty failed to abate, income inequality was exacerbated, and annual budget deficits and the accompanying
national debt skyrocketed (see DiNitto, in press).

The Clinton administration's policy has been referred to as "enterprise economics," in which the government invests in human capital (education and training of
workers), technology (communication systems), and infrastructure (transportation
systems) that affect a broad spectrum of people (Dye, 1998). Although it is difficult to
know the exact impact of this policy, during the late 1990s, the country's economic
picture was much brighter, with employment high and inflation low. Federal budgeting involves considerable use of "smoke and mirrors," but deficits and the debt were
also abating as Republicans and Democrats finally came to some agreement over balancing the budget. Even in these good times, some Americans remain outside the economic mainstream. They have been referred to as the *underclass* (Wilson, 1987),
those who remain the concern of the public sector and who rely especially on the social policies called public assistance.

There have long been ideological differences among Americans over the role of
government in social welfare. For example, those who wished to prevent government
intervention in health care programs (the American Medical Association prominent
among them) claimed that publicly sponsored health care programs would propel the

country to socialism. But during the 1930s (the New Deal era), Republicans and Democrats banded together to ease the financial hardship faced by so many. During the 1960s (the era of the Great Society), Congress and the President again tried to alleviate poverty for those who had not benefitted from the affluence of the previous decade.

In the last few decades, rifts over social policy have become increasingly apparent. In 1994, Republicans offered a 10-point "Contract with America" to represent their conservative budgetary and social agenda. Democratic President Bill Clinton vetoed two major welfare reform bills delivered by the Republican-controlled Congress because he thought they were too punitive. In 1996, he finally approved a major reform, but he was still unhappy with some provisions, such as denying most aid to immigrants residing legally in this country. On the other hand, he supported provisions limiting the time that families can receive Temporary Assistance for Needy Families (TANF), the program that replaced AFDC. Some of his closest social welfare advisers quit in protest over the new law.

Opinion polls also show that the American public holds different views about public assistance policy, but often, responses fluctuate based on what questions are asked. For example, Americans say they want to help those in need, even though many claim to disdain welfare programs (Weaver, Shapiro, & Jacobs, 1995).

One might say that Republicans and conservatives favor limited social programs, Democrats and liberals support greater intervention, and libertarians believe in a hands-off approach. These are overly simplistic descriptions. A Republican may be conservative on spending issues but support abortion or gay rights, which are considered traditional liberal positions (DiNitto, in press). A Catholic Democrat may want to expand the food stamp program, toughen work requirements for TANF recipients, and overturn the right to an abortion. Within both major political parties, there are conservatives, liberals, and moderates.

Politics in the United States can rightfully be called special interest politics. Individuals and groups often pool their resources by donating to political action committees (PACs) to support candidates who share their positions. To garner the money to run for political office, candidates become beholden to special interest groups. Big-money politics breeds corruption. Some candidate or organization is always being investigated for violating campaign contribution rules. We might assume that elected officials would prefer not to be at the mercy of special interests. We can also assume that proposed ethics and campaign finance reform legislation frequently fails in Congress because few candidates have figured out how to do without special interest money.

Groups supportive of social welfare legislation may not have the biggest coffers, but they still form PACs. The National Association of Social Workers' PAC is called Political Action for Candidate Election. Social workers and other groups act as proxies for the poor, children, and other disenfranchised groups who cannot easily represent themselves in the political process (Keller, 1981). Nonetheless, they are sometimes accused of being more concerned about their own professional interests than those of their clients.

The media play a key role in the development of social policy. Everyone knows the media's ability to bring social problems and proposed solutions to the public's attention (Dye & Zeigler, 1991; Hewitt, 1996). Prior to mass means of communication, it was difficult to mobilize Americans behind issues. Today, Americans are bombarded with so much media coverage that they have probably become desensitized to many social issues (DiNitto, in press). Many people seem to be afflicted by some type of social problem, and many of them want to see government do something about it. The media are said to have a liberal bias, but never before have there been so many conservative commentators to challenge the positions of liberals.

Other influences shaping social policy are the relationships among the public, not-for-profit (voluntary), and private (proprietary) sectors. The once sharp distinctions among them have been blurred. The inability of governments and voluntary organizations to solve social problems has led to privatization—allowing profit-making entities to provide services, such as residential programs for people with disabilities and even child protective services, once thought to be the clear purview of state and local governments (Kamerman & Kahn, 1989). Some people think that privatization results in governments abrogating their responsibilities. Others believe that private entities can do the job at least as well and more efficiently. In a capitalist society, entrepreneurs are constantly seeking new ventures. The foray into social welfare, like other ventures, can be motivated by profit as well as the desire to do good.

To quote James Madison (in Hamilton, Jay, & Madison, 1929) on class distinctions, "the most common and durable source of factions has been the various and unequal distribution of property. Those who hold and those who are without property have ever formed distinct interests in society" (p. 43). Americans voice support for programs to help those in need, but few want to give up too much to help others (Noble & Melville, 1989). What is perhaps surprising is that Americans in upper-income brackets tend to be the most liberal on many social welfare issues. For example, in a 1996 public opinion poll, those earning $75,000 or more each year were more likely than those who earned less to oppose cuts in social spending and restrictions on abortions, and they were most supportive of school busing (Saad, 1996).

Race has also had a profound effect on social policy. Slavery was abolished in 1865, but the "separate but equal" clause of the Constitution supported racial segregation until 1954, when it was struck down by the U.S. Supreme Court in *Brown v. the Board of Education of Topeka, Kansas.* The Civil Rights Act of 1964 was another milestone in securing opportunity regardless of an individual's race or national origin. Affirmative action programs in schools and in workplaces followed, but in the 1990s, the call was for an end to race-based preferences. Black Americans, those of Hispanic origin, and other ethnic groups have made considerable social and economic progress, but one need only look at the income of these groups to see that they still do not earn the same as whites, even with the same education (Housing and Household Economics Statistics Division, 1996). Social spending cuts are often considered direct affronts to these groups because these programs help offset the economic effects of discrimination. Many people feel that preferential treatment may no longer be in order but that affirmative action is still needed to ensure that people of all ethnic and racial groups have a fair chance.

Gender must also be considered in social policy analysis. From the bedroom to the boardroom and from the state legislature to the houses of Congress, gender politics is a sensitive issue. Women continue to earn less than men even when they work full-time at the same jobs. Because women's poverty rates are much higher, they are most of the adults in public assistance programs. The more generous social insurance legislation of the 1930s was written with men as the primary breadwinners in mind (Gordon, 1990, 1994). The same legislation built on states' efforts to help women through the more penurious public assistance programs, primarily Aid to Dependent Children (which later became AFDC). The driving force behind welfare reform has been the large numbers of children born to unmarried mothers, combined with the lack of support these children receive from their fathers. The feminist political movement has resulted in some gains, such as the Equal Pay Act of 1963 and the 1972 Title IX education amendments to the 1964 Civil Rights Act. For many women, the crowning touch would be an equal rights amendment to the U.S. Constitution.

Many more issues including the aging of the population, the deterioration of the inner cities, and violence in communities should be included in this review of the context of social policy. All these issues have a direct bearing on social policy.

SOCIAL POLICY FUNCTIONS OF GOVERNMENTS

Social policy is made by federal, state, and municipal governments and entities such as school districts and hospital districts. Federalism is the constitutional division of powers among the federal and state governments. The Constitution grants the federal government 18 powers, including the power to tax and spend for the "general welfare" and the power granted by the "necessary and proper" clause, which allows the federal government to do many things it deems necessary (Dye & Zeigler, 1995). The Constitution also reserves powers for the states (and the people). Social welfare functions are generally considered among the states' powers, although local governments were initially responsible for assisting those in need.

During the latter 1800s and early 1900s, heavy industrialization, urbanization, immigration, and World War I brought rapidly changing conditions and many social problems (Dye, 1998; Dye & Zeigler, 1995). The states' role in social welfare grew rapidly during the Progressive Era (1900 to 1919) as local governments needed assistance with these mounting concerns. States passed child labor laws; instituted mothers' aid for women whose husbands died, deserted, or became disabled; adopted workers' compensation laws; and provided aid to poor people who were elderly or blind (Axinn & Levin, 1997; Day, 1997).

Dual federalism, which emphasized separate functions for the federal and state governments, changed to *cooperative federalism,* as the federal government ventured into the social policy arena (Dye, 1998; Jost, 1996). The federal Children's Bureau was established in 1912 to address the problems of the country's youngest citizens. The Sheppard-Towner Act of 1921 allowed the bureau to establish maternal and child health clinics. This was a beginning, but the defining event that led the federal government to exercise the major role it does today in social policy was the Great Depression.

The stock market crash of 1929 and the Great Depression that followed caused widespread suffering. The federal government's initial response was temporary strategies—soup kitchens and public works (jobs) programs. The more permanent strategies came in President Roosevelt's New Deal, embodied in the Social Security Act of 1935. The act made the federal government a full partner with the states in alleviating poverty through public assistance programs. Using the model the states had adopted, the program established for poor families with children was called Aid to Dependent Children. The programs for people who were poor and aged or blind were Old Age Assistance and Aid to the Blind, respectively. More important, the federal government adopted a new strategy to prevent poverty through the national social insurance program called Old Age Insurance or Social Security retirement. It also adopted an unemployment compensation program to be largely administered by the states. The act contained additional provisions to assist the states in providing for maternal and child health and welfare. The Social Security Act cast the federal government's net quite wide in addressing social policy issues. None of this could have been accomplished without the introduction in 1913 of the federal income tax, which gave the federal government a large source of revenues that could be tapped to address these problems (see Dye, 1998).

Federal intervention increased in the 1950s. Many more workers were included under the Social Security retirement program. Social Security Disability Insurance was established for people who became disabled during their working years. The federal government also stepped in to help the states by adding a public assistance program called Aid to the Permanently and Totally Disabled.

The federal government increased its role in social policy again during the 1960s with its War on Poverty and the programs of the Great Society. These strategies began emerging during the Kennedy administration, but it was President Johnson whose rhetoric included the war analogy. Some of the experimental strategies of the war, which varied from community to community, did not survive. Others remain well-known today, none more than the Head Start preschool program. The Great Society programs also included the Food Stamp Program (FSP) to assist poor and low-income individuals and families to obtain an adequate diet, the Medicaid program to help certain categories of poor people gain access to medical care, and the Medicare program to provide health care access to virtually all the population age 65 and older.

Except for some administrative costs paid by the states, the FSP is funded by the federal government, which also sets eligibility rules. The program is available to more poor and low-income Americans than any other public assistance program. Medicaid, the most expensive of all the public assistance programs, is a joint federal-state program and relies on funding and rule making by both the federal and state governments. Medicare, a social insurance program, is the most highly centralized and entirely under federal purview.

Beginning in the 1950s, the federal government embraced another role by providing social services to families receiving public assistance (Kahn, 1979; Morris, 1979). This role expanded in the 1960s, with the hope that social services could help AFDC parents address the personal problems that might have prevented them from leaving the welfare rolls. The federal government also stepped up its role in helping the states provide services for people with mental retardation and mental illnesses through the Mental Retardation Facilities and Community Mental Health Centers Construction Act of 1963. It ventured further into social services for older people with the Older Americans Act in 1965.

In 1974, Old Age Assistance, Aid to the Blind, and Aid to the Permanently and Totally Disabled were transformed into the Supplemental Security Income (SSI) program. Under SSI, the federal government now sets eligibility requirements, makes a basic payment to all recipients, and does most of the program administration. This federalization was intended to bring an end to the unequal treatment of poor people who were aged, blind, or otherwise disabled across the states. Many states still supplement the federal minimum, but once again, the federal role in public assistance had grown.

In 1965, national defense consumed 43% of the federal budget, and social welfare (social insurance, health, and public assistance), 24%. By 1975, defense was 26% and social welfare, 42% (DiNitto, in press). Political scientist Aaron Wildavsky (1979) calls this the "revolution no one noticed." But eventually the revolution was noticed by critics such as George Gilder (1981) and Charles Murray (1984). Both contend that many of the country's social welfare problems can be blamed on social policy itself. They believe that public assistance (primarily AFDC) has emasculated men in their role of breadwinner, causing them a personal loss of self-esteem and a loss of worth to society. They blame these programs for family breakup and entrapment in lives of degradation and despair.

Gilder's work caught the attention of President Reagan, who wanted to turn back to the states much of the role the federal government had assumed in social welfare, an approach known as the New Federalism or devolution. Reagan successfully combined many smaller categorical grant programs for specific functions into block grants for broader functions. These block grants allow the states more flexibility in determining how the money is spent. President Bush also encouraged devolution, looking to the states as laboratories to test new approaches to AFDC. President Clinton went even further, helping to make many of the experiments federal policy by signing the Personal Responsibility and Work Opportunity Reconciliation Act of 1996. The act changed AFDC, a categorical entitlement program, into the block grant called TANF. Other attempts to make block grants of major public assistance programs such as the Food Stamp Program have failed. There is no doubt, however, that the era of public assistance devolution has arrived.

The federal government continues to retain full responsibility for Social Security and Medicare, the major insurance programs. But there has been a good deal of talk about privatization. Even if employees were allowed to invest only a portion of their Social Security taxes privately, this would still be a radical departure from the way Social Security has operated. The possibility is a whittling away of the government's role in both social insurance and public assistance.

State Government's Role

Prior to federal intervention, growing social problems caused states to aid local governments with a number of social welfare programs. Even with the Social Security Act, the states maintained key roles in financing public assistance and social service programs and determining eligibility requirements and the payments or services to be provided. In the ensuing years, the federal government took on more social welfare responsibilities. For several decades, federalization was the prevailing social policy philosophy. But the growth of public assistance programs, particularly AFDC, resulted in deep dissatisfaction with this approach. As states tried to cope with AFDC's perceived failure, they invented new approaches—everything from limiting payments to families who had more children while on AFDC and cutting benefits to families whose children missed too much school, to allowing AFDC families to keep more job earnings while still receiving benefits and allowing them to save money for education or to start a business. While Congress argued over President Clinton's proposed Health Security Act and members of Congress offered their own health care proposals, the states were taking concrete steps to cover more individuals and families through managed health care arrangements and laws requiring employers to cover more employees. Presidents Reagan and Bush and many members of Congress were convinced that less federal red tape would allow the states to deliver public assistance and social service programs better. The country had embarked on this era of "devolutionist federalism."

One program that some states and localities continue to operate without federal help is General Assistance (GA) or General Relief. Following the Social Security Act, GA expenditures dropped considerably as the federal government stepped in to help. GA programs vary widely from place to place, but they continue to have an important function by helping people who do not qualify for federal or federal-state social welfare programs. Traditionally, these have been needy people who did not qualify for AFDC, Old Age Assistance, Aid to the Blind, or Aid to the Permanently and Totally Disabled. They were able-bodied adults who were not receiving unemployment insurance and were unable to find work and individuals who could not pay their medical bills (MacIntyre, 1964). A recent study of California's GA program describes many recipients as people with mental disabilities, immigrants, and individuals recently released from correctional facilities (Moon & Schneiderman, 1995). There is still a need to fill in the cracks of social welfare programs, but it appears that many jurisdictions are cutting back on GA benefits (Moon & Schneiderman, 1995).

Local Government's Role

Early relief in the United States consisted of communities compensating families that took in needy people, "outdoor relief" provided to people in their own homes, and "indoor relief" in institutions such as almshouses or workhouses. Once the key public player in social welfare, local governments now have the smallest role. Today, local jurisdictions' primary tasks are public safety (police and fire protection) and public school education. Local governments do provide some support for local social service programs, such as community mental health centers, shelters for women victimized by spousal violence, and senior citizens centers. Many cities operate some type of social welfare or social service department, and some offer GA even if their state does not have a GA program.

LEGISLATIVE, EXECUTIVE, AND JUDICIAL AUTHORITY IN SOCIAL POLICY MAKING

Social policy is made by federal, state, and local legislative bodies, by the executive authority of elected officials (the president, governors, and other state and municipal officials) and appointed officials (agency heads), and by the judiciary (the Supreme

Court and other federal, state, and municipal courts). This system of checks and balances may not make for a speedy policy process, but it does help to ensure that policy issues get thorough consideration in a pluralistic, democratic society.

Legislative Processes

Both branches of Congress have a number of committees and subcommittees that are responsible for social policy. Many of the largest social programs (Social Security, Medicare, Medicaid, TANF, SSI) come under the jurisdiction of the House Committee on Ways and Means. The House Committee on Agriculture, with its Subcommittee on Department Operations, Nutrition, and Foreign Agriculture, is responsible for food stamps and many other nutrition programs. The Senate Committee on Finance oversees Social Security, family policies, and health care. The Senate also has a Committee on Agriculture, Nutrition, and Forestry. Many other congressional committees are also responsible for parts of social policy.

It may be comforting to know that so many hands are involved, but this complex system can make for a social welfare system with overlapping and even contradictory policies. Some of this results from the different ideologies of the major political parties. It can also result from regional differences. For example, states with heavy agricultural interests are particularly concerned about the programs of the U.S. Department of Agriculture. States with large immigrant populations pay close attention to legislation affecting the U.S. Immigration and Naturalization Service and immigrants' entrance and social welfare benefits.

In addition to the legislation they generate, state legislatures must often respond to laws that Congress has passed and other federal mandates. For example, when Congress passed the Personal Responsibility and Work Opportunity Reconciliation Act of 1996, state legislatures had to transform their AFDC programs to make them conform to the new TANF program legislation or risk losing their funding.

States are often unhappy with legislative directives from the federal government, especially when they are unfunded. For example, when the federal government expands the required categories of Medicaid-eligible individuals, each state must generate the match money to serve them, even if the state would not have chosen to do so.

The federal and state governments have different social policy traditions. Congress has instituted automatic cost of living adjustments (COLAs) in the Social Security, SSI, and Food Stamp programs. States rarely choose to make automatic adjustments in public assistance programs. There are also different social welfare traditions among the states. Some states, often those in the Northeast, are known for a more generous orientation to public assistance programs, whereas the poorer states of the South have a different reputation.

Municipal governments (city councils, county commissions) also deliberate about social programs. Although the financial stakes are smaller, citizen participation in local policy making is often the greatest because it is closest to home. Some cities run elaborate social welfare programs, as might be expected in a place like New York City where considerable resources are directed to public aid. Many municipalities are much smaller and have limited funds to distribute among many worthy causes. For local social service programs, even a few thousand dollars of operating funds are important. Local elected officials might want to support all these programs, but because they cannot really do enough for any of them, many appoint a group of citizens to study the requests and make funding recommendations. This might deflect some of the heat local officials feel when a group feels slighted by the council or commission's budget decisions.

The budget of any government is its most important policy statement because this is where it spends the revenue it generates. Many individuals and groups try to influence the allocation of the scarce monetary resources available. Each year the Office of Management and Budget, part of the Executive Office of the President, works with federal agencies to develop a budget for the following year. Based on this work, the President presents a budget for the operation of the entire federal government to Congress. Congress then does its work through House and Senate budget committees and a joint Congressional Budget Office as well as House and Senate Appropriations Committees and subcommittees. Appropriations acts must be passed by both houses and signed by the President. Wildavsky (1988) calls this legislatively centered, decentralized, and fragmented process one that "distinguishes the American budgetary process from that of any other democratic nation" (p. viii).

Although the media reports the bitter battles that often ensue in passing a budget, much federal spending is considered uncontrollable because so many legislatively mandated programs are in place. Many of them are social welfare programs, primarily the large social insurance programs, which are hardly likely to be eliminated or even reduced by much. The President's proposed budget for fiscal year 1999 was $1.7 trillion (Office of Management and Budget, 1998), making the federal government very big business. State and local budgets are much smaller, but sometimes the smaller the stakes, the more bitter the battles.

Actions of the Executive Branch

Elected government executives—the President, governors, and mayors—also make social policy decisions. The President and governors can veto legislation, although the respective legislative body may overturn these vetoes with sufficient votes. Elected government heads also make policy through executive decisions. Examples are President Harry S. Truman's decision to desegregate the military and President Clinton's order to establish a uniform policy of nondiscrimination against gay men and lesbians in federal government employment. Executive orders have also been used to deny federal contracts to employers who practice gender discrimination and for many other purposes.

The executive branch is composed of agencies responsible for administering government functions. At the federal level, the vast Department of Health and Human Services is but one of the agencies responsible for carrying out social policy. The Departments of Agriculture, Labor, and Justice, the independent Social Security Administration and Legal Services Corporation, and many other entities also administer social policy. The states have their own bureaucratic agencies for administering social policy. Some have a large social welfare umbrella agency that encompasses many public assistance and social services functions. Others use a more decentralized approach with many separate agencies to carry out health, public assistance, protective services, vocational rehabilitation, and other functions.

Elected government executives appoint agency heads who oversee the operation of these social welfare agencies. These appointed officials and their agency employees make policy in the form of rules and regulations that must be developed when a piece of legislation lacks the specificity to be implemented. Many of these rules and regulations are published in the *Federal Register* or similar state publications or are otherwise made available for public review. Sometimes, it takes years before rules and regulations are issued, reviewed, contested, revised, and finally put into place. The Rehabilitation Act of 1973 was the first to provide certain protections for people with disabilities, but not until 1977 were implementing regulations issued (World Institute on Disability, 1992). Many other agency decisions are not subject to formal review, but they become standard operating procedures that can have a profound effect on social policy.

The Decisions of the Courts

When people are unhappy with a policy decision, they may appeal to the courts, and when they disagree with a lower court decision, they try to appeal to a higher court. The Supreme Court is the ultimate authority. It plays a critical role in social policy. For example, in 1968, it ruled that "man-in-the-house rules" could not be used to "flatly deny" children AFDC, and in 1979, it ruled that it was unconstitutional to provide AFDC benefits to unemployed fathers but not to unemployed mothers. The U.S. Supreme Court has also played a major role in the quest to end racial discrimination and in the right to obtain an abortion. Without these decisions, social policy might be quite different from what it is today.

The role of judges is to interpret the laws and the constitutions of the federal and state governments, but there are conservative justices, liberal justices, and those who are sometimes conservative and sometimes liberal. Many Supreme Court decisions are split. That is why the high court offers majority and minority opinions with its rulings. The president makes nominations to the Supreme Court and other federal courts, and the Senate decides whether or not to approve them. This is serious business because the judges are permitted to serve for life. Dye and Zeigler (1995) call the nine Supreme Court justices the most elite of policy makers.

PLURALISM AND INCREMENTALISM

With all the players and processes involved, it is no wonder that social policies are overlapping and conflicting. This mass of social policy may be difficult for the public to comprehend and for people in need to traverse, but many people get to see some of their desires enacted. This system may be preferable to highly centralized policy making, which may leave some people out entirely. Such an approach may also prevent large social policy errors from occurring.

Another safeguard is that at all levels, social policy making is largely incremental (Lindblom, 1959). There is good reason for this. Neither policy makers nor anyone else usually knows with certainty what a major policy change will mean in the present or in the future. By funding demonstration programs, allowing states to obtain waivers from federal requirements to try new approaches, and relying on private groups to execute their own initiatives, governments are able to avoid the costly mistakes that might ensue from major shifts in policy paradigms. Many people have portrayed the change from AFDC to TANF as a radical departure from long-held federal policy, yet many states had tried these approaches before the Personal Responsibility and Work Opportunity Reconciliation Act was passed.

In 1993, President Clinton's proposed Health Security Act recommended a sweeping change of the nation's health care system. Other national health care proposals have been introduced in Congress, and all have failed. Instead, Congress and the states have made many more modest changes—expanding Medicaid eligibility, offering tax incentives to employers who provide employee health care benefits, and adding the Child Health Insurance Program in 1997 to cover more low-income children. Policy making is not a single event. Policy is constructed and reconstructed time and time again, but the wheels of policy making turn slowly.

In summary, political, economic, and social institutions affect social policy development, and social policy affects these institutions. Federal, state, and local governments share functions in making and carrying out social policy, but the balance of responsibilities among the three levels of government continues to shift with the times. The legislative, executive, and judicial branches of government all play important roles in this process. In a pluralistic and democratic society like the United States, pol-

icy making is decentralized and fragmented, resulting in overlapping and even conflicting policies. Policy making is also incremental. Whatever the virtues of incremen-
talism, social policy making almost always moves slowly.

REFERENCES

Axinn, J., & Levin, H. (1997). *Social welfare: A history of the American response to need* (4th ed.). White
    Plains, NY: Longman.
Bureau of the Census, U.S. Department of Commerce. (1997). *Statistical abstract of the United States:
    1997* (pp. 1318-1321). Washington, DC: Government Printing Office.
Committee on Ways and Means, U.S. House of Representatives. (1996). *1996 Green book: Background
    material and data on programs within the jurisdiction of the Committee on Ways and Means* (pp. 372-
    373). Washington, DC: Government Printing Office.
Day, P. J. (1997). *A new history of social welfare* (2nd ed.). Boston: Allyn & Bacon.
DiNitto, D. M. (in press). *Social welfare: Politics and public policy* (5th ed.). Boston: Allyn & Bacon.
DiNitto, D. M., & Gustavsson, N. (1998). The interface between family practice and family policy. In C.
    Franklin & C. Jordan (Ed.), *Family practice brief systems methods for social work* (pp. 341-388). Pacific
    Grove, CA: Brooks/Cole.
Dye, T. R. (1998). *Understanding public policy* (9th ed.). Upper Saddle River, NJ: Prentice Hall.
Dye, T. R., & Zeigler, H. (1991). *American politics in the media age* (4th ed.). Pacific Grove, CA: Harbrace.
Dye, T. R., & Zeigler, H. (1995). *The irony of democracy: An uncommon introduction to American politics*
    (10th ed.). Pacific Grove, CA: Harbrace.
Gilder, G. (1981). *Wealth and poverty.* New York: Bantam.
Gordon, L. (1990). *Women, the state, and welfare.* Madison: University of Wisconsin Press.
Gordon, L. (1994). *Pitied but not forgotten: Single mothers and the history of welfare.* New York: Free
    Press.
Hamilton, A., Jay, J., & Madison, J. (1929). *The federalist; or, the new constitution.* London: Dent. (Re-
    printed from *The Federalist,* No. X, November 23, 1787)
Hewitt, C. (1996). Estimating the number of homeless: Media misrepresentation of an urban problem.
    Journal of Urban Affairs, 18(3), 431-447.
Housing and Household Economics Statistics Division, Bureau of the Census, U.S. Department of Com-
    merce. (1996). TIPS Table 15, unpublished data.
Jost, K. (1996, September 13). The states and federalism. *Congressional Quarterly Researcher,* pp. 795-
    815.
Kahn, A. (1979). *Social policy and social services.* New York: Random House.
Kamerman, S., & Kahn, A. J. (1989). *Privatization and the welfare state.* Princeton, NJ: Princeton Univer-
    sity Press.
Keller, B. (1981, April 16). Special treatment no longer given advocates for the poor. *Congressional Quar-
    terly Weekly, 39*(16), 659-664.
Lindblom, C. (1959). The science of "muddling through." *Public Administration Review, 19,* 79-88.
MacIntyre, D. M. (1964). *Public assistance: Too much or too little.* Ithaca: New York State School of Indus-
    trial and Labor Relations, Cornell University.
Moon, A., & Schneiderman, L. (1995). *Assessing the growth of California's General Assistance pro-
    gram. Berkeley: California Policy Seminar,* http://www.sen.ca.gov/ftp/sen/committee/STAND-
    ING/HEALTH/home/rear02.htm.
Morris, R. (1979). *Social policy of the American welfare state: An introduction to policy analysis.* New
    York: Harper & Row.
Murray, C. (1984). *Losing ground: American social policy, 1950-1980.* New York: Basic Books.

Noble, J., & Melville, K. (1989, January/February). The public's social welfare mandate. *Public Opinion,* pp. 45-49, 59.

Office of Management and Budget, Executive Office of the President. (1998). *Budget of the United States government, fiscal year 1999.* Washington, DC: Government Printing Office.

Olasky, M. (1992). *The tragedy of American compassion.* Washington, DC: Regnery Gateway.

Olasky, M. (1996). *Renewing American compassion.* New York: Free Press.

Piven, F. F., & Cloward, R. (1971). *Regulating the poor: The functions of public welfare.* New York: Random House.

Saad, L. (1996, May). Issues referendum reveals populist leanings. *The Gallup Poll Monthly.*

Weaver, R. K., Shapiro, R. Y., & Jacobs, L. R. (1995). Welfare (The polls-trends). *Public Opinion Quarterly, 59*(4), 606-627.

Wildavsky, A. (1979). *Speaking truth to power: The art and craft of policy analysis.* Boston: Little, Brown.

Wildavsky, A. (1988). *The new politics of the budgetary process.* Glenview, IL: Scott, Foresman.

Wilson, W. J. (1987). *The truly disadvantaged: The inner city, the underclass, and public policy.* Chicago: University of Chicago Press.

World Institute on Disability. (1992). *Just like everyone else.* Oakland, CA: Author.

CHAPTER THREE

Economic Dimensions of Social Policy

JANE WALDFOGEL

*T*his chapter examines the economic context in which social policy in the United States is formulated and implemented. It traces the historical growth of expenditures on social programs and describes current social welfare spending with reference to the major program areas to which resources are allocated. It compares social spending in the United States with other countries and asks whether spending on social welfare is sufficient or inadequate. In discussing this issue and examining wider questions of social welfare allocation, reference is made to the principles economists use to decide issues of social spending. These principles are concerned with efficiency, equity, and other social goals. As will be shown, economists differ in the way they relate these principles to current economic realities, social welfare programs, and social expenditure.

THE ECONOMIC CONTEXT OF SOCIAL POLICY

Social welfare programs are designed to promote economic security by protecting individuals from risks that could potentially face anyone in a market society. These risks include the loss of income due to one's own unemployment, injury, disability, or retirement; the loss of income due to a family member's unemployment, injury, disability, retirement, or death, for individuals who are dependent children or spouses; inadequate income to afford an extraordinary and irregular purchase such as health care or education; and income poverty.

Programs to insure individuals against these types of risk are present in virtually all industrialized countries, although, of course, individual countries vary a great deal in the type of programs they provide and in the generosity of those programs. And many countries go beyond these narrow aims to promote other goals, such as equality of opportunity or social inclusion.

What principles are used to decide when government intervention is justified and what types of programs are warranted? Governments do not intervene unless it is generally agreed that there is a problem. Economists refer to this as the need to identify a market failure, which basically means that "if it isn't broken, don't fix it." However, even when there is an agreed-upon problem, before government intervenes, it must also be agreed that government as opposed to private intervention is the best solution and that government intervention will not do more harm than good. Two basic principles play a key role in these decisions.

The first principle is economic efficiency, which has three different aspects. Macro-efficiency is concerned with the effect of the overall level of social welfare expenditures on the economy; micro-efficiency considers the relative merits of spending on one social program versus others; and incentives efficiency has to do with potential adverse effects of social welfare policy on individuals' behavior (Barr, 1998). In making decisions about social welfare policy, then, one would want to minimize to the extent possible the adverse effects of those decisions on the overall economy (macro-efficiency) and on individuals' decisions about employment, savings, and so on (incentive efficiency), and one would want to be sure to allocate expenditures where they could do the most good, relative to other social welfare expenditures (micro-efficiency) as well as to other non-social welfare expenditures (macro-efficiency).

The second principle underlying social welfare policy is equity. Economists typically distinguish two types of equity: vertical equity or redistribution, which is the principle that a social welfare system should redistribute income from those who have more to those who have less; and horizontal equity or fairness, which is the principle that similarly situated people should be treated equally (Barr, 1998). Thus, all else equal, one would tend to prefer social welfare policies that help make the poor better off and that treat individuals fairly. One would also prefer programs that make their intended recipients better off; this form of equity gain is sometimes referred to as *target efficiency*.

What happens when these principles collide? Obviously, trade-offs must be made (Okun, 1975), but social theorists disagree on how to resolve this question. Liberal theorists such as John Rawls (1972) place equity and social justice first and would promote equity even at the price of some efficiency losses. Conservative theorists such as Milton Friedman (1962) see efficiency as primary and worry a great deal about adverse incentives and also about restrictions on personal freedom; they therefore tend to have a much more skeptical view of social welfare programs.

Other principles that are relevant to the design of social welfare programs tend to vary by country and over time. In the United States, one important goal of social welfare policy has been to promote equality of opportunity. In the 19th century, universal public schools were introduced as a way to help integrate immigrants into American society, and more recently, in the 1960s, reducing racial inequality was a key goal of the War on Poverty. As another example, in much of Europe currently, an important goal of social policy is to promote social solidarity and social inclusion. Thus, in many European countries, social policy aims to reduce income inequality and relative poverty as well as absolute poverty.

Generally speaking, the size, structure, and generosity of a country's social welfare system will reflect how these questions about efficiency and equity, and about other social goals, have been answered over time. A country's social welfare system will also reflect that society's assumptions and norms, for instance, about gender or family responsibility. A good example of how efficiency, equity, and other concerns interact to shape social welfare policy arises when we consider the decision whether to provide services universally or to target them to low-income or other specific groups (Garfinkel, 1982; Titmuss, 1968). If the aim of a social welfare program is to reduce poverty, for instance, then it seems obvious that the best way to deliver the program would be to target it to those who are poor. This has the advantage of targeting the benefits to those who need them most, which would improve both efficiency and equity. However, income testing also imposes costs. Identifying poor people and ensuring that benefits are provided only to them creates administrative costs for the system and stigma for the recipients. Stigma is costly in that it may diminish recipients' well-being and may also deter some potential recipients from taking up the benefit. Income testing can also create adverse work incentives. Because, to maintain targeting, families who work and earn more must then have their benefits reduced, there is an incentive for families to keep their earnings low. In the extreme case, if benefits are reduced dollar for dollar as earnings rise, families have an incentive not to work at all (or to work "off-the-books"). This kind of "poverty trap" impedes the efficiency of the program and also lowers families' well-being relative to what it might be under a better designed program.

Universal benefits, in contrast, impose much lower administrative costs, do not stigmatize their recipients, and do not have large adverse effects on work effort, because they are provided to all residents regardless of income or other characteristics. They also have the advantage of promoting social solidarity and social inclusion. However, universal benefits are also likely to do a poorer job of redistributing income because they provide benefits to rich and poor alike. Of course, the extent to which they are redistributive will depend on the extent to which they are funded through progressive taxation.

Indicator targeting offers an attractive intermediate solution to the targeting versus universalism dilemma. If, for instance, families with children are at much higher risk of poverty than other families or households, then the presence of children could be used as an indicator, and benefits could be targeted accordingly. Compared to income targeting, this kind of targeting costs much less to administer, does not stigmatize recipients, and poses fewer problems in terms of adverse incentives, although one might worry about fertility effects. However, it may be less efficient in terms of reaching its intended targets. Thus, whether this kind of indicator targeting makes sense from a target efficiency and equity perspective will depend on what share of families with children are poor and on what share of poor people live in families with children. In the extreme case, if all families with children were poor and all poor people were found in families with children, targeting to families with children would be the most efficient way to target resources to the poor. In the United States today, about one sixth of families with children are poor, and about two thirds of poor people are found in families with children. Therefore, although entirely replacing income testing with indicator targeting would not be warranted, some additional targeting to families with children might be.

HOW MUCH DOES THE UNITED STATES SPEND ON SOCIAL PROGRAMS?

In 1994, the United States spent over $1.4 trillion on social welfare programs. Even when one takes the overall size of the U.S. economy into account, this figure is a large amount, representing one fifth of the country's gross domestic product or GDP. The GDP represents the total amount of goods and services produced in a country each year. The figure of $1.4 trillion is about two thirds of all the money spent by federal, state, and local governments. It is important to note that this figure, and the figures reported below, capture only a portion of the American social welfare system. As is customary in analyses of social welfare expenditures, these figures do not include private social welfare expenditures (such as spending on health insurance by individuals and employers) nor do they include tax expenditures (such as the Earned Income Tax Credit, child care tax credits, and tax deductions for mortgage interest and property tax payments). If these expenditures were included, the American social welfare system would look even larger.

The historical data on total social welfare expenditures and on these expenditures as a share of GDP, shown in Table 3.1, allow us to place the current figures in historical perspective. Table 3.1 shows a dramatic increase in total expenditure levels over time;

TABLE 3.1   Social Welfare Expenditures in the United States, 1929-1994

	Total Federal, State, and Local Expenditures (in millions of dollars)	Expenditures as a Percentage of Gross Domestic Product (GDP)
1929	3,921	3.9
1940	8,795	9.2
1950	23,508	8.8
1955	32,844	8.5
1960	52,293	10.0
1965	77,175	11.0
1970	145,856	14.2
1975	290,080	18.2
1980	492,213	18.1
1985	731,874	17.8
1990	1,048,809	18.5
1994	1,434,645	21.0

SOURCE: *Social Security Bulletin*, Annual Statistical Supplement, 1981, Table 1; *Social Security Bulletin*, February 1990, Vol. 53, No. 2, Table 2; and *Social Security Bulletin*, Fall 1997, Vol. 60, No. 3, Table 1.
NOTE: Expenditures are expressed as a share of gross national product (GNP), instead of GDP, for the years 1929 and 1940.

however, the total expenditure figures must be interpreted cautiously because they are not adjusted for inflation nor for increases in the size of the population. Therefore, Table 3.1 also shows expenditures as a share of GDP. This percentage provides a better measure of how much government is spending on social welfare as a share of the total size of the economy.

In 1929, the earliest year shown for which comparable data are available, social welfare spending by government at all levels amounted to under 4% of GDP. By 1940, that share had more than doubled, reflecting the increase in spending at the federal level after the passage of the Social Security Act of 1935. Spending as a share of GDP did not rise again until the War on Poverty in the 1960s, which resulted in a jump in the share of GDP spent on social welfare from 11% in 1965 to over 14% in 1970 and over 18% in 1975. Spending on social welfare programs then held steady from the mid-1970s until the 1990s, when the share increased only slightly, to 21% in 1994. But, as we shall see below, the distribution of expenditures by type of program changed a good deal over this period.

Expenditures by Type of Program

Although the public often thinks of social welfare as public assistance or welfare, social welfare includes a much broader range of programs. One of these is social insurance, which covers the risks of unemployment, injury, disability, or death provided on a universal basis to all individuals who have worked and paid into the social security system. In addition to what is termed *welfare,* a wide range of other means-tested programs are also included in the definition of social welfare. These programs are targeted to needy individuals and families and include educational assistance, housing, food stamps and medical services.

Until fairly recently, education was the largest social welfare program as a share of GDP. As we can see in Table 3.2, it was not until 1960 that spending on social insurance exceeded spending on education for the first time, and it was not until 1980 that spending on social insurance began to take up twice as large a share of the GDP as education.

The increase in spending on social insurance has been driven by demographic, economic, and political factors: the increasing share of the population that is over retirement age, rapidly rising health care costs for retirees, and rising levels of retirement benefits, reflecting an increased willingness on the part of Congress to spend money on older Americans.

In contrast to social insurance, spending on public assistance or welfare has risen much more gradually and today constitutes only about 3.5% of GDP, about a third of the share taken up by social insurance. Spending on public assistance, like spending on social insurance, is affected by demographic, economic, and political changes. The rising share of children living in female-headed families, who are at greater risk of poverty due to the lack of a second earner; economic downturns such as the Great Depression in the 1930s; and political changes such as the welfare expansions of the 1970s or the welfare cutbacks of the 1980s all have had an effect on the share of GDP that is allocated to public assistance.

As noted earlier, education was the largest single component of the social welfare system until the 1960s, and at 5% of GDP, it continues to take up about a quarter of all social welfare spending today. The remaining categories—health and medical, veterans, housing, and other—are less important, together making up only about 2.5% of GDP and only a little over one tenth of overall social welfare spending.

Thus, only a small share of social welfare expenditures (about 16%) is spent on public assistance or welfare. The largest single item, and the one that is growing most rapidly, is social insurance, which in the United States is mainly composed of retirement and health care benefits for the elderly.

How Do U.S. Expenditures Compare to Those of Other Countries?

Another useful way to place U.S. social welfare expenditures in context is to compare them to social welfare expenditures by other Western industrialized countries. Table 3.3 shows social welfare expenditures as a share of GDP for 21 countries that are members of the Organization for Economic Cooperation and Development (OECD) at

TABLE 3.2   Expenditure on Major Types of Social Welfare Programs in the United States as a Percentage of Gross Domestic Product (GDP), 1929-1994

	Social Insurance	Public Aid	Health and Medical	Education	Veterans, Housing, and Other
1929	0.3	0.1	0.3	2.4	0.8
1940	1.3	3.8	0.6	2.7	0.8
1950	1.8	0.9	0.8	2.5	2.8
1955	2.4	0.8	0.8	2.8	1.7
1960	3.7	0.8	0.9	3.4	1.2
1965	4.0	0.9	0.9	4.0	1.2
1970	5.3	1.6	0.9	5.0	1.4
1975	7.7	2.6	1.0	5.1	1.8
1980	8.5	2.7	1.0	4.5	1.4
1985	9.0	2.4	0.9	4.2	1.3
1990	9.0	2.6	1.1	4.5	1.3
1994	10.0	3.5	1.2	5.0	1.3

SOURCE: *Social Security Bulletin*, Annual Statistical Supplement, 1981, Table 1; *Social Security Bulletin*, February 1990, Vol. 53, No. 2, Table 3; and *Social Security Bulletin*, Fall 1997, Vol. 60, No. 3, Table 2.

NOTE: Expenditures are expressed as a share of gross national product (GNP), instead of GDP, for the years 1929 and 1940.

three points in time, 1960, 1975, and 1990. Table 3.3 ranks countries by the share of their GDP that they dedicated to social welfare spending in 1990 (the most recent year for which comparable data are available). As in the earlier tables, the figures in this table refer only to public spending and do not include tax expenditures.

Table 3.3 shows that the U.S. share of GDP devoted to social welfare—20.1%—is well below the OECD average of 27.9%; indeed, the United States ranks 17th out of the 21 countries on this measure, with only four countries spending less as a share of their economy. Moreover, the U.S. ranking has not changed much over time: in 1960, only four countries spent a lower share of GDP on social welfare than the United States, and in 1975, only three countries did. If private spending and tax expenditures were included in this table, the U.S. ranking would be higher, but the United States would still be outspent by many other countries.

JUDGING THE ECONOMIC IMPACT OF SOCIAL WELFARE EXPENDITURES

With spending on social welfare at an all-time high in the United States, and yet low by international standards, how are we to judge whether we are now spending too much

TABLE 3.3 Government Social Welfare Expenditure as a Percentage of Gross Domestic Product (GDP) in Organization for Economic Cooperation and Development (OECD) Countries, 1960, 1975, and 1990 (countries ranked by percentage in 1990)

Rank	Country	1960	1975	1990
1	Sweden	15.6	27.4	39.6
2	Norway	11.0	23.2	35.5
3	Netherlands	12.8	29.3	34.4
4	Denmark	9.0	27.1	33.9
5	Finland	14.9	21.9	33.8
6	France	14.4	26.3	31.9
7	Belgium	NA	28.7	30.6
8	Austria	17.4	26.0	29.9
OECD	AVERAGE	12.3	21.9	27.9
9	United Kingdom	12.4	19.6	27.6
10	Germany	17.1	27.8	27.5
11	Italy	13.7	20.6	26.7
12	Canada	11.2	20.1	25.5
13	Ireland	11.3	22.0	25.2
14	Spain	NA	NA	23.8
15	Portugal	NA	NA	20.8
16	Switzerland	8.2	19.0	20.5
17	United States	9.9	18.7	20.1
18	New Zealand	12.7	19.0	19.8
19	Greece	NA	10.0	19.5
20	Australia	9.5	17.3	17.7
21	Japan	7.6	13.7	15.3

SOURCE: Kamerman and Kahn (1997), Table 4.1, p. 94.
NOTE: 1990 figures for Greece, Italy, and New Zealand are from 1985; 1990 figure for Switzerland is from 1984.

or too little on social welfare? In this section, three possible tests are discussed that can be used to decide this issue. The first test concerns macro-efficiency, that is, whether social welfare spending has negative effects on the economy as a whole. The second concerns possible adverse incentives associated with social welfare spending. The third test takes into account the well-being of the intended targets of the social welfare expenditures, that is, those who are the recipients of social welfare benefits and participants in the programs. Returning to the framework outlined at the start of the chapter, one can think of the first two tests as reflecting concerns about efficiency and the third as reflecting concerns about equity (as well as target efficiency), keeping in mind that trade-offs between the two are unavoidable.

Measuring the impact of the welfare state on economic efficiency is no easy task. Many analysts take it as given that strong economic performance in the United States is due at least in part to the fact that its welfare state is smaller and its labor market less tightly regulated than those of other Western industrialized nations, but the comparative evidence on such effects is not very strong (Blank, 1994; Burtless, 1994).

Looking within the United States, there is not much evidence of large adverse effects of social welfare expenditures on our economy over time. Most analysts would agree with Lampman (1985) that if there is a point at which welfare state spending would interfere with the smooth functioning of the economy, we have not reached it in the United States. This is not to say that such a point could not be reached (see, e.g., Freeman, Topel, & Swedenborg's 1997 work on Sweden) but rather that we have not come close to it.

There has been a great deal of work, and controversy, in recent years on the potential adverse effects of welfare on family formation. Charles Murray (1984) and other conservatives have argued forcefully that the American social welfare system creates perverse incentives that encourage out-of-wedlock childbearing and divorce and thus lead to the formation and maintenance of female-headed families. But evidence of such effects is lacking (see Moffitt, 1998, for the most recent review). Thus, most scholars have concluded that social welfare programs have had little or no effect on recipients' family formation decisions (Ellwood, 1988; Garfinkel & McLanahan, 1986).

There has also been a great deal of research on the effects of welfare on work incentives, and here the evidence of adverse effects is stronger (Blank, 1997). The issue, however, is not so much whether too much or too little is being spent on welfare as how that spending is allocated. As a result, the welfare system has undergone a series of reforms to improve work incentives, with most states now using both positive and negative incentives ("carrots and sticks") to reward work effort.

We also have some evidence with regard to equity, and here, we can more clearly address the question of whether we are now spending too little or too much on social welfare. If we can agree that a desired outcome of social insurance spending is to reduce economic insecurity and poverty among older Americans, then the increased spending on social insurance seems to be money well-spent, because it has reduced the poverty rate among those over 65 from nearly 30% in 1966 to just over 10% today (Kamerman & Kahn, 1998). The poverty statistics for older Americans also suggest that although spending for social insurance is now at record-high levels, we may not be spending enough or we may be spending inefficiently. Even after receiving social insurance, about 25% of the elderly poor (constituting about 10% of all elderly) are still poor (Danziger & Weinberg, 1994). If we want to eliminate poverty among older Americans, we will have to either spend more or shift some spending from the non-poor elderly to the poor elderly. However, this latter option would run the risk of undermining Social Security's universal appeal.

What are we to make of the spending on public assistance? We now spend more on means-tested public assistance, as a share of our economy, than at any point since the Great Depression, and yet, poverty rates among families with children remain stubbornly high. One in five children in the United States is poor, and for children under the age of 6, the rate is one in four (Kamerman & Kahn, 1998). Public assistance is not making much of a dent in the problem. In 1990, only about 6% of poor female-headed families were moved out of poverty by public assistance (Danziger & Weinberg, 1994).

Not everyone agrees that these high child poverty rates mean that we are spending too little on public assistance. Some would argue that aid itself may increase poverty in the long run by, for example, inducing young women to have children out of wedlock. However, it is clear in an accounting sense that if we spent more on public assistance and raised benefit levels for poor families, then at least in the short run, the incomes of poor families would be higher. This is not to say that public assistance is the only, or even the best, strategy to raise the incomes of poor families; as we shall see below, many countries use universal benefits to fight child poverty. Here, although cross-national comparisons can be perilous, the comparative data are certainly suggestive. Deborah Mitchell (1991) used data held by the Luxembourg Income Study to compare the social welfare systems of 10 industrialized countries across an array of measures and found that the United States ranked last in its effectiveness in reducing the poverty rate (the share of the population in poverty) and the poverty gap (the amount that would be needed to raise poor families' incomes up to the poverty line) and next to last in reducing income inequality (as measured by the Gini coefficient). In a study focused on families with children, Lee Rainwater and Tim Smeeding (1996) studied 18 industrialized countries participating in the Luxembourg Income Study and found that the U.S. social welfare system did the poorest job of bringing families with children out of poverty. Rainwater and Smeeding found that the high level of child poverty in the United States compared to other countries reflects not just the fact that many children live in single-parent families or families with low earnings but also the fact that the U.S. social welfare system does a poorer job of alleviating child poverty among these families. These results makes sense, given the relatively low amount spent on social welfare in the United States as compared to other countries, as shown in Table 3.3 (Smeeding, O'Higgins, & Rainwater, 1990). In social welfare, as in other domains, the old adage holds: You get what you pay for.

In thinking about the adequacy of spending on social welfare, it is important not to forget the smaller components of the system. For instance, health and medical expenditures make up only a small share of the social welfare system, reflecting the fact that the United States, unlike most other industrialized nations, has no system of universal health insurance. Although many Americans receive coverage privately, through their employers or through policies they purchase on their own, at any given point in time, an estimated 15% of Americans have no health insurance, and an even higher percentage (about 20%) lack health insurance at some point during the year (Bureau of the Census, 1996). Whether it would be better, in terms of both efficiency and equity, to move toward a universal system of health insurance in the United States continues to be actively debated. For an excellent overview on this issue, see Fuchs (1997).

A second example of an area in which the United States lags behind other countries is in the provision of universal benefits for families with young children. Most other industrialized countries have some form of universal child allowance or child benefit. This allowance is typically provided to families with children of all ages, but it plays a particularly important role for families with preschool-age children, who can use the allowance to offset the costs of a parent staying at home or to offset the cost of child care. In addition, most other countries provide other universal supports to families with young children, including paid maternity leave and publicly provided or subsidized child care for preschool-age children (Kamerman & Kahn, 1997). In the United States, in contrast, virtually all benefits for young children are targeted, although not necessarily to the lowest income families. Cash welfare benefits and a broad range of in-kind benefits (including day care programs such as Head Start and nutritional programs such as the Women, Infants, and Children program and Food Stamps) are targeted to poor families, as is the Earned Income Tax Credit for those with earnings. However, there is also an array of nonrefundable tax credits and tax deductions that mainly benefit nonpoor families because they can be claimed only by families who pay income taxes and, in the case of mortgage interest and property tax deductions, only by families that own property.

Would it be advantageous for the United States to move toward a universal early childhood allowance or some other type of universal early childhood program? Advocates of early childhood intervention point to the potential benefits in terms of child health and development, particularly in light of what we now know about the importance of children's experiences in the preschool years. Moreover, to the extent that young children are at disproportionately high risk of poverty, establishing a benefit for them could be an effective form of indicator targeting, with potentially much lower administrative and stigma costs than targeting on the basis of low income. However, there would also be costs entailed in moving toward more universal benefits for young children, and thus the merits of such a move depend on both efficiency and equity concerns. If the money for a universal early childhood allowance came from other programs where the spending was less effective, then it would be an improvement in terms of efficiency. Whether incentives would be improved is a more complicated question, because a universal program could avoid some of the adverse incentives of targeted welfare programs but might introduce others (for instance, fertility incentives) that might or might be not be seen as positive. Whether equity would be improved is a complicated question as well. If the new program was less redistributive than the ones it replaced, then equity would be adversely affected. However, if the program was at least as redistributive, then equity would be improved because social solidarity and social inclusion would be enhanced with all families receiving the same universal benefit.

SOCIAL SPENDING: TOO MUCH OR TOO LITTLE?

Although social welfare spending has increased dramatically in the United States since 1929, the share of our economy that is devoted to social welfare continues to be low by international standards. Although we now spend one fifth of every dollar in our economy on the "welfare state," most modern industrialized nations spend more.

It has also been shown that contrary to popular perceptions, most social welfare spending in the United States does not go to welfare. Cash and other forms of assistance to the poor make up only a small share (16%) of social welfare expenditures and a tiny share (3.5%) of the total economy. The largest component of the welfare state, and the one that is growing most rapidly, is social insurance that benefits the retired and the disabled: It now makes up about half of social welfare expenditures. Indeed, social insurance alone now takes up 10% of GDP, as much as the entire welfare state took up in 1960.

It is also clear from this review that there are no easy answers to whether the right amount is being spent on the social welfare system. The answer depends on which programs and which populations are being considered. Spending on social insurance for the elderly, for instance, has been high enough to substantially reduce poverty among its target population, whereas spending on public assistance and other programs for children has not.

Whether more or less should be spent on social welfare also depends on how much weight one places on efficiency versus equity concerns. Nevertheless, it is fair to conclude that there is little evidence in terms of efficiency that too much is being spent on the social welfare system, and some evidence in terms of equity that too little is being spent. Of particular concern in this regard are the programs such as public aid that seem to be inadequately funded as well as the programs such as universal health insurance and universal child allowances that do not exist at all.

Ultimately, an assessment of the social welfare system will also be affected by what we see as the aims of social welfare policy. We tend to think of those aims fairly narrowly, as we saw above, whereas many European countries are now moving to a broader conception that includes notions of reducing social exclusion and inequality. If, in the future, we decided as a nation that we wished to achieve those aims, and to assess the adequacy of our system in those terms, we would probably find that our current spending levels and patterns are even more inadequate than they appear today.

REFERENCES

Barr, N. (1998). *The economics of the welfare state* (3rd ed.). Oxford, UK: Oxford University Press.

Blank, R. (Ed.). (1994). *Social protection versus economic flexibility: Is there a tradeoff?* Chicago: University of Chicago Press.

Blank, R. (1997). *It takes a nation: A new agenda for fighting poverty.* Princeton, NJ: Princeton University Press.

Bureau of the Census. (1996). Dynamics of economic well-being: Health insurance, 1993-1995. *Current Population Reports.* Washington, DC: Government Printing Office.

Burtless, G. (1994). Public spending on the poor: Historical trends and economic limits. In S. Danziger, G. Sandefur, & D. Weinberg (Eds.), *Confronting poverty: Prescriptions for change* (pp. 51-84). Cambridge, MA: Harvard University Press.

Danziger, S., & Weinberg, D. (1994). The historical record: Trends in family income, inequality, and poverty. In S. Danziger, G. Sandefur, & D. Weinberg (Eds.), *Confronting poverty: Prescriptions for change* (pp. 18-50). Cambridge, MA: Harvard University Press.

Ellwood, D. (1988). *Poor support.* New York: Basic Books.

Freeman, R., Topel, R., & Swedenborg, B. (1997). *The welfare state in transition: Rethinking the Swedish model.* Chicago: University of Chicago Press.

Friedman, M. (1962). *Capitalism and freedom.* Chicago: University of Chicago Press.

Fuchs, V. (1997). *Who shall live: Health, economics, and social choice* (2nd ed.). River Edge, NJ: World Scientific Publishing.

Garfinkel, I. (1982). *Income-tested transfers: The case for and against.* New York: Academic Press.

Garfinkel, I., & McLanahan, S. (1986). *Single mothers and their children: A new American dilemma.* Washington, DC: Urban Institute Press.

Kamerman, S. B., & Kahn, A. J. (1997). *Starting right: How America neglects its youngest children and what we can do about it.* New York: Oxford University Press.

Kamerman, S. B., & Kahn, A. J. (1998). *Poverty and income distribution* (Mimeo). New York: Columbia University School of Social Work.

Lampman, R. (1985). *Balancing the books.* Washington, DC: National Conference on Social Welfare.

Mitchell, D. (1991). *Income transfers in ten welfare states.* Aldershot, UK: Avebury.

Moffitt, R. (1998). *Welfare, the family, and reproductive behavior: Research perspectives.* Washington, DC: National Academy Press.

Murray, C. (1984). *Losing ground: American social policy 1950-1980.* New York: Basic Books.

Okun, A. (1975). *Equality and efficiency: The big trade-off.* Washington, DC: The Brookings Institution.

Rainwater, L., & Smeeding, T. (1996). *Doing poorly: The real income of American children in comparative perspective* (Working Paper No. 127). Walferdange: Luxembourg Income Study.

Rawls, J. (1972). *A theory of justice.* Oxford, UK: Oxford University Press.

Smeeding, T., O'Higgins, M., & Rainwater, L. (Eds.). (1990). *Poverty, inequality, and income distribution in comparative perspective: The Luxembourg Income Study.* Washington, DC: The Urban Institute.

Titmuss, R. M. (1968). Universal and selective social services. In *Commitment to welfare* (pp. 113-123). London: George Allen & Unwin.

CHAPTER FOUR

Policy Analysis

BRUCE JANSSON

Policy selection lies at the heart of the policy-making process. Confronting policy issues or problems, policy practitioners and advocates must develop policy alternatives to address them, then select a preferred alternative in the course of policy deliberations. This process is commonly called *policy analysis* (Patton & Sawicki, 1993; Weimer & Vining, 1992).

After discussing the rational approach to policy analysis and the criticisms made of this approach, the chapter concludes that pure approaches or models seldom exist. Rather, values, data collection, and political considerations usually influence policy analysis, even if the relative emphasis on them differs between situations and among policy analysts.

THE RATIONAL APPROACH

The rational approach to policy analysis came of age in the 1960s as economists and systems analysts assumed major roles in policy selection (Heineman, Bluhm, Peterson, & Kearny, 1997). Rationalists were perturbed by the lack of rigor in the selection of policies in governmental and corporate settings, believing that empirical data were rarely used to compare and contrast policy alternatives or to evaluate existing policies (Meltsner, 1976). With the support of such government officials as Robert McNamara and Lyndon Johnson, ambitious projects were undertaken known as planning, programming, and budgeting systems; zero-based budgeting; and management by objectives. The first approach identified major objectives of government programs, requiring that alternative methods of achieving them be subjected to rigorous empirical analysis before making policy choices. Zero-based budgeting proposed periodically erasing existing policies and programs so that an array of policies could be compared to ascertain which of them would best achieve specific policy goals. Management by objectives is a process of rigorously defining an organization's objectives and developing program, budget, and policy strategies that will effectively achieve them. Spurred by these early efforts, the rational approach to policy selection has dominated the policy field in subsequent decades in academic settings and in some governmental arenas. Indeed, about 30 journals currently focus on policy analysis from a rational perspective (Einbinder, 1996).

The basic logic of the rational approach is described by a decision-making matrix that can be used in organizational, corporate, or governmental settings (Jansson, 1998; Patton & Sawicki, 1993). After studying a problem or issue, analysts identify objectives they wish to achieve and then operationalize them into one or more criteria. They identify policy alternatives, selecting the one that best meets the criteria. Assume, for example, that staff in a hospital want to increase responsiveness of services to Hispanic patients when few Hispanic medical staff or translators exist. They identify four alternative policy options: offering a cultural course for medical staff, creating a computerized list of Spanish-speaking employees (who can be mobilized to assist in specific cases), hiring interpreters, and recruiting 40 bilingual undergraduate volunteers from local colleges. They select four criteria: cost, effectiveness in helping patients with translations, political feasibility, and ease of implementation. Because they have identified multiple criteria, they must weight them, ranking them with numbers that cumulatively total 1.0 to establish the relative importance of each of them. (They rank cost as .3, effectiveness in helping patients with translations as .3, political feasibility as .2, and ease of implementation as .2). Drawing on the informed estimates of organizational consultants and existing research, they rank the four options from 1 (worst) to 10 (best) with respect to each of the criteria: Hiring more interpreters ranks worst (1) whereas creating the computerized list of Spanish-speaking employees gets the best score (8). They derive a score for each policy option with respect to each criterion by multiplying the rankings of the four options on each of the criteria by the weight of the criteria. After totaling the scores of each option, they select the option of recruiting 40 bilingual undergraduate volunteers because its total score (7.8) exceeds the other policy alternatives.

When using a rational approach to social policies in governmental contexts, a single criterion, such as efficiency, effectiveness, cost-effectiveness, and cost-benefit criteria, is often used. When using *efficiency* as a criterion, policy makers select the alternative that is least expensive; when using *effectiveness,* they select the alternative that brings the best outcomes. They might compare two job-training strategies for welfare recipients, for example, choosing the one that most effectively removes recipients from the rolls. Or they might identify several outcomes, such as the extent to which recipients leave the rolls and the level of earnings of graduates 6 months later, selecting the job training option that yields the best aggregate benefits.

Rationalists sometimes couple several criteria into a single measure. In the case of *cost-effectiveness* criteria, for example, they examine both the cost and the effectiveness of policy alternatives, selecting the policy option that is both efficient and effective (Chambers, Wedel, & Rodwell, 1992). Under this approach, a job training strategy for welfare recipients that placed many of them in jobs at a relatively low cost per placement would receive a high score as compared with a strategy that was equally effective but more costly. *Cost-benefit* analyses aim to measure the net benefits to society when the costs to society are compared with the benefits to society (Weimer & Vining, 1992). Analysts estimate the costs of a policy alternative by gauging how much it costs and estimating its *opportunity costs*. The opportunity cost is the interest that could have been earned on the funds had they not been expended. They then estimate the value of the benefits rendered to society by the policy alternative, such as (in the case of a job training strategy for recipients) increases in tax revenues from enhanced job earnings and averted welfare payments for recipients who leave the rolls. Analysts then compare the ratio of costs to benefits: A policy alternative with a 1:1 ratio, where costs equal benefits, would be regarded as inferior to a policy alternative with a 1:5 ratio, where society receives benefits far exceeding the cost of a policy option.

Although comparisons of policy alternatives in the context of one or more criteria often yield important findings, policy analysts provide a relatively static analysis of dynamic phenomena. Many analysts use a systems framework to study complex phenomena and to gauge the likely effects of specific policies. Take the case of the welfare dependency of single heads of households, for example, as portrayed in Figure 4.1, which identifies an array of factors that, singly and in tandem, influence the likely outcomes of the Personal Responsibility and Work Opportunities Act of 1996 (Jansson, 1998). Susceptible populations (on the left of Figure 4.1) are people not currently on the rolls but at risk (in varying degrees) of becoming recipients. Neither susceptible or current recipients are homogenous populations; as the typology in Figure 4.1 suggests, they include recipients with different skill levels, job experience, levels of disability, motivation to leave the rolls, and longevity on the rolls. These various factors describe, singly and in tandem, the likelihood that specific people will obtain and keep jobs. Nor is postwelfare experience understandable in simple terms, because it involves work activity for varying lengths of time, at different levels of remuneration, and with varying levels of state subsidies for short or extended periods. The welfare issue is associated, moreover, with various indirect effects; as rolls diminish, for example, local costs associated with foster care, homelessness, and general relief may

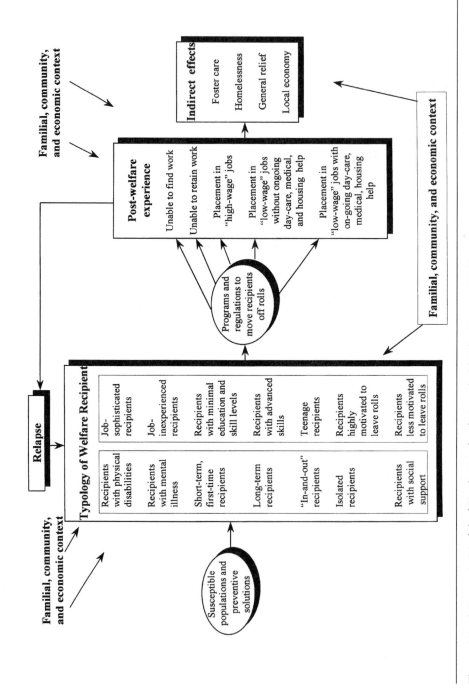

Figure 4.1. A Dynamic Model of Single Heads of Household Who Become Welfare Recipients

SOURCE: Jansson (1999).

increase if large numbers of former recipients only find jobs that pay them at or near the minimum wage.

A dynamic view of such problems as welfare, moreover, requires that contextual factors be included, such as familial, community, and economic ones (see Figure 4.1). Recipients live in families and communities whose cultures, patterns of interaction, and characteristics may profoundly influence the outcomes of welfare policies. The ability of recipients to obtain assistance from relatives, such as help with child care or financial assistance, may influence the ability of recipients to survive on low wages. Economic realities, such as up- or downturns in a local economy, can facilitate or frustrate efforts to diminish the size of rolls. The decisions of thousands of employers to hire—or not to hire—welfare recipients powerfully influence the ability of government to reduce the rolls. Indeed, many employers may not hire recipients unless given substantial and ongoing subsidies.

Were policy analysts desirous of analyzing the likely effects of the Personal Responsibility and Work Opportunity Reconciliation Act, they would have to examine complex interactions between the various elements of Figure 4.1 (Wolch & Sommer, 1997). Moreover, they would need to identify possible contingencies, such as the effects of an economic upturn on the one hand and an economic downturn on the other hand. The power to predict likely outcomes of the Act becomes weaker as the complexity of interactions *and* the range of possible future events increases. Yet, modeling and simulations of likely policy outcomes in the context of a systems framework are often preferable to statical analyses that only examine the interactions of several factors.

The Role of Research

The rubric of policy analysis includes research into the causes of specific social problems, because analysts' perceptions of these causes powerfully shape the kinds of policy options they will consider. Reanalyzing data reported by Herrnstein and Murray (1994) in *The Bell Curve,* sociologists at the University of California at Berkeley contended, for example, that welfare dependence stems from a system of inequality that places certain people at particular risk of welfare dependence (Fischer et al., 1996). These sociologists disputed Herrnstein and Murray's contention that welfare dependence was primarily caused by intelligence, arguing that *cognitive skills*—a term they preferred to *intelligence*—are themselves caused by such environmental factors as parental home and the adolescent community. Women who enter adolescence with multiple and interacting deficits in their environments, such as coming from low-income families, being tracked into noncollege classes in school, and living in communities with primarily low-paying service jobs, are more likely than others to become welfare recipients, no matter what their innate abilities. The

Berkeley sociologists' analysis led them to support an array of interventions in communities and schools, as well as job training and educational programs for recipients themselves.

If correlational data provide important insights into the causes of social problems, other strategies are used by policy analysts, as well. They compare people with a social problem with people who do not have that problem to infer from their differences why certain people develop the problem. They follow people through time to discover when they develop a problem, for example, following teen women over time to discern why some of them become pregnant and join welfare rolls. They evaluate existing programs to find clues to a problem's causes. If an evaluation of job training programs discovers, for example, that a program that offers expansive child care benefits yields better outcomes than other programs, a policy analyst might deduce that inadequate child care is a cause of welfare dependency. Policy analysts get information directly from people who are experiencing a specific problem, by observing them (as in anthropological studies) or by interviewing them (Jansson, 1998).

Epidemiological research in public health also provides useful insights to policy analysts who seek measures to prevent social problems (Bloom, 1981). It identifies negative factors that place people at varying degrees of risk of developing a problem as well as strengths or environmental supports that immunize some people from developing specific problems. These findings, in turn, are linked to research on interventions, whether to diminish or reduce at-risk factors or to bolster strengths or environmental supports. Policy analysts seek preventive strategies that focus resources on true positives (people who will develop a problem) rather than false positives (people with at-risk signs who do not develop a problem) or false negatives (people lacking at-risk signs who develop a problem).

Marketing research is also used by policy analysts. As Aaron, Mann, and Taylor (1994) note, values profoundly shape the actions and choices of people that policies aim to help, influence, or regulate, even if academics and policy analysts often "take values, habits, and social norms as given [and] beyond analysis and the reach of public policy" (p. 1). Influenced by economists to emphasize incentives, analysts often assume that mere provision of services or resources will suffice, not sufficiently considering how consumers' values and norms profoundly shape how they respond to specific services, resources, or opportunities. Analysts use survey research, focus groups, and client satisfaction studies to obtain data about perceptions, values, and desires of potential or actual users of social programs (Kotler, 1989).

Other empirical techniques are available to policy analysts. They can use multiple regression techniques to predict future trends, such as using historical trends, to predict future rates of crimes (Gupta, 1994). They can use decision trees to illuminate the relative merits of alternative choices (Behn & Vaulpel, 1982). They can use geographical analysis to locate specific problems and to analyze their causes (Maguire,

1991; Queralt & Witte, 1998). They can use the Delphi technique to elicit policy alternatives, criteria, and rankings from informed experts (Gupta, 1994). They can use needs assessment techniques to gauge the incidence, prevalence, and location of specific social problems (Mayer, 1985).

Policy analysis that is grounded in use of empirical data has many advantages. By basing policy selection on data, policy analysts can avoid selection that is based on best guesses, tradition, professional wisdom, or political considerations. An empirical approach forces policy analysts to structure their inquiry systematically. It fosters critical discussion of options, criteria, rankings of options, and choices by publicly disclosing assumptions and data. It can be used in agency as well as governmental settings (Kettner, Moroney, & Martin, 1990).

CRITICISMS OF THE RATIONAL MODEL

Despite its currency in academic, think-tank, and government settings, critics cite political, value-based, and methodological problems with the rational model of policy analysis. Rationalists usually assume that decision makers will use their analytic findings to make policy choices, whether in organizational or legislative settings, but this assumption is often incorrect (Heineman et al., 1997). Mann and Ornstein (1995) contend, for example, that Congress does not usually make important health policy decisions in a rational way, responding instead to political pressures from interest groups, partisan competition, or ideology. A dramatic example of indifference to empirical data was demonstrated when President Bill Clinton decided in 1998 not to allow Donna Shalala, Secretary of Health and Human Services, to announce public funding of sterilized needles to drug addicts, even though scientific evidence demonstrated that this policy would markedly reduce transmission of the HIV virus without stimulating additional use of drugs, as was alleged by many conservatives. Often ignored when they conflict with ideological preferences or strongly held beliefs, rationalists' arguments are often overridden, as well, when legislators and political leaders believe the findings conflict with their political interests. Indeed, such a leader as Lyndon Johnson *began* his analysis with political questions, not even considering policy initiatives until he was convinced that he could build sufficient support for them. Most legislators and political leaders have scant knowledge of research, economics, or statistics, making them unlikely to read technical analyses.

Indeed, many political scientists contend an "iron triangle" of interest groups, bureaucrats, and legislators often shapes policy on the basis of interests and tradition (Smith, 1988). When rationalists seek to eliminate a specific program on grounds that it is ineffective, for example, they are often opposed by the program's defenders, whose resources and power would decline if it were eliminated.

Public opinion can also promote opposition to rationalists' arguments, as illustrated by widespread indifference to technical arguments opposing the death penalty and gun control in specific jurisdictions, not to mention investing of resources in job training and child care to help welfare recipients leave the rolls.

Politics shapes policy analysis in other ways, as well. Desirous of enacting policies that bring political benefits—and wanting to enact policies when windows of opportunity exist—public officials seldom wait for extended technical analyses of alternative policies. Indeed, Smith (1988) likens policy innovation to surfing, as politicians try to ride waves of media coverage and public opinion that support specific innovations, afraid that the waves will dissipate if they fail to move rapidly. Public officials often develop policies in uncharted areas before extensive evaluative or social science data exist, forcing policy analysts to choose between policy options with scant information. Few people could accurately predict in 1996, for example, the likely effects of the Personal Responsibility and Work Opportunity and Reconciliation Act because only the scattered precedents of waiver programs in various states preceded its enactment.

As the study by Herrnstein and Murray (1994), which was described earlier, suggests, participants in policy debates often opportunistically use data to support positions that they held *before* they commenced their policy analysis. Already believing that welfare recipients were parasites and should be dealt with in a punitive fashion, Herrnstein and Murray (1994) marshaled empirical data to support this position, even though many social scientists subsequently criticized their research methodology.

Other critics question whether rationalists overstate the scientific nature of their work, because values intrude at many points (Hawkesworth, 1988; Jansson, 1990). Analysts use conceptual lenses to order reality, such as ecological, medical, deviance, or other perspectives (Rubington & Weinberg, 1989). These lenses powerfully influence their perceptions of problems, the kinds of variables they include in their research, and their interpretation of data. As some advocates of rational approaches concede, the selection and weighting of criteria are primarily determined by values, ideology, or political considerations. Different analysts use different—and conflicting—criteria that reflect their value premises when examining welfare policy. If some conservative analysts, for example, prioritize rapid reduction of welfare rolls, relatively liberal analysts are more likely to favor improving the economic condition of recipients over an extended period. Liberal analysts are less likely to want reduction in rolls at the price of erosion of the economic condition of recipients, framing welfare reform as an antipoverty initiative rather than as a cost-saving device. Whereas some welfare analysts use a short time frame to compare alternatives, selecting alternatives that demonstrate success in a year or less, other analysts advocate longer time frames.

Interpretations of data are also shaped by values. When faced with ambiguous data, analysts must decide whether "the glass is half full or half empty." In the case of evaluations of programs, for example, data rarely suggest overwhelming success, even when statistically significant differences exist between control and experimental groups. Deciding where to establish minimum thresholds of success required to declare a policy to be meritorious is a value-laden enterprise. Nor is it easy to decide whether adverse side effects of a policy possess sufficient magnitude to rescind it. In the case of evaluations of guaranteed income, for example, analysts differed regarding whether heightened divorce rates that accompanied a guaranteed income constituted sufficient grounds for rejecting the policy itself.

The values of analysts also shape how they define specific social problems. If some analysts define poverty in absolute terms, such as subscribing to the market-basket approach of the federal government, others define it in relative terms by focusing on the extent of economic disparities between different social classes. In each case, the analysts must decide what thresholds must be exceeded to bring someone into poverty—also a value-laden choice. As Rein (1983) notes, "the facts we attend to depend upon the construction we impose on reality" (p. 86). Indeed, the decision that a condition in the external world is or is not a "problem" is highly shaped by cultural and value considerations, as history and comparative studies amply reveal. If reading and learning disorders were not commonly viewed as problems in the 1960s, for example, they were widely seen as major problems three decades later.

When viewing the same data, moreover, analysts may interpret their findings in strikingly different fashion. Take the example of the failure of most job training programs to markedly improve earnings of former welfare recipients over an extended period when compared with welfare recipients not receiving any job training (Grubb, 1996). Most short-term earnings improvements erode with time, meaning that trainees in the long term tend to have incomes roughly commensurate with people who were not trained. This adverse finding prompts some people to abandon training altogether or to rely on job placement and referral programs. Others contend these negative findings should lead to *increased* public funding of job training and remedial education, contending that the ineffectiveness of past programs stems from their short-term and fragmented nature. Grubb (1996) advocates that many low-income people receive an extended sequence of training and education, often spread over many years, that yields credentials that have been demonstrated to catapult people into jobs that pay relatively high wages.

Ethical objections have been raised against some technical approaches. Cost-benefit studies can yield findings, for example, that discriminate against certain kinds of populations. When applied to programs to assist populations that cannot work, such as terminally ill people, cost to benefit ratios are likely to be relatively high because these people cannot produce monetary benefits to society by working (Heineman et al., 1997).

The work of policy analysts is also influenced by political realities. When identifying policy options, for example, analysts frequently do not consider options that lack political feasibility, such as drastic shifts from the status quo. When they work in legislative or bureaucratic settings—or conduct analysis under contract in academic settings—the views of their sponsors often influence their work, perhaps focusing them toward certain policy options that sponsors favor.

DIFFERENT MODELS—OR VARIATIONS ON A THEME?

A strong case can be made, then, that policy analysis remains an art rather than a science (Bardach, 1996; Heineman et al., 1997; Majone, 1989). It often contains rational elements, such as sophisticated use of data to illuminate social issues and to select policy options. Indeed, with the explosion of social science, economic, and medical research, most policy analysts *have* to use some data to buttress their case if their arguments are to merit consideration by decision makers.

But the relative emphasis given to rational, value, and political factors varies between analysts and specific analytic projects. Value-based analysts are likely to identify value-focused criteria and policy options that conform with their personal beliefs (Gil, 1981; Moroney, 1985). Whereas analysts in conservative think tanks often select policies that advance devolution, rights, and choice, analysts in liberal think tanks are more likely to favor policy options that promote equality, social justice, and fairness. To the extent that analysts use legal arguments to support or oppose specific policy options, they use normative criteria drawn from legal precedents or the Constitution, such as opposing (or supporting) on constitutional grounds a policy that legalizes euthanasia (Turnbull, 1985).

Legislative aides and some civil servants are likely to emphasize political criteria. When circumstances favor it, such as when tidal shifts in public opinion occur or when the balance of power changes markedly in a legislative setting, they may support policy options that propose sweeping changes from the status quo (Brown, 1990; Kingdon, 1997). More typically, they favor incremental shifts because these are less likely to attract opposition from people and groups who support existing policies (Lindblom, 1968).

University-based and some think-tank analysts are more likely to emphasize rational analysis. Emancipated from the political process, possessing resources and time to complete sophisticated studies, and working in a setting that accords quantitative work considerable prestige, they frequently develop extended research projects.

Yet, few of these analysts can escape values or political realities—and most of them have to use data at some point. Rather than distinct models of policy analysis, then, perhaps different analysts place differing emphasis on rational, political, and value-focused criteria. Different emphases can be used sequentially and iteratively. Perhaps policy analysts begin with a rational model that locates specific options and produces data to determine their relative merit. Then, perhaps the analysts decide to factor political realities into their analysis as they realize that their preferred (rational) option has virtually no chance of selection. Then, perhaps they decide to include a value-based criterion, even (again) shifting their choice. Or perhaps the inclusion of political and value-based criteria leads them to include new options in their analysis, thus enriching their deliberations.

Different emphases may exist within a specific analytic project when complex proposals are developed in legislative settings. Take the development of a federal shelter program as discussed by Jansson (1998), where a policy practitioner develops a multifaceted piece of legislation that includes a mission for the program, locating the program in the federal bureaucracy, determining its auspices, and determining myriad other policies. With respect to some of these policy choices, political considerations will likely prevail, such as when a powerful faction will oppose the legislation, no matter its overall merit, if a certain policy is chosen. With respect to other issues, legislators may be willing to be governed by rational considerations. With respect to yet other issues, values may predominate. So policy analysts need to be agile, emphasizing different kinds of criteria as they engage in different projects. If they want decision makers to use their products, moreover, they need to place their work in a broader political and cultural context. Policy analysis is embedded in a larger policy-making process that includes agenda building, policy analysis, policy enactment, policy implementation, and policy assessment (Jansson, 1998). If policy analysts want their work to influence decisions within this broader context, they need to include important stakeholders in their projects from the outset and at multiple points during it, both to gain insights and to increase the chances that their work will influence decisions. They need to disseminate their results to advocacy groups and decision makers in a manner that makes a convincing case (Bardach, 1996). In short, excessively narrow definitions of policy analysis that emphasize only technical skills place analysts in a restrictive niche. To avoid relegating their work to the sidelines of the policy-making process, policy analysts need to couple their technical skills with political, interactional, and value-clarifying ones.

REFERENCES

Aaron, H., Mann, T., & Taylor, T. (Eds.). (1994). *Values and public policy.* Washington, DC: The Brookings Institution.

Bardach, E. (1996). *The eight-step path of policy analysis (a handbook for practice)*. Berkeley, CA: Berkeley Academic Press.

Behn, D., & Vaulpel, J. (1982). *Quick analysis for busy decision makers*. New York: Basic Books.

Bloom, M. (1981). *Primary prevention: The possible science*. Englewood Cliffs, NJ: Prentice Hall.

Brown, R. (1990). *The logic of congressional action*. New Haven, CT: Yale University Press.

Chambers, D., Wedel, K., & Rodwell, M. (1992). *Evaluating social programs*. Boston: Allyn & Bacon.

Einbinder, S. (1996). Policy analysis. In National Association of Social Workers (Ed.), *Encyclopedia of social work* (19th ed., pp. 1849-1855). Silver Springs, MD: National Association of Social Workers.

Fischer, C., Hout, M., Jankowski, M., Lucas, S., Swidler, A., & Voss, K. (1996). *Inequality by design*. Princeton, NJ: Princeton University Press.

Gil, D. (1981). *Unraveling of social policy* (3rd ed.). Cambridge, MA: Schenkman.

Grubb, W. (1996). *Learning to work*. New York: Russell Sage Foundation.

Gupta, D. (1994). *Decisions by the numbers*. Englewood Cliffs, NJ: Prentice Hall.

Hawkesworth, M. (1988). *Theoretical issues in policy analysis*. Albany: State University of New York Press.

Heineman, R., Bluhm, W., Peterson, S., & Kearny, E. (1997). *The world of the policy analyst*. Chatham, NJ: Chatham House.

Herrnstein, R. J., & Murray, C. (1994). *The bell curve: Intelligence and class structure in American life*. New York: Free Press.

Jansson, B. (1990). Blending social change and technology in macro-practice: Developing structural dialogue in technical deliberations. *Administration in Social Work, 14,* 13-28.

Jansson, B. (1999). *Becoming an effective policy advocate: From policy practice to social justice*. Belmont, CA: Wadsworth.

Kettner, P., Moroney, R., & Martin, L. (1990). *Designing and managing programs*. Newbury Park, CA: Sage.

Kingdon, J. (1997). *Agendas, alternatives, and public choices*. Boston: Little, Brown.

Kotler, P. (1989). *Principles of marketing* (4th ed.). Englewood Cliffs, NJ: Prentice Hall.

Lindblom, C. (1968). *The policy making process*. Englewood Cliffs, NJ: Prentice Hall.

Maguire, D. (1991). An overview and definition of GIS. In D. Maguire, M. Goochild, & D. Rhind (Eds.), *Geographical information systems: Principles and applications: Vol. 1. Principles* (pp. 9-20). New York: John Wiley.

Majone, G. (1989). *Evidence, argument, and persuasion in the policy process*. New Haven, CT: Yale University Press.

Mann, T., & Ornstein, N. (1995). *How Congress shapes health policy*. Washington, DC: The Brookings Institution.

Mayer, R. (1985). *Policy and program planning*. Englewood Cliffs, NJ: Prentice Hall.

Meltsner, A. (1976). *Policy analysts in the bureaucracy*. Berkeley: University of California Press.

Moroney, R. (1981). Policy analysis within a value theoretical framework. In R. Haskins & J. Gallagher (Eds.), *Models for analysis of social policy* (pp. 78-101). Norwood, NJ: Ablex.

Patton, C., & Sawicki, D. (1993). *Basic methods of policy analysis and planning*. Englewood Cliffs, NJ: Prentice Hall.

Queralt, M., & Witte, A. (1998). A map for you? Geographic information systems in the social services. *Social Work, 43,* 455-469.

Rein, M. (1983). Value-critical policy analysis. In D. Callhan & B. Jennings (Eds.), *Ethics, the social sciences, and policy analysis* (pp. 83-111). New York: Plenum.

Rubington, E., & Weinberg, M. (1989). *The study of social problems* (4th ed.). New York: Oxford University Press.

Smith, H. (1988). *The power game: How Washington works*. New York: Ballantine.

Turnbull, H. (1981). Two legal analysis techniques and public policy analysis. In R. Haskins & J. Gallagher (Eds.), *Models for analysis of social policy* (pp. 153-173). Norwood, NJ: Ablex.

Weimer, D., & Vining, A. (1992). *Policy analysis: Concepts and practice*. Englewood Cliffs, NJ: Prentice Hall.

Wolch, J., & Sommer, H. (1997). *Era of welfare reform*. Los Angeles: Southern California Inter-University Consortium on Homelessness and Poverty.

CHAPTER FIVE

Policy Practice

DEAN PIERCE

The policy-making involvement of direct service providers in social welfare, education, and health care settings has dramatically increased over the past decade and a half. Although policy making was previously regarded as the domain of politicians and professional planners, today, teachers, nurses, mental health professionals, and social workers have become deeply involved in the process of policy formulation and implementation.

For example, one study about teachers and school reform identified three groups of educational professionals who contribute to reform. These include the professionals who believe in reform, those who actively embrace and support reform, and those who actually become involved in making school reforms through engaging in the policy process (Bank & Hall, 1997). In addition, the use of decentralized decision making and shared governance in schools leads to successful and ongoing policy change in which teachers play an active part (Bank & Hall, 1997).

In the field of mental health, professionals have also become more involved in policy practice. The positive consequences of their involvement have also been recognized and analyzed. For example, in writing about the involvement of professionals in policy making, Smith and Meyer (1987) note that one "theme has been the significant impact that mental health professionals can have on the law directly (by participating in the legal system as witnesses and consultants)" (p. 658).

Holtzman (1985) points to both an impetus toward and an example of professional involvement in policy making and implementation. In discussing the impact of federal budget cuts during the Reagan administration, he notes that after the initial shock and disbelief had worn off, political opposition from professionals who had previously not engaged in policy debates grew more active. Psychologists, psychiatrists, nurses, social workers, and social scientists all began to express strong opposition to the cuts and exerted pressure on the administration for restoration.

As a result of their involvement, some budget cuts were in fact restored, and the most outrageous proposals and actions were effectively countered. As a result of the protests of thousands of individuals and professional organizations, the harshest impacts of the cuts were mitigated.

Nursing was one of the first professions to reassess the role of providers in policy making. Discussing the way nurses began to engage in policy making, Wieczorek (1985) pointed out that nurses gradually began to realize that they needed power in their places of employment. They came to believe that power should be based on the level of knowledge, skill, experience, and area of responsibility of professionals. Today, nurses are having a significant impact on government health policy by being highly active in the political and legislative arenas. Nurses are now more extensively involved in making policy related to nursing practice, health care reimbursement practices, and laws and regulations affecting the health of the people they serve.

Debates about the role of social workers in policy making have a long history. In their conception of practice, some of the founders of social work linked an analysis of social conditions to the need for social policy action. However, within a few decades, social work educators and practitioners came to view policy as a set of laws, regulations, and rules that guided social work practice. They accepted that these laws and regulations were made chiefly by actors other than social workers. Their conception of policy was limited to the analysis and understanding of written policies. Only a few social work planners and policy analysts were engaged in policy making. By and large, most social work practice was thought to take place outside the policy-making realm.

By the early 1980s, however, several authors offered a different perspective on policy in social work. During this time, several models of what Jansson (1984) has termed policy practice were published. Examples include those of Jansson (1984, 1994), Pierce (1984), Wyers (1991), Flynn (1992), and Schorr (1985). Building on the notion that policies come from identifiable social and political processes (Burns, 1956; Gilbert & Specht, 1974), these authors began to explore ways in which social workers could analyze and create social policies that were in line with the values of the profession and the needs of clients. Most of these models clearly identified steps in policy analysis, development, and implementation.

In spite of this re-emergence of the concept that policy action is a natural part of social work practice, some models, such as that of Jansson (1984) or Flynn (1992), emphasize policy analysis, formal written policies, and highly structured policy-making processes to the exclusion of policy action, informal unwritten policies, and less formally structured policy-making processes. Other writers place more emphasis on these informal aspects. Wyers (1991) concludes that at least five overlapping perspectives about policy practice have emerged. These include social workers as policy experts or specialists, change agents in internal or external work environments, the connection or conduit through which policy is implemented and integrated in practice, and actual makers and interpreters of policy. Hence, ideas about policy practice range from those that encompass only some social workers dealing with limited types of policies (Burch, 1996; Johnson, 1994) to those that call on all social workers to become involved in an unlimited range of policy-related activities (Figueira-McDonough, 1993; Holosko & Au, 1996; McInnis-Dittrich, 1994; Weick & Saleeby, 1995).

Today, many writers on policy practice take a very broad view of the involvement of social workers in the field. For example, Wyers (1991) contends that policy practice in social work involves all practitioners, including those engaged in direct practice. Policy practice is a responsibility of frontline social workers and supervisors in either public or private settings. However, to be effective, this requires that direct service practitioners understand and be able to analyze the effects of policy decisions on clients. It also requires that they participate in the formulation and modification of social policies. Practitioners should be especially sensitive to policies that are harmful to clients. To achieve these goals, practitioners must be active at multiple policy levels including the personal, the organizational, the community, and the legislative.

Several recent developments have reinforced the idea that the professional activities of every social worker include those related to making and implementing policy. In addition, it has been argued that social workers should encourage their clients and the wider community to engage in policy action. The *NASW Code of Ethics,* for example, calls for social workers to promote public participation in policy making, engage in social and political action themselves, and advocate for programs and policies that promote the rights of and confirm equity and social and economic justice for all people.

Moreover, the latest standards of the Commission on Accreditation of the Council on Social Work Education strongly connect policy to practice. The *Curriculum Policy Statement* of the Commission on Accreditation (1994) states, in its discussion of the purposes of social work, that the profession is committed to: "The pursuit of policies, services, resources, and programs through organizational or administrative advocacy and social or political action, to empower groups at risk and to promote social and economic justice" (pp. 97, 135).

POLICY PRACTICE

For line workers and generalist practitioners, a policy model must incorporate positive values and attitudes about engaging in policy-making activities. This model must build a policy frame of reference that values the importance of integrating policy and practice. A model of this kind must also focus on knowledge of specific policies and policy-making processes that are grounded in the social worker's practice. It must develop policy analysis and intervention skills that lead to policy-related practice activities.

It was noted earlier that no one has expected policy making to play a role in direct social work practice. For this reason, direct practitioners need to learn about policy practice and also adopt a frame of reference that lends support to the emerging professional expectation that they incorporate policy in their practice. Above all, they need a positive attitude toward policy (Gitterman & Miller, 1989).

The conventional understanding of the role of social workers and nurses in policy making assumes that it is an *inactive* one. Someone other than the worker makes policy, and the worker adheres to it. A second way of viewing the relationship between policy making and practice has assumed a *reactive* role for the worker. While others initiate the analysis and development of policy, workers might be consulted about their input (Gilbert & Specht, 1974; Holosko & Au, 1996). The third view includes an expectation that all workers must engage in policy making. In other words, workers are expected to be *proactive* about their role in policy making (Pierce, 1984; Mason, Talbott, & Leavitt, 1993).

Unfortunately, these competing expectations pose a potential role conflict for social workers, nurses, and other social welfare professionals. Whereas some institutions expect inaction on the part of workers, the profession itself now calls for a more proactive stance. Hence, in their professional education and ongoing professional socialization, social workers require a policy frame of reference that values making policy and supports realistic policy interventions.

IDENTIFYING POLICIES OF CONCERN

The practitioner also must define and identify policies as broadly as possible. Moreover, such policies should be evaluated in relation to the purposes and values of the profession. In addition, all policies that may be relevant to the worker's clients should be identified, including informal and unwritten as well as formal written policies. Table 5.1 helps identify and systematize all the elements that compose an analysis of policies of concern. It may be used by policy practitioners to identify these policies of concern for different groups of clients.

TABLE 5.1   POLICIES OF CONCERN

NAME OF CONSUMER _____

Policy focus derived from social work purposes and values to: 1. Enhance social functioning 2. Meet basic human needs 3. Achieve social justice	Informal Unwritten					Formal Written				
	Personal Policies (or practices)			Group Policies (Or Practices)		Organizational Policies		Social Policies (Law)		Social Welfare Policies (Bureaucratic Regulations)
	Social Worker	Colleague	Consumer	Informal Group of Colleagues	Consumer Group	Professional Association	Social Agency	Local Community	Soc. at Large	
1. Addresses emotional, intellectual, vocational, environmental, spiritual, and social needs										
2. Addresses basic physiological and safety needs										
3. Policies by which the system operates itself										

57

Smith and Meyer (1987) note the importance of ethics for all professionals to follow in meeting their obligations to clients, other professionals, and society. To meet their ethical obligations, social workers should be familiar with policies that enhance social functioning and meet basic human needs, and they should be able to explain how policy-making systems work. These activities enable social workers to fulfill their fundamental duties of strengthening people's capacities for effective functioning, providing them with optimum living conditions, and creating just service-delivery programs and services.

Policy practice is applied across a range of systems that deal with the resource needs and rights of social welfare consumers. Mason et al. (1993) identify four spheres of political action for nurses, including the workplace, government, professional organizations, and the community. For social workers, Pierce (1984) identifies policies in five areas: personal, group, service agency, regulating bureaucracies, and laws. These are listed in the categorization of policies of concern shown in Table 5.1.

Informal, unwritten policies of individuals and small groups, sometimes referred to as *practices,* are just as important as the formal policies that are the primary focus of policy analysis. Informal policies can have a major impact on the way formal policies are developed and implemented. They are the consistent patterns or plans that guide how these individuals or groups consistently allocate their resources (knowledge, time, networks) in practice. Examples include a worker who places job security above social action or the social worker who does not involve certain clients such as unwed fathers in his or her practice. The personal policies of social work colleagues can also have a critical impact on performance. An example is the medical colleague who does not respect and consistently undermines social work services or the psychiatrist who assigns social workers only certain duties. The personal policies of individual clients have an equally important effect on policy practice. Clients whose policies result in cooperation with social workers obviously facilitate the effective implementation of programs whereas those whose policies create conflict obviously impede the process.

Small groups that have informal policies include groups of clients, such as families or youth gangs. In addition, informal work groups also have policies. Examples of these policies are rules of communication in a family or the rules that determine gang membership and behavior.

Typically, the policies of organizations, whether these are professional associations or service-delivery agencies and the social or social welfare policy of laws, statutes, court decisions, and bureaucratic regulations, have received the bulk of attention. Thus, practitioners should determine the specific bureaucratic and professional organizations, social and other service agencies, and state and federal laws that deal with their clientele.

POLICY-MAKING PROCESSES AND POLICY MAKERS

Identifying all policies related to professional purposes across a range of systems is the first part of the practitioner's policy knowledge base. The second aspect of the policy practitioner's knowledge base involves understanding policy-formulation processes and the people who use them to make policy. By applying system ideas to the clusters of policy-making entities used to identify policies of concern (personal, group, organizational, social, and social welfare), an analytical framework can be developed for worker use.

The framework uses system ideas of input, process, output, and feedback and can be applied to understanding specific policy-making entities, including individuals, groups, agencies, legislatures, and bureaucracies. Input, of course, is the ideas about policy that are used in the system's policy-making process. These include experiences, knowledge, values, assumptions, existing policies, and policies from other systems. Identifiable individuals guide this process.

The system's output or product is its policy, whether the practices of a worker, an agency rule, a law, or a bureaucratic regulation. Small-group policy outputs include family rules as well as small-group rules. Regarding organizational policies, outputs include board decisions, manuals of policy and procedures, and annual plans. Outputs derived from social policies include laws, court decisions, and local ordinances. Social welfare policy outputs include bureaucratic regulations.

In addition to providing knowledge of the policy practice process, the framework identifies points for practitioner participation in the policy making of each system and highlights those places where practitioners can provide feedback. Major opportunities for the modification or revision of policy include the amendment of laws, hearings to assess the impact of policies, and, of course, systematic evaluation research.

Examples of these various components of the policy-making process are summarized in Table 5.2. As may be seen from this table, the policy-making process takes place at various levels, including the personal, group, organizational, and social. At the social welfare level, a variety of legislative and regulatory/bureaucratic mechanisms are used to promote policy formulation and implementation.

ANALYSIS AND ACTION

A great deal has been written about approaches that are useful in policy analysis (Iatridis, 1997). Policy analysis involves researching and obtaining as much information about policies as possible. It includes managing data and information about problems and policies and understanding the wider, social, economic, and political dimensions of policies.

TABLE 5.2   Types of Policy-Making Processes

Personal Policy Making	Group Decision Making	Organizational Policy Making	Legislative Process	Development of Bureaucratic Regulations
Data collection Identification of concern	Problem solving in the context of a variety of modes of group interaction	Board member actions	Bill drafted	Review of issue or law by staff
Development of statement of concern, issue, or problem		Issue identification	Committee hearing and testimony	Interpretation by legal counsel
Reflection on possible policies		Data collection by committee or staff	Bill revisions	Publication of proposed regulation
Selection of a policy to allocate resources		Placement on agenda	Legislative debates	Hearings (public input)
		Board discussion and hearings	Membership vote	Final draft of regulations
		Board vote or decision		Regulation publication

In addition to analyzing policies, policy practitioners are engaged in shaping policies and ensuring that they are implemented. A range of skills that are valuable in getting a particular policy adopted has also received scholarly attention recently (Haynes & Mickelson, 1996; Holosko & Au; 1996; Jannson, 1994). One way to think about policy analysis and action is to define them in terms of specific behaviors or activities a social worker would use in a given policy-making arena.

Analyzing and writing policy uses research and evaluation skills. As shown in Table 5.3, efforts to shape the policy of other systems include guiding, influencing, cooperating and collaborating, testifying, lobbying, advocating, and monitoring. As this table reveals, policy practitioners can engage in a great variety of direct policy-making activities.

These policy practice-related activities are not used in a single system or in isolation from one another. Moreover, analysis and action are not separate functions, as workers think about, write, and take action on policy-making simultaneously. It is important that the interdependence of the various components of policy practice be linked to each other in a coherent way. Table 5.4 provides a visual summary of how these different components operate simultaneously at the various levels of policy practice. In turn, policy practices at the personal, group, organizational, social, and social welfare levels interact in a dynamic way to generate the worker's desired policy.

TABLE 5.3 Illustrations of Policy-Related Activities

Policy-Related Activities	*Illustrative Behaviors*
Analyzing policy	Analyzing, researching, searching for information about policies, detecting policy issues, managing data and information about problems and concerns, evaluating system outcomes
Policy shaping	
Interpreting or guiding	Teaching, enabling, supporting decisions, providing expert knowledge, instructing, consulting with groups or agencies, helping others decide
Influencing or persuading	Changing policy of others, presenting issues, using coercion, providing information
Collaboration	Networking, coalition building, maintaining contacts with decision makers
Testifying	Preparing testimony, public speaking, responding to questions, preparing and delivering critiques of regulations
Lobbying	Contacting decision makers, presenting policy proposals, seeking support
Advocating (class)	Assertively presenting the cause of a class of clients for consideration
Monitoring	Keeping up to date on bureaucratic regulations, responding to calls for public input
Direct policy making	
Policy-related self-assessment	Examining practice in relation to policy issues, changing one's own policy
Implementing	Putting policy into operation, making changes as feasible
Official policy makers	Holding political office, participating on committees, being a political activist, serving on boards, holding office in associations, leading other policy-related interest groups

STRENGTHENING POLICY PRACTICE

Policy practice offers many exciting opportunities for human service personnel, including administrators, managers, and professionals. It strengthens their voice in their efforts to create just and effective social service programs and delivery systems. Social welfare personnel and professionals must no longer rely on only a few of their members to engage in policy-making activities. Policy practice, with analysis and action directed at every level of policy making, not only increases the number of workers involved, it also expands the scope and quantity of policies receiving attention from professionals.

TABLE 5.4   Worker Activities According to Policy-Making Clusters

Analyzing, influencing or persuading, interpreting or guiding	—	Personal Policy	
Analyzing, influencing or persuading, interpreting or guiding, collaborating	—	Group Policy	
Analyzing, influencing or persuading, participating, lobbying, testifying, implementing, collaborating, advocating	—	Organizational Policy	Worker's Desired Policy
Analyzing, participating, class advocating, testifying, lobbying, collaborating	—	Social Policy (law)	
Analyzing, monitoring, testifying, advocating, collaborating	—	Social Welfare Policy (bureaucratic regulations)	

Although the policy practice curriculum, both in accreditation standards and in publications about teaching skills, appears to be increasingly centered on analysis and intervention, greater attention needs to be paid to ongoing socialization and learning. Social welfare associations should greatly expand their conference and workshop offerings on policy practice. Continuing education on specific ways to analyze and influence policy making should be offered to all social welfare and health care professionals. With an ever strengthened place for policy practice within the human service professions, social welfare is much more likely to achieve social and economic justice for its consumers.

REFERENCES

Bank, B. J., & Hall, P. M. (1997). *Gender, equity, and schooling.* New York: Garland.

Burch, H. A. (1996). *Basic social policy and planning: Strategies and practice methods.* New York: Haworth.

Burns, E. M. (1956). *Social security and public policy.* New York: McGraw-Hill.

Commission on Accreditation. (1994). *Handbook of accreditation standards and procedures* (4th ed.). Alexandria, VA: Council on Social Work Education.

Figueira-McDonough, J. (1993). Policy practice: The neglected side of social work intervention. *Social Work, 38*(2), 179-188.

Flynn, J. (1992). *Social agency policy: Analysis and presentation for community practice.* Chicago: Nelson Hall.

Gilbert, N., & Specht, H. (1974). *Dimensions of social welfare policy.* Englewood Cliffs, NJ: Prentice Hall.

Gitterman, A., & Miller, I. (1989). The influence of the organization on clinical practice. *Clinical Social Work Journal, 17*(2), 151-164.

Haynes, K. S., & Mickelson, J. S. (1996). *Affecting change: Social workers in the political arena.* New York: Longman.

Holosko, J., & Au, E. (1996). Social and public policy analysis: A niche for social work practice. *Journal of Health and Social Policy, 7*(3), 65-73.

Holtzman, W. H. (1985). Role of private initiative in public policy and practice. In R. A. Kasschau & L. P. Ullman (Eds.), *Psychology research public policy and practice* (pp. 124-152). New York: Praeger.

Iatridis, D. S. (1997). Policy practice. In J. L. Edwards (Ed.), *Encyclopedia of social work* (19th ed., pp. 1855-1866). Washington, DC: National Association of Social Workers.

Jansson, B. S. (1984). *Theory and practice of social welfare policy: Processes and current issues.* Belmont, CA: Wadsworth.

Jansson, B. S. (1994). *Social welfare policy: From theory to practice* (2nd ed.). Monterey, CA: Brooks/Cole.

Johnson, A. K. (1994). Teaching students the task force approach: A policy-practice course. *Journal of Social Work Education, 30*(3), 336-347.

Mason, D. J., Talbott, S. W., & Leavitt, J. K. (1993). *Policy and politics for nurses* (2nd ed.). Philadelphia: Saunders.

McInnis-Dittrich, K. (1994). *Integrating social welfare policy and social work practice.* Pacific Grove, CA: Brooks/Cole.

Pierce, D. (1984). *Policy for the social work practitioner.* New York: Longman.

Schorr, A. (1985). Professional practice as policy. *Social Service Review, 59,* 178-196.

Smith, S. R., & Meyer, R. G. (1987). *Law, behavior, and mental health* (pp. 658). New York: New York University Press.

Weick, A., & Saleeby, D. (1995). Supporting family strengths: Orienting policy and practice toward the 21st century. *Families in Society, 76*(3), 141-149.

Wieczorek, R. R. (1985). *Power, politics, and policy in nursing.* New York: Springer.

Wyers, N. L. (1991). Policy-practice in social work: Models and issues. *Journal of Social Work Education, 27*(3), 241-250.

CHAPTER SIX

The Impact of Social Policy

PRANAB CHATTERJEE

JOHN SINCLAIR

There is increasing recognition today that social policies and programs should be carefully evaluated to determine whether they do in fact meet their stated objectives. Although it has often been assumed that social policies have a positive impact, this assumption has been called into question by many critics of government social programs. This chapter discusses the ways in which the impact of social policies can be assessed. It describes the principles and techniques used in different types of evaluation. Although evaluation research has become increasingly sophisticated, values and ideologies continue to play an important role in deciding which policy approaches work best.

THE LOGIC OF IMPACT ANALYSIS

Rossi and Freeman (1985, 1993) observe that there are four phases of social policy evaluation. These are needs assessment, selection of a program to respond to needs, impact evaluation, and cost-benefit analysis. After outlining the four phases of evaluation, they discuss many experimental, quasi-experimental, and time series designs that can be used for program evaluation. Mohr (1995) singled out the idea of impact evaluation and called it an attempt to isolate the direct effects of a policy (or, more precisely, a program derived from a policy) apart from any confounding environmental effects. Earlier, Suchman (1967) suggested that a program is a form of social experiment, and any evaluation of it leads to the conclusion that the program does or does not produce given social ends. Following Suchman's ideas, Riecken and Boruch (1974) listed ways of evaluating the impact of social experiments, many of which can be construed as preludes to new forms of social policy. Schalock (1995), using these contributions, defined impact analysis or outcome-based evaluation as "evaluation that uses valued and objective person-referenced outcomes to analyze a program's effectiveness, impact, or benefit-cost" (p. 5). Suchman (1967), in his earlier work, had stated that if any one program does not produce given social ends, one should conclude that it is a case of *program* failure. However, if it seems that a substantial number of programs, all similar in nature, do not produce given ends, then it indicates a case of *theory* failure. By theory failure, Suchman meant that the theory that generated the program (as an intervention to bring about change) has been developed on faulty premises.

Both Rossi and Suchman's groundwork about impact analysis (of social programs and their parent policy or theory) rest on the assumption that quantitative analysis and multivariate design will produce knowledge about the impact of social policies and programs. Ask a typical policy analyst, academic, or program administrator about the impact of social policy, and one will be provided with a sheaf of statistics supporting one perspective or another. This has come to be regarded as not just natural but the most appropriate response. On the matter of overemphasis on numbers, Zerbe (1998) has observed, "Hard numbers drive out soft" (p. 429).

Designing Impact Analysis: Some Issues

For example, an intervention designed to improve economic conditions in an urban neighborhood might well appear to be very successful, until one becomes aware that a regional upturn in the economy has occurred throughout the evaluation period and, although the neighborhood economy is much improved, it has, in fact, lagged far behind the rapid growth evident across the rest of the region. To reliably sort out program effects from environmental and other confounding influences is a daunting task. The significant achievements of impact analysis have been to spark an awareness of the need for such an analysis, if program effectiveness is ever to be convincingly established, and to offer a cookbook of strategies for attempting to achieve valid statistical evaluations.

Perhaps the best case for the use of quasi-experimental designs in impact analysis was made by Campbell (1969), when he proposed that the evaluation of a policy in one state, province, or country is possible by comparing the post-tests in two near-identical states, provinces, or countries, where one has experienced a policy and the other has not. However, this form of impact analysis often requires doing two case studies, which defeats the entire purpose of quasi-experimentation with valid samples and controls.

Impact analysis typically suggests a spectrum of research approaches from experimental to quasi-experimental and strongly recommends that the evaluator sticks as close to the classic controlled experiment and statistical analysis strategies as possible. Of course, it is rarely possible to approach these conditions in social experimentation and evaluation, and so the main thrust of an impact analysis is on quasi-experimental strategies and somewhat less powerful statistical analyses. The notion of qualitative strategies is usually dismissed as neither rigorous nor practical enough to warrant consideration.

The product resulting from an impact analysis is a methodologically and statistically sophisticated document detailing relationships and relative levels of importance among a number of variables. In keeping with the values of science in the modern age, it is widely accepted that rigorous attention to methodological and statistical norms will produce an objective analysis of the program under study, so the resulting information may safely be used to determine the fate of a particular policy and the fates of all those stakeholders on which it has an impact.

Information of this statistical kind has become the lingua franca of decision makers for many easily appreciated reasons. It is a manageable way to consider very large numbers, whether dollars or populations. It appears to offer a nearly irrefutable assessment, apparently devoid of bias or ideology. It is not presented as personal or emotional but rather as dispassionate and objective. It does indeed provide one of the most useful approximations available of valid grounds for a judgment as to the effect of a particular policy or program. And it allows for the easy flow of information from one venue to another, for example, from the budget office to the program designers to states, counties, and beyond.

The methodological and statistical achievements of impact analysis have, however, contributed to certain strategies for the evaluation of policy (Rossi & Freeman, 1985). Crane (1982, pp. 86-88) suggested that a useful impact analysis clearly depends on the formulation of evaluative hypotheses, which may take the following form:

Null hypothesis: The true effect is zero.
Alternative hypothesis: The true effect is at least equal to the threshhold effect.

Mohr (1995), using Deniston's (1972a, 1972b) ideas, listed further elements of impact evaluation, as he defined a problem relative to a given policy or program as *some predicted condition that will be unsatisfactory without the intervention of the program and satisfactory, or at least more acceptable, given the program's intervention* (italics ours). Yet troubling questions persist. To be statistically malleable, complex phenomena must be reduced to measurable form. Where this is not possible (as it frequently is not), *indicators* must be developed. That is, one kind of information must be made to substitute for another. So, for example, educational level or occupational title is often used as a proxy for income or socioeconomic status because respondents to surveys are loath to reveal their actual earnings. One potential difficulty arises when indicators are used, not as indicators but as actual measures. The potential for misunderstanding inherent in the process is important enough that it has lead to the establishment of nationwide panels charged with the production of increasingly more reliable indicators.

For example, there are no existing measures that are called "measures of the impact of social policy." However, the Human Development Index (HDI), developed by the United Nations, can be used as a somewhat direct measure of conditions in a society, and it can then be speculated whether this outcome is due to a certain kind of social policy. The HDI represents three equally weighted indicators of quality of human life: longevity, as shown by life expectancy at birth; knowledge, as shown by adult literacy and mean years of schooling; and income, as purchasing power parity dollars per capita (United Nations Development Programme, 1994). Using 0.875 as a boundary, 35 states from Canada through Portugal could be said to rate high as welfare societies in 1993. In contrast, using the same outcome measure, 10 countries from the former planned economies of Eastern Europe are rated below the 0.875 threshold. The data are presented in Table 6.1.

The data from Table 6.1 can now be placed in the design parameters shown in Table 6.2. In this posttest-only design, the impact of economic and social policies show that market-oriented policies produce higher HDI levels than planning-oriented policies. The data presented in Table 6.1 are standardized data and can be placed in almost any design parameters. Statistical impact analysis works well with such data.

Perhaps a "better" form of impact analysis would emerge if the HDI measures were available for Time 1 and Time 2, and then one could see where the planned economies were at Time 1 and whether their gain or loss is greater or less than those of market economy societies. This better design would be called a pretest-posttest design (Campbell & Stanley, 1963; Cook & Campbell, 1979; Mohr, 1995).

A still better design for impact analysis would emerge if prestest-postest measures were available for societies that were comparable to the societies described in Table 6.1 at Time 1 but that did not experience any industrial development, as market economy societies and planned economy societies did. Actually, this effort can be simulated by going back to the post-only design (as shown in Table 6.2). Take, for example, the case of Afghanistan, which has not experienced any form of industrialization or social policy, and note its HDI level in 1993 (which is 0.229). Then, look at its ethnically similar neighboring societies, Uzbekistan or Turkmenistan or Tajikistan, and look at their HDI levels in 1993 (0.679, 0.695, and 0.616, respectively, as reported by

TABLE 6.1   Market Versus Planned Economy Societies and Their Human Development Index (HDI), 1993

State	HDI	State	HDI
Market economy societies:			
Canada	0.951	Denmark	0.924
Switzerland	0.926	Belgium	0.929
Japan	0.938	Iceland	0.919
Austria	0.928	Finland	0.935
Sweden	0.933	Luxembourg	0.895
Norway	0.937	New Zealand	0.927
France	0.935	Israel	0.908
Australia	0.929	Barbados	0.908
United States	0.940	Ireland	0.919
Netherlands	0.938	Italy	0.914
United Kingdom	0.924	Spain	0.933
Germany	0.920	Hong Kong	0.909
Greece	0.909	Argentina	0.885
Cyprus	0.909	Costa Rica	0.884
Bahamas	0.895	Uruguay	0.883
SouthKorea	0.886	Chile	0.882
Malta	0.886	Singapore	0.881
Portugal	0.878		
Former planned economy societies:			
Czech Republic	0.872	Russia	0.804
Slovakia	0.864	Bulgaria	0.773
Hungary	0.855	Belarus	0.787
Latvia	0.820	Ukraine	0.719
Poland	0.819	Lithuania	0.719

SOURCE: United Nations Development Programme (1996).

the United Nations Development Programme, 1996). Such data can be grouped together for a posttest-only design to see the impact of economic and social policies driven by forced industrialization and planned economy (see Table 6.3).

The existence of standardized data on nations, as shown above, make it possible to do several types of statistical analysis: time series observation, posttest-only observation, and several types of quasi-experimental observation.

TABLE 6.2   Impact of Economic and Social Policies in Market Versus Planned Societies, With Posttest Measures

Market economy societies	Time 1	Time 2 (1993)
($N_1 = 35$)	(Undetermined)	(Higher in Human Development Index)
Planned economy societies	Time 1	Time 2 (1993)
($N_2 = 10$)	(Undetermined)	(Lower in Human Development Index)

However, data like those presented in Table 6.1 cannot be used to show within-nations outcomes, because HDI indicators do not exist about within-nation groups. Thus, when one is interested in seeing whether policies targeted to a region only within a nation have had any impact, one has to resort to other indicators, which are often not comparable to the HDI levels.

Lack of acceptable and standardized outcome measures is one principal problem in impact analysis. However, there are other problems as well. Coleman (1975) had listed them in the following terms:

For policy research,

(1) partial information available at the time an action must be taken is better than complete information after that time;

(2) the ultimate product is not a "contribution to existing knowledge" in the literature, but a social policy modified by the research results;

(3) results that are with high certainty approximately correct are more valuable than results which are more elegantly derived but possibly grossly incorrect;

(4) it is necessary to treat differently policy variables which are subject to policy manipulation, and situational variables which are not;

(5) the research problem enters from outside any academic discipline, and must be carefully translated from the real world of policy or the conceptual world of a client without loss of meaning; and

(6) the existence of competing or conflicting interests should be reflected in the commissioning of more than one research group, under the auspices of different interested parties where possible. Even in the absence of explicitly conflicting interests, two or more research projects should be commissioned to study a given policy problem. (pp. 22-34)

Ideological Biases in Impact Analysis

But beyond methodological considerations lie questions of another order. There is, for example, a growing literature regarding the value-laden nature of the ostensibly objective evaluation process. Every aspect of evaluation reflects a decision made, of-

TABLE 6.3   Four Societies, Where Three Have Had Economic and Social Policies, With Posttest
                 Measures

Three societies with industrialization and economic and social policies ($N_1 = 3$)

Time 1 (Undetermined)	Time 2 (1993) (Higher in Human Development Index)	
	Uzbekistan	0.679
	Turkmenistan	0.695
	Tajikistan	0.616

One society without industrialization and without economic or social policies ($N_2 = 1$)

Time 1 (Undetermined)	Time 2 (1993) (Lower in Human Development Index)	
	Afganistan	0.229

ten according to a particular perspective or value system. When one measures poverty, for example, what is it that is being measured? Income, perhaps. But income relative to what?

Orshansky developed the federal poverty thresholds in 1964 for the Social Security Administration (Fisher, 1997). They are based on what has been termed the economy budget, that is, the amount a careful homemaker would spend on food for a family of a particular size for "temporary or emergency use when funds are low." This decision was to locate the American standard of poverty below the level of "minimum comfort" and even below the level of "minimum adequacy" at the level of "minimum subsistence."

The problem is, this measure presumes the family in question has access to a working stove connected to utilities, owns a substantial collection of cookware, and has a working refrigerator, not to mention having the opportunity to learn nutritious cooking techniques and basic budgeting and shopping strategies. It seems that at the levels of poverty often addressed in evaluation reports, few of these assumptions are valid, and yet, they remain the de facto standard of American poverty.

Serious attempts at redefining poverty, either according to different levels of income or from different perspectives (for example, poverty defined as the inability to afford satisfactory housing as opposed to simply affording shelter of any kind or, most notably, the ability to financially support a socially rewarding lifestyle as opposed to affording simple existence) have been the subject of intense debate since the turn of the century. The United States has produced 60 different "poverty levels" since the 1900s (Fisher, 1996).

EFFECTIVENESS ANALYSIS

One simple question can be derived from the above discussions. It can be stated in the following form: Is a given policy, and program(s) generated from that policy, effective? Obviously, such a question about effectiveness requires clarity of goals (or ends to be achieved) of social policy.

The idea of effectiveness analysis is borrowed from the field of organizational studies and, more specifically, from the concept of organizational effectiveness (Cameron & Whetten, 1983; Mintzberg, 1993; Price, 1968, 1972). In effectiveness analysis, one sees organizational behavior as rational goal-directed behavior and begins the analysis of effectiveness by assessing how much of the goal has been or is being reached by the organization. This model originates in the classic works of Max Weber (1947) and is called the rational model of organizational studies (Haas & Drabek, 1973). Building on this model, Price (1972) proposed that organizations with single goals are likely to be more effective than organizations with multiple goals. Similarly, he suggests that organizations with a high degree of goal specificity are more likely to be effective than organizations that have diffuse goals, and so on. Also building on this model, Etzioni (1964) proposed that effectiveness can be studied from two perspectives: a goal perspective and a systems perspective. The goal perspective tries to decipher the organizational goals and then attempts to assess whether or how much of the goals have been reached. In this context, often, it becomes important to differentiate between *stated goals* and *pursued goals*. That is, the organization may claim that it is in business to pursue Goal X, but in reality, it is pursuing Goal Y. The second perspective proposed by Etzioni, the systems perspective, calls for a comparative perspective to assess the impact of organizations. Here, one assesses the impact of two or more similar organizations in the pursuit of similar ends and attempts to come to some conclusions about which one is more effective and why.

Most of the reasoning behind the studies of rational bureaucracies and their effectiveness can be transferred to the study of impact analysis of social policy. Here, one just needs to substitute *social policy* for *organization*. After all, the implementation of social policy often requires a rational bureaucracy, where the policy sets the goal, and the organization responsible for program execution attempts to attain that goal.

The lessons learned from the studies of organizational effectiveness can be used in the studies of policy effectiveness (assuming that the concept of effectiveness is similar to that of impact). These lessons are that policy goals are often not clearly stated, that there may be multiple and conflicting goals set by a social policy, and that there may be two or more cultural contexts, with the same form of policy execution producing different outcomes due to the cultural context in which they are executed (Boje, Gephart, & Thatchenkery, 1996; Haas & Drabek, 1973; Newstrom & Davis, 1993).

Taking these issues into account, Hudson (1997) has commented that "there can be no effectiveness unless there is change, [and] a measure of effectiveness is a measure of change" (pp. 70-71). He has also offered a set of equations that formally assess change with a probabilistic model.

The term, goal analysis, was popularized by Mager (1972). In his small but comprehensive work, he outlines how to decipher attainable goals, ensure that these are the goals being pursued, and do impact analysis of a program or policy behind that program.

EFFICIENCY ANALYSIS

In organizational behavior, the concept of efficiency analysis has long been popular. It was formally introduced by Taylor (1987) and can be referred to as an early form of cost-benefit analysis. Taylor showed that an organization could be effective but not necessarily efficient, especially if the unit cost of production is too high or if the goals of production cannot be met within a specified time period.

The lessons learned from efficiency analysis (Haas & Drabek, 1973; Newstrom & Davis, 1993) are already used by Rossi and Freeman (1985) as they offered designs for cost-benefit evaluation. They can be translated to policy analysis by asking, first, whether the policy under question is effective but not necessarily efficient and, second, whether the policy under question is effective, but not useful under the time constraints?

MANIFEST AND LATENT BENEFICIARIES OF SOCIAL POLICY

Clearly, the concept and effects of poverty are complex and troublesome issues for researchers of all kinds, and particularly for policy makers. There are issues on at least two additional levels that are more troubling still. Since the early 1970s, social scientists have begun examining the policy process in a reflexive manner that has generated several important new insights.

Among these important insights is the notion, now supported through research, that policies may state program goals or identify target populations that are not the actual focus of the policy. That is, social policy is directed at both manifest beneficiaries—for example, the poor or minorities—and at what may be termed latent beneficiaries—for example, providers of services or policy makers themselves (Chatterjee, in press). This process is common enough in a variety of contexts. In fact, the entire edifice of gentlemanly compromise that has produced such an impressive history of social development in America is grounded in the shared willingness of elected representatives to allow such fictions to pass, as often as not, without question.

The question of who benefits by given social policies has been dealt with from several perspectives in recent times. Bartik (1991) has used it in relation to policies intended to promote regional and local economic development. Clotfeller (1991, 1992) has asked this very question in great detail about policies that create and support the nonprofit sector in market economies.

An examination of recent American social welfare policy may help make clear some of the more important issues. For example, in an environment that is perceived by many as increasingly apt to blame the beneficiaries of welfare, it has also been increasingly fashionable to discuss the wealth of opportunity that awaits only ambition and personal commitment to hard work. A policy outgrowth of these two streams of thought has been the recent drive for welfare reform under its many names, such as welfare-to-work, workfare, and so on.

The idea publicly put forth is that the beneficiaries of the programs will be the presently poor who prepare diligently for new careers and pull themselves up with a helping hand from the government. By limiting the amount and the duration of benefits available, legislatures expect to eliminate or curtail the culture of poverty, welfare dependency, work aversion or avoidance, and other problems of recent welfare strategies. This public message has been well-received and oft repeated. However, it fails to tell the whole story.

For example, who are the beneficiaries of this program? The manifest beneficiaries, of course, are the poor, who will finally be given just what they need, no less and no more, to succeed in America. But what of what we have termed the latent beneficiaries, those who stand to benefit from the program but not as publicly? Earlier welfare strategies created an entire industry of service providers and program administrators (as well as the hundreds of college and professional programs to train them, and the thousands of professors to staff those programs and institutions to evaluate them, etc.). The present approach will benefit the career training industry and whatever bureaucratic mechanism becomes necessary to monitor the quality of its work.

Private industry is likely to benefit from the sudden influx of recently trained, poorly experienced, low-cost workers created by the welfare reform effort. Those who currently provide services to low-paid workers without government benefits, such as child care, insurance, medical care, and other industries, will see their market expanding.

A further step away from the manifest beneficiaries are the institutions and individuals who theorize, consult, and write about social problems, as well as those who conduct research. With so many new and untried interventions in the field, it will be a bonanza for those who can produce the kinds of research and theoretical products deemed most useful to policy makers and others with a stake in welfare change.

Finally, the legislators themselves stand to benefit. By appealing to a natural tax-payer instinct to save money by reducing government, they have frequently been able to solidify their political position. By reducing benefits to the poorest, least politically powerful groups, they have been able to do so with little risk.

The same process of identifying latent beneficiaries may be applied to any social welfare legislation, whether it originates from Left or Right, conservative or liberal. It is important to do so to understand fully why social welfare policy takes the form it does, who supports its passage and implementation, and what the real stakes are in an evaluation process. It may make little difference to policy makers if a program is perceived to fail its manifest beneficiaries, so long as latent beneficiaries are pleased with the results.

Of late, a number of social theorists have written in essential agreement with Charles Lemert's (1997) assessment of the social policy process: "The more sensible post-modernists, being generally respectful of much in modernity, are rigorously skeptical of the prospects that modernity's grand ideals ever will, or ever were truly meant to, become the true *manifest* structure of world things" (p. 75). That is, there is a widening realization that policy is not infrequently created for reasons other than those offered publicly by policy makers themselves.

STAKEHOLDER-BASED ANALYSIS

The concept of stakeholder-based analysis, like effectiveness and efficiency analysis, has also been popular in studies of organizational behavior (Cooperrider & Dutton, 1998; Harrison & Shirom, 1998). Here the critical question is: Who wants to know about the impact of a given policy? It is entirely possible that groups such as policy makers, politicians, disinterested social scientists, and others, using their various tool-bags, conclude that a given policy is not very effective. On the other hand, those involved with the policy's target population or those who are one of the beneficiaries of the programs generated by a given policy may hold a very different position than the groups mentioned above. Nowakowski (1987), shifting the "who wants to know" question, offered plans to do research taking the client's perspective in question. In the discipline called organizational development, which is usually located in business schools and where training is offered to individuals who would serve as consultants to various organizations, a similar approach is called *appreciative inquiry* (Cooperrider, 1986; Srivastava & Cooperrider, 1990). An important point in appreciative inquiry is to study a client's organization in such a way that the client benefits from the consultant's (the organization developer) knowledge but does not get alienated if the consultant makes some constructive criticisms.

Translated to the realm of impact analysis of social policy, appreciative inquiry would mean a study of social policy that is sensitive to the needs of clients who commissioned the study, who may be stakeholders in the programs derived from that policy and who may be beneficiaries of some or all parts of that policy's execution.

Impact Analysis or Satisfaction Analysis?

We could proceed to contrast these strategies across the entire evaluation process. However, it is important to note that the whole concept of impact analysis as analysis by impartial third-party scientists to see whether a given policy X produces outcome Y should be differentiated from the question whether given policy X produces satisfaction in given group G and whether given group G wants the programs derived from that social policy continued. What we have here will suffice to make the real point, which is that several of the attempts to define a new evaluation process really amount to attempts to shift the ability to define concepts and standards from policy makers to those who must live with policy consequences. This work is more than simply political in nature (although, clearly, it could reduce or bolster the influence of groups espousing any number of ideological or political views). Rather, it represents a serious-minded attempt to get inside the black box at the heart of so many important social policy questions. That is, the developing strategies attempt not only to discover what policies work, but why they work, and in what contexts, what their meaning is to each class of stakeholder, and what approaches may best be applied in which particular contexts.

Use of Focus Groups

The concept of the *focus group* originated in the 1930s (Rice, 1931), and it was developed to gather specific types of information from key informants in a group setting. Typically, it is a group somewhere between 7 and 10 members in size, selected by the researcher (Krueger, 1988). In this group, the researcher creates a relaxed atmosphere to elicit information about certain subjects. The discussions carried on in this group become an important source of data for the researcher. Roethlisberger and Dickson (1939) used a version of the focus group during their famous studies of employee participation and productivity. Merton, Fiske, and Kendall (1956) produced the first book on the subject, and they outlined how the focus group is an important tool for policy research. Krueger (1988) has outlined how focus groups can be used before a program begins, corresponding with the idea of needs assessment in the sequence described by Rossi and Freeman (1985, 1993). They can also be used during a program, in what Rossi and Freeman have called program monitoring. Then, they can be used after a program, which Rossi and Freeman have called impact evaluation. However, it is entirely possible that focus groups may yield information that is different from formal, multivariate, instrument-generated information captured through a pretest-posttest design or a posttest-only design.

The use of focus groups is comparable with what is called the *Delphi method,* where selected purposive groups are used for community-level agenda building (Linstone & Turoff, 1975).

THE INTERPRETIVE MODEL IN POLICY RESEARCH

It has become increasingly common for conscientious theorists to recommend that researchers employ a variety of approaches in conducting policy evaluations (Porter, 1995). A particularly eloquent statement of the case from a more general perspective than simply policy studies has been made by Robert Alford (1998). He has suggested that there are three paradigms of inquiry, and they are multivariate, interpretive, and historical. At the macrolevel, the multivariate model studies *structure,* the interpretive method studies *culture,* and the historical method studies *context.* In the multivariate model, knowledge is obtained through *data,* in the interpretive model through *observation,* and in the historical model through *evidence.* The following case example illustrates how impact evaluation from a different paradigm may lead to different forms of outcome.

An Example From Delinquency Research

A metropolitan city (in the United States) gets a large grant to set up a delinquency prevention program, and the program is to be administered through its park district. The theory behind the program is the opportunity theory of Cloward and Ohlin (1964), which suggests that the reason for delinquent behavior by working- and lower-class youth is their lack of opportunity. Given proper opportunity, the theory further suggests, delinquent behavior in working- and lower-class youth is likely to be reduced. Arnold (1964) pronounced that this was a failed idea, and Lewis (1966) claimed that working-class and lower-class youth are products of a culture of poverty.

Influenced by this theory, a city sets up a program where about 150 teenagers are recruited in a program of delinquency prevention. The program consists of counseling by young adult counselors two to three times a week, participation in recreational group work throughout the week, and a stipend of a few hundred dollars a month. A multivariate program evaluation is shown in Table 6.4.

TABLE 6.4 Pretest-Posttest Comparison in Delinquency Prevention: An Example

	Time 1	Time 2 (about a year later)
Program group	x_1	x_2
A comparable group	x_3	x_4

In this multivariate (the research included other variables besides x) pretest-posttest model, x represented the rate of being apprehended by juvenile authorities. At Time 1, it was found that

$$x_1 = x_3;$$

that is, apprehension rates in the Program Group and the Comparison Group are approximately equal.

However, at Time 2, it was found that

$$x_2 > x_1; x_2 > x_3; x_2 > x_4; \text{ and } x_1 = x_3 = x_4 \text{ (approximately)}.$$

This multivariate model of policy and program analysis leads to the conclusion that the program is not effective. In fact, it seems to increase delinquency and certainly does not lead to delinquency reduction.

However, an interpretive model of study, done by a series of open-ended interviews with program staff and coupled with some observations of interactions between the program staff and the counselors in the program, revealed the following scenario: The counselors are not professionally trained to help people. They are young adult members from the same community in their early twenties, some of whom are graduates of a nearby community college. The counselors have developed a work group themselves, and a work group culture has formed. Within that work group culture, the counselors often brag about their clients and take pride in the fact that their clients are indeed very tough, perhaps even tougher than the clients of their peer counselors. One of the secretaries said the following about these counselors: "Boy, they treat those kids [teenagers in the Program Group who are targets of intervention] like some rich people treat their Doberman-Pinschers!"

The statement by a secretary is indeed a very important symbolic statement: The work group culture of the counselors, themselves only a few years older than the teenagers in the program, has created a status system. Within that status system, a program teenager confers status on his counselor by being "bad," "tough," and more unruly than others. They are rewarded by their counselors for being deviant. Whatever the counselors do during their formal interaction with these teenagers toward delinquency reduction, the culture of the work group and the status system within that work group give an important message to the inner-city youth, and that message is that they are to be rewarded for their "toughness."

The case makes clear, we think, the usefulness of an interpretive model in program and policy evaluation. A particularly eloquent statement about it from a more general perspective than policy studies has been made by Alford (1998):

> The emphasis on the multivariate [quantitative] paradigm as the only "real" social science is impoverishing, a mark of the insecurity of the discipline, not a sign of its scientific maturity . . . (p. 4)
>
> Developing coherent arguments that recognize historical processes, symbolic meanings, and multivariate relations is the best way to construct an adequate explanation of a complex social phenomenon. (p. 19)

CONCLUSION

These considerations may encourage reflection on what the most significant impact of recent social welfare policy in America might be. That is, it has become increasingly evident to observers from many political points of view that the policy and policy evaluation process is not objective in the sense science is usually taken to be. Statistics, alone, may mask more than they reveal; any meaningful evaluation of the impact of social welfare policy must, as a matter of course, incorporate sophisticated statistical analysis, provide historical perspective on the problem being addressed and previous attempts at solutions, and provide rigorously collected and analyzed qualitative data from the perspective of every stakeholder (that is, beneficiary) group involved. Furthermore, an effective evaluation of policy impact must first seek to unearth and clearly state the goals of the policy under consideration from the point of view of all those who supported it and worked for its passage and implementation.

REFERENCES

Alford, R. A. (1998). *The craft of inquiry.* New York: Oxford University Press.

Arnold, R. (1964). Mobilization for youth: Patchwork or solution? *Dissent, 11,* 347-354.

Bartik, T. J. (1991). *Who benefits?* Kalamazoo, MI: W. E. Upjohn Institute.

Boje, D. M., Gephart, R. P., Jr., & Thatchenkery, T. J. (Eds.) (1996). *Postmodern management and organization theory.* Thousand Oaks, CA: Sage.

Cameron, K., & Whetten, D. A. (1983). *Organizational effectiveness: A comparison of multiple models.* New York: Academic Press.

Campbell, D. T. (1969, April). Reforms as experiments. *American Psychologist, 24,* 409-429.

Campbell, D. T., & Stanley, J. C. (1963). *Experimental and quasi-experimental designs in research.* Chicago: Rand McNally.

Chatterjee, P. (in press). *The dispensation of surplus.* Washington, DC: NASW Press.

Clotfeller, C. T. (1991). *Economic challenges in higher education.* Chicago: University of Chicago Press.

Clotfeller, C. T. (Ed.). (1992). *Who benefits from the nonprofit sector?* Chicago: University of Chicago Press.

Cloward, R., & Ohlin, L. E. (1964). *Delinquency and opportunity.* New York: Free Press.

Coleman, J. S. (1975). Problems of conceptualization and measurement in studying policy impacts. In K. M. Dolbeare (Ed.), *Public policy evaluation.* Beverly Hills, CA: Sage.

Cook, T. D., & Campbell, D. T. (1979). *Quasi-experimentation: Design and analysis issues for field studies.* Chicago: Rand McNally.

Cooperrider, D. L. (1986). *Appreciative inquiry: Toward a methodology for understanding and enhancing organizational innovation.* Unpublished Ph.D. thesis in the Department of Organizational Behavior, Case Western Reserve University, Cleveland, OH.

Cooperrider, D. L., & Dutton, J. E. (1998). *Organizational dimensions of global change.* Thousand Oaks, CA: Sage.

Crane, J. A. (1982). *The evaluation of social policies.* The Hague: Kluwer-Nijhoff.

Deniston, O. L. (1972a). *Evaluation of disease control programs.* Washington, DC: U.S. Department of Health, Education, and Welfare, Public Health Service, Health Services and Mental Health Administration, Communicable Disease Center.

Deniston, O. L. (1972b). *Program planning for disease control programs.* Washington, DC: U.S. Department of Health, Education, and Welfare, Public Health Service, Health Services and Mental Health Administration, Communicable Disease Center.

Etzioni, A. (1964). *Modern organizations.* Englewood Cliffs: Prentice Hall.

Fisher, G. M. (1996, Summer). Relative or absolute: New light on the behavior of poverty lines over time. *GSS/SSS Newsletter,* pp. 10-12.

Fisher, G. M. (1997, Winter). The development and history of the behavior of poverty lines over time. *GSS/SSS Newsletter,* pp. 6-7.

Haas, J. E., & Drabek, T. E. (1973). *Complex organizations: A sociological reader.* New York: Macmillan.

Harrison, M., & Shirom, A. (1998). *Organizational diagnosis and assessment.* Thousand Oaks, CA: Sage.

Hudson, W. (1997). Assessment tools as outcome measures in social work. In E. J. Mullen & J. L. Magnabosco (Eds.), *Outcomes measurement in the human services* (pp. 68-80). Washington, DC: NASW Press.

Krueger, R. A. (1988). *Focus groups: A practical guide for applied research.* Newbury Park, CA: Sage.

Lemert, C. (1997). *Postmodernism is not what you think.* Malden, MS: Blackwell.

Lewis, O. (1966). *La vida: A Puerto Rican family in the culture of poverty—San Juan and New York.* New York: Random House.

Linstone, H. A., & Turoff, M. (1975). *The Delphi method: Techniques and applications.* Reading, MA: Addison-Wesley.

Mager, R. F. (1972). *Goal analysis.* Belmont, CA: Lear Siegler/Fearon.

Merton, R. K., Fiske, M., & Kendall, P. L. (1956). *The focused interview.* Glencoe, IL: Free Press.

Mintzberg, H. (1993). *Structure in fives: Designing effective organizations.* Englewood Cliffs, NJ: Prentice Hall.

Mohr, L. B. (1995). *Impact analysis for program evaluation.* Thousand Oaks, CA: Sage.

Newstrom, J. W., & Davis, K. (1993). *Organizational behavior: Human behavior at work.* New York: McGraw-Hill.

Nowakowski, J. (1987). *The client perspective on evaluation.* San Francisco: Jossey-Bass.

Porter, T. M. (1995). *Trust in numbers: The pursuit of objectivity in science and public life.* Princeton, NJ: Princeton University Press.

Price, J. (1968). *Organizational effectiveness: An inventory of propositions.* Homewood, IL: Richard Irwin.

Price, J. (1972). The study of organizational effectiveness. *The Sociological Quarterly, 13,* 3-15.

Rice, S. (1931). *Methods in social science.* Chicago: University of Chicago Press.

Riecken, H. W., & Boruch, R. F. (Eds.). (1974). *Social experimentation: A method for planning and evaluating social intervention.* New York: Academic Press.

Roethlisberger, F. J., & Dickson, W. J. (1939). *Management and the worker.* Cambridge, MA: Harvard University Press.

Rossi, P., & Freeman, H. (1985). *Evaluation: A systematic approach*. Beverly Hills, CA: Sage.

Rossi, P., & Freeman, H. (1993). *Evaluation: A systematic approach*. Newbury Park: CA: Sage.

Schalock, R. L. (1995). *Outcome-based evaluation*. New York: Plenum.

Srivastava, S., & Cooperrider, D. (1990). *Appreciative management and leadership*. San Francisco: Jossey-Bass.

Suchman, E. A. (1967). *Evaluative research: Principles and practice in public service and social action programs*. New York: Russell Sage Foundation.

Taylor, F. (1987). The principles of scientific management. In J. M. Shafritz & J. S. Ott (Eds.), *Classics of organization theory*. Chicago: Dorsey. (Original work published 1916)

United Nations Development Programme. (1996). *Human development report 1996*. New York: Oxford University Press.

Weber, M. (1947). *The theory of social and economic organization*. New York: Free Press.

Zerbe, R. O. (1998). Is cost-benefit analysis legal? Three rules. *Journal of Policy Analysis and Management, 17*(3), 419-456.

PART TWO

The History of Social Policy

Part II of this book summarizes more than three hundred years of history, focusing on the way government has formulated policies that affect the well-being of America's diverse peoples. Chapter 7 provides an account of social policy during the Colonial era and the early years of the Republic, showing how the Poor Laws dominated government action in the field. It also describes the ways in which slavery and policies towards native Americans caused great harm. It dramatically illustrates the point that social policies are not always benevolent but that they can be used for malignant purposes.

Chapter 8 highlights a period of activist government intervention intended to enhance the well-being of citizens. Known as the Progressive Era, this period in the nation's history witnessed considerable expansion of government involvement that resulted in improved working conditions for poor people, particularly in industrial occupations. It was also characterized by the expansion of the social services and the enactment of legislation that afforded a greater measure of protection to children and other vulnerable groups.

Chapter 9 shows how the involvement of government in social welfare increased during the 1930s—a period known as the New Deal. Faced with mass unemployment resulting from the Great Depression, the Roosevelt administration introduced various measures to meet the needs of the unemployed and poor. Although the job training and placement programs which were central to the New Deal were eventually disbanded, the Social Security Act of 1935 continues to function today, providing social protection to millions of Americans.

As shown in the following chapter, the Johnson administration's Great Society programs perpetuated the trend towards the expansion of government involvement in social welfare which had begun on a significant scale during the Progressive Era. These programs strengthened the existing social services and introduced new programs such as Medicare and Medicaid. They also encouraged local participation in poverty alleviation and recognized in law the Civil Rights Movement's struggle against racism and oppression. These developments fostered the integration of millions of African Americans into the nation's political life.

The last chapter in Part II traces the efforts of the Reagan administration to halt the apparently inexorable trend towards ever increasing government involvement in social welfare. It shows how budgetary retrenchments, privatization, contracting of services and other radical policy innovations reshaped social policy in America. It also considers how the Clinton administration has intervened in the social policy arena, reacting to complex pressures and, at the same time, seeking to implement a New Democrat social policy agenda.

CHAPTER SEVEN

Social Policy From Colonial Times to the Civil War

PHYLLIS J. DAY

*T*hroughout history, social policy's evolution has been a repetition of past ideologies rather than forward movement. As our nation developed, based on European policies toward "outsiders" and the disadvantaged, two patterns emerged. The first was colonialism along North America's east coast, beginning with the Dutch East India Company and English merchants and settlers. The second, often ignored, was Spanish invasions in areas touched by the Gulf Stream in the South and up from Central America in the Southwest.

The latter brought *conquistadores* and Catholic priests, the first seeking gold, the second, souls. Established self-supporting Native American communities were wiped out, their people starved and decimated by enormous tributes demanded by the conquerors. Priests tended the welfare of this newly poor population in missions based on Catholic social policy: hospices for the needy, alms for the poor, hospitals for the sick, and shelter for the aged, homeless, or dependent. By the 1600s, there were 3,000 Catholic missionaries in the Southwest, their missions the major social welfare system (Day, 1997).

SOCIAL POLICY UNDER COLONIAL RULE

In Florida and the Caribbean, as early as 1502, Spanish-appointed governors set up forced labor systems that promised wages, "protection," and Christian instruction for Native American laborers. In reality, this meant starvation and work slavery often resulting in death. Runaways were killed, others committed suicide, and multitudes died from overwork and disease (Morgan, 1993). By the end of the 1600s, most native populations in the area were extinct (Morgan, 1993). As in the Southwest, social welfare depended on Catholic missions.

Meanwhile, northern colonists entered into a vast experiment: the Protestant work ethic reinforced by Puritan morality. The Dutch East India Company, needing satisfied workers, required each settlement to provide preachers, schoolmasters, and "comforters" of the sick, unhappy, ill, and disabled. The church collected donations and fines for alms; church and Company encouraged neighbors to set up mutual aid societies and help one another. Courts, Company, and church established and controlled schools. The able-bodied poor—vagabonds and idlers—were "bonded" to *patroons,* often for life, in return for their keep.

After ousting Dutch rulers, colonists brought Elizabethan Poor Laws to America, laws expressly intended to control the laboring poor: Poor relief was a by-product, to keep them working. Religion and governance were inseparable; their major social and economic theme was wealth as morality and poverty as immorality. Even the "worthy poor"—aged, disabled, children—should work to their full capacities.

Slavery and Indenture

Social policies legitimated both harsh colonial poor laws and the institutions of slavery and indenture, which provided two of the country's most important labor groups. Enforced work "taught" morality to slaves and indentured servants while adding to their masters' wealth, and masters supported them. Other poor people depended on colonial poor relief systems. In the agricultural South, slaves were property by law, as any animal was property. Providing for them, then, was not social policy but animal husbandry that kept them able to work, produce, and reproduce. Not all slave owners agreed, but slave holding itself gave the institution legal, moral, and social legitimation.

About half of all white immigrants in the colonial era—a quarter million people, half of them women—came to America as indentured servants (Hymowitz & Weissman, 1980). Some came willingly, selling their indentures, or legal work bonds, to ship captains in return for passage to America. Colonists bought the bonds, often of entire families, although captains could and did separate husbands from wives and children from their parents. Children could not be sold, but they could be "given" to colonists to work for their keep, boys usually until age 18 and girls to age 21.

However, forced indenture was common: America became a dumping ground for England's unwanteds—paupers, beggars, criminals (many charged with small offenses and given the choice of death or deportation), political dissidents (such as the Irish), and dependent or unwanted children. England deported 300 to 400 children ages 10 to 15 as indentured servants (Compton, 1980). "Newlanders" or "man-stealers" provided more, kidnaping people to sell off to America. Indenture usually lasted from 5 to 7 years, although it was doubled for political dissenters.

Colonial Poor Relief

In the colonies, churches, private philanthropy, and local governments merged to help the worthy poor, reform the nonworking poor, and control the workforce. Work became a social, civic, and religious obligation, and those who failed it—nonworking, able-bodied persons, vagabonds, rogues, criminals, unwed pregnant women and poor women with children—were considered dangerous to community safety and morality. Like criminals, they were branded, flogged, put in stocks and pillories, auctioned off to the highest bidder or "sold" to the lowest bidder, banished or "warned out," or even hanged.

Colonies depended on private citizens and associations to take care of special groups such as the insane, blind, deaf, and retarded. In addition, religions, craft societies, and ethnic groups developed mutual aid systems and even almshouses for their own needy people: for example, Quakers gave alms, sent Friendly Visitors to the sick and old, and established the Friends Almshouse in 1713. Service to the country elicited new social policies: Veterans' pensions were established shortly after the American Revolution, and the Marine Hospital Service was begun in 1789.

American Poor Laws had three major tenets: local responsibility, family responsibility, and categorization of the poor.

Local responsibility. By 1636, Plymouth and Massachusetts were "placing" the poor to work, and by 1642, all towns had to supply their basic necessities (Day, 1997). Town supervisors investigated the poor to determine their worthiness and dispensed poor relief from monies collected from poor taxes, church and private donations, and fines for such errors as refusing to work at harvest time, selling at short weight, not attending church, or bringing a pauper into town. Eligibility for poor relief depended on owning property or having lived in the town a set number of years. Newcomers were ineligible for poor relief. If they wanted to settle, they had to prove they would not become town dependents. By 1725, strangers had to register with town councils within 20 days or leave, and by 1767, many town councils forbade immigration without permission. In 1793, Massachusetts, required people to stay 5 years without being warned out before they were granted residency status (Grob, 1976).

Relatives' responsibility. By 1675, laws required families to enforce community social, moral, and economic customs. They had to "take in" and support poor or ill relatives and to provide bond for immigrating relatives in case they became poor. All children under age 21 had to live with families to ensure their moral upbringing, and
those without families were placed to work for their keep or, if from the upper classes,
indentured to learn a trade.

Classification of the poor. Following the English model, colonial towns categorized
their poor and dependent into three categories: worthy poor, unworthy poor, and dependent children.

Worthy poor were widows, the incapacitated or ill, and the aged: poor through no
fault of their own. "Outdoor" relief, which allowed them to remain in their homes,
was an option, but placement with relatives was preferred. If neither was possible,
they were sold to the lowest bidder—those who would charge the town the least for
their care. Often, this became a business, with profits gleaned from cutting back food,
clothing, shelter, and medical care. Mortality among those sold was so high that, at
least in larger towns, almshouses were built to offer alternative care. However, these
too were run as businesses, with results similar to the private care homes.

The unworthy poor were able-bodied nonemployed men and women, including
widows; vagrants, idlers, and strangers; and the mentally retarded. Reasons for their
poverty were irrelevant, but the cause was usually considered to be personal defect
and often crime. Male paupers could be put to work on town projects until completed, then "auctioned off," often for life, with proceeds going to the town. Women,
along with their children, were "farmed out" to local homes, or, if they could not be
placed, "warned out" to other towns or into the forests, where many simply disappeared. As early as 1639, 8 years after Boston was settled, courts could return the
poor to their former towns or deport them from the country. Workhouses and houses
of correction proliferated during the 1700s, increasingly popular for placement because they could force inmates to work to help earn costs of their care.

Dependent children included orphans, children born out of wedlock, unwanted
children, and children of the poor, all of whom communities "owned." An overriding
concern was that children not follow their parents into poverty. By 1641, courts could
bond them out: In Virginia, for example, two children from every poor family could
be indentured to flaxhouses for piecework, their wages paid to the town (Day, 1997).
Courts sold most poor children to families to work for board and room, with the expectation that they would receive a Christian education and that boys would learn to
read and girls would learn housekeeping. Often, these children were considered
cheap labor, ill-used or worked to death by their "hosts." Runaways, incorrigibles,
and "criminal children" went to workhouses or jails (later reform schools). The idea
of childhood was unknown, and children were punished as adults, up to and including hanging.

The Institution as Social Policy

From colonial days, towns preferred to place their poor or deviant people in institutions, which enforced work and morality, rather than provide outdoor relief, admittedly more humane. Despite proof otherwise, institutions were thought to be cheaper: their "pay-by-the-head" schemes more easily budgetable, and inmates' work, whether inside or contracted out, more likely to reduce town costs. However, as supervisors profited on costs by reducing inmates' food, heat, clothing, and medical care, mortality rates skyrocketed. Investigations found these institutions to be inhumane, places of "filth and misery, and the most degrading, unrelieved suffering" (Grob, 1976, p. 16).

In the 1700s, first almshouses and then workhouses, houses of correction, and penal institutions spread across the country, warehouses for society's unwanted people. Unsegregated by sex, age, physical condition, or reason for incarceration, the worthy poor (aged, ill, physically disabled) were housed with vagabonds, rogues, and idlers; criminals; able-bodied women; dependent children from ages 1 month to 14 years, often placed with their mothers; and the "insane" (Day, 1997). Obstreperous or violent inmates were whipped, chained, or shackled and often left to die in their own excrement. Many of the aged or ill died quickly, and only 3% of children under age 1 survived (Grob, 1976).

After the American Revolution, outdoor relief remained common and acceptable in the South, but in the North, almshouses and workhouses increased and diversified, becoming forerunners of hospitals, mental hospitals, orphanages, reform schools, and penitentiaries. Sections set aside for the ill and insane became the first public hospitals. Later, with the medical profession's growth, these became teaching hospitals for new treatments. Medical customs and faith, rather than science, dictated treatments, the most common of which included bleeding, violent purges, heavy doses of mercury-based drugs, and the use of opium. People who went to public hospitals had about a 50/50 chance of dying. Experimental treatments on them, if successful, could be transferred to paying patients. Women (and women slaves in the South) were particularly vulnerable after the ovum was discovered in 1824. Although women slaves were rarely afflicted with upper-class "women's problems," exploration of their organs offered new explanations for those ills.

The first law for the so-called insane, in 1676, was intended to protect towns from their bizarre behavior, often thought to be demonic possession. Although families were responsible for the insane at first, they often whipped and beat them to get rid of "devils"; shackled them in outside pens, basements, or attics without heat despite the cold northern winters; and neglected their most basic care. Whether to better their conditions or get rid of the victims, almshouses became the answer, although treatment was just as horrific. Almshouses began to segregate the insane from other inmates and so became the first insane asylums. They attracted researchers, among them Benjamin Rush, who nearly a century later instituted private asylums where "moral treatment" was available to paying patients. Although inhumane by today's standards, these asylums were still better than almshouse care.

Almshouses and workhouses also set institutional patterns for both juvenile and adult offenders. The industrial reformatory movement began with the New York House of Refuge for boys in 1825. Intended to reform inmates through moral training, religion, and labor, it used indeterminate sentencing at the discretion of judge or reformatory administrator, along with "organized persuasion" rather than coercive restraint. In like manner, penitentiaries, first established by Quakers in 1823, took the able-bodied poor from almshouses, workhouses, and jails and tried to rehabilitate them through silence, isolation, and meditation. Along with later penology and prison models, these became standards for prison and corrections. Philanthropists Isaac Hopper and John Augustus brought the concept of probation, Hopper helping discharged prisoners find work, Augustus supervising offenders charged with minor offenses to keep them from imprisonment.

FROM THE REVOLUTION TO THE CIVIL WAR

The Enlightenment era surrounding the American Revolution, although it fermented with new ideas, had little effect on social policies for the poor or unwanted. Abetted by the new Constitution, the nation continued to violate treaties with Native Americans and other non-Caucasians, to enslave Africans and retain slavery (though Africans and their descendants were redefined as two thirds of a person), and to deny equal rights to women and to unpropertied workers: In northern factories, laborers worked when owners dictated, depending on charities or starving when factories closed. For all intents and purposes, throughout a massive change in government, social policies still focused on work morality for the poor and exclusion of rights for the "different."

The context changed, of course, through expansion to the West, burgeoning immigration, and leadership in international trade. A cycle of wars and depressions followed the Revolution, the worst in 1815-1819, reaching a peak in 1819 with 500,000 workers unemployed and whole families starving or freezing to death in the northern winter (Mencher, 1967). At times, a third of the labor force was unemployed, and wages fell 30% to 50% (Compton, 1980). Yet, despite unemployment and minuscule wages, the monied elite still issued reports blaming the poor for "idleness, ignorance, spend-thriftiness, hasty marriages, use of pawnbrokers, lottery, houses of prostitution and gambling" (Mencher, 1967, pp. 527-528).

New York's Secretary of State J. V. N. Yates believed intemperance to be the major cause of poverty, estimating in 1824 that it affected two thirds of the poor. Yet, after blaming the poor and calling for better ways to control them, he reported only 27%

of those he studied could actually work—the others were old, ill, disabled, or children (Yates, 1824). Social policy in the 1800s was a split reality: One part pondered the causes and cures of poverty, another *was* poverty, illness, the drudgery and dangers of work, and brutal punishments for the nonworking or different. Two trends in social policy strengthened: a trend toward state rather than local authority, first seen when states required counties to build poorhouses and to use state standards; and a trend toward institutionalization as the answer to every social problem.

The number of immigrants, mostly from the impoverished classes of Europe, rose steadily from 129,000 in the 1820s to 540,000 by the end of the 1830s, peaking at more than 1.75 million in the 1850s. Six million people came to America between 1820 and 1860 (Coll, 1972). Moreover, in the United States, migration from farms to cities increased with the new technologies of the Industrial Revolution. The urban population grew at a rate of 40% to 50% per decade. In New York state alone, the urban population grew from 5.5% in 1796 to 27.4% in 1855 (Seller, 1984). As the proportion of wage laborers increased, employers could lower wages more drastically.

Almshouses in immigration ports, supported (unwillingly) by local towns, were the first stop for poverty-stricken or ill immigrants. Not until 1847 did the Board of Immigration collect taxes and impose fines on immigrants, crews, and ships to support almshouses or reimburse local communities for outdoor relief, medical help, education, transportation, and job placement (Compton, 1980). Cities became human warrens of crowding, disease, plagues, crime, and unemployment, with little if any minimum sanitation or safety standards. By 1859, one out of every 20 urban residents lived in cellars, averaging 6 to 20 per room, with an estimated 10,000 abandoned, orphaned, or runaway children living in the streets (Hymowitz & Weissman, 1980).

The depression of 1837-1838 broke the back of private charity and gave impetus to new social reform, not only for poverty-related problems but on such issues as the morality of slavery, women's suffrage, and temperance. A women's movement arose, enabled in part by the decline of the extended family, where single women were expected to care for children. Among its leaders were the Grimké sisters of Georgia, Elizabeth Cady Stanton, Susan B. Anthony, and Sojourner Truth, who began to speak out publicly for women's rights and the emancipation of slaves. Frederick Douglass, freed slave and orator, joined them at Seneca Falls, New York, where the first women's conference was held in 1848.

While men studied and supported poverty reform movements, women became active in them as friendly visitors. In New York, Robert Hartley established the Association for Improving the Condition of the Poor, which divided the city into wards where friendly visitors investigated needs and distributed relief and friendly advice. The Association led the way to planned giving, cooperation among agencies, and accurate record keeping, and it became the model for later charity organization societies. At first opposed to almsgiving, the Association made that a major purpose when data collected by friendly visitors proved poverty was caused by society's institutions. The Association became the poor's advocate, opening health dispensaries, crippled children's hospitals, public bathhouses, and asylums for the care and instruction of children (Mencher, 1967).

In 1840, Dorothea Dix began to investigate conditions of the mentally ill in Massachusetts asylums and, pleading the state had moral and legal obligations to them, gained state care. She pursued her cause in other states, which refused responsibility. However, her proposal to the U.S. Congress to use proceeds of set-aside public lands to care for the indigent mentally ill was passed as the Ten Million Acre Bill of 1848, with an additional 2.5 million acres to support the indigent deaf. President Franklin Pierce vetoed the legislation in 1851, saying that the federal government could not impinge on states' rights and that the bill would open the door for all indigents seeking federal aid.

By 1830, there were more than 100 private charities, among them organizations for Freedmen, Chinese, Finnish Women, the Polish Women's alliance, Female Guardian Society, Homes for the Friendless, Mission to Children of the Disabled, and the American Temperance Society. Religious groups played their part: Protestants advocated better housing, sanitation, and moral improvement; gave religious tracts along with food and clothing; and established first the Young Men's Christian Association in 1851, which served rural boys in the cities, and in 1866 in Boston the first Young Women's Christian Associations. Irish and Italian Catholics began highly successful outdoor relief programs for immigrants and built orphanages, schools, and hospitals. For their newcomers, Jews set up mutual aid societies especially for education and work.

Reformers demanded special schools for the blind, deaf, and retarded and campaigned for better treatment of criminals, delinquents, and the mentally ill. Public schools, always a goal in the colonies, became firmly established by the middle 1800s. Their purpose, in addition to education, was to provide supervision for children and take them out of the men's job market. Reform schools based on new penology principles trained the incorrigible to conform to society and work rules, readying them for labor in the Industrial Revolution.

Three social movements set the stage for the social work profession today: the Charity Organization Societies, the Child-Saving Movement, and the Settlement House movement. The first two reached fruition in the middle 1800s, the latter at the turn of the century. Charity Organization Societies developed in all the larger cities, with structures and processes modeled on the Association for Improving the Condition of the Poor. Originally aimed at cooperation and referral among city agencies, partly to prevent "double-dipping" by the needy, the Societies developed procedures for charity distribution, registered the city's poor, worked with police to clean up city crime and delinquency, and collected and collated accurate data, leading to more reform. Programs for training social workers began under their auspices as the major professional associations of the time.

The thousands of children roaming city streets led Charles Loring Brace in 1853 to establish the Child-Saving Movement. He believed that no help should be given that kept pauper families together, and he determined to relocate children with families in the West so that they could learn the benefits of hard work in a new environment. Over the next 20 years, haphazardly and without follow-up, his agents took (often kidnapped) over 50,000 children, loaded them into freight trains, and shipped them west, where they were picked over and chosen stop after stop. Unfortunately, many were taken for cheap labor, mistreated, and overworked. Many ran away, got lost, died, or simply disappeared.

Saving children became a hallmark of the times, spreading through public and private charities. It led to provision of nurseries and day care for poor children, new health care, and food distribution. An orphanage movement began, taking children from almshouses. Work morality was the major emphasis, with rigid discipline, work schedules, and harsh punishments. However, the orphanages were run on the almshouse profit-making model, with mortality rates of about 20% (Compton, 1980).

Women and Non-White Populations

Social policies continued to oppress women and people of color throughout this era. Some white women won victories in education and the professions, and women migrating to the West had citizen rights because of their scarcity. However, most women remained subservient to male rule. Poor women were considered almost as prostitutes, selling their labor and being used sexually by men of the upper class. Women of color underwent inhumane treatment: hard work, being bred for children sold away as slaves, rape, mutilation, and, of course, death, because owners could inflict any punishment on their property.

Because of cotton production's importance, slave imports continued until 1859, with breeding programs to produce prime workers. Prices of "good slaves" rose from $300 in 1820 to over $1,000 in 1859, and the slave population grew from 1.5 million to almost 4 million (Bennett, 1966). Rebellions begun by folk leaders such as Gabriel Prosser, Denmark Vesey, and Nat Turner in the early 1800s were brutally put down, and state slave codes dictated proper behavior and forbade assembly and education. The Missouri Compromise of 1829 ensured continuance of slavery in the South, ordering that any new free state be matched with a new slave state. Updated in 1850, the Compromise mandated a new and harsher Fugitive Slave Law. In 1857, the Dred Scott decision reaffirmed that slaves were property, and although escaped slaves flocked to join the Union army, Lincoln ordered them returned to their owners. Free people of African descent were present from 1826, but even in the North, they had no citizen rights.

Every treaty with Native Americans was broken as they were systematically robbed of their lands. Andrew Jackson, perhaps the most anti-Native American President, signed the Indian Removal Act of 1830, which led to the infamous Trail of Tears, where thousands of the more than 70,000 Native Americans sent beyond the Allegheny River died. The westward movement brought an estimated 250,000 white settlers between 1840 and 1860, encouraged by legislation such as the Kansas-Nebraska Act of 1854 and the Homestead Act in 1863, and the bison-based economy of the Plains societies was destroyed by hunters riding the transcontinental railroad, completed in 1869.

Southwest and Mexican Hispanics were also in the path of white settlers, whose encroachment included the annexation of Texas in 1845. This precipitated the Mexican War of 1845, ending with the Treaty of Guadalupe Hidalgo in 1848, in which the United States commandeered Texas, New Mexico, and the California coast. Border clashes continued, led by Mexican hero Juan Cortina against local militia and the Texas Rangers, but white squatters continued their assault on Mexican territory, and the white migration wave soon reduced the Southwest Spanish culture to peonage.

Although a smaller group, Chinese people also bore the brunt of race hatred in America. Men shanghaied from China after the devastation of the Opium Wars in the mid-19th century became American debt slaves, and, although nominally free, were put to work in gold mines and on the railroad until its completion. The Oriental Exclusion Acts of 1880 effectively ended any rights they had in the United States until after World War II.

CONCLUSION

In the Civil War, the real issue was the states' rights to profit in international trade: unrestricted shipping of cotton based on slave labor for the South or using the South's cotton for manufacturing in the North by the laboring poor. This battle for profit, overlaid on the yeasty mix of civil, moral, and religious reform of the 1800s, exploded into war with ourselves. Yet, basically, it was a logical outcome: a result of the 400-year-old experiment in work ethic morality that wed wealth to the use of others as cogs in the profit-making machine. Social policies throughout that time rose and fell according to what was required for profit. Perhaps this experiment and its success were necessary to build our nation. How would we know?

EFERENCES

Bennett, L. J. (1966). *Before the Mayflower: A history of the Negro in America.* Chicago: Johnson.

Coll, B. (1972). Public assistance in the United States: Colonial to 1860. In E. W. Martin (Ed.), *Comparative development in social welfare.* London: Allen & Unwin.

Compton, B. (1980). *Introduction to social welfare and social work: Structure, function, and process.* Homewood, IL: Dorsey.

Day, P. J. (1997). *A new history of social welfare* (2nd ed.). Needham Heights, MA: Allyn & Bacon.

Grob, G. N. (Advisory Ed.). (1976). Maryland report on almshouses. In *State and public welfare in nineteenth century America.* New York: Arno.

Hymowitz, C., & Weissman, M. (1980). *A history of women in America.* New York: Bantam.

Mencher, S. (1967). *From poor house to poverty programs.* Pittsburgh: University of Pittsburgh Press.

Morgan, T. (1993). *Wilderness at dawn: The settling of the North American continent.* New York: Simon & Schuster.

Seller, M. (1984). *Immigrant women.* Philadelphia, PA: Temple University Press.

Yates, J. V. N. (1824). Report of the secretary of state in 1824 on the relief and settlement of the poor. In *34th annual report of the State Board of Charities of the State of New York, 1900* (Vol. 1, pp. 939-963).

CHAPTER EIGHT

Social Policy and the Progressive Era

JOHN M. HERRICK

From the 1890s to the 1920s, there were many attempts at social, political, and economic reform. This era has come to be called the Progressive Era. Its beginning and ending dates are debated by scholars, as are the motives of the Progressive reformers and the final legacy of reformist measures.

It is impossible to understand the Progressive Era and Progressivism without some understanding of changes in American society during the period. From the late 19th to the early 20th century, urbanization was under way. By 1916, about half of the population of nearly 100 million resided in urban areas of at least 8,000 people (Coll, 1969). Large-scale industrial enterprises developed, creating national markets that determined prices (North, 1966). Small businesses often struggled to compete. Complex transportation systems emerged, linking major markets and serving as means for farmers to get goods into the national marketplace. Large industrial producers needed workers, many of whom had to develop specialized skills. Contests between labor and capital characterized the era. Immigration brought workers of many nationalities into urban and rural areas, sometimes upsetting the status quo.

Political responses to change varied. Democratic, Republican, Progressive, and Socialist parties offered voters visions for coping with new realities in the Progressive Era. There was considerable legislative innovation and commotion, much of it the legacy of earlier Populist concerns aimed at making government more responsive to "the people." Progressives wanted the direct election of senators, a federal income tax, the initiative and referendum, and women's suffrage (Goldman, 1956).

Responses to a changing society were complex, and their purposes and functions are debated by scholars. Most often the Progressive Era is seen as a period when reforms attempted to grapple with social change by seeking social policy responses that would promote market stability by providing measures of protection and security for those seen as vulnerable to the vicissitudes of social change—workers, women, families, and children (Davis, 1967).

INTERPRETING THE PROGRESSIVE ERA

Early scholars of the Progressive Era generally saw the period as a time in which liberal reformers battled against conservative interests in efforts to win opportunities for common people as opposed to corporate interests led by greedy, heartless, if not un-American, corporate elites. Vernon Louis Parrington's (1927) *Main Currents in American Thought* and Beard and Beard's (1927) *The Rise of American Civilization,* written from a liberal-progressive paradigm, saw the Progressive Era as a time when democratic interests attempted to wrest power from monopolistic, corporate, conservative elites. Popular sentiment, fueled by sensationalistic, *muckraking journalism*—a term coined by Theodore Roosevelt and exemplified by Upton Sinclair's *The Jungle* and Frank Norris's *The Octopus,* portrayals of gigantic, inhumane meat processors and greedy railroads—helped create popular demand for reforms aimed at protecting public health and creating more equitable economic opportunities for small producers and consumers. Parrington and others writing from the liberal-progressive perspective saw the Progressive Era as a time in which democratic reform was possible, an era of potential realization of the aspirations of common men and women, unlike earlier periods of conservative consolidation and increasing domination by corporate interests. Progressives sought opportunities for realization of the American dream. They wanted a democratic society that reflected egalitarian ideals. For Parrington and others, the Progressive Movement consisted of many reformist thrusts, often spearheaded by middle-class reform-minded academics, writers, and representatives of emerging professions such as social work who were seeking means to promote social, economic, and political democracy.

Writing after World War II, a group of influential historians reassessed the Progressive Era and found the motives of Progressives to be suspect. Richard Hofstader, a prominent historian, won a Pulitzer Prize for his *Age of Reform: From Bryan to FDR,* written in 1955, in which he concluded that Progressives' motives could be best explained by profound status anxiety as their social status was threatened by social change. David W. Noble's (1958) *The Paradox of Progressive Thought* found Progressive thought to be more backward- than forward-looking as it idealized a simplistic Jeffersonian, agrarian past while it rejected the complexity of modern industrial society. As such, it searched for an idealized past that ignored contemporary conflict and complexity. Hofstader and his colleagues may be characterized as representing a neo-conservative perspective that was critical of Progressives and the Progressive Era. They saw American history as the story of the remarkable persistence of a basic consensus about means and ends. Criticizing the liberal-Progressive genre as emphasizing struggles between people and large, special interests, their studies found that profound consensus characterized the American past, a shared normative framework that allowed differences and struggles but always within a basic, shared set of assumptions about the purposes and ends of American institutions, a shared liberal consensus.

Hofstader assessed the Progressive Movement through the words of its leading proponents and found it unrealistic and narrow in its objectives, led by middle-class reformers who were alienated from contemporary social change. Progressives did not appeal to immigrants and reflected class notions of propriety and safety (Goldman, 1956). They longed for a simpler, less complex age than the complex industrial economic society that confronted them. George E. Mowry (1951), studying *California Progressives,* found reformers attempted to retain the prerogatives of social class as their authority and status were threatened by emerging corporate power elites. Informed by highly individualistic values, they were more concerned about their own status than in making substantive structural changes in American society. Recent research finds that the view of Progressive reformers may be too simplistic. Because many reformers were women, women's changing status informed their activities. Reform, in effect, emancipated some women reformers and served as a socially acceptable activity that was socially beneficial (Skocpol, 1992, 1996).

Still other historians, influenced by the behavioral sciences, studied the rise of complex organizations and bureaucracies in the Progressive Era. They found increasing professionalization in many fields such as social work, where helping became a refined technique. These developments downplayed individualistic values, and they stressed the importance of rational planning to promote efficiency. This outcome contrasted sharply with the nostalgic pining of some Progressive Era thinkers for a simpler, more agrarian society. Proponents of what Samuel P. Hays (1959) called the "Gospel of Efficiency" wanted a rationally planned, technically efficient society in contrast to a loosely arranged, decentralized society.

Robert Wiebe (1962), in *Businessmen and Reform: A Study of the Progressive Movement,* saw the drive for business regulation in the Progressive Era not as an attempt to curtail the power of large corporations to create more democratic opportunities for small business, but rather as a rationally planned strategy to eliminate competition that contributed to economic instability. Efficiency and economic stability that could avoid the destructive financial upheavals of the past were in the best interests of both business and government. Wiebe found that whereas business often opposed unions and social insurance, it often supported economic regulation. In his *Search for Order, 1877-1920,* Wiebe (1967) argued that middle-class Progressives wanted to promote social order through the creation of new organizational arrangements most often characterized by bureaucracy. Out of the fragmented, divisive past of the late 19th century, they created arrangements for conducting society's affairs that would characterize the 20th century, particularly through the use of complex administrative structures.

Other interpreters of Progressivism saw it as fundamentally conservative and nonreformist. Gabriel Kolko (1963), the most influential of the New Left historians of the Progressive Era, argued in *The Triumph of Conservatism: A Reinterpretation of American History, 1900-1916,* that reform meant the political rationalization of the status quo. Whatever business deemed best for itself was seen as consistent with the general welfare of America. Economic regulation of business during the Progressive Era, he found, was often directed by leaders of businesses targeted for regulation. Larger businesses shared a common consensus with leading politicians about the necessity of maintaining social and economic norms that would protect property relationships. Kolko argued that a shared ethos of political capitalism shaped Progressive reforms and American society in the 20th century (Grob & Billias, 1972; Weinstein, 1968).

Recent scholarship has questioned the motives of Progressive Era reformers, especially their assumptions that social policy enactments could transform intended beneficiaries into semblances of the middle-class reformers themselves (Mink, 1995). This created inevitable class, gender, cultural, and racial tensions, especially because much social policy was generated and supported by women (Skocpol, 1996). Furthermore, when reforms were implemented by states and municipalities, administrators' decisions were informed by local values and standards, creating idiosyncratic results (Ladd-Taylor, 1994; Lasch-Quinn, 1997; Mink, 1995; Muncy, 1991).

These conflicting interpretations of the Progressive Era reflect ongoing scholarly debate about the meaning and function of reform in American history. They demonstrate the complexity and futility of attempting to explain Progressive Era reforms simplistically. Historiographic complexity should inform our attempt to understand its important social policy legacy.

STUDIES FOR REFORM

The Progressive Era coincided with the publication of some pioneering American studies of social conditions, which would be used by reformers to argue for a variety of policies and programs that they hoped might ease the condition of the poor and those who were seen as in need of assistance. Progressive Era reformers believed that social problems would be resolved by the use of professionals, by experts who could work through government to improve well-being (Lasch-Quinn, 1997). These studies emulated earlier ones done in England, such as Charles Booth's (1902) multivolume *Life and Labour of the People of London,* which brought the existence of considerable poverty to the attention of British policy makers. Robert Hunter's (1904) study of poverty in the United States, *Poverty,* estimated that 10 million Americans out of a total population of 82 million were poor, according to a normative income standard he developed (Leiby, 1978). Patterson (1986) suggested Hunter's poverty estimate was conservative, even though it was a pioneering effort. Hunter struggled with the conceptualization of poverty. He acknowledged that many people were poor temporarily whereas others were more or less permanently poor, mainly because of their own sloth. They deserved little if any public assistance. Hunter also understood the relationship between economic upheaval and the creation of temporary poverty among the otherwise employable. His portrayal of deserving and undeserving poor and the causes of poverty contributed to long-standing discussion and debate about the nature of poverty and its amelioration.

Perhaps the most important Progressive Era survey of American social conditions was completed under the direction of Paul U. Kellogg, a journalist, social reformer, and friend of many social workers. His *Pittsburgh Survey* (1909-1914) was supported by the Russell Sage Foundation, which later financed other social welfare studies. Paul Kellogg saw the *Pittsburgh Survey* as more than a social scientific experiment to assess contemporary social problems. It was meant to be a springboard for social action that would address the problems studied. Its findings were often cited in state efforts to develop workmen's compensation programs and industrial safety campaigns. Kellogg went on to serve as founder and editor of *The Survey,* an important magazine devoted to social welfare issues, from 1909 until 1952. Kellogg was active in the National Conference of Charities and Corrections and its Committee on Occupational Standards, which studied working conditions and made many policy recommendations on worker's compensation, industrial health, and limits on hours of labor. It was these recommendations that were incorporated into the platform of the Progressive Party in 1912, which also called for the prohibition of child labor and minimum wages for female workers. *The Survey* became an important venue for many reformers and their causes. The American Association for Labor Legislation, an important source of social policy advocacy, reported on its activities in *The Survey,* and Kellogg printed articles on discrimination against immigrants and Negroes, on tenement safety concerns, on the need for more parks and playgrounds and better hospitals, on the need for juvenile courts, on social insurance programs and how they could protect workers from sickness and accidents and even protect them in old age, and on women's suffrage (Chambers, 1971; Coll, 1969; Woodroofe, 1971).

MAJOR REFORMS OF THE PROGRESSIVE ERA

Progressive reforms were difficult to achieve because prevailing theories of government held that the federal government generally did not possess the constitutional authority to enact social policy reforms. Consequently, the states were the arenas for contests to enact social policy reform (Coll, 1969).

Such reforms were not easily won. In 1905, the Supreme Court held in *Lochner v. People of the State of New York* that a New York state law limiting the hours of workers in the baking industry was unconstitutional. The court held that baking was not a dangerous or unhealthy occupation. If public safety could not be shown to be at risk, the Court would not interfere with employees' and employers' liberty of contact. Some state courts did, however, uphold state laws establishing maximum 12-hour workdays for women (Moss, 1996).

In 1908, reversing its 1905 Lochner decision, the Supreme Court in *Muller v. State of Oregon* upheld Oregon's 10-hour workday law for women. It did so by relying on a brief submitted by Louis D. Brandeis, social reformer and later a Supreme Court judge, which introduced sociological information about the ill effects of harsh working conditions on workers. It presented research showing the effects of lengthy workdays on women workers. The Russell Sage Foundation and the National Consumers' League supported the American Association for Labor Legislation by distributing the brief to supporters of regulation of working conditions. The Muller decision encouraged other judicial rulings protecting women in the workplace. By 1917, 41 states had enacted laws regulating women's working conditions, setting hours and conditions of work (Abramovitz, 1996).

Some states studied minimum wage laws affecting women and minors. In Massachusetts, a commission was established that investigated working conditions in specific industries and then recommended minimum wage scales for them. In 1910, the Russell Sage Foundation created a Committee on Women's Work. Mary Van Kleeck, a skilled social researcher, spearheaded the committee's authoritative studies of the impact of low wages on women and how they contributed to women's poverty (Bremner, 1956). The U.S. Bureau of Labor's influential *Report on Conditions of Women and Child Wage Earners in the United States,* published from 1910 to 1913, found that there were no agreed-on standards governing women's wages. Reflecting concern about exploitation of women workers, Mary van Kleek observed, "It is the worker nearest starvation who is most likely to accept starvation wages" (Bremner, 1956, p. 238).

By 1917, the momentum for minimum wage legislation was stalled. Little headway was made at the state level, and opposition by commercial interests contributed to lack of action. After World War I, opposition to minimum wage legislation continued. In 1923, the U.S. Supreme Court in *Adkins v. Children's Hospital* held a District of

Columbia minimum wage law to be unconstitutional because it interfered with the right of contract. Abramovitz (1996) argued that, in general, protective laws aimed at women actually limited women's opportunities by confining their labor to specific occupations that often paid low wages. These laws maintained a "sex segregated labor market" and "channeled women back into the home" (p. 188), Abramovitz maintained. The lack of success in creating solid standards to regulate wages reflects the differential success of Progressive social policy efforts owing to the relative timeliness of some reforms and not others at the state level.

Housing

Investigation of social conditions in urban areas led to many policy responses aimed at providing measures to improve housing. New York, Chicago, and Boston saw many successful efforts to reform living conditions of the poor, most notably in efforts to demolish unsafe tenements or to strengthen housing codes aimed at strengthening safety measures. New York City's Tenement House Law of 1901 and Chicago's ordinance of 1902, which was largely the result of Jane Addams and her Hull House colleagues' skillful advocacy, are examples of successful Progressive Era housing reforms. By 1917, 40 cities and 11 states had new tenement house codes and regulations that attempted to improve sanitary conditions (Bremner, 1956).

The idea of public housing, which was attacked vehemently by those who felt provision of housing was not a government responsibility, was proposed by the American Federation of Labor (AFL) in 1914. At its national convention, the AFL resolved that the federal government provide loans to cities to finance construction of municipal housing. In 1915, Massachusetts adopted a constitutional amendment that allowed the state to construct low-cost housing (Bremner, 1956). Although the number of public housing efforts begun in the Progressive Era was modest, they became precedents for government subsidization of housing during the 1930s in response to the Great Depression (Lubove, 1963).

Child Welfare and Mothers' Pensions

Campaigns to "save" children have long been part of reform efforts in the United States. Progressive Era reformers continued these efforts, and between 1900 and 1917, there were numerous enactments by municipalities and states that created juvenile courts, improved recreational opportunities by creating parks and playgrounds, extended periods of compulsory school attendance, and established standards that would protect children's health. The crusade against child labor, as Bremner (1956) has noted, was one of the areas where Progressive reformers achieved considerable success. John Spargo's (1906) *The Bitter Cry of the Children* alerted sympathetic readers that there were over 2 million child laborers in the United States. Jane Addams told the National Conference of Charities and Corrections in 1903 that many working boys and girls would grow up without schooling or skills they could use in the marketplace. She felt this would lead to unproductive, wasted lives (Bremner, 1956).

Child welfare reformers were acutely aware of arguments by those who supported continuation of child labor, most notably that children's wages were necessary for support of families, particularly for single mothers. Part of the Progressive counterargument was that if laboring fathers were paid living wages, this would reduce the need for child welfare. The notion that workers had a right to a living wage that would enable their families to enjoy the "promise of American life" would be used by social reformers throughout the 20th century. If industry could pay male workers less than living wages, the unarticulated assumption was that the wages of wives and children would supplement a family's income. Because they were viewed as nonprimary breadwinners, it was seen as acceptable to pay women and children lower wages. As competitors in the labor market, women and children would also decrease men's wages, leading to a result that primarily benefitted employers. By 1900, 28 states had adopted laws regulating child labor and more followed during the Progressive Era. In 1904, a National Child Labor Committee was formed. Among its founders were Felix Adler, active in New York campaigns to improve tenements, and Jane Addams and Lillian Wald from the social settlements. The National Child Labor Committee conducted studies of child welfare and created state organizations to lobby for more effective child welfare legislation and recommended standards governing child labor, including a minimum age of 14 in the manufacturing industry (Bremner, 1956).

In 1909, after persistent lobbying by the Child Labor Committee, a White House Conference on the Care of Dependent Children was held. It urged creation of a federal children's bureau that would investigate children's welfare throughout the nation. Supported by President Theodore Roosevelt, a Children's Bureau in the Department of Labor and Commerce was created in 1912.

In 1916, child labor reformers succeeded in passing federal legislation attacking child labor. The law mandated that the items produced using child labor were prohibited from interstate commerce. Shortly, therefore, the courts held the federal law to be unconstitutional. In the 1920s, child labor reformers lobbied for a constitutional amendment prohibiting child labor. Their efforts were unsuccessful, as a loose coalition of anti-reform groups, reflecting the conservatism of the 1920s, succeeded in preventing state ratification of the amendment. This proved to be a bitter defeat for reformers and symbolized the reactionary conditions of the 1920s as the nation reassessed its priorities after World War I. It is noteworthy, however, that by 1930, all states had created some form of child protection laws (Day, 1997).

The White House Conference of 1909 also recommended that whenever possible children should not be removed from their homes despite the presence of poverty. Although the Conference did not support public relief for families, in 1911, Illinois became the first state to provide support for needy single mothers of young children. Illinois' experience was scrutinized by reformers, some fearful that public relief would be open to fraud and corruption (Leiby, 1978). Despite these reservations, 20 states had adopted mothers' pension laws by 1913, and by 1926, all but 8 states had enacted them (Patterson, 1986). Southern states with the greatest number of African American residents were the last states to adopt mothers' pension laws (Abramovitz, 1996). Mothers' pensions were eventually seen as acceptable forms of outdoor relief. They often had means tests that limited assistance only to women who were "fit" physically, mentally, and morally. Having an illegitimate child could prevent a mother from receiving aid. Widows with young children were the preferred recipients. Levels of mothers' pension support varied across states, and it is questionable whether assistance was adequate for achieving even a modest standard of living (Lubove, 1986; Moss, 1996; Patterson, 1986; Skocpol, 1992). The 1919 White House Conference on Children reported that assistance to women was inadequate for raising children in many states, resulting in the need for outside employment (Abramovitz, 1996).

Mothers' pension laws were precedent-setting. With them, government agreed to support certain women and their children, clear recognition that family life was superior to institutional residency for some needy children. They also allowed public supervision of mothers and their children to ensure that public assistance was having its intended result of family stability. Maternalist social norms, reflecting middle-class ideals of appropriate female behavior, influenced the administration of mothers' pensions. Social workers and others hired to determine eligibility for assistance and to monitor its effects through supervision and casework enforced dominant norms that have characterized much discretionary social policy (Coll, 1969; Gordon, 1994; Mink, 1995; Skocpol, 1996).

Linda Gordon (1994) found that single or divorced women were seen as unworthy of assistance in most states, evidence of the strength of social norms supporting traditional views of the family. She argued that worker's compensation, whose beneficiaries were primarily men, eventually became seen as an entitlement program, less open to discretionary determination of eligibility than mothers' pensions, primarily because of gender bias. Nevertheless, by 1926, only five states continued to give assistance only to widows, and some jurisdictions gave support to divorced mothers or to women whose husbands were incapacitated or imprisoned (Day, 1997). Clearly, mothers' pensions were only palliative. They did little to address fundamental causes of social inequality and poverty, but they did demonstrate widespread public awareness and support for needy mothers and children. However inadequate mothers' pensions were, however few mothers of color were assisted, however pensions reflected maternalist bias, they did support family life and often removed women from the labor market, at least temporarily. When mothers had to work outside the home to supplement public assistance, they were forced to join the ranks of temporary, low-paid, female workers, thereby supplying labor demand and enforcing social norms regulating women's work. In the 1930s, mothers' pensions became important precedents for federal efforts to support women and children during the Great Depression.

Workmen's Compensation

During the Progressive Era, reformers saw workingmen's insurance as a rational response to the growing recognition of the dangers of the workplace. Industrial accidents claimed lives and created loss of wages because of injury. The U.S. Bureau of Labor and the Russell Sage Foundation conducted comparative studies of foreign social insurance systems. The idea of creating public insurance to protect people from life's vicissitudes was supported by many reformers. Isaac M. Rubinow's (1913) *Social Insurance* became an influential source of ideas for reformers. The Progressive Party's "Social and Industrial Justice" recommendations in its 1912 platform called for old age and unemployment insurance.

Before workmen's compensation, workers' assistance for job-related injuries was uncertain (Bremner, 1956). They might be covered under employer or private insurance, or they could attempt to use common law remedies by suing employers, an expensive and uncertain process. Statistics on the number of industrial accidents in 1913 revealed at least 25,000 fatalities and injuries. Between 1909 and 1913, 30 state commissions studied workers' accidents and recommended systems of workmen's compensation. By 1920, all states except 6 and the District of Columbia had passed workers' compensation laws (Day, 1997). They were often supported by reform-minded organizations such as the American Association for Labor Legislation as well as the occasional nemeses of labor, the National Association of Manufacturers and the National Civic Federation.

From 1911 to 1920, over 40 states enacted workers' compensation laws. Most did not offer the level of benefits thought adequate by the American Association for Labor Legislation, which included compensation at two thirds of wages for total disability. Why were workers' compensation laws so widely adopted? One explanation is that workers' compensation laws were seen by business as more acceptable than the uncertainties resulting from liabilities incurred because of workers' common law negligence cases (Moss, 1996). Within the emerging culture of corporate capitalism, workers' compensation statutes came to be accepted as appropriate rationalizations of marketplace uncertainty. However enthusiastic the support for workers' compensation, state laws initiated in the Progressive Era most often excluded agricultural and domestic laborers, many of whom were women and African Americans (Alston &

Fearie, 1985; Moss, 1996). Although workers' compensation laws signaled willingness by states to enact legislative protection, they did not offer universal coverage for all workers. They often did not provide compensation for occupational diseases, nor did they provide benefits sufficient to provide for an adequate standard of living. Furthermore, most state laws were voluntary, so that employers could elect not to provide compensation insurance for their workers. About 30% of workers in states with compensation laws in 1920 were not covered (Bremner, 1956).

Health Insurance and Unemployment Insurance

Progressive reformers, feeling some justifiable success with the enactment of workers' compensation statutes, turned to health insurance as a solution to the many problems created by illness. Even though prominent reformers such as Jane Addams and Paul Kellogg saw health insurance as a logical goal that complemented other reforms, they did not anticipate the strength of opposition to the notion. Insurance companies, labor, medical and dental associations, drug producers, and other powerful interests opposed public health insurance, sometimes arguing that it was un-American, an especially potent argument after World War I (Chambers, 1967; Day, 1997). In retrospect, it seems curious that so many Americans have objected to the idea of public health insurance, even though they generally agreed that workers' compensation was acceptable. Unemployment insurance was also controversial. By 1930, not a single state had enacted unemployment insurance (Patterson, 1986). It was only in 1932 that Wisconsin passed legislation of this kind (Skocpol & Ikenbery, 1995). Even during the Progressive Era, there was widespread fear that unemployment insurance might encourage carelessness or idleness despite the arguments of some reformers.

The Elderly

Care of the aged was another issue Progressive Era reformers included in their policy agenda. The 1912 Progressive Party platform recommended establishment of social insurance that would cover the elderly. By 1914, only Arizona had a modest form of old age pension, with eligibility quite circumscribed. Very few workers in private employment had any form of old age protection, indicating the strongly held belief that it was the responsibility of individuals to save for their old age. When public health insurance was opposed, support for old age pensions was weakened. During the 1920s, several states adopted forms of old age pensions, setting precedents for federal policies during the 1930s as the nation responded to the Depression (Day, 1997).

THE LEGACY OF THE PROGRESSIVE ERA

Social policy reflects the possible, and the parameters of the possible are most often decided by elites whose beliefs determine allocation of resources to those who are economically and socially vulnerable. Progressive Era reformers seldom proffered structural solutions to the social problems they studied. Most often, they offered remedies whose effect would only support those in need periodically and temporarily (Patterson, 1986).

There were, of course, Progressive Era policy initiatives that had widespread effect on the political system. The long struggle for women's suffrage could claim victory in 1919, the same year the Volstead Act became federal law and brought prohibition of the manufacture and sale of alcoholic beverages. Prohibition was supported by some social reformers and derided by others. Its impact was felt by New York City settlement workers, whose neighborhoods, often teeming with immigrants, did not understand the rationale for Prohibition and often ignored it (Herrick, 1970).

Progressive reform was mainly an urban phenomenon. Social policy reformers were urban-focused and reflected the views of their times. Child labor and its elimination, a central concern of pre-World War I reform, targeted children working in industry, not the 60% of child laborers working in rural agricultural labor. Protecting women workers from unsafe and exploitive working conditions also focused on industrial workers, not women working in rural areas. Debates about the legacy of Progressive reforms, particularly its meaning for women, enrich our understanding of the era.

Progressive reformers generally shared a "new" view of poverty, which broke from older beliefs that saw poverty as the result of individual character flaws. Rather than emphasizing personal rehabilitation as the main solution to poverty, they felt reform of the social conditions linked to poverty could prevent it. Consequently, they focused their energies on housing reform, eliminating dangers to workers, regulating working conditions, eliminating child labor, and providing workmen's compensation, aid to women with children, and old age pension laws. To create a more just and humane society and to preserve social order, Progressive reformers, many of whom were women, realized that reducing dependency and strengthening families necessitated policy changes aimed at ameliorating conditions that, if left unattended, could lead to social instability. Although the Progressives never did achieve comprehensive social insurance, their accomplishments foreshadowed the social policy enactments of the 1930s. Even selectively modest old age assistance and mothers' pensions were precedents for social insurance initiatives in the 1930s.

According to prominent historian Arthur Schlesinger, Jr. (1957), World War I brought the generation of Progressive reformers to maturity. Much of their domestic program had been enacted as legislation and regulations. Reformers associated with the Progressive Party had by 1916 become disillusioned with President Wilson's stance on domestic reform and were absorbed with international issues as the nation moved toward war. Most opposed Wilson, and the decline of the Progressive Party is seen by many historians as symbolic of the waning of liberal reform and the end of the Progressive Era (Margulies, 1969). Henry F. May (1959), analyzing intellectual history from 1912 to 1917, characterized the end of the Progressive Era as "The End of American Innocence," a diminishing of the American "belief in Progress," which had been implicitly assumed by Progressive social reformers. Clearly, although some Progressive social policies had been enacted, the 1920s witnessed a general retreat from social policy development, which would not resurface until the era of the Great Depression. Some reformers continued to express hope that the unfinished business of the Progressive Era, such as wholesale prohibition of child labor and the provision of social insurance, would someday be addressed. However, it took massive economic breakdown before the nation created a new reform agenda (Chambers, 1967).

REFERENCES

Abramovitz, M. (1996). *Regulating the lives of women: Social welfare policy from colonial times to the present* (rev. ed.). Boston: South End Press.

Adkins v. Children's Hospital of District of Columbia, 261 U.S. 525 (1923).

Alston, L. J., & Fearie, J. P. (1985). Labor costs, paternalism, and loyalty in southern agriculture: A constraint on the growth of the welfare state. *Journal of Economic History, 45,* 95-117.

Beard, C., & Beard, M. E. (1927). *The rise of American civilization.* New York: Macmillan.

Booth, C. (1902). *Life and labour of the people in London.* New York: Macmillan.

Bremner, R. H. (1956). *From the depths: The discovery of poverty in the United States.* New York: New York University Press.

Chambers, C. A. (1967). *Seedtime of reform: American social service and social action.* Ann Arbor: University of Michigan Press.

Chambers, C. A. (1971). *Paul U. Kellogg and the survey.* Minneapolis: University of Minnesota Press.

Coll, B. (1969). *Perspectives in public welfare: A history.* Washington, DC: Government Printing Office.

Davis, A. (1967). *Spearheads for reform: The social settlements in the Progressive Era, 1890-1914.* New York: Oxford University Press.

Day, P. J. (1997). *A new history of social welfare* (2nd ed.). Boston: Allyn & Bacon.

Goldman, E. (1956). *Rendezvous with destiny.* New York: Vintage.

Gordon, L. (1994). *Pitied but not entitled: Single mothers and the history of welfare, 1890-1935.* New York: Free Press.

Grob, G. N., & Billias, G. A. (Eds.). (1972). The progressive movement: Liberal or conservative? In G. N. Grob & G. A. Billias (Eds.), *Interpretations of American history* (Vol. 2, pp. 159-176). New York: Free Press.

Hays, S.P. (1959). *Conservation and the gospel of efficiency: The progressive conservation movement, 1890-1920.* Cambridge, MA: Harvard University Press.

Herrick, J. M. (1970). *A holy discontent: The history of the New York City social settlements in the interwar era, 1919-1941.* Unpublished Ph.D. dissertation: University of Minnesota.

Hofstader, R. (1955). *The age of reform: From Bryan to FDR.* New York: Vintage.

Hunter, R. (1904). *Poverty.* New York: Macmillan.

Kellogg, P. U. (1909-1914). *The Pittsburgh survey* (6 vols.). New York: Charities Publication Committee.

Kolko, G. (1963). *The triumph of conservation: A reinterpretation of American history, 1900-1916.* Chicago: Quadrangle Books.

Ladd-Taylor, M. (1994). *Mother-work: Women, child welfare, and the states, 1890-1930.* Urbana: University of Illinois Press.

Lasch-Quinn, E. (1997). Progressives and the pursuit of agency. *Reviews in American History, 25,* 253-257.

Leiby, J. (1978). *A history of social welfare and social work in the United States.* New York: Columbia University Press.

Lochner v. People of the State of New York 198 U.S. 45 (1905).

Lubove, R. (1963). *The progressives and the slums: Tenement house reform in New York City, 1890-1917.* Pittsburgh, PA: University of Pittsburgh Press.

Lubove, R. (1986). *The struggle for social security, 1900-1935.* Pittsburgh, PA: University of Pittsburgh Press.

Margulies, H. (1969). Recent opinion on the decline of the progressive era. In M. Plesur (Ed.), *The 1920s: Problems and paradoxes* (pp. 39-58). Boston: Allyn & Bacon.

May, H. (1959). *The end of American innocence: A study of the first years of our own time, 1912-1917.* Chicago: Quadrangle Books.

Mink, G. (1995). *The wages of motherhood: Inequity in the welfare state, 1917-1942.* Ithaca, NY: Cornell University Press.

Moss, D. A. (1996). *Socializing security: Progressive era economists and the origins of American social policy.* Cambridge, MA: Harvard University Press.

Mowry, G. E. (1951). *The California progressives.* Berkeley: University of California Press.

Muller v. State of Oregon, 208 U.S. 412 (1908).

Muncy, R. (1991). *Creating a female dominion in American reforms, 1890-1935.* New York: Oxford University Press.

Noble, D. W. (1958). *The paradox of progressive thought.* Minneapolis: University of Minnesota Press.

Norris, F. (1929). *The octopus: A story of California.* Port Washington, NY: Kennikat.

North, D. (1966). *Growth and welfare in the American past: A new economic history.* Englewood Cliffs, NJ: Prentice Hall.

Parrington, V. (1927). *Main currents in American thought* (3 vols.). New York: Harcourt, Brace & World.

Patterson, J. (1986). *America's struggle against poverty.* Cambridge, MA: Harvard University Press.

Rubinow, I. M. (1913). *Social insurance, with special reference to American conditions.* New York: Holt.

Schlesinger, A. M., Jr. (1957). *The crisis of the old order, 1919-1933.* Boston: Houghton Mifflin.

Sinclair, U. (1906). *The jungle.* New York: The Jungle Publishing Co.

Skocpol, T. (1992). *Protecting soldiers and mothers: The political origins of social policy in the United States.* Cambridge, MA: Harvard University Press.

Skocpol, T. (1996). The trouble with welfare. *Reviews in American History, 24,* 641-646.

Skocpol, T., & Ikenbery, G. R. (1995). The road to social security. In T. Skocpol (Ed.), *Social policy in the United States* (pp. 136-166). Princeton, NJ: Princeton University Press.

Spargo, J. (1906). *The bitter cry of the children.* New York: Macmillan.

Weinstein, J. (1968). *The corporate ideal in the liberal state, 1900-1918.* Boston: Beacon.

Wiebe, R. H. (1962). *Businessmen and reform: A study of the progressive movement.* Cambridge, MA: Harvard University Press.

Wiebe, R. H. (1967). *The search for order. 1877-1920.* New York: Hill & Wang.

Woodroofe, K. (1971). *From charity to social work in England and the United States.* Toronto: University of Toronto Press.

CHAPTER NINE

Social Policy of the New Deal

LESLIE LEIGHNINGER
ROBERT LEIGHNINGER

Scholars consider the New Deal a defining moment in American public life (Bordo, Goldin, & White, 1998). A major change in American attitudes toward government and the economy took place, they say, and social policies were formulated that were to define public life for the rest of the century. Others scholars, although not denying the changes, point out the continuities underlying them (Dubofsky, 1992). It seems fair to conclude, however, that the efforts of Franklin Roosevelt's government to pull the country out of a catastrophic depression produced a degree of creative experimentation in social policy that has never been equaled.

Interpretations of the social and political meaning of the New Deal are numerous and varied. The standard liberal view of an overthrow of conservative business domination and the inauguration of a new era of rights for common working people prevailed into the 1960s (Schlesinger, 1957). But by the end of the decade, revisionist historians had begun painting a very different picture of the triumph of capitalism and the maintenance of the status quo despite apparent upheaval (Bernstein, 1969).

Since then, more complicated analyses have been made of the many political and economic forces contending during the period. Some see the emergence of a "broker state," within which a variety of interests compete (Lowi, 1969). A related perspective, sometimes called *corporatism,* sees advances in the security and welfare of common people being achieved because it was in the economic interests of the holders of wealth and power (Ferguson, 1989).

One particularly interesting account focuses on state capacity and party alignment in the formation and implementation of New Deal policy. In this view, the government can have some autonomy in what does and does not become policy. The state is not simply responding to popular forces or powerful interest groups (Finegold & Skocpol, 1995).

Still other analysts have focused on the ways in which New Deal policies were shaped by assumptions about gender, race, and class. These historians picture a national agenda that in many ways ignored the needs of women (especially single mothers), African Americans and other minorities, and chronically low-paid workers (Gordon, 1994; Jones, 1985; Patterson, 1994; Sitkoff, 1984; Smith, 1995).

In documenting specific New Deal policy initiatives, this chapter will try to see how these interpretations might improve understanding of policy formation and successful implementation. It will look particularly at the relationships of federal, state, and local government, public and private interest, and centralized and decentralized administration. It will also look at the roles of minorities and women as they participated in and were affected by New Deal policy making.

ECONOMIC REFORMS

Initial blame for the Depression fell on bankers and financiers, so the first reform efforts included the Securities Act of 1933, the Securities Exchange Act of 1934, and the Banking Acts of 1933, 1934, and 1935. They all aimed at curbing reckless speculation. But it was clear that agriculture and industry would need major support. The Agricultural Adjustment Act and the National Industrial Recovery Act were both enacted in Roosevelt's first "hundred days."

The central strategy of the Agricultural Adjustment Act was to bring farm prices up by reducing production. This, in turn, would boost farmers' incomes so that they might buy more farm machinery, thus helping the industrial sector recover. Farmers were paid subsidies for not producing. Soil conservation was another hoped-for result.

Farmers themselves had lobbied for programs that maintained high levels of production and dumped the result overseas. Cutbacks were against all their instincts. But the program was made law and found wide support. It remains the basis for modern farm policy. The reason for this success, despite strong skepticism from a powerful interest group, say Finegold and Skocpol (1995), was that the Department of Agriculture had strong institutions and relationships that could both create a successful policy and implement it effectively. Its Bureau of Agricultural Economics with its partners in the land grant colleges across the South and West was accustomed to thinking holistically about American agriculture and its role in the world market. The

Department could take a larger view. It also had working relationships with farmers through the Agricultural Extension Service and Experiment Stations. Thus, it could ground its theories in practical experience. The southern congressmen who controlled key committees could see the benefits for their constituents, so the passage of the Act was speedy.

Sharecroppers and tenant farmers were important casualties of the Agricultural Adjustment Act. The price supports paid to landowners under the Act were rarely shared with their farm workers. The result was a massive uprooting of poor farmers and a boost to large landowners. When lawyers tried to protect sharecroppers, the latter were fired (Biles, 1994). The Resettlement Administration and Farm Security Administration tried to compensate for this forced migration but could do little.

There was no similar state capacity in the business sector. Efforts to mobilize the economy during World War I had been ad hoc and managed by corporate executives who returned to private life after the war, leaving nothing behind. The National Industrial Recovery Act brought such executives back together and, with labor leaders, they attempted to gain agreements in each industry on which production levels, prices, and wages would return the economy to health. This became the National Recovery Administration, and its symbol was the blue eagle with the motto, "We do our part."

There were, however, no established relationships or organizations for implementing the National Industrial Recovery Act. Noncompliance was widespread, and the policy was a total failure. Some say it may even have delayed recovery (Finegold & Skocpol, 1995). Both statutes were declared unconstitutional by the conservative Supreme Court. The basic policy of the Agricultural Adjustment Act was quickly revised to avoid further challenges. The National Industrial Recovery Act was abandoned.

One part of the National Industry Recovery Act had a rebirth, however. Its section 7a was the first federal guarantee of collective bargaining, and the act also regulated minimum wages and maximum hours. Subsequent legislation resurrected and strengthened these provisions. The Wagner National Labor Relations Act of 1935 was in part a response to the loss of section 7a. Crucial to the Act's development was the emergence of a new industrial unionism, soon to be embodied in the Congress of Industrial Organizations (CIO), and the mobilization of the Keynesian left wing of the New Deal following the Supreme Court's rulings. These two groups coalesced around beliefs in a planned economy, the redistribution of income, and the necessity of expanding mass consumption (Fraser, 1989). Growing business opposition to Roosevelt following the breakup of the National Recovery Administration pulled him closer to labor. Also, the increased number of liberal urban Democrats in Congress after the 1934 elections established a more favorable climate for progressive labor legislation (Finegold & Skocpol, 1995).

The Wagner Act strengthened labor's right to organize and engage in collective bargaining. Policy makers believed that this spur to unionization would lead to wage increases and thus to increased consumption. Union membership did grow. Yet, because of opposition to the Act by southern farm interests, tenant farmers, both black and white, were excluded from its provisions.

The Fair Labor Standards Act proved more difficult to pass. This legislation represented the chance to reinstall the wage and hours protections and a child labor prohibition included in the National Industry Recovery Act. In fact, Secretary of Labor Frances Perkins had kept a version of the standards bill in her desk drawer as a hedge against the demise of the National Recovery Administration. When the bill was introduced in 1938, it encountered heavy resistance from business and farm interests. The women's reform network of the New Deal had been active in the Act's development, especially the child labor ban, and along with labor interests carried out a strong lobbying effort (Ware, 1981). The legislation passed but in a weakened form. Again, agricultural along with other workers were excluded from certain provisions in the Act. The last major legislation of a waning New Deal, the Fair Labor Standards Act, along with the Wagner Act, managed nonetheless to give some support to the emergence of the modern labor movement in the 1930s.

The New Deal also carried out an important experiment in federally backed regional planning, through a program initiated by the Tennessee Valley Authority Act of 1933. The Authority focused on the Tennessee River valley area, an economically underdeveloped part of the South involving seven states, which were faced with continued problems of flooding and soil erosion. The program set up an independent corporation to construct dams, carry out flood control, build power plants, and produce and sell electrical power. It also sought to improve the welfare of the people of the region and to do this through a process emphasizing decentralized decision making and grassroots democracy.

Like many New Deal reforms, the Tennessee Valley Authority produced a mixed record. As implemented, the stress on grassroots democracy led to local control by southern whites bent on excluding African Americans from most benefits. Blacks received the least skilled and lowest-paid construction jobs and were denied admission to training programs (Sitkoff, 1984). Members of the board debated the appropriate balance between government and business in regional planning; while the Tennessee Valley Authority public power system prevailed over the private utility companies, it favored the interests of large commercial farmers over those of tenants and sharecroppers (Bernstein, 1969; Olsen, 1985). Yet, the program made major contributions to the region, including construction of nine huge dams; the electrification of the entire Tennessee Valley; and, by altering water levels, the elimination of malaria as a serious health problem (Biles, 1994).

RELIEF

One of the most pressing challenges of the New Deal was to do something for the phenomenal number—25% of the U.S. population in 1933—left unemployed by the Depression. This was "a disaster without equal in the twentieth century" (Bordo et al., 1998, p. 7). Over a million people wandered the country seeking work. Many cities and states, particularly in the South, provided little or no aid to their out-of-work citizens. Shelby County, Tennessee, spent more on golf course maintenance than relief (Biles, 1994). Private social agencies and those cities that attempted to provide aid found their resources woefully inadequate. Early calls by social workers and others for federally financed relief had been rebuffed by President Hoover. Roosevelt, who as governor of New York had established a statewide relief system, was far more receptive.

In early 1933, Congress appropriated an initial $500 million for a federal relief effort. Roosevelt established the Federal Emergency Relief Administration (FERA) and put social worker Harry Hopkins, former head of the New York State program, in charge. Shrewd, hard-driving, and with genuine humanitarian impulses, Hopkins quickly built a massive federal/state program to get relief out as fast as possible. While the FERA put greatest emphasis on emergency work relief programs, a good amount of money was expended on cash relief to the needy, including single mothers (Gordon, 1994; Trattner, 1994).

Hopkins tried to steer a path that avoided the potential of corruption in state administration of relief as well as the intensive casework-screening approach of private social agencies. To increase federal control, he bypassed existing state welfare departments and set up separate state relief organizations. He also ruled that federal relief was to be administered solely by public agencies; however, in an attempt to enhance the professionalism of welfare services, he approved regulations calling for supervision of relief workers by trained social workers (Jansson, 1997). Despite all this, the FERA was in some ways a traditional relief program; for example, recipients of both work and cash relief had to undergo a means test. Yet, overall, the FERA spent about $4 billion and affected some 20 million people (Trattner, 1994). Its public works programs were its greatest and most tangible contribution (Olsen, 1985).

Work relief was championed by many, even though it might be more expensive, because it would allow workers to retain their skills and their self-respect. In the process, they might perform needed services and construct useful public facilities. Economic advisers, particularly Alvin Hansen, supported public works programs because they believed, following John Maynard Keynes, that public investment would encourage greater private investment (Rosenof, 1997).

The first such program, and one of the most popular of the New Deal, was aimed at youth. The Civilian Conservation Corps (CCC) recruited young men ages 17 to 28 to stop soil erosion, plant trees, fight forest fires, create parks, build or repair roads and bridges, and do other work in rural and suburban areas. Next, the Public Works Administration (PWA) was given the task of constructing traditional, heavy-duty public works projects: dams, tunnels, airports, and larger public buildings. Harold Ickes, Secretary of the Interior, was chosen to direct the program. It became clear almost immediately, however, that the agency was not going to have enough of an impact on unemployment soon enough to relieve the misery of the Depression because large projects required careful planning and relied on skilled workers and heavy machinery. As the winter of 1933 approached, the Civil Works Administration (CWA) was created to employ more unskilled laborers in labor-intensive projects such as road building. The CWA lasted only until March of 1934, but it provided useful experience for the creation of the Works Progress Administration (WPA) the following spring.

The WPA engaged in construction of public facilities but provided other services as well. It staffed clinics, supervised playgrounds, preserved historic records and buildings, revived traditional crafts, excavated archeological sites, painted pictures, produced plays and concerts, and recycled clothing and toys. Under the WPA, the National Youth Administration (NYA) helped students stay in school by providing part-time jobs, offered vocational training to out-of-school youth, and oversaw construction projects similar to those of the other agencies.

The Depression, the ecological disaster in the Dust Bowl of the Midwest, and the New Deal's own agricultural policies displaced many farm families. The Department of Agriculture began a variety of programs to aid destitute farmers, later consolidated in the Resettlement Administration and still later run by the Farm Security Administration. These included loans to small farmers; organization of farm cooperatives, camps for migrant workers, and planned suburban greenbelt towns; and efforts to move urban families back to the land and to relocate farmers from marginal and depleted land to communities where they might farm successfully. The Farm Security Administration did much to explain the reality of rural poverty to the rest of the nation through a photography program that employed the talents of Walker Evans, Dorothea Lange, and Gordon Parks.

The organization and administration of federal relief programs varied widely. FERA monies were allocated to state and local governments, half as matching grants and half at Hopkins's discretion. Hopkins used the discretionary funds to maximize state donations, rewarding states for spending more of their own money on relief (Wallis & Oates, 1998). The Civilian Works Administration was centrally organized; workers were recruited and paid directly from Washington. The WPA was run through state and city offices with strong central leadership. Local sponsorship of projects was required, and local financial participation was encouraged but negotiable. In contrast, PWA projects were locally initiated and designed. They were financed by a combination of federal grants and local money. Part or all of the local portion could be loaned by PWA. The projects were reviewed by PWA for financial and structural soundness, but Washington made no attempt to dictate what projects communities should want nor how they should look (Williams, 1939).

The CCC was a very unusual collaboration of government branches. The Department of Labor recruited participants; the Departments of Agriculture and Interior chose the projects for them to work on, some of which involved the National Park Service; and the training, billeting, and supervision of the "boys" was done by the Army.

The programs for farmers were all fairly centralized. Rexford Tugwell, head of the Resettlement Administration, was the major New Deal voice for national planning. Participants were screened by social workers and their conduct monitored (Alanen & Elden, 1987). One observer found considerable parallels between the ideology and administration of New Deal resettlement efforts and those of Mussolini (Ghirardo, 1989).

Most of the relief programs maintained policies of nondiscrimination, but enforcement was another matter. African Americans often had difficulty qualifying for aid under the FERA and, once qualified, received less money than whites (Jones, 1985). Jobs in the WPA were supposed to be awarded without discrimination, but state and local managers were usually allowed to do as they pleased (Wye, 1992). Aubrey Williams, National Youth Administration administrator, was more aggressive in enforcing nondiscrimination and in targeting black colleges and vocational training programs for support. He employed the noted African American educator Mary McLeod Bethune to direct a Division of Negro Affairs.

Particularly strong on civil rights was the PWA's Ickes. He desegregated the public areas of the Interior Department and hired black professional and clerical staff. He allocated half of PWA's housing projects to blacks, although he did not try to desegregate them in the South. Because PWA projects were locally initiated, the PWA had no control over what was proposed, but an estimated $40 million worth of schools, hospitals, and libraries for African Americans in the south was approved (Sitkoff, 1984).

Although CCC Director Robert Fechner was a segregationist and tried to inhibit recruitment of African Americans, the organization was 11% black by 1938. Over 40,000 black enrollees learned to read in the CCC. Also participating were 80,000 Native Americans (Biles, 1994; Leake & Carter, 1988).

The National Youth Administration did not make enrollment of women a priority, but it did not discourage them. By 1941, half of its ranks were female. Women played little role in the PWA because it concentrated on heavy construction. But the FERA had a Women's Division, the CWA had women's projects, and the WPA had a Division of Women's and Professional Projects, all directed by Ellen Woodward (Swain, 1994). These projects tended to support traditional women's roles: sewing, child care, nursing, clerical work. But the New Deal gave more prominence to women in leadership positions—including the first woman Cabinet officer, Secretary of Labor Frances Perkins—than any earlier administration.

The impact of work relief on the reduction of unemployment and stimulation of the economy was slow but substantial. Millions of people had been kept working, and their families fed. The CCC saved millions of acres of land from erosion and trees from forest fires, as well as planting 3 billion new trees. It refurbished and extended national parks and added over 800 state parks for our enjoyment. Although the record of rural resettlement was modest, it rescued many farm families and migrant workers from disaster and included the propagation of soil conservation and scientific farming methods (Biles, 1994; Cannon, 1996). The greenbelt communities remain as models of safe, healthy, comfortable places that nurture family growth and community life.

The FERA ended in 1935. When full employment returned, sped by preparations for the Second World War, the rest of these programs were closed. But their effects survive 60 years later. The FERA set important precedents for the public assistance titles of the Social Security Act. The combined building legacy of the various agencies of the New Deal is the least noticed but perhaps the most important accomplishment of its relief approach. There is scarcely a community that was any size in the 1930s that does not contain a school, civic building, park, waterworks, or other public structure contributed by one of these agencies, and most are still in use (Federal Works Administration, 1946; Leake & Carter, 1988; Public Works Administration, 1939).

SOCIAL SECURITY AND INSTITUTIONALIZED PUBLIC WELFARE

Early in 1935, in what would become a frequently quoted statement, Roosevelt declared that "the Federal Government must and shall quit this business of relief." The President and Hopkins had never intended public cash relief to be an ongoing federal responsibility. Although they saw continuation of federal work relief as an important tool in combating unemployment, even this could be terminated once employment levels had sufficiently recovered. At the same time, Roosevelt and his advisers realized the necessity of establishing permanent programs to deal with shortcomings in the American economic system. These ideas led to three interrelated policy developments in 1935: the closing down of the FERA, the formation of the WPA, and the creation of what is arguably the most long-lasting contribution of the New Deal—the social insurance and public assistance programs of the Social Security Act.

To end federal involvement in relief, or "the dole," responsibility for general cash relief was transferred from the FERA to the states. Although it was clear that states had less resources for this job, the WPA was expected to take up the slack through its expanded jobs program. Social workers and their organizations vociferously opposed these policy decisions, arguing that neither the WPA nor states and localities could handle all those in need. They saw federal funding of general relief as the necessary cornerstone of a permanent federal welfare program, but this proposal was rejected by the Roosevelt administration (Coll, 1995; Leighninger, 1987).

To structure a program to protect people, particularly workers and the elderly, "against the hazards and vicissitudes of life," Roosevelt had established a Committee on Economic Security (CES) in 1934. Frances Perkins chaired the committee; Hopkins was one of its members. A large advisory group included employers, labor leaders, social workers, and representatives of civic groups. The Committee was further supported by a technical board headed by Arthur Altmeyer, an economist from Wisconsin. Control of the process rested largely in the hands of Perkins and Edwin Witte, another Wisconsin economist, who held the powerful job of the Committee's executive director. Thus, many groups had input, although some more than others, in the creation of the Social Security Act (Coll, 1995). Together, they attempted to develop a politically, economically, and administratively feasible national economic security program.

When Roosevelt spoke of protecting workers and the elderly, he had in mind a social insurance program along the lines of those created earlier in Europe and promoted by an American social insurance movement since the early 1900s. Two versions of unemployment insurance were debated, one a state system developed in Wisconsin, with employer funds providing the resources; the other a federal program financed by general revenues. Witte, an author of the Wisconsin legislation, was influential in getting this model adopted by the Committee on Economic Security. The federal incentive for states' adoption of the program was a new 5% payroll tax on employers. If a state enacted employer-based insurance, the federal government would forgive the tax (Berkowitz, 1991).

Providing for the security of the elderly was a more politically charged issue. By the mid-1930s, the Townsend Plan had achieved wide publicity. Devised by a California physician, the plan proposed payment of a flat grant of $200 a month to everyone over 60. Financed by federal taxation, the measure would bolster the economy by requiring recipients to spend the entire amount within 30 days. This and other solutions to the problems of the elderly, such as Louisiana Senator Huey Long's Share Our Wealth program, captured public interest far more than a social insurance program. This helped lead to the creation of two mechanisms for supporting the elderly: social insurance and a federal-state old-age public assistance measure. The latter received far more acceptance than the former during passage and implementation of the Social Security Act (Leiby, 1978).

To assure passage of a permanent program of social insurance for the elderly, Roosevelt strongly influenced the Committee on Economic Security to recommend a plan financed by taxes on employers and employees. This peculiarly American approach contrasted with the European system of support through general revenues but resonated with American values of hard work and self-help. By tying old age insurance to a contributory system, and designating that taxes would be kept in a separate trust fund, Roosevelt felt he had insulated the program from future attempts by Congress to change appropriation levels (Achenbaum, 1986; Berkowitz, 1991). Thus, the opportunity to use general taxes to create real income redistribution and a higher level of aid for the elderly was lost. Also, due in part to pressure from southern congressmen, the Act omitted coverage for agricultural and domestic workers (a large proportion of the African American workforce).

In addition to old age assistance, public assistance programs were created for two other categories: children in families with one caretaker and people who were blind. All three programs were joint endeavors, with states receiving matching funds from the federal government. It was up to the states to apply for participation. Acceptance was predicated on the existence of a specific state agency to implement the program, applying uniform policies and procedures throughout the state (an attempt to avoid local control over public relief). As shaped by congressional debate, dominated by southern Democrats, certain aspects of the proposed public assistance titles were toned down. Within certain general restrictions, states would be in charge of eligibility standards, could impose such requirements as good moral character, and were free to set minimum levels of payment (Coll, 1995).

The final shape of the Social Security Act thus established a two-tier system for dealing with poverty and dependence. The insurance titles of the legislation were universal entitlements covering workers or former workers; the public assistance titles were means-tested programs with residency requirements, designed primarily for people considered unemployable. To use Berkowitz's (1991) terms, the lower tier was predicated on a poor law notion of assistance based on location, the higher tier on assistance based on occupation.

The nature of the public assistance titles reflected the thinking of prominent social workers in and out of government. This was particularly true of the development of Aid to Dependent Children (ADC), in which Katharine Lenroot, chief of the U.S. Children's Bureau, was very influential. The Committee on Economic Security asked the Children's Bureau to present a proposal for aiding dependent children. Assisted by former Bureau head Grace Abbott, Lenroot set up a program similar to existing state mothers' pensions. ADC, like those pensions, assumed that widowed, deserted, and other single women caring for children should be given a stipend to enable them to stay at home rather than work. In what some historians have labeled a "maternalistic" approach by white women of privilege, Lenroot suggested that ADC should include careful investigations of applications for relief and that the program should be staffed by skilled caseworkers (Gordon, 1994; Mink, 1995).

Although the Children's Bureau developed ADC, it was not successful in its bid to gain administrative responsibility for the program. However, it did receive control over a system of public child welfare services. Instead, ADC, along with Old Age Assistance and Assistance to the Blind, was assigned to the new Social Security Board, under a Bureau of Public Assistance. The Bureau's director was Jane Hoey, a trained social worker who had worked with Hopkins in New York. One of Hoey's major concerns was to develop a professionalized public social service, using professional social workers wherever possible. Her goal was not so much the provision of in-depth casework services as the development of a fair and adequate system of assistance. Hoey battled with state officials over issues of patronage in hiring public assistance staff, discrimination against African American and Hispanic applicants, and inadequate grant levels. Because much of the control over ADC was lodged in the states, Hoey had to rely mostly on persuasion in these endeavors (Leighninger, 1987). The Social Security Amendments of 1939 improved things by mandating merit systems for state public assistance personnel and increasing the federal match for ADC payments.

The story of the development and implementation of ADC underscores the fact that women played important roles in New Deal policy making, particularly regarding labor standards and public welfare. Frances Perkins's position as Secretary of Labor gave her influence over a broad spectrum of policies. Like many women activists, she received invaluable support from Eleanor Roosevelt. Yet, New Deal programs for women generally provided less security and lower coverage than those for men. The gendered nature of New Deal social policies has come under increasing scrutiny (Mettler, 1998). Perspectives on the influence of gender in policy development range from the fairly single-faceted gender lens of Linda Gordon to the more comprehensive approach of analysts like Suzanne Mettler, who sees gender-specific policies as emerging out of a complex interplay of "institutional factors, political imperatives, and unintended consequences of policy design" (p. xii).

IMPACT OF NEW DEAL POLICIES

The New Deal had a major impact, not only in dealing with the immediate challenge of the Great Depression, but in other areas of life as well. Its impact can be felt in the development of the nation's infrastructure, in its social welfare policies, in housing, and in civil rights.

Infrastructure

A vast amount of physical and cultural infrastructure was built in the 10 years that the PWA and other agencies were in operation. We are still using most of it almost 70 years later. Washington National Airport, Hoover Dam, the Triborough Bridge, Skyline Drive, Key West Overseas Highway, major parts of Brooklyn College, The Citadel, and universities across the country are just a few examples. The impact on our education, health, commerce, and recreation was immense (Short & Stanley-Brown, 1939). Ironically, even New Dealers came to question the cost effectiveness of work relief (Patterson, 1986) without ever factoring into this calculation the long-term value of what was built.

Social Insurance, Health, and Welfare Policies

The Social Security Act created two long-lasting responses to economic insecurity: institutionalized entitlements to old age and unemployment insurance and more traditional public assistance measures. The first favored male workers and former workers and was legitimized by stressing recipient contributions to the system. The second concentrated on women and children and was sanctioned by the more tenuous criterion of need. Widows and survivors were soon added to Social Security, and a large proportion of women now benefit from the program. Yet, public welfare, with its smaller, less stable, and more stigmatized provision of aid, has remained the dominant program for poor women and minorities. A system of national health care benefits would have mitigated the situation, but such a system was politically unachievable during the New Deal era and was to prove equally elusive in future decades.

Housing

A two-tiered housing policy emerged from the New Deal, one part hugely successful, the other a dismal failure. For the middle-class home buyer, low-interest mortgages from the Federal Housing Administration, a PWA offshoot, made the American dream of a single-family home a reality. For the working poor, PWA offered the first public housing in America: well-planned, well-built, and well-appointed. Its first occupants were the envy of even middle-class apartment dwellers (Straus & Wegg, 1938). But the attempt to continue this standard of building failed. The Wagner-Steagall Housing Act of 1937 was passed only after being gutted by southern senators. The result was that the agency it created, the U.S. Housing Authority, could construct only cheap, boring, easily worn-down housing projects, forever stigmatized as "poor-people's housing" (Radford, 1996).

Civil Rights

African Americans, particularly southern sharecroppers, were hit harder than most citizens by the Depression, and they received far less help from the New Deal than they needed. But they did receive help. Jobs through New Deal agencies such as the

PWA were a key to the survival of many black families. Federal employment of African Americans tripled in the 1930s, including the professional ranks of lawyers, engineers, economists, and scientists (Biles, 1994). It was also important that federal programs established policies of apportioning jobs to African Americans in proportion to their presence in the population and made some attempt to enforce these policies. All of these measures raised African American expectations for future progress.

Ickes and Williams and their African American appointees Robert Weaver and Mary McLeod Bethune, along with Will Alexander of the Farm Security Administration, First Lady Eleanor Roosevelt, and others, were visible to the nation in support of civil rights. A political basis for later challenges to segregation was under construction. And it is not unimportant to that challenge that seven of eight Roosevelt appointees to the Supreme Court would support it (Biles, 1994; Sitkoff, 1984).

THE NEW DEAL AND SOCIETY

Abe Fortas, who held various positions in the federal government during and after the 1930s, describes the New Deal not as a radical change, but as "a successful effort to salvage the existing way of life, using objectives, procedures, and methods that were in existence" (Louchheim, 1983, p. 225). It is true that many elements of the New Deal program drew on prior policies; Roosevelt worked within the context of a capitalist system, a federal form of government, and American values of hard work, self-help, and limited government interference. Yet, all these factors were stirred around and some transformed by the onset of the Depression and subsequent attempts to deal with it. An air of excitement hung in the nation's capital during the New Deal years; great numbers of talented young people were drawn to Washington to improvise and innovate (Louchheim, 1983). These innovations often drew on existing political and economic arrangements, yet in the process, these arrangements were modified and recast.

The relationship between federal, state, and local governments shifted in interesting ways. Contrary to current critics of "big government," although the federal government grew and took on more responsibilities, this did not diminish state or local powers. Federal programs encouraged state and local participation, creating stronger governments at all levels (Wallis & Oates, 1998). Localities were enabled to do things they wanted to do but could not manage without national support. But, rather than turning all control over to localities, some federal direction and oversight was retained. The importance of this can be seen in efforts, not always successful, to prevent local discrimination and graft.

The United States retained its capitalist system, yet that system now had to accommodate a more powerful labor movement. New rules regulated the labor-capital relationship. Social Security provided protections beyond the capacity (or willingness) of the private sector. Comprehensive economic planning measures achieved some success and would be revived during World War II.

On the other hand, as Patterson (1994) has noted, the New Deal did relatively little to change long-term structural causes of poverty: low-paid and irregular employment, discrimination against minorities, and women's inequality in the workplace. It abandoned tenant farmers in the interest of promoting agribusiness. It produced two-tiered programs, such as those in welfare and housing, that greatly benefited the middle class while stigmatizing the poor.

During the New Deal, there was a national change in attitudes about the relationship of government to the economy. The Great Depression, and the country's slowness to recover from it, convinced people that a balanced budget and an unobstructed market were inadequate and even inappropriate responses to their problems. Forceful government intervention was needed. The many successes of that intervention produced a new confidence in government efficacy that lasted another four decades. And this tended to obscure for a while the failures and inadequacies of New Deal programs. But the confidence gradually eroded and came to be replaced by an equally lop-sided belief: that governments, particularly big ones, can do nothing right. A closer look at the myths and the realities of New Deal programs could give us the confidence and wisdom to construct more effective policies in the future.

REFERENCES

Achenbaum, W. A. (1986). *Social security: Visions and revisions.* New York: Cambridge University Press.

Alanen, A. R., & Elden, J. Y. (1987). *Main street ready-made: The New Deal community of Greendale, Wisconsin.* Madison: State Historical Society of Wisconsin.

Berkowitz, E. D. (1991). *American's welfare state: From Roosevelt to Reagan.* Baltimore, MD: Johns Hopkins University Press.

Bernstein, B. J. (1969). The New Deal: The conservative achievements of liberal reform. Reprinted in M. Dubofsky (Ed.), *The New Deal: Conflicting interpretations and shifting perspectives* (1992), (pp. 1-24). New York: Garland.

Biles, R. (1994). *The New Deal and the South.* Lexington: University of Kentucky Press.

Bordo, M. D., Goldin, C., & White, E. N. (Eds.). (1998). *The defining moment: The great depression and the American economy in the twentieth century.* Chicago: University of Chicago Press.

Cannon, B. Q. (1996). *Remaking the agrarian dream: New Deal rural resettlement in the mountain west.* Albuquerque: University of New Mexico Press.

Coll, B. D. (1995). *Safety net: Welfare and Social Security, 1929-1979.* New Brunswick, NJ: Rutgers University Press.

Dubofsky, M. (1992). Not so "turbulent years": Another look at the American 1930s. In M. Dubofsky (Ed.), *The New Deal: Conflicting interpretations and shifting perspectives* (pp. 123-146). New York: Garland. (Original work published 1979)

Federal Works Administration. (1946). *Final report on the WPA program. 1935-1943.* Washington, DC: Government Printing Office.

Ferguson, T. (1989). Industrial conflict and the coming of the New Deal: The triumph of multinational liberalism. In S. Fraser & G. Gerstle (Eds.), *The rise and fall of the New Deal order, 1930-1980* (pp. 3-31). Princeton, NJ: Princeton University Press.

Finegold, K., & Skocpol, T. (1995). *State and party in America's new deal.* Madison: University of Wisconsin Press.

Fraser, S. (1989). The "labor question." In S. Fraser & G. Gerstle (Eds.), *The rise and fall of the New Deal order, 1930-1980* (pp. 55-84). Princeton, NJ: Princeton University Press.

Ghirardo, D. Y. (1989). *Building new communities: New Deal America and fascist Italy.* Princeton, NJ: Princeton University Press.

Gordon, L. (1994). *Pitied but not entitled: Single mothers and the history of welfare, 1890-1994.* New York: Free Press.

Jansson, B. S. (1997). *The reluctant welfare state: American social welfare policies—Past, present, and future* (3rd ed.). Pacific Grove, CA: Brooks/Cole.

Jones, J. (1985). *Labor of Love, labor of sorrow: Black women, work, and the family from slavery to the present.* New York: Vintage.

Leake, F. E., & Carter, R. S. (1988). *Roosevelt's tree army: A brief history of the civilian conservation corps.* St. Louis, MO: National Association of Civilian Conservation Corps Alumni.

Leiby, J. (1978). *A history of social welfare and social work in the United States.* New York: Columbia University Press.

Leighninger, L. (1987). *Social work: Search for identity.* Westport, CT: Greenwood.

Louchheim, K. (Ed.) (1983). *The making of the New Deal: The insiders speak.* Cambridge, MA: Harvard University Press.

Lowi, T. J. (1969). *The end of liberalism: Ideology, policy, and the crisis of public authority.* New York: Norton.

Mettler, S. (1998). *Dividing citizens: Gender and federalism in new deal public policy.* Ithaca, NY: Cornell University Press.

Mink, G. (1995). *The wages of motherhood: Inequality in the welfare state.* Ithaca, NY: Cornell University Press.

Olsen, J. S. (1985). *Historical dictionary of the New Deal.* Westport, CT: Greenwood.

Patterson, J. T. (1986). *America's stuggle against poverty, 1990-1985).* Cambridge, MA: Harvard University Press.

Patterson, J. T. (1994). *America's struggle against poverty, 1900-1994.* Cambridge, MA: Harvard University Press.

Public Works Administration. (1939). *America builds: The record of PWA.* Washington, DC: Government Printing Office.

Radford, G. (1996). *Modern housing for America: Policy struggles in the New Deal era.* Chicago: University of Chicago Press.

Roosevelt, Franklin D. Annual Message to Congress, January 4, 1935, in Carothers, D. (1937), *Chronology of the Federal Emergency Relief Administration.* Research Monograph 6. Washington, DC: U.S. Works Progress Administration, Division of Research.

Rosenof, T. (1997). *Economics in the long run: New Deal theorists and their legacies, 1933-1993.* Chapel Hill: University of North Carolina Press.

Schlesinger, A. M. (1957). *The age of Roosevelt.* New York: Houghton-Mifflin.

Short, C. W., & Stanley-Brown, R. (1939). *Public buildings: A survey of architecture of projects constructed by federal and other governmental bodies between the years 1933 and 1939 with the assistance of the Public Works Administration.* Washington, DC: Government Printing Office. (The first half of this volume was reprinted by DeCapo Press, New York, 1986.)

Sitkoff, H. (1984). The impact of the New Deal on black southerners. In J. C. Cobb & M. V. Namorato (Eds.), *The New Deal and the South* (pp. 117-134). Jackson: University of Mississippi Press.

Smith, S. L. (1995). *Sick and tired of being sick and tired: Black women's health activism in America, 1890-1950.* Philadelphia: University of Pennsylvania Press.

Straus, M. W., & Wegg, T. (1938). *Housing comes of age.* New York: Oxford University Press.

Swain, M. H. (1994). *Ellen S. Woodward: New Deal advocate for women.* Jackson: University of Mississippi Press.

Trattner, W. I. (1994). *From poor law to welfare state: A history of social welfare in America* (5th ed.). New York: Free Press.

Wallis, J. J., & Oates, W. E. (1998). The impact of the New Deal on American federalism. In M. D. Bordo, C. Goldin, & E. N. White (Eds.), *The defining moment: The great depression and the American economy in the twentieth century* (pp. 155-180). Chicago: University of Chicago Press.

Ware, S. (1981). *Beyond suffrage: Women in the New Deal.* Cambridge, MA: Harvard University Press.

Williams, J. K. (1939). *Grants-in-aid under the PWA.* New York: Columbia University Press.

Wye, C. G. (1992). The New Deal and the Negro community: Toward a broader conceptualization. In M. Dubofsky (Ed.), *The New Deal: Conflicting interpretations and shifting perspectives* (pp. 247-269). New York: Garland.

CHAPTER TEN

Social Policy and
the Great Society

MICHAEL REISCH

Between 1940 and 1960, economic growth, a progressive income tax, and modestly redistributive policies provided many Americans with a better life and hope for a brighter future. The Gross National Product increased over 150%, and unemployment ranged between 3% and 5%. The social policies of the New Deal, particularly the Social Security Act, helped maintain a floor on workers' spending power. These policies contributed substantially to the physical transformation of cities and laid the foundation for the post-war growth of suburbs (Patterson, 1994).

Dramatic demographic shifts accompanied this rapid economic expansion, especially the northern migration of over 4 million African Americans. These phenomena changed the character of American cities and the impact of social policies introduced in the 1930s. Yet, their long-term implications were little understood by policy makers at the time (Lemann, 1991).

By the end of the Eisenhower years, however, the boom that fueled the post-war recovery had begun to subside. The economies of northern and midwestern states began to decline, increasing industrial unemployment among semiskilled blue-collar workers. Although over two thirds of Americans still lived in cities affected by this decline, the growth of suburbs and the appearance of universal material well-being fostered by the media, particularly television, contributed to the increasing "invisibility of the poor" (Harrington, 1962). A quarter century after the passage of the Social Security

Act, severe and chronic poverty lurked below the surface of the nation's well-being, particularly in urban ghettos and isolated rural areas. The recognition that the New Deal had not solved the problem of poverty was a major factor in the emergence of the War on Poverty programs described in this chapter.

BACKGROUND TO THE WAR ON POVERTY

The repressive political climate of the Cold War and McCarthyism abetted efforts to roll back the New Deal (Andrews & Reisch, 1997). Social activism declined, and openly anti-welfare political attitudes reemerged (Jones, 1992). Social policy advances of this period, such as the expansion of Social Security and the growth of private family service and mental health agencies, largely aided middle-income people. The perception grew, however, that the preponderance of tax dollars was being spent on increasing numbers of "undeserving" urban welfare recipients. This resentment of the urban poor, which later undermined federal anti-poverty efforts in the 1960s, resulted from a shift in the racial composition of the welfare rolls (Danziger & Weinberg, 1994; Edsall, 1991; Quadagno, 1994).

Michael Harrington's (1962) classic exposé, *The Other America,* and other lesser known works such as Harry Caudill's (1963) *Night Comes to the Cumberlands,* forced Americans to rediscover those segments of the country bypassed by modern economic and social progress. In what Harrington termed "The Other America," over 40 million people lived in poverty, about one third of them children. Poverty moved to the front page for the first time since the Great Depression (Patterson, 1994).

Images of Poverty

Prior to the New Deal, the nation's conception of poverty in the United States was closely linked to individually focused, often moral explanations. Several factors shaped this view of poverty: the expectation of chronic material scarcity, the physical proximity of social classes in urban environments, and the extent of social interaction between the poor and nonpoor components of the population (Reisch, 1996). Although the Depression changed many attitudes about poverty, it did not eliminate societal prejudices toward the poor, particularly those from racial or ethnic minority groups. As a consequence, social welfare programs continued to reflect pre-New Deal myths about the poor and to stigmatize those who received public assistance (Axinn & Stern, 1988).

Nor did New Deal policies eliminate poverty or unemployment, which remained as high as 17% in 1939. Four specific factors contributed to the decline in poverty between 1940 and 1960: wage increases, the growth of two-earner households, the increase in income from private pensions and investments, and the impact of government transfers such as social insurance and public assistance programs. The primary beneficiaries of these advances were white workers and the elderly, who began to leave urban areas in the post-war decades. Poverty seemed to disappear because aggregate economic growth, the structure of suburbs, and the images of American society conveyed by popular culture masked its persistence (Axinn & Stern, 1988; Danziger & Weinberg, 1994). The "rediscovery of poverty" around 1960, which inspired the Great Society programs of the 1960s, must be understood in this context.

The War on Poverty thus rested on misconceptions about the extent of poverty and misinterpretations of contemporary analyses of poverty and the poor (Harrington, 1962; Lewis, 1966). The popular "culture of poverty" thesis assumed that the poor were different from the nonpoor and, by implication, somehow inferior in terms of their values and behaviors. These differences, it was argued, were transmitted from generation to generation. By defining the needs of low-income people as the product of individual or cultural deficiency, rather than institutional or resource deficiency, poverty came to be viewed as a normal state for large segments of the urban population (Ryan, 1971). This justified existing patterns of resource distribution.

In the late 1950s, however, new perspectives on social problems emerged within American universities that also shaped social policy responses to poverty in the 1960s. In such areas as juvenile delinquency and urban poverty, academics propagated a new structuralist perspective that focused on issues of opportunity rather than pathology. This view initially caused a schism between its proponents (largely sociologists) and mainstream social workers, who tended to regard family dysfunction as the source of deviant behavior. Despite these differences, the work of Lloyd Ohlin and Richard Cloward inspired the development of a new kind of social service organization in cities like New York and Chicago (Lemann, 1988-1989). Initiatives implemented by the Kennedy and Johnson administrations emulated this model and reinvigorated the community organization component within the social work profession (Reisch & Wenocur, 1986).

Initiatives by the Kennedy Administration

The 1960 presidential campaign brought these issues to the attention of the American people, primarily through the speeches of Senator John F. Kennedy beginning with the West Virginia primary. Consciously evoking Franklin Roosevelt, Kennedy repeatedly referred to the hunger and deprivation he had seen (Matusow, 1984). Ironically, the poignancy of rural deprivation distorted the nation's efforts to deal with problems that had structural and not personal causes.

A major influence on the Kennedy administration was the Ford Foundation's Grey Areas Project, which funded community action agencies that focused on initiatives to address the physical and social needs of low-income urban residents. Another was Mobilization for Youth, a New York City project originally designed and implemented in the late 1950s by the Henry Street Settlement. By 1960, Mobilization for Youth was an independent agency and, in 1962, the Kennedy Administration created a package of $12.6 million for the program (Gillette, 1996).

Economists such as John Kenneth Galbraith and Walter Heller, whose ideas emphasized the expansion of economic opportunity rather than income support, also influenced Kennedy's anti-poverty efforts. The creation of the Area Redevelopment Agency in 1961 brought increased federal attention and funding to economically depressed regions. The Manpower Development and Training Act of 1962 continued the American trend of stressing employment over public assistance, a trend that led to a series of welfare reforms over the next three and a half decades.

Continuing the pattern of social policies established during the New Deal, President Kennedy also proposed legislation designed to maintain the level of consumption of low-income families, both the working poor and the welfare poor. These included the extension of Aid to Families With Dependent Children (AFDC) benefits to the children of unemployed workers, an increase in the minimum wage, and the expansion of public housing projects. A complementary approach appeared in the 1962 Public Welfare Amendments, which increased federal support for the public social services (Jones, 1992; Patterson, 1994).

Prior to this legislation, with the exception of child welfare services, social services had been omitted from the original Social Security Act. In 1956, however, the federal government began to reimburse states for one half of the social services they provided welfare recipients. These matching funds provided inadequate incentives for many states, and few chose to take advantage of the government's offer. The 1962 amendments attempted to address this problem by providing a higher federal matching rate (75%) and incorporating a social services strategy into broader federal efforts to combat poverty. Initially, this prevention-oriented strategy appeared to offer greater likelihood of reducing poverty, particularly in the African American community. Under less sympathetic administrations, it led to punitive policies that mandated work to receive benefits (Katz, 1989).

The 1962 amendments emphasized preventive and rehabilitative services through the expansion of eligibility for services to former and potential welfare recipients with a particular emphasis on family preservation, another recurring theme of social policy. Other key components included the development of services to the elderly, particularly the elderly poor; limitations on workers' caseloads; support for individual counseling and information and referral services; and the introduction of case management via individualized service plans. Financial incentives included authorization for state governments to contract for services, the absence of a ceiling on federal expenditures for social services, and permission for states to conduct home visits to determine clients' eligibility (Gillette, 1996).

Separating Services From Income Support

Despite its preventive focus, this service strategy did not stem the growth of welfare caseloads. Between 1962 and 1967, welfare rolls increased by nearly 50%. The social activism of welfare rights organizations and relaxed eligibility requirements were not the sole causes of this increase. Basic flaws in the service strategy itself undermined its intentions. As later studies revealed, the low level of public assistance provided insufficient support for clients to take advantage of services (Bell, 1983; Katz, 1989; Patterson, 1994).

The 1967 amendments attempted to correct this problem by further strengthening the social service provisions within public welfare, with a new emphasis on a work-based alternative to welfare. The amendments placed greater emphasis on moving clients from welfare to work through job training and child care in addition to counseling. Yet, the new Work Incentive Program ultimately made public assistance more restrictive through the initiation of "workfare" requirements. It also had little impact on labor force participation among AFDC recipients.

Changes in the administration of social services abetted this new policy focus. Perhaps the most important organizational shift was the formal separation of the administration of federally funded social services from the administration of cash assistance. This occurred as a result of the Department of Health, Education, and Welfare reorganization that created the Social and Rehabilitation Service. Regulations mandating this separation first appeared in 1972, but local governments split their administration as early as 1969 (Patterson, 1994).

Proponents of separation asserted that it would promote better relationships between social service workers and clients because workers would no longer have the ability to deny cash benefits to clients. They also argued that many of the problems of welfare recipients were merely the result of poverty, not pathology. Requiring all clients to receive social services, they argued, perpetuated the view of clients as humans in need of fixing, rather than financial assistance (Gillette, 1996; Ginzberg & Solow, 1974).

From the federal government's perspective, separation had desirable fiscal consequences as well. Since 1962, the costs of public social services had increased dramatically, largely because the states had transferred their service expenditures to the public sector to take advantage of the 75% match. Separation prevented states from claiming this rate for the administrative costs of cash assistance programs, which had a lower matching rate of 50%.

Despite efforts in the late 1960s and early 1970s to curtail social services spending, AFDC rolls more than doubled in 5 years, while federal spending for social services increased by over 500%. A combination of factors produced this dramatic surge in expenditures. These included vague legislative definitions of a social service, liberal eligibility requirements, and sophisticated applications of the law's purchase of service authority by the states (Derthick, 1975).

A similar pattern emerged in the area of mental health policy. The Community Mental Health Centers Act of 1963 emphasized prevention over treatment and a community- rather than institution-based approach to mental health services. Yet, in some ways, the movement for deinstitutionalization spawned by this legislation inadvertently worsened the plight of the chronically mentally ill and contributed to the growing problem of homelessness in the 1980s and 1990s (Blau, 1992).

THE WAR ON POVERTY AND THE GREAT SOCIETY

In January 1964, 2 months after the assassination of President Kennedy, President Lyndon Johnson proclaimed an "unconditional" War on Poverty in his first State of the Union Address. Soon, the *Economic Report of the President* proposed a broad range of economic and social policies designed to achieve this lofty objective. Acknowledging the complexity of a problem like poverty, the Johnson administration's legislative package included economic stimuli, full employment programs, urban and rural rehabilitation, expanded educational and labor opportunities for youth and adults, new health care programs, and increased assistance for the elderly and the disabled (Danziger, 1991; Gillette, 1996).

The primary instrument of the War on Poverty was the Economic Opportunity Act. This legislation created such programs as the Job Corps, VISTA, Upward Bound, the Neighborhood Youth Corps, Community Action, Head Start, Legal Services, Foster Grandparents, and the Office of Economic Opportunity. Later that year, the landmark Civil Rights Act further promoted an equal opportunity agenda through the prohibition of racial, ethnic, or gender discrimination in employment and the establishment of the Equal Employment Opportunity Commission. In three whirlwind years, the Johnson administration augmented these efforts.

In 1965, through the enactment of Medicare and Medicaid, Congress created a mandatory program of hospital insurance, an optional program of physician care for the elderly and the disabled, and federal/state health insurance for low-income people. In the same year, Congress established the Department of Housing and Urban Development, funded an array of services for the aged through the Older Americans Act, and created the Food Stamp Program under the auspices of the Department of Agriculture. In addition, the Elementary and Secondary School Education Act overturned long-standing precedents and directed federal aid to local schools to equalize educational opportunities for children. The Voting Rights Act sought to equalize political opportunities by expanding on the Civil Rights Act and prohibiting the denial of the right to vote (Matusow, 1984).

In 1966, the Model Cities Act targeted certain urban areas with comprehensive services. Emphasizing the concept of community control, funds for Model Cities would pass through municipal governments, yet were controlled by boards composed equally of elected officials, low-income people, and representatives of community organizations. Shortly, this proved to be an explosive formula, and tensions between largely white politicians and African American and Latino activists escalated. This conflict weakened support for the Great Society agenda, which collapsed in 2 years under the pressures of foreign war and inflation (Lemann, 1988-1989). Despite these emerging tensions, the Housing and Urban Redevelopment Act of 1968 expanded federal funding for low-income housing and, through Section 8 housing, enabled poor tenants to rent apartments outside of stigmatized and increasingly ghettoized projects. Additional growth in this area occurred in 1974 through the Housing and Community Development Act.

The Idea of the Great Society

After Johnson's landslide victory over Barry Goldwater in November 1964, he unveiled the concept of the Great Society in his 1965 State of the Union address. Drawing on a deep reservoir of public support, his own well-honed legislative skills, and the support of large Democratic majorities in Congress, Johnson pushed through a social policy agenda second only to Roosevelt's (Ginzberg & Solow, 1974).

From the outset, the Great Society was closely linked with a civil rights agenda, the movement toward community control, and efforts to ameliorate the plight of poor children. Its centerpiece was the creation of semi-autonomous community action programs in virtually every city in the United States. Together with VISTA and local legal assistance services established under the Equal Opportunity Act, the community action programs increased the role of community residents in shaping the policies and programs that affected their lives. They developed alternative centers of political power in low-income urban neighborhoods.

Opposition to such programs soon emerged among some big city mayors, who regarded the community action programs as a potential threat to their political dominance (Katz, 1989; Matusow, 1984). In their view, efforts to empower low-income communities threatened to alter the political balance of power. The egalitarian implications of the Great Society initiatives led to attacks on anti-poverty programs, even popular and successful ones like Head Start, particularly in southern states such as Mississippi. Both rural and urban conservative critics of the Office of Economic Opportunity and the Great Society alleged that these programs promoted a socialist agenda. As early as 1966, conservative Democrats joined Republicans in calling for major reductions in federal spending for such purposes (Quadagno, 1994).

Yet, despite their radical image, the policies of the Johnson Administration did not constitute a fundamental shift away from traditional approaches to the problem of poverty for several reasons. First, changes in public assistance policies and the development of programs within the Office of Economic Opportunity such as the Job Corps emphasized employment incentives and training over income maintenance. This was in line with the long-standing American preference for employment over welfare. Second, the federal government provided states with financial incentives to develop social services leading to self-care and self-support. This reinforced American values such as political decentralization, individualism, and self-reliance. Third, even the policy shift (at least in theory) from a subsistence to a prevention focus occurred primarily for reasons of cost-efficiency and out of a reluctance to expand public assistance benefits. In fact, the planning and community development components of the OEO spurred nearly as much opposition as its expectation of "maximum feasible participation" by community residents. The underlying assumption of all such policies, however, was that economic growth, rather than resource distribution, was the key to solving urban problems (Gillette, 1996).

In the late 1960s, however, several developments underscored the insufficiency of this strategy. Cities such as Detroit and Newark erupted in a series of increasingly violent disturbances. Welfare rolls grew rapidly in the midst of an era of prosperity. Organized welfare recipients and urban residents took seriously the government's promise of "maximum feasible participation" by the community in the design and implementation of so-called community action programs (Moynihan, 1969). Fearing a challenge to their political power from both alarmed middle-income residents and newly organized low-income groups, conservative urban politicians persuaded the federal government to dismantle or cut many anti-poverty initiatives, particularly Community Action (Lemann, 1988-1989). In an increasingly conservative political climate, the policy emphasis shifted from inducements to coercive pressures to seek employment (Edsall, 1991; Katz, 1989; Patterson, 1994).

At the same time, by the mid-1960s, the nature of U.S. economic growth itself intensified the poverty and isolation of urban populations. Even at the height of the War on Poverty, a late 1966 study revealed that a majority of Americans earned less than was needed to live a "decent life." This created the appearance that urban problems were beyond solution—the consequence of a growing urban "underclass"—and provided the justification for the retreat of social policy from addressing the needs of urban communities (Katz, 1989).

The attack on the urban poor in the late 1960s coincided with a major shift in the locus of American economic and political power—a shift that went initially unnoticed. Large corporations began to shift the base of their manufacturing operations away from the traditional urban areas of the Northeast and Midwest (the so-called Rust Belt cities) to the newer cities of the Sun Belt, to suburban areas that soon ringed older cities, and to factories abroad. Ironically, efforts to undermine the Great Society also affected the bulk of the nation's population, including the middle class (Midgley, 1992).

Beginning with the 1968 election, these economic shifts were accompanied by political changes of considerable magnitude. The power of states in which the old New Deal coalition (which consisted of organized labor, white ethnics, African Americans, and intellectuals) did not exist increased as their populations and economic bases expanded (Matusow, 1984). Such states, in which unions were weak and racial minorities scarce, supported increasingly anti-urban, anti-social welfare policies at the local and national levels (Edsall, 1991). As social policies since the 1930s had left considerable discretion to state governments in establishing eligibility and benefits, this power shift (Sale, 1976) exacerbated existing disparities in income among regions. As multinational corporations and their political allies grew stronger, the decline in the power of unions and the social movements of the 1960s removed an effective counterweight and a force for progressive social policy development. Simultaneously, "white flight" from urban centers weakened the tax base of cities and created the "fiscal crisis of the state" (O'Connor, 1973), best exemplified by the budget problems encountered by New York and Cleveland in the mid-1970s.

The policies of the Johnson administration exacerbated these developments. By refusing to choose between the "guns" of the Indochina war and the "butter" of the Great Society, Johnson brought about an increase in inflation. This slowed economic growth, diminished support for anti-poverty programs, and fostered renewed receptivity to arguments that again explained poverty in personal rather than structural terms (Ginzberg & Solow, 1974; Katz, 1989; Lemann, 1988-1989). The continuing militancy of welfare recipients and community action leaders, the spread of civil unrest in urban ghettos, and the growing cost of public assistance further contributed to this political shift. In the 1968 election, Richard Nixon eked out a narrow victory by effectively exploiting these fears and resentments and appealing to racial and class resentments in carefully coded language (Matusow, 1984).

Welfare Rights and the War on Poverty

Between 1966 and 1973, as the Civil Rights Movement shifted its focus to northern cities, a social movement of welfare recipients, the National Welfare Rights Organization, transformed the political debate over welfare and economic justice. Led by Dr. George Wiley, a chemist and former organizer with the Congress of Racial Equality, and inspired by the anti-poverty strategy developed by Richard Cloward and Francis Fox Piven, the National Welfare Rights Organization sought to organize welfare recipients to fight on their own behalf (Kotz & Kotz, 1977; Piven & Cloward, 1977; West, 1981).

In a few years, the National Welfare Rights Organization reframed the national debate over poverty. Unlike the liberal creators of the Great Society programs, whose benign paternalism was frequently its target, the Organization argued that poor people were entitled to public aid as a matter of legal and human rights. Their philosophy and tactics "pushed the post-war welfare state to new limits. They also articulated a historically remarkable theory of citizenship . . . and [thereby] reconfigured familiar Anglo-American ideas about rights and obligations" (Kornbluh, 1997, p. 103).

An alliance between the National Welfare Rights Organization and the Office of Economic Opportunity-sponsored Community Legal Services produced a legal strategy to create a constitutional right to subsistence that complemented the National Welfare Rights Organization's confrontational political tactics. Spearheaded by the Center for Social Welfare Policy and Law, this approach initially met with considerable success. In 1966, 10 years after the Warren Court had hinted its receptivity to arguments recognizing the unconstitutionality of wealth-based discrimination, the Court established the principle that such discrimination was equivalent to "invidious" racial discrimination. This expanded the concept of fundamental rights to include those rights not explicitly listed in the Constitution. Inspired by these rulings, welfare rights advocates forged a strategy to convince the Court to find a "right to live" within the Equal Protection Clause of the 14th Amendment. Relying on natural law tradition and universalist arguments, advocates sought to eradicate the distinction between positive and negative rights. By 1968, prospects looked hopeful that this bold strategy would prevail (Bussiere, 1997).

Yet, the strategy ultimately failed for two reasons. Ironically, the initial successes of welfare rights advocates, which relied on a selective, maternalist ideology and a judicially oriented approach, contained the seeds of this failure. At the organizational level, their strategy failed because National Welfare Rights Organization leaders increasingly resisted the use of a maternalist argument in support of welfare rights. This resistance also produced internal conflicts within the Organization between male founders such as Wiley and female grassroots leaders such as Johnnie Tillmon (West, 1981).

The principal explanation for the failure of the National Welfare Rights Organization, however, lies in the advocates' legal strategy, not their ideology. Their court victories led to natural rights being defined as mere statutory entitlements rather than constitutional guarantees. Thus, in the late 1960s, just as anti-poverty programs were beginning to lose their broad base of public support in the aftermath of civil disturbances, judicial decisions neutralized the universal appeal of advocates' arguments and limited their redistributive potential (Bussiere, 1997; West, 1981).

In addition, the Court's focus on procedural rather than substantive rights and its definition of welfare as a statutory rather than a constitutional entitlement made welfare recipients dependent on the political whims of elected officials. By the early 1970s, this approach succeeded in getting 6 million more people on public assistance and significantly increasing both total welfare spending and average benefit levels. Yet, in the long run, it inadvertently "tended to set different groups of poor people against each other in the pluralist political arena . . . in a fierce competition for diminishing public resources" (Bussiere, 1997, p. 119). It fostered a climate in which advocates for disadvantaged groups were ill prepared to defend against the anti-welfare policies of the Reagan-Bush era. The failure of the legal War on Poverty thus resulted from the same philosophical limitations of the Great Society programs. These included an emphasis on procedural rights (opportunity) instead of group outcomes, a negative conception of liberty, and hostility to the role of local communities.

SOCIAL POLICIES UNDER NIXON, FORD, AND CARTER

Although he initially maintained many of the social policies of the Johnson administration, President Nixon sought to continue the war in Indochina and simultaneously control inflation by reducing the domestic side of the federal budget. A major component of his strategy was to shift administration of anti-poverty programs to states and localities. Between 1968 and 1972, grants to states for services increased by over one third to $500 million. These funds were to be controlled largely by elected officials rather than community action programs or residents.

Nixon also tried to replace AFDC with a Family Assistance Program that would provide a guaranteed annual income. In 1970, the Family Assistance Program failed in Congress—the victim of a unique coalition of liberals and conservatives (Moynihan, 1973). In 1972 and 1973, however, Congress passed the State and Local Fiscal Assistance Act and the Comprehensive Employment and Training Act. This legislation established the concept of revenue sharing and led ultimately to the dismantling of the Office of Economic Opportunity, effectively ending the Great Society concept (Ginzberg & Solow, 1974; Katz, 1989; Matusow, 1984; Patterson, 1994).

The most significant social policy accomplishments of the Nixon administration, however, were the Social Security Amendments of 1972, which centralized and standardized aid to the disabled and low-income elderly and indexed benefits to inflation. Other programs, such as food stamps, child nutrition, and railroad retirement, were also linked to Cost-of-Living Adjustments (or COLAs). These reforms prompted predictions that official poverty might be eliminated by 1980.

In 1971 and1972, in another attempt to curtail the growth of federal social services expenditures, the Nixon administration proposed a controversial ceiling of $2.5 billion, effective 1973. Only 10% of these funds, to be distributed to the states on the basis of their population, could be used for services to former or potential welfare recipients (Bixby, 1990; Derthick, 1975). This controversy ultimately led to the passage of Title XX of the Social Security Act in January 1975. This legislation reinforced the popular concept of federal *revenue sharing,* which provided states with maximum flexibility in planning social services while promoting fiscal accountability.

During the Ford and Carter administrations, Title XX shaped the direction of both public and nonprofit social services. It sought to alter the provision of social services to low-income people without creating any new programs, guided by four basic principles. These were, first, the prevention, reduction, or elimination of welfare dependency and, second, the prevention or remediation of abuse, neglect, or exploitation of children and vulnerable adults (through emphasizing family preservation, rehabilitation, and reunification). Two other principles were the prevention or reduction of inappropriate institutional care through the provision of alternative forms of assistance and targeting at least 50% of state funds to low-income people.

In the late 1970s, the implementation of Title XX led to a rapid increase in federal social service expenditures at a time when economic stagnation undermined government's ability to sustain these costs. The combination of a legislatively imposed spending ceiling and the increased rate of inflation, however, froze state Title XX budgets and undermined efforts to develop innovative and comprehensive forms of services. In addition, fiscal inefficiency, program redundancy, uneven regulations and standards, and lack of integration often plagued state programs developed under Title XX (Gilbert, 1977). The growing power of suburban legislators led to a disproportionate distribution of benefits to middle-income families, further undermining the legislation's original intent to target programs for the inner-city poor. The final battle of the War on Poverty, an attempt to develop a national social services strategy, failed largely due to insufficient resources and a lack of political commitment (Edsall, 1991; Katz, 1989).

In sum, there was a general failure during the Nixon, Ford, and Carter administrations to assist the growing proportion of low-income and working-class families who were left behind in rapidly declining older cities. During the 1970s, the country's tax structure at all levels had become increasingly regressive. Reflecting an anti-poor, anti-urban bias, states and local governments froze revenues. An example of this is Proposition 13 in California. In addition, government failed to adjust the size of public assistance payments to keep pace with high rates of inflation. Even prior to the anti-welfare policies of Presidents Reagan and Bush, the plight of low-income populations had become increasingly grave (Edsall, 1991; Jones, 1992; Katz, 1989; Patterson, 1994).

THE IMPACT OF THE GREAT SOCIETY ON SOCIAL POLICY

In conjunction with sustained economic growth, the anti-poverty policies of the Great Society produced a decline in the official poverty rate from 19% in 1964 to 11.1% in 1973. The poverty rate was nearly one half what it was at the end of the Eisenhower era. Between 1959 and 1969, the per capita incomes of the bottom 20% of households increased faster than those of any other groups, while real median family income grew by 40% (Danziger & Weinberg, 1994).

Yet, the decline in poverty varied significantly among demographic groups. Throughout the 1970s, poverty continued to decline among the elderly, largely as a consequence of benefit indexing and Medicare. A virtual freeze on AFDC benefits after 1973, however, and a decline in the purchasing power of wages produced a steady increase in poverty among children, particularly children of color. Thus, despite continuing growth in social spending in the 1970s, economic stagflation and unevenly distributed social policies prevented further reductions in poverty. By 1980, the rate had risen to 13% (Patterson, 1994).

There are several ways of interpreting these developments. Conservative critics of government social spending, such as Charles Murray (1984), argue that government policies from 1950 to 1980 produced negligible social benefits and, in fact, harmed those they sought to assist. The critics assert that economic growth and not government intervention produced any reduction in poverty that occurred during this period. This view became popular during the Reagan administration, leading to deep cuts in anti-poverty programs (Katz, 1989).

A liberal perspective on the War on Poverty (Danziger, 1991; Lemann, 1988-1989) asserts that a combination of anti-poverty and growth-promoting economic policies achieved some success in reducing poverty, established a stronger safety net, and cushioned the poor from the economic shocks of the 1970s. Social spending increases particularly benefitted the elderly, whose poverty rate plummeted between 1960 and 1980 as a result of the passage of Medicare and Medicaid, the expansion of Social Security benefits, and the creation of a broad network of social services for the aged. "Poverty rose during the 1970s primarily among those groups for whom spending did not accelerate," such as children and single adults (Danziger, 1991, p. 53). Neoliberals agree with conservatives that Great Society programs such as Model Cities were wasteful or counterproductive, but they support the liberal view that the underlying goals were worthwhile (Keisling, 1984).

Radical perspectives on this period (Abramovitz, 1992; Piven & Cloward, 1995; Quadagno, 1994) maintain that the rise and fall of social spending in the 1960s and 1970s occurred for several reasons. One was the desire of the government to dampen growing social unrest by controlling access to the labor market and its benefits. Another was the use of social spending to reinforce prevailing gender roles regarding work and the family. A third influence was institutional racism, a perspective shared by some liberal analysts as well (Edsall, 1991). These analyses argue that social action, not government benevolence, produced modest reforms, and that ultimately, egalitarian goals run counter to what O'Connor (1973) termed the *accumulation function* of capitalist political economies.

The Great Society's Influence on Social Service Delivery

The new direction of social policy inspired by the Great Society also had several significant implications for the design and implementation of social services. In the late 1960s and early 1970s, many nonprofit agencies became the beneficiaries of government contracting of mandated, publicly funded services under various rubrics, including community participation and control, decentralization, the "new Federalism," or revenue sharing. In fact, the primary motives were cost efficiency and political expediency.

Initially, this policy shift increased the accessibility of services to those most in need and began to reverse the trend since the late 1930s among nonprofits toward serving primarily a white, middle-income clientele. Rapidly, these agencies became to depend largely on government revenues to maintain fiscal solvency. Beginning in the mid-1970s, this reliance on public funds began to backfire (Gilbert, 1977).

As economic growth stalled, social service providers encountered growing numbers of clients with increasingly complex and chronic problems. At the same time, economic stagnation and declining political support for social spending led to a withdrawal of government support for programs directed at the effects of poverty. Increasing racial and class stratification exacerbated these trends in the 1980s (Katz, 1989).

As urban areas became more dramatically divided along income and racial lines, nonprofit community-based organizations that served low-income areas had fewer sources of potential income. Consequently, when policymakers promoted the concepts of privatization and agency self-sufficiency beginning in the late 1970s, nonprofit organizations lacked the resources to respond effectively to the burgeoning social costs being thrust upon them. This hampered their ability to respond to dramatic increases in homelessness and drug abuse (Blau, 1992).

In sum, policy changes in the 1970s altered the government's role in social service delivery and further compounded the effects of the formal separation of income maintenance and services. These included an increase in the public use of the private sector through contracting and greater decentralization policy planning, which produced more variations in the scope, coverage, and quality of services. Another development was more universal coverage in child care and family planning programs. Finally, policy changes in the 1970s resulted in the creation of block grants by the

Carter administration, which combined formerly categorical programs into broad programmatic areas and established a ceiling on total state expenditures in return for increasing state control of spending patterns. The last development was particularly significant in the 1980s, when political leaders tried to dismantle the remnants of the Great Society.

REFERENCES

Abramovitz, M. (1992). The Reagan legacy: Undoing race, class, and gender accords. In J. Midgley (Ed.), *The Reagan legacy and the American welfare state* [Special issue]. *Journal of Sociology and Social Welfare, 22*(4), 91-110.

Andrews, J., & Reisch, M. (1997). Anti-communism and social work: An historical analysis. *Journal of Progressive Human Services, 8*(2), 29-49.

Axinn, J., & Stern, M. (1988). *Dependency and poverty: Old problems in a new world.* Lexington, MA: Lexington Books.

Bell, W. (1983). *Contemporary social welfare.* New York: Macmillan.

Bixby, A. K. (1990, February). Public social welfare expenditures, 1965-1987. *Social Security Bulletin, 53,* 10-26.

Blau, J. (1992). *The visible poor: Homelessness in the United States.* New York: Oxford University Press.

Bussiere, E. (1997). *(Dis)entitling the poor: The Warren court, welfare rights, and the American political tradition.* University Park: The Pennsylvania State University Press.

Caudill, H. (1963). *Night comes to the Cumberlands: A biography of a depressed area.* Boston: Little, Brown.

Danziger, S. (1991, September-October). Relearning lessons of the war on poverty. *Challenge,* pp. 53-54.

Danziger, S., & Weinberg, D. (1994). The historical record: Trends in family income, inequality, and poverty. In S. Danziger, G. D. Sandefur, & D. H. Weinberg (Eds.), *Confronting poverty: Prescriptions for change.* Cambridge, MA: Harvard University Press.

Derthick, M. (1975). *Uncontrollable spending for social services grants.* Washington, DC: The Brookings Institution.

Edsall, T. (1991). *Chain reaction: The impact of race, rights, and taxes on American politics.* New York: Norton.

Gilbert, N. (1977). The transformation of social services. *Social Service Review, 53*(3), 75-91.

Gillette, M. (1996). *Launching the war on poverty: An oral history.* New York: Twayne.

Ginzberg, E., & Solow, R. M. (Eds.). (1974). *The great society: Lessons for the future.* New York: Basic Books.

Harrington, M. (1962). *The other America: Poverty in the United States.* New York: Penguin.

Jones, J. (1992). *The dispossessed: America's underclasses from the Civil War to the present.* New York: Basic Books.

Katz, M. (1989). *The undeserving poor: From the war on poverty to the war on welfare.* New York: Pantheon.

Keisling, P. (1984, December). Lessons of the Great Society. *The Washington Monthly,* pp. 50-53.

Kornbluh, F. (1997). To fulfill their "rightly needs": Consumerism and the national welfare rights movement. *Radical History Review, 69,* 76-113.

Kotz, N., & Kotz, M. (1977). *A passion for equality: George Wiley and the movement.* New York: Norton.

Lemann, N. (1988-1989, December-January). The unfinished war. *Atlantic Monthly,* Parts I & II, pp. 37-56, 53-68.

Lemann, N. (1991). *The promised land: The great black migration and how it changed America.* New York: Knopf.

Lewis, O. (1966). *La Vida: A Puerto Rican family in the culture of poverty—San Juan and New York*. New York: Random House.

Matusow, A. J. (1984). *The unravelling of America: A history of liberalism in the 1960s*. New York: Harper & Row.

Midgley, J. (Ed.). (1992). The Reagan legacy and the American welfare state [Special issue]. *Journal of Sociology and Social Welfare, 22*(4).

Moynihan, D. P. (1969). *Maximum feasible misunderstanding*. New York: Free Press.

Moynihan, D. P. (1973). *The politics of a guaranteed income: The Nixon administration and the family assistance plan*. New York: Random House.

Murray, C. (1984). *Losing ground: American social policy, 1950-1980*. New York: Basic Books.

O'Connor, J. (1973). *The fiscal crisis of the state*. New York: St. Martin's.

Patterson, J. (1994). *America's struggle against poverty, 1990-1994* (2nd ed.). Cambridge, MA: Harvard University Press.

Piven, F. F., & Cloward, R. (1977). *Poor people's movements: How they succeed, why they fail*. New York: Vintage.

Piven, F. F., & Cloward, R. (1995). *Regulating the poor: The functions of public welfare* (rev. ed.). New York: Vintage.

Quadagno, J. (1994). *The color of welfare: How racism undermined the war on poverty*. New York: Oxford University Press.

Reisch, M. (1996). Urbanisation et politique sociale aux Etats-Unis, *Revue M,* Nos. 85-86, Paris, 9-14.

Reisch, M., & Wenocur, S. (1986). The future of community organization in social work: Social activism and the politics of profession-building. *Social Service Review, 60*(1), 70-91.

Ryan, W. (1971). *Blaming the victim*. New York: Vintage.

Sale, K. (1976). *Power shift: The rise of the southern rim and the challenge to the eastern establishment*. New York: Random House.

West, G. (1981). *The national welfare rights movement: The social protest of poor women*. New York: Praeger.

CHAPTER ELEVEN

Social Policy: Reagan and Beyond

DAVID STOESZ

F ollowing a half century of liberal hegemony in social policy, the Reagan presidency represented the recrudescence of American conservatism. Beginning with the Social Security Act of 1935, liberals had crafted an ideology that eclipsed conservative designs in public philosophy up to that time, at least with respect to domestic policy. Further elaborated during the Great Society of the mid-1960s, liberalism was so ascendent that few would have prophesied its demise. Even Republican presidents, such as Nixon, affirmed the American welfare state and further expanded its provisions. Yet, the liberal plan to replicate the northern European welfare state in the United States was not to be. The Reagan presidency pushed social policy to the Right, away from unconditional federal entitlements and toward temporary state-managed, work-oriented benefits—in the words of one commentator: "the work-ethic state" (Kaus, 1992). In this fundamental shift, the United States paralleled Great Britain, leading the way to a new formulation of social policy among the industrialized nations (Yergin & Stanislaw, 1998).

ANTECEDENTS TO THE REAGAN ERA

The conservative assault on the liberal welfare state was waged on both philosophical and programmatic fronts. In the most sweeping of philosophical treatments, Rose and Milton Friedman (1988) posited three epochs in the "tides of man": the rise of laissez-faire during the 19th century (Adam Smith tide); the rise of the welfare state during the 20th century (the Fabian [Marxist] tide); and the resurgence of free markets during the coming century (the Hayek tide). In naming the latter after Frederich von Hayek, the Friedmans honored a philosopher, little known to liberals, who not only foretold the demise of communism, but also predicted the globalization of capitalism. Hayek would become a cornerstone of the intellectual foundations to the most influential institutions promoting conservatism in America: the Department of Economics at the University of Chicago and the Heritage Foundation in Washington, D.C.

Conservative strategy was abetted by academics who had reservations about liberal social policy in general and welfare policy in particular. George Gilder (1981) suggested that liberal social programs induced dependency on the part of the poor; what the poor needed most was not more government programs, but "the spur of their own poverty" (p. 118). Charles Murray (1984) proposed even more draconian measures: "scrapping the entire federal welfare and income support structure for working-aged persons, including Aid to Families with Dependent Children, Medicaid, Food Stamps, Unemployment Insurance, Workers Compensation, subsidized housing, disability and the rest" (pp. 227-228). More moderate, Lawrence Mead (1986) proposed making receipt of welfare conditional on specific behavioral standards. Although the research and conclusions of Gilder, Murray, and Mead were hotly disputed by liberal scholars, conservatives were securing the endorsements of neoconservatives, former liberals like Daniel Patrick Moynihan (1988), who had become disillusioned with the liberal direction of social policy.

The conservative case against the welfare state would have consisted of little more than ideological sniping had not wealthy individuals and corporations funded the establishment of a network of policy institutes to promote their agenda. During the 1980s, policy institutes, or think tanks, that subscribed to conservative philosophy blossomed around the nation. The American Enterprise Institute, the Heritage Foundation, and the Cato Institute of Washington, D.C., were complemented by the Manhattan Institute of New York City, the Hoover Institution of Stanford, and the Hudson Institute in Indianapolis (Smith, 1991). Assuming an aggressive stance compared to the more staid liberal institutes, such as the Brookings Institution, the conservative think tanks viewed their mission as if it were a crusade. Writing shortly after the Reagan presidential election victory, a Heritage vice president observed that conservative think tanks could "deploy formidable armies on the battlefield of ideas—forces which [conservative] traditionalist movements previously lacked" (Pines, 1982, p. 254).

THE REAGAN PRESIDENCY

The conservative strategy against the welfare states was threefold: (a) end liberal dominance in social policy; (b) whenever possible, reroute public policy through the states or the private sector, and (c) preclude the prospect of a resurgence in social entitlements (Blumenthal & Edsall, 1988). The end of the millennium would demonstrate how enormously successful conservatives had become in redefining public philosophy, although few would have credited a compliant Democratic Party with much of this transformation. An example of Democratic sclerosis can be found in testimony preceding the first Reagan legislation targeting liberal social programs, the 1981 Omnibus Budget and Reconciliation Act (OBRA). Democrats were so bewildered by the conservative legislative assault that when the administration's new director of the Office of Management and the Budget, David Stockman, "cooked" the budget numbers affirming the soundness of the Reagan proposal, the House leadership was completely hoodwinked.

By 1983, the consequences of the 1981 OBRA were clear. Some 408,000 families had been terminated from welfare; benefits had been reduced for another 299,000. Among the casualties were the working poor. About 35% of adults who persisted in working while on public assistance were removed from the program. In addition to cuts in cash welfare, OBRA consolidated many categorical programs into block grants, in the process cutting appropriations. Accompanying the construction of the Social Services block grant, for example, was a 25% reduction in funding (Stoesz, 1996).

The most profound impact of the Reagan presidency on social policy were the 1983 amendments to the Social Security Act. To block a rapidly hemorrhaging trust fund, Reagan established a bipartisan commission under the direction of Alan Greenspan to restore the program's health. The suggestions of the Greenspan Commission, later adopted by Congress, promised to keep Social Security solvent well into the 21st century. The 1983 amendments to Social Security were incremental adjustments, but the consequences of these changes had radical implications. Modest changes included advancing the age of eligibility for benefits, increasing the federal withholding tax, including federal and nonprofit employees in the program, a 6-month delay in benefit increases, and modification in the indexing formula. Altogether, the Commission assured that Social Security would generate unprecedented surpluses in anticipation of the retirement of baby boomers. They also spelled the end of pay-as-you-go, placing Social Security financing on a reserve basis. Conveniently, the surplus generated by the 1983 Social Security amendments cushioned the massive federal budget deficits that grew during the subsequent decade.

The most incisive strike against the welfare state promulgated during the Reagan presidency was the Family Support Act (FSA) of 1988. Foremost, the FSA mandated that mothers on public assistance who did not have exempting conditions would be required to participate in education or training activities or find work in exchange for benefits. It incorporated incentives as well as penalties: The carrot consisted of the Job Opportunities and Basic Skills (JOBS) program, which included "transitional benefits" (the continuation of child care, Medicaid, and transportation for 1 year after securing a job); the stick was the termination of benefits for recipients who refused to participate in "welfare-to-work." The FSA was budgeted at only $3.34 billion over 5 years. During this period, states were encouraged to obtain federal waivers for innovative demonstrations designed to wean poor mothers from public assistance and assist them in becoming economically self-sufficient (Stoesz & Karger, 1989).

The Reagan legacy extended far beyond these legislative triumphs, however. His vice president took the White House, and although the Bush presidency was limited to one term, it witnessed an underappreciated addition to social policy: the Americans With Disabilities Act (ADA). Liberals praised the implementation of ADA because it extended civil rights to people with disabilities; conservatives lauded ADA for a different reason. Unlike traditional disability programs, such as Supplemental Security Income, which assumed that people with disabilities would need assistance because they could not participate in activities such as work, ADA evolved from a different orientation: those with disabilities were entitled to be involved in the mainstream—indeed, would insist on it. Rather than being unable to work, the ADA portrayed those with disabilities as being capable employees if only barriers to the labor market were removed.

Another legacy of the Reagan presidency was its influence on the Democratic Party. Reflecting on the failed presidential candidacies of Jimmy Carter in 1980, Walter Mondale in 1984, and Michael Dukakis in 1988, Charles Peters (1983), editor of the *Washington Monthly,* coined the term *neoliberalism* in proposing an alternative to the welfare liberalism that had guided the Democratic Party. "We still believe in liberty and justice and a fair chance for all, in mercy for the afflicted, and help for the down and out," wrote Peters, attempting to pull Democrats to the Right, "but we no longer automatically favor unions and big government or oppose the military and big business" (p. 34). Peters was not alone among progressively oriented Democrats who perceived the party as having moved too far to the Left.

THE CLINTON PRESIDENCY

Success of the conservative ideological juggernaut led Democratic leaders to reassess the party's adherence to welfare liberalism. During the late 1980s, several prominent Democrats—Paul Tsongas, Richard Gephardt, Sam Nunn, and Bill Bradley—founded the Democratic Leadership Council (DLC) to pull the party toward the center. The

DLC hired Al From as its political director and soon established a think tank, the Progressive Policy Institute (PPI), under the direction of Will Marshall, as its intelligence incubator. The DLC and PPI scored a major victory when the Democratic presidential ticket featured two additional founders: Bill Clinton and Al Gore. After a decade of frustration, Democrats had found the key to the White House. Success, however, entailed one significant concession: abandoning welfare liberalism.

Much of Clinton's presidential victory was attributed to his claim to be a "new Democrat," one who eschewed sentimental liberalism as much as retrograde conservatism. As a Democratic nominee, Clinton had identified himself as pursuing a "new covenant," that would reflect a "third way" in American politics. As President, however, Clinton proved less capable of moving beyond his ubiquitous references to change and toward the institutionalization of a post-liberal and post-conservative orientation to social policy. Indeed, the tentativeness of Clinton's control of the executive branch was conspicuous during the ill-fated initiatives of 1993.

Confronted, on entering the White House, by the massive deficits generated during the Reagan-Bush era, Clinton found little fiscal room for his investment strategy to rebuild the nation's physical and social infrastructure. Clinton resolved the dilemma by siding with Federal Reserve Chairman Alan Greenspan, who advised against massive tax increases that would be necessitated by major new federal initiatives. Accordingly, Clinton's 1993 budget consisted of much line-item reshuffling with only token allocations for those projects that had identified candidate Clinton as a "new" Democrat. The primary exception was a major expansion of the Earned Income Tax Credit for low-wage workers, an income-subsidy program long favored by conservatives as an alternative to welfare. Clinton's 1993 budget squeaked through a Democratic Congress by single votes in both houses, the slimmest margin in the history of the republic.

A minimalist budget notwithstanding, 1993 would become most associated with failed health care reform. The Clinton Health Security Act (HSA) was the product of a protracted and elaborate planning process managed by White House adviser and corporate savant, Ira Magaziner, and overseen by First Lady Hillary Rodham Clinton. HSA was designed as a national health insurance program that would be administered by health alliances, which would subscribe large numbers of members over entire regions. By extending a Health Maintenance Organization approach to health care to the entire population, HSA was an industry-friendly proposal. The requirement that employers would have to finance much of the initiative and the elimination of small health insurers spelled the demise of the HSA, however. In the face of the increasingly bitter opposition by the business community, Clinton admitted defeat of the HSA. Years later, planners of the HSA would be fined by the courts for having plotted the scheme in violation of federal requirements that such planning be open to the public.

The 1993 budget and health reform initiatives were soon overshadowed by the 1994 mid-term congressional election debacle. White House ineptitude and Democratic intransigence in Congress bred contempt among voters, who took revenge at the polls, electing the first Republican-controlled Congress in 40 years. A shocked Clinton took stock of his political fortunes and quickly veered Right. After the disastrous 1994 congressional election, Clinton showed his conservative colors by announcing in his 1996 State of the Union address that "the era of big government is over." Democrat survivors in Congress were heartened by Clinton's embrace of an increase in the minimum wage, elevating it in two stages to $5.15/hour; yet any suspicion of the President's inherent liberal tendencies was soon dashed. After vetoing two welfare reform proposals forwarded by a conservative Congress, Clinton signed the third. Thus, on the eve of his 1996 reelection campaign, Clinton appeared to sacrifice the well-being of America's poor children on the altar of his reelection.

In signing the 1996 Personal Responsibility and Work Opportunity Reconciliation Act (PRWORA), Clinton cashiered the 60-year-old entitlement for poor families. Aid to Families With Dependent Children (AFDC) was replaced with Temporary Assistance for Needy Families (TANF), a block grant that was devolved to the states. In place of the open-ended entitlement, states would receive finite funding, the amount predicated on caseload levels of the early 1990s. Beyond a few requirements—states must have 75% of one adult from two-parent households in the labor market by 1997, 25% of single heads-of-household in the labor market by 1997, and 50% of single heads-of-households working by 2002—states were free to exercise latitude in managing their block grants. PRWORA established a 5-year lifetime limit on receipt of welfare and allowed the states to establish shorter time limits. The only funding restriction was that 80% of the block grant had to be committed to "maintenance of effort," in other words, to welfare recipients (Karger & Stoesz, 1997).

Response to PRWORA was immediate and volatile. The conservative reaction to federal welfare reform was euphoric. Since passage of the FSA in 1988, some 40 states had received federal waivers to experiment with welfare reform, most of which focused on pushing mothers on public assistance into the labor market. Conservatives touted state and local welfare reforms, which reduced caseloads sharply, increasing earnings of welfare recipients, and leaving localities and states with substantial savings. Contrary to liberal fears that welfare reform would provoke a "race to the bottom" in which states would compete in lowering benefits to make welfare less and less desirable, states tended to retain benefit levels; some, such as Wisconsin, actually increased programs to help welfare recipients find and keep jobs (Vobejda, 1998). In the absence of evidence indicating otherwise, conservatives were free to pronounce welfare reform a uniform success, in terms of both the increasing work experience of welfare beneficiaries and the absence of the disastrous consequences voiced by liberal critics.

Liberals, on the other hand, were horrified. Speaking for many, Peter Edelman (1997), an advocate for the poor as well as husband of Children's Defense Fund founder and director Marian Wright Edelman, condemned PRWORA as "the worst thing that Bill Clinton has done." Citing evidence of tentative attachment to the labor market, liberal policy analysts contended that the benefits of welfare-to-work were temporary and that long-term consequences were cause for much less optimism, particularly once time limits were considered (Stoesz, 1997). If, as conservatives claimed, the benefits were universal, liberals contended that was largely because states had not tracked those families who had left public assistance voluntarily nor those who had been terminated involuntarily from aid. Although state welfare demonstrations did yield positive outcomes, liberals pointed out, these were quite modest over the long run and vaulted relatively few families out of poverty (Friedlander & Burtless, 1995; Gueron & Pauly, 1991).

The counterpoint to welfare reform was Clinton's concern for the middle-class and affluent. In signing the Balanced Budget Act of 1997, Clinton called the bluff of congressional Republicans by offering to eliminate the budget deficit within 5 years. Although this made for lusty rhetoric, the reality was more problematic. By shifting most of the budget balancing to the last few years of the plan, the Act not only seemed unrealistic, but it also made tax concessions to the wealthy in the billions of dollars. As had been the case since the Reagan presidency, much of the budget balancing was afforded by the massive surplus generated by the 1983 Social Security reforms. In his 1998 State of the Union address, Clinton promised to divert any federal budget surplus resulting from budget balancing to the Social Security trust fund so that baby boomers would be assured of benefits on their retirement. Not a few observers wondered how increasing Social Security funds that had already been credited to deficit reduction could also generate additional revenues to keep the program solvent into the next century. Indeed, if Social Security were removed from Clinton's budget-balancing calculations, the federal budget remained in the red through the beginning of the 21st century, after which it would spill red ink when the baby boomers retired.

In fairness, the Clinton presidency featured a number of progressive policies. Immediately on entering office, the President reversed several abortion-restrictive executive orders. Clinton's adherence to affirmative action was unshakable, even when states and localities reversed their commitment to equality by race and gender. The Clinton presidency oversaw the establishment of "empowerment zones" to reverse the deterioration of urban and rural regions, a long-overdue increase in the minimum wage, and the extension of health care to the nation's poor children. And the Clinton Americorps initiative reacquainted tens of thousands of Americans with the virtues of volunteerism while providing essential services to disadvantaged communities. Compared to earlier initiatives, such as Johnson's War on Poverty, however, Clinton's initiatives appeared modest if not puny. Aside from general policy achievements, such as the Balanced Budget Act, the Clinton presidency proved unable to mount a social policy achievement on a par with the ADA, signed into law by President Bush.

As President, Clinton behaved as the quintessential moderate Republican. His social policy reinforced the work ethic, while diminishing welfare entitlements. Tax policy afforded modest wage subsidies to the working poor; at the same time, it provided much larger rebates to the affluent. The administration's social policy innovations were small-scale and overshadowed by reversals (the demise of the welfare entitlement) or inaction (the failure to reform social insurance, particularly Medicare and Social Security). Just at the point when Clinton seemed poised to use an anticipated budget surplus for program innovation, he opted to reinforce Social Security instead. Even that action appeared dubious as the presidency was rocked by sex scandals. Despite Clinton's two-term presidency—the first since Franklin Delano Roosevelt—the Democratic Party seemed unable to attract promising politicians. Except for the vice president and first lady, Clinton's following of new young Democrats appeared to be small. After he signed the 1996 welfare reform legislation on the eve of his presidential campaign, the primary question regarding a Clinton reelection was not whether it represented a second term of the Clinton presidency, but whether it was actually the fifth term of Ronald Reagan.

THE FUTURE OF SOCIAL POLICY

The millennium found American social policy in a period of transformation. Since the 1980s, the policy template of welfare liberalism—federally assured benefits available unconditionally as an open-ended entitlement—seemed an artifact of the New Deal and the War on Poverty. To reform the welfare state, the Reagan/Bush administrations introduced a conservative direction in social policy, one that clearly resonated with American voters. Rather than revive liberalism, Clinton actually furthered the conservative momentum in public policy. Liberal human services professionals, for their part, reacted defensively to conservatism in Congress and the White House. Social policy advocates defended the American welfare state, whenever possible protecting the more vulnerable public assistance program while keeping a wary eye on the social insurances. Despite the opportunities to redefine social policy so that it would be more consonant with a service and information-oriented post-industrial environment, the liberal reflex was to defend the industrial era welfare state (Gans, 1995).

At the end of the decade, three broad themes were shaping American social policy: privatization, the "new paternalism," and social investment.

Privatization. Arguably the most enduring consequence of the conservatism introduced by the Reagan presidency has been privatization, "the act of reducing the role of government, or increasing the role of the private sector, in an activity or in the ownership of assets" (Savas, 1987, p. 3). The issue of privatization is integral to the nation's political economy: Under democratic capitalism, most consumers obtain needed goods and services from the market. When markets fail, however, government programs have evolved to provide essential goods and services. Advocates of privatization observe that government programs operated under public bureaucracies are less than optimal, often unresponsive to the needs and demands of consumers. Their prescription is to transform public utilities held by government bureaucracies into private markets.

Momentum to privatize social programs was propelled by the President's Commission on Privatization (1988) empaneled by President Reagan. The Commission reported favorably on several government functions that were amenable to privatization, including low-income housing, education, and Medicare, among others. Subsequently, a critical examination of privatization revealed improved services at lower cost in some instances, but producing conclusive evidence was devilishly tricky (Donahue, 1989). Ambiguous data notwithstanding, the privatization impulse continued to influence social policy.

Since passage of Medicare and Medicaid in 1965, American health care has become increasingly commercialized, with for-profit health and human services firms exploiting markets in child care and welfare, education, and corrections (Stoesz, 1986). During the early 1990s, New Jersey and Texas verged on putting major pieces of the welfare bureaucracy out to bid to the corporate sector. A bipartisan committee reviewing Social Security reforms produced three reports, each of which called for varying degrees of privatization. The 1996 federal welfare reform not only allowed for contracting with for-profit firms for the first time, but also encouraged private religious organizations to provide services to the welfare poor.

New paternalism. In requiring welfare recipients to engage in education and training or secure employment, the FSA of 1988 introduced reciprocity into social policy: in exchange for benefits, beneficiaries would be held accountable for a standard of conduct (Mead, 1986). Because the Act encouraged states to obtain federal waivers to demonstrate experiments in welfare reform, several added to the list of behaviors necessary to obtain public assistance. Recipients of aid were required not only to find work, but also to assure school attendance and vaccinations for their children, identify paternity of children receiving benefits, and practice family planning. (This is a de facto requirement as a result of imposing the "family cap," refusing additional benefits for children born after a household head becomes eligible for aid.) Reciprocity thus represented a marked shift away from unconditional provision of benefits; "government is moving away from freedom and toward authority as its basic tool in social policy" (Mead, 1992, p. 181).

As state experiments in welfare reform were consolidated in the 1996 federal welfare reform, the implication of "the new paternalism" became more evident. In the words of Lawrence Mead, the new paternalism marked a new era in poverty policy: "Government is seeking to supervise the lives of poor citizens who are dependent on it, often in return for supporting them" (Mead, 1997, p. 1). Although the new paternalism was long on rhetorical mileage, its programmatic outcomes were less convincing. A review of various demonstration programs intended to increase earnings, improve school attendance, enhance child support, and reduce teen pregnancy concluded that "the imposition of conditions for receipt of welfare yields modest results at best; at worst, the consequences are downright perverse" (Stoesz, 1997, p. 68). Evidence notwithstanding, the new paternalism so resonated with mainstream American values that reciprocity continued to shape welfare policy.

Social investment. In response to an increasingly conservative political environment, many liberal policy advocates began to reorient their prescriptions to advance social justice. James Midgley (1995), for example, has proposed social development as a basis for social policy: This is "a process of planned social change designed to promote the well-being of the population as a whole in conjunction with a dynamic process of economic development" (p. 25). So configured, social development is consistent with the strategy of investing in social infrastructure advanced by Robert Reich (1991).

> Well-trained workers and modern infrastructure attract global webs of enterprise, which invest and give workers relatively good jobs; these jobs, in turn, generate additional on-the-job training and experience, thus creating a powerful lure to other global webs. As skills increase and experience accumulates, a nation's citizens add greater and greater value to the world economy—commanding ever-higher compensation and improving their standard of living. (p. 265)

By integrating social policy with economic development, proponents of social investment attempted to reclaim ground in the public policy debate lost to conservatives since the 1980s.

The Individual Development Account (IDA) initiative promoted by Michael Sherraden (1991) illustrates the social investment approach to social policy. IDAs are tax-exempt matching accounts that are reserved for finishing college or vocational school, purchasing a home, establishing a business, or supplementing a pension. As opposed to income support strategies that have characterized American poverty policy since the New Deal, IDAs represent an investment strategy, a more effective mechanism to leverage the poor out of poverty. Through IDAs, the investment of the poor in their future is matched with an investment from an external source. By the late 1990s, IDAs were being demonstrated in 13 sites nationwide in the "Downpayment on the American Dream" initiative funded by $8 million in foundation grants. These policy strategies—privatization, the new paternalism, and social investment—bear the imprint of conservatism, although with varying consequences. Thus, the ideological move to the Right, introduced by the Reagan presidency, continues to influence American social policy.

REFERENCES

Blumenthal, S., & Edsall, T. (1988). *The Reagan legacy.* New York: Pantheon.

Donahue, J. (1989). *The privatization decision.* New York: Basic Books.

Edelman, P. (1997, March). The worst thing Bill Clinton has done. *Atlantic Monthly,* pp. 23-29.

Friedlander, D., & Burtless, G. (1995). *Five years after.* New York: Russell Sage Foundation.

Friedman, M., & Friedman, R. (1988). The tide in the affairs of men. In A. Anderson & D. Bark (Eds.), *Thinking about America.* Stanford, CA: Hoover Institution.

Gans, H. (1995). *The war against the poor.* New York: Basic Books.

Gilder, G. (1981). *Wealth and poverty.* New York: Basic Books.

Gueron, J., & Pauly, E. (1991). *From welfare to work.* New York: Russell Sage Foundation.

Karger, H., & Stoesz, D. (1997). *American social welfare policy* (3rd ed.). New York: Longman.

Kaus, M. (1992). *The end of equality.* New York: Basic Books.

Mead, L. (1986). *Beyond entitlement.* New York: Free Press.

Mead, L. (1992). *The new politics of poverty.* New York: Basic Books.

Mead, L. (1997). (Ed.). *The new paternalism: Supervisory approaches to poverty.* Washington, DC: Brookings Institution.

Midgley, J. (1995). *Social development: The developmental perspective in social welfare.* London: Sage.

Moynihan, D. (1988). *Came the revolution.* San Diego: Harcourt Brace Jovanovich.

Murray, C. (1984). *Losing ground: American social policy, 1950-1980.* New York: Basic Books.

President's Commission on Privatization. (1988). *Privatization: Toward more effective government.* Washington, DC: Author.

Peters, C. (1983). A new politics. *Public Welfare, 18,* 12-14.

Pines, B. (1982). *Back to basics.* New York: William Morrow.

Reich, R. (1991). *The work of nations.* New York: Knopf.

Savas, E. (1987). *Privatization.* Chatham, NJ: Chatham House.

Sherraden, M. (1991). *Assets and the poor.* Armonk, NY: M. E. Sharpe.

Smith, J. (1991). *The idea brokers.* New York: Free Press.

Stoesz, D. (1986, July-August). Corporate welfare. *Social Work, 31*(4), 245-249.

Stoesz, D. (1996). *Small change: Domestic policy under the Clinton presidency.* New York: Longman.

Stoesz, D. (1997, March-April). Welfare behaviorism. *Society,* pp. 68-77.

Stoesz, D., & Karger, H. (1989, March-April). When welfare reform fails. *Tikkun,* 23-25, 118-122.

Vobejda, B. (1998, February 16). Fewer welfare recipients. *Washington Post Weekly,* p. A-1.

Yergin, D., & Stanislaw, J. (1998). *The commanding heights.* New York: Simon & Schuster.

PART THREE

Social Policy and the Social Services

Part III is the largest of the book, containing twelve chapters that range over a number of social service and social policy fields. It discusses a number of social services that are included in most conventional accounts of social policy and social welfare. These include child welfare, programs for the elderly, social security, services to people with disabilities and "welfare," as means-tested income support programs are popularly known. It also examines activities that are not conventionally grouped with the mainstream social services. These include employment policies and services, correctional services, and urban development policies and programs. Part III also includes an overview of health, education, and housing, which are very large fields of social policy endeavor and are often thought to require separate and more substantial analysis. However, to ensure that the book is as comprehensive as possible, these services are included in Part III although, of course, they cannot be covered in great detail.

Each chapter in this part of the book follows a standard format in which the historical evolution of each social service field is briefly described; the current legislative and administrative arrangements pertaining to service delivery in each field is outlined; and the social, political and economic factors influencing policies and service delivery are considered. Each chapter also discusses the issues arising out of the descriptive account of each social service field. As will be seen, social services policy formulation and delivery raise complex and often contentious disagreements about which approaches are the most effective ways of meeting human needs.

CHAPTER TWELVE

Child and Family Welfare Policies and Services: Current Issues and Historical Antecedents

KATHERINE BRIAR-LAWSON

JEANETTE DREWS

Vulnerable children have been among the most marginalized and underserved populations throughout the history of the United States. Their families and the systems that serve them often fail them. Policy makers have not deemed vulnerable children or their families as primary human resource investments, despite the predictable challenges and human costs that are consequences associated with their vulnerability. Consequently, the living conditions of many children in some U.S. communities rival those of children in developing nations.

Child and family policy in the United States has been characterized as residual, crisis-driven, and often child saving rather than family strengthening (Lindsey, 1994). Such policy strategies have created high-cost human and fiscal outcomes that could have been avoided with relatively low-cost investments in vulnerable children and families (Bruner, 1993).

This chapter explores some of the policy and program challenges facing child and family welfare in the next century while addressing the historical antecedents to U.S.

policy responses to children and families. Special attention is placed on child protection and child welfare systems and their relation to poor children and families.

FAMILIES AS FOUNDATIONS FOR SOCIAL WELFARE

Families perform 90% of all the caregiving, counseling, education, child protection, health care, and policing in the nation and around the world, yet many remain unaided as they strive to support their dependent members. In the United States, since the late 1700s, parents have been charged with the protection and education of their children. During the 1800s, children might be taken away from their parents simply because of their poverty. In 1874, the Society for the Prevention of Cruelty to Children was formed to protect them from maltreatment. Mother's pensions for poor families, child labor protections, infant and maternal feeding and health programs, and public schooling all emerged as Progressive Era innovations to assist vulnerable children.

Although the 1935 Social Security Act required the protection of children as a focus of public social services, it was not until the discovery of the battered child syndrome in 1962 that child maltreatment emerged as a prominent policy and practice concern across the nation (Brissett-Chapman, 1995). Since then, states have developed a continuum of supportive, supplemental, and substitute care services (Kadushin, 1980). These include family supports through child abuse prevention initiatives; child protection including investigation of reports; family preservation services promoting placement prevention and intensive family services; kin and nonkin foster families as well as group care services with reunification supports; adoption, guardianship, and independent living programs.

Legislation governing child protection and child welfare systems in the United States includes the 1974 Child Abuse Prevention and Treatment Act (CAPTA). This Act established the National Center on Child Abuse and Neglect and mandated coordinated practices in prevention, identification, and treatment of abused and neglected children. States received funds to develop reporting systems for investigations and to engage guardians ad litem serving as court-based advocates for the children. Since the passage of CAPTA, there have been a number of amendments to strengthen prevention and reporting.

In recent years, safety and risk assessments have dominated much of the practice in child protection services. Safety assessment is conducted to determine if the child is in imminent danger. Risk assessment addresses the persistence and prevalence of the factors that affect safety. Safety and risk factors include domestic violence, mental illness, substance abuse, homelessness, environmental conditions, history of abuse, age of the child, skills of the caretaker, special needs of the child (such as developmental disabilities), and medical challenges. Many safety and risk assessment tools have been developed to counter the incident- and offense-based focus of investigations; only a few focus on family resilience, strengths, or cultural and community assets.

Law Enforcement Versus Social Work-Based Child Protection

Debates are intensifying over the underlying practice and policy paradigms for child protection. One school of thought focuses on children's legal rights, with abusive parental behaviors seen as crimes requiring police-like rather than social work-style investigations (Pelton, 1989). Child welfare has served as the centerpiece of social work since its inception as a profession, yet lawsuits and ineffective investigatory practices have led to litigiously oriented rather than social work-operated systems of child protection.

Another school of thought is reflected in the work of the National Association of Public Child Welfare Administrators (NAPCWA, 1998). This association has issued a guide for family-centered risk assessment and child protection services. States such as North Dakota, Florida, Kentucky, and Missouri have moved to replace formal investigations and substantiation of abuse practices with family-centered services. In North Dakota, according to Schmidt (1997), services and supports have been provided to vulnerable parents referred to Child Protection. These services have been deemed promising, with fewer subsequent referrals to the child protection system and better child and family outcomes (Schmidt, 1997). Such service approaches are in keeping with research studies that show that when biological parents receive the support they need, improved child welfare outcomes may result (Emlen, Lahti, Downs, McKay, & Downs, 1977; Fanshel & Shinn, 1978; Gambrill & Stein, 1981; Kinney, Madsen, Fleming, & Haapala, 1977).

Family Preservation and Family-Centered Practice

Many states and counties have experimented with family preservation services to address placement prevention and reunification. Such family preservation initiatives have varied in intensity, duration, worker-family ratios, and skills of workers. So far, mixed results have emerged (Fraser, Pecora, & Haapala, 1991). Legislation that has helped to reinforce family preservation services includes the Indian Child Welfare Act of 1978, the Adoption Assistance and Child Welfare Act of 1980, and the Family Preservation and Support Services provisions of the Omnibus Reconciliation Act of 1993. Among other mandates, the Indian Child Welfare Act requires that active efforts be pursued to ensure that Indian children remain with their families and that tribal courts oversee decision making regarding Indian children.

The Adoption Assistance and Child Welfare Act of 1980 requires that "reasonable efforts" be pursued to ensure that children remain with their families. This Act requires that preplacement efforts attempt to divert children from going into out-of-home care, that reunification be expedited, and that permanent alternative supports through adoption, kinship care, and guardianship be provided if reunification is not possible. This Act helped to spawn a number of family preservation demonstration projects, including Homebuilders of Federal Way in Washington (Kinney et al., 1977).

The Family Preservation and Support Services provisions of the Omnibus Reconciliation Act promote cohesive strategies to build community-based family supports and preservation strategies. As a result, some communities are experimenting with neighborhood teams of child protection and child welfare workers who collaborate with other service providers in decision making and family-centered interventions.

About 15% of the children who are referred for abuse and neglect go into foster or group care. High caseloads among child welfare workers, inadequate reunification services, and parental difficulty in follow-through with court-ordered case plans have created long stays in foster care, especially for children who are poor and of color. Disruptions in foster placements have increased over the years, signaling rising behavioral, health, and parenting challenges among abused and neglected children.

THE CHILD WELFARE CRISIS

In 1995, the General Accounting Office (GAO) declared that the foster care system was in crisis because of the sharp increases of children in care. In addition, over 30 state systems are experiencing varying forms of class action litigation involving child welfare. Moreover, other systems may be facing class action litigation affecting juvenile justice, school districts, and institutions for the mentally ill and developmentally disabled children. In 1997, rising numbers of children "adrift" and even "aging out" in foster care led the U.S. Children's Bureau and Congress to enact the Adoption and Safe Families Act. This Act sets time limits for children in care so that permanency planning decisions are made within 12 months of systems entry or when the child spends 12 out of 18 months in out-of-home care.

Permanency planning has long been a concern of child welfare reformers. This Act expedites permanency decisions and upholds children's rights to a permanent family. It is expected to place extraordinary burdens on already stressed systems and families. Parents, challenged by addiction, poverty, and lack of resources, are required to quickly mobilize and use services to eliminate safety and risk factors while making rapid interpersonal and behavioral change. It is anticipated that many more children will be freed for adoption under the new law.

Adoption has long been part of the child welfare system. In recent years, attention has been diverted away from adoptive services to child protection, family preservation, kinship, and foster and group care services. Nonetheless, adoption dissolution rates have been a concern of the child welfare system for some time (Barth, Berry, Yoshikami, Goodfield, & Carson, 1988). Such disruptions, although often preventable, have not been the focus of much child welfare innovation. Thus, new adoption preservation practices and approaches are expected to emerge in the near future.

Kinship foster care enables children to be placed with relatives, who may, in fact, become legal guardians. Kinship care has accelerated the use of extended family members for out-of-home placements. In some states, up to half of the children in out-of-home care may be in kinship arrangements (Hegar, 1998).

Paralleling the principles of "reasonable efforts" in placement prevention are other policy principles such as a child's right to the "least restrictive" environment, to the "least intrusive" interventions, and to supports that ensure "normalization" and "mainstreaming." Some of these principles have been reinforced, if not introduced, by movements on behalf of children with special needs. Laws such as the Education for All Handicapped Children Act of 1975 and its reauthorization in 1990 as the Individuals With Disabilities Act require that states provide education, special supports, and services to meet the needs of all children and to provide these supports and services in the least restrictive environment. Thus, children who might have been sent to institutions, including residential treatment, for care and schooling are instead attending local public schools.

Child Abuse and Neglect and Co-Occurring Symptoms

The past decade has witnessed a doubling of reports of abuse and neglect (Brissett-Chapman, 1995). Some might argue that reporting systems have improved. Others might contend that rising rates of poverty, inequality, and underemployment are the key contributors to family stress and an epidemic of abuse and neglect (Lindsey, 1994). Still others might argue that the increasing detection and surveillance systems such as hospital screening for substance-exposed newborns and drug-using mothers have escalated the reporting rates.

Correlates and risk factors for abuse and neglect are increasingly being mapped and studied. Nonetheless, the paucity of policy and service reforms addressing co-occurring symptoms and factors that accompany abuse and neglect is indicative of the insufficient research base that drives child welfare policy, programs, and practices

(Austin, 1998). For example, it is estimated that between 50% and 80% of all child welfare families have substance abuse as a presenting problem (Curtis & McCullough, 1993; Murphy et al., 1991). In many cases, referral resources for families are inadequate; child welfare families do not have first call on these resources. For example, few states have enacted policies enabling drug-using pregnant mothers to have priority access to substance abuse treatment beds. Thus, despite the evidence for substance abuse-related neglect and maltreatment, few substance abuse treatment systems are tailored to meet the needs of these families. Few integrative policies and service delivery systems have been explicitly crafted that simultaneously address co-occurring symptoms.

Evidence that 50% of child welfare families may have domestic violence occurring with child maltreatment warrants far greater interdependence among the service systems addressing domestic violence and child abuse victims (Aron & Olson, 1997). Instead, the philosophical clashes between child welfare and domestic violence service providers often make such close articulation of services and supports problematic. Philosophical differences stem from the belief that abused women need to leave the perpetrator at any cost; child welfare workers may be addressing the family as a unit and the services needed to keep it intact.

Differential Policies and Services for Children in Mental Health, Developmental Disabilities, and Child Welfare Systems

Children who are poor and of color are disproportionately found in the child welfare system. Recent guidelines developed by NAPCWA (1998, p. 17) for child protection practice suggest that families of color are disproportionately reported for abuse and neglect. These families of color also may receive harsher and more pessimistic assessments (NAPCWA, 1998).

In some states, children from nonpoor, nonminority families may be served in the mental health or developmental disabilities service systems. Families with children who have mental or physical disabilities are less likely to be blamed or punished and to receive police-like services than those in the child welfare system. Instead of a "rescue and place" response, the mental health and disabilities service systems have often sought to provide special supports to help families accommodate the challenging behaviors of their children. In contrast, substitute care often has dominated the child welfare system. This may be in part because most federal child welfare funding, through Titles IVB and IVE of the Social Security Act, supports out-of-home rather than in-home services.

One study found that nearly half the children being served by the foster care system reveal mental health problems as severe as those children being served by the mental health systems (Trupin, Tarico, Low, Jemelka, & McClellan, 1993). However, specialized care is not systematically pursued for this child welfare group unless litigation has forced specialized mental health treatment. There are no uniform national practices or policies ensuring that the mental health, developmental disabilities, health, and income support needs of children are systematically addressed regardless of which system they enter. In fact, a differential response, based on class, income, and ethnicity may be evident in many states and communities (Lindsey, 1994).

In some communities, an abused child with developmental and mental health challenges might enter a variety of systems. If the child is first seen for mental health or developmental disabilities, the focus may be on services and specialized care. If the child enters the child welfare system due to abuse, the goal may be safety, requiring placement. Specialized or "tailored and individualized" care may never be provided. Whereas child welfare workers are faced with finding adequate "beds" or placements, case managers in disabilities or mental health systems may devise individualized and tailored services so that these children can be mainstreamed to maximize their potential.

Policies governing children with disabilities mandate specialized care ranging from institutions, skilled nursing facilities, intermediate care facilities, and community-based group homes to family-based individualized support services. Similarly, children with mental health challenges may receive individualized home and community-based service options. Some of the most innovative practices have emerged with tailored, "wrap around services" that allow emotionally disturbed children to remain in their own homes and classrooms.

Many child victims of abuse and neglect also have co-occurring symptoms of mental illness and even disabilities. However, neither policy makers nor service providers have ensured that all children, regardless of which system they enter, receive similar rights to individualized, tailored services, homelike settings, trained foster parents, and services delivered by professionals with expertise and requisite professional preparation.

Collaborative Practices

The rise of collaborative practices and attempts at service integration is in part a response to children and families caught in these "cross systems." Categorical policy and service strategies have resulted in piecemeal approaches to families. Moreover, families may have as many as 14 service providers all working with various needs. Each of these providers is governed by a different set of policies, services, and funding streams, often contradicting each of the other providers. As a result, some states require that service providers collaborate on service plans and even pool funds to ensure that children receive the requisite services from all relevant providers.

The rise of school-based collaboratives represents one of the more promising strategies to build more cohesive, integrated, and comprehensive interventions (GAO, 1992; Tetleman, 1996). In fact, when child protection workers are linked to classrooms and have resources to address abuse and neglect, such as emergency income assistance, the diversion rates are as high as 87% (Tanoury, Saunders, & Lusk, 1996). Research on effectiveness regarding collaborative practices and outcomes for children and families is spotty. Despite the high correlation of poverty with abuse and neglect, neither child welfare workers nor allied health, mental health, substance abuse, and domestic violence service providers have income- and job-generating tools in their skill and resource repertoire. Thus, much of their work is consigned to symptom-focused problem remediation rather than the mobilization of income, jobs, and occupational ladders. This is particularly problematic given welfare terminations and the absence of living wages for families. As Lisabeth Schorr has argued, we cannot service our way out of poverty (Weiss, 1995). Yet, the primary response of the social work community has been toward service rather than income- and job-generating investment strategies.

Violence to Children by Systems Designed to Serve Them

Violence to children may not just occur in the home but in systems designed to serve them. At the community systems level, for example, children who have been abused and neglected may face problematic out-of-home placements. Paradoxically, they may become harmed in some of these placements and deprived of requisite mental health and related services. Thus, the trauma of abuse and neglect may be compounded by the trauma of placement in foster or group care along with a succession of failed or injurious placements. Many well-intended foster parents across the nation are insufficiently prepared for the challenges of caring for children whose abuse and neglect require intensely therapeutic and skilled care, as well as multiple services and supports.

Biological parents face systems challenges just as their children do. The court orders many parents into services that may not be available to them. Thus, despite policy mandates for expedited permanency, the reality is that, for some, services such as counseling, substance abuse treatment, and parenting classes may not be available. Consequently, children who might have been reunited with their parents are denied such reunification and move to adoption.

The chain of harmful experiences for children may have ripple effects and compounding consequences for their lifetime. This chain begins with abuse and neglect along with co-occurring factors such as parental substance abuse, domestic violence, and mental illness. The chain may continue with unsatisfactory foster or group care or poor reunification experiences, along with concomitant school failure. If their traumas go untreated, these children move through adolescence and adulthood with painful scars (Gustavsson & Segal, 1994). High rates of incarcerated individuals were once abused children; numbers of homeless adults were once foster care children (Sosin, Piliavin, & Westerfelt, 1991). Moreover, there is a high prevalence of sexual abuse among help seekers, and studies indicate that over half of adult females may have been victims. In fact, one study found that up to 90% of women who have alcohol and substance abuse problems were sexually abused (Ladwig & Anderson, 1992). This has led Conte (1995) to argue that social work practitioners who do not screen for such violence are in effect committing a form of malpractice.

School-based corporal punishment is another source of violence to children. Physical punishment as a disciplinary intervention has been found to be unnecessary, ineffective, and harmful (Corrigan, 1996). Many states have outlawed corporal punishment in schools. None have outlawed all forms of corporal punishment, even though alternative and more effective forms of discipline are widely known and available.

Several authors, such as Gil (1970) and Lindsey (1994), argue that poverty is violence against children. Such claims are reinforced by recent research on brain and behavioral development. Poverty poses grave danger to children's healthy development (Duncan, Huston, & McLoyd, 1998).

POVERTY AND ITS RELATION TO CHILD AND FAMILY WELFARE

The United States is undergoing the highest income inequality in its history. As the predictable stresses of poverty, unemployment, underemployment, substance abuse, mental illness, intergenerational violence, and insufficient parenting skills take their toll on parents, they, in turn, may neglect, harm, and even maim their children or the elderly in their care (Briar, 1988). Rather than promoting investments, such as individual development accounts or dependent care or family allowances, the United States is the only industrialized nation that does not provide social insurance for children or families. Welfare assistance was born out of the mother's pension movement to ensure that no full-time caregiver should also be a full-time employee and thus forced to place a child in an institution. Although unevenly enacted across the states, mother's pensions were the forerunners of the federally provided Aid to Dependent Children associated with the 1935 Social Security Act. Now succeeded by Temporary Assistance to Needy Families (TANF), benefits are time-limited and employment-based.

Because wages have never been based on family income needs, many parents work full-time and are still poor. Work-contingent income supplements through Earned Income Tax Credits are the primary boost enabling some working parents to rise above the poverty income threshold. The debates preceding the policy decisions that established TANF failed to include the importance of intergenerational care-giving roles of families or the costs associated with institutionalizing dependent members so that family caregivers can meet assistance-based work requirements. Further discounted in those debates were the stresses of many impoverished single parents, usually women, who must juggle work and care-giving responsibilities with limited resources. Often, these families have no car, no health insurance, problematic and costly child care, and stress-related illness; many are victims of domestic violence. Consequently, it is predicted that the numbers of children in foster care and homeless shelters will increase as TANF time limits exacerbate the stresses of joblessness and as the removal of income supports takes its toll (Digre, 1997; Edelman, 1997).

Poor children suffer higher incidences of adverse health, developmental disabilities, and other outcomes than nonpoor children. Even with safety-net programs, poor children do not fare as well as those whose families are not poor (Chase-Lansdale & Brooks-Gunn, 1995). Income deficits have stronger effects on cognitive and verbal ability test scores than on indices of emotional health in childhood years (Brooks-Gunn & Duncan, 1997).

Adverse birth outcomes are more prevalent for poor unmarried mothers with low levels of education. Poor women (ethnic minorities as well as Caucasians) are more likely to have a low birth weight baby than nonpoor women (Starfield, 1992).

Inadequate prenatal supports foster low birth weight babies, who in turn may have cognitive and related physical impairments and disabilities. Even if well born, babies born into poverty are 1.3 times as likely as their nonpoor counterparts to experience learning disabilities and developmental delays. Brooks-Gunn and Duncan (1997) report that poverty often affects children's cognitive development immediately after birth. Moreover, they found that chronically poor children (living in poverty 4 years or more) scored consistently lower on numerous cognitive assessments than children who were never poor. The long-term effects of poverty on cognitive development remain unknown. Research findings suggest that income may be an important determinant of completed schooling, and it appears that income during the early childhood years matters most (Duncan et al., 1998).

Poor children suffer from emotional and behavioral problems more frequently than do nonpoor children (Brooks-Gunn & Duncan, 1997). In fact, children in persistently poor families have more behavior problems than those who have never been poor. Poor children demonstrate more internalizing behaviors, such as anxiety, social withdrawal, and depression, as well as externalizing behaviors, such as aggression, fighting, and acting out, than children who have never been poor. Furthermore, short-term poverty (being poor in 1 out of 4 years) is also associated with more behavioral problems, but its effects are not as great as with those who are persistently poor. Like their children, parents who are poor are likely to be less emotionally and physically healthy than those who are not poor (Adler, Boyce, Chesney, Folkman, & Syme, 1993). Moreover, the compounding effects of poverty, such as having fewer resources to address children's cognitive, health, and emotional needs, aggravate family capacity to nurture children's development and heighten the stresses that often lead to abuse, neglect, depression, substance abuse, and domestic violence.

TANF is expected to aggravate children's poverty, as an estimated 1 million children are expected to be affected by growing impoverishment. As time limits on public assistance end and some parents are unable to find work, families will struggle to cope in any way they can. They may turn to crime or move into living situations that heighten the prospects of children entering the child welfare system. Thus, during this century, public assistance, a chief instrument of child welfare, has come full circle. Assistance initiated to protect children from out-of-home care due to poverty is now replaced with employment requirements attached to time-limited assistance. Nonetheless, TANF causalities will increase the demands on already overwhelmed and crisis-driven child welfare systems and add to child and family trauma instead of ameliorating it. For those who acquire and sustain employment, the results may be beneficial (Golden, 1992).

CURRENT LEGISLATION AND ADMINISTRATIVE FEATURES

One of the institutional symbols of the century-long struggle for child protection and well-being is the U.S. Children's Bureau. Established in 1912 to investigate child labor and to advocate for income supports for poor children, the U.S. Children's Bureau has been a source of advocacy and policy making for child welfare and for social work with their families.

Despite increasing budget and staff cuts, the Children's Bureau oversees all the policies and funding affecting child welfare systems. Federal funds are funneled through state and county funding streams. These channels include Title XX of the Social Security Act, which provides block grants to the states for social services. Titles IV-E and IV-B of the Social Security Act primarily support substitute or out-of-home child welfare services.

TANF has caused a devolution of federal policy frameworks and entitlements for impoverished children and families. This has raised concerns that similar devolutions would occur with child welfare programs and the quality assurance mandates that govern Title IV-B funds and audits.

Rather than devolution, more federal frameworks for practice and quality assurance are needed in child welfare. For example, currently, each state interprets the federal definition of abuse and neglect differently. Therefore, children in various parts of the country experience varying degrees of protection and services. A federal role is needed to ensure that there is a more uniform standard of safety and protection. For example, children in out-of-home care in one state might receive in-home services if they were to live in another state. Moreover, although neglect constitutes almost half of the child protection reports, emotional abuse constitutes the most vague and poorly addressed aspect of child maltreatment. Thus, much more federal initiative is required to build a national foundation for child welfare.

Family rights to preservation and the accompanying freedom from intervention seems contradictory to a policy and practice emphasis on safety and protection. Much of the public and many service providers remain confused about these apparently opposing service goals. For this reason, there may be a pendulum-like swing in public sentiment and law privileging family intactness over child safety and vice versa. Nevertheless, most child welfare practice involves safety considerations in the context of family services and child permanency.

Every state operates child protection, foster and group care, and adoptive services, but there is also a patchwork of public and private voluntary services for abused and neglected children across the nation. Increasingly, the functions of child protection, foster care, and adoption are being contracted out to voluntary social service agencies. Managed care has prompted states and localities to design alternative service delivery systems, to privatize much of the child welfare system, and to manage the cost.

Pressure to provide the most effective and time-limited services, along with the pressure of lawsuits, has helped to reinforce efforts to reprofessionalize child service systems. Reprofessionalization has led to a decade of partnerships between schools of social work and public child welfare. These partnerships have involved training for frontline staff, research, practica, faculty staff exchanges, curricular developments, and demonstration projects. In fact, at this time, it is estimated that there are over 80 partnerships among schools and agencies in the nation. In addition, there are statewide consortia of universities and state agencies, as well as regional partnerships (Zlotnick, 1998b). Partnership movement facilitators include IV-E funding, growing child welfare crises, increased child fatalities, and commitments by child welfare administrators and schools of social work to reprofessionalize the system (Briar-Lawson, Schmid, & Harris, 1997). The partnership movement has been seen as a way to counter the decline in the numbers of social workers in public child welfare. Once, over 28% of all staff in public human service agencies were social workers; now, in some states, less than 3% have this background (Zlotnick, 1998a). Ongoing funding under IV-B, section 426 of the Social Security Act, designated for schools of social work, has also helped to nurture the partnerships and accountability of social work to the child welfare field.

Collaborative efforts by advocates and organizations help to shape national directions for child welfare. Among the key collaborators are the National Association of Public Child Welfare Administrators, the Association of Public Human Services (formerly known as the American Public Welfare Association), the National Association of Social Workers, the Council on Social Work Education, the Child Welfare League of America, the American Humane Association, and the Children's Defense Fund. These organizations work together to lobby for child welfare funding, new legislation, child welfare staffing, and systems supports.

In addition, several foundations have been at the center of child welfare system reform. The Annie E. Casey Foundation has invested in a collaborative community response to child welfare families and promotes grassroots neighborhood service and partnership approaches. The Edna McConnell Clark Foundation has focused on family preservation models and optimal outcomes; more recent investments have been in multitrack child protection systems involving diversion and alternative service responses to low- and moderate-risk families by public health and related service providers. The W. K. Kellogg Foundation has examined an array of neighborhood initiatives and has also invested in a number of adoption preservation innovations. The DeWitt Wallace and Danforth Foundations have supported effective parent paraprofessional services in schools.

Reforms are also under way in countries like Sweden. The Swedish government, having made corporal punishment illegal, now works to aid families with the tools of child rearing so that the risk of abuse and neglect is reduced. Simultaneously, families in Sweden receive preventive and early intervention rather than just remedial services. For example, families are able to request respite care for exhaustion. This is provided by a contact family, which can offer an array of respite and socially supportive services to both children and families. Devised to prevent the need for entry into the child welfare system, the contact family program has demonstrated a sound and effective way to reach vulnerable families (Andersson, 1993).

Current Issues and Controversies

Human service systems such as child welfare are hard-pressed to achieve effective outcomes. First, rule-driven, bureaucratized services tend to impede desired individualized and enfranchising helping approaches. Second, child welfare service paradigms may be based on outdated and flawed assumptions. Third, services are ineffective because people who deliver the services are often not educationally and professionally prepared for the job.

The need for an overhaul is clear. The reform of the child welfare system may require much more data-driven and pilot-driven approaches (Austin, 1998). Because many of the underlying challenges and problems stem from inattention to poverty and economic insecurity, such reforms will undoubtedly involve a reintegration of service and income supports (Berns, 1998; Jones & Levy, 1998).

TABLE 12.1   Child Welfare Paradigms

Necessary Conditions	Promotion and Prevention	Early Intervention	Crisis Services
Intensive use of self-help and mutual assistance	Neighborhood colleges (how not to take stress out on family)	Former clients trained as case aides and parent aides to build family capacity and serve as drug addiction treatment aides	Professionals help families organize, using the Mori Family Group Conference model
Paraprofessionals	Parents Anonymous Indigenous community members provide information and referral services and supports; parent-led Family Resource Centers	Kinship care fostered early with stipends to aid in care arrangements; Swedish family contract programs are replicated; exhaustion and need for respite are legitimate bases for seeking help	Aides assist with homemaking, service follow-through, reunification, adoption assistance, and respite; neighbors and family members are deputized, trained, and supported as aides to help with case closure, boosters, relapse; contracts are signed
Economic and occupational investments	Occupational ladders are developed		Economic and employment needs are assessed as stresses that reinforce the abuse and neglect patterns; intensive services involve up to 40 hours a week with aides, providing in-home or wrap-around services in foster home or group care; intergenerational family supports are focus of services

NEW CENTURY CHALLENGES

In the next century, child welfare paradigms may need to be governed by new principles, programs, and approaches. These include family capacity building and preventive supports rather than punishment. This may also include occupational ladders for economically disenfranchised parents and intensive services co-delivered by former

TABLE 12.1 Continued

Necessary Conditions	Promotion and Prevention	Early Intervention	Crisis Services
Professionals	Serve as consultants, facilitators, grant writers, advocates; redesign system of prevention	Build capacity of contract families and paraprofessionals; test models for effective service delivery	Every professional in a health and human service system does "case finding"; assesses risks of neglect and abuse based on co-occuring symptoms (such as substance abuse, mental illness, domestic violence, disabilities)
Service ethics	Bills of rights are developed regarding the quality of treatment; confidentiality	Quality of treatment indices guide practice	Parents experience more help-giving rather than antagonistic relationship with child welfare staff
Research and evaluation	Role of parents as frontline service providers is documented; effectiveness and outcome studies are integral to the new frontline service designs	Pilots in preventive and early intervention services are designed and tested throughout the nation; each child who enters the child welfare system receives a case staffing to see which preventive service failed to reach them; lessons are derived so that new outreach approaches are developed	Entire system is data and outcome driven; families are enfranchised to help guide research and system design changes

clients trained as paraprofessional case aides, parent aides, reunification aides, and foster and adoption support aides. Over half of the tasks that once were performed by social workers in the Homebuilders project in Washington state can be performed by parents (Apple et al., 1997). The rise of self-help groups such as Parents Anonymous, and the use of neighborhood colleges to support parents in stress reduction strategies, reflects attempts to build more family helpful and child protective strategies into communities. The high rates of system reentry of children reunited with their families suggest that many families may be chronically vulnerable and may need ongoing supports much like families with children with disabilities. Thus, long-term, low-cost support systems may need to be devised to reflect family and child protection needs. Table 12.1 outlines some of the possible elements and frameworks for promoting prevention, early intervention, and remedial or crisis service approaches.

REFERENCES

Adler, N. E., Boyce, T., Chesney, M. A., Folkman, S., & Syme, S. L. (1993). Socioeconomic inequalities in health: No easy solution. *Journal of the American Medical Association, 269,* 3140-3145.

Andersson, G. (1993). Support and relief: The Swedish contact person and contact family program. *Scandinavian Journal of Social Welfare, 2,* 54-62.

Apple, K., Berstein, S., Fogg, K., Fogg, L., Haapala, D., Johnson, E., Johnson, R., Kinney, J., Natoli, J., Price, D., Roberts, K., Robinson, K., Steele, T., Trent, E., Trent, M., Trent, V., Smith, R., & Vignec, R. (1997). Walking the talk in the neighborhoods: Building professional/natural helper partnerships. *Social Policy, 27*(4), 54-61.

Aron, L. Y., & Olson, K. K. (1997). *Efforts by child welfare agencies to address domestic violence: The experiences of five communities.* The Urban Institute: http://www.urban.org/welfare/aron3.htm.

Austin, D. M. (1998, July). *A report on progress in the development of research resources in social work.* Austin, TX: School of Social Work..

Barth, R. P., Berry, M., Yoshikami, R., Goodfield, R. K., & Carson, M. L. (1988). Predicting adoption disruption. *Social Work, 33*(3), 227-233.

Berns, D. (1998). *Working papers on TANF, family preservation and poverty eradication.* Colorado Springs, CO: El Paso County Department of Human Services.

Briar, K. (1988). *Social work with the unemployed.* Silver Springs, MD: National Association of Social Workers.

Briar-Lawson, K., Schmid, D., & Harris, N. (1997, Spring). Improving training, education, and practice agendas in public child welfare: First decade. *Public Welfare, 55,* 4-7.

Brissett-Chapman, S. (1995). Child abuse and neglect: Direct practice. In *Encyclopedia of social work* (19th ed., pp. 353-366). Alexandria, VA: National Association of Social Workers.

Brooks-Gunn, J., & Duncan, G. J. (1997). The effects of poverty on children. *The Future of Children: Children and Poverty, 7*(2), 55-71.

Bruner, C. (1993). *Toward outcome-based accountability: Readings on constructing cost-of-failure/return-on-investment analysis of prevention initiatives.* Des Moines, IA: Child and Family Center.

Chase-Lansdale, P. L., & Brooks-Gunn, J. (Eds.). (1995). *Escape from poverty: What makes a difference for children?* New York: Cambridge University Press.

Conte, J. (1995). Child sexual abuse overview. In *Encyclopedia of social work* (19th ed., pp. 402-408). Alexandria, VA: National Association of Social Workers.

Corrigan, D. (1996). An educator's view on expanding partnerships. In K. Hooper-Briar & H. A. Lawson (Eds.), *Expanding partnerships for vulnerable children, youth, and families.* Alexandria, VA: Council on Social Work Education.

Curtis, P. A., & McCullough, C. (1993). The impact of alcohol and other drugs on the child welfare system. *Child Welfare, 72*(6), 533-542.

Digre, P. (1997). *Impact of proposed federal welfare changes on child protection: Executive summary.* Unpublished document, Los Angeles, CA.

Duncan, G., Huston, A., & McLoyd, V. (1998). *Growing up poor: The effects on achievement, parenting, and child care.* A Congressional Breakfast Seminar: Consortium of Social Science Associations.

Edelman, P. (1997, March). The worst thing Bill Clinton has done. *Atlantic Monthly,* pp. 43-58.

Emlen, A, Lahti, J., Downs, G., McKay, A., & Downs, S. (1977). *Overcoming barriers to planning for children in foster care*. Portland, OR: Regional Research Institute for Human Services, Portland State University.

Fanshel, D., & Shinn, E. (1978). *Children in foster care: A longitudinal investigation*. New York: Columbia University Press.

Fraser, M., Pecora, P., & Haapala, D. (1991). *Families in crisis*. New York: de Gruyter.

Gambrill, E. D., & Stein, T. J. (1981). Decision making and case management: Achieving continuity of care for children in and out of home placement. In A. N. Maluccio & P. A. Sinanoglu (Eds.), *The challenge of partnership: Working with parents of children in foster care* (pp. 109-139). New York: Child Welfare League of America.

General Accounting Office. (1992). *Integrating human services: Linking at-risk families with services more successful than system reform efforts*. Washington, DC: Government Printing Office.

General Accounting Office. (1995). *The foster care crisis*. Washington, DC: Government Printing Office.

Gil, D. (1970). *Violence against children*. Cambridge, MA: Harvard University Press.

Golden, O. (1992). *Poor children and welfare reform*. Westport, CT: Auburn House.

Gustavsson, N. S., & Segal, E. A. (1994). *Critical issues in child welfare*. Thousand Oaks, CA: Sage.

Hegar, R. L. (1998). The cultural roots of kinship care. In R. L. Hegar & M. Scannapieco (Eds.), *Kinship foster care: Policy practice and research*. New York: Oxford University Press.

Jones, S. J., & Levy, J. Z. (Eds.) (1998). *Preparing helping professionals to meet community needs*. Alexandria, VA: Council on Social Work Education.

Kadushin, A. (1980). *Child welfare services* (3rd ed.). New York: Macmillan.

Kinney, J. M., Madsen, B., Fleming, T., & Haapala, D. (1977). Homebuilders: Keeping families together. *Journal of Clinical and Counseling Psychology, 43,* 667-673.

Ladwig, G. B., & Anderson, M. D. (1992). Substance abuse in women: The relationship between chemical dependency of women and reports of physical and/or sexual abuse. In C. M. Sampelle (Ed.), *Violence against women: Nursing, research, education, and practice issues* (pp. 167-180). New York: Hemisphere.

Lindsey, D. (1994). *The welfare of children*. New York: Oxford University Press.

Murphy, J. M., Jellinek, M., Quinn, D., Smith, G., Poitrast, F. G., & Goshko, M. (1991). Substance abuse and serious child maltreatment: Prevalence, risk, and outcome in a court sample. *Child Abuse & Neglect, 15,* 197-211.

National Association of Public Child Welfare Administrators (NAPCWA). (1998, October). *Child protection guidelines*. Washington, DC: American Public Human Services Association.

Pelton, L. H. (1989). *For reasons of poverty: A critical analysis of the public child welfare system in the United States*. New York: Praeger.

Schmidt, D. (1997, June). *Child protection innovations*. Presentation at the Children's Bureau Permanency Planning Conference, Washington DC.

Sosin, M. R., Piliavin, I., & Westerfelt, H. (1991). Toward a longitudinal analysis of homelessness. *Journal of Social Issues, 46,* 157-174.

Starfield, B. (1992). Child and adolescent health status measures. *The Future of Children, 2*(2), 25-39.

Tanoury, T., Saunders, M. A., & Lusk, M. W. (1996) In partnership with families, schools, and communities: Using Title IV-A emergency assistance funds. In K. Hooper-Briar & H. Lawson (Eds.), *Expanding partnerships for vulnerable children, youth, and families* (pp. 833-891). Alexandria, VA: Council on Social Work Education.

Tetleman, E. (1996). Implications for national policymakers. In K. Hooper-Briar & H. Lawson (Eds.), *Expanding partnerships for vulnerable children, youth, and families* (pp. 298-304). Alexandria, VA: Council on Social Work Education.

Trupin, E. W., Tarico, V. S., Low, B. P., Jemelka, R., & McClellan, J. (1993). Children on child protective service caseloads: Prevalence and nature of serious emotional disturbance. *Child Abuse and Neglect, 17,* 345-355.

Weiss, C. (1995). Nothing as practical as good theory: Exploring theory-based evaluation for comprehensive community initiatives for children and families. In J. Connell, A. Kubish, L. Schorr, & C. Weiss

(Eds.), *New approaches to evaluating community initiatives: Concepts, methods, and context* (pp. 65-92). New York: Aspen Institute.

Zlotnick, J. (1998a). *Historical analysis of the implications of federal policy: A case study of access to IV-E funds to support social work education*. Unpublished dissertation, University of Maryland, Baltimore.

Zlotnick, J. (Ed). (1998b). Title IV-E partnerships continue to grow. In *Partnerships for child welfare (Vol. 5, No. 6, p. 10). Alexandria: VA: Council on Social Work Education*.

CHAPTER THIRTEEN

Income Maintenance and Support: The Changing Face of Welfare

JILL DUERR BERRICK

At the turn of the 20th century, the economic circumstances of most single mothers in the United States was, at best, insecure. As we approach the millennium, reflections on the economic protections afforded single mothers is not substantially improved. Over the course of several decades, local, state, and federal policies have been designed to assist unmarried women and their families, yet, many of these mothers still struggle to offer their children sufficient protection from the vicissitudes of poverty.

In recent years, in particular, the United States has seen a profound change in the nature and degree of economic assistance provided to poor children and their families. In 1996, the federal government introduced a new approach to financial support with passage of the Personal Responsibility and Work Opportunity Reconciliation Act (P.L. 104-193 or PRWORA). This legislation, heralded as "ending welfare as we know it," significantly altered the historic design of income assistance in the United States, shifting responsibility for support from the federal government to state and local entities. Variously called the devolution revolution (Kingsley, 1996; Weaver, 1996) or the new federalism (Corbett, 1996), the new approach to policy gives a large degree of flexibility and considerable authority to smaller levels of government for the design of poor people's income support. Largely untested as a means of reducing poverty, the new welfare program instead reflects social values that center on the desirability of work, marriage, and positive parenting. These values have held currency throughout U.S. social history, and a close reading of previous approaches to economic support provides a context for the contemporary design of welfare efforts. Today's income maintenance program for poor families is both a departure from and a return to previous policies attempted in this country. The new program, Temporary Assistance to Needy Families (TANF), provides time-limited cash assistance to poor families, with reciprocal obligations required of mothers. Because TANF offers few real protections from a capricious labor market, the consequences for poor families are, as yet, undetermined.

THE HISTORICAL EVOLUTION OF WELFARE

Less than a century ago, single mothers had few socially appropriate avenues for supporting their children economically. Work was considered anathema to good parenting and was discouraged among "good" girls (Gordon, 1994). Instead, children were often forced into the labor market by circumstance, providing important financial support to the family during hard times (Gensler, 1996). With the introduction of child labor laws, children's employment prospects were severely curtailed, leaving single mothers as principal household earners. As many women and children faced destitution, legislators in a few states responded to the appeal for help and developed cash assistance programs to support women whose husbands had died, deserted, or divorced them. These mothers' pensions quickly gained popularity across much of the country. The purpose of financial support was to supplant the loss of income from the primary breadwinner—the father—and to encourage mothers to remain at home to parent their children (Abramovitz, 1988; Gordon, 1994). Aid was conditional and was provided to those mothers who could show their worthiness to a social worker or other community helper. Women who gave birth to "illegitimate" children, women of color, and women who had relationships with men outside of marriage were often considered undeserving of aid. Their children were sometimes removed from their homes and institutionalized, or the family was left to fend for itself in abject poverty (Abramovitz, 1988).

Mothers' pensions programs expanded dramatically across the country, particularly from 1910-1920. But in the 1930s, states were overwhelmed by rapidly rising caseloads in their mothers' pension programs as the country fell into a deep economic depression. Faced with rising costs and reduced capacity to fund mothers' pensions through government aid, state and local officials turned to the federal government for fiscal relief. The Social Security Act of 1935 launched several federally supported programs in aid of the poor, with Aid to Dependent Children, or ADC, specifically targeted to single parents (i.e., poor women) with children. With the introduction of ADC (renamed AFDC in 1950), income support for poor families became a shared obligation between the federal, state, and local governments.

The AFDC program changed little from the 1930s through the 1950s; however, over time, the characteristics of AFDC families changed considerably. Whereas the majority of caregivers on aid in the early years of the program were widowed, deserted, or divorced, by the 1970s, the AFDC caseload included large and rapidly growing numbers of never-married women (GAO, 1994; Rein, 1982). In the early years, welfare participants also were dominated by Caucasians—primarily due to state and local policies that precluded the participation of women of color (Abramovitz, 1988; Bell, 1965; Quadagno, 1994). In later decades, however, the AFDC caseload included large numbers of women of color, with disproportionate use of aid by African American families (Quadagno, 1994). These changes were accompanied by shifts in the labor force participation of women outside of AFDC. Rather than shun work, women were joining the labor market in droves. By 1983, more than 70% of U.S. women worked or were regularly looking for work (Ellwood, 1988).

Mirroring the changes outside of AFDC, federal policies in the 1960s, '70s, and '80s brought a new emphasis to employment within the AFDC program. With each iteration of reform, new policies were overlaid onto AFDC, with an increasing emphasis on work participation among welfare recipients. The WIN demonstration of 1969, WIN II (1972), and the JOBS program of 1988 all reflected an increased orientation toward employment (Bane & Ellwood, 1994; Coll, 1995; Ellwood, 1988; Pappas, 1996). Yet, funding constraints limited the number of AFDC parents allowed to participate, and overall, each of the programs proved only modestly effective in supporting women's transitions from welfare to work (Gueron & Pauly, 1991).

By the early 1990s, changes in the characteristics and circumstances of women on aid, and shifting perspectives in public opinion (Blendon, 1995; Farkas, 1995; Farkas & Johnson, 1995; Weaver, Shapiro, & Jacobs, 1996), compelled state and federal lawmakers to reconsider the basis of the AFDC program. On August 22, 1996, President Clinton signed PL 104-193, ushering in a new era of welfare in the United States.

WHAT'S NEW ABOUT WELFARE? CURRENT LEGISLATIVE AND ADMINISTRATIVE ARRANGEMENTS

With the passage of the Personal Responsibility and Work Opportunity Reconciliation Act, welfare has substantially shifted from its original intent. The 60-year old AFDC program was abolished and replaced with a new program whose name conveys the meaning behind assistance. Temporary Assistance to Needy Families, or TANF, includes several requirements that reshape the symbols and provisions of public assistance for poor families. The entitlement to aid has been abolished, and eligibility for assistance is now conditional and time limited, withdrawal from aid is expected to be rapid, and employment is the preferred passage to economic self-sufficiency.

Block Grants

Prior to the implementation of TANF, all poor, single-parent families who met income and asset tests were eligible to receive cash assistance. The entitlement to AFDC guaranteed that the poorest families could receive assistance until their personal income rose above a predetermined threshold, or until their youngest child turned 18. Funding for aid was provided through a combined federal/state contribution. When AFDC caseloads grew, state officials applied to the federal government for increased funding; significant expenditure increases were largely controlled through incremental benefit reductions or, in times of low unemployment, reduced caseloads.

Under TANF, the entitlement to aid has been abolished. States receive an annual block grant of funding from the federal government that replaces AFDC, JOBS, and Emergency Assistance. State governments are required to maintain their financial commitment to welfare families by allocating between 75% and 80% of the funding they were providing in the early 1990s. This "maintenance of effort" ensures that states will not withdraw their support entirely from the TANF program. Nevertheless, the combined federal and state expenditures may be insufficient if the TANF caseload rises above the block grant allocation. Should this occur, state and local authorities will be fully responsible for the additional financial burden. Given this financial disincentive, states may reduce costs either through benefit reductions, time limits, or targeting strategies (Berrick, in press).

Time Limits

In addition to changes in the funding formula for TANF, recipients are now restricted to aid for a maximum of 60 cumulative months, regardless of the age of their child or the poverty status of the family. States are given latitude to reduce time limits further, and many states have adopted more restrictive policies (Gallagher, Gallagher, Perese, Schreiber, & Watson, 1998; U.S. Department of Health and Human Services, 1997). States are permitted to exempt up to 20% of their caseload and are given full discretion to determine which families should be released from the time limit requirements. Costs for exemptions beyond 20%, however, must be borne by the states.

Work Requirements

In addition to time limits, states are now required to impose work requirements on recipients who have received assistance for 2 years. Work includes either unsubsidized or subsidized employment; other types of activities allowable as work include on-the job training, work experience, community service, up to 12 months of vocational training, or providing child care to individuals participating in community service. Single parents are required to work 20 hours per week; two-parent families must work 30 hours per week.

Economic Sanctions and Penalties

The TANF program may also be distinguished from its predecessor, AFDC, by the conditional environment of aid. Without an entitlement to assistance, low-income families must now prove their capacity to abide by set rules of conduct to qualify. Errors in judgment or behavior may be met with harsh economic penalties designed to correct the behavior and impose compliance. For example, unmarried minor parents may not receive aid unless living with an adult or in an adult-supervised setting; sanctions may apply for failure to submit to procedures that establish paternity, for births of additional children while on aid, and if children are not immunized or do not regularly attend school. Unless the penalty is overturned at the state level, adult recipients are barred from aid for life if they are convicted of a drug felony.

Income Restrictions

In addition to the behaviors that may disqualify an individual from aid, whole categories of families may be restricted from assistance at state discretion. For example, legal immigrants may be barred from accepting TANF due to their citizenship status.

Safety Net Provisions

Although a number of the TANF features may result in income restrictions for families, some program elements may offer significant opportunities that were formerly unavailable. TANF gives state governments considerable discretion to develop work and training programs that match the needs of their welfare population. Block grant funds may be used to offer job clubs and other work preparation activities as long as annual budgets allow. Such activities may better prepare welfare recipients for the demands of the labor market, offering improved skills and employment support.

Although job training and support may be crucial in obtaining employment, many welfare critics have argued that women cannot remain in the labor market if they cannot access supportive services such as child care or health insurance (Polit & O'Hara,

1989). Child care is a critical requirement of working mothers, and given that about half of all children on welfare are under age 6 (U.S. House Ways and Means Committee, 1996), the child care needs of these families can be substantial. PL 104-193 significantly expands child care funding, offering greater child care accessibility and affordability for many families.

Beyond child care, health insurance is also critical to employment retention. Families who previously moved from AFDC to work often faced significant obstacles to economic self-sufficiency because health insurance was not available (Edin & Lein, 1997). The Balanced Budget Act of 1997 created the State Children's Health Insurance Program (S-CHIP) to expand health insurance for low-income children. Developed as part of Title XXI of the Social Security Act, this new law offers states new funding opportunities and program flexibility to offer expanded health insurance coverage for families with incomes below 200% of the poverty level. With program expansions such as these, many more families will have access to health coverage.

And finally, under AFDC regulations, earned income was taxed at very high rates, reducing the economic allure of work. The TANF guidelines now offer states significant latitude to set these rates at various levels to induce greater work participation among welfare recipients.

Through economic benefits and sanctions, the TANF provisions encourage women to work outside of the home, and they support appropriate parenting practices. More subtle is the symbolic message that low-income women should raise children within the context of heterosexual marriage. Indeed, the legislation itself targets marriage as the foundation of a "successful society" and an "essential institution. . . which promotes the interests of children" (H.R. 3734, Section 101, p. 1). The emphasis on marriage and positive parenting diverge little from the foundations of the AFDC program; the emphasis—indeed, the requirement—that women work, sets TANF apart from previous efforts at reform.

SOCIAL, POLITICAL, AND ECONOMIC FACTORS INFLUENCING TANF POLICY

The success of TANF largely depends on sustained growth in the national economy and low unemployment rates. In 1998, the U.S. unemployment rate hovered around 4.5% (U.S. Department of Labor, 1998). In this rapidly expanding economy, jobs have been more plentiful than ever. But measuring success solely by whether recipients become employed may be short-sighted. For example, in California's widely touted Greater Avenues to Independence (GAIN) welfare-to-work JOBS program, 30% of AFDC recipients participating in the program were working a year later, compared to 27% of recipients who did not participate in the program; differences in annual earnings between the two groups were about $271 per year (Riccio & Friedlander, 1992). Another welfare-to-work program was studied by the Manpower Demonstration Research Corporation (MDRC) in 1998 in Los Angeles County, California. Data from the preliminary report show that 43% of the participants were employed 6 months following participation in the program, compared to 32% of control families. The difference in earnings between the two groups was $407 (MDRC, 1998).

Although these figures were heralded as evidence of great success, very few families' incomes had risen above the poverty level. Therefore, if TANF's success is based on the number of families entering the workforce, it will be judged against a standard profoundly different from the criterion of poverty reduction (Corbett, 1993). Many families are likely to find jobs following participation in TANF; some may also be diverted from applying for assistance either because of perceived or actual restrictions on aid. Yet, the financial prospects of many of these very low-income families are not likely to be appreciably better once they obtain employment (Pavetti, 1993). Low educational attainment, few job skills, little work history, and other social and personal barriers collude to push women into welfare. Welfare reform is not necessarily targeted to change these characteristics, and therefore, with few differences in women's circumstances following a period on aid, their continued economic insecurity is inevitable.

In spite of diverse views about the intended and unintended effects of welfare reform, proclamations about TANF's accomplishments have already been heard across the political spectrum. In 1997, President Clinton observed, "I think it's fair to say the debate is over. We know now that welfare reform works" (Broder, 1997). Indeed, reductions in the welfare caseload have been dramatic since the reform bill was passed. At its peak in 1994, welfare supported 14.4 million individuals on aid (U.S. DHHS, 1998). In 1998, only 8.4 million children and adults collected welfare checks; some states experienced still more dramatic caseload reductions. Wisconsin saw an 82% reduction in caseload size from 1993 to 1998; other states saw equally striking changes in caseload size. How much of the change can be attributed to the reformed program, and how much to the strength of the economy or other unmeasured factors, will likely be debated for years.

NEW ISSUES

As welfare reform unfolds at the dawn of the new century, welfare administrators, policy makers, advocates, and researchers are watching the program as it affects women and children. The program could have highly beneficial effects if women find work and family incomes rise. Income is closely correlated with a number of positive benefits for children (Duncan & Brooks-Gunn, 1997; Haveman & Wolfe, 1995), and improved economic conditions may mean better neighborhoods, better schools, improved health and nutrition, and improved parenting.

For some families, welfare reform may have little if any impact on their income, their family life, or their personal behavior. Again, looking to the previous incarnation of welfare reform in the shape of the GAIN program, dramatic positive or negative effects were rare. Instead, the standard of living for most program participants did not change appreciably after participation in that program (Riccio & Friedlander, 1992). For welfare recipients in general, evidence from the earlier AFDC program indicates that the majority left welfare voluntarily within 2 years (Ellwood, 1988), although more worrisome is the finding that avenues off of welfare to work were the most unstable predictors of future reliance on aid (Pavetti, 1993). Families who previously used AFDC may continue to use TANF as a transitional safety net program, yet their access to the program's benefits may be severely curtailed if their spells on aid accumulate over time.

Along with the positive and neutral effects of reform, some families are sure to suffer in a TANF environment. What is unclear, of course, is the size and scope of this population and the types of effects families are likely to experience. Unlike AFDC, TANF offers families greater opportunities to experience increased poverty simply because the income support provided by welfare reform rests on more precarious standards than before. Benefit reductions, program sanctions, and, of course, time limits will reduce family income, thereby creating greater challenges to the healthy development of welfare's children.

Women who cannot find work, those who are unable to force their adolescent children to school, or women with unintended pregnancies, for example, may experience much worse public assistance conditions than other women, and their family's poverty may deepen considerably. Women who are challenged to locate or retain employment may have little prior work history, low educational attainment, health or mental health conditions, or substance abuse problems. Numerous studies describe the special challenges of AFDC recipients (Leon & Weissman, 1993; Meyers & Lukemeyer, 1995; U.S. Department of Health and Human Services, 1992, 1994; Vega et al., 1993; Zill, Moore, & Nord, 1991). The growing number of elderly relative caregivers who currently provide support to low-income children may face particular challenges in a reformed welfare environment (Minkler, Berrick, & Needell, in press).

When family income falls, the effects for children are not likely to be positive. Family poverty is associated with increased rates of maltreatment (Garbarino & Kostelny, 1992; U.S. DHHS, 1996), increased health conditions (Brooks-Gunn, Duncan, & Maritato, 1997; Halpern, 1993), poorer educational attainment (Benedersky &

Lewis, 1994; Pagani, Boulerice, & Tremblay, 1997; Smith, Brooks-Gunn, & Klebanov, 1997), and other adverse outcomes. Because women's participation in TANF is dependent on their poverty status, the conditions for child rearing will already be strained; families who see further reductions in income assistance may face especially precarious conditions.

CONCLUSION

The new structure of the welfare program in the United States brings with it great anticipation. The effects of reform have been very positive for state and local government administrators, who have had great latitude to shape their program according to community needs and who have had a significant infusion of funding to craft a welfare program that is customized to their political and social constituents. Some welfare programs will be efficiently operated and humanely organized, and some will offer opportunities for training and work support that welfare recipients otherwise might not have received. For women on aid, changes in the welfare program may also be embraced with enthusiasm. Many women on welfare condemned the previous era of income support, and features of the new program will likely suit the personal circumstances of thousands—if not millions—of poor women. TANF brings new reciprocal obligations that recipients work in exchange for cash support and that they abide by social conventions as defined by law. Some of these notions may indeed find favor with large numbers of people in the welfare population.

But the anticipation about reform is also guided by the voices of advocates who, during the congressional debates over reform, weighed in with predictions of dire consequences including increased poverty, homelessness, child maltreatment, and poor nutrition for the children caught in the overhaul of federal poverty policy (Kamerman & Kahn, 1997). Although some or all of these effects may or may not occur, it is clear that the massive impacts that had been predicted earlier have not as yet appeared. Delays in program implementation and the time lags expected before families hit the limits of eligibility may postpone the realization of negative effects for some time.

Whether it is the delayed effects of implementation, or states' inability to measure effects, the implications for social workers are the same. As welfare reform unfolds, social work practitioners, policy makers, and researchers should make concerted efforts to follow the effects of welfare reform. Assumptions about the positive or null effects of reform could have the dangerous consequence of inspiring complacency rather than diligence. Thoughtful attention to the needs of poor families will be critical during this time of great transition, and social workers may play a large role in ensuring that poor children are not left behind in the era of reform.

REFERENCES

Abramovitz, M. (1988). *Regulating the lives of women: Social welfare policy from colonial times to the present*. Boston: South End Press.

Bane, M. J., & Ellwood, D. (1994). *Welfare realities: From rhetoric to reform*. Cambridge, MA: Harvard University Press.

Bell, W. (1965). *Aid to dependent children*. New York: Columbia University Press.

Benedersky, M., & Lewis, M. (1994). Environmental risk, biological risk, and developmental outcome. *Developmental Psychology, 30*(4), 484-494.

Berrick, J. D. (in press). Personal responsibility, private behavior, and public benefits: Targeting social welfare in the United States. In N. Gilbert (Ed.), *Targeting social benefits*. New York: Transaction Books.

Blendon, R. J. (1995). *Survey on welfare reform: Basic values and beliefs; support for policy approaches; knowledge about key programs*. Menlo Park, CA: The Henry J. Kaiser Family Foundation.

Broder, J. M. (1997, August 17). Big social changes revive the false god of numbers. *New York Times,* Section 4, p. 14.

Brooks-Gunn, J., Duncan, G., & Maritato, N. (1997). Poor families, poor outcomes: The well-being of children and youth. In G. Duncan & J. Brooks-Gunn (Eds.), *Consequences of growing up poor*. New York: Russell Sage Foundation.

Coll, B. D. (1995). *Safety net: Welfare and Social Security, 1929-1979*. New Brunswick, NJ: Rutgers University Press.

Corbett, T. (1993). Child poverty and welfare reform: Progress or paralysis. *Focus, 15,* 1-17.

Corbett, T. (1996). The new federalism: Monitoring consequences. *Focus, 18*(1), 3-25.

Duncan, G., & Brooks-Gunn, J. (Eds.). (1997). *Consequences of growing up poor*. New York: Russell Sage Foundation.

Edin, K., & Lein, L. (1997). *Making ends meet: How single mothers survive welfare and low-wage work*. New York: Russell Sage Foundation.

Ellwood, D. T. (1988). *Poor support*. New York: Free Press.

Farkas, S. (1995). *Public attitudes toward welfare and welfare reform*. New York: Public Agenda.

Farkas, S., & Johnson, J. (1995). *The values we live by: What Americans want from welfare reform*. New York: Public Agenda.

Gallagher, L. J., Gallagher, M., Perese, K., Schreiber, S., & Watson, K. (1998). *One year after federal welfare reform: A description of state Temporary Assistance for Needy Families (TANF) decisions*. Washington, DC: Urban Institute.

Garbarino, J., & Kostelny, K. (1992). Children in dangerous environments: Child maltreatment in a context of community violence. In D. Cicchetti & S. L. Toth (Eds.), *Child abuse, child development, and social policy*. Norwood, NJ: Ablex.

General Accounting Office. (1994). *Families on welfare: Sharp rise in never-married women reflects societal trend*. Washington, DC: Author.

Gensler, H. (Ed.). (1996). *The American welfare system: Origins, structure, and effects*. Westport, CT: Praeger.

Gordon, L. (1994). *Pitied but not entitled: Single mothers and the history of welfare*. New York: Free Press.

Gueron, J. M., & Pauly, E. (1991). *From welfare to work*. New York: Russell Sage Foundation.

Halpern, R. (1993). Poverty and infant development. In C. H. Zeanah (Ed.), *Handbook of infant mental health*. New York: Guilford.

Haveman, R., & Wolfe, B. (1995). *Succeeding generations*. New York: Russell Sage Foundation.

Kamerman, S., & Kahn, A. (1997). *P.L. 104-193: Challenges and opportunities*. New York: Cross-National Studies Research Program, Columbia University School of Social Work.

Kingsley, G. T. (Autumn, 1996). Perspectives on devolution. *Journal of the American Planning Association, 62*(4), 419-426.

Leon, A. C., & Weissman, M. M. (1993). *Analysis of NIMH's existing epidemiological catchment area data on depression and other affective disorders in welfare and disabled populations*. Washington, DC:

U.S. Department of Health and Human Services, Office of the Assistant Secretary for Planning and Evaluation.

Manpower Demonstration Research Corporation (MDRC). (1998). *The Los Angeles Jobs-First GAIN evaluation: Preliminary findings on participation patterns and first year impacts.* http://www.acf.dhhs.gov.

Meyers, M. K., & Lukemeyer, A. (1995, December). *A statistical profile of disabilities and health conditions in the California AFDC population.* Paper presented at The Role of Social Services in Welfare Reform Forum, Public Policy Institute of California, San Francisco.

Minkler, M., Berrick, J. D., & Needell, B. (in press). Impacts of welfare reform on California grandparents raising grandchildren: Reflections from the field. *Journal of Aging and Social Policy.*

Pagani, L., Boulerice, B., & Tremblay, R. (1997). The influence of poverty on children's classroom placement and behavior problems. In G. J. Duncan & J. Brooks-Gunn (Eds.), *Consequences of growing up poor.* New York: Russell Sage Foundation.

Pappas, A. (1996). Welfare reform: Child welfare or the rhetoric of responsibility? *Duke Law Journal, 45,* 1301-1328.

Pavetti, L. (1993). *The dynamics of welfare and work: Exploring the process by which women work their way off welfare.* Ph.D. dissertation, Harvard University.

Polit, D., & O'Hara, J. (1989). Support services. In P. Cottingham & D. T. Ellwood (Eds.), *Welfare policy for the 1990s.* Cambridge, MA: Harvard University Press.

Quadagno, J. (1994). *The color of welfare: How racism undermined the War on Poverty.* New York: Oxford University Press.

Rein, M. (1982). *Dilemmas of welfare policy: Why work strategies haven't worked.* New York: Praeger.

Riccio, J., & Friedlander, D. (1992). *GAIN: Program strategies, participation patterns, and first-year impacts in six counties.* New York: Manpower Demonstration Research Corporation.

Smith, J., Brooks-Gunn, J., & Klebanov, P. (1997). Consequences of living in poverty for young children's cognitive and verbal ability and early school achievement. In G. Duncan & J. Brooks-Gunn (Eds.), *Consequences of growing up poor.* New York: Russell Sage Foundation.

U.S. Department of Health and Human Services, Office of Inspector General. (1992). *Functional impairments of AFDC clients.* Rockville, MD: Author.

U.S. Department of Health and Human Services. (1994). *Patterns of substance use and substance-related impairment among participants in the Aid to Families with Dependent Children program.* Washington, DC: Author.

U.S. Department of Health and Human Services. (1996). *Results of the third national incidence study on child maltreatment in the United States.* Washington, DC: National Center on Child Abuse and Neglect.

U.S. Department of Health and Human Services, Office of the Assistant Secretary for Planning and Evaluation. (1997). *Setting the baseline: A report on state welfare waivers.* Washington, DC: Author.

U.S. Department of Health and Human Services. (1998). *Change in welfare caseloads.* http://www.acf.dhhs.gov/news/caseload.html.

U.S. Department of Labor. (1998). *Economy at a glance.* http://stats.bls.gov:80/eag.table.html.

U.S. House Ways and Means Committee, House of Representatives. (1996). *Government green book.* Washington, DC: Author.

Vega, W. A., Noble, A., Kolody, B., Porter, P., Hwang, J., & Bole, A. (1993). *Profile of alcohol and drug use during pregnancy in California.* Sacramento: California Department of Alcohol and Drug Programs.

Weaver, R. K. (1996, Summer). Deficits and devolution in the 104th Congress. *Plubius—The Journal of Federalism, 26*(3), 45-85.

Weaver, R. K., Shapiro, R. Y., & Jacobs, L. R. (1996). *Public opinion on welfare reform: A mandate for what? Looking before we leap: Social science and welfare reform.* Washington, DC: Brookings Institution.

Zill, N., Moore, K. A., & Nord, C. W. (1991). *Welfare mothers as potential employees: A statistical profile based on a national survey.* Washington, DC: Child Trends.

CHAPTER FOURTEEN

Social Security

MARTHA N. OZAWA

Throughout its history, Social Security has expanded its coverage of people and increased its benefit levels. These changes have been progressive and incremental and have received strong public support. But since the late 1970s, the public has been more and more concerned about Social Security's financial viability. To stem the tide of public concern, the 1977 amendments to the Social Security Act changed the benefit-computation rules and increased the tax rates and taxable earnings base. The 1983 amendments raised the normal retirement age, subjected up to half the benefits to income taxes, moved cost-of-living-adjustment payments (COLAs) from July to January, and covered federal and nonprofit employees. The 1994-1996 Advisory Council on Social Security reported that the long-range financial condition of Social Security worsened, in spite of the comprehensive reform under the 1983 amendments. Some members of the Council placed other aspects of Social Security under close scrutiny, as well. For example, they warned that under a pay-as-you-go financing system, such as the current one, future generations of beneficiaries will have unfavorable rates of return on their contributions and that the current preferential treatment of one-earner couples over two-earner couples in the provision of benefits no longer makes sense in light of the growing labor force participation of women.

A 1994 public opinion poll indicated that about two thirds of those below age 55 do not have confidence in the Social Security system, compared with less than one third of those 55 and older (Baggette, Shapiro, & Jacobs, 1995). In a comprehensive survey on Social Security, 93% of the respondents agreed that "working Americans are beginning to lose faith in whether Social Security benefits will be available when they retire" (Friedland, 1994, p. 5).

With such a volatile political situation as a backdrop, this chapter discusses the principles and provisions of Social Security, its emerging problems, and current proposals for reform.

The U.S. Social Security system includes social insurance programs to provide economic security for elderly people, disabled workers, and workers' dependents and survivors. Specifically, the system includes (a) Old-Age and Survivors Insurance (OASI), established under the Social Security Act of 1935 and its 1939 amendments to provide cash benefits for retired workers, dependents, and survivors; and (b) Disability Insurance (DI), enacted through the 1956 amendments, designed to provide cash benefits for disabled workers and their eligible family members.

During calendar year 1997, Old-Age, Survivors, and Disability Insurance (OASDI) benefits, amounting to $362 billion, were paid to retired and disabled workers and their families and to survivors of deceased workers. A total of 44 million were receiving OASDI benefits at the end of December 1997. In 1997, an estimated 147 million people worked in jobs covered by the OASDI program and paid Social Security taxes (Board of Trustees, 1998).

BASIC PRINCIPLES

Social Security provides benefits as an earned right without a means test or income test. Contributions are compulsory, unless workers are specifically exempt, such as those whose state employers have not opted to have public employees participate in Social Security. The provision of Social Security benefits is predicated on two principles: (a) individual equity, relating benefits directly to beneficiaries' prior earnings, and (b) social adequacy, providing larger benefits to low-wage workers in relation to their contributions and extra benefits to auxiliary beneficiaries (for example, children, dependent parents, and spouses with no earnings of their own) without added contributions.

Social Security funding is based on the principles of pay-as-you-go financing and compulsory contributions from employees, employers, and self-employed workers. However, the 1983 amendments included the provision to build up the trust fund's assets in anticipation of the large number of baby boomers who will reach retirement age starting in 2010.

PROVISIONS

Old Age and Survivors Insurance

To be eligible for OASI benefits, workers must be either fully insured or currently insured. To be fully insured, one must have earned the minimum amount of quarters of coverage, 40. In 1998, workers received 1 quarter of coverage for each $700 of covered annual earnings, with no more than 4 quarters credited to an individual in 1 year. The amount of earnings needed to gain a quarter of coverage increases at the rate of the increase in the average wages.

The normal retirement age is 65. It will increase gradually to age 67 by the year 2027 for those who attained age 62 in 2022. By 2027, the full actuarial reduction in benefits at age 62 will increase to 30% from the current 20%.

To be currently insured, one must acquire 6 quarters of coverage in the 13-quarter period ending the calendar quarter of death, disability, or 62nd birthday. This status entitles the worker's surviving spouse and children to survivors' insurance benefits, plus a lump-sum payment of $255 for burial expenses.

To be eligible for disability benefits, one must be both fully insured and disability insured. Being disability insured requires that workers earn a certain number of quarters of coverage, depending on their age. However, only the fully insured status is required for workers whose disability is caused by blindness.

All Social Security benefits are based on the primary insurance amount (PIA), which is derived in two steps. First, the worker's average indexed monthly earnings (AIME) is obtained, which is calculated by (a) indexing the taxable earnings for each year from 1951 and after to the average wage level in the second year before age 62, disability, or death; summing indexed earnings (and unindexed earnings in years after age 60); and dividing the sum by the number of months elapsed after 1950 (or age 21, if later) through age 61 (or the year before the year of disability or death). The 5 years of lowest earnings are dropped from the calculation of AIME (fewer dropout years apply to disabled workers). The benefit computation period is 35 years (fewer years apply to disabled workers).

The PIA is then calculated on the basis of the AIME. For people who retired at age 62 in 1998, the PIA is calculated as follows:

$$\text{PIA} = 90\% \text{ of the first } \$477 \text{ of AIME} + 32\% \text{ of the next}$$
$$\$2,398 \text{ of AIME} + 15\% \text{ of AIME in excess of } \$2,875$$

The bend points ($477 and $2,875) increase each year at the rate of the increase in the average wage. Benefits for workers who retire earlier than the normal retirement age are subjected to actuarial reductions in the PIA, a 20% reduction for those retiring at age 62 and pro rata reductions for those retiring at ages 63 and 64.

Eligible auxiliary members of a retired worker's family are each entitled to benefits equivalent to 50% of the PIA. But spouses who claim auxiliary benefits before age 65 face an actuarial reduction unless an eligible child is present. In addition, when spouses receive pensions based on their own federal, state, or local government work not covered by Social Security, their Social Security benefits are reduced by an amount equal to two thirds of their public pensions. Total family benefits may not exceed the maximum family benefit.

Widows or widowers of insured workers are entitled to 100% of the deceased spouse's PIA if they claim benefits at age 65 or later. Widows and widowers can claim benefits as early as age 60 (or age 50 if disabled), although the benefits are subjected to actuarial reduction in their benefits.

Children under age 18 (or under 19 if still in high school) and the surviving spouse who is caring for them are entitled to survivors' insurance benefits. Each eligible survivor is entitled to benefits equal to 75% of the PIA, but the maximum-family-benefit rule applies. When the youngest child reaches age 18, benefits for the surviving spouse cease, but if any child has a disability that originated in childhood (before age 22), benefits for the child and caretaker parent continue without an age limit.

Disability Insurance

To receive disability benefits, a worker must be unable to engage in any substantial gainful activity because of a severe physical or mental impairment that is expected to last for at least 12 months or to result in death. Education, work experience, and age are taken into account in determining disability. Disability beneficiaries must accept rehabilitation services offered by state rehabilitation agencies if the Social Security Administration determines that these services are likely to be successful.

Eligible disabled workers are entitled to monthly benefits equal to the PIA. Eligible children and the spouse caring for a child under age 18 or children who became disabled before age 22 are each entitled to 50% of the PIA. The total family benefits may not exceed the disability maximum family benefit.

Unless they recover medically from their disability, disabled people generally are allowed to continue to receive benefits for up to 9 months while they test their ability to work. Benefits are not terminated until the second month following the earliest month after the trial work period in which the individual engages in substantial gainful activity or is determined by the Social Security Administration to be able to engage in substantial gainful activity.

Other Rules for OASDI Beneficiaries

Earnings test. There is an earnings test for OASI beneficiaries. Beneficiaries age 65 to 69 could earn up to $14,500 in 1998 without a reduction of their benefits. On earnings exceeding this amount, there was a $1 reduction for each $3 earned. A lower exempt amount ($9,120 in 1998) and a higher reduction rate ($1 for each $2 earned) applied to beneficiaries age 62 to 64. There were no earnings restrictions for those age 70 and older. Disabled worker beneficiaries were not subjected to the earnings test; instead, the rule regarding substantial gainful activity applies.

Taxes on benefits. As was mentioned earlier, the 1983 amendments required beneficiaries with incomes of more than $25,000, if single, and $32,000, if married, to include up to 50% of their benefits in their taxable income. The Omnibus Budget Reconciliation Act of 1993 further required beneficiaries with incomes of more than $34,000, if single, and $44,000, if married, to include up to 85% of their benefits in their taxable income. Revenues from the 1983 amendments are credited to the OASDI Trust Funds, and those from the 1993 Act are credited to the Hospital Insurance Trust Fund. In 1998, 25.7% of all beneficiaries were affected, and the aggregate amount of taxes was 3.7% of the aggregate amount of Social Security benefits (U.S. House of Representatives, 1998, p. 41).

Financing

OASDI is financed by payroll taxes on employers, employees, and the self-employed. The payroll tax is authorized by the Federal Insurance Contribution Act up to the maximum taxable earnings ($68,400 in 1998). The tax rate of 6.2% for OASI and DI combined is levied on employees and employers, totaling 12.4% of the payroll. The self-employed pay at the 12.4% rate. Allocation of the payroll tax is as follows: 5.35% for OASI and 0.85% for DI. In 2000, the tax rate for OASI will decrease by 0.05% and that for DI will increase by 0.05%.

EMERGING PROBLEMS

Financial Problems

Because Social Security benefits are paid for basically on a pay-as-you-go basis, whether future generations of retirees will be adequately supported through Social Security is largely a demographic issue. Likewise, the tax rate at which future generations of workers will have to pay Social Security taxes to provide benefits for future retirees is largely a demographic issue.

According to data compiled by the Board of Trustees (1998) of the OASDI Trust Funds, the number of OASI beneficiaries (mostly elderly people) per 100 covered workers—the dependency ratio—will increase from 26.4 in 1990 to 48.3 in 2075. Under a strict pay-as-you-go basis, the increase in the dependency ratio, while maintaining the level of benefits relative to wages, will result in an increase in the tax rate by 83% from 1990 to 2075. The financial problem stemming from the growing dependency ratio will not disappear, even after the baby-boom generation passes away, because the proportion of children will continue to decline (Bosworth, 1997).

To compound the situation, it is expected that the aging of the population itself will cause the rate of economic growth to decline (General Accounting Office, 1998). Indeed, the Social Security's Board of Trustees projected that the rate of growth in the gross domestic product will decline to 1.3% by 2020, compared with 2.2% from 1989 to 1997 (General Accounting Office, 1998). Thus, in the future, Social Security financing will be adversely affected not only by the growing elderly population, but by the adverse impact of the aging of the population on economic growth.

In addition, the trend toward early retirement has aggravated the financial condition of Social Security. The average age for men at first receipt of Social Security benefits declined from 68.7 in 1950 to 63.7 in 1991; the age for women declined from 68.0 in 1950 to 63.5 in 1991 (Steuerle & Bakija, 1997).

The Board of Trustees (1998) determined that the long-term financial solvency of OASDI is worsening by (a) comparing the annual income rates and cost rates for OASI, DI, and the combination of the two (income included only payroll taxes and income taxes on Social Security benefits and excluded income from the OASDI Trust Funds assets) and (b) evaluating actuarial conditions of the OASI fund, the DI fund, and the combination of the two, all in terms of the percentage of the taxable payroll. All data presented below are based on the intermediate assumptions established by the Office of the Actuary in the Social Security Administration.

Table 14.1 shows the average annual rates of income and cost for OASI, DI, and the combination (OASDI) during the three consecutive 25-year periods: 1998-2022, 2023-2047, and 2048-2072. In the coming decades, the annual cost rate will exceed the annual income rate at an accelerating rate. The average OASI cost rate during the second and third 25-year periods will exceed the income rate by 3.99 percentage points and 4.90 percentage points, respectively, of the taxable payroll. Put another way, during the second 25-year period, the cost rate, on average, will exceed the income rate by 35%, and during the third 25-year period, it will exceed the income rate by 43%. The extent of imbalance between the income and cost rates for DI will be as great, with the cost rate exceeding the income rate by 32% in the second 25-year period and by 39% in the third 25-year period. The imbalance between these two rates involving OASDI as a whole will be 35% in the second 25-year period and 42% in the third 25-year period.

Table 14.2 shows the actuarial status of the OASI Trust Fund, the DI Trust Fund, and the combination of the two during the incremental periods of years: 25 years from 1998 to 2022, 50 years from 1998 to 2047, and 75 years from 1998 to 2072. Note that in Table 14.2, rates of income and cost relate to the present value of the aggregate income and cost during the selected periods. In contrast, the rates in Table

TABLE 14.1 Summarized Annual Income Rates and Cost Rates for 25-Year Subperiods, by Trust Fund, Under Intermediate Assumptions, Calendar Years 1998-2072 (as a percentage of the taxable payroll)

Subperiod	Old Age and Survivors Insurance			Disability Insurance			Combined		
	Income Rate	Cost Rate	Balance	Income Rate	Cost Rate	Balance	Income Rate	Cost Rate	Balance
1998-2022	10.95	10.61	0.34	1.82	1.97	-.16	12.76	12.58	0.18
2023-2047	11.29	15.28	-3.99	1.84	2.43	-.59	13.13	17.71	-4.58
2048-2072	11.44	16.34	-4.90	1.85	2.57	-.72	13.29	18.91	-5.62

SOURCE: Board of Trustees (1998), Table II.F14, p. 112.

TABLE 14.2 The State of Trust Funds: Summarized Income Rates and Cost Rates for Valuation Periods, by Trust Fund, Under Intermediate Assumptions, Calendar Years 1998-2072 (as a percentage of the taxable payroll)

Periods	Old Age and Survivors Insurance			Disability Insurance			Combined		
	Income Rate	Cost Rate	Actuarial Balance	Income Rate	Cost Rate	Actuarial Balance	Income Rate	Cost Rate	Actuarial Balance
25 years: 1998-2022	11.82	11.07	0.75	1.91	2.05	-.14	13.73	13.12	0.61
50 years: 1998-2047	11.61	12.68	-1.07	1.88	2.19	-.30	13.49	14.86	-1.37
75 years: 1998-2072	11.57	13.38	-1.81	1.88	2.26	-.38	13.45	15.64	-2.19

SOURCE: Board of Trustees (1998), Table II.F15, p. 113.

14.1 relate to the average annual rates of income and cost, with no regard to the interest income from the trust funds.

Table 14.2 indicates that except in the first 25-year period, the OASI Fund will have an actuarial imbalance: 1.07% of the taxable payroll during the coming 50 years and 1.81% of the taxable payroll during the coming 75 years. Thus, looking into the 75-year time frame, income has to increase by 1.81% of the taxable payroll—or 15.6% of the projected income—immediately. Otherwise, the OASI Trust Fund will be out of balance. In the same vein, income to pay for DI benefits must increase by 20.2% of the projected income to meet the actuarial balance in the DI Trust Fund for the coming 75 years. OASI and DI together will require an increase of 16.3% of the projected income—or 2.19% of the taxable payroll. In short, somehow, the OASDI system's income must increase by 16.3%, starting now, to strike an actuarial balance in the coming 75-year period. If the action is delayed, the rate of the payroll tax will have to increase even more.

Specifically, the following events are expected to take place (Koitz & Kallmann, 1998). At the end of 1997, the OASDI Trust Funds had assets of $655 billion. Assets are expected to grow to almost $3.8 trillion by the end of 2020 (in nominal dollars). However, the financial viability of OASDI will begin to deteriorate as early as 2013. In particular, beginning in 2013, OASDI expenditures will be higher than the income from taxes (payroll taxes plus taxes on benefits). At that time, OASDI will need to resort to using a part of the interest due to the trust funds on U.S. Treasury's special issues, in addition to tax income, to meet the benefit obligations. Beginning in 2021, OASDI spending will exceed the total income (tax income plus interest on U.S. Treasury's special issues). At this point, OASDI will have to begin to use the trust fund assets. In 2032, the trust fund assets will be exhausted. At that time, the trust fund income will be sufficient to pay only 72% of the benefits. Because the rate of growth in benefit obligations will continue to increase faster than the rate of growth in tax income, the percentage of the benefits that can be paid with current income will continue to decline, dropping to about two thirds at the end of the 75-year period, and it is expected to continue to drop after that.

Inter- and Intracohort Inequity

Social Security has been criticized for its inter- and intracohort inequity in benefits in relation to contributions—the "money's worth" issue. Findings from a study by Steuerle and Bakija (1997), presented in Table 14.3, are informative.

The findings indicate that future cohorts of beneficiaries will have a worse money's worth in Social Security benefits than did past beneficiaries. For example, the average-wage, single man who retired in 1960 received $36,500 more in retirement benefits during his lifetime than what he paid into the OASI program, whereas his

TABLE 14.3 Lifetime Old Age and Survivors Insurance Benefits, Taxes, and Net Transfers (in thousands of constant 1993 dollars)

Year Cohort Turns 65	Single Male			Single Female			One-Earner Couple			Two-Earner Couple[a]		
	Low Wage	Average Wage	High Wage	Low Wage	Average Wage	High Wage	Low Wage	Average Wage	High Wage	Low/Low Wage	Average/Low Wage	High/Average Wage
1960												
Benefits	30.1	45.5	50.6	45.7	69.0	76.7	66.3	98.9	111.0	76.8	102.0	122.1
Taxes	4.0	9.0	13.8	4.3	9.6	14.6	4.0	9.0	13.8	8.4	13.3	23.4
Net transfers	26.1	36.5	36.8	41.4	59.4	62.1	62.3	89.9	97.2	68.4	88.7	98.7
1980												
Benefits	54.3	90.2	114.6	80.8	134.3	170.1	129.3	209.9	264.3	146.9	208.4	273.2
Taxes	22.9	51.0	71.9	24.2	53.9	76.1	22.9	51.0	71.9	47.2	75.2	125.7
Net transfers	31.4	39.3	42.7	56.6	80.5	94.4	106.4	158.9	192.4	99.7	133.3	147.5
1995												
Benefits	58.0	95.7	133.6	80.6	132.9	185.5	134.9	223.4	305.4	155.2	226.6	312.6
Taxes	45.4	100.8	170.7	47.2	104.8	179.0	45.4	100.8	170.7	92.5	148.0	275.5
Net transfers	12.6	-5.1	-37.1	33.4	28.1	6.5	89.5	122.5	134.7	62.6	78.6	37.1
2010												
Benefits	69.0	115.2	175.9	93.6	156.1	238.4	154.6	258.8	388.6	178.9	261.7	394.2
Taxes	68.2	151.5	310.8	70.4	156.5	322.4	68.2	151.5	310.8	138.6	221.9	467.3
Net transfers	0.9	-36.3	-135.0	23.2	-0.4	-84.1	86.5	107.3	77.7	40.3	39.8	-73.1
2030												
Benefits	84.0	139.6	220.3	113.7	189.0	298.1	187.4	312.8	493.0	215.9	316.5	498.1
Taxes	88.1	195.8	468.8	91.3	202.8	485.4	88.1	195.8	468.8	179.4	287.1	671.6
Net transfers	-4.1	-56.2	-248.5	22.5	-13.8	-187.3	99.3	117.0	24.2	36.5	29.4	-173.5

NOTE: All amounts are discounted to the present value at age 65 using a 2% real interest rate. Adjustments for chance of death in all years after age 21. Includes actuarial value of all OASI workers, spousal, and survivors benefits payable over a lifetime. Includes both employer and employee portions of the OASI payroll tax. Couples are assumed to be the same age and to have two children born when the parents are age 25 and 30. Assumes retirement at the OASI normal retirement age. Projections are based on the intermediate assumptions from the 1993 OASDI Board of Trustees report. The OASI tax rate is assumed to be set at 10.65% after 1992.
a. Low/low means that both spouses are low-wage earners; high/average means that one spouse is a high-wage earner and the other is an average-wage earner.
SOURCE: Steuerle & Bakija (1997), p. 47.

counterpart who will retire in 2030 is expected to receive lifetime benefits that are $56,200 less than his lifetime contributions. This pattern will persist regardless of the earnings level or family structure. This is an indication of intercohort inequity.

The finding also indicates that within a cohort of beneficiaries, the following categories received a better money's worth: female workers over male workers, one-earner couples over two-earner couples, and high-wage earners over low-wage earners—at least until 1980. By 1995, the money's worth for high-wage earners had become worse than that for low-wage earners.

Table 14.4 further illustrates the preferential treatment of one-earner couples over two-earner couples. From the table, it is clear that one-earner couples with the identical maximum AIME as two-earner couples, with each spouse earning half the maximum, receive larger benefits either when both are alive or when only one is alive. The difference in benefits when only one is alive is especially pronounced in favor of one-earner couples (see also Burkhauser, 1979; Burkhauser & Holden, 1982; General Accounting Office, 1996; Holden, 1997; Meyer, 1996; Olson, 1994; U.S. House of Representatives, 1992a, 1992b).

When the provision of survivors' benefits was established in 1939, lawmakers meant to ensure that widows could sustain their lives. But this provision, although well intended, is rapidly becoming obsolete as the labor force participation of women increases.

PROPOSALS FOR CHANGE

The foregoing discussion indicates that the Social Security system, which is financed on a pay-as-you-go basis, with contingency funds, will eventually become insolvent. During the coming 75 years, the deficit will be 2.19% of the taxable payroll (Board of Trustees, 1998). Furthermore, because of the sustaining phenomenon of the aging of the population (more retirees, compounded by the higher benefits they will claim, and for more years), meeting the actuarial balance in the OASDI Trust Funds in successive 75-year periods will require additional infusions of resources into the trust funds (Ball, 1998). It is estimated that a shift of one year in a 75-year period would increase the actuarial deficit by about 0.08% of the taxable payroll (1994-1996 Advisory Council on Social Security, 1997). Thus, the main policy issue is this: How can the system be made financially solvent and fair for future generations of workers and retirees?

The 1994-1996 Advisory Council on Social Security (1997) made three different recommendations for reforming the Social Security system. However, one aspect of all these proposals is the same: The system should invest part of Social Security contributions in the equity market, so that the Social Security system not only can establish

TABLE 14.4   Monthly Benefits For One-Earner Couples With the Maximum Average Indexed Monthly Earnings ($4,144) and Two-Earner Couples with Half the Maximum Each ($2,072): Couples Claiming Benefits at Age 65 in 2001

	One-Earner Couple, With Husband Earning $4,144 per Month Throughout His Life	Two-Earner Couple, With Each Earning $2,072 a Month Throughout Their Lives
Benefit when both spouses are alive	$2,081	$1,880
Benefit when only one spouse is alive	$1,387	$ 940

SOURCE: Board of Trustees (1998), p. 67; Mercer (1997), pp. 24-25.
NOTE: Couples are assumed to be the same age and to retire at age 65.

the actuarial balance for the immediate 75-year period and succeeding 75-year periods, but can increase the money's worth ratios for younger generations (Gramlich, 1996a).

The first approach, called the Maintain Benefits plan, attempts to preserve the benefit provisions of the current system as much as possible. It proposes the following:

1. Extend Social Security coverage to all state and local workers.
2. Change the current system of taxing benefits to simply taxing Social Security benefits in excess of what the worker paid in.
3. Change the Consumer Price Index, as announced by the Bureau of Labor Statistics in March 1996.
4. Increase, from 35 to 38 years, the period over which AIME are computed.
5. Redirect to the OASDI Trust Funds the revenues from the taxation of Social Security benefits; these revenues are currently going to Hospital Insurance Trust Fund.
6. Invest 40% of the assets of the OASDI Trust Funds in stocks.
7. Increase the OASDI payroll tax rate in 2045 by 0.8 percentage points for employees and employers.

These measures are all designed to eliminate the 75-year actuarial deficit in OASDI for the coming 75-year period and beyond while leaving the benefit provisions generally untouched.

The second approach, called the Individual Accounts plan, aims to meet the actuarial balance by reducing Social Security benefits by 30% for average workers, 22% for low-wage workers, and 32% for high-wage workers and to establish individual accounts financed by extra contributions from employees, equal to 1.6% of the taxable payroll. The annuity benefits derived from the accounts would make up for the programmed 30% reduction in Social Security benefits (Ball, 1998). The first four measures of the Individual Accounts plan are the same as the has the same four measures (1, 2, 3, and 4) as the Maintain Benefits plan. In addition, it proposes the following:

5. Change the formula for calculating the PIA by gradually reducing the second and third multiplying factors from 0.32 and 0.15 to 0.224 and 0.105, respectively, by 2030.
6. Increase the normal retirement age to 67 by 2011 and index it thereafter to increases in life expectancy.
7. Reduce the benefits for aged spouses from 50% to 33% of the PIA in 2016.
8. Gradually replace the benefit for the surviving spouse under the current system with the highest of own PIA, spouse's PIA, or 75% of the combined benefits if both were alive, phased in over the coming 40 years (This measure is intended to minimize the preferential treatment of one-earner over two-earner couples under the current system).
9. On enactment of the proposal, require all workers to contribute an extra 1.6% of their taxable earnings to an Individual (retirement savings) Account.

The third approach, called the Personal Security Accounts plan, is a departure from the Social Security system. Its aim is to transform OASDI into a two-tier system, with the first tier providing a flat-amount benefit (equivalent to 65% of the poverty line) and the second tier consisting of large-scale individualized retirement accounts, financed by 5 percentage points of the OASDI employee payroll tax. In effect, this plan would transform Social Security into a combination of defined-benefit and defined-contribution programs. Because the Personal Security Accounts plan introduces a defined contribution program (that is, advance funding for future generations of beneficiaries), it would incur a sizable transaction cost. Also, it incorporates a clear notion of the "privatization" of Social Security because the individualized accounts would be totally controlled by individuals who would invest money and consume the proceeds starting at age 62 for all purposes, including bequeathing them to heirs. To accomplish all these goals, the plan's first four measures are the same as measures 1 and 3 of both the Maintain Benefits and Individual Accounts plans and measures 6 and 8 of the Individual Accounts plan. In addition, the Personal Security Accounts plan proposes the following measures:

5. Gradually replace the current PIA formula with a basic benefit ($4,101 in 1996[1] and wage-indexed thereafter) for workers under age 55 in 1998. Provide past service credits for workers 25 to 54 in 1998. Retain the current PIA formula for disability and young survivor beneficiaries. Provide 50% of the full flat benefit for aged spouses.
6. Beginning in 1998, subject 50% of OASDI benefits to income tax (100% of flat benefit) and credit the tax income solely to the OASDI Trust Funds. Eliminate the current $25,000/$32,000 thresholds between 1998 and 2007. No revenue transfer to the hospital fund.
7. Eliminate the earnings test at the normal retirement age.

8. Redirect 5 percentage points of the OASDI employee payroll tax to personal security accounts of workers under age 55 in 1998. Proceeds from the accounts would not be taxed.

To pay for the transition costs, the personal security accounts plan would adopt the following:

1. Increase the payroll tax rate by 0.76 percentage points for employees and employers, each year from 1998 to 2069 (or an equivalent tax of another form).
2. Borrow additional funds ($1.9 trillion) from the General Fund of the U.S. Treasury from 2002 to about 2034, to be paid back with interest by 2070.

The Maintain Benefits and Personal Security Accounts plans are at two ends of the continuum of reform proposals. The Maintain Benefits plan would attempt, as much as possible, to maintain the current basic principles and provisions of Social Security and, at the same time, to infuse more funds into the system by investing up to 40% of the assets accumulated in the OASDI Trust Funds and increasing the OASDI payroll tax rate by 0.8 percentage points in 2045. In contrast, the Personal Security Accounts plan would revolutionize the Social Security system. In essence, it is designed to provide a basic floor of income, which is lower than the poverty line, and let individual OASDI taxpayers develop and manage their own individualized retirement accounts, which are similar to the current IRAs and 401(k) plans, through registered security firms. To make personal security accounts a reality, a sizable transition cost would be incurred.

The Individual Accounts plan falls in the middle between the Maintain Benefits and Personal Security Accounts plans. It would shrink the scope of Social Security benefits by about 30%, finance the benefits by the current 12.4% payroll tax, and let taxpayers make up for the reduction in benefits with annuity benefits derived from individualized accounts (which would be run by the government in a manner similar to the Federal Employees Thrift Savings Plan), which would be funded by an additional 1.6% payroll tax levied on employees.

DISCUSSION

What would be the anticipated effects of the proposed plans on future Social Security beneficiaries? This section compares the effects of the Maintain Benefits and Personal Security Accounts plans in relation to several policy issues.

Money's Worth

Whether future Social Security beneficiaries will receive favorable returns on their Social Security contributions will depend on the extent to which the OASDI Trust

Funds are invested in the equity market collectively or through individualized accounts, instead of in U.S. Treasury's special issues as is currently done. The difference in real rates of return between these two investment instruments is estimated to be 4.7%, 7% from equities minus 2.3% from U.S. Treasury's special issues (1994-1996 Advisory Council on Social Security, 1997). Thus, it is anticipated that both the Maintain Benefits and Personal Security Accounts plans would generate considerably higher rates of return than does the current system, with the Personal Security Accounts plan outperforming the Maintain Benefits plan, according to the Office of the Actuary of the Social Security Administration (1994-1996 Advisory Council on Social Security, 1997). The better performance of the security accounts plan would be a result of the investment of huge sums of money in the equity market from the start of its implementation: 5 percentage points of the current 12.4% payroll tax that would be put into individualized accounts, an additional 1.52% payroll tax, and the $1.9 trillion borrowed from the Treasury at a rate for U.S. Treasury's special issues (Mashaw & Marmor, 1996). Privatization per se would not be responsible for the higher rates of return; rather, the magnitude of the investment in equities would account for the higher rates of return (Ball, 1998; Mashaw & Marmor, 1996; Mitchell & Zeldes, 1996).

The effectiveness of investing money in the equity market was demonstrated by Feldstein (1997) and Feldstein and Samwick (1996), who reported that because the rate of return on equities considerably exceeds that on the U.S. Treasury's special issues, the benefits that can be financed by the existing 12.4% payroll tax could eventually be financed by mandatory contributions of only 2.1% of the taxable payroll, which would be invested through mandatory individualized retirement accounts. The transition cost, estimated by Feldstein (1997), would require an additional 1.5% of the taxable payroll during the early part of the transaction. Because fewer resources would be available for internal redistribution under the Personal Security Accounts plan than under the Maintain Benefits plan, the distributive effects of benefits on two-earner versus one-earner couples would be different: Under the Personal Security Accounts plan, two-earner couples would fare better; under the Maintain Benefits plan, one-earner couples would fare better. In essence, this anticipated effect under the Personal Security Accounts plan would undo the often criticized special treatment of one-earner couples under the current system. Also, the Personal Security Accounts plan would do better in terms of money's worth ratios for younger workers than for older workers, whereas the Maintain Benefits plan would do better for older workers than for younger workers, at least over the next four decades (1994-1996 Advisory Council on Social Security, 1997). In addition, single workers would fare better under the Personal Security Accounts plan than under the Maintain Benefits plan (Gramlich, 1996b).

The rate of national savings is directly related to economic growth (Gramlich, 1997; Solow, 1956). Thus, the relationship between the privatization of Social Security and national savings is a hotly debated issue. Advocates of the privatization of Social Security argue that a plan like the Personal Security Accounts, which would privatize a large part of Social Security, would result in greater national savings (see Kerry & Simpson, 1995; Kuttner, 1984; Wheeler & Kearney, 1996; Ycas, 1994). But economists say otherwise. Any decrease in borrowing by the U.S. Treasury from the OASDI Trust Funds must be offset by an increase in its borrowing from the public, leaving the federal government's gross debt largely unchanged. Thus, unless the government cuts spending or the public increases its savings, there would be no change in the amount of national savings (Bosworth, 1995; General Accounting Office, 1998; Mashaw & Marmor, 1996; Mitchell & Zeldes, 1996).

On the other hand, favorable secondary effects might occur: that is, if the OASDI program did not lend its excess income to the U.S. Treasury, but instead invested it in stocks (as under the Maintain Benefits plan) or if workers are allowed to invest 5 percentage points of their payroll taxes through individualized accounts (as under the Personal Security Accounts plan), then smaller amounts of money would go to the Treasury. The result would be the exposure of the true scope of the federal deficit (or surplus). Such an exposure might force legislators to refrain from increasing spending and result in a real increase in national savings (Mitchell & Zeldes, 1996). A study by the Congressional Research Service (Kallman & Koitz, 1998) indicated that the 1999 estimated surplus of $80 billion could be transformed into a $37 billion deficit if all revenues that accrue to Social Security were taken out of the calculation of the surplus. The public might also increase its savings as a result of beneficial experiences in individualized accounts, in the same way that 40l(k) plans stimulate personal savings (Bernheim, 1996; Wise, 1997).

Internal Redistribution

Currently, a complex system of internal redistribution of financial resources operates in three ways. First, financial resources are redistributed from later to earlier generations of retirees. Second, a horizontal redistribution takes places from two-earner couples to one-earner couples and from workers without auxiliary beneficiaries to those with such beneficiaries. Third, a vertical redistribution occurs from high-wage workers to low-wage workers. (This vertical redistribution is offset by the higher mortality rate of low-wage earners than of high-wage earners; Garrett, 1995). These redistribution schemes would be maintained in the Maintain Benefits plan.

Because the Personal Security Accounts plan would divert a large amount of financial resources to individualized accounts, the plan would have few financial resources to redistribute, beyond providing flat-amount benefits (Burtless, 1998; Mashaw & Marmor, 1996; Panel on Assumption and Methods, 1997). In short, the Personal Security Accounts plan would minimize the social adequacy principle and emphasize the individual equity principle. On the other hand, the Personal Security Accounts plan could draw a clear line between benefits provided according to the social adequacy principle and benefits provided according to the individual equity principle. Under the Maintain Benefits plan, it would be difficult to see where social adequacy ends and individual equity begins in benefit provisions.

Differential Risks

High returns on contributions through equity investments are always accompanied by high risks. The outcome of investing financial resources through individualized accounts, as envisioned by the Personal Security Accounts plan, would affect individuals immediately, directly, and fully, whereas the collective investment of OASDI Trust Funds assets, according to the Maintain Benefits plan, could spread the risk both within a generation and between generations (General Accounting Office, 1998).

Burtless (1998) demonstrated that intercohort differences in rates of return could be considerable. His study, involving the experience of 88 hypothetical workers whose earnings increased 1% a year and who contributed 2% of their wages to individualized retirement accounts throughout their working lives, showed that the percentage of wages that could be replaced by annuities purchased with the accumulated assets in the individualized retirement accounts differed enormously, depending on when the workers entered the workforce. The highest replacement rate (40%) was obtained by the worker who entered the workforce in 1926 and retired in 1965, whereas the lowest rate (7%) was obtained by the worker who entered the workforce in 1881 and retired in 1920.

Within a cohort of retirees, the outcome of their investments is expected to vary, depending on individual investment behaviors. For example, several studies found that women are consistently more averse to risk and thus are less likely than men to invest in stocks and more likely to invest in money market accounts, certificates of deposits, and bonds (Bajitelsmit, Bernasek, & Jianakoplos, 1996; Hinz, McCarthy, & Turner, 1997; Poterba & Wise, 1996). Also, more educated people and those with high incomes or greater wealth are more aggressive and sophisticated investors than are others (Diamond, 1996; Poterba & Wise, 1996). Therefore, the distribution of the proceeds from investments is significantly more unequal than that of Social Security benefits, to the advantage of the rich and the sophisticated.

More generally stated, because the Personal Security Accounts is a defined contribution plan, the level of retirement benefits, beyond the flat amount benefits, would be directly related to the investment behavior of individuals. In contrast, because the Maintain Benefits plan is a defined-benefit plan, the level of benefits under it would be defined under the law. This crucial difference in these two plans would be directly related to the differential degrees of uncertainty in retirement income.

Problems in Implementation

The Maintain Benefits and Personal Security Accounts plans would face different sorts of problems in their implementation. Because the Personal Security Accounts plan would be established in the form of individualized accounts, the problems in its implementation would include overhead costs, administrative costs, and paperwork. A study of the Chilean privatized system of retirement accounts showed that the administrative costs are 13% of the program expenditures, which is high by U.S. standards (Koitz, 1998; Kritzer, 1996; Myers, personal communication, January 28, 1999; Superintendencia de Administratodoras de Fondos de Pensiones, 1996). In addition, the bookkeeping required of employers might be horrendous, error rates in misreporting the wages withheld might be considerably higher among small employers than among large ones, and fees imposed by security firms on transactions of stocks and bonds by low-wage earners would be high. Among workers covered by Social Security, 56% have annual taxable earnings of only $18,000 or less, producing a deduction of $900 or less at 5% (Ball, 1998). Few well-established brokerage firms would find it in their interest to open accounts for low-wage and average-wage earners.

Because the Personal Security Accounts plan would create large-scale individualized accounts, the public might eventually demand that they should be permitted to use the accumulated assets in the accounts not only for retirement purposes, but for other vicissitudes of life, such as financing children's education and paying medical bills (Heclo, 1998). The word *individualized* invokes the idea of "it's my money." Legislators would find it difficult to resist such demands.

The Maintain Benefits plan would face different kinds of problems. It proposes to invest up to 40% of the assets of OASDI Trust Funds in passive ways; that is, an expert investment board would invest the huge amount of money in several index funds and would have no voting rights in any fund. These restrictions are supposed to ensure that the board's actions would not interfere with economic transactions in the private sector. However, it might be difficult to restrain Congress from influencing the investment of a fund under government control (Feldstein, 1997).

Impact on Future Development

Assuming that the Personal Security Accounts and Maintain Benefits plans are implemented, what impact would they have on the future development of Social Security? As the scope of individualized accounts held by high-wage earners becomes far larger than the scope of the first-tier provision, the public interest in upgrading the first tier would wane; instead, political pressures would increase to expand the second tier of Personal Security Accounts: the individualized accounts. If the second tier was expanded, it is likely that the future Social Security system would be in a dual form, with rich retirees drawing retirement income mainly from their individualized accounts and poor retirees drawing retirement income from first-tier, flat-amount benefits, supplemented by Supplemental Security Income. This situation would mark the beginning of the destruction of the Social Security system in the United States (Mashaw & Marmor, 1996).

On the other hand, under the Maintain Benefits plan, the generational issue in paying for the Social Security benefits of future retirees would continue to exist. The plan's expert investment board would have to start investing the funds' assets immediately and effectively so that future generations of workers would not need to pay Social Security taxes at increasingly high rates. Moreover, the board would need to be aware of the aging phenomenon that tends to increase the cost rates persistently, even though the 1994-1966 Advisory Council on Social Security (1997) reported that all three proposals took this aging phenomenon into account.

THE FUTURE

The idea of mandatory privatization of Social Security is sweeping the world. A system of individualized accounts is already in operation in Australia and some Latin American countries. Sweden allows individuals to shift part of their payroll taxes into private accounts (Feldstein, 1997). Japan is thinking about the adoption of a system similar to the Personal Security Accounts plan.

In the final analysis, however, it is up to the public to choose between the systems envisioned by advocates of the Maintain Benefits and Personal Security Accounts plans. In a broad sense, both plans reflect the two polls of the American ideology: collectivism and individualism (see Heclo, 1998; Wheeler & Kearney, 1996). Should the Social Security system reflect the American value of developing a sense of community and be designed to make old-age income more secure for the largest number of elderly people though internal redistribution, if necessary? Or should it embody the American value of individual responsibility to meet one's own economic needs in old age? Should the Social Security system provide predictable, stable amounts of retirement income? Or should it incorporate, in its design, market fluctuations in returns on contributions? Finally, should the Social Security system be the first defense against economic insecurity in old age, on which other layers of protections can be built? Or should it be just one of many ways through which individuals seek retirement income security?

Three decades ago, Titmuss (1970), a leading British welfare-state theoretician, stated that the type of social welfare program that a society adopts affects how the society develops. He argued that the British were given a chance to develop a sense of community by choosing a nonmarket approach to collecting and distributing blood, whereas the United States rejected such an opportunity by choosing the market mechanism to collect and distribute blood. An analogy can be drawn to the current debate on the reform of Social Security. It will be the public's choice. Altmeyer (1966), one of the founders of American Social Security, said that the Social Security Act is a living document. It is up to each generation to perfect it.

NOTE

1. The full flat-amount benefit of $410 would be paid to individuals with 35 or more years of covered employment. For individuals who do not work a full career, half the flat-amount benefit would be earned with 10 years of covered employment, with a 2% increment for each additional year of work up to 25 years.

REFERENCES

Altmeyer, A. J. (1966). *The formative years of Social Security.* Madison: University of Wisconsin Press.

Baggette, J., Shapiro, R. Y., & Jacobs, L. R. (1995). The polls-poll trends: Social security—An update. *Public Opinion Quarterly, 59,* 424-425.

Bajitelsmit, V. L., Bernasek, A., & Jianakoplos, N. A. (1996). *Gender differences in pension investment allocation decisions* (Working paper in Economics and Political Economy). Fort Collins: Department of Economics, Colorado State University.

Ball, R. M. (1998). *A commentary on the current Social Security debate.* Washington, DC: Author.

Bernheim, D. (1996). *Rethinking saving incentives.* Stanford, CA: Stanford University, Department of Economics.

Board of Trustees, Federal Old-Age and Survivors Insurance and Disability Insurance Trust Funds. (1998). *1998 annual report of the Board of Trustees of the Federal Old-Age and Survivors Insurance and Disability Insurance Trust Funds.* Washington, DC: Government Printing Office.

Bosworth, B. (1995, January). *The Social Security fund: How big? How managed?* Paper presented at a meeting of the National Academy of Social Insurance, Washington, DC.

Bosworth, B. (1997). What economic role for the trust funds? In E. R. Kingson & J. H. Shulz (Eds.), *Social security in the 21st century* (pp. 156-177). New York: Oxford University Press.

Burkhauser, R. V. (1979). Are women treated fairly in today's Social Security system? *The Gerontologist, 19,* 242-249.

Burkhauser, R. V., & Holden, K. C. (Eds.). (1982). *A challenge to Social Security: The changing roles of women and men in American society.* New York: Academic Press.

Burtless, G. (1998, June 18). The role of individual personal saving accounts in Social Security (Testimony before the Subcommittee on Social Security Committee on Ways and Means, U.S. House of Representatives). Washington, DC: Government Printing Office.

Diamond, P. A. (1996). Proposals to restructure Social Security. *Journal of Economic Perspectives, 10,* 67-88.

Feldstein, M. (1997, July-August). The case for privatization. *Foreign Affairs, 76,* 24-38.

Feldstein, M., & Samwick, A. (1996). *The transition path in privatizing Social Security* (Working paper No. 5761). Cambridge, MA: National Bureau of Economic Research.

Friedland, R. B. (1994). *When support and confidence are at odds: The public's understanding of the Social Security program.* Washington DC: National Academy of Social Insurance.

Garrett, D. M. (1995). The effects of differential mortality rates on the progressivity of Social Security. *Economic Inquiry, 33,* 457-475.

General Accounting Office. (1996). *Social security: Issues involving benefit equity for working women* (GAO/HEHS-96-55). Washington, DC: Author.

General Accounting Office. (1998). *Social security financing: Implications of government stock investing for the trust fund, the federal budget, and the economy* (GAO/AIMD/HEHS-98-74). Washington, DC: Author.

Gramlich, E. M. (1996a). Different approaches for dealing with Social Security. *American Economic Review, 86,* 358-362.

Gramlich, E. M. (1996b). Different approaches for dealing with Social Security. *Journal of Economic Perspectives, 10,* 55-66.

Gramlich, E. M. (1997). How does Social Security affect the economy? In E. R. Kingson & J. H. Schulz (Eds.), *Social security in the 21st century* (pp. 147-155). New York: Oxford University Press.

Heclo, H. (1998, September). Political risk and Social Security reform. *Social Security Brief* (No. 1). Washington, DC: National Academy of Social Insurance.

Hinz, R. P., McCarthy, D. D., & Turner, J. A. (1997). Are women conservative investors? Gender differences in participant-directed pension investment. In M. S. Gorden, O. S. Mitchell, & M. M. Twinney (Eds.), *Positioning pensions for the twenty-first century* (pp. 91-103) Philadelphia: University of Pennsylvania Press.

Holden, K. C. (1997). Social security and the economic security of women: Is it fair? In E. R. Kingson & J. H. Schulz (Eds.), *Social security in the 21st century* (pp. 91-104). New York: Oxford University Press.

Kallman, G., & Koitz, D. (1998). *Social security: The protect Social Security account* (CRS Report for Congress, 98-799 EPW). Washington, DC: Congressional Research Service.

Kerry, B., & Simpson, A. K. (1995, May 23). How to save Social Security. *New York Times,* p. A17.

Koitz, D. (1998). *Ideas for privatizing Social Security* (CRS Report to Congress 96-504 EPW). Washington, DC: Congressional Research Service.

Koitz, D., & Kallmann, G. (1998). *The financial outlook for Social Security and Medicare* (CRS Report for Congress, 95-543 EPW). Washington, DC: Congressional Research Service.

Kritzer, B. E. (1996). Privatizing Social Security: The Chilean experience. *Social Security Bulletin, 59*(3), 45-55.

Kuttner, R. (1984). *The economic illusion: False choices between prosperity and social choice.* Philadelphia: University of Pennsylvania Press.

Mashaw, J. L., & Marmor, T. R. (1996, November-December). The great social scare. *American Prospect, 29,* 30-37.

Meyer, M. H. (1996). Making claims as workers or wives: The distribution of Social Security benefits. *American Sociological Review, 61,* 449-465.

Mitchell, O. S., & Zeldes, S. P. (1996). Social security privatization: A structure for analysis. *American Economic Review, 86,* 363-367.

1994-1996 Advisory Council on Social Security. (1997). *Report of the 1994-1996 Advisory Council on Social Security: Vol. 1. Findings and recommendations.* Washington, DC: Author.

Olson, L. K. (1994). Women and Social Security: A progressive approach. *Journal of Aging & Social Policy,* 6, 43-56.

Panel on Assumption and Methods, 1994-1996 Advisory Council on Social Security. (1997). Social Security and the future of U.S. fertility. *Population and Development Review, 23,* 208-213.

Poterba, J. M., & Wise, D. A. (1996). *Individual financial decision in retirement saving plans and the provision of resources for retirement* (Working paper No. 5762). New York: National Bureau of Economic Research.

Solow, R. M. (1956, February). A contribution to the theory of economic growth. *Quarterly Journal of Economics,* pp. 65-94.

Steuerle, C. E., & Bakija, J. M. (1997). Retooling Social Security for the 21st century. *Social Security Bulletin, 60*(2), 37-60.

Superintendencia de Administradoras de Fondos de Pensiones. (1996, November). *Boletin Estadistico* (No. 132).

Titmuss, R. M. (1970). *Gift relationship: Human blood to social policy.* London: Allen & Unwin.

U.S. House of Representatives, Committee on Ways and Means. (1998). *1998 green book: Background material and data on the programs within the jurisdiction of the Committee on Ways and Means.* Washington, DC: Government Printing Office.

U.S. House of Representatives, Select Committee on Aging, Subcommittee on Retirement Income and Employment. (1992a). *How well do women fare under the nation's retirement policies: A report by the chairman and ranking Republican.* Washington, DC: Government Printing Office.

U.S. House of Representatives, Select Committee on Aging, Subcommittee on Retirement Income and Employment. (1992b). *How will today's women fare in yesterday's traditional retirement system?* Washington, DC: Government Printing Office.

Wheeler, P. M., & Kearney, J. R. (1996). Income protection for the aged in the 21st century: A framework to help inform the debate. *Social Security Bulletin, 59*(2), 3-19.

Wise, D. A. (1997). Retirement against the demographic trend: More older people living longer, working less, and saving less. *Demography, 34,* 83-95.

Ycas, M. A. (1994). The challenge of the 21st century: Innovating and adapting Social Security systems to economic, social, and demographic changes in the English-speaking Americas. *Social Security Bulletin, 57*(4), 3-9.

CHAPTER FIFTEEN

Social Policy and the Elderly

FERNANDO M. TORRES-GIL
VALENTINE VILLA

The contemporary nature of social policy and the elderly in the United States involves a unique amalgam of history, politics, public benefits, and demographic
trends. These factors, in turn, have come to shape public discourse and actions for
older people, caregivers, and all who are approaching old age. The aging population,
elders as a political force, and the pending age wave will make issues of social policy
and the elderly a top domestic concern for much of the next century, even more so
than in the past.

Social Security, Medicare, and the aging of the baby-boomer cohort are at the core
of contemporary controversies about how individuals, government, the private sector, and society at large respond to aging and the alteration of existing social policies
for the elderly. This chapter examines the factors affecting policies and programs for
the elderly and the major issues facing social policy by describing historical developments, the politics of aging, and the current set of public entitlements and services for
the elderly.

HISTORICAL OVERVIEW: THE POLITICS OF AGING

The United States is unique among nations in the area of social policies predicated on
age and the influence of senior citizens in politics and public policy. In part, this is due

to the tripartite American political system (executive, judicial, legislative), which makes for a permeable structure allowing interest groups and organized lobbies to "work the system" toward their own ends. Our sense of a civic culture and, as de Tocqueville (1945) astutely observed, the tendency of Americans to be involved have created a climate whereby organized constituencies can have a powerful influence on laws and political decisions. More than most groups, the elderly exemplify interest group politics and have benefitted from a host of entitlements, services, and legislative protections that have given them a prominent place in society. In contrast, nations with parliamentary and authoritarian forms of government do not have a politics of aging, although many do have generous social welfare programs for the elderly. Although some nations, such as Canada, Australia, and France, are beginning to see pensioners mobilize, only the United States has seen an inextricable link among politics, old age, and social policy developments.

Population aging is hardening this link. Today, about 33 million people—one eighth of the total population—are 65 years and older. About half of the nation's population is 34 and older. Between 1900 and 1994, the elderly population increased elevenfold, compared with only a 3-fold increase for those under age 65 (Bureau of the Census, 1996). The growth of the older population has made the needs and desires of older people quite visible to elected officials, especially given their high rates of registration and voting (Binstock & Day, 1996). The greatest impact of population aging, however, is yet to come. By 2010, baby boomers will be reaching retirement; and when they become senior citizens (assuming we continue to use current definitions of old age), the population of older people will double to about 75 million.

Historical Developments

The politics of aging represents the coming of age of older people as a political force and the rise of social policies predicated on age as a primary criterion. This was not always so. When the nation was founded, life expectancy at birth was about 35 years, and by the mid-1800s, it had increased to about 42 years (Bureau of the Census, 1996). Thus, it comes as no surprise that there were few very old people in those societies. Throughout much of human civilization, older people (who might be in their 40s, depending on life expectancy) were few and privileged. In agrarian societies, those few who survived into old age acquired a measure of status and authority (Williamson, Evans, & Powell, 1982). In more sophisticated societies such as ancient China, gerontocracies developed where those in power were invariably the very old. Elders with authority were usually men with wealth; rarely did women (with Sparta being one of the few exceptions) and the poor acquire influence in their old age. The advent of industrialization and modern societies in the 19th and 20th centuries, with movement toward cities and away from rural areas, broke down the inherent advantages of old age. Social mobility, the ascendancy of private property, industrial specialization, and urbanization served to break down customs of respect and value of elders. In such times, individualism and physical abilities became highly prized, and older people and those with disabilities were often at the mercy of families, neighbors, and communal organizations.

Throughout history, regardless of whether societies were agrarian or urban and regardless of the extent of gerontocracies, old age was not a basis for collective organizing and political actions. The advent of a politics of aging, whereby older people advocated on behalf of older people for the purpose of creating old-age laws, is a phenomenon unique to the United States in this century. While the United States moved from its agrarian roots toward cities and westward expansion, older people, especially the poor, frail, and those unable to compete, relied on the vagarious willingness of their children, neighbors, and local charities to give aid. Poverty among elderly people without those safety nets was widespread, and by the 1930s, old age was synonymous with being poor. There were a few exceptions. Civil War veterans and widows did receive pensions, and some industries such as railroads, provided retirement benefits. But generally, retirees and the elderly were dependent on others.

The Great Depression was a paradigm shift from historical ambivalence toward elders to the rise of social policies for older people. The elderly were most vulnerable to the vagaries of economic dislocation and forced migration and found themselves cast adrift. Older people and middle-class families lost their homes, life savings, and a sense of stability. The radicalization of older people and the subsequent advent of social policies for the elderly took place in the depths of the Great Depression. As early as the 1920s, a group called the Fraternal Order of the Eagles campaigned on behalf of old-age pensions. By the 1930s, others followed that example, especially in areas with a high proportion of retirees (Day, 1990). California was prominent as a place where both individuals and organizations began to use the economic problems of older Americans for political organizing. Upton Sinclair's campaign for governor in 1933, with his "end poverty in California" agenda, rallied retirees with a promise to provide a $50-per-month pension. The Townsend movement in the early 1930s, based in Long Beach, California, gained national notoriety. Dr. Francis Townsend proposed to give people 65 and older $200 a month, on condition that it be spent within 30 days (Williamson et al., 1982). Those and other efforts highlighted the isolation and social vulnerability of older people and gave impetus to President Franklin Roosevelt's proposal for a national social insurance plan. The passage of the Social Security Act of 1935 represented the culmination of historical and demographic forces that gave shape to a social policy predicated, in part, on attaining old age. Paradoxically, the signing of the Social Security Act did not include representatives of the pension movements, whose advocates considered Social Security too tame. In fact, the passage of the Social Security Act had multiple goals: to provide a national safety net, to mitigate radical tendencies, to open up the labor force to younger workers, and to give elderly people some measure of security. For whatever reasons, the stage was set for the philosophical and political acceptance of age as a basis of eligibility in social policies. Older people were then considered the "deserving poor," and political organizing around pensions, as well as national attention to the plight of the elderly, gave impetus to a politics of aging that would shape social policy for the next 60 years.

POLICIES AND PROGRAMS FOR THE ELDERLY

Since the 1930s, a plethora of policies have been created to serve older people and their families. They range from entitlement programs to social services to volunteer and advocacy programs and involve a separate service delivery system for the elderly. Few other constituency groups (with the possible exception of veterans) enjoy such a dedicated set of programs and benefits, and none have policies predicated on age.

Entitlements

Entitlement programs constitute the bedrock of social policies for the elderly. Social Security, Medicare, and Medicaid guarantee access to benefits, depending on eligibility and contributions, and provide a social safety net for most older Americans and their families. Yet, entitlement programs are at the heart of heated political debates about the future of social policies for the elderly.

The Social Security Act of 1935 established the basic federal old-age benefits program and a federal-state system of unemployment insurance (Schulz, 1988). Since its inception, Social Security has come to exemplify a "social contract," whereby older people expect the federal government (and the public) to provide a measure of retirement security in their old age, regardless of economic circumstances. The Social Security Act has evolved and expanded dramatically in subsequent years: In 1939, survivors' and dependents' benefits were added (Old Age and Survivors Insurance). In 1956, Social Security was expanded to include disability insurance to protect severely disabled workers (Old Age, Survivors, and Disability Insurance). In 1965, Medicare was added, establishing a comprehensive health program for the elderly (Old Age, Survivors, Disability, and Health Insurance). Indexing of earnings used to compute benefits was legislated in 1972 (Schulz, 1988).

Today, about 145 million workers and their employers pay taxes on wages. In 1998, the tax rate was 6.2% for workers and 6.2% for employers on salaries up to $68,400, with a Medicare tax of 1.45% paid by workers and employers on all salaried income. The money collected from payroll taxes goes to pay monthly benefits to more than 44 million beneficiaries, including 27.3 million retired workers, 3.4 million dependents of retirees, 4.5 million disabled workers, and 7.2 million survivors of workers ("Americans Discuss Social Security," 1998). In 1997, Social Security paid out about $367 billion in benefits—the largest single federal expenditure, accounting for 20% of the total federal budget ("Americans Discuss Social Security," 1998).

Medicare and Medicaid, both passed in 1965, constitute a national health care system for older people and the poor. Together, they represent the second-largest portion of the federal budget, costing $351 billion in 1996. Medicare is the federal program providing health care insurance for seniors and people with disabilities. Often called Part A, it provides benefits financed by compulsory payroll taxes (1.45% on all income). Medicare covers all people age 65 and older who are eligible for Social Security or Railroad Retirement benefits, are age 65 or older and the spouse or former spouse of an eligible person, have been receiving Social Security disability benefits for at least 2 years, or have end-stage renal (kidney) disease. Supplementary medical insurance, often called Part B, is a voluntary program for non-hospital health care financed by participant premiums ($43.80 per month in 1998) and a matching contribution by the federal government out of general revenue.

Medicaid, enacted in 1965 as Title XIX of the Social Security Act, is a means-tested program for people in need. Medicaid is not limited to older people; rather, it is a state and federally funded program that provides health insurance to people with low-incomes who meet certain eligibility requirements. It pays for health care services deemed "medically necessary," including physician visits, hospital and nursing home care, adult day health services, home health care, and hospice care. Although initially intended for the very poor, regardless of age, Medicaid has become a de facto nursing home and long-term care program for older people who have spent down their assets to qualify. Given the high costs of nursing homes (averaging $30,000 to $40,000 a year), 70% to 80% of the elderly cannot afford to stay in a nursing home (Schulz, 1988). Medicaid will pay for such care when private assets are exhausted. This "spend down" provision has enabled—or forced—middle-income elderly to become impoverished to qualify for Medicaid-financed nursing home care.

By 1996, Medicare was providing health insurance for 38 million people who were elderly or disabled, and Medicaid provided coverage for 36 million low-income people (Pear, 1998). Medicare and Medicaid accounted for one third of national health spending in 1996, making those programs, along with Social Security, an extraordinarily visible segment of national social policy. These entitlement programs affect the lives of most Americans, directly or indirectly, and thus are highly political and personal issues for the elderly, their caregivers, and their families. Medicare and Medicaid also represent an "industrial health complex" that feeds a huge conglomerate of hospitals, nursing homes, medical suppliers, pharmaceutical companies, and health care professionals. Proposals to restructure these programs, then, becomes a matter of great national importance.

Public Benefits and Social Services

Although highly visible, Social Security, Medicare, and Medicaid are not the sole components of social policy for the elderly. A host of public benefits and social services provide crucial support to older people, their families, and caregivers. In particular, two programs have an important impact on the economic and social welfare of the aged. Social Security's Disability Insurance (DI) program and the Supplemental Security Income (SSI) program provide benefits to people who have severe long-term disabilities. The DI program became part of the Social Security Act in 1956. Disability protections under the DI program are provided to disabled insured workers and their dependents, disabled widows and widowers of insured workers, and adult (age 18 or older) sons and daughters who become disabled before age 22 of insured disabled, retired, or deceased workers (Schulz, 1988). The Supplemental Security Income program (SSI), authorized in 1972 under Title XVI of the Social Security Act, provides cash benefits to aged, blind, or disabled individuals whose income and resources are below certain levels. It is administered by the federal government and financed from general revenues. In 1996, SSI and DI together paid about $60 billion annually to 9 million disabled beneficiaries. Another 1.6 million nondisabled dependents of DI beneficiaries also received benefits (GAO, 1996).

The Older Americans Act (OAA) of 1965, as amended, constitutes a small but elaborate set of social and supportive services for the elderly. Unlike entitlement programs, the OAA is administered through a national network of state and local area agencies on aging. The OAA, funded for about $1.2 billion in 1998, authorizes grants to state and community programs for the provision of ombudsman services, legal assistance, housing and transportation services, and employment training, as well as grants to Native American tribes. A popular component of the OAA is support for congregate and home-delivered meals (Meals-on-Wheels). Separate housing and transportation subsidies, albeit small in scale, are provided through the Department of Housing and Urban Development and the Department of Transportation. Taken together, these services enable older people to stay in their homes and communities. The senior citizen centers developed through the OAA provide a social network and focal point for senior citizens to socialize, eat, and receive various forms of assistance. The prevalence of local and state offices on aging gives older people an important infrastructure for advocacy, community organizing, and political visibility.

One more important source of social services for older people is Title XX of the Social Security Act (Social Services Block Grants). In 1974, Title XX was included in the Social Service Amendments to the Social Security Act, and funds are authorized according to the size of state populations (Gelfand, 1988). States, in turn, are required to design their own packages of service and define their eligible populations. Among services for the aging provided by Title XX are adult day care, foster care, homemaker services, and in-home supportive services.

Taken together, these benefits and social services constitute a set of social policies that provide a substantial system of services and programs giving older and disabled people and their families a wide measure of support. State and local governments depend heavily on these federal disbursements to cope with the costs of social services to older people. Although not all of these policies are strictly age-based, older people benefit immeasurably from their status as a deserving group and their ability to confront elected officials when these programs are threatened with cutbacks.

Volunteer, Advocacy, and Projections

Alongside these social supports lies another set of programs and activities that exemplify the success older people have enjoyed in seeking public sympathy and crafting social policies. A host of volunteer programs provide older people with a variety of opportunities to contribute their time and energies to civic activities. The Retired Senior Volunteer Program (RSVP), the Foster Grandparent program, the Senior Companion program, and the Service Corp of Retired Executives (SCORE) enlist and use the talents, experiences, and goodwill of older people who wish to help others. Advocacy by the elderly is encouraged and incorporated in many policies and programs, including the OAA, state Offices on Aging, and national organizations such as the American Association of Retired Persons. Educational programs for older people include gerontology education at the community, college, and university levels and the growing ElderHostel national education program for retirees.

In addition, older people enjoy a variety of legal and civil rights, safeguards, and legal protections. Ageism and fears that people will be discriminated against as they age have led to the passage of laws such as the Age Discrimination Employment Act of 1967. The Act provides protections for people 40 to 70 years of age who are seeking employment. It covers people in the private and nonfederal sectors and has also abolished mandatory retirement for most federal employees. In 1986, amendments to the Act outlawed mandatory retirement at the age of 70.

THE NEW AGING: CHANGES AND PRESSURES ON SOCIAL POLICIES

Given this historical and descriptive overview, what do we make of the constellation of policies and programs for the elderly? What does it tell us about the nature of social policy and politics toward the elderly? What are the factors and forces likely to bring change?

Over the last 60 years, older people have seen the development of an enviable set of benefits, programs, laws, and services. In many ways, social policy for the elderly has been extraordinarily successful. During the Great Depression, poverty rates among the elderly climbed as high as 70%. By 1995, poverty rates for people 65 and older had dropped to 10.5% (American Association of Retired Persons, 1996). Older people have sophisticated lobbies in Washington, D.C., in state capitals, and in their local communities that have given them the ability to promote an expansion of benefits and protect their programs. However, those programs and services, by their very nature, are also a complex, fragmented and increasingly controversial component of social policy. Older people and their families—especially those who are poor, illiterate, and non-English speaking—find it difficult to access the multitude of agencies, eligibility criteria, and forms required to receive services. The proliferation of services and programs has created a vast and unwieldy system. Yet, even with the size and expenditures devoted to programs that benefit older people, directly or indirectly, there are still wide gaps. The elderly, for example, find themselves spending the same proportion of their incomes on health care as was the case before Medicare and Medicaid were enacted (Villers Foundation, 1987). Medicaid, SSI, and Title XX do not provide help to middle-income families struggling with the high costs of social, health, and long-term care. Most individuals and families prefer home- and community-based services to hospital and nursing home care; yet, unless they qualify for Medicaid, they must take care of themselves or do without. In addition, the move toward devolution of federal responsibility to state and local governments has led to the consolidation of social services to include programs for older people, the disabled, and those needing long-term care, and thus the identity of old-age programs has been eroded. The success of social policies predicated on age and geared toward the elderly, then, has sown the seeds of profound changes.

What does all of this say about the nature of policy and politics toward the elderly? Will public attitudes and social policy continue to support existing programs and benefits for the elderly? What are the forces that may change both the public perception of the elderly and the nature of social policies for older people?

Several trends have created a major crossroads in the politics and policies of aging: the demographic imperative, the graying of the federal budget, the aging of the baby boomers, and generational tensions. Together, these trends are leading toward another paradigm shift in social policy and aging, moving us into a new historical period in the politics of aging (Torres-Gil, 1992). The first two historical periods can be characterized as the Young-Aging and the Modern Aging periods. In the Young-Aging period (pre-1930), like much of human history, older people, with some exceptions, did not expect or receive age-based support. With the 1930s came the Modern Aging period, a dramatic growth and acceptance of aged-based social policies. We are now witnessing a move toward a New Aging period. The earlier successes in responding to the needs of older people stemmed from the economic vulnerability that elicited public sympathy. During this period, the 1930s to the 1990s, there was little opposition to or concern about expanding programs for the elderly. Their high propensity to vote and sophisticated lobbying made them a powerful force, alongside other well-known interest groups (e.g., the American Medical Association, the National Rifle Association). By the 1990s, however, public opinion toward older people, their entitlements, and their use of political clout began to show discernible change. This New Aging period and a paradigm shift in social policy will be heavily influenced by three forces: longevity, diversity, and generational claims.

Longevity involves life expectancy and a redefinition of old age. Life expectancy continues to increase. Today, life expectancy at birth is about 76 years, although there continue to be gender and racial differences, with women living longer than men and some racial groups having lower life expectancy. Yet, we can expect longer life expectancy not only at birth but after reaching age 65. The number of centenarians has more than doubled since 1980 (Bureau of the Census, 1996). This increased longevity is altering social views about old age. Sixty-five years of age is no longer considered "old," and we are seeing healthy and active people among those 70 to 80 years of age. In the New Aging period, we will see a trend to alter the years at which one is considered middle aged and old. At the same time, longevity is forcing a rethinking of eligibility ages. If we are living longer and staying healthier, does it still make sense to use age 65 as an eligibility criterion for Medicare and full benefits under Social Security, age 60 to qualify for the Older Americans Act, and age 50 to join the American Association of Retired Persons?

Diversity relates to the tremendous heterogeneity in the American population. Differences involve race, ethnicity, and language, as well as economic disparities and lifestyle choices. The growth of the minority population (e.g., Hispanic, Asian/Pacific Islander, African American, Native American) is well documented. This will mean a much different America in the next century. For example the percentage of non-Hispanic whites may drop from 79.9% in 1980 to 49.9% by 2080 ("Profile of Tomorrow's New U.S.," 1986). The diversification of the United States will also see social and family changes. Women continue to outlive men, and the trends toward fewer children and continued geographic and social mobility will reinforce alternative lifestyles and households. More people will live alone and apart from family members, and three- and four-generation households will also be common. Single-parent families and grandparents caring for grandchildren will abound. The continued prevalence of economic disparities will haunt social policy in the next century. More people will do well, but more families will be poor as well. The baby-boom cohort, for example, although it is a relatively privileged generation socially and economically, has at least 18 million members (out of 75 million) who are considered "at-risk" today because they do not own homes, are single women, or have low-education levels. Thus, in the next century, baby-boomer retirees will be both well-off and poor. Diversity will further complicate how social policy responds to the needs of an aging population.

Generational claims are leading to the more immediate controversies and policy debates. The United States is facing an unprecedented situation involving distinct cohorts of age groups within its population. These generations of individuals, born around the same period and sharing historical events and life-long experiences, also tend to have differing views about the role of government and politics in their lives: The New Deal generation includes today's elderly and the greatest proponents for Social Security and Medicare. The baby-boomer generation has greater antipathy toward big government, big business, and big labor and has greatly influenced popular culture. Generation X (those currently in their teens and 20s) and the baby boomlet cohort (those in the primary and secondary grades) are today's youth and tomorrow's workers. Thus, generational claims will greatly influence social policy and aging, because each cohort may view old age differently and have different views about today's public programs for the elderly. As important, members of each generation must support their elders' retirement through productivity and taxes and prepare for their own aging.

By the 1990s, generational debates became quite visible with fears of "generational warfare" and inequity; new interest groups (e.g., the Concord Coalition, Americans for Generational Equality, the Third Millennium) argued that the elderly were receiving too much and at the expense of younger generations. Propelling these fears was the growing recognition that longevity and the aging of the baby boomers would put unsustainable pressures on public entitlements. The "graying of the federal budget" had become such that, by 1994, one third of the federal budget was expended on benefits to older Americans, even though older people constituted only about 13% of the population. Thus, curtailing the costs of Social Security, Medicare, and Medicaid increasingly consumed the energies of elected officials at the federal and state levels. Generational claims began to exemplify a changing public and political attitude toward the programs of the Modern Aging period and set the stage for what may be major reforms in Social Security and Medicare.

CONTEMPORARY DEBATES AND THE FUTURE OF SOCIAL POLICY

Longevity, diversity, and generational claims are interacting with a host of demographic, social, and political forces to reshape our views of old age, how older people are viewed as a political force, and how to promote social policy for the elderly. These changes are reflected in the policy debates around Social Security and Medicare and give important clues about the future direction of social policy. Social Security continues to enjoy widespread support among all ages and cohorts, but there are growing concerns that it will be unable to pay benefits to future generations of retirees. Although Social Security trust funds held more than $600 billion in U.S. Treasury Bonds in 1998, those surpluses will be insufficient for the baby boomers approaching retirement. By 2013, payments to beneficiaries will no longer equal incoming revenues, and the federal government will have to begin repaying interest and principal on treasury bonds. By 2033, the trust funds will be depleted, and new sources of revenue will be needed, although payroll taxes will still provide 75% of needed revenues at that time. Medicare is also facing severe fiscal problems and is expected to become financially insolvent by 2008. The continuing rise in health care and nursing home costs and the lack of long-term care will be a severe drain on the public and private sectors when baby boomers become old.

The pressures on Social Security and Medicare have led to a host of dramatic proposals to restructure entitlement programs and revise the social contract. For the first time in Social Security's venerable history, bipartisan support is growing for some form of "privatization" of Social Security that includes investing trust funds in the private market and allowing individuals to use part of their payroll taxes for "individual security accounts." The Bipartisan Commission to Reform Medicare is entertaining proposals to raise the eligibility age, impose means-testing, increase premiums, and move beneficiaries into managed care. State and local governments continue to consolidate and merge old-age services into agencies serving multiple populations.

How these proposals and trends eventually unfold is uncertain. What is clear is that public attitudes toward the elderly have changed dramatically. Although the public strongly supports Social Security, Medicare, and most programs for the elderly (especially the poor elderly), younger cohorts increasingly voice skepticism that they will not receive those benefits, and thus they are more open to ideas of privatization. Public and private encouragement to save and prepare for one's own retirement is exemplified in the dramatic growth of 401(k) plans and stock market investments. The vaunted political power of the elderly no longer carries the same collective influence or pressure on politicians. The heyday of senior power may have been the passage and dismissal of the Medicare Catastrophic Coverage Act of 1988 when, within 1 year, the Congress passed and repealed legislation to protect seniors from the high cost of health care at the price of higher premiums for upper-income people. Since then, diversity and a public backlash to the apparent material and economic gains of the elderly has diminished public sympathy for social policies based solely on old age.

What future changes might occur in social policy for the elderly? How might the politics and policies of aging respond to aging in the next century? Any expansion of social policy for the elderly, especially in health and long-term care, may well see the use of need (low income, poverty level), disability (limitations in activities of daily living), and old-old age (75 years and older) as the essential criteria. Programs for the elderly may move toward a merging of social services for people with similar vulnerabilities (e.g., the blind, disabled, homeless). Future cohorts of individuals may, in fact, not want to take advantage of senior citizen programs such as senior citizen centers. Healthy and affluent people in their 70s and 80s will be more interested in recreation and travel within intergenerational groupings.

This somewhat optimistic scenario, however, cannot detract from a possible return to a politics of aging. If younger cohorts are unable to save and invest well for their retirement, if we face economic recession in the early part of the next century, if the stock market should perform badly, and if entitlement programs and social, health, and long-term care services are not available for individuals and families in their old age, we may see a return to renewed political demands by the elderly for expanded benefits and programs.

The future of social policy for the elderly remains unclear, but the history and current programs make for a storied and successful model of interest group lobbying and public response to what have been very real needs of older people. The pressures facing social policies today will force fundamental changes, but the aging of the population and the doubling of older people will ensure that social policy for the elderly and the politics of aging will remain important elements in social welfare policy.

REFERENCES

American Association of Retired Persons. (1996). *A profile of older Americans.* Washington, DC: Author.

Americans Discuss Social Security. (1988). *Making sense of Social Security* (a discussion starter). Washington, DC: Author.

Binstock, R., & Day, C. (1996). Aging and politics. In R. Binstock & L. George (Eds.), *Handbook of aging and the social sciences.* New York: Academic Press.

Bureau of the Census. (1996). 65 + in the United States. In *Current Population Reports, Special Studies,* (pp. 23-190). Washington, DC: Government Printing Office.

Day, C. (1990). *What older Americans think: Interest groups and aging policy.* Princeton, NJ: Princeton University Press.

de Tocqueville, A. (1945). *Democracy in America.* New York: Vintage.

General Accounting Office. (1996, October). *Social security disability: Alternatives would boost cost-effectiveness of continuing disability reviews.* Washington, DC: Author.

Gelfand, D. (1988). *The aging network: Program and services* (3rd ed.). New York: Springer.

Pear, R. (1998, January 13). Spending on health grew slowly in 1996. *The New York Times,* National edition, p. A9.

Profile of tomorrow's new U.S. (1986, November 24). *U.S. News and World Report,* p. 32.

Schulz, J. (1988). *The economics of aging* (4th ed.). Dover, MA: Auburn House.

Torres-Gil, F. (1992). Toward a new politics of aging in America. *In-Depth: A Journal for Values and Public Policy, 2*(3), 37-38.

Villers Foundation. (1987). *On the other side of easy street: Myths and facts about the economics of old age.* Washington, DC: Author.

Williamson, J., Evans, L., & Powell, L. (1982). *The politics of aging: Power and policy.* Springfield, IL: Charles C Thomas.

CHAPTER SIXTEEN

Social Policy and Health Care

J E N N I E   J A C O B S   K R O N E N F E L D

Federal involvement in health is a fairly new occurrence in U.S. history. Although a few laws and special concerns were passed prior to the 20th century, the bulk of the federal legislation that has health impact has been passed since 1900, and most of it has actually been passed in the past 50 or so years. This chapter will first review the history of federal government involvement in health care and health concerns, including a review of some of the major pieces of legislation that affect health: both their historical development and their current features. The next section will discuss the importance in the health care arena of such values as freedom of choice, protection of the private sector, and aversion in the United States to socialized models of health care and rationing of care. The final section will discuss current controversies in the U.S. health care system about how to restructure health care delivery.

REVIEW OF HISTORICAL EVOLUTION OF POLICIES

This section reviews the historical evolution of health care policies in the United States. It outlines developments before and during the Second World War, changes in the role of the federal government during the Kennedy and Johnson administrations, and subsequent changes through the 1980s.

Health Care Policy Through the End of World War II

Neither public health nor health care was an important part of the role of the federal government from the founding of the republic to the time of the Civil War. Most books mark the beginning of federal involvement in health care with the passage of a law in 1798, the Act for the Relief of Sick and Disabled Seamen, which provided health services for this group by imposing a 200-cent per month tax on seamen's wages to pay for their medical care (Kronenfeld & Whicker, 1984; Lee & Benjamin, 1993). Shortly thereafter, arrangements were made to care for sick and disabled seamen in most major coastal seaports, through the building of what later became known as the Merchant Marine hospitals and later the Public Health Service Hospitals.

During and after the Civil War, the role of the federal government in health was only gradually expanded as major changes in the overall involvement of the central government in many activities took place. At other governmental levels, most states began to establish departments of public health, and by 1909, such agencies were established in all the states. Corresponding to this, local health departments also grew in size and responsibility in most areas. In 1902, a separate health act was passed, clarifying federal health functions and recognizing the expansion of the activities of the Marine Hospital Services by renaming it the Public Health and Marine Service of the United States. This Act legitimated the dominant role of the federal government in public health by specifying a system of communications among state and territorial health officers.

One major piece of federal legislation was passed in 1906, the Federal Food and Drug Act. Although the initial legislation was focused more on regulating the adulteration and misbranding of food and drugs with an aim of protecting the pocketbook of consumers as much as their health, this Act became the basis for most of the present-day regulation of testing, marketing, and promotion of both prescription and over-the-counter medications.

Another major piece of legislation was the Maternity and Infancy Act, also known as the Sheppard-Towner Act. This Act was passed in 1921 and provided grants to states to help them develop health services for mothers and their children. This legislation has served as a prototype of federal grants-in-aid programs in health. This Act proved to be quite controversial, generating criticism and opposition from conservative groups and from medical groups such as the American Medical Association (AMA), which openly called the Sheppard-Towner Act "an imported socialistic scheme." Adding to the controversy was the Act's requirement that services provided under its aegis be available for all residents of a state, regardless of race. This particular piece of legislation was allowed to lapse in 1929, although many of the functions of the Act were resumed under the Social Security Act in 1935 (Skocpol, 1992; Wallace, Gold, & Oglesby, 1982).

From the 1930s on, the role of the federal government expanded both generally and in health, first with the Depression, then with World War II, and then gradually with major programs to help support the building of hospitals, the training of health personnel, research into important diseases and health care concerns, and, gradually, the provision of insurance and funds for health care. One of the most important pieces of legislation in this time period was the passage of the Social Security Act of 1935, arguably the most significant piece of domestic legislation related to health passed up to that point in time. It did not include health care services for the elderly, although early drafts of the legislation had included such provisions. They were removed due to the threatened opposition of the AMA. The Act did solidify the principle of federal aid to the states for public health and welfare assistance, as had been started by the Sheppard-Towner Act, and it included federal grants to the state for maternal and child health and crippled children's services (Title V) and for public health (Title VI). The program for crippled children represented a new thrust in federal legislation. Included were demonstration monies that became the foundation of experience for innovative project grant amendments in later legislation.

Consumer protection in the drug arena was further expanded by the passage of the Food, Drug, and Cosmetic Act in 1938. This Act required manufacturers to demonstrate the safety of drugs before marketing them. Other programs of the 1930s and early 1940s included a temporary program instituted during World War II to pay for maternity care of wives of Army and Navy enlisted men. Some experts have concluded that this program was responsible for an improvement in infant and maternal health during World War II. Although the program was discontinued after the war ended, its success became one factor considered in later debates about national health insurance.

One major accomplishment in this era was the beginning of a major role for the federal government in health research. The U.S. Public Health Service Hygienic Laboratory, established in 1901, was converted into the National Institute of Health in 1930 with the passage of the Ransdell Act. This Act, along with the ongoing activities of the laboratory, marked a departure from the originally constricted federal role of providing services to merchant seamen or directly affecting epidemics. With this Act, the federal government edged into general health activities and began a very small role in manpower training (Kronenfeld & Whicker, 1984; Strickland, 1978).

A second act also expanded the federal role in health research. The first categorical institute within the overall NIH framework was created as part of the focus on cancer begun with the passage of the National Cancer Institute Act in 1937 (Raffel, 1980; Strickland, 1978). NCI was authorized to award grants to nongovernmental scientists and institutions, provide fellowships for the training of scientists and clinicians, and fund direct federal government cancer research. Representing a break with tradition, providing federal funds to nongovernmental institutions and scientists became a pattern for all federal support of biomedical research.

A major separate federal involvement in the direct provision of health care services applied to veterans. The Veterans Act of 1924 codified and extended the role of the federal government in the provision of health care services to veterans. That Act extended medical care to veterans not only for treatment of disabilities associated with military service, but also for other conditions requiring hospitalization. Preference was given to veterans who could not afford private care. In 1930, the Veterans' Administration was created as an independent U.S. government agency to help disabled soldiers and handle other veterans' matters such as pensions.

A major piece of legislation, the Public Health Service Act, was passed in 1944 and became the foundation for most public health legislation after World War II, including the large expansion of hospital building funded under the Hill-Burton Amendment. The Hill-Burton Act provided grants to help states to make an inventory of existing hospitals and health centers, to survey the need for the construction of additional health facilities, and, after state surveys were completed, to build new hospitals.

Title IV of the Public Health Service legislation relocated the National Cancer Institute to the Public Health Service, where it became part of the newly created subdivision labeled the National Institutes of Health. The Heart Institute was added as another specific institute in 1946, and now, there are institutes to deal with most major categories of diseases, as well as ones linked to specific segments of life (the National Institute of Aging and the National Institute of Child Health and Human Development) and general medical issues.

Expansion of the Federal Role in Direct Provision of Services During the Kennedy-Johnson Years

Many major federal health policy developments occurred during the Kennedy and Johnson years. The most important was the passage of the Medicare and Medicaid programs as amendments to the Social Security Act. The first amendment increasing the federal role in directly paying for health services was the Kerr-Mills Act in 1960, which established a new program of medical assistance for the aged. Federal aid was given to states to pay for medical care for medically indigent people 65 years of age and older. State participation was optional. The program became the forerunner of Medicaid and was implemented in 25 states before the passage of Medicare and Medicaid.

The Social Security Amendments of 1965 established the Medicare program, the program of national health insurance for the elderly, through a new title, XVIII. It also established a special program of grants to the states for medical assistance to the poor through title XIX (Medicaid).

For the Medicare program, Part A of the title provided basic protection against the cost of hospital and certain post-hospital services. Inpatient hospital services of up to 90 days during any episode of illness, and psychiatric and inpatient services for up to 190 days in a lifetime, were included. Extended care services, such as nursing home care, were covered for up to 100 days during any episode of illness. Some home health services and hospital outpatient diagnostic services were covered initially (and these areas were expanded over time with new amendments). Part B provided supplemental medical insurance benefits and was a voluntary insurance program, financed by premium payments from those enrolled, along with matching payments from general Social Security revenues. Initially, enrollment was very high (over 90%), and now, it is generally above 98%. Physician and related services, such as X-rays, laboratory tests, supplies, and equipment were covered, as were additional home health services. Claims and payment were not handled directly by the Social Security Administration but were paid through fiscal intermediaries such as Blue Cross-Blue Shield in many parts of the country. Institutional providers had to meet conditions of participation, such as utilization reviews, which were aimed at ensuring a minimum quality of service. This program is an important departure from many earlier federal health programs in that it provides direct services to citizens, through a fiscal intermediary, but not through states and localities, as had been the case with many other federal health-related programs. It was consistent with the model of Social Security, however, in which direct payments were sent to individuals from the federal government.

The Medicaid program is more complex in its administrative structure, although it follows a more standard pattern of joint federal-state programs with a matching component in terms of funding. Medicaid was started as a program of medical assistance to public welfare recipients, with participation by any particular state voluntary. Thus, from the beginning, there was variability in coverage and amounts of services funded across the states, as well as in participation.

Under Medicaid, all states were initially required to provide at least five basic services: inpatient hospital care, outpatient hospital services, other laboratory and X-ray services, skilled nursing home services, and physician services. A large number of optional services, such as optometry services, could be made available, along with more essential mental health coverage, ambulance transportation, and dental care.

Health Care Policy Changes From 1968 to 1980

Amendments to the Medicare and Medicaid legislation began only a few years after the initial passage, with many having either the goal of extending the program or amount of services provided or modifying the institutional eligibility requirements and reimbursement schedules. The 1967 amendments featured expanded coverage for durable medical equipment and podiatry, for example. In 1972, new services such as chiropractics and speech pathology were added to Medicare, and family planning services were added to Medicaid. Eligibility was increased by adding to Medicare people who were eligible for cash benefits under the disability provisions of the Social Security Act for at least 24 months. In addition, Medicare services were extended to people who required hemodialysis or renal transplants for chronic renal disease, a program later known as the ESRD (end-stage renal disease) program.

The 1972 amendments were also the first to address the growing costs of the Medicare program by establishment of Professional Standards Review Organizations (PSROs) to address problems of cost, quality case control, and medical necessity of services.

In 1976-1977, a separate agency, the Health Care Financing Administration, was established to assume the primary responsibility for implementing the Medicare and Medicaid programs. Policy changes focused on antifraud and abuse efforts in 1977 and cost control measures in 1978. Details are available from other sources (Kronenfeld, 1997; Longest, 1994). The 1980 Omnibus Budget Reconciliation Act or OBRA '80 included extensive modifications in Medicare and Medicaid, with 57 separate sections, many focused on controlling costs.

Two important programs dealt with education for health professionals and mental health concerns. The Health Professions Educational Assistance Act of 1963 authorized direct federal aid, mostly in the form of construction funds, to medical, dental, pharmacy, and other health professional schools, as well as scholarship and student loan aid to their students. In the mental health area, the 1963 Mental Retardation Facilities and Community Mental Health Centers Construction Act provided assistance through grants for construction of research centers and grants for facilities for the mentally retarded. In addition, assistance was provided for construction of community health centers.

The basic Public Health Service legislation (although passed in 1944) has been amended many times, with new responsibilities added and old ones deleted. Constant shifting and changing of the organizational structure and location of the service has continued from 1967 to the present day, reflecting the crisis-oriented development of health policy in the United States. A typical response to a problem, either new or newly articulated, is to create a new bureau, restructure a bureau, or move a bureau around. Restructuring is further driven by the turnover of presidential administrations and political appointees within the bureaucracy. New administrations enter with fresh ideas about how to reorganize the bureaucracy in what they hope will be a more rational manner. As an example, the 12 years between 1967 and 1979 saw eight major reorganizations of the Public Health Service and related federal health activity. Tracing all of these detailed shifts can become tedious and is well covered in books that focus on this topic (Kronenfeld, 1997; Kronenfeld & Whicker, 1984; Longest, 1994; Raffel, 1980).

The division of the Public Health Service the least affected by organizational relocation and structural turmoil has been the National Institutes of Health. Most of the changes there have been the addition of new functions and new institutes in additional research areas. Although the creation of each new institute has involved the movement of some grants and research away from older institutes, reorganizational shifts have been minimized compared to some of the other divisions. Not totally coincidentally, research promulgated and funded by this division has been regarded as one of the more successful areas of national health policy.

One interesting fact about many of the new programs enacted during this time period is that few, even Medicaid, were directly administered by the federal government. Medicare was one of the very few exceptions. Many of the other programs involved grants to states or to private health-related agencies. Grant-in-aid programs grew during the Johnson administration (excluding Medicare and Social Security) from $7 billion at the beginning of the presidency of John F. Kennedy in 1961 to $24 billion in 1970 (Lee & Benjamin, 1993). These types of programs became the prototypical type of involvement of the federal government in health care. Federal funds for biomedical research, health personnel development, hospital construction, health care financing, and a large range of categorical programs all grew in this time period, which saw an expanding role for the federal government in health care.

CURRENT PROGRAMS AND ADMINISTRATIVE FEATURES

This section reviews how current health care policies developed during the Reagan, Bush, and Clinton administrations.

Reagan Administration Efforts

The series of amendments in Medicare and Medicaid noted above set the stage for the Reagan administration's efforts in health. Reagan pushed for a significant reduction in federal domestic social expenditures, including those on health care. Revenue-sharing funds were eliminated, and block grants were created for what had been many separate category-specific programs (Lee & Benjamin 1993). The Omnibus Budget and Reconciliation Act of 1981 included extensive budget reductions and program revisions for the Public Health Service. One major change was a move away from specific categorical grants dealing with special programs and diseases to the consolidation of these programs under block grants. Budget cuts were included in the block-grant process. Total funding for the programs in each block grant was reduced by 21%. Given inflation, the real size of the cuts was probably closer to 30%.

Concern over rapidly rising costs led to diagnosis-related groups (DRGs), and Medicare payment reform increased the amount of federal regulation of hospitals as a way to control costs, although this was a regulatory solution at odds with much of the philosophical orientation of the Reagan presidency. The new system made payments to hospitals based on predetermined rates per discharge for DRGs as contrasted to the earlier cost-based system of reimbursement.

A recent summary of this system argues that inpatient hospital care use declined initially and then stabilized in 1987 while outpatient hospital care continued to increase, as did costs for physician care (Edwards & Fisher, 1989). Many analysts contend that piecemeal reforms of the health care system generally lead to disappointing results after a few years.

The other major area of reform within the Medicare program has been control of physician costs through a new physician payment program. Although it was begun in 1989, the legislation was implemented in the 1990s. The Health Care Financing Administration was directed to begin implementing a resource-based relative value scale using a system initially developed by Hsiao (Hsiao, Yntema, Braun, & Becker, 1988). Previously, physicians had been paid on the basis of what their charges were for various services. By 1996, payments for family physicians were increased by almost 30%, whereas payments for procedure-oriented specialties dropped a similar amount (McIlrath, 1996). Changes were gradual from 1992 to 1996. The implementation of this new payment program led some physicians to argue that the health care system is becoming increasingly bureaucratic, limiting the options for practice in the name of cost control.

More in line with the overall philosophy of his administration, health planning was eliminated under Reagan. The Omnibus Budget and Reconciliation Act of 1981 also included an elimination of all federal funds for Health Maintenance Organizations (HMOs). All new HMO funds were eliminated in 1982. This may also appear a contradictory move, given the emphasis in the Reagan administration on a pro-competition model of health care. The stance of the Reagan administration, however, was that federal funds were unnecessary to stimulate competition and that private market forces would be sufficient to facilitate HMO growth. Renamed and broadened to managed care, growth in this type of organization has continued, accelerating in the second half of the Clinton years.

Implications of Changes During the Reagan-Bush Administrations

The period from 1969 until the present has been an era of controversy regarding the appropriate role of the federal government in health care. This was especially true during the Bush presidency and Clinton's first term due to the pressure of the growing federal debt and the need to constrain growth in all government programs, including health care. The conflict included more than Medicare and Medicaid. The federal role in funding training and development of health professionals grew from a minuscule one to a substantially greater effort by the late 1970s. Expansion of the federal role ended and substantial retrenchment began with the Reagan administration.

The amendments to the Public Health Service Act again illustrate the turmoil and rapid changes that have occurred at times in both health legislation and health agency structure. Instability has undercut the development of a coherent and chronologically consistent federal policy. Often, shifts in administration, as with the shift to the Reagan administration, have changed the role of the federal government vis-à-vis states, local governments, and private health-related organizations. During the 1980s, the federal government moved, in a relatively short time span, from providing HMOs with financial and organizational assistance to a more neutral role in terms of actual support even though the approach was still viewed positively by many in important health policy positions within the administration. Whereas the federal categorical grant programs had encouraged local health departments to develop a multitude of specialized and separately organized programs, often independent of the state health department, the block grant procedure forced local health departments to work through their state units and encouraged consolidation rather than separation of program functions. These federally required and rapid shifts in program focus and in state-local relationships have been deleterious to ongoing continuity in agencies and to smooth administrative functioning. Chaotic federal changes have led to a public perception that state and local health officials are ineffective managers. In reality, the atmosphere of chaotic changes and crisis development of policy is federal in origin.

Clinton Achievements and Failures

Clinton was elected to his first term as President in November, 1992 and started a discussion of health care reform with a goal of improving access to health care for all while containing costs. To accomplish this, a special task force was created. Although the creation of such a task force could have been productive, most experts now agree that the task force became problematic, with the attempt at openness and discussion backfiring (Blendon, Brodie, & Benson, 1995; Kronenfeld, 1997; Starr, 1994). The public became confused, the initial momentum needed to push reform was lost, and negative ads by some interest groups further lowered the chances of the reform plan passing (Johnson & Broder, 1996).

Although major health care reform did not pass, some new legislation has been passed in the 1990s. A new commission has been formed to deal with border health issues, and a Freedom of Access to Clinic Entrances law was passed for abortion clinics. Definitions of dietary supplements were clarified by new legislation, and small changes in Medicare and Medicaid (often clarifying benefits and improving fraud control efforts) have been passed. Federal health, primary care, and prevention programs were consolidated by a new Health Centers Act in 1996. The Ryan White Act, which deals with AIDS, has been expanded. Minor improvements in access were passed, one requiring that annual lifetime caps on mental health benefits be the same as those for physical illness. Another prohibited employers who offer health insurance from excluding an employee because that person has very high health care expenses and removes the limitations on pre-existing conditions when people switch jobs and therefore health insurance. Most important, some of the public's concerns about the growth of managed care, which followed the failure of major health care reform, were covered under a bill that required health insurance companies to allow overnight hospital stays for maternity visits.

One of the trends in U.S. health care today is the growth of managed care in all parts of the country. Terms are not always clear in the HMO-managed care areas, but managed care is a broader term that covers point-of-enrollment plans and preferred provider plans. This includes the switch of many state Medicaid programs to a managed care approach and the encouragement of managed care within the Medicare program. About two thirds of all households are now enrolled in managed care plans under this broadened definition, versus only 39% in 1994 (Jensen, 1996). Consumer satisfaction has been declining, however. Consumers are concerned about care that is denied, inability to see specialists, and limitations on certain drugs. This chapter will return to the issue of managed care in the next sections.

State Child Health Insurance Program (CHIP)

The largest expansion of health coverage since the passage of Medicare and Medicaid in 1965 is the State Child Health Insurance Program, created by the Balanced Budget Act of 1997. Over a span of 5 years, beginning in Fiscal Year 1998, $24 billion will become available to cover health care for children. Some sources estimate that free or low-cost health insurance may become available to up to half of the nation's children (Kilborn, 1997). As with Medicaid, this is a joint federal-state program, and states have several options as to how to implement the plan. Some will do so by adding more children to Medicaid, mostly those whose families earn too much to qualify for cash welfare benefits. Gradually, states can add children whose families earn up to 300% of the federal poverty level. States can also require children to enter their managed care plans or set up special programs. States must first develop an implementation plan and have it approved by the federal government. As of fall 1998, all states except Washington and Wyoming had developed or were in the process of developing plans. About 20 states plan to expand Medicaid, 14 are developing new programs, and most of the others are combining the two approaches. The ultimate success of the program will depend both on specifics designed by states and on implementation issues. Recent studies have indicated that as many as 4.7 million children are eligible for current Medicaid but are not enrolled (Aston, 1998; Reschovsky & Cunningham, 1998).

POLITICAL, SOCIAL, AND ECONOMIC FACTORS THAT INFLUENCE HEALTH CARE

Many different types of factors influence the organization of health care in the United States. Health care policy is part of broad social policy, and the overall beliefs of the country are reflected in its health care system. In the past, certain values have been central to the health care system. These have included a right to choose the provider, a basic principle in the early Medicare legislation; protection of the private sector; and an aversion to "socialized" models of care and the concept of rationing of care, such as programs in countries like Great Britain. Another important value in the United States has been an emphasis on technology.

As discussed in more detail in the next section, the growth of managed care has already changed the concept of the right to choose a provider; other new factors include the changing importance of employment-based insurance and the push by employers to limit their costs for health insurance. Many employers now offer only one plan, and many of these plans limit choice of provider. These trends have not led to elimination of the private sector, and, in fact, the past decade has seen a growth of for-profit companies in the HMO field and in the hospital field. Except for physicians, the private sector continues to be protected. Some experts think that by 2020, a majority of physicians will work for groups, rather than being self-employed as most physicians were in 1950. This is one area in which the U.S. health care system is currently evolving.

Given the basic ideological orientation of the United States toward capitalism, as well as the greater U.S. emphasis on the independent role of local and state governmental units, an effort to avoid a centralized or government-controlled medical care system is not surprising. Unlike other countries with capitalist economies, all of which have some form of comprehensive universal health insurance, the United States has not seen this as a value for most of the last half-century. Similarly, rationing as a way to allocate limited resources is not a popular idea in the United States. Instead of explicit rationing, the allocation of health care resources relies on implicit rationing, which includes allocation of services on the basis of the possession of health insurance, a good job (with health insurance), and income and its ability to purchase non-insurance supported care.

Last, the United States has long been a culture enamored of new technology in many areas. This is also true of health care. The United States has the most technologically sophisticated health care, and this is widely available rather than carefully controlled. Whether the U.S. health care system of the future will continue to reflect high technology is not clear. One way to control costs is to limit access to the most expensive technology, and this is an unsolved dilemma in the U.S. health care system.

CURRENT CONTROVERSIES: ACCESS, MANAGED CARE, HOSPITALS, MEDICARE, AND MEDICAID

What is likely to happen to the U.S. health care system in the future, given the failure of the most recent attempt at major health care reform under the Clinton administration, and what will be the federal role? Most of the major problems of the health care system that were discussed in 1992, at the beginning of the debate about major health care reform, still remain at the end of the 1990s. Small incremental reforms have been passed, of which the child health provisions may have the largest impact on access to care, but major overall reform or restructuring of the U.S. health care system has not occurred. Some reports indicate that more adults are lacking health insurance. The failure to pass reform legislation has not caused major problems to disappear. Access to health care is still a major issue, fears of increased costs abound, and problems in funding of Medicare and Medicaid are real.

Given the presence of divided government for the second Clinton term (one party in the White House, another controlling at least one branch of Congress), most experts have not expected major federally led changes in health care, with the exception of some attention to the issue of the Medicare trust fund. Given the Monica Lewinsky scandal and the attention that it diverted from other congressional business, few health issues were addressed in 1998, even those that experts felt in January were almost certain of passage, such as legislation to deal with consumer concerns about HMOs. Some experts believe that we are beginning to observe major restructuring, led not by federal legislation but by reaction to the need to cut costs and control growth. Relationships in the health care market are in the midst of major changes. Competitive market forces are dominating the system. Two important aspects of this restructuring are growth of HMOs and managed care and the emergence of new organizational structures among physicians, hospitals, and insurers, resulting in a redefinition of the role of the hospital ("Complexity Defines," 1996).

Many experts agree that "health policy in the United States is increasingly focusing, either by design or by default, on managed care as a means of controlling costs" (Luft & Greenlick, 1996, p. 445). Although at their best, HMOs can foster preventive care and apply a population-based epidemiological approach to determining use of health care, much of the literature on the benefits only applies to older, group-model HMOs, not the newer forms of managed care (Luft & Greenlick, 1996). It is unclear to what extent many of the cost savings of HMOs were linked to specific historical and environmental factors and thus may not apply to newer HMOs based on less sharply defined models in different kinds of health care environments. Connected to this issue is the growth of concern by the public about limitations on care, denied hospital and other coverages, and restrictions placed on physicians. Federal legislation was passed to restore the option of in-hospital stays for normal deliveries. Legislation on gag rules for physicians (rules that limit what physicians are allowed to tell their patients in HMOs about alternative treatments not typically supported by the HMO) had been expected to pass, as well as a law dealing with restrictions on hospitalization for breast cancer surgery (McIlrath, 1996). This did not occur before the 1998 congressional elections. Recent books by journalists have stressed the concerns about quality of care in HMOs and argued that managed care works only for people who need routine care and checkups, not for those with serious or chronic illnesses (Anders, 1996). It is ironic that the fears some Americans had of the proposed Clinton health plan (forcing consumers into alliances and HMO-type models, severing the pre-existing relationships between patients and doctors) are now occurring as part of the growth of managed care.

Managed competition, or the idea that within each market, networks with different and distinct organizational cultures and internal cultures would form and compete, is becoming the new organizational structure of the future, including major questioning of the hospital's role in the new health care system ("Complexity Defines," 1996). Most observers agree that the acute care hospital is undergoing a process of rapid, fundamental change (Cassil, 1996; Robinson, 1994; Shortell, Gillies, & Denvers, 1995; Stoeckle, 1995). Hospital occupancy rates are down in most parts of the country, hospitals are not staffing their facilities to serve the maximum number of beds, and most facilities are diversifying into ambulatory diagnostic and surgery centers. But this change is not government-driven but rather the workings of the marketplace. In the real world of health care delivery today, some of the best assumptions of managed competition (that consumers would be able to recognize the differences between plans and make plan selections based on comparative value) may not hold. Some experts argue that the structure of the market does not encourage consumer choice because of the paucity of purchasing coalitions for small employers and the lack of standardized benefits, as well as the lack of options that employers provide to employees ("Complexity Defines," 1996). Shortell, Gillies, and Anderson (1994) argue that a reinvention process will be necessary for the community hospital, and that this process will be to make itself more invisible, hidden within the context of an integrated health system operating as part of a community care network.

As much as some experts believe that the next half-decade or decade will focus on nongovernmental actions, some pressures from within the federal government will also drive health care policy. One subject of continuing government consideration is the Medicare program. Medicare finances health care now for 38 million elderly or disabled Americans. The trust fund that pays for hospital care, financed out of a fixed payroll tax, will run out of money in the next few years if no further changes in the program occur. The doctor trust fund is set up differently and has unlimited access to the federal Treasury's general revenue, as well as receiving funds from Medicare recipients in the form of premiums paid each month. Medicare is not only large, but it has become central to budget negotiations over the last decade because it is growing faster than other parts of government. Something will have to occur, and fixing Medicare is likely to be a major topic of debate, if not by the end of the Clinton administration, then in the next decade. Although one of the short-term ways to deal with the program is to cut Medicare spending, it is not clear that this is a politically acceptable solution. Congress could freeze Medicare payments to hospitals and doctors, but this also has limitations.

Medicaid presents other complex issues, especially with the welfare reform legislation passed in 1996. Some see that legislation as the first wave of a movement called devolution or new federalism, which provides states with more flexibility in how welfare-related programs work and how much they are funded. Clinton was able to preserve most of the Medicaid program as a federal guarantee in 1996. However, some experts predict that Republicans will call for deeper tax and program cuts in the future, although the Children's Health Insurance Program represents an increase in services to some of the near poor (Stevenson, 1997; Verhovek, 1997).

Several different health policy experts have argued that the current situation features special contradictions. Employers of all sizes have reduced the choice of health care plans available to their workers. Traditional fee-for-service medicine is on the decline, but now due to marketplace impetus rather than government manipulation. One health policy expert argues that "what we're getting is managed care but without the consumer protection and patients' rights that people have a right to expect" (Starr, cited in Toner, 1996, p. 3). Drew Altman, president of the Kaiser Foundation, states "there are a lot of people out there who feel, or should feel, that they fought off the government monster only to find themselves faced with changes in the marketplace that they care about a lot more" (Altman, cited in Toner, 1996, p. 3).

This section has mentioned some current trends in managed care and competition, the formation of integrated systems of care, and Medicare problems. None of these trends or solutions will resolve one of the major concerns that began the health care reform debate in 1992, problems of access to care. Whether these trends will even hold down rising costs in health care is unclear. In Medicare, the aging of the population and the growth in the number of the elderly insured by Medicare will represent a major pressure point on the health care delivery system, even if some short-term reforms in Medicare financing occur. Some of those reforms (limitations on payments to hospitals and HMOs) may cause financial and thus perhaps quality problems in the newly emerging managed competition approach. Where do these trends leave government, and what is its role in the future U.S. health care delivery system? The presidential election of 2000 will help to answer this question.

REFERENCES

Anders, G. (1996). *Health against wealth*. Boston: Houghton Mifflin.

Aston, G. (1998, June 5). Getting insurance for kids. *American Medical News*, pp. 5-6.

Blendon, R. J., Brodie, M., & Benson, J. (1995). What happened to Americans' support for the Clinton health plan? *Health Affairs, 14*, 7-23.

Cassil, A. (1996, November 11). Hospitals can expect anything but status quo. *AHA News*, p. 1.

Complexity defines relationships in increasingly competitive marketplaces. (1996, November). In *Health care financing and organization news and progress* (pp. 1-4). Washington, DC: Alpha Center.

Edwards, W. O., & Fisher, C. R. (1989). Medicare physician and hospital utilization and expenditure trends. *Health Care Financing Review, 11*, 111-116.

Hsiao, W. C., Yntema, D. B., Braun, P., & Becker, E. (1988). Resource based relative values: An overview. *Journal of the American Medical Association, 260*, 2347-2353.

Jensen, J. (1996, October 7). HMO satisfaction slipping. *Modern Healthcare*, pp. 86-88.

Johnson, H., & Broder, D. S. (1996). *The system: The American way of politics at the breaking point*. Boston: Little, Brown.

Kilborn, P. T. (1997, September 21). States to provide health insurance to more children. *The New York Times*, pp. 1, 22.

Kronenfeld, J. J. (1997). *The changing federal role in U.S. health care policy*. Westport, CT: Praeger.

Kronenfeld, J. J., & Whicker, M. L. (1984). *U.S. national health policy: An analysis of the federal role*. New York: Praeger.

Lee, P. R., & Benjamin, A. E. (1993). Health policy and the politics of health care. In S. J. Williams & P. R. Torrens (Eds.), *Introduction to health services* (4th ed.). Albany, NY: Delmar.

Longest, B. B., Jr. (1994). *Health policymaking in the United States*. Ann Arbor, MI: AUPHA Press.

Luft, H. S., & Greenlick, M. R. (1996). The contribution of group and staff-model HMOs to American medicine. *Milbank Quarterly, 74*, 445-467.

McIlrath, S. (1996, December). HCFA issues final RBRVS rules. *American Medical News*, pp. 1, 26-47.

Raffel, M. W. (1980). *The U.S. health system: Origins and functions*. New York: John Wiley.

Reschovsky, J. D., & Cunningham, P. J. (1998, August). CHIPing away at the problem of uninsured children. *Issue Brief, Center for Health System Change*, No. 14, pp. 1-4.

Robinson, J. C. (1994). The changing boundaries of the American hospital. *The Milbank Quarterly, 72*, 259-268.

Shortell, S. M., Gillies, R. R., & Anderson, D. (1994). The new world of managed care: Creating organized delivery systems. *Health Affairs, 13*, 46-64.

Shortell, S. M., Gillies, R. R., & Denvers, K. J. (1995). Reinventing the American hospital. *The Milbank Quarterly, 73*, 131-160.

Skocpol, T. (1992). *Protecting soldiers and mothers: The political origins of social policy in the United States*. Cambridge, MA: Harvard University Press.

Starr, P. (1994). *The logic of health care reform*. New York: Penguin.

Stevenson, R. W. (1997, January 12). Sharp differences and compromise are likely on budget. *The New York Times*, p. 12.

Stoeckle, J. D. (1995). The citadel cannot hold: Technologies go outside the hospital, patients and doctors too. *The Milbank Quarterly, 73*, 131-160.

Strickland, S. (1978). *Research and the health of Americans: Improving the public policy process*. Lexington, MA: Lexington Books.

Toner, R. (1996, November 24). Harry and Louise were right, sort of. *The New York Times*, Section 4, Editorials and Op-ed, pp. 1, 3.

Verhovek, S. H. (1997, January 12). Legislators meet, surprised at limit on shift of power. *The New York Times*, pp. 1, 12.

Wallace, H., Gold, E. M., & Oglesby, A. C. (1982). *Maternal and child health practices: Problems, resources, and methods of delivery* (2nd ed.). New York: John Wiley.

CHAPTER SEVENTEEN

Housing Policy

KEVIN FOX GOTHAM

JAMES D. WRIGHT

The history of federal housing policy in the United States is much more than a history of government programs pertaining to physical shelter, real estate, and home
building. As the famous poet Robert Frost once remarked, "home is the place where,
when you have to go there, they have to let you in" (Jackson, 1985, p. 73). As Frost
recognized, housing is not just a dwelling and a place to live; it is a symbol of personal
worth, social status, and security. The selection of a home represents the selection of a
neighborhood, which, in turn, can influence the nature of one's friends and styles of
social interaction with them. In addition to lifestyle and social status, housing and
neighborhood heavily influence the types and kinds of jobs and cultural amenities to
which one has access. Moreover, housing and neighborhood not only determine the
quality of schools children attend but the quality of other public services including fire
and police protection, parks and recreation, and transportation. As many scholars
have recognized, housing policy affects a broad range of public and private activities
including housing availability, affordability, quality, real estate and banking activities,
taxation policy, local building codes and zoning, subdivision regulations, and insurance laws (Bratt, Hartman, & Meyerson, 1986; Logan & Molotch, 1987; Squires,
1993). Indeed, in the case of housing policy, it is important to understand just how the
programmatic orientation of federal housing policy plays a crucial role in structuring
market relations and reinforcing the trajectories of social inequality, including uneven
metropolitan development, homelessness, and poverty.

The institutional structure of housing and housing policy is an underresearched component of social stratification and inequality. This is a significant omission given that housing is the average household's single largest expenditure and asset. As a key source of investment for many American families, housing represents the most visible insignia of social rank and prestige that people present to the larger world. Moreover, housing is the physical entity that defines families, which are, in turn, the most basic unit of society. In addition, housing reflects and reinforces the polarization of race and social class in the larger society, a process that few scholars acknowledge in empirical studies on the causes and consequences of social stratification. As the gap between the haves and the have-nots continues to widen in the United States, racial minorities and the poor will likely face a higher incidence of poor physical conditions, overcrowding, and severe housing cost burdens. Recent years have witnessed a sharp increase in the number of working poor families needing housing assistance at the same time that federal aid has declined (U.S. Department of Housing and Urban Development, 1998). Yet, racial minorities and the poor face more than a higher rate of unaffordable, dilapidated, and overcrowded housing. Housing patterns tend to reinforce the segregation of classes and races, which simultaneously perpetuates educational segregation and impedes access to employment opportunities and upward mobility for disadvantaged groups. In this way, housing expresses and perpetuates the stratification of classes and races that exists within the society as a whole.

This chapter is organized into four sections. We begin by examining the historical development of federal housing policy from the 1930s through the 1970s. We focus on the origin of New Deal housing programs, including the creation of the Federal Housing Administration (FHA) through the Housing Act of 1934 and the beginnings of public housing via the Housing Act of 1937. Our historical narrative then traces the development of federal housing policies and programs through the immediate post-World War II era. We focus on the 1949 Housing Act, which promised a "decent home and suitable living environment" for all citizens and embraced other policy initiatives pertaining to public housing and suburban home building. Next, we explore the creation of the cabinet-level Department of Housing and Urban Development (HUD) in 1965; passage of the Housing Act of 1968, which established the Section 235 and Section 236 programs; and President Nixon's 1973 moratorium on public housing construction and housing subsidies.

In the second section of the chapter, we examine legislative and administrative arrangements pertaining to housing policy from the 1970s to the present. The centerpiece of all federal housing policy since the 1970s has been retrenchment, privatization, and devolution of authority, responsibility, and funds from the federal government to state governments and, then, to local municipalities. We examine the content, evolution, and significance of the Section 8 program, the 1987 McKinney Homeless Assistance Act, the 1990 Cranston-Gonzalez National Affordable Housing

Act, the 1992 Housing and Community Development Act, and other housing-related programs.

The third section of the chapter explores the major population and demographic trends affecting the formulation and implementation of federal housing policy. First, we examine the impact of increasing poverty and homelessness, abandonment, and escalating housing costs on housing policy. Second, we investigate the impact of racial discrimination and residential segregation on federal housing policy. Third, we examine the consequences of the federal government's heavy reliance on the private sector to address housing problems.

The last section and conclusion explore some of the major issues arising from our descriptive account. We examine recent programmatic developments on the federal level, the implications of current policy trends, and future directions in housing policy. Our discussion addresses two major questions: First, can increasing housing mobility through the Section 8 housing voucher program be an effective anti-poverty strategy? Second, what are the current policy concerns surrounding public housing (e.g., tenant self-management and the recent emphasis on mixed-use and mixed-income residents)? In conclusion, we address the limitations of market-centered strategies and discuss policy recommendations for meeting the housing needs of U.S. citizens.

HISTORICAL REVIEW OF FEDERAL HOUSING POLICY, 1930s-1970s

The Housing Acts of 1934 and 1937 marked the beginnings of federal involvement in housing and finance markets, subsidizing suburban development, and policy formulation. The Housing Act of 1934 created the FHA and provided mortgage insurance guarantees to encourage banks to make loans for single-family homes for middle-income people. Designed and run by representatives of the real estate and banking industries, the FHA was created to salvage the home-building and finance industries, which had collapsed in the early years of the Great Depression (Checkoway, 1984; Weiss, 1987, Chapter 6). The FHA, and later the Veterans Administration (created in 1944), lowered down payments on homes from 30% to less than 10%, established minimum standards for home construction, and eliminated lending institutions' risk in providing mortgage financing by lowering interest rates (FHA, 1959; Radford, 1996, pp. 179-180).

During the 1930s, the FHA, along with the Federal Home Loan Bank Board and the Home Owners Loan Corporation, introduced the long-term, self-amortizing mortgage with uniform payments spread over the life of the housing debt, as well as extended national appraisal norms and training to realtors, builders, developers, and banks throughout the United States (Jackson, 1980, 1985; Mitchell, 1985). The effect of this new mortgage system was to fully amortize all home loans and reduce the average monthly payment, thereby substantially increasing the number of families who could buy a home. As a result of the FHA's home-building and home-ownership subsidies, housing starts rose from 93,000 in 1933 to 332,000 by 1937, to 619,000 per year by 1941. After World War II, the numbers increased substantially, and by 1972, the FHA had helped 11 million families become homeowners (Jackson, 1985, p. 205). Indeed, from the 1930s to 1959, the FHA (1959) proudly proclaimed that it had financed three out of every five homes purchased in the United States. Thus, the long-term effect of the establishment of the FHA and the modern mortgage system was to transform a nation of renters (52% of the population) before the 1930s into a nation of homeowners (65%) by the mid-1980s (Bartelt, 1993).

The 1937 Housing Act established the public housing program to provide rental units to low-income households through local public housing authorities (McDonnell, 1957; Quercia & Galster, 1997). The 1937 Act decentralized the administration of public housing and empowered local communities to create local housing authorities with the legal power of eminent domain to acquire privately owned land for slum clearance and rehousing (Bauman, 1987; Hoffman, 1996; Jackson, 1985; Marcuse, 1986). Interestingly, public housing was originally conceived as temporary way station for working-class families on the road to upward mobility and home ownership (Bauman, 1987). However, following World War II, population and demographic changes affecting the United States and opposition from real estate interests gradually transformed public housing into modern-day asylums for the poorest of the urban poor (Bauman, Hummon, & Muller, 1991; Gelfand, 1975; Hoffman, 1996; Keith, 1973). Real estate and building interest groups such as the National Association of Home Builders and the National Association of Real Estate Boards successfully lobbied Congress to impose budget cuts on public housing from the 1930s onward, and production was curtailed throughout the ensuing decades (Bratt, 1986; Hays, 1985). Moreover, local officials and real estate interests in many cities prevailed in getting public housing located away from affluent white neighborhoods and built near poor and deteriorating areas of the inner city (Henderson, 1995; Hirsch, 1983; Kirp, Dwyer, & Rosenthal, 1995).

The decentralized nature of public housing coupled with the tendency to segregate public housing tenants by race also served to reinforce racial residential segregation and concentrate poor minorities, especially African Americans, in central cities throughout the United States. Up to 1964, almost all housing authorities segregated their public housing residents by race. Although Title VI of the Civil Rights Act of 1964 banned discrimination in housing receiving federal assistance, programmatic changes in public housing tenant selection during the 1960s reinforced racial segregation in public housing. Many cities adopted a "freedom of choice" tenant selection policy that allowed prospective tenants to choose among housing projects when an opening became available. However, in direct violation of federal law, many housing authorities maintained a separate waiting list for each project and refused to take affirmative steps to undo segregation in their projects. The segregating impact of public housing was reinforced by the passage of the Brooke Amendments in 1969, 1970, and 1971, which capped public housing rental costs at 25% of income and opened up admission to welfare recipients. Although the purpose of the Brooke Amendments was to open public housing to more poor families, the legislation also reduced the amount of funds available for maintenance and upkeep. Caught between increasing costs and declining rents, the public housing stock deteriorated rapidly, projecting an image of social disaster and impoverishment.

By the 1970s, public housing was being criticized by scholars for creating "vertical ghettos," concentrating poverty, and reinforcing the chasm between the predominantly white suburbs and the increasing black inner city—an image that Reynolds Farley and associates referred to as "Chocolate City, Vanilla Suburbs" (Farley, Schuman, Bianchi, Colasanto, & Hatchett, 1978). From 1944 to 1951, nonwhite families represented between 26% and 39% of all public housing tenants. This percentage increased substantially over the decades that followed. In fact, by 1978, over 60% of the residents of public housing were African Americans (Bratt, 1986). Recent research suggests that despite a modest decline in racial segregation in public housing since the 1970s, the majority of African American public housing residents live in poor, racially isolated neighborhoods whereas white tenants typically live in less isolated neighborhoods (Goering, Kamely, & Richardson, 1997). Today, for family public housing projects, the typical African American family household lives in a project that is 85% African American with 80% of the tenants below the federal poverty level. In contrast, the typical white family household lives in a project that is 60% white with 74% of the tenants below the poverty level (Goering et al., 1997). Empirical research by Massey and Denton (1993), Goering et al. (1997), and Wright, Rubin, and Devine (1998) suggest that the pattern of racial isolation in public housing exacerbates residential segregation and the concentration of the disadvantage in adjacent neighborhoods. These and other findings corroborate recent research showing that racial segregation in housing is fundamental to the structuring of market relations and patterns of capitalist investment and disinvestment that have created the class and racial geography of American metropolitan areas (Massey & Denton, 1993; Wright et al., 1998).

The FHA's housing subsidies, which were established during the 1930s, also had a major impact on post-World War II migrations of middle-income whites to suburban areas and the concentration of low-income, mostly African American families, in deteriorating inner cities. Racial minorities, especially African Americans, were officially excluded from FHA subsidies and segregated by the agency's refusal to underwrite mortgages in predominantly minority areas (Myrdal, 1944). From the 1930s through the 1950s, the FHA's underwriting manuals considered African Americans to be "adverse influences" on property values and warned against the "infiltration of inharmonious racial or nationality groups" in racially homogeneous all-white neigh-borhoods (FHA, 1936, 1952). The FHA alerted land developers and realtors that "if a neighborhood is to retain stability it is necessary that properties shall continue to be occupied by the same social and racial classes. A change in social or racial occupancy generally leads to instability and a reduction in values" (FHA, 1936, p. 233).

Local and national real estate boards followed the lead of the FHA in adopting a code of ethics stating that "a Realtor should never be instrumental in introducing into a neighborhood . . . members of any race or nationality . . . whose presence will clearly be detrimental to property values in that neighborhood" (Helper, 1969, p. 201). Agency officials, realtors, land developers, banks, and appraisers all embraced the be-lief that the highest appraisal value goes to homes in all-white neighborhoods, with lesser values to homes in racially mixed neighborhoods, and still lesser values in all-black neighborhoods. Although the FHA's underwriting manual was revised in the 1950s and 1960s to delete explicit reference to racial groups, the agency continued to trumpet the merits and necessity of maintaining and creating racially homogeneous neighborhoods (Abrams, 1965; FHA, 1952, 1959; Massey & Denton, 1993). As a re-sult, the housing policies and practices of the FHA influenced lending and home mortgage financing decades after the Second World War, thus subsidizing suburban housing construction, contributing to and exacerbating neighborhood deterioration in inner cities, and institutionalizing a racially segregated housing market on a na-tional scale (Oliver & Shapiro, 1995; Squires, 1993; Weiss, 1987).

The Housing Act of 1949 promised a "decent home and suitable living environ-ment for every American family." The Act authorized construction of 810,000 public housing units over the next 6 years and provided the legal regulations (eminent do-main) and funding for large-scale slum clearance through the new urban renewal pro-gram (Hoffman, 1996; Weiss, 1980). Urban renewal used the model of federal fund-ing and local decision-making provided in the 1937 Housing Act, and it empowered localities to create urban renewal authorities to designate and clear "blighted" areas (Gelfand, 1975; Wilson, 1966). The Housing Act of 1954 broadened the urban re-newal program, increased funding for FHA home-financing activities, and estab-lished the first specific housing for elderly citizens through the public housing pro-gram. Due to opposition from the real estate industry and conservative members of Congress, public housing never came close to the construction levels provided in 1949 (810,000 units). By 1960, only 250,000 units had been made available, and by 1979, only about 1 million total units had been built across the nation (Mitchell, 1985). The urban renewal program destroyed thousands more units than it replaced and became the target of intense civil rights protest from leaders who labeled it "black removal" due to the large number of African American residents and neighborhoods cleared under the guise of urban renewal (Bayor, 1989; Gans, 1962; Jacobs, 1961; Kleniewski, 1984; Weiss, 1980).

Three major programmatic developments in the 1960s transformed the role of federal involvement in housing and the implementation of housing policy. First, HUD was established in 1965 to coordinate and streamline the federal government's housing-related activities and programs. HUD was designed to replace the old Housing and Home Finance Agency, which had been the umbrella of all federal housing agencies and programs since World War II. Second, the passage of Title VIII of the Civil Rights Act of 1968 established the national goal of fair housing and provided the first administrative mechanisms to combat housing discrimination through litigation.

Third, the 1949 goal of a "decent home" for every American family was reaffirmed in the Housing Act of 1968 (Keith, 1973, pp. 165-167). Praised as a solution to the urban riots and housing shortages plaguing the nation, the 1968 Act signaled the beginnings of a long-term shift in federal housing policy away from dispensing aid to local housing authorities for building public housing to providing direct supply-side subsidies to the private sector to stimulate homeownership for the poor (Bratt & Keating, 1993; Hays, 1985; Mitchell, 1985; Schafer & Field, 1973). The 1968 Act directed the FHA to relax standards so that the poor could obtain mortgages for homeownership (e.g., the Section 235 program) or rent subsidies (e.g., the Section 236 program), allowing them to move into affordable apartments rather than public housing. After decades of underwriting mortgages for middle-income, mostly white families in the suburbs, the FHA was required by the 1968 Act to shoulder the risk of making loans to money lenders in inner-city areas. The homeownership provision provided lending institutions with mortgage insurance and reduced the homeowners' housing costs by making payments directly to the lenders on behalf of the owners (Hays, 1985). The newly created Government National Mortgage Association (Ginnie Mae) was the conduit for the housing subsidy, whereas the Federal National Mortgage Association (Fannie Mae) was to provide a secondary market for the federally insured mortgages (Bratt & Keating, 1993; Hays, 1985). The 1968 Housing Act programs were designed to attract private lenders and developers to participate in supplying low-cost housing for poor people. However, reports of scandals in the programs provided the impetus for the discontinuation of the housing subsidy programs and the decision by the Nixon administration to impose a moratorium on all federally subsidized and public housing construction in 1973.

FEDERAL HOUSING POLICY SINCE THE 1970s

Shrinking federal housing resources, declining supplies of public housing units as a result of demolition, lax enforcement of fair housing and anti-discrimination statutes, and increased reliance on market-centered strategies (e.g., tax subsidies, privatization, etc.) have been the core features of housing policy since the 1970s (Gotham, 1998a; Hays, 1994; Rubin, Wright, & Devine, 1992). During this time, virtually all federal housing programs that provide housing to low-income residents, through new construction or rehabilitation, have witnessed severe cutbacks and defunding. Plans are currently under way, and have been since the 1980s, to demolish, convert, or privatize substantial portions of the existing federally subsidized housing stock (Hartman, 1986; Koebel, 1997). In recent years, Congress has resolved to end subsidies for public housing construction, repeal the Housing Act of 1937, which created the public housing system, and end all subsidies to local housing authorities (Quercia & Galster, 1997).

A major centerpiece of federal housing policy since the 1970s has been the Section 8 program, established through the Housing and Community Development Act of 1974. The Section 8 program works by allowing local housing authorities to issue housing vouchers to low-income renters to give to landlords, who then receive rental subsidies from HUD to keep rents at affordable levels. Participating landlords charge the approved "prevailing market rate" for apartments; low-income tenants pay 30% of their income for rent, and HUD pays the rest. Low-income renters use the housing voucher to search for affordable housing that meets HUD-approved minimum quality standards. The Section 8 program has remained the major centerpiece of all federal housing policy since the 1970s (Hays, 1985; Mitchell, 1985; Salsich, 1996). Other federal housing subsidy programs include the Low Income Housing Tax Credit, established in 1986 to encourage the private sector to build low-income housing, as well as the 1990 Cranston-Gonzalez National Affordable Housing Act and the 1992 Housing and Community Development Act, which provide block grants to states and local governments to subsidize low-income housing construction and rental and homeowner assistance.

The only major legislative response to the scarcity of accessible and affordable low-income housing for homeless people has been the 1987 McKinney Homeless Assistance Act. Increasing homelessness during the 1980s (Wright, 1989) prompted the passage of the McKinney Act to provide shelter to homeless and near-homeless low-income citizens (Adler, 1991). Amendments in 1988, 1990, 1992, and 1994 have expanded the scope, reach, and funding of the original McKinney Act, so that programs reach the mentally ill, homeless veterans and children, rural homeless people, and other needy citizens. Currently, the McKinney Act consists of a series of programs, including emergency shelter, transitional housing, job training, health care, education, and permanent housing. However, in recent years, funding and support for McKinney Act programs, like other low-income housing assistance programs, have decreased, and attempts have been made to repeal the authorization of the original act. A number of program evaluations of the McKinney Act conducted in 1995 and 1996 found that the homeless programs aided in providing permanent housing at reasonable costs for significant numbers of homeless people (Fuchs & McAllister, 1996). However, all these program evaluations noted that resources allocated to McKinney programs are insufficient to meet demand and that lack of funding severely limits the programs' effectiveness.

In sum, since the 1970s, the focus of federal housing policy has undergone a dramatic transformation. The Reagan, Bush, and Clinton administrations have continued the shift to privatization, decentralization, and retrenchment begun in the 1970s by embracing an explicit goal of minimizing federal involvement in housing provision (Bartelt, 1993; Rubin et al., 1992). Federal expenditures for subsidized housing, which peaked at $31.5 billion in 1978, fell to $13.3 billion in 1982, $9.5 billion in 1987, and $6 billion in 1989. During the Reagan and Bush administrations, federal appropriations for low-income housing were cut by 80%—the most severe cuts endured by any major federal program (Boger, 1996). Federal dollars to finance construction of new low-income housing units were reduced from $4 billion in 1981 to only $400 million in 1987. In September 1996, President Clinton signed legislation providing no new Section 8 housing vouchers, and plans are currently under way to privatize all public housing and demolish 100,000 public housing units over the next 5 years without any guarantee of one-for-one replacement with housing units or vouchers (DeParle, 1996; Nitschke, 1996). These steps on the federal level have climaxed a two decade-long transformation of federal housing policy that has included privatizing federally supported mortgage markets, substituting housing vouchers for public housing construction, partially privatizing remaining public housing projects while unilaterally demolishing others, tightening eligibility requirements, and, most important, drastically reducing federal spending on housing.

POPULATION AND DEMOGRAPHIC TRENDS
AFFECTING FEDERAL HOUSING POLICY

A major trend affecting federal housing policy is increasing poverty and homelessness in the face of escalating housing costs and declining supplies of low-income housing units in U.S. cities (Devine & Wright, 1993; Wright & Rubin, 1991). As numerous studies have documented, inner-city housing costs have been increasing more rapidly than people's incomes, creating an affordability gap for low- and even moderate-income households (Stone, 1993). Moreover, stagnating and declining incomes, rising housing costs, and dwindling supplies of affordable housing units have contributed to increasing homelessness and near-homelessness in many U.S. cities (for an overview, see Shlay & Rossi, 1992). Studies in New Orleans (Devine & Wright, 1997), Kansas City (Gotham, 1998a), Philadelphia (Bartelt, 1993), and other cities document that many urban residents are on the edge of homelessness, whereas others are paying a huge portion of their income for rent. In addition to increasing homelessness, a related trend affecting housing policy is the growth in the number of poor families who live in substandard or overcrowded conditions (Gotham, 1998a). As a result of retrenchment and devolution in federal housing policy, the social problems of increasing homelessness, overcrowding, and downward mobility are now common features of many U.S. cities.

In addition to the problems of housing availability and affordability, racial residential segregation continues to be a tenacious and enduring feature of metropolitan housing markets and public housing, despite the passage of fair housing and a host of anti-discrimination statutes (Denton, 1994; Massey & Denton, 1993). Scholarly analyses indicate that high levels of racial residential segregation cannot be explained by individual or group housing preferences or socioeconomic differences between whites and African Americans (Farley, 1995; Horton & Thomas, 1998). Rather, racial discrimination remains an institutionalized feature of the housing industry that cuts across a variety of public agencies and private firms, including landlords, bankers, real estate agents, and government officials (Feagin, 1994; Yinger, 1995). Racial discrimination in housing today is somewhat different than it was decades ago. State and federal laws make official discrimination illegal, and a few African American families now live, or have tried to reside, in historically white neighborhoods in almost all U.S. cities (Darden, 1994; Keating, 1994). However, informal patterns and institutionalized mechanisms of housing discrimination remain a persistent and undeniable characteristic of American society. Institutional housing discrimination refers to actions prescribed by the norms of public agencies, private firms, and social networks of actors within the housing industry that have a differentiated and negative impact on members of a subordinate racial group (Feagin, 1994). For example, much research has documented that housing prices and rents are generally higher for racial minorities, especially African Americans, than for whites (even when income is controlled) and that conventional loans for home purchases and remodeling are available to whites while racial minorities are forced to buy with cash, on contract, or through federal loan programs (Brown & Bennington, 1993; Horton & Thomas, 1998; Squires & Velez, 1987). Similarly, a vast array of housing data indicate that whites are the overwhelming beneficiaries of single-family suburban housing whereas African Americans and other racial minorities are likely to be restricted to multifamily projects, conventional public housing units, and deteriorating and substandard housing in inner cities (Goering et al., 1997; Massey & Kanaiaupuni, 1993; Oliver & Shapiro, 1995).

Trends in housing affordability, overcrowding, homelessness, poverty, and persistent racial residential segregation have been exacerbated by the federal government's increasingly heavy reliance on the private sector to address housing problems. Interestingly, most federally assisted housing in the United States, unlike that in other industrialized nations, is provided by the private sector (Sternlieb & Hughes, 1991). In many European nations, by contrast, a third or more of all units are owned and operated by government housing authorities (Quercia & Galster, 1997). Since the New Deal, home builders, bankers, and other housing and real estate interests have been more or less unified in their opposition to federal intervention in the housing market, particularly where that intervention involves subsidies or programs for low-income citizens (Hays, 1985). Throughout the post-war era, conservative politicians and real estate elites attacked public housing as a "socialist" program and opposed it on the grounds that it would put the government in competition with private housing construction and real estate (Bratt, 1986; Keith, 1973). In the 1960s and 1970s, the National Association of Real Estate Boards continued to resist new housing subsidy programs for the poor at the same time it championed an expansion of FHA resources to benefit upper- and middle-income homeowners and real estate and home-building interests (Hays, 1985). Since its inception in 1965, HUD programs have relied mainly on the private housing market for the production, distribution, and rehabilitation of low-income and public housing (Bratt & Keating, 1993).

IMPLICATIONS AND FUTURE DEVELOPMENTS IN FEDERAL HOUSING POLICY

In recent years, the Section 8 program has been promoted by public officials as a promising anti-poverty strategy to increase housing mobility for low-income, inner-city residents. Others have championed the program as an effective vehicle for deconcentrating racial minorities and creating racially mixed and economically mixed neighborhoods (Keating, 1994). According to promoters, the Section 8 program enables low-income residents and racial minorities to leave high-poverty areas and segregated neighborhoods to move to middle- and high-income areas and racially integrated neighborhoods. The potential benefits of increasing housing mobility through the Section 8 program supposedly include greater access to employment opportunities, quality schools, reduced crime, enhanced cultural amenities and entertainment venues, and enrichment of the lives of white, middle-class residents through increased interaction with more diverse groups of people (Briggs, 1997; Burby & Rohe, 1989; Rosenbaum, 1991, 1995). A number of localities, such as Camden, New Jersey; Kansas City, Missouri; Chicago, and Yonkers, New York, are experimenting with housing mobility in this way.

Despite the fanfare, there is little evidence to indicate that increasing housing mobility through Section 8 vouchers and certificates is an effective anti-poverty strategy or housing desegregation strategy. On the one hand, one study found that modest racial mixing can be achieved through Section 8 if home counseling and information services are provided to recipients (Finkel & Kennedy, 1992). On the other hand, in a case study of Washington, D.C., Hartung and Henig (1997) found that whereas vouchers and certificates scatter subsidized tenants into suburbs better than conventional public housing, these suburbanized tenants nonetheless tend to concentrate in areas whose socioeconomic status and proportions of white residents are below average. McDonnell's (1997) analysis of the Section 8 program revealed a negative relationship between the size of a city's African American population and the likelihood of city participation in the Section 8 program. McDonnell found that devolution of low-income housing programs from the federal to local level perpetuates and exacerbates prevailing patterns of racial residential segregation and housing discrimination. Similarly, in a case study of Kansas City, Gotham (1997) found that the Section 8 program served to reinforce housing segregation, channeling low-income African Americans into predominantly African American neighborhoods in the inner city and dispersing low-income whites to white neighborhoods in suburban areas. Moreover, like the public housing program, the Section 8 program has encountered NIMBY (not in my backyard) protests in some cities, including Boston and Kansas City, from local residents opposed to locating subsidized housing residents in their neighborhoods (Gotham, 1998b; Hoffman, 1996).

In addition, the Section 8 program has been the target of intense criticism by housing and civil rights activists throughout the country due to persistent and multiyear waiting lists for embarrassingly few vouchers (Gotham, 1998a). The average waiting time nationwide for Section 8 housing vouchers is over 2 years, and many housing agencies have much longer waits (Finkel et al., 1996). As of 1995, the Housing Authority of Kansas City, Missouri, had a 3-year waiting list of over 1,200 people for Section 8 housing units ("U.S. Aid," 1996). In Chicago, the waiting list is more than 5 years, with the number of applications running as high as 10,000 in recent years, according to a recent HUD (1998) report. The Section 8 program gives a few qualifying low-income people inadequate resources to compete with other needy citizens for a dwindling supply of affordable housing. Not surprisingly, studies throughout the country indicate that many residents fail to use their vouchers because of an inability to locate quality housing and the dearth of landlords willing to participate in the voucher program (Gotham, 1998a; Salsich, 1996). In addition, although inadequate funding clearly impedes the effectiveness of the Section 8 voucher program, the program's greatest weakness is its focus on increasing the housing "choice" for low-income residents rather than addressing the problem of housing affordability that many low-income citizens face (Hartung & Henig, 1997; Hoffman, 1996).

In addition to the recent emphasis on the Section 8 program, HUD (1995) has proposed that public housing authorities adopt policies that promote tenant self-management, mixed-use and mixed-income residents, and scattered-site low-income housing. Public housing authorities in Chicago, St. Louis, New Orleans, and Seattle, among other cities, are currently experimenting with mixed-income housing that includes both public and private units (Quercia & Galster, 1997). Another key element in the transformation of public housing authorities is the decentralization of management by adopting site-by-site needs analysis, site-based budgets, and market-based leasing. In addition, increased demolition of existing public housing units is part of a larger process of reconstruction that involves converting larger projects into small-scale communities as a vehicle for promoting self-sufficiency among tenants (HUD, 1996). It is too early to tell whether these efforts at self-sufficiency will be successful, but the early indications are not encouraging.

CONCLUSION

Today, housing policy in the United States is at a crossroads. On the one hand, housing conditions as a whole are better than 50 years ago, and various federal housing programs and subsidies have enabled millions of families to become homeowners (Apgar, DiPasquale, Cummings, McArdle, & Fernald, 1990). Since the 1930s, federal intervention in housing markets has been an effective policy stimulating private-sector housing construction and improving the quality of home building in this country. Indeed, despite trends toward devolution and retrenchment in federal housing provision, the federal commitment to housing remains enormous when tax expenditures and credit enhancements for homeownership and housing construction are considered. On the other hand, the goal of a decent home in a suitable living environment, which Congress adopted almost 50 years ago, remains elusive and unattainable for millions of American families, both those who are homeless and those living in marginal, overcrowded, or otherwise substandard conditions. Only about a third of households below the poverty line receive either Section 8 or direct housing assistance, and escalating housing costs and affordability are still a problem for homeless people and other low-income citizens (Salsich, 1996).

Interestingly, the bulk of federal intervention in housing-tax laws, which allow mortgage interest and property taxes to be deducted, continues to benefit upper- and middle-income homeowners at the expense of the needy (Salsich, 1996). According to President Clinton's 1993 budget, the tax expenditures for the mortgage interest deduction, deferral of capital gains on reinvestment in multiple homes, and other tax deductions on housing amounted to over $74.7 billion. In contrast, direct federal appropriations and expenditures for low-income housing for 1993 amounted to $18 billion. Interestingly, the subsidies derived from the mortgage interest deduction continue to be weighted in favor of upper-income families. A study of 1988 tax receipts found that over half of the savings from the mortgage interest deduction is concentrated among those with incomes in the 92nd percentile or higher. Thus, the vast majority of federal tax expenditures and appropriations benefit those who least need housing assistance (Salsich, 1996).

In contrast to federal tax expenditures for middle- and upper-income groups, many of the federal government's housing programs fail to meet the housing needs of low-income residents. Inadequate funding and tendency to attack the symptoms of homelessness (i.e., substance abuse, mental illness), rather than its causes (lack of affordable housing) hampers the effectiveness of the McKinney Act programs. Moreover, although the 1990 Cranston-Gonzalez Housing Act and the 1992 Housing and Community Development Act emphasize homeownership and tenant-based assistance, these programs have been underfunded and fail to satisfy the housing needs of low-income people. In addition, a recent HUD report found that an estimated 12.5 million rental households that qualify for HUD housing aid are unable to get it because the department does not have the funding to help them. Congress has rejected requests to give more needy citizens housing assistance at the same time that the number of affordable apartments for low-income families dropped by 900,000 from 1993 to 1995. These ominous developments are compounded by other housing trends indicating a 24% increase in the number of working poor families needing housing assistance from 1991 to 1995 (HUD, 1998). As HUD Secretary Andrew Cuomo remarked during the release of the 1998 HUD report,

> Our report shows that growing numbers of men and women who serve the fast food we eat, who clean the offices where we work, who watch our children in day care centers, and who perform many other low-wage jobs aren't paid enough to house their families in safe and decent conditions. Without housing assistance, they live on the edge of homelessness, struggling desperately each month to put food on the table and to keep a roof over their families' heads. (www.hud.gov/pressrel/pr98-178.html)

Many of the policy recommendations being put forth by scholars and researchers to remedy the nation's housing problems are based on market-centered strategies designed to increase housing options for the poor and stimulate greater private-sector participation in the production of housing. However, we believe that scholarly debates must move beyond discussions of the relative merits of market-centered housing policies and expose the conservative thrust of public policy, which seeks to convince us of the beneficence of the private market. In particular, the recent focus on opening up supposedly free and benevolent housing "markets" through various federal tax credits, or Section 8 vouchers and certificates, ignores the fact that markets are not necessarily open to all those who wish to participate as buyers and sellers. What unites these otherwise different tax incentives and subsidies is that they are all based on the notion that market forces will cure housing ills if only the barriers to investment and growth are removed. However, despite more than two decades of ostensibly open housing markets, anti-discrimination ordinances, and the universal adoption of market-centered housing policies, markets in metropolitan areas throughout the United States routinely fail to adequately provide quality housing for all citizens. The history of housing policy indicates that market-based stratagems have never been successful in revitalizing cities, ameliorating poverty and disinvestment, or providing housing for the needy (Katz, 1986). What market-centered policies have traditionally been quite successful at is distributing wealth and income upward, reinforcing the segregationist tendencies of the private market, and perpetuating geographic patterns of investment and disinvestment. Thus, we believe that the faith that scholars, policy researchers, and elected officials place in market-centered policies to remedy the problems of housing affordability, homelessness, and segregation is misplaced. As the history of federal housing policy shows, the problems, instead, are market-induced (Gotham, 1998a; Squires, 1993).

Given the massive cutbacks in HUD's budget over the last two decades and the general anti-poor sentiment in the nation, it is unlikely that there will be any increased housing expenditures or substantial new housing programs on the federal level in the near future. New and innovative housing policies and programs, although necessary and laudable, are unlikely to meet with much support and enthusiasm from government officials given the current political climate. Thus, housing advocates should try to protect current government funding and shore up political support for existing housing programs while calling for additional policies to increase the supply of low-income housing. Another approach could be to coordinate existing housing programs with local social service agencies, schools, and other educational services. In addition, housing advocates could concentrate their efforts on state and local governments to tap new sources of government funding and support. However, although the above initiatives are important for attacking the housing problems of the poor, such efforts, by themselves, will not be sufficient to address the major population and demographic trends and programmatic changes that are contributing to increased abandonment, escalating housing costs, and deterioration of the inner-city housing stock. Thus, we believe that the goal of providing decent and affordable housing to low-income people does not lie just in housing programs themselves but, rather, in an effort to coordinate housing programs with a comprehensive welfare policy. As we see it, the housing problems of low-income people can only be addressed through a comprehensive program that includes the creation of jobs that provide a living wage, adequate benefits for those who cannot work, access to affordable health care, and increased supply of affordable housing.

REFERENCES

Abrams, C. (1965). *The city is the frontier.* New York: Harper & Row.

Adler, W. C. (1991). *Addressing homelessness: Status of programs under the Stewart McKinney Act and related legislation.* Washington, DC: National Coalition for the Homeless.

Apgar, W., DiPasquale, D., Cummings, J., McArdle, N., & Fernald, M. (1990). *The state of the nation's housing, 1990.* Cambridge, MA: Joint Center for Housing Studies of Harvard University.

Bartelt, D. (1993). Housing the underclass. In M. Katz (Ed.), *The underclass debate: Views from history* (pp. 118-157). Princeton, NJ: Princeton University Press.

Bauman, J. F. (1987). *Public housing, race, and renewal: Urban planning in Philadelphia, 1920-1974.* Philadelphia: Temple University Press.

Bauman, J. F., Hummon, N. P., & Muller, E. K. (1991). Public housing, isolation, and the urban underclass. *Journal of Urban History, 17*(3), 264-292.

Bayor, R. H. (1989). Urban renewal, public housing, and the racial shaping of Atlanta. *Journal of Policy History, 1*(4), 419-439.

Boger, J. C. (1996). Race and the American city. In C. Boger & J. W. Wegner (Eds.), *Race, poverty, and American cities.* Chapel Hill: University of North Carolina Press.

Bratt, R. G. (1986). Public housing: The controversy and contribution. In R. G. Bratt, C. Hartman, & A. Meyerson (Eds.), *Critical perspectives on housing* (pp. 362-377). Philadelphia: Temple University Press.

Bratt, R. G., Hartman, C., & Meyerson, A. (Eds) (1986). *Critical perspectives on housing.* Philadelphia: Temple University Press.

Bratt, R. G., & Keating, W. D. (1993). Federal housing policy and HUD: Past problems and the future prospects of a beleaguered bureaucracy. *Urban Affairs Quarterly, 29*(1), 3-27.

Briggs, X. de S. (1997). Moving up versus moving out: Neighborhood effects in housing mobility programs. *Housing Policy Debate, 8*(1), 195-234.

Brown, J., & Bennington, C. (1993). *Racial redlining: A study of racial discrimination by banks and mortgage companies in the United States.* Washington, DC: Essential Information, Inc.

Burby, R., & Rohe, W. M. (1989). Deconcentration of public housing: Effects on residents' satisfaction with their living environments and their fear of crime. *Urban Affairs Quarterly, 25*(1), 117-141.

Checkoway, B. (1984). Large builders, federal housing programs, and postwar suburbanization. In W. K. Tabb & L. Sawyers (Eds.), *Marxism and the metropolis: New perspectives in urban political economy* (2nd ed., pp. 152-173). New York: Oxford University Press.

Darden, J. T. (1994). African American residential segregation: An examination of race and class in metropolitan Detroit. In R. D. Bullard, J. E. Grigsby, III, and C. Lee (Eds.), *Residential apartheid: The American legacy* (pp. 82-94). Los Angeles: UCLA, Center for African American Studies.

Denton, N. A. (1994). Are African Americans still hypersegregated? In R. D. Bullard, J. E. Grigsby, III, & C. Lee (Eds.), *Residential apartheid: The American legacy* (pp. 49-81). Los Angeles: UCLA, Center for African American Studies.

DeParle, J. (1996, October 20). Slamming the door. *The New York Times Magazine,* pp. 52-57, 68, 94, 105.

Devine, J. A., & Wright, J. D. (1997). Losing the housing game: The leveling effects of substance abuse. *American Journal of Orthopsychiatry, 67*(4), 618-631.

Devine, J. A., & Wright, J. D. (1993). *The greatest of evils: Urban poverty and the American underclass.* New York: Aldine De Gruyter.

Farley, J. E. (1995). Race still matters: The minimal role of income and housing cost as causes of housing segregation in St. Louis, 1990. *Urban Affairs Review, 31*(2), 244-254.

Farley, R., Schuman, H., Bianchi, S., Colasanto, D., & Hatchett, S. (1978). Chocolate city, vanilla suburbs: Will the trend toward racially separate communities continue. *Social Science Research, 7,* 319-344.

Feagin, J. R. (1994). A house is not a home: White racism and U.S. housing practices. In R. D. Bullard, J. E. Grigsby, III, & C. Lee (Eds.), *Residential apartheid: The American legacy* (pp. 17-48). Los Angeles: UCLA, Center for African American Studies.

Federal Housing Administration. (1936). *Underwriting manual.* Washington, DC: Government Printing Office.

Federal Housing Administration. (1952). *Underwriting manual.* Washington, DC: Government Printing Office.

Federal Housing Administration. (1959). *The FHA story in summary, 1934-1959.* Washington, DC: Government Printing Office.

Finkel, M., Climaco, C. G., Elwood, P. R., Feins, J. D., Locke, G., & Popkin, S. J. (1996). *Learning from each other: New ideas for managing the Section 8 certificate and voucher programs.* Washington, DC: U.S. Department of Housing and Urban Development.

Finkel, M., & Kennedy, S. D. (1992). Racial/ethnic differences in utilization of section 8 existing rental vouchers and certificates. *Housing Policy Debate, 3*(2), 463-508.

Fuchs, E., & McAllister, W.(1996). *The continuum of care: A report on the new federal policy to address homelessness.* Gaithersburg, MD: Community Connections.

Gans, H. (1962). *Urban villagers.* Glencoe, IL: Free Press.

Gelfand, M. I. (1975). *A nation of cities: The federal government and urban America, 1933-1965.* New York: Oxford University Press.

Goering, J., Kamely, A., & Richardson, T. (1997). Recent research on racial segregation and poverty concentration in public housing in the United States. *Urban Affairs Review, 22*(5), 723-745.

Gotham, K. F. (1997). *Constructing the segregated city: Housing, neighborhoods, and racial divisions in metropolitan Kansas City, 1880-2000.* PhD dissertation, Department of Sociology, University of Kansas, Lawrence.

Gotham, K. F. (1998a). Blind faith in the free market: Urban poverty, residential segregation, and federal housing retrenchment, 1970-1995. *Sociological Inquiry, 68*(1), 1-31.

Gotham, K. F. (1998b). Suburbia under siege: Low-income housing and racial conflict in metropolitan Kansas City. *Sociological Spectrum, 18*(4), 449-483.

Hartman, C. (1986). Housing policies under the Reagan administration. In R. G. Bratt, C. Hartman, & A. Meyerson (Eds.), *Critical perspectives on housing* (pp. 362-377). Philadelphia: Temple University Press.

Hartung, J., & Henig, J. (1997). Housing vouchers and certificates as a vehicle for deconcentrating the poor. *Urban Affairs Review, 32,* 403-419.

Hays, R. A. (1985). *Federal government and urban housing: Ideology and change in public policy.* Albany: State University of New York Press.

Hays, R. A. (1994). Housing privatization: Social goals and policy strategies. *Journal of Urban Affairs, 16*(4), 295-317.

Helper, R. (1969). *Racial policies and practices of real estate brokers.* Minneapolis: University of Minnesota Press.

Henderson, P. H. (1995). Suburban visions and the landscape of power: Public housing, suburban diversity, and participation in metropolitan Baltimore. In M. L. Silver & M. Melkonian (Eds.), *Contested terrain: Power, politics, and participation in suburbia* (pp. 195-210). Westport, CT: Greenwood.

Hirsch, A. R. (1983). *Making the second ghetto: Race and housing in Chicago, 1940-1960.* Cambridge, UK: Cambridge University Press.

Hoffman, A. V. (1996). High ambitions: The past and future of American low-income housing policy. *Housing Policy Debate, 7*(3), 423-446.

Horton, H. D., & Thomas, M. E. (1998). Race, class, and family structure: Differences in housing values for black and white homeowners. *Sociological Inquiry, 68*(10), 114-136.

Jackson, K. T. (1980). Race, ethnicity, and real estate appraisal: The Home Owners Loan Corporation and the Federal Housing Administration. *Journal of Urban History, 6*(4), 419-452.

Jackson, K. T. (1985). *Crabgrass frontier: The suburbanization of the United States.* New York: Oxford University Press.

Jacobs, J. (1961). *The death and life of great American cities.* New York: Vintage.

Katz, M. (1986). *In the shadow of the poorhouse: A social history of welfare in America.* New York: Basic Books.

Keating, W. D. (1994). *Suburban racial dilemma: Housing and neighborhoods.* Philadelphia: Temple University Press.

Keith, N. S. (1973). *Politics and the housing crisis since 1930.* New York: Universe Books.

Kirp, D. L., Dwyer, J. P., & Rosenthal, L. A. (1995). *Our town: Race, housing, and the soul of suburbia.* New Brunswick, NJ: Rutgers University Press.

Kleniewski, N. (1984). From industrial to corporate city: The role of urban renewal. In W. K. Tabb & L. Sawyers (Eds.), *Marxism and the metropolis: New perspectives in urban political economy* (2nd ed.) New York: Oxford University Press.

Koebel, C. T. (1997). Housing conditions of low-income families in the private unassisted housing market in the United States. *Housing Studies, 12*(2), 201-213.

Logan, J., & Molotch, H. (1987). *Urban fortunes: The political economy of place.* Berkeley: University of California Press.

Marcuse, P. (1986). The beginning of public housing in New York. *Journal of Urban History, 12*(4), 353-390.

Massey, D. S., & Denton, N. A. (1993). *American apartheid: Segregation and the making of the underclass.* Cambridge, MA: Harvard University Press.

Massey, D., & Kanaiaupuni, S. N. (1993). Public housing and the concentration of poverty. *Social Science Quarterly, 71*(1), 109-122.

McDonnell, J. (1997). The role of "race" in the likelihood of city participation in the United States public and section 8 existing housing programs. *Housing Studies, 12*(2), 231-245.

McDonnell, T. (1957). *The Wagner Housing Act: A case study of the legislative process.* Chicago: Loyola University Press.

Mitchell, J. P. (Ed.). (1985). *Federal housing programs: Past and present.* Rutgers: State University of New Jersey Press.

Myrdal, G. (1944). *An American dilemma: The Negro problem and modern democracy.* New York: Harper Torchbooks.

Nitschke, L. (1996, February 21). Housing overhaul still looking for a home in GOP Congress. *Congressional Science Quarterly,* pp. 423-431.

Oliver, M. L., & Shapiro, T. M. (1995). *Black wealth, white wealth: A new perspective on racial inequality.* New York: Routledge.

Quercia, R. G., & Galster, G. (1997). The challenges facing public housing authorities in a brave new world. *Housing Policy Debate, 8*(3), 535-569.

Radford, G. (1996). *Modern housing for America: Policy struggles in the New Deal era.* Chicago: Chicago University Press.

Rosenbaum, J. (1991). Black pioneers: Do their moves to the suburbs increase economic opportunity for mothers and children. *Housing Policy Debate, 4*(1), 1179-1213.

Rosenbaum, J. (1995). Changing geography of opportunity by expanding residential choice: Lessons from the Gautreaux program. *Housing Policy Debate, 6*(1), 231-270.

Rubin, B. A., Wright, J. D., & Devine, J. A. (1992). Unhousing the urban poor: The Reagan legacy. *Journal of Sociology and Social Welfare, 19*(1), 111-148.

Salsich, P. W. (1996). A decent home for every American: Can the 1949 goal be met? In J. C. Boger & J. W. Wegner (Eds.), *Race, poverty, and American cities* (pp. 343-372). Chapel Hill: University of North Carolina Press.

Schafer, R., & Field, C. G. (1973). Section 235 of the National Housing Act: Homeownership for low-income families? In J. Pynoos, R. Schafer, & C. W. Hartman (Eds.), *Housing urban America* (pp. 460-471). Chicago: Aldine de Gruyter.

Shlay, A. B., & Rossi, P. H. (1992). Social science research and contemporary studies of homelessness. *Annual Review of Sociology, 18,* 129-160.

Squires, G. D. (1993). The political economy of housing: All the discomforts of home. *Research in Urban Sociology, 3,* 129-157.

Squires, G. D., & Velez, W. (1987). Neighborhood racial composition and mortgage lending: City and suburban differences. *Journal of Urban Affairs, 9*(3), 217-232.

Sternlieb, G., & Hughes, J. W. (1991). Private market provision of low-income housing: Historical perspectives and future prospects. *Housing Policy Debate, 2*(2), 123-156.

Stone, M. (1993). *Shelter poverty: New ideas on housing affordability.* Philadelphia: Temple University Press.

U.S. aid to house the poor declines. (1996, June 2). *Kansas City Star,* p. B1.

U.S. Department of Housing and Urban Development. (1995). *HUD's reinvention: From blueprint to action.* Washington, DC: Government Printing Office.

U.S. Department of Housing and Urban Development. (1996). *Public housing that works.* Washington, DC: Government Printing Office.

U.S. Department of Housing and Urban Development. (1998). *Rental housing assistance—the crisis continues.* Washington, DC: Government Printing Office.

Weiss, M. A. (1980). The origins and legacy of urban renewal. In P. Clavel, J. Forester, & W. W. Goldsmith (Eds.), *Urban and regional planning in an age of austerity* (pp. 53-79). New York: Pergamon.

Weiss, M. A. (1987). *Rise of the community builders: The American real estate industry and urban land planning.* New York: Columbia University Press.

Wilson, J. Q. (Ed.). (1966). *Urban renewal: The record and the controversy.* Cambridge: MIT Press.

Wright, J. D. (1989). Address unknown: Homelessness in contemporary America. *Society, 26,* 45-53.

Wright, J. D., & Rubin, B. A. (1991). Is homelessness a housing problem? *Housing Policy Debate, 2*(2), 937-956.

Wright, J. D., Rubin, B. A., & Devine, J. (1998). *Beside the golden door: Policy, politics, and the homeless.* Hawthorne, NY: Aldine de Gruyter.

Yinger, J. (1995). *Closed doors, opportunities lost: The continuing costs of housing discrimination.* New York: Basic Books.

CHAPTER EIGHTEEN

Social Policies and Mental Health

JAMES W. CALLICUTT

In the United States, the provision of services to mentally ill people and their families is inextricably tied to mental health policy. In this chapter, I will identify and briefly discuss some of the major issues dealing with the organization and delivery of services in the mental health field vis-à-vis mental health policy. In addition, I will review the historical evolution of services for the mentally ill; describe the current mental health service system; identify, define, and discuss the major forces that interact in formulating and forging mental health policy; and finally examine the major issues and trends in this arena.

MENTAL ILLNESS AND MENTAL HEALTH

It is impossible to discuss the term *mental illness* without at the same time considering the concept of *mental health*. Mental illness is a synonym for mental disorder, which is defined as

> Impaired psychosocial or cognitive functioning due to disturbances in any one or more of the following processes: biological, chemical, physiological, genetic, psychosocial or social. Mental disorders are extremely variable in duration, severity, and prognosis, depending on

the type of affliction. The major forms of mental disorder include *mood disorders, psychosis, personality disorders, organic mental disorders,* and *anxiety disorder.* (Barker, 1995, p. 231)

Mental health, on the other hand, defies uniform definition. Vague and imprecise, the notion has multiple meanings that differ with the context. For example, in one instance, it may be used as a euphemism for mental illness; in another, it may be used to indicate emotional or psychological well-being; and in yet a third, it may be used to mean both well-being and mental illness (Callicutt, 1987; Callicutt & Lecca, 1983). It is interesting to note how terminology and rhetoric change over time in the broad arena of social welfare, including the field of mental illness. In part, terminology is changed with a conscious effort to destigmatize the population served. For example, insane asylums became mental hospitals, then psychiatric institutes, and subsequently behavioral health care facilities. Also, we talk about a mental health service system rather than a mental illness service system. Consequently, in this chapter, I will at times use the terms mental illness and mental health interchangeably.

HISTORICAL EVOLUTION OF SERVICES FOR THE MENTALLY ILL

Cruel, harsh, and inhumane treatment, reflecting the views of society about the causes of mental illness, characterized the care of the mentally ill for centuries. The mentally deranged, thought to be possessed of demons or spirits, were subjected to devices of coercion and restraint including manacles, chains, and whips to instill fear and awe and to promote discipline and order, and thus restore reason (Callicutt, 1987).

Colonial America

Sparsely populated, with a largely rural, agrarian economy, colonial America provided care for the mentally ill by the family or community primarily on an ad hoc, informal basis (Grob, 1994). The methods of caring for dependent people, including the "distracted" and the poor, were basically modeled after England's Poor Laws. According to Deutsch (1949), provision for the mentally ill in colonial America was characterized by punishment, indifference, and oppression. In contrast, Grob (1973) observed that "all that can be said is that each community, depending on its circumstances, improvised or attempted to do the best that it could under prevailing conditions" (p. 12).

Mentally ill people were first received by the Pennsylvania Hospital, the first general hospital in America, completed in 1756. There, in the cellar, they were confined by chains attached to the cell walls (Deutsch, 1949). In Williamsburg, Virginia, the first state hospital for the mentally ill was opened in 1773. Subsequently, state hospitals for the mentally ill were established throughout the United States, and they continue to provide the bulk of inpatient services in the public sector.

Moral Treatment

Moral treatment, the treatment of mental patients with kindness and consideration, rather than as subhuman and incurable, is associated with the names of Vincenzo Chiarugi, an Italian; Phillipe Pinel, a Frenchman; and William Tuke, an Englishman. Benjamin Rush and Dorothea Dix, Americans, also merit inclusion in this discussion. While presiding over a large mental hospital, Chiarugi (1759-1820), a physician in Florence, Italy, put his ideas into effect, arguing that "medical personnel had a moral duty to treat the mentally ill as individuals and to treat them tactfully and humanely" (Cockerham, 1989, p. 19).

Pinel (1745-1826), also a physician, asserted that mental patients would respond favorably to kindness and sympathy administered in the context of firm guidance (Cockerham, 1989). After being appointed as a physician to the insane asylum of Bicetre in 1779, Pinel went from cell to cell unchaining the 53 male lunatics. He ordered beatings and other forms of physical abuse stopped; "food was improved and the patients were treated with a new drug: kindness" (Cockerham, 1989, p. 21). Often, the responses of the patients were dramatically salutary. Three years later, Pinel instituted the same reforms at the women's mental institution in Paris (Callicutt, 1987). Pinel articulated the philosophy and precepts of moral treatment.

At virtually the same time, William Tuke, a layman, obtained formal support from Quakers in York, England, to start an institution that would offer gentle and wholesome treatment to fellow believers (Deutsch, 1949). Then, in 1796, the Retreat was established in York (Glover, 1984). There, chains were prohibited; patients were treated as guests rather than inmates. Exercise and work, along with a family environment, were emphasized. Firm guidance emanating from the physician, clinician, and/or superintendent of the mental hospital was a hallmark of the ideology of treatment.

Earlier, in America, Benjamin Rush (1745-1813) a physician considered to be the father of American psychiatry (Deutsch, 1949), played a prominent role in improving the care of the mentally ill. In 1783, he adopted kinder and more humane treatment practices at the Pennsylvania Hospital than were usually accorded mental patients. In this process, Rush gave attention to employing well-qualified attendants to serve as friends and companions to the lunatics. Rush's positive impact on the treatment of the mentally ill is undeniable. Yet, he was a product of his time: He practiced bloodletting and invented treatment devices including the "tranquilizer, which consisted of a chair to which the patient was strapped hand and foot, together with a device for holding the head in a fixed position" (Deutsch, 1949, p. 79). Although his approaches were not completely consistent with the philosophy of moral treatment as espoused by Chiargui, Pinel, and Tuke, Rush's contributions were remarkable.

Born in Hampden, Maine, Dorothea Lynde Dix (1802-1887) earned acclaim as "one of the most famous women in American history" as a "teacher, writer, social reformer, religious poet, nurse [and] friend to the poor" (Stroup, 1986, p. 123). Frail and subject to periods of physical and mental collapse, Dix displayed a sensitivity and zeal that were forged into a consuming force of advocacy for the mentally ill when, after conducting Sunday school services for women offenders, she found seriously mentally ill prisoners in unheated quarters in the East Cambridge, Massachusetts, jail. She gathered facts about the callous and inhumane confinement of the mentally ill in institutions including agencies, jails, and private homes. In presenting memorials (speeches citing the facts that she had collected) to many state legislatures, she succeeded in establishing asylums for the care of the mentally ill. Ironically, Dorothea Dix's efforts resulted in part in the expansion of large state hospitals together with the increasing popularity of the view that insanity was incurable. This contributed to custodial functions becoming more dominant, and moral treatment declining. Certainly moral treatment was never applied universally in America, where it was practiced primarily by private hospitals "or by only the most progressive public asylums" (Cockerham, 1989, p. 21). Unquestionably, Dorothea Dix's work had a profound impact on mental health policy in the United States, with the effects and implications continuing today.

Early 20th Century

In the late 1800s, state hospitals continued to increase in number and size. Overcrowding "due to the large influx of poor immigrants and the emptying of jails and almshouses into the state facilities at the urging of Dorothea Dix" contributed to the failure of state hospitals (Krauss & Slavinsky, 1982, p. 70). Again, custodial care became the overriding role of state mental institutions.

Marking a milestone in the course of care of the mentally ill, a New Haven, Connecticut, businessman, Clifford Whittingham Beers, in 1908 published his remarkable autobiography, *A Mind That Found Itself*. This book dramatically chronicled the abusive and harsh treatment he received when hospitalized in 1900 for 3 years for manic-depressive mental illness (Beers, 1913). Also, in 1908, he played a major role in establishing the Connecticut Society for Mental Hygiene and was named its executive secretary (Deutsch, 1949). The next year, the National Committee for Mental Hygiene was founded primarily as the result of Beers's vision, energy, and talents. This citizen's movement identified mental illness as a problem requiring government intervention (Langsley, Berlin, & Yarvis, 1981). It evolved into the National Mental Health Association, a major advocacy organization in the mental health and mental illness arena.

In the 1920s, demonstration child guidance clinics were established throughout the country, financed as a project of the Commonwealth Fund (Stroup, 1960). Predicated on the concept that by meeting the mental health needs of children, adult psychopathology would be prevented, this movement employed an interdisciplinary team-staffing model consisting of a psychiatrist, psychologist, and psychiatric social worker (Callicutt, 1983).

World Wars I and II

As Deutsch (1949) notes, "It is one of the grotesque ironies of history that wars, with their frightful carnage in lives lost and wrecked, do tend to give impetus to various health movements" (p. 317). In this context, the high incidence of mental disorder in the military and the recognition of the need to deal with this issue in terms of the war effort, led to the formation of a division of neurology and psychiatry as part of the office of the Surgeon General. The responsibility for organizing this division was allocated to the National Committee for Mental Hygiene. Screening, diagnostic and treatment services, and the development of facilities were among the major functions of the division of neurology and psychiatry (Deutsch, 1949).

During World War II, psychiatric disorders caused over a million draft registrants to be rejected for military service by August 1, 1949, according to testimony by the director of the Selective Service System (Deutsch, 1949). Similarly, during the period from January 1, 1941, through December 31, 1945, about 1 million patients with neuropsychiatric disorders were admitted to U.S. Army hospitals (Menninger, 1947). These experiences provided an impetus for the federal government regarding policies of mental illness and mental health as presented in a subsequent section of this chapter.

Community Mental Health Movement

Penetration of the concepts of public health into the field of mental health was identified as "mental health's third revolution" by Hobbs (1964). Hobbs identified the names of Pinel, Tuke, Rush, and Dix with mental health's first revolution (see previous discussion of moral treatment), and the name of Sigmund Freud and the consequent preoccupation with intrapsychic life with mental health's second revolution (Hobbs, 1964).

The community mental health movement, embracing the concepts of public health, including the early identification and treatment of mental disorders and attention to the realm of prevention, represented, in part, an outcome of the publication, *Action for Mental Health*. This report of the Joint Commission on Mental Illness and Health (1961), sponsored by 36 organizations making up the Commission, was a political and ideological document setting forth recommendations of experts after a 5-year study. In 1963, Congress passed the Mental Retardation Facilities and Community Mental Health Centers Construction Act. This legislation committed "the federal government to help support easily accessible and locally controlled mental health centers" and "reflected the objective of modern treatment to support mental patients in their own communities" (Cockerham, 1989, p. 280). Although the initial legislation excluded staffing grants, provision for staffing was included in subsequent amendments.

To receive federal funds, local centers were mandated to provide five essential elements of service. Four of these elements were clinical or direct service in nature: inpatient, outpatient, 24-hour emergency, and partial hospitalization services. The remaining element—consultation and education—was nonclinical or indirect in nature. Through this service component, mental health centers provided services to schools, social service agencies, professional groups including the clergy, and the general public.

By 1982, there were 691 community mental health centers in the United States, up from about 300 in 1972. One of the expectations of the community mental health movement was to reduce admissions to state hospitals and serve patients more effectively and at less cost in the community. However, a well-recognized shortcoming was, for the most part, the failure of publicly funded centers to serve the chronic mental patient.

Deinstitutionalization

Deinstitutionalization is defined as "the process of releasing patients, inmates, or people who are dependent for their physical and mental care from *residential care facilities*, presumably with the understanding that they no longer need such care or can receive it through community-based services" (Barker, 1995, p. 93). Community mental health centers were expected to be the lynch pin in the deinstitutionalization of mental patients. Although state hospital admissions fell, and outpatient and partial care admissions increased dramatically (as discussed in my subsequent discussion of the de facto mental health system), there is evidence that community mental health centers had little impact in the remarkable reduction of the number of patients populating state hospitals (Isaac & Armat, 1990).

Explosion of Private Psychiatric Hospital Services

Dramatic increases in the number of private psychiatric hospitals, from 150 to 462, accompanied by an increase in the number of psychiatric beds in these facilities, occurred between 1970 and 1990 (Redick, Witkin, Atay, & Manderscheid, 1994). Accounting for only 2.7% of inpatient beds in 1970, by 1990, these hospitals had 44,871 beds for 16.5% of the total of 524,878 for all mental health organizations (Redick et al., 1994). Legislative and judicial decisions combined with funding policy changes based, in part, on cost containment issues, and the scandalous abuses of some private psychiatric hospitals in their unethical practices relating to filling beds without regard to patients' needs for inpatient treatment, have resulted in the consolidation, downsizing, and closing of many of these hospitals (Callicutt, 1997; Sharkey, 1994.) Thus, the trend involving the expansion of private psychiatric hospitals has now been reversed.

Managed Care

Currently, managed care is recognized as a potent, even dominant force relative to the provision of services across the full spectrum of health and mental health services. As Ross and Croze (1997) observed, "Today, both the public and private sectors are attempting to manage care in an effort to deliver appropriate care that meets the patient's clinical needs under a fixed budget" (p. 359). Managed care is further discussed elsewhere in this volume.

It is clear that there are many issues including accessibility to services and underservice as mental health care is extended further under the umbrella of managed care. There are hazards in terms of potential abuses, but there are challenges and opportunities to develop broader, better integrated, and more effective systems of mental health care (Mechanic, 1999).

THE CURRENT MENTAL HEALTH SYSTEM

A wide array of mental health programs and services proliferate across the United States today. They provide services to individuals and, to a lesser extent, families on a selective basis. The concept of *system* embraces the notion of interdependent or interrelated parts forming a unified or organized whole (Anderson & Carter, 1990). Rather than having a unified whole, the extant programs and services often are disjointed, fragmented, and lacking in cohesion. As they are driven by political, philosophical, professional, and ideological forces that may be neutral or even antagonistic instead of supportive of the development of an authentic, organized mental health system, it is reasonable to assume that what exists is basically a nonsystem (Callicutt,

1997). Nevertheless, there is wide recognition that the broad scope of mental health services—provided under public, not-for-profit, and for-profit corporate and proprietary auspices in a multiplicity of settings—results in the existence of a de facto mental health service system (Bevilacqua, 1991; Regier, Goldberg, & Taube, 1978).

Components of the Mental Health System

Now, I will identify and briefly describe the major components of the mental health system. The two major components of the mental health system are inpatient care and outpatient care. Partial care is also an important category.

Inpatient. "Around-the-clock care is indicated when people are so seriously mentally disturbed that they pose a significant threat to themselves or others" (Callicutt, 1987, p. 126). The 22-year period from 1970 to 1992 showed a major change in the number of psychiatric beds in mental health organizations providing inpatient and/or residential treatment services. From an estimated 524,878 psychiatric beds in 1970, the number decreased by 48% to 270,867 in 1992 (Redick, Witkin, Atay, & Manderscheid, 1996). This occurred while the number of mental health organizations with inpatient and/or residential treatment services doubled. This startling drop reflected decreases in the number of beds in state and county mental hospitals, which accounted for about four fifths of the beds in 1970 but only one third of all psychiatric beds in 1992 (Redick et al., 1996).

Decreases in inpatient and residential treatment beds are related to the deinstitutionalization movement, increases in outpatient services, increases in the number of community mental health centers, and the use of psychotropic medications. Influences of managed care and other cost-containment policies and measures are also discerned in the reduction in inpatient beds.

Outpatient. I have asserted that outpatient services are the backbone of the mental health system (Callicutt, 1987). More extensive and effective use of outpatient care has both averted admissions to inpatient facilities and shortened inpatient stays (Callicutt, 1997).

Outpatient treatment options include short-term, individual counseling or therapy, group and family therapy, extended supportive treatment, medication, and case management services. These and other services are available to a wide range of patients reflecting a broad spectrum of mental health problems (Callicutt, 1997).

Outpatient service settings include child and family guidance clinics, community mental health centers, outpatient departments of freestanding mental health agencies, and private practice offices of mental health professionals, including social workers, psychologists, and psychiatrists. Furthermore, primary care clinicians also treat a large number of patients with mental health problems.

As shown in Figure 18.1, a stunning shift has occurred in patient care episodes—a duplicated count of the number of people under care throughout the year—in mental health organizations from 1955 to 1992. In 1955, inpatient episodes accounted for 77% of a total of 1.7 million episodes, whereas outpatient episodes claimed the remaining 23%. Remarkably, in 1992, outpatient episodes were 68% of a total of 8.8 million episodes. Inpatient episodes were 26%, and partial care episodes were 6%.

Partial care. Falling between inpatient care and outpatient care, partial care involves day or night partial care or partial hospitalization. Rehabilitation, habitation, and education programs are now included in this classification.

Major Mental Health Settings

This section describes the principal settings in the specialty mental health system. It includes those organizations designed to provide mental health services per se as distinct from the general health care system, which also includes mental health services.

Community mental health centers. Passage of the Mental Retardation Facilities and Community Mental Health Centers Construction Act of 1963 (known as the CMHC Act) and its later amendments was a powerful stimulant to the growth in the number of community mental health centers, from 205 in 1969 to 789 in 1980 (Lecca, 1983). However, the Omnibus Budget Reconciliation Act of 1981, passed during the Reagan administration, changed the course of federal financial support of community mental health centers from direct funding to the provision of block grants to the states, which would then allocate the funds. Although the federal initiative of providing staffing and construction grants was discontinued, we continue to experience the influence of the funding support that stimulated the development of community mental health centers from 1963 to 1981. The organization, structure, and funding of centers varies from state to state, as does the funding of mental health programs from state sources (Callicutt, 1987).

The de jure policy of deinstitutionalization (discussed in a previous section and discussed further in a subsequent section on policies) had a positive impact on the development of community mental health centers, originally mandated to provide five essential elements of service: inpatient, outpatient, and 24-hour emergency services; partial hospitalization; and consultation and education. Later amendments to the CMHC Act of 1963 provided for staffing grants and added other service requirements. These requirements no longer apply, as federal funds come to the states via block grants.

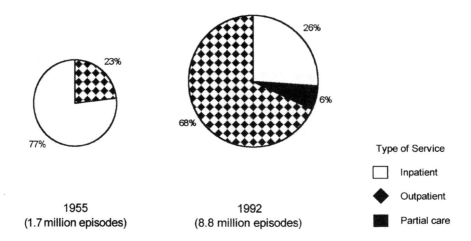

Figure 18.1. Patient Care Episodes in Mental Health Organizations in 1955 and 1992
SOURCE: Reprinted from Redick et al. (1996, p. 96).

Department of Veteran Affairs. In 1992, the Department of Veterans Affairs (formerly the Veterans Administration or VA) provided psychiatric services to veterans at 162 VA medical centers. The number of inpatients at the end of 1969 was 51,696, dropping to 18,531 in 1992 (Redick et al., 1996). During this same time, the number of outpatient additions rose from 16,790 to 144,591, and partial case additions increased from 3,500 to 14,391. VA medical centers accounted for 9% of the 2.3 million inpatient and residential treatment care episodes and 8% of the 6.0 million outpatient case episodes in all mental health organizations in 1992 (Redick et al., 1996). (See Price, 1997, for a more detailed discussion of mental health services for veterans.)

State and county mental hospitals. From 1970 to 1992, the number of state and county mental hospitals declined from 310 to 273. Even more telling, for the same period, the number of beds in these facilities shrunk from 413,066 to 93,058. In 1970, state and county hospitals accounted for almost 79% of inpatient beds available in all mental health organizations, whereas in 1992, their proportion had decreased to 34.4%. Still, in 1992, these facilities had 83,180 inpatient residents, nearly 39% of the inpatient and residential treatment residents in all mental health organizations (Redick et al., 1996). Again, although the number of hospitals, wards, and beds has dropped precipitously and the number of inpatient additions and inpatient residents likewise has declined, state and county mental hospitals continue to play a vital role in the care of the seriously mentally ill and the poor. Lutterman (1994) indicated that state mental health agencies provide planning, policy making, and other functions in addition to direct client care services. In 1993, states operated 256 state hospitals, 22 fewer than in 1980, reflecting a concurrent shift from state hospital to community-based services (Lutterman, 1994).

Private psychiatric hospitals. The number of private psychiatric hospitals increased markedly between 1970 and 1992, from 150 to 475, with all of them providing inpatient care (Redick et al., 1996). In 1992, outpatient services were offered by 198 of these hospitals. Private psychiatric hospitals accounted for only 2.7% of inpatient beds in 1970, but in 1990, they had 44,871 beds, 16.5% of the total of 524,878 beds for all mental health organizations (Redick et al., 1994) As mentioned previously, 1992 saw a decline in the number of beds in private psychiatric hospitals to 436,684 and an accompanying marked decline in the number of inpatient residents, from 32,268 in 1990 to 24,053 in 1992.

Psychiatric units in general hospitals. Nonfederal general hospitals with psychiatric units increased from 796 in 1970 to 1,674 in 1990, then dropped to 1,616 in 1992 (Redick et al., 1996). Similarly, the number of inpatient additions increased from 478,000 in 1969 to 959,893 in 1990, declining to 951,121 in 1992. Here, again, an upward trend has halted and appears to have reversed. It seems that the previous shift in the locus of mental health care to nonfederal general hospitals is unsettled and problematic at this point.

Residential treatment centers. Residential treatment centers for emotionally disturbed children, which numbered 261 in 1970, nearly doubled to 501 in 1990, then declined to 497 in 1992 (Redick et al., 1996). Also, the number of beds nearly doubled, from 15,129 to 29,756 in 1990 and 30,089 in 1992.

In 1992, these facilities had 27,754 inpatients at the end of the year, up from 13,489 in 1969 and accounting for 12.9% of all inpatient and residential treatment center additions (Redick et al., 1996).

Other organizations. Freestanding psychiatric partial care organizations and multiservice mental health organizations, which include community mental health centers unless they are part of psychiatric or general hospitals, are included in this category. In 1992, there were 1,613 such organizations, with about one third providing inpatient services, 1,309 providing outpatient services, and most (1,434) providing partial care services.

Freestanding psychiatric outpatient clinics. The number of freestanding psychiatric outpatient clinics declined from 1,109 in 1970 to 743 in 1990 but increased to 862 in 1992. Outpatient additions decreased from 538,426 in 1969 to 464,499 in 1992, but these facilities cared for 16% of the outpatient care episodes in mental health organizations in 1992 (Redick et al., 1996).

Nontraditional settings and innovative services. As mentioned previously, mental health professionals in private practice settings play an important role in the mental health service system. Systematic service statistics are not available relative to this component of care. In addition, the role of primary care clinicians is clearly recognized, with Regier et al. (1978) observing that 54.1% of people with mental disorders received services in the outpatient/primary care medical sector. Primary care clinicians (e.g., general practitioners, family practitioners, pediatricians, and internists) frequently are the sole source of care for people with mental disorders (Manderscheid, Rae, Narrow, Loch, & Regier, 1993).

Staffing: The Mental Health Professions

Traditionally, the recognized core mental health professions are psychiatry, psychology, mental health nursing, and social work. (See Callicutt & Price, 1997, for a fuller discussion of these four mental health core professions.) In addition, other important patient care professions involved in the provision of mental health services have been clearly acknowledged. For example, Dial et al. (1992) discuss marriage and family therapy, clinical mental health counseling, and psychosocial rehabilitation in the context of developing areas of practice. More recently, school psychology has been included in "An Update on Human Resources in Mental Health," published in *Mental Health, United States, 1996* (Peterson et al., 1996). The revival of the practice movement in sociology is also outlined (Peterson et al., 1996).

In 1992, there were 585,972 full-time equivalent staff employed in all mental health organizations. Table 18.1 shows the number and percentage distribution of these positions by staff discipline, for selected years from 1972 to 1992. In 1992, among the traditional core professions, registered nurses accounted for 13.4%; social workers, 9.7%; psychologists, 4.3%; and psychiatrists, 3.9%. Each of the core professions increased substantially in numbers for the years reported. Social work alone showed increased percentages for all of the years reported.

It is obvious that the specialty mental health industry uses a broad array of human resources in staffing organizations. Expanded use of personnel from the various professions is likely to produce both competition and conflict among the patient care professions as this process continues.

MENTAL HEALTH POLICY

As mentioned previously, mental health service provision is a reflection of mental health policy. For the most part, public mental health policy is a product of legislative, regulative, and judicial processes—that is, laws, regulations, and court decisions (Callicutt, 1997). In addition, customs and mores of the community shape public policy.

TABLE 18.1 Number (and percentage distribution) of Full-Time Equivalent Staff[a] in All Mental Health Organizations, by Staff Discipline: United States, Selected Years, 1972-1992[b]

Staff Discipline	1972		1978		1986[b,c]		1990		1992	
	Number[d]	(Percentage)	Number	(Percentage)	Number	(Percentage)	Number	(Percentage)	Number	(Percentage)
All staff	375,984	(100.0)	430,051	(100.0)	494,915	(100.0)	563,619	(100.0)	585,972	(100.0)
Patient care staff	241,265	(64.2)	292,699	(68.1)	346,630	(70.1)	415,719	(73.8)	432,866	73.9
Professional patient care staff	100,886	(26.9)	153,598	(35.8)	232,481	(47.0)	273,374	(48.5)	305,988	(52.5)
Psychiatrists	12,938	(3.4)	14,492	(3.4)	17,874	(3.5)	18,818	(3.3)	22,803	(3.9)
Other physicians	3,991	(1.1)	3,034	(0.7)	3,868	(0.8)	3,865	(0.7)	3,949	(0.7)
Psychologists[d]	9,443	(2.5)	16,501	(3.8)	20,210	(4.1)	22,825	(4.0)	25,000	(4.3)
Social workers	17,687	(4.7)	28,125	(6.5)	40,951	(8.3)	53,375	(9.5)	57,136	(9.7)
Registered nurses	31,110	(8.3)	42,399	(9.9)	66,180	(13.4)	77,635	(13.8)	78,588	(13.4)
Other mental health professionals (bachelor's degree and more)	17,514	(4.7)	39,363	(9.2)	56,245	(11.4)	84,071	(14.9)	102,162	(17.4)
Physical health professionals and assistants	8,203	(2.2)	9,684	(2.3)	27,153	(5.5)	12,785	(2.3)	16,350	(2.8)
Other mental health workers (less than bachelor's degree)	140,379	(37.3)	139,101	(32.3)	114,149	(23.1)	142,345	(25.3)	126,878	(21.7)
Administrative, clerical, and maintenance staff	134,719	(35.8)	137,352	(31.9)	147,885	(29.9)	147,900	(26.2)	153,106	(26.1)

SOURCE: Reprinted from Redick et al. (1996, p. 119). Those authors list the following source: published and unpublished inventory data from the Survey and Analysis Branch Division of State and Community Systems Development, Center for Mental Health Services.

a. The computation of full-time equivalent staff is based on a 40-hour workweek.

b. For 1986, some organizations had been reclassified as a result of changes in reporting procedures and definitions. For details, see text.

c. Includes data for Community Mental Health Centers in 1978. In 1986, 1990, and 1992, these staff are subsumed under other organization types. Data for the centers are not shown separately.

d. For 1972 to 1978, this category included all psychologists with a B.A. degree and above; for 1986 to 1990, it included only psychologists with an M.A. degree and above.

Beyond these forces, there is also the impact of program spending patterns in both the public and voluntary sectors in further contouring mental health policy and services.

Making a useful distinction between de jure and de facto public policy, Kiesler and Sibulkin (1987) observe, "*De jure* policy is intentional in nature and usually legislated into law. The *de facto* policy is the net outcome of overall practices whether the outcome is intended or not" (p. 27). In this context, the de jure mental health policy of the United States is deinstitutionalization and its presumed concomitant, community-based care emphasizing outpatient services. However, de facto mental health policy, shaped by the underfunding of community-based programs and resources, has led, in part, to the flood of homeless mentally ill people, an unintended negative consequence of deinstitutionalization (Callicutt, 1997). This tragic national phenomenon is attributed, in part, to the misguided efforts of civil libertians to "free" the mentally ill (Grob, 1994; Isaac & Armat, 1990; Kuhlman, 1994; Rochefort, 1997; Torrey, 1988). Isaac and Armat (1990) assert that psychiatry, as well as the law, abandoned the mentally ill and contributed to the surge of mentally ill people "in the streets." As discussed earlier, the United States has a de facto mental health system; also, we have a de facto mental health policy.

Federal Government Leadership and Initiatives

The states historically have played a prominent role in providing care for the mentally ill and consequently in the establishment of mental health policy (see Hudson & Cox, 1991). World War II created an increased awareness of the high cost of mental illness coupled with the potential effectiveness of psychiatric intervention. This set the stage for the passage of the National Mental Health Act of 1946, which provided for the funding of research, the training of professional personnel, and assistance to the states in establishing pilot and demonstration projects and studies. It focused on the cause, diagnosis, treatment, and prevention of mental disorders. In 1949, the National Institute of Mental Health was formed, after funds were appropriated to carry out the Act's provisions. This agency has had a major impact on the development of the mental health system in the United States.

As a result of the Mental Health Study Act of 1955, the Joint Commission on Mental Illness and Health was formed to study the problems of mental and emotional illness. A series of important monographs was published by the commission. Its final report, *Action for Mental Health* (Joint Commission on Mental Illness and Health, 1961), listed the major barriers to the development of mental health programs and recommended the establishment of full-time mental health clinics and general hospital psychiatric units, the development of intensive psychiatric treatment centers, increased recruitment of professional personnel, and investment in long-term basic research.

Based on experience, including the successful treatment of military personnel on the front lines, new community mental health centers focused on treating the patient in the community, not in an isolated institution away from family, job, and friends (Callicutt, 1987). The intent was to provide seed money for initiating programs, with the expectation that the state and local community would cover the operating costs as federal support was withdrawn.

In 1977, President Jimmy Carter signed Executive Order No. 11793 establishing the President's Commission on Mental Health "to review the mental health needs of the Nation and to make recommendations to the President as to how the Nation might best meet these needs" (President's Commission on Mental Health, 1978, p. 1). After holding public hearings across the country, the Commission submitted its report in 1978.

The Commission suggested that 15% of the population, rather than the previous estimate of 10%, needed mental health services. However, estimates of prevalence rates in 1990 suggested that 40.4 million people experienced a nonaddictive mental disorder, with an additional 10.9 million people affected by an addictive disorder (Bourdon, Rae, Narrow, Manderscheid, & Regier, 1994). Other recommendations addressed the needs of underserved populations including the chronically mentally ill and racial and ethnic minorities. Subsequently, the Mental Health Systems Act of 1980 authorized the continuation of grants for community mental health centers and for special populations. Case management was stressed for the chronically mentally ill who were discharged or diverted from inpatient facilities. Also, it required that performance contracts be executed.

The Omnibus Budget Reconciliation Act of 1981, passed under the Reagan Administration, provided that federal funds would be cut by 25% and be allocated directly to the states, which have the responsibility for distributing them. This legislation set a different tack relative to the course of mental health policy and the interface of the federal government and the states. Individual states have considerable mental health policy leeway, in terms of the influence of the state mental health agency director, office of the governor, and state legislators, as well as local elected officials, boards, and staff members in molding, interpreting, directing, and implementing decisions regarding program funding and service provisions (Fellin, 1996).

Other federal policy initiatives have been directed to specific populations, especially the chronically mentally ill. Community support programs were developed, and service emphases included the "clubhouse" mode for the rehabilitation of ex-mental patients, with Fountain House in New York City being the first. A psychosocial rehabilitation model was used, like the one developed in Madison, Wisconsin, and known as Assertive Community Treatment, which is replicated with variations throughout the country (Fellin, 1996).

Other federal legislation targeting the chronically mentally ill and focusing on states establishing an organized community-based system of care is the State Comprehensive Mental Health Services Plan Act of 1986 (PL 99-660) (Fellin, 1996).

Patterns of funding for programs including Medicare and Medicaid also have affected patient care, shifting many elderly patients from state hospitals to nursing homes or board and care homes in the community. In some respects, the operative term is transinstitutionalization rather than deinstitutionalization.

Role of the Courts

Judicial decisions have had a profound impact on mental health policy. Only a few instances will be mentioned to highlight the significance of the court's influence. For example, when the courts held that people who were involuntarily committed should receive care according to the concept of the least restrictive alternative, this principle challenged mental health professionals to determine the need for institutional treatment as opposed to a form of community care; it also required that similar consideration be given to the range of limitations and restrictions in structuring a person's care in the hospital (Crain, 1983; Shannon, 1997).

In another important decision, the courts have also held that patients may not be exploited for their work in mental institutions. If they work, this must be done voluntarily, and they must be compensated (Crain, 1983).

In 1971, a federal court found that the Alabama state mental health facility was providing woefully inadequate care and the court (*Wyatt v. Stickney,* 1971) subsequently conducted an extensive bearing, ultimately resulting in the stipulation of an array of treatment conditions to provide an acceptable treatment program (Shannon, 1997). A broad array of treatment issues were addressed, including the right to be free from excessive or unwarranted medication and a right to informed consent before the use of invasive procedures such as electroconvulsive treatment. In this case, the least restrictive alternative issue was spelled out (Shannon, 1997).

Many other court decisions speak to issues such as the insanity defense, competence to stand trial, and diversion of mentally ill offenders. In addition, there are decisions affecting the potential liability of mental health professions; for example, the question of the "duty to warn" when the professional has direct knowledge that a patient might pose a risk to harm someone (Shannon, 1997). These examples illustrate the enormous impact of the courts in forming mental health policy.

ISSUES AND TRENDS

In this section, I will underscore some of the basic issues in the sphere of mental health policy. Likewise, selected trends will be highlighted. First and foremost, inpatient and residential treatment services—in terms of the number of facilities, number of beds, number of treatment episodes, and length of stay—is declining. This trend started in 1955, and the locus of patient care has shifted from inpatient to outpatient as a consequence of the deinstitutionalization movement and the use of psychotropic medications. Sadly, we are continuing to witness the spectacle of "The Tragic Odyssey of the Homeless Mentally Ill" (Torrey, 1988). The forces involved in this problem are complex: political, economic, philosophical, ideological, and more. Although the need to house the homeless is obvious, the need to provide treatment resources for those suffering from mental and/or addictive disorders is also apparent. We are not yet close to adequately addressing this problem.

The environment of managed mental health care is a current reality, but its parameters are not fixed. Although this movement is, in fact, inexorable, its effects are uncertain. We can safely predict that the competition for managed care contracts will be keen, as the stakes are high. Special provision should be made to ensure that severely and persistently mentally ill people will receive the necessary treatment and community support services to permit them to have a reasonably safe and acceptable life in the community. Although this is an appropriate goal, inpatient care should be accessible when needed. Not every acute mental disturbance is responsive to community-based interventions.

People with addictive disorders by and large require treatment services. People involved in crimes related to substance abuse are taxing the resources of state and federal prisons in the United States. In 1993, drug offenders made up 30% of newly sentenced inmates, as opposed to 7% in 1988 (Turnbo & Murray, 1997). As noted by Turnbo and Murray (1997), "Because of the deinstitutionalization of the mentally ill, the criminal justice system now increasingly has become the destination of mentally ill and developmentally disabled individuals" (p. 298). This unsettling trend should compel policy makers to make mental health treatment services available to this group. However, it seems that elected officials are responding to their constituents' views, which support the building and maintenance of prisons at the expense of providing an adequate range of treatment services. Advocacy organizations must be more aggressive in educating the public as well as pushing for policy reforms.

Advances in the neurosciences offer one foundation for optimism regarding the treatment of people with mental disorders. New, more effective medications offer increased hope of providing mental stability for people with schizophrenia, depression, anxiety, or bipolar affective disorders. Wilson (1997) asserts, "Neuroscience now provides an essential perspective regarding the causes and treatments of mental disorders." He concludes, "Effective humanistic treatments for mental illness will be heavily influenced by neuroscientific research" (p. 105). Here, the call is for policy makers and funding organizations to continue, and even increase, support for neuroscientific research. Furthermore, social research legitimately has a claim for funding (Millard, 1997) in terms of the potential impact in preventing and combating mental illness.

Perhaps one of the more compelling issues deals with the balance between the mentally ill person's right to treatment and the right to refuse treatment. This complex equation at one point seemed to pit the fields of mental health law, fueled by the passion of the Civil Rights Movement, against the ideology involving psychiatry's responsibility to provide appropriate treatment services to the mentally disordered. As lawyers fought to free people from confinement related to mental problems, it is suggested that the psychiatrists acquiesced to the onslaught of the mental health bar (Isaac & Armat, 1990). Shannon (1997) captures the essence of the issue, placing it within our cultural context:

> As greater knowledge is acquired about the diagnosis and treatment of serious mental illness, the courts and judicial system will eventually catch up. Unfortunately, however, there is often a time lag between medical learning and judicial acceptance of new developments. As old stigmas and inaccurate assessments of serious mental illnesses as somehow not being real diseases fade away, the courts and advocates will likely become more attuned to appropriate treatment needs. (p. 66)

Judicial decisions, then, will continue to be prominent in the mental health policy arena, and thus, will affect the system of mental health service delivery.

REFERENCES

Anderson, R. E., & Carter, S. (1990). *Human behavior in the social environment: A social system approach* (4th ed.). New York: Aldine de Gruyter.

Barker, R. L. (1995). *The social work dictionary* (3rd ed.). Washington, DC: National Association of Social Workers.

Beers, C. W. (1913). *A mind that found itself* (3rd ed., rev.). Norwood, MA: Plimpton.

Bevilacqua, J. J. (1991). Overview of state mental health policy. In C. G. Hudson & A. J. Cox (Eds.), *Dimensions of state mental health policy* (pp. 73-83). New York: Praeger.

Bourdon, K., Rae, D., Narrow, W., Manderscheid, R. W., & Regier, D. (1994). National prevalence and treatment of mental and addictive disorders. In R. W. Manderscheid & M. A. Sonnenschein (Eds.), *Mental health United States, 1994* (CDHHS Publication No. SMA 94-3000, pp. 22-51). Washington, DC: Government Printing Office.

Callicutt, J. W. (1983). Contemporary settings and the rise of the profession in mental health. In J. W. Callicutt & P. J. Lecca (Eds.), *Social work and mental health* (pp. 30-41). New York: Free Press.

Callicutt, J. W. (1987). Mental health services. In A. Minnehan et al. (Ed.), *Encyclopedia of social work* (pp. 125-135). Silver Spring, MD: National Association of Social Workers.

Callicutt, J. W. (1997). Overview of the field of mental health. In T. R. Watkins & J. W. Callicutt (Eds.), *Mental health policy and practice today* (pp. 1-16). Thousand Oaks, CA: Sage.

Callicutt, J. W., & Lecca, P. J. (1983). The convergence of social work and mental health services. In J. W. Callicutt & P. J. Lecca (Eds.), *Social work and mental health* (pp. 3-10). New York: Free Press.

Callicutt, J. W., & Price, D. H. (1997). Personnel: The professionals and their preparation. In T. B. Watkins & J. W. Callicutt (Eds.), *Mental Health policy and practice today* (pp. 69-85). Thousand Oaks, CA: Sage.

Cockerham, W. C. (1989). *Sociology of mental disorders* (2nd ed.). Englewood Cliffs, NJ: Prentice Hall.

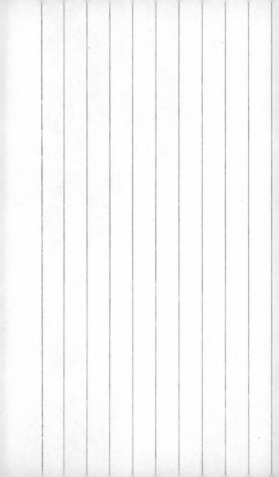

Crain, P. M. (1983). Civil law. In J. A. Talbott & S. R. Kaplan (Eds.), *Psychiatric administration: A comprehensive text for the clinician-executive* (pp. 369-383). New York: Grune & Stratton.

Deutsch, A. (1949). *The mentally ill in America* (2nd ed.). New York: Columbia University Press.

Dial, T. H., Pion, G. M., Cooney, B., Hohout, J., Kaplan, K. O., Ginsberg, L., Merwin, E. I., Fox, J. C., Ginsberg, M., Staton, J., Cawlson, T. W., Windermuth, V. A., Blankertz, L., & Hughes, R. (1992). Training of mental health providers. In R. W. Manderscheid & M. A. Sonnenschein (Eds.), *Mental health, United States, 1992* (CDHHS Publication No. SMA-92-1942, pp. 142-162). Washington, DC: Government Printing Office.

Fellin, P. (1996). *Mental health and mental illness: Policies, programs, and services.* Itasca, IL: F. E. Peacock.

Glover, M. R. (1984). *The retreat York: An early experiment in the treatment of mental illness.* York, UK: William Sessions.

Grob, G. N. (1973). *Mental institutions in America.* New York: Free Press.

Grob, G. N. (1994). *The mad among us: A history of the care of America's mentally ill.* New York: Free Press.

Hobbs, N. (1964). Mental health's third revolution. *American Journal of Orthopsychiatry, 34,* 822-833.

Hudson, C. G., & Cox, A. J. (Eds.). (1991). *Dimensions of state mental health policy.* New York: Praeger.

Isaac, R. J., & Armat, V. C. (1990). *Madness in the streets: How psychiatry and the law abandoned the mentally ill.* New York: Free Press.

Joint Commission on Mental Illness and Health. (1961). *Action for mental health.* New York: Science Editions.

Kiesler, C. A., & Sibulkin, A. E. (1987). *Mental hospitalization: Myths and facts about a national crisis.* Newbury Park, CA: Sage.

Krauss, J. B., & Slavinsky, A. T. (1982). *The chronically ill psychiatric patient and the community.* Boston: Blackwell Scientific Publications.

Kuhlman, T. L. (1994). *Psychology on the streets: Mental health practice with homeless persons.* New York: Brunner/Mazel.

Langsley, D. G., Berlin, F. N., & Yarvis, R. M. (1981). *Handbook of community mental health.* Garden City, NY: Medical Examination Publishing.

Lecca, P. J. (1983). Current trends in mental health services and legislation. In J. W. Callicutt & P. J. Lecca (Eds.), *Social work and mental health* (pp. 11-29). New York: Free Press.

Lutterman, T. C. (1994). The state mental health agency profile system. In R. W. Manderscheid & M. A. Sonnenschein (Eds.), *Mental health, United States, 1994* (CDHHS Publication No. SMA 94-3000, pp. 165-187). Washington, DC: Government Printing Office.

Manderscheid, R. W., Rae, D. S., Narrow, W. E., Loch, B. E., & Regier, D. A. (1993). Congruence of service utilization estimates from the epidemiologic catchment area project and other sources. *Archives of General Psychiatry, 50,* 108-114.

Mechanic, D. (1999). *Mental health and social policy: The emergence of managed care* (4th ed.). Boston: Allyn & Bacon.

Menninger, W. C. (1947). Psychiatric experience in the war, 1941-1946. *American Journal of Psychiatry, 103,* 577-586.

Millard, D. W. (1997). Research into social factors in mental health. In T. R. Watkins & J. W. Callicutt (Eds.), *Mental health policy and practice* (pp. 107-128). Thousand Oaks, CA: Sage.

Peterson, B. D., West, J., Pincus, H. A., Kohout, J., Pion, G. M., Wicherski, M. M., Vandivort, W. R., Palimeter, M., Merwin, E. J., Fox, J. C., Clawson, T. W., Rhodes, K. K., Stockton, R., Ambrose, J. P., Blankertz, L., Dwyer, K. P., Stanhope, V., Fleischen, M. S., Goldsmith, H. F., Witkin, M. J., Atay, J. E. & Manderscheid, R. W. (1996). An update on human resources in mental health. In R. W. Manderscheid & M. A. Sonnenehein (Eds.), *Mental health, United States, 1996* (CDHHS Publication No. SMA 3098, pp. 168-204). Washington, DC: Government Printing Office.

President's Commission on Mental Health. (1978). *Report to the president* (Vol. 9). Washington, DC: Government Printing Office.

Price, D. H. (1997). Mental health services to America's veterans. In T. R. Watkins & J. W. Callicutt (Eds.), *Mental health policy and practice today* (pp. 209-234). Thousand Oaks, CA: Sage.

Redick, R. W., Witkin, M. J., Atay, J. E., & Manderscheid, R. W. (1994). Highlights of organized mental health services in 1990 and major national and state trends. In R. W. Manderscheid & M. A. Sonnenschein (Eds.), *Mental health, United States, 1994* (CDHHS Publication No. SMA 94-3000, pp. 99-125). Washington, DC: Government Printing Office.

Redick, R. W., Witkin, M. J., Atay, J. E., & Manderscheid, R. W. (1996). Highlights of organized mental health services in 1992 and major national and state trends. In R. W. Manderscheid & M. A. Sonnenschein (Eds.), *Mental health, United States, 1996* (CDHHS Publication No. SMA 96-3098, pp. 90-137). Washington, DC: Government Printing Office.

Regier, D. A., Goldberg, J. D., & Taube, C. A. (1978). The de facto U.S. mental health services system: A public health perspective. *Archives of General Psychiatry, 35,* 685-693.

Rochefort, D. A. (1997). *From poorhouses to homelessness: Policy analysis and mental health care* (2nd ed). Westport, CT: Auburn House.

Ross, E. C., & Croze, C. (1997). Mental health policy and practice today. In T. R. Watkins & J. W. Callicutt (Eds.), *Mental health policy and practice today* (pp. 346-361). Thousand Oaks, CA: Sage.

Shannon, B. (1997). The impact of the courts on mental health policy and services. In T. R. Watkins & J. W. Callicutt (Eds.), *Mental health policy and practice today* (pp. 49-68). Thousand Oaks, CA: Sage.

Sharkey, J. (1994). *Bedlam.* New York: St. Martin's.

Stroup, H. S. (1960). *Social work: An introduction to the field.* New York: American Book Co.

Stroup, H. (1986). *Social welfare pioneers.* Chicago: Nelson-Hall.

Torrey, E. F. (1988). *Nowhere to go.* New York: Harper & Row.

Turnbo, C., & Murray, D. W., Jr. (1997) The state of mental health services to criminal offenders. In T. R. Watkins & J. W. Callicutt (Eds.), *Mental health policy and practice today* (pp. 298-311). Thousand Oaks, CA: Sage

Wilson, W. H. (1997). Neuroscientific research in mental health. In T. R. Watkins & J. W. Callicutt (Eds.), *Mental health policy and practice today* (pp. 89-106). Thousand Oaks, CA: Sage.

Wyatt v. Stickney, 325 F. Supp. 781 (M.D. Ala. 1971), 334 F. Supp. 1341 (M.D. Ala. 1972), 344 F. Supp. 373 (M.D. Ala 1972), 344 F. Supp. 387 (M.D. Ala 1972), aff'd sub nom., Wyatt v. Aderholt, 503 F.2d 1305 (5th Cir. 1974).

CHAPTER NINETEEN

Social Policies for People With Disabilities

MARY F. HAYDEN

The purpose of this chapter is to discuss the dominant social policies for people with disabilities. Social policy is defined as the government's planning, decision making, and allocation of public resources through which the relationships of individuals with disabilities—the governed—are regulated by their government. I will first discuss the major forces that influence social policy. Second, I will provide a brief historical overview of the dominant policies and services for people with disabilities and discuss their major characteristics. Finally, I will discuss the current issues and controversies within the realm of policy development for people with disabilities.

UNDERLYING FORCES

Social policies for people with disabilities are derived from federal laws that are influenced by three major forces: social altruism, deinstitutionalization, and shifts in power relationships. These forces provide the impetus for nearly every law enacted by Congress and nearly every regulation that an executive agency of the federal government has adopted to implement an act of Congress (Turnbull & Barber, 1986). To understand these forces is to understand the history and rationale of social policy and people with disabilities.

Social Altruism

Altruism is the "devotion to others or to humanity, as opposed to selfishness" (English Language Institute of America, 1971). Social altruism is a collective effort by the majority to improve the lives of other people, who are part of a minority. When social altruism is expressed through law, it is based on the legal principle of parens patriae; that is, the government is responsible for individuals who are unable to take care of themselves without assistance (Turnbull & Barber, 1986). For people with disabilities, many policies are based on the principle of *parens patriae* and are motivated by social altruism. As a result, these policies are based on the belief that the government, a state or federal bureaucrat, professional, or some other "expert" knows what is best for individuals with disabilities. Policies based on social altruism are paternalistic in nature and, as a result, impose the majority's values and beliefs on others.

Deinstitutionalization

Institutionalization has been a long-standing policy in the United States, based on social altruism that went astray. Although the intent of the institutions was to provide care and treatment, there is ample documentation that people who have been institutionalized are subject to abuse, neglect, and poor medical care (Blatt & Kaplan, 1974; Hayden, 1997; Wisconsin Coalition for Advocacy, 1986). Indeed, the treatment of people with disabilities can be depicted as one of "the country's most shameful oversights," which caused the handicapped to live "shunted aside, hidden, and ignored" (*Alexander v. Choate,* 1985, pp. 287, 295-297). As Ash (1993) observed, "The only difference between a halo and a noose is the distance of twelve inches" (p. 195).

Deinstitutionalization was a term first applied to concerted social policy and demonstrably effective social commitments to increase access to real communities for people with mental retardation and other developmental disabilities. The effects of those commitments are most commonly characterized by statistics that show the average daily census of state institutions. Between 1967 and 1997, deinstitutionalization led to a 75.5% reduction in the population of people with mental retardation living in large (16 people or more), state-operated, mental retardation and psychiatric institutions, from 228,500 to 55,894 (Anderson, Polister, Prouty, Lakin, & Sandlin, 1998). However, an additional 37,726 people with mental retardation were living in large, non-state institutions, and 24,958 people were living in nursing homes in 1997 (Anderson, Polister, Prouty, & Lakin, 1998; Prouty & Lakin, 1998). In addition, more than half of the residents of all settings in Arkansas, Illinois, Mississippi, and Oklahoma lived in large institutions; nationally, 27.3% of all residential service recipients lived in settings of 16 or more residents (Prouty & Lakin, 1998).

Traditionally, planning and service provision are viewed as the territory of experts. The quality of life that people with disabilities experience is dependent on expert opinion, rather than on their own definitions of what they desire. In addition, service planning is about designing programs and deciding where "to put people," rather than developing person-centered approaches to program planning and service delivery. Although traditional views still permeate policy development and service provision, new approaches are being developed to shift power from professionals, parents, direct care staff, and service providers to the individuals. One such approach is called supported living.

The principles of supported living include control over one's own home and personal space; freedom to shape one's daily life; choice in one's services, service providers, and service goals; autonomy as desired from formal service systems through opportunities to use and pay for the "natural supports" from family, friends, neighbors, and the generic services of one's community; and assistance in building and sustaining meaningful, enjoyable, and personally rewarding relationships in the community. Supported living focuses on empowering people to decide how they want to live and on providing them with the necessary supports to follow through with their decisions:

> In the supported living ideal, individuals needing support and those providing support view themselves in a partnership, where planning is done *with* rather than *for* and in which people with disabilities have a strong and respected role in deciding how and where they want to live. When people do not use words to communicate, people who support them listen to their behavior and record and recall their preferences. (Lakin, Hayden, & Burwell, 1996, p. 2)

HISTORICAL OVERVIEW

Prior to the 20th century, social welfare generally was considered the responsibility of families and charitable organizations. Local, county, and state governments intervened only as a last resort. The only type of assistance that most people with disabilities received was that provided in the almshouses and poorhouses. However, innovative services such as foster care and community placement were being developed and implemented on a small scale in selected states (Braddock, 1998).

The establishment of the first publicly financed residential school program in Boston in 1848 was the initial benchmark in the provision of services for people with mental retardation and other developmental disabilities (Braddock, 1998). This was also the benchmark for the beginning of a series of policies such as sterilization, institutionalization, and guardianship, policies that reinforced the belief that people with disabilities are dependent and need to be segregated from the general population. However, by 1920, special education was present and, in addition, professionals in the field of mental retardation were calling for a comprehensive array of community services for people with mental retardation (Scheerenberger, 1983). However, the country moved away from social reform during the 1920s (May, 1964). The stock market crash of 1929, which was followed by the Great Depression, only continued to reinforce the idea that families and charity organizations were responsible for people in distress.

The inauguration of Franklin D. Roosevelt in 1933 was the beginning of a dramatic change in this country's perspective on the federal government's responsibility to its citizens. During his tenure, the most important piece of federal legislation directly benefitting people with developmental disabilities, the Social Security Act of 1935, was passed, and, as a result, social policy for people with disabilities became formalized and would be interpreted through the Act, its subsequent amendments, and other federal laws passed after this point in time.

Social Security Act

The precursor of the Social Security Act of 1935 was a federal program to provide Civil War pensions to disabled veterans and widows and orphans of veterans. The Act created a social insurance program designed to pay retired workers age 65 or older a continuing income after retirement. Of its original titles, only Title V, the Maternal and Child Health and Crippled Children's Services, provided immediate direct assistance to people with developmental disabilities (Boggs, Hanley-Maxwell, Lakin, & Bradley, 1988). Initially, the emphasis of Maternal and Child Health and Crippled Children's Services was on orthopedic impairments, but by the 1940s and 1950s, children with cerebral palsy and epilepsy were more frequently reported as receiving services. In the mid-1950s, these services focused on early diagnosis and evaluation of young children with retardation.

In 1950, the Social Security Act was amended to create Aid to the Permanently and Totally Disabled. This was a program of federal aid to states for categorical cash assistance. In 1974, it was replaced by Supplemental Security Income (SSI). The SSI program (Title XVI) provides cash assistance to people who are aged, have disabilities, or are blind, and who meet standards of financial need. In addition, SSI has paid benefits to children with disabilities since the program's inception.

In 1954, the Social Security Act was amended to provide benefits to disabled workers age 50 to 65 and disabled adult children. Over the next 2 years, Congress broadened the scope of the program and, in 1957, it created Social Security Disability Insurance. This program covered disabled workers under age 50 and adults disabled in childhood, who are the survivors or dependents of covered workers who have died, retired, or have themselves become disabled.

The Medicaid program was enacted as Title XIX of the Social Security Act amendments of 1965. Initially, the program was created to provide medical assistance to certain individuals and families with low incomes and resources. It is a jointly funded cooperative venture between the federal and state governments to assist states in the provision of adequate medical care to eligible needy people. Today, Medicaid is essentially three programs: a health insurance program for low-income people, a long-term care program for people who are elderly and those with disabilities, and a specialized service program for individuals with developmental disabilities and mental illness (Braddock, 1998).

In 1995, there were 36,281,586 Medicaid recipients in the United States (Hemp, Braddock, & Westrich, 1998). Of this number, 47.3% were children, 21% were adults, 11.4% were "aged," 4.2% were other people, and 16.2% were people with all types of disabilities. Of the 16.2%, 4.9% were individuals with developmental disabilities. In the same year, $120 billion was spent on Medicaid (Hemp et al., 1998). Of this amount, 41.6% was spent on people with all types of disabilities. Of the 41.6%, 15.7% was spent on those with developmental disabilities.

Medicaid also plays a key role in financing long-term care through the Intermediate Care Facility/Mentally Retarded programs and Home and Community Based Services Waiver programs (Braddock & Hemp, 1996). In 1996, 71% of the total long-term care resources allocated for mental retardation and developmental disability services in this country consisted of federal-state Medicaid funding (Braddock, 1998).

The Medicare program (Title XVIII) was enacted in 1972 and provides health insurance to people who are 65 years old, people with disabilities, and people with permanent kidney failure. It has two parts. Part A provides coverage of inpatient hospital services, skilled nursing facilities, home health services, and hospital care. Part B pays for the cost of physician services, outpatient hospital services, medical equipment and supplies, and other health services and supplies.

Intermediate Care Facility/ Mentally Retarded Program

In 1967, the Intermediate Care Facility/Mentally Retarded program was authorized under Title XI of the Social Security Act. In 1971, the Intermediate Care and Skilled Nursing Facilities programs were combined under Title XIX. Three primary outcomes of the legislation appear to have been intended by Congress (Prouty & Lakin, 1998):

1) to provide substantial federal incentives for upgrading the physical environment and the quality of care and habilitation being provided in public mental retardation/developmental disability institutions; 2) to neutralize the above-mentioned incentives for states to place persons with mental retardation or developmental disabilities in nonstate nursing homes and/or to certify their state inceptions as Skilled Nursing Facilities; and 3) to provide a program for care and habilitation ("active treatment") specifically focused on the needs of persons with Mental Retardation or Developmental Disabilities rather than upon medical care. Many proponents of this new program also saw it as a way to enlist the federal government in assisting states with their rapidly increasing state institution costs. (pp. 75-76)

The desired outcomes were not actualized. Conditions at state-operated institutions did not provide active treatment or improve the care and treatment or quality of life of people living in state-operated institutions (Hayden, 1997). The program also created incentives for states to maintain institutions, rather than to create community options. As a result, states diverted funds that could otherwise have been spent on community program development. Moreover, the program promoted private, community-based Intermediate Care Facility/Mentally Retarded institutions (Prouty & Lakin, 1998). In addition, the program promoted organizational inefficiency and individual dependency by promoting a single uniform standard for care and oversight of residents of these institutions, whatever the nature and degree of their disabilities and/or their capacity for independence (Prouty & Lakin, 1998). Although these regulations were later amended to include smaller institutions, research suggests that less intensively regulated and more flexible models of residential support produce superior outcomes at equal or lower cost than small Intermediate Care Facility/Mentally Retarded institutions (Conroy, 1996).

Home- and Community-Based Services Waiver Program

Beginning in 1981, Home and Community-Based Services Waiver programs became available to states to provide services to individuals with mental retardation and other developmental disabilities who would be at risk of placement in intermediate care facility/mentally retarded institutions or nursing facilities. State programs developed under this authority permitted substantial latitude to states to pursue the goals of supported living. Although state waiver programs have been provided primarily in group homes, some states have begun to shift the focus of waiver program services to serve more people in their own home, their family's home, or an adult foster care home and to provide a broader range of services tailored to individuals' needs and preferences (General Accounting Office, 1996). In addition, the waiver program has permitted states to pursue various objectives, such as closing many large and small intermediate care facility/mentally retarded institutions, expanding services to people previously in state-financed programs, and including people not previously served.

As a result of the waiver program, many states during the late 1980s sought opportunities to expand Medicaid-financed community services by decreasing their use of intermediate care facility/mentally retarded group home models, which were governed by institutional standards that were wholly inconsistent with supported living principles. In addition, states were also interested in being able to serve people with mental retardation and other developmental disabilities who might not be eligible for intermediate care/mentally retarded facilities and, therefore, not eligible for home and community-based services on certain technical grounds, such as not needing "active treatment."

Medicaid Community-Supported Living Arrangements

In 1990, Congress enacted Section 1930 of Title XIX of the Social Security Act, establishing the Community-Supported Living Arrangements program, as a special initiative to provide supported living services to Medicaid-eligible individuals with developmental disabilities for a 5-year period. The supported living approach to long-term care presented a substantial contrast to the institutional living and congregate care that has dominated social policy for people with disabilities.

The Community-Supported Living Arrangements program permitted targeting of services to specific groups and geographic areas, removed demonstration of intermediate care facility/mentally retarded or nursing home level-of-care need as a condition of eligibility, allowed each state to develop its own quality assurance plan within defined federal guidelines, and provided flexibility in the services provided. States were authorized to provide personal care assistance; training and habilitation to increase integration, independence, and productivity; 24-hour emergency assistance; assistive technology and adaptive equipment; support services for community participation; and other services consistent with Community Supported Living Arrangements program goals if approved by the Secretary of Health and Human Services. Total federal expenditures for the program were capped.

The Community-Supported Living Arrangements program brought a clearer focus, higher expectations, and new opportunities to individualized community services. One legacy of the program was its contribution as a catalyst of supported living. It provided direct and important expansion of supported living in at least six states and stimulation to the development and expansion of supported living in all Community Supported Living Arrangement states, with particularly notable and lasting effects (Lakin et al., 1996). In addition, the program showed the potential of federal influences and incentives to plant the seeds of substantial system change within long-term care.

The Community-Supported Living Arrangements program heightened attention to the distance between the ideals of the emerging systems of support and the common practices in the traditions of congregate care. These discrepancies were found in the program's efforts to move from models of supervision to needed support, from rules to protect safety to negotiations of balance between safety and personal freedom, from being accountable for clear and fixed expectations of government entities to being responsive to the changing preferences of service recipients (Lakin et al., 1996). Although each state provided stories about the difficulties of making these transitions, all participants felt their supported living was the only acceptable future in service delivery for people with disabilities.

Rehabilitation Act of 1973

Section 504 (PL 93-112) of the Rehabilitation Act prohibits any recipient of any federal financial assistance from discriminating against a person with a disability solely because of his or her disability. In addition, the section states that public schools must provide each handicapped child with a free, appropriate education, conduct nondiscriminatory testing, place children in the least restrictive environment, and guarantee due process (Turnbull & Barber, 1986).

Sections 501 and 503 (PL 93-516) under Title V of this law stated that people with disabilities applying for employment or employed by an organization under federal contract were entitled to equal opportunity and could not be subjected to discrimination. Section 503 provided assistance to people with disabilities in obtaining federal employment and sought to improve the hiring, placement, and advancement of these individuals (Turnbull & Barber, 1986).

The Rehabilitation Act was called "the cornerstone of the civil rights movement of the mobility-impaired" (*ADAPT v. Skinner,* 1989). However, the Section had a number of problems, such as the statutory language, the limited extent of its coverage, inadequate enforcement mechanisms, and erratic judicial interpretations (*Helen L. et al. v. Albert L. DiDario,* 1995). As a result, the section did not adequately combat the problems of discrimination that people with disabilities were continuing to face.

Education for All Handicapped Children Act (PL 94-142)

The Education for All Handicapped Children Act was passed in 1975 and was later renamed the Individuals with Disabilities Education Act (IDEA) in 1990. The initial law was driven by a coalition of parents and educators seeking public education for children with disabilities who lived with their families. IDEA gave children with disabilities the right to a free, appropriate public education. IDEA has had a successful impact on deinstitutionalization; many children who would have been placed in separate schools and institutions 25 years ago are able to remain at home and are educated in their neighborhood schools.

Although significant progress has been made, the status of children with disabilities continues to fall short of the original law. Twice as many children with disabilities drop out of school. Dropouts do not return to school and, as a result, have difficulty finding jobs and often end up in the criminal justice system. Also, many children with disabilities are excluded from the curriculum and assessments used with their nondisabled counterparts and, as a result, their opportunity to meet higher standards of performance is limited (IDEA, 1997).

The 1997 amendments to IDEA included a number of changes that were to remedy these and other problems that contribute to the barriers children with disabilities face. These changes included raising the expectations for children with disabilities; increasing parental involvement in the education of their children; including children with disabilities in assessments, performance goals, and reports to the public; and supporting quality professional development for all personnel who are involved in educating children with disabilities.

Americans with Disabilities Act (P.L. 101-336)

In 1990, the Americans with Disabilities Act was enacted to eliminate discrimination against people with disabilities in the areas of employment, transportation, public accommodations, public services, and telecommunication. The Act is the most comprehensive civil rights law ever enacted, and its purpose is the following:

> (1) to provide a clear and comprehensive national mandate for the elimination of discrimination against individuals with disabilities; (2) to provide clear, strong, consistent, enforceable standards addressing discrimination against individuals with disabilities; (3) to ensure that the Federal Government plays a central role in enforcing the standards established in this Act on behalf of individuals with disabilities; and (4) to invoke the sweep of congressional authority, including the power to enforce the fourteenth amendment and to regulate commerce, in order to address the major areas of discrimination faced day-to-day by people with disabilities (PL 101-336, Section 1 (b) Sec. 1)

With the passage of the Americans with Disabilities Act, people with disabilities enjoy a degree of anti-discrimination protection comparable to that of women and members of other minority groups. Since its enactment, a series of court cases have further defined the parameters of the Act. For example, a recent Supreme Court decision ruled that prisons fall under the jurisdiction of the Act (Title II) (*Pennsylvania Department of Corrections et al. v. Ronald R. Yeskey,* 1998). Other cases are requiring substantial desegregation under the Act (i.e., *Kathleen S. v. Department of Public Welfare,* 1998; *Helen L. et al. v. DiDario,* 1995).

Personal Responsibility and Work Opportunity Reconciliation Act

Until 1996, the Social Security Act did not contain a separate definition of disability for children. A child was considered disabled if she or he had a medically determinable impairment or a combination of impairments that was of comparable severity to an impairment that would disable an adult. In 1991, a new policy of functional equivalence to its medical listings and an Individualized Functional Assessment for evaluating disability in children were incorporated into the Social Security Insurance regulations.

In 1996, the Personal Responsibility and Work Opportunity Reconciliation Act changed the definition of disability for children. The new definition set a higher standard of severity than the previous law, and children can now qualify only through more restrictive medical listings. Specifically, the definition requires that a child have a physical or mental condition or conditions that can be medically proven and that result in marked and severe functional limitations, that the medically proven physical or mental condition or conditions must last or be expected to last at least 12 months or be expected to result in death, and that a child may not be considered disabled if she or he is working at a job that the Social Security Administration considers to be substantial work.

The Act also eliminated the Individualized Functional Assessment and certain other provisions of the Social Security Act's regulations. As a result, children must prove a higher level of severity than before. The largest group affected by elimination of the Individualized Functional Assessment are children with serious mental, emotional, and behavioral disorders (Bazelon Center, 1998).

There were about 1 million children receiving SSI benefits as of December 1996 (Apfel, 1998). A redetermination process was conducted, and, as of May 30, 1998, initial redeterminations were issued for 245,349 children. Of these children, 54.1% continued to receive SSI benefits. For those children who lost these benefits as a result of the changes due to welfare reform, an amendment to the Balanced Budget Act ensured that they remain eligible for Medicaid benefits. However, they still lost their cash benefits, and, as a result, many families will face significant health care costs, including premiums, deductibles, and co-payments.

For example, some expenses may not be covered by a family's private health coverage, or the child may exceed the lifetime maximum for certain services. The SSI cash benefits could have paid for these expenses. In addition, if specialized medical care is only available far from home, there may be other major expenses that the family has to incur while the child is hospitalized (i.e., transportation and lodging). In the past, families with private insurance have used their SSI benefits to pay for these expenses; now, they will have to find other means of assistance.

CURRENT ISSUES AND CONTROVERSIES

Current issues and controversies surrounding social policies for people with disabilities include waiting lists, aging, managed care, and self-advocacy.

Waiting Lists

In 1987, a national survey of state directors of the Association for Retarded Citizens found 139,673 individuals with mental retardation waiting for residential services and day/vocational programs (Davis, 1987). A later study found 102,261 people with mental retardation waiting for residential services and day/vocational programs (Hayden & DePaepe, 1994). Current research indicates that the demand for community services and support is growing (Prouty & Lakin, 1997). Davis and Lloyd (1998) conducted a follow-up interview in 1997 and found that the number of community services requested by families across the country in the 48 states that reported data was 223,562.

Over the 9 years between 1987 and 1996, there was an average annual increase of 3% in the number of people receiving residential services, but an average annual increase of 4% in individuals requesting such services. At the rate and direction we are currently moving, we are not 9 years from a solution; we are 9 years from chaos (Lakin, 1998). Without massive infusions of new resources or substantial change in the ways we provide services and allocate resources, in 9 years, circumstances will be substantially worse than at present. As the baby-boom generation ages over the next 10 to 30 years, growing demand for developmental disabilities services will severely strain state capacities.

Aging Society

The significantly improved longevity in the United States and the demographics of the baby-boom generation will contribute to the increased need for basic health care and long-term care services in the future (Hemp et al., 1998). In the decade between 1982 and 1992, the number of people with disabilities age 65 and over in the United States increased by nearly 21%, compared to an overall U.S. population increase of only 10% (Hardwick, Pack, Donohoe, & Aleska, 1994). In addition, the declining fertility rate, which reduces the number of working-age taxpayers entering the workforce, will place a strain on public support of long-term care. By 2010, 14% of the U.S. population will be 65 or older, and this group will increase to over 20% of our population in the year 2030 (Bureau of the Census, 1996). As our society ages, federal and state governments seek strategies to control the cost of delivery of service. Managed care is one of these strategies.

Managed Care

Medicaid managed care is similar to managed care in the private insurance market in that it consists of a range of health care models that use primary care practitioners to control and coordinate the delivery of services (Hemp et al., 1998). It is becoming a fast-growing program. In 1991, 9.5% of the total Medicaid population was enrolled in some type of managed care program; by 1997, 47.8% of the total population was enrolled in these programs (Health Care Financing Administration, 1998). However, the majority of these beneficiaries are women and children rather than people with disabilities (Hemp et al., 1998). Only 21 states have plans that involve individuals with all types of disabilities. Three of the states have plans specifically for people with developmental disabilities. Several issues are critical to individuals with developmental disabilities and their families. These issues include the following:

> Consumers must be concerned about non-discrimination and about the structure of plans and the appropriate services required by individuals with developmental disabilities. There are also important issues for individuals with developmental disabilities related to the techniques and practices of managed care. These include the management of plans and participation of service providers, the technique of service substitution, the appropriate structuring of risk, and care management. Quality assurance for individuals with disabilities is an area of concern both in terms of the development of appropriate standards to govern managed care and in assuring access to needed acute health care and long-term care services. Finally, consumers have to work to stay informed about and involved in the ongoing implementation of managed care. (Hemp et al., 1998, p. 83)

Institutional Bias of Long-Term Care

The Medicaid program is the single most important public program in the United States for people with developmental disabilities. It finances the majority of long-term care through Intermediate Care Facilities/Mentally Retarded and Home & Community-Based Services programs, as well as nursing facilities. The majority of expenditures are spent on the Intermediate Care Facilities/Mentally Retarded program, although the majority of people are recipients of the Home & Community-Based Services Waiver program (Lakin, Polister, & Prouty, 1998). Opponents of the Intermediate Care Facilities/Mentally Retarded program assert that the program creates direct incentives for maintaining people in state institutions; diverts funds that could otherwise be spent on community program development into institution renovations, promotes the development of private Intermediate Care Facilities/Mentally Retarded institutions for people leaving state institutions, and promotes organizational inefficiency and individual dependency (Prouty & Lakin, 1998). There has been a great deal of interest in changing the institutional bias in the service delivery of long-term care. One attempt to make this change is the Medicaid Community Attendant Services Act (CASA), a bill that was introduced on June 24, 1997 (HR 2020).

The purpose of the bill is to amend Title XIX of the Social Security Act to provide for coverage of qualified community attendant services under the Medicaid program. Under the bill, any person who is entitled to nursing home placement or the Intermediate Care Facilities/Mentally Retarded program will have community-based attendant services furnished (a) on an as-needed basis that is agreed to by the individual; (b) in a home or community-based setting, which may include a school, workplace, or recreation or religious facility; (c) under either an agency-provider model or other models (i.e., vouchers, direct cash payment, individual provider model, consumer-directed agency model); and (d) the furnishing of which is selected, managed, and controlled by the individual. In addition, backup and emergency attendant services must be available, 24 hours a day, 7 days a week. Health-related tasks can be delegated to or performed by unlicensed personal attendants. Moreover, a state program must allow for co-payment or cost sharing for people with higher socioeconomic status.

The Community Attendant Services Act would establish a national program of community-based attendant services for people with disabilities, based on functional needs and without regard to age or disability. The Act would redirect long-term care dollars to encourage community-based attendant services instead of institutional services and, as a result, would fundamentally change our long-term care system by redirecting the institutional bias that now exists within it.

Self-Advocacy Movement

The self-advocacy movement is an international civil rights movement led by and for people with developmental disabilities and is one part of the broader disability rights/independent living movement (Shoultz, 1996). It originated in Sweden in the 1960s and started in the United States in 1974. Self-advocacy can range from one individual advocating on his or her own behalf to "independent groups of people with disabilities working together for justice by helping each other take charge of our lives and fight discrimination" (Self-Advocates Becoming Empowered, 1991).

As a result of this movement, there has been increased participation of people with disabilities in policy developments, such as Americans with Disabilities Act and the Community Attendant Services Act. Also, service agencies have policies promoting choice and self-expression, and the federal government is supporting initiatives that provide individuals with more choice and individualized supported living, such as the Community-Supported Living Arrangements program. Finally, people with disabilities are demanding that their service delivery systems be transformed into a self-determination support system. Indeed, state service delivery systems are moving more toward supported-living models, where individuals with disabilities have more control over how services and supports will be provided to them.

For state service systems to change, states will have do business in a different manner. Transformation will need to occur at the policy level and at the personal level. Policy makers, service providers, families, and individuals with disabilities will need to find new ways to work together through the adoption of new values. As a result, service delivery will shift from a menu of programs to self-directed options based on the priorities set by individuals and their "circle of support." If cost savings continue to occur, other states will be interested in implementing this model. Indeed, self-determination may be a win-win situation for everyone concerned. On the one hand, people with disabilities will have greater control over their own lives. On the other hand, policy makers will be able to cost-effectively meet the growing demand for individualized supported living.

REFERENCES

ADAPT v. Skinner, 881 F.2d at 1205 (3rd Cir. 1989) (concurring opinion).

Alexander v. Choate, 469 U. S. 287, 296 (1985).

Anderson, L., Polister, B., Prouty, R. W., & Lakin, K. L. (1998). *Services provided by state and nonstate agencies in 1997.* In R. Prouty & K. C. Lakin (Eds.), *Residential services for persons with developmental disabilities: Status and trends through 1997* (pp. 69-104). Minneapolis: University of Minnesota, Research and Training Center on Community Living, Institute on Community Integration.

Anderson, L., Polister, B., Prouty, R. W., Lakin, K. L., & Sandlin, J. (1998). In R. Prouty & K. C. Lakin (Eds.), *Residential services for persons with developmental disabilities: Status and trends through 1997* (pp. 69-104). Minneapolis: University of Minnesota, Research and Training Center on Community Living, Institute on Community Integration.

Apfel, K. S. (1998, July 7). Testimony of Commissioner Apfel given before the Senate Finance Committee, Subcommittee on Social Security and Family Policy. Washington, DC.

Ash, M. (1993). *The Zen of recovery.* New York: Jeremy P. Tarcher/Perigee.

Bazelon Center for Mental Health Law. (1998, February, 28). *Children's SSI Program* [On-line]. Available: http://www.bazelon.org/kidssi.html.

Blatt, B., & Kaplan, F. (1974). *Christmas in purgatory: A photographic essay on mental retardation.* New York: Human Policy Press.

Boggs, E. M., Hanley-Maxwell, C., Lakin, K. D., & Bradley, V. J. (1988). Federal policy and legislation: Factors that have constrained and facilitated community integration. In L. W. Heal, J. I. Haney, & A. R. Novak Amado (Eds.), *Integration of developmentally disabled individuals into the community* (2nd ed., pp. 245-271). Baltimore, MD: Paul H. Brookes.

Braddock, D. (1998). Mental retardation and developmental disabilities: Historical and contemporary perspectives. In D. Braddock, R. Hemp, S. Parish, & J. Westrich (Eds.) *The state of the states in developmental disabilities* (5th ed., pp. 3-21). Washington, DC: American Association on Mental Retardation.

Braddock, D., & Hemp, R. (1996). Medicaid spending reductions and developmental disabilities. *Journal of Disability Policy Studies, 7*(1), 1-32.

Bureau of the Census. (1996, December). *Population estimates program, population division.* Washington, DC: Government Printing Office.

Conroy, J. W. (1996). The small ICF/MR program: Dimensions of quality and cost. *Mental Retardation, 34*(1), 13-26.

Davis, S. (1987). *A national status report on waiting lists of people with mental retardation for community services.* Arlington, TX: Association for Retarded Citizens of the United States.

Davis, S., & Lloyd, J. C. (1998). The list grows on and on. *TASH Newsletter, 24,* 17-19.

English Language Institute of America. (1971) *The living Webster encyclopedic dictionary of the English language.* Chicago: Author.

General Accounting Office. (1996, July 22). *Medicaid: Waiver program for developmentally disabled is promising but poses some risks* (GAO/HEHS-96-120). Gaithersburg, MD: Author.

Hardwick, S. E., Pack, P. J., Donohoe, E. A., & Aleska, K. J. (1994). *Across the states, 1994: Profiles of long-term care systems.* Washington, DC: AARP Public Policy Institute.

Hayden, M. F. (1997). Class-action, civil rights litigation for institutionalized persons with mental retardation, and other developmental disabilities: A review. *Mental and Physical Disability Law Reporter, 21,* 411-423.

Hayden, M. F., & DePaepe, P. A. (1994). Waiting for community services while living at home: The impact on persons with mental retardation and other developmental disabilities. In M. F. Hayden & B. H. Abery (Eds.), *Challenges for a service system in transition: Ensuring quality community experiences for persons with developmental disabilities.* Baltimore, MD: Paul H. Brookes.

Health Care Financing Administration. (1998). *National summary of Medicaid managed care programs and enrollment* [On-line]. Available: http://www.hcfa.gov/medicaid/omchmpg.html.

Helen L. et al. v. Albert L. DiDario 46 F3d 325 (3d Cir, 1995).

Hemp, R., Braddock, D., & Westrich, J. (1998). Medicaid, managed care, and developmental disabilities. In D. Braddock, R. Hemp, S. Parish, & J. Westrich (Eds.), *The state of the states in developmental disabilities* (5th ed., pp. 67-89). Washington, DC: American Association on Mental Retardation.

IDEA. (1997, September 30). IDEA O97: *General Information* [On-line]. Available: http://www.ed.gov/offices/OSERS/IDEA/overview.html.

Kathleen S. v. Department of Public Welfare, 1998 U. S. Dist. LEXIS 9558 (June 26, 1998).

Lakin, K. C. (1998). Perspectives: On the outside looking in: Attending to waiting lists in systems of services for people with developmental disabilities. *Mental Retardation, 36,* 157-164.

Lakin, K. C., Hayden, M. F., & Burwell, B. (1996). *Final report: An evaluation of implementation of the Medicaid Community Supported Living Arrangements (CSLA) program in eight states.* Minneapolis: University of Minnesota, Center on Community Living, Institute on Community Integration.

Lakin, K. C., Polister, B., & Prouty, R. W. (1998). Utilization of and expenditures for Medicaid institutional and home and community based services. In R. Prouty & K. C. Lakin (Eds.), *Residential services for persons with developmental disabilities: Status and trends through 1997* (pp 69-104). Minneapolis: University of Minnesota, Research and Training Center on Community Living, Institute on Community Integration.

May, E. (1964). *War, boom, and bust.* New York: Time.

Pennsylvania Department of Corrections et al. v. Ronald R. Yeskey, 118 F. 3d 168 (June 15, 1998).

President's Panel on Mental Retardation. (1962). *A proposed program for national action to combat mental retardation.* Washington, DC: U.S. Superintendent of Documents.

Prouty, R. W., & Lakin, K. C. (Eds.). (1997). *Residential services for persons with developmental disabilities: Status and trends through 1996.* Minneapolis: University of Minnesota, Research and Training Center on Community Living, Institute on Community Integration.

Prouty, R., & Lakin, K. C. (Eds.). (1998). *Residential services for persons with developmental disabilities: Status and trends through 1997.* Minneapolis: University of Minnesota, Research and Training Center on Community Living, Institute on Community Integration.

Scheerenberger, R. C. (1983). *A history of mental retardation.* Baltimore, MD: Paul H. Brookes.

Self-Advocates Becoming Empowered. (1991). *Self-advocacy by persons with disabilities: Ideas for creating a national organization.* Minneapolis: University of Minnesota, Research and Training Center on Community Living.

Shoultz, B. (1996). More thoughts on self advocacy: The movement, the group, and the individual. *TASH Newsletter, 22,* 22-25.

Turnbull, H. R., & Barber, P. A. (1986). Federal laws and adults with developmental disabilities. In J. A. Summers (Ed.), *The right to grow up: An introduction to adults with developmental disabilities* (pp. 255-285). Baltimore, MD: Paul H. Brookes.

Wisconsin Coalition for Advocacy. (1986). *The "active treatment" myth: People with developmental disabilities trapped in Wisconsin institutions.* Madison: Author.

CHAPTER TWENTY

Social Policy and the Correctional System

MARGARET SEVERSON

No single chapter can accurately report the historical and present-day complexities of the correctional system in the United States. This system is not a single definable entity; it is a complex array of infinite physical and philosophical influences, designs, services, products, and functions. Likewise, a simple list of the social policies driving the vast assortment of correctional prototypes would read like a catalogue of schizophrenic special interests. The sheer number and magnitude of these policies must be understood as affecting separate and joint parts of a system that, as the 21st century looms ever closer, might be said to be not so much correctional as insurrectional. Although the violent prison disturbances of 20 and more years ago at Attica and Santa Fe have thankfully not become commonplace, the uprisings of the 1990s are of the political and philosophical kinds. As will be seen, since the founding of this nation, the politics of punishment has in some ways come full circle.

The modern-day correctional system, narrowly defined for the purposes of this chapter as including only jails and prisons, operates on two sometimes contradictory levels. Although federal, state, and local legislation and judicial rules and case law may regulate the lives of both the governed and the governors in these institutions, these regulations are carried out via intrasystem functions that are obscure and generally attract public scrutiny only over piecemeal issues and publicized revolts. Many examples of this exist: the bait and switch of determinate sentencing, given the disparity between the length of one's delivered prison sentence and the actual time served due to intrasystem allocation of good-time credits; the admonition against incarceration of the mentally ill and the advent of mercy bookings that occur when access to the mental health system is denied or curtailed; the officially declared functions of jails and prisons; and the internal pressures and procedures that exist to force the institution to turn a profit.

As the terms are commonly construed, prisons are federal or state-sponsored—although not necessarily owned and/or operated—facilities constructed to house prisoners who have been convicted of a crime and sentenced to a period of punishment, of isolation from society. Jails are facilities intended primarily for the purpose of housing pretrial detainees who have been assessed as presenting a continuing risk of danger to society and/or of flight from the jurisdiction of the court and who have been unable to post the bail required to assure the court of their presence at trial. Although burgeoning prison populations have to some extent altered these traditional jail functions, so that jails now carry out many of the same punishment and isolation duties, the mission of the pretrial detention facility is to act as the safekeeper of the accused so that justice, allegedly a blind justice at that, can be served through the means of a speedy trial and the rendering of the procedural process due each defendant.

Over time, because of their distinct official roles, different forces have shaped the look of prisons and jails in the United States. Increasingly, however, in the booming industry of corrections, the line between the pretrial and postconviction milieu is blurred; a prisoner in either environment is still a prisoner. Where necessary in the limited confines of this chapter, the distinctions between the two will be made, but readers are encouraged to keep their eyes on the driving policy issues that affect both types of organizations rather than focusing narrowly on the system types and thereby missing the bigger picture.

THE EVOLUTION OF CORRECTIONAL SERVICES: SOCIAL POLICY AND THE DEVELOPMENT OF JAILS AND PRISONS

It has been suggested that as a matter of public policy, prisoners are supposed to live in poverty (Sykes, 1958), and in the early days of incarceration in this country, austerity was often used as an excuse for unconscionable environmental conditions. Through most of the 18th century, deterrence was the guiding principle when it came to the handling of criminals. Banishment, brutal handling of prisoners, and the frequent use of barbaric forms of punishment and execution ultimately gave way in the late 1700s to a treatment philosophy espoused in Pennsylvania by the Quakers, who opposed the undisciplined management and violent conditions of the Philadelphia jail. In 1790,

the Pennsylvania Prison Society opened the Walnut Street Jail, the first prison to operate with the philosophy that the proper objective of punishment was rehabilitation.

In the 1820s, the first large prisons opened in the United States: the Auburn State
Prison in New York and the Pennsylvania prisons located in Pittsburgh and Philadelphia. The organization and treatment philosophies of these early prisons were centered around differing beliefs about the impact of social influences and the principles
of resocialization as they affect the individual person. The Auburn prison, a congregate system, had prisoners sleeping alone but working alongside each other every day,
albeit in total silence. In contrast, the Pennsylvania prisons operated so that prisoners
were totally segregated from each other for the duration of their sentences (Rothman,
1998). The emphasis of each system on preventing communication between prisoners, believing that such contact would defeat the rehabilitation objective, meant that
external control mechanisms such as architectural design and types of work projects
became the "treatment" influences. This can be contrasted with the rehabilitative efforts made in the late 19th and 20th centuries, when treatment of the individual became a more popular form of trying to achieve rehabilitation. In any case, like many
individual treatment experiments of the 20th century, these early programming endeavors in the prisons in New York and Pennsylvania have been declared failures in ac-
complishing their rehabilitative objectives. The failure of these prison models is, in
part, attributed to the rise in mental health problems among isolated prisoners, as
seen in suicides, self-mutilations, and other self-destructive and unusual behaviors,
and to the "bizarre, obsessive prison practices" that grew out of desperate attempts to
enforce silence in the institutions (Fogel, 1975, p. 56).

While model prisons were being discussed and developed in the 19th century, the
proliferation of local jails was paid little notice. In fact, local jail conditions were often
every bit as deplorable as those found in state prisons, but because they were deemed
to be short-term holding facilities, policy-making and advocacy efforts were instead
directed toward the operations of the larger institutions (Welch, 1991). Even today's
references to jail reform speak primarily to reformation of mid-20th century jail management strategies and are largely a result of judicial intervention as opposed to being
the products of the righteous indignation of social reformers. One notable exception
merits attention.

Since the late 1600s, a variety of state and local laws have authorized the incarceration of the seriously mentally ill individual. In one example bearing startling resem-
blance to events happening some 200 years later in the 1990s, the governor of Virginia was forced to approve the confinement of mentally ill people in the
Williamsburg jail in 1773, because of the unavailability of appropriate psychiatric
services elsewhere in the area (Deutsch, 1937).

In the mid 1800s, these practices came to the attention of Dorothea Dix, a former
school teacher turned progressive social reformer, who led the campaign to remove

mentally ill people from prisons, jails, and almshouses and place them instead into special hospitals (Deutsch, 1937). Dix's work is looked on as being the type of advocacy that lies at the very roots of the social work profession, and, in fact, by the end of the 19th century, she and her colleagues succeeded in witnessing the creation of a number of psychiatric hospitals into which mentally ill people could be diverted. Still, more than 100 years later in 1999, similar laws and/or practices—known generally as protective custody authorizations—serve to undo Dix's efforts (Torrey et al., 1992). Despite her pioneering advocacy work, if there is one connecting thread that ties together the penal philosophies and practices of colonial America and those of the 20th century, it surely has to do with the jails and prisons being used as repositories for those with severe and persistent mental illnesses.

Other social policies were also helping to shape the operations of the country's penal systems in the 19th century. The prison at Auburn charged its 6,000 to 8,000 annual spectators a fee to tour the penitentiary; these fees were applied to the prison's budget (Fogel, 1975). Elsewhere, while enlightened reformers like Edward Livingston, Alexis de Tocqueville, and Jeremy Bentham were working to instill humanitarian interests in the prisons in the United States and other areas of the world, in some states, money making/money saving missions became the driving force behind correctional policy. In post-Civil War America, after what the late scholar Mark Carleton (1971) called "the most decisive event in the history of southern penology" (p. 13), the southern state legislatures were confronted with a growing prisoner population consisting of former slaves and an accompanying increase in expenses associated with providing these prisoners with the basic necessities of life. By the 1880s, all of the southern states, Nebraska, and the New Mexico Territory turned to convict leasing and/or a contract system of prison management to cut costs and, ideally, to make money (Carleton, 1971). Under these systems, private operators were allowed to either enter into a lease with the state for inmate labor or contract with the state to actually operate the prison itself. Vestiges of these private management schemes, which include private mental health interests, are seen in today's proliferation of private correctional operations. Furthermore, the legacies of the convict leasing/contract systems include the underlying tensions that lie between present-day correctional policies and political agendas: Are prisoners players or pawns? Are they subjects or objects?

In the 20th century, social policy practitioners, in part led by the former president of the American Association of Social Workers, Kenneth Pray, had the opportunity to contribute to the development of the modern correctional era. Instead, the development of contemporary penal policies and practices was forfeited to criminal justice and behavioral science experts. Rehabilitation through therapeutic treatment, particularly through the use of psychotherapy, has been emphasized (McNeece, 1995). Although a few social workers such as Pray, who also served as dean of the Pennsylvania School of Social Work, advocated for penal reforms and for social work professionals to provide treatment services to prisoners, the social work practice and academic communities never wholly embraced this cause. Pray (1951) suggested that the "disciplined skill [of casework] in helping individuals make an adequate and satisfying social adjustment within relatively narrow limits is the distinctive potential contribution of professional social work to prison administration" (p. 207). Instead, social workers nested in the standards and guidelines for the profession as Mary Richmond expressed them: They were to work with individuals, helping them to help themselves (Fox, 1983). Social work was work destined to be done elsewhere, not in prison, and certainly with more amenable patients. Furthermore, David Fogel (1975), social worker, criminologist, and proponent of the justice model for corrections, suggests that "the prison monolith was basically unshaken by the entry of professionals; rather, it absorbed social workers, psychologists, psychiatrists, teachers, chaplains, and others to help insulate itself from criticism" (p. 61).

All in all, the social policies driving corrections up through the third quarter of this century, including those that emphasized the popular rehabilitation ideals of corrections, seem largely to have been inspired by penologists and politicians. Even professionals eager to provide the treatment services thought to be the key to true prisoner rehabilitation approached this task with the unrealistic idea that ultimately jailers would be replaced by nurses, and judges by psychiatrists: professionals who would treat and cure rather than punish the individual (Fogel, 1975).

THE IMPACT OF POLITICAL, JUDICIAL, ECONOMIC, SOCIAL, AND CULTURAL FACTORS ON CORRECTIONAL POLICIES AND PRACTICE

The most recent correctional population data compiled by the U.S. Department of Justice reveals that at midyear 1997, about 1,725,842 people were incarcerated in prisons and jails in the United States, a rate of 645 people per 100,000 U.S. residents (Gilliard & Beck, 1998a). Two thirds of these prisoners were incarcerated in federal and state prisons throughout the country. The remaining one third were held in local jails; jails across the nation were operating at 97% of their rated bed capacities, despite the fact that nearly 20,000 new jail beds became available during the 12-month period between July 1, 1996, and June 30, 1997. In addition to those residing inside these physical institutions, over 70,000 more offenders were being supervised in a variety of jail alternative programs (Gilliard & Beck, 1998a). Thousands more were managed under correctional supervision via probation and parole services.

These numbers offer a glimpse of what the range of contemporary correctional policies and practices in the United States might be. Although social policy ordinarily serves as the driving force behind actual practice, this assumption is suspect where corrections is concerned. A key issue in the 1990s and in the last quarter of the 20th century is whether, in the correctional arena, practice is instead driving policy.

As the number of people locked up continues to increase at an alarming rate, the policies driving correctional services are seen in the outcomes of three primary and interrelated courses of action. The first of these courses—for these purposes, labeled public commitments—is shaped by a variety of social pressures and contributions. Perhaps more than ever before, corrections falls victim to the whims of politics. "Lock 'em up" is a favored stance, realized through the enactment of truth-in-sentencing laws and in certain forms of involuntary detention and treatment. Pressure from crime victims (read voters) has made it easier for elected officials and elected judges to err on the conservative side of sentencing. The federal courts in particular, called on to determine the constitutionality of legislation and to safeguard human rights for all, including the incarcerated and their victims, have reacted to and wrought their own brand of force, as seen in the 15 years of judicial activism in prison and prisoner case law.

The second course encompasses environmental and material considerations. Included here are the efforts to conserve tangible corrections resources such as the number of custodial beds, the number of trained correctional personnel, and the amount of physical space required by institutions. These efforts have been made through legislative activity at all levels of government.

Finally, the third direction, containment, is related to the ever-increasing incarcerated population and the social and fiscal costs associated with incarcerating so many people. These containment issues have also been addressed through various pieces of legislation and service-delivery system configurations.

Not surprisingly, given their inherently contradictory natures, the process and results of the activities springing from these three policy catalysts are mixed, and one might conclude that some have played out with a zero-sum result. A look at a few of many such legislative and administrative strategies is illustrative.

Public Commitments

Political forces. Smart politicians always include the anti-crime agenda as part of their campaign platform. Regardless of the veracity of the claim, proclaiming oneself a champion of public safety is an expedient way to gain favor among voters. For those politicians who are in the position of being able to pursue get-tough-on-crime legislative strategies, their motivations seem to have been influenced more by emotional public opinion than by reasoned analysis of the facts and the potential consequences of the pending legislation. California's Polly Klass murder case, which instigated the popular three-strikes laws, has led to a rapidly increasing and unmanageable prison population. Megan's Law, Section 170101(d) of the Violent Crime Control and Law

Enforcement Act of 1994 (42 USC 14071(d); Lehman & Labecki, 1998) which calls for sexual offender notification, has raised concerns about privacy, stigma, and treatment effectiveness. Kansas's sexual offender law, upheld by the U.S. Supreme Court in *Kansas v. Hendricks* (1997), changed the standards for involuntary detention and treatment and has raised issues about both treatment effectiveness and the relationship between dangerousness and mental illness. All of these legislative actions are timely examples of the politicization of correctional policies. Further evidence of political pressures driving correctional policies are the truth-in-sentencing laws. These also have their origins in the Violent Crime Control and Law Enforcement Act of 1994, which requires states, in exchange for federal funds, to pass legislation mandating that prisoners serve a minimum of 85% of their sentences, and in the Prisoner Litigation Reform Act of 1995, which both curtailed the litigious activities of the jailhouse lawyer and limited the power of the federal courts to declare whole systems unconstitutional and/or continue, ad infinitum, their supervision of such systems via long-standing consent decrees.

It is practically unimaginable for a politician to speak aloud of the inadvisability of continuing to lock up even the minimalist offender. When one considers as a whole the restrictive legislation mentioned above and the rapidly increasing incarcerated population, in fact, it is becoming more clear that the tax-paying populace must at some point call a halt to the expense of incarcerating the high-cost inmate. Included here are the mentally ill, aging, and/or physically infirm people, many of whom could be better served, with more fiscal responsibility, in and/or by another system.

Victims' rights. Victims, as a group and a status, have gone from being an afterthought to a force to be reckoned with in the last two decades. The directives of the Victim and Witness Protection Act (U.S. Congress, 1982), Victims of Crime Assistance Act (U.S. Congress, 1984), the Violent Crime Control and Law Enforcement Act (U.S. Congress, 1994), and the Attorney General's office have ensured that the needs of crime victims are addressed from a variety of fronts. Aside from being informed of the perpetrator's status at significant stages of the criminal justice process, victims have also been victorious in asserting their rights to a more personal justice. In the United States, we now have a national crime victims agenda, an Office for Victims of Crime (the federal government's advocacy resource for victims of crime), financial support for victim assistance and compensation programs, and initiatives to ensure the fair treatment of victims in the legal system and in other areas of public life (Adams, 1997).

"Broken windows." Some scholars are "convinced that there are too many prisoners and prisons in the United States today not because we overuse imprisonment but . . . because in the past we have not been willing enough to imprison serious offend-

ers" (Block, 1997, p. 10). In their "broken windows" thesis, criminologists Wilson and Kelling (1982) argued that crime erodes neighborhoods and pulls apart communities that are already struggling to maintain some measure of stability. As Blagg and Smith (1989) explain,

> Instead of social workers and community activists "mobilizing" the poor and disadvantaged, the forces of law and order are invited to step in and fill the "vacuum" left by the lack of appropriate social authority: the police become the guardians of a collapsing moral order. (p. 16)

In this philosophy, a policy of zero tolerance for even the slightest criminal activity is in order if troubled communities are to be morally reclaimed. Furthermore, the assertion is made that too many criminals are committing too many crimes because sentencing practices over the last 50 years have not been harsh enough. Case law regarding the rights of prisoners and the standards of confinement "leave policymakers with only the weakest instrument (sentence length) for increasing the severity of punishment . . . [and] policy initiatives aimed at increasing the unpleasantness of prison life would likely be a cost-effective method of fighting crime" (Block, 1997, p. 13). Finally, Block suggests instituting a more draconian sentencing structure of imprisonment, one that mandates imprisonment for all convictions for violent crimes, and he surmises that this is likely to justify its cost and ultimately lead to a reduction in the prison population.

Judicial activism. The role of the courts in shaping social policy in corrections has filled volumes, and even then true justice has not been done in describing the justice delivered. Suffice it to say that many of the policy/practice changes witnessed in corrections over the last three decades have been as a direct result of judicial intervention. Although we have seen more activist days in the federal courts, litigation seeking prison reforms is still being filed in this country.

The federal courts did not involve themselves in prison operations until the late 1960s, when, in many cases, deplorable conditions of confinement and individual cases of maltreatment came to the attention of judges who were reading the Eighth Amendment's prohibition of cruel and unusual punishment with new energy (Ackerman, 1991). The bloody prison riots, the unsafe conditions, the growing number of prisoner suicides and mentally disturbed inmates seen over the next 15 years spurred the courts into a reformation mind-set. Not long after the courts confirmed prisoner rights to basic medical care, they found prisoners had the same rights to basic mental health care (see, e.g., the prison cases of *Ruiz v. Estelle,* 1980, and *Ramos v. Lamm,* 1980, and the jail cases of *Campbell v. McGruder,* 1978, *Bell v. Wolfish,* 1979, and *Tittle v. Jefferson County Commission,* 1992).

Although court activism has forced correctional systems to change their operational and treatment policies, it has been unable to change the course and pace of population and institutional growth. Regardless of the amount of activity in the courts, the larger the correctional system becomes, the greater the burden will be to effectively manage it. Not only do the courts have less ability to do so now, in part due to the legislative constraints put on judges via the Prisoner Litigation Reform Act of 1995, the judges may not have the legal and political support to carry on in the change-agent fashion that made judicial intervention so interesting to watch in the 1970s and 1980s.

Conservation of Resources

Trained correctional personnel. The last two decades of corrections have brought about a professionalization of the rank and file. Contributors to this elevation in status are the development of a variety of nationally recognized standards for the operation and management of correctional facilities, such as those promulgated by the American Correctional Association (1991), and the enactment of various state-established standards for certification of correctional officers. Professional and trade journals, as well as conferences designed to assist officers and managers in doing their jobs more efficiently, are commonly available. The federal government subsidizes training and technical assistance opportunities and a resource clearinghouse for state and local corrections professionals through its National Institute of Corrections, which has separate jail, prison, and community corrections divisions. Slowly, the tattered picture of the knucklehead turnkey is being replaced by one of an educated and skilled manager of people. Confidence in the quality of correctional personnel has led to a new unit management philosophy, in which governance of the institution is allocated among key staff members who are empowered to make decisions about the management of their inmate-populated living units.

Physical space and the availability of beds. A "new generation" correctional philosophy has emerged in the last 20 years. It suggests that changes in the physical design of jails and prisons will force changes in management practices, which will, in turn, result in changes in inmates' behaviors (Zupan & Menke, 1991). These new generation facilities are replacing the old linearly designed institutions. The latter made adequate supervision and surveillance of inmates, which would maximize the safety of the inmate and the institution, very difficult to accomplish and also required a considerable number of staff members to perform these duties. Furthermore, old-style institutions were designed with a premium placed on housing space while neglecting the need for program areas. The new institutions are streamlined in that supervision is easier to provide because the officer stands in closer proximity to the prisoners; program space is built in, so that program and living areas often merge within a certain physical boundary. When designed well, these newer institutions can provide better operational and personal security, supervision, and more program opportunities while requiring fewer staff employees. Finally, although many new generation-style facilities were designed to house inmates in single-occupancy cells, conversion to two-person cells has been accomplished with minimal disruption to the operation and the safety goals of many of these institutions.

But, like other advances made through more humanistic correctional policies, these advances in environmental design are threatened by the use of the correctional facility as a political tool. A few examples are illustrative. In the early 1990s, several state legislatures considered the possibility of "hot-racking" inmates to make maximum use of prison beds. Under this scheme, borrowed from the military, each bunk could accommodate three prisoners if they were assigned specific 8-hour sleeping shifts. Other correctional agencies determined that a return to the fortress prisons of the past would serve them well, resulting in the "super-max" prisons commonly found and touted in the state and federal systems. These locked-down institutions minimize staff-inmate and inmate-inmate verbal and physical contact and are reminiscent of the early prison era in this country. Litigation alleging that the environmental deprivation experienced in these prisons results in severe mental health problems has been argued and, in one recent well-known California class action suit, *Madrid v. Gomez* (1995), has resulted in system changes.

Containment of the Growth in Correctional Populations

Alternative sentencing and diversion programs. In light of the steadily increasing correctional population, legislators and criminal justice experts have worked to reevaluate what types of crimes require incarceration of the perpetrator and whether alternatives to incarceration are feasible. As a result, programs authorized by local legislation and judicial approval include house arrest, electronic monitoring, community service, victim-offender mediation, and diversion into mental health and/or substance abuse programs, halfway houses, and day treatment centers. Good-time credits, granted often solely on the authority of the incarcerating agency, also serve to get people out of institutions more quickly so that bed space is freed for more serious offenders. Many jurisdictions no longer support the incarceration of people convicted of misdemeanors, unless they have committed a politically volatile crime, such as drunk driving or domestic assault, or have an apparent mental illness for which other services cannot be as easily accessed. Eligibility for early release and diversion programs may be determined by a mental health or corrections professional who has been vested with the duty to reliably predict each particular prisoner's propensity to commit a new and more serious offense.

Rehabilitation/habilitation strategies. Despite controversial assessments of the outcomes of various offender treatment programs (see, e.g., Lipton, Martinson, & Wilks, 1975; Martinson, 1974; these works are often cited with bringing to a halt to the individual treatment philosophy in corrections), work, educational, and therapeutic opportunities are offered, especially to convicted prisoners, in the hope that these will reduce their risk of reoffending. In the 1990s, correctional managers are invested in being able to offer these types of services in their institutions as much or more for the purpose of keeping inmates busy as for habilitation reasons—relying on the notion that the busy inmate is a tired inmate, and the tired inmate won't create trouble in the institution. It is in the rehabilitation area where jail and prison programmatic differences are most pronounced; social policies that speak to what services must be provided inmates differ according to whether the person has been tried and convicted and the length of time the person is to be incarcerated. The length of time and degree of control the state exercises over the movements of an individual directly corresponds to the amount of control the state can and, in some cases, must exert over that person.

Even though mental health programs are still available in prisons, having survived critical research findings, actually attracting and employing mental health professionals in corrections has proven difficult. In 1965, a national survey of correctional institutions revealed that a total of 167 "social workers or counselors" were working in penal institutions in this country, or one for every 846 prisoners. Furthermore, there was only one psychologist for every 4,282 inmates and one psychiatrist for every 2,436 inmates (President's Commission on Law Enforcement, 1967, p. 178). A National Institute of Mental Health (1991) survey completed 25 years later revealed little change: Only 297 social workers were employed in prison mental health services throughout the United States in 1988. A survey published by the National Association of Social Workers and completed in 1991 showed that only 1.3% of its members identified the correctional setting as the site of their primary practice, a drop from 1.5% in 1988 (Gibelman & Schervish, 1993). Furthermore, this same survey revealed that those providing social work services in correctional settings were most likely to hold bachelor degrees in social work, leading the authors to comment that this "reinforces the view that clients with the most complex and intractable socioeconomic and psychosocial problems are served by the least educated members" of the profession (Gibelman & Schervish, 1993, p. 64-65).

CURRENT ISSUES AND CONTROVERSIES

Corrections is an industry that serves clients on both the front and back steps of the criminal justice system. The industry itself is both shaping and being shaped by correctional policy. Because of its dual roles as grantor and grantee, it is an enduring institution even though the ultimate social objective might be said to be to no longer need (so many) prison and jail beds. Aside from the ambiguities inherent in the correctional industry's mission, there are social policy ambiguities that perpetuate the proliferation and perhaps overutilization of correctional beds. The guiding policies of these two forces come together in the nonexhaustive list of critical issues discussed in the following pages.

Incarceration of Mentally Ill People

At the forefront of any discussion of social policy and corrections stands the issue of the transinstitutionalization of the mentally ill. Soon after the first wave of deinstitutionalization in the United States, when state hospitals downsized subsequent to the passage of the Mental Retardation Facilities and Community Mental Health Centers Construction Act (U.S. Congress, 1963), researchers began remarking about the possibility that a criminalization process involving people with mental illness had resulted from this shift in government policy (Abramson, 1972; Teplin, 1983). The reduction in the nation's state hospital patients from 559,000 in 1955, when the total national population was 165 million, to a patient population of 72,000 out of the 250 million people nationally in 1994 (Lamb & Weinberger, 1998), meant that mentally ill people were going somewhere, because they were not all being served in their communities.

The bulk of the research into the incarceration of severe and persistently mentally ill people has been completed within the last 10 years. Steadman, Fabisiak, Dvoskin, and Holohean (1987) found that 8% of inmates required immediate psychiatric treatment and another 16% of those evaluated required some type of periodic mental health service. Jones (1989) found that the number of mentally ill offenders ranged from 900,000 to 1.5 million in the United States, depending on how the term *mental illness* was defined. Steadman (1990) suggested that, in 1988, 679,000 jail admissions involved people with severe mental illnesses, and up to 672,000 releases from jails into the community that same year were people "who were severely mentally ill upon admission" (p. 1). Overall, the percentage of incarcerated people with mental disorders is significantly higher than the percentage of people with mental disorders residing in the general population (Steadman & Veysey, 1997). In part, the "urgent problem" (Lamb & Weinberger, 1998, p. 483) of the increasing number of severe and persistently mentally ill people housed in local jails is attributable to the perception that jails are safe havens when there are inadequate community-based mental health services available to those who need them.

The last two decades of the deinstitutionalization movement have been marked by the closing of some state hospitals and the downsizing of patient capacity in others, the promise of effective and comprehensive treatment interventions within the community through local mental health agencies, rising costs of inpatient psychiatric treatment, and the failure to provide local communities with the funds and expertise to deliver on the promises of reformers. The fallout from this change process—this movement from hospitalization to community treatment—has been that jails have become "the recycling station for some deinstitutionalized persons" (Briar, 1983, p. 388). Mercy bookings, charging a seriously mentally ill person with a crime for the sole purpose of gaining access to a jail bed, have become the order of the day in some areas with limited mental health resources.

Although there has been more recognition of and credence given to this transinstitutionalization phenomenon in recent years, it has coincided with the greater social importance placed on managed health care systems. In an effort to cut costs and deliver constitutionally adequate health care, increasing numbers of jails and prisons are contracting with private health care providers to manage their institutional medical and mental health departments. As a result, public mental health agencies such as community mental health centers and state psychiatric facilities must find ways to work cooperatively and collaboratively with profit-motivated corporations. In a time of fierce competition for diminishing fiscal resources, although it may be difficult to keep the professional focus on the care and treatment of those with mental illness no matter where they reside, public and private systems must find ways to do so.

Correctional Treatment

Ten years ago, Steadman, McCarty, and Morrissey (1989) proposed five principles for planning effective mental health services in jails. Included was the suggestion that the care and treatment of mentally disturbed inmates should be seen as a community issue and services should be developed and provided with this axiom in mind. What Steadman et al. and others have proposed are interventions that are initiated before the person is brought to jail (diversion), holistic treatment programming if incarcerated (Severson, 1992), and discharge planning in anticipation of, and community case management services after, the inmate's release.

For state and federal prisoners, the possibility and value of longer term, more intensive treatment services has been recognized and, in fact, has been supported both by legislation and case law. Some have advocated for a community mental health model of service delivery in prisons (Center for Mental Health Services, 1995), allowing for both inpatient and outpatient interventions.

Complicating the process of bringing these schemes to reality, however, are the legislative and judicial actions that make targeting dollars and therapeutic efforts to the seriously mentally ill population more difficult. For example, sexual offender treatment laws such as those in effect in Kansas (see *Kansas v. Hendricks,* 1997) require the state to dedicate expensive inpatient psychiatric beds and adequate numbers of mental health professionals to treat a condition for which a cure—or even symptom reduction—is elusive. The double bind that these types of laws create is seen as follows: Mental health professionals must effectively treat pedophiles, at least to the extent of showing they are no longer dangerous, in order for hospital beds to be made available, only to have those beds filled again with the questionably treatable pedophile. The burden falls on the mental health professional to treat the (perhaps untreatable) sex offender as well as the treatable mentally ill person, but the clearer legislative mandate is geared toward the more difficult objective. It may be redundant, then, to suggest that social policies guiding corrections must also prioritize by both need and potential the objectives of intervention.

Women Prisoners

The number of women in prison is climbing at an alarming rate. In 1997, for the second year in a row, women outpaced men in terms of the increase in the number incarcerated (6.2% increase in women prisoners; 5.2% increase in men) (Gilliard & Beck, 1998b). Even worse, and serving as an ominous warning for the near future, is the growth in the number of female juvenile arrests in recent years. Between 1989 and 1993, there was a 23% increase in these arrests, more than double the increase for males (Prescott, 1997). It can be said of women more than of men that they do not enter prison alone—at least not in a metaphysical sense; indeed, they are accompanied by the knowledge that imprisonment isolates them from their children. Furthermore, they present unique mental health and social challenges within the corrections environment and are met with different standards of care and intervention. Teplin, Abram, and McClelland (1996) found that over 80% of the incarcerated women in their jail sample met the criteria for one or more lifetime psychiatric disorders; 17% of these women were diagnosed with a severe psychotic or affective disorder. Teplin, Abram, and McClelland's (1997) data also reveal that less that one fourth of females with severe mental disorders received services while incarcerated.

Correctional facilities, particularly jails, rarely have available to women programs that are comparable to those provided male inmates. Furthermore, when such programs are available, they are often based on the same models used to treat males (Veysey, 1997). In addition, research has clearly illustrated the fact that women bring with them into the correctional facility gender-dominant histories of being victims of sexual and physical abuse and domestic assault, as well as the problems associated with being single parents, being pregnant, and/or having to physically if not emotionally separate from their children while serving out their prison sentences (Center for Mental Health Services, 1995).

Racial Disparities

Without supposing anything in a discussion about the relationship between racial group membership and incarceration, the statement the numbers make is unmistakable. People belonging to a racial minority group are locked up in greater numbers and in greater percentages that ever before. Whereas the incarceration of white individuals in prisons has declined over the 6-year period from 1990 through 1996 (50.1% to 47.9%), that of persons of African American descent has steadily risen during the same time period (48.6% to 49.4%) (Gilliard & Beck, 1998b). By the end of 1996, there were more black males in prisons across the country than white males (Gilliard & Beck, 1998b).

Regarding the "racialisation of crime" in Britain and in the United States, Blagg and Smith (1989) suggest that the "dominant tradition in social work of perceiving black families as essentially pathological, inadequate, and unstable" (p. 24) has worked its way into the suggestion that criminality springs from a culture of "frustrated aspirations amongst black youth" (p. 26). At least one of the dangers with this thinking about culture is that it can lead to entire communities being identified as "criminally inclined" (p. 26) and thus lead to differential treatment based on this assumption. This differential treatment affects not only how law enforcement operations are carried out, but also the social and economic perceptions of the neighborhood, potentially resulting in lost business opportunities, a decline in the types of social activities that support youth and families, and a weakening of other fundamental neighborhood supports.

Certainly, any interdiction into the racialization of the correctional system must begin before getting to the front steps of the system itself, that is, by increasing understanding of and tolerance for expressions of racial and cultural diversity in the world community. This diversity must be considered when planning the physical, educational, commercial, and service components of communities, components that will support children and youth as they search for ways to express their differences.

Once one is found on the steps of the system, however, at the point of contact with law enforcement and then carrying on throughout the adversarial process, work must continue to create social policies making a color-blind, justice-seeking approach to correctional system management the norm.

Alternative Sanctions and Diversion

In terms of serving the needs of people with mental illnesses, diversion programs screen defined groups of detainees for mental disorder; use mental health professionals to evaluate them; negotiate with system players, including the courts "to produce a mental health disposition as a condition of bond, in lieu of prosecution, or as a condition of a reduction in charges (whether or not a formal conviction occurs); and link the detainee directly to community-based service" (Steadman, Morris, & Dennis, 1995, p. 1630). In addition, diversion for the purposes of conserving correctional beds for the most serious offenders, saving money, and enhancing system efficiency has been discussed for many years. Fogel (1975) reviewed the early research on the impact of early institutional release on recidivism and concluded that recidivism rates did not appear to either decline or increase with probation or early release. In any case, the diversion of those with mental illnesses to more appropriate treatment milieus represents the humanitarian sentiments of some segments of the public. By completing the collaborative loop that ties together the community and the correctional system, diversion programming helps ensure continuity of care, reduces the extent of disruption in the system and in the individual's and families' lives, and can be accomplished "without significant additional costs" (Center for Mental Health Services, 1995, p. 42).

However, even if one might agree on the importance of diversion programs and/or on alternative sanctions for convicted offenders, where their "time" or "diversion" can be accomplished is not without its own controversy, even among social workers. McKinney (1992) suggested that sentencing otherwise unqualified people to perform community service in lieu of serving time could be interpreted as social workers allowing their "hard-fought achievement of having our clients served by fully prepared professionals to be undermined" (p. 262).

Certainly, talk of diversion programming also quickly becomes a hotbed of political and special interest activity. It is an area of continuing controversy fueled, in part, by media exploitation of violent incidents involving mentally ill people, which, but for the sensationalizing presence of a mental illness, might have otherwise found their way to the middle section of the nightly news or the back page of the local paper. Still, it is an area of social policy that must be addressed in the near future, as jails and prisons fill with habitual offenders and others serving longer sentences as a result of truth-in-sentencing laws, tighter drug enforcement policies, and the wielding of victims' power.

THE FUTURE OF CORRECTIONAL SOCIAL POLICIES AND SOCIAL SERVICES: CHALLENGES

> *The extent to which the existing social system works in the direction of the prisoner's deterioration rather than his rehabilitation; the extent to which the system can be changed; the extent to which we are willing to change it—these are the issues which confront us and not the recalcitrance of the individual inmate.*

> Sykes, 1958, p. 134

And so we have come full circle in this chapter. Much remains to be done in the correctional realm. Although advances in inmate management, staff professionalism, and physical security of institutions have been realized, the humanistic aspects of corrections still require much work. The dangers that lurk ahead are the very same dangers that plagued the past: allowing punishment for profit to be a guiding concept in correctional management; assuming these institutions are endless resources that can continue to absorb and banish society's misfits as well as society's ill-fits with an "out of sight, out of mind" perspective; using corrections as a political tool to be wielded as a reward or as a punishment depending on who's inquiring. Sykes was right: The social policy issues of the future and our focus must be on creating systemic change, not on producing change in any given (recalcitrant) individual.

The presumptive sentencing practices of the last two decades of the 20th century, particularly those mandating certain sentences for drug, sex, and multiple felony convictions, promise to keep the population of jails and prisons increasing. Those increases will necessarily include more people with mental illnesses and will mean significantly higher societal costs—fiscal and social—the costs of locking up a substantial number of young black males, increasing numbers of women, and hoards of juveniles.

History has repeated itself. Sixteen years ago, Briar (1983) remarked that jails are among society's most enduring institutions and suggested that the jail's "uses and its future, should be a major issue in social work communities across the United States" (p. 393). There is little doubt that the social policies driving and guiding corrections are major issues with which social workers must grapple; the question remains when we shall choose to do so.

REFERENCES

Abramson, M. F. (1972). The criminalization of mentally disordered behavior: Possible side-effects of a new mental health law. *Hospital and Community Psychiatry, 23*(4), 101-107.

Ackerman, H. A. (1991). The New Jersey jail crisis: The judicial experience. *Rutgers Law Review, 44,* 135-164.

Adams, A. (1997). *Victims of Crime Act of 1984 as amended: A report to the President and the Congress.* Washington, DC: U.S. Department of Justice Office of Justice.

American Correctional Association. (1991). *Standards for adult detention facilities* (2nd ed.). Laurel, MD: Commission on Accreditation for Law Enforcement.

Bell v. Wolfish, 441 U.S. 520 (1979).

Blagg, H., & Smith, D. (1989). *Crime, penal policy, and social work.* Essex, UK: Longman.

Block, M. K. (1997, July). *Supply side imprisonment policy.* Presentations from the 1996 Annual Research and Evaluation Conference, Washington, DC. http://www.ncjrs.org (http://www.ncjrs.org/txtfiles/165702.txt)

Briar, K. H. (1983). Jails: Neglected asylums. *Social Casework: The Journal of Contemporary Social Work, 64*(7), 387-393.

Campbell v. McGruder, 580 F.2d. 521, 188 U.S. App. D.C. 258 (D.C. Cir. 1978).

Carleton, M. T. (1971). *Politics and punishment: The history of the Louisiana state penal system.* Baton Rouge: Louisiana State University Press.

Center for Mental Health Services. (1995). *Double jeopardy: Persons with mental illnesses in the criminal justice system* (A report to Congress). Rockville, MD: U.S. Department of Health and Human Services.

Deutsch, A. (1937). *The mentally ill in America.* New York: Doubleday, Doran.

Fogel, D. (1975). *". . . We are the living proof . . ." The justice model for corrections.* Cincinnati, OH: W. H. Anderson.

Fox, V. (1983). Foreword. In A. R. Roberts (Ed.), *Social work in criminal justice settings* (pp. ix-xv). Springfield, IL: Charles C Thomas.

Gibelman, M., & Schervish, P. H. (1993). *Who we are: The social work labor force as reflected in the NASW membership.* Washington, DC: National Association of Social Workers.

Gilliard, D. K., & Beck, A. J. (1998a, January). Prison and jail inmates at midyear 1997. In *Bulletin,* Bureau of Justice Statistics. Washington, DC: U.S. Department of Justice.

Gilliard, D. K., & Beck, A. J. (1998b, August). Prisoners in 1997. In *Bulletin,* Bureau of Justice Statistics. Washington, DC: U.S. Department of Justice.

Jones, W. (1989). Mentally ill offenders. *American Jails, 3,* 47-56.

Kansas v. Hendricks, 117 S.Ct. 2072, 138 L.Ed.2d 501 (1997).

Lamb, H. R., & Weinberger, L. E. (1998) Persons with severe mental illness in jails and prisons: A review. *Psychiatric Services, 49*(4), 483-492.

Lehman, J. D., & Labecki, L. S. (1998) Myth versus reality: The policies of crime and punishment and its impact on correctional administration in the 1990s. In T. Alleman & R. L. Gido (Eds.), *Turnstile justice: Issues in American corrections* (pp. 42-70). Saddle River, NJ: Prentice Hall.

Lipton, D., Martinson, R., & Wilks, J. (1975). *The effectiveness of correctional treatment: A survey of treatment evaluation studies.* New York: Praeger.

Madrid v. Gomez, 889 F.Supp. 1146 (N.D. Cal. 1995).

Martinson, R. (1974) What works?—Questions and answers about prison reform. *The Public Interest, 35,* 22-54.

McKinney, C. M. (1992). Why do we remain silent? *Social Work, 37*(3), 261-262.

McNeece, C. A. (1995). Adult corrections. In *Encyclopedia of social work* (19th ed., Vol. 1, pp. 60-68). Washington, DC: National Association of Social Workers.

National Institute of Mental Health. (1991). *1988 inventory of mental health services in state adult correctional facilities.* Washington, DC: U.S. Department of Health and Human Services.

Pray, K. L. M. (1951). Social work in the prison program. In P. W. Tappan (Ed.), *Contemporary corrections* (pp. 204-210). New York: McGraw-Hill.

Prescott, L. (1997). *Adolescent girls with co-occurring disorders in the juvenile justice system.* Delmar, NY: Policy Research.

President's Commission on Law Enforcement and Administration of Justice. (1967). *The challenge of crime in a free society.* Washington, DC: Government Printing Office.

Ramos v. Lamm, 639 F.2d 559 (10th Cir. 1980), cert. denied, 450 U.S. 1041, 101 S. Ct. 1759, 68 L.Ed.2d 559 (1981).

Rothman, D. J. (1998). The invention of the penitentiary. In T. Flanagan, J. W. Marquart, & K. G. Adams (Eds.), *Incarcerating criminals: Prisons and jails in social and organizational context* (pp. 15-23). New York: Oxford University Press.

Ruiz v. Estelle, 503 F.Supp. 1265 (S.D. Texas 1980), aff'd in part, 679 F.2d 1115 (5th Cir. 1982), cert. denied, 40 U.S. 1042 (1983).

Severson, M. (1992). Redefining the boundaries of mental health services: A holistic approach to improving inmate mental health. *Federal Probation, 56*(3), 57-63.

Steadman, H. J. (1990). Introduction. In H. J. Steadman, *Jail diversion for the mentally ill; Breaking through the barriers; Effectively addressing the mental health needs of jail detainees* (pp. 1-9). Washington, DC: National Institute of Corrections.

Steadman, H. J., Fabisiak, S., Dvoskin, J., & Holohean, E. J. (1987). A survey of mental disability among state prison inmates. *Hospital and Community Psychiatry, 38,* 1086-1090.

Steadman, H. J., McCarty, D. W., & Morrissey, J. P. (1989). *The mentally ill in jail: Planning for essential services.* New York: Guilford.

Steadman, H. J., Morris, S. M., & Dennis, D. L. (1995). The diversion of mentally ill persons from jails to community-based services: A profile of programs. *American Journal of Public Health, 85*(12), 1630-1635.

Steadman, H. J., & Veysey, B. M. (1997). Providing services for jail inmates with mental disorders. In *Research in brief.* Washington, DC: National Institute of Justice.

Sykes, G. M. (1958). *The society of captives: A study of a maximum security prison.* Princeton, NJ: Princeton University Press.

Teplin, L. A. (1983). The criminalization of the mentally ill: Speculation in search of data. *Psychological Bulletin, 94*(1), 54-67.

Teplin, L. A., Abram, K. M., & McClelland, G. M. (1996). Prevalence of psychiatric disorders among incarcerated women. *Archives of General Psychiatry, 53,* 505-512.

Teplin, L. A., Abram, K. M., & McClelland, G. M. (1997). Mentally disordered women in jail: Who receives services? *American Journal of Public Health, 87*(4), 604-609.

Tittle v. Jefferson County Commission, 10 F.3d 1535 (11 Cir. 1994), en banc, vacating a contrary opinion appearing at 966 F.2d 606 (11th Cir. 1992).

Torrey, E. F., Stieber, J., Ezekiel J., Wolfe, S. M., Sharfstein, J., Noble, J. H., & Flynn, L. M. (1992). *Criminalizing the seriously mentally ill: The abuse of jails as mental hospitals.* Arlington, VA: National Alliance for the Mentally Ill and Public Citizen's Health Research Group.

Veysey, B. M. (1997). *Specific needs of women diagnosed with mental illnesses in U.S. jails.* Unpublished manuscript.

U.S. Congress. (1963). P.L. 88-164. *Mental Retardation Facilities and Community Mental Health Centers Construction Act of 1963.*

U.S. Congress. (1982). P.L. 97-291. *The Victim and Witness Protection Act of 1982.*

U.S. Congress. (1984). *Victims of Crime Assistance Act* (VOCA).

U.S. Congress. (1994). P.L. 103-322. *The Violent Crime Control and Law Enforcement Act of 1994.*

U.S. Congress. (1996). *Prisoner Litigation Reform Act of 1995.*

Welch, M. (1991). The expansion of jail capacity: Makeshift jails and public policy. In J. A. Thompson & G. L. Mays (Eds.), *American jails: Public policy issues* (pp. 148-162). Chicago: Nelson-Hall.

Wilson, J. Q., & Kelling, G. L. (1982, March). Broken windows: The police and neighborhood safety. *The Atlantic Monthly,* pp. 29-38.

Zupan, L. L., & Menke, B. A. (1991). The new generation jail: An overview. In J. A. Thompson & G. L. Mays (Eds.), *American jails: Public policy issues* (pp. 180-194). Chicago: Nelson-Hall.

CHAPTER TWENTY-ONE

Employment Policy and Social Welfare

MICHELLE LIVERMORE

For the majority of people in the United States, work provides enough resources to ensure their own welfare. For others, however, jobs that provide an income adequate enough to support a family are elusive. This chapter addresses the mechanisms by which the U.S. government has acted to maximize work and the benefits of work to individuals. Current employment policies are reviewed in a historical context.

A range of policies exist to intervene in labor market processes to benefit individuals. In the most general terms, strategies promoting the welfare of workers either address factors affecting the supply of and demand for workers or they regulate the treatment, wages, or benefits of workers. Like all markets, labor markets are seen by neoclassical economists as regulated by two forces: supply and demand. The supply of labor includes the number and characteristics of workers. Related employment strategies focus on improving worker quality and linking workers to employers. They include education and training programs and job search and placement assistance. The demand for labor includes the amount and type of labor needed by an employer for production. Demand-side strategies attempt to increase employers' ability and desire to hire workers. These include macroeconomic policies that aim to improve the market and subsequently create jobs, employer tax credits that reward employers for hiring certain categories of workers, and policies aimed at preventing discrimination.

Regulatory policies focus on preventing worker exploitation and ensuring workers against job loss. This includes job loss protection, worker safety, and benefits and wage protection.

The history of employment policy in the United States involves a mix of these three types of policies. The first three sections of this chapter discuss each type of policy as implemented in the United States. The final section summarizes current issues and controversies related to these policies.

LABOR SUPPLY POLICY

Augmenting the quantity or quality of the labor supply is the most common employment policy strategy implemented in the United States. Such policies include employment training and job placement strategies.

Employment Training

Numerous employment and training programs exist in the United States with the goal of increasing the skills of current and potential workers. These include comprehensive high schools, vocational education classes and schools, apprenticeship programs, the military, community colleges, colleges, universities, and targeted employment training programs. The focus of this section is on targeted employment and training programs. Although all of the institutions mentioned above are relevant to the welfare of individuals in society, the latter have been most closely associated with social welfare policy because they specifically target individuals having difficulty in the labor market. Also, Chapter 22 in this book discusses educational policy in the United States in more detail.

Federal intervention focusing on employment training emerged during the War on Poverty. Policies implemented during this era were based on assumptions that unemployment was an individual problem because jobs were plentiful. Therefore, targeting the poor was seen as the most effective strategy to combat unemployment as policy makers strove to promote equality of opportunity. Human capital theory, on which this type of policy is based, posed that training would remedy individual deficiencies that prevented full labor market participation (Mucciaroni, 1990).

Employment and training programs begun during this period were small and fragmented. The 1962 Manpower Development and Training Act (MDTA) sought to prepare unemployed and displaced blue-collar workers for the new high-skilled jobs being created by the economy through vocational and on-the-job training, testing, counseling, job placement services, and living allowances (Janoski, 1990). The Economic Opportunity Act of 1964 created its own manpower development system under the Office of Economic Opportunity, which used community action agencies to provide a centralized outreach point for employment training and placement, with specialized skills training provided by independent contractors (Janoski, 1990). Later that decade, the Work Incentive Program was implemented to increase the work effort of recipients of Aid to Families with Dependent Children (AFDC). From 1967 until 1989, the program required public assistance recipients to register for work and training program unless they had young children. Although training and placement were the intentions of the program, only rarely did these activities follow registration (Bane & Ellwood, 1994).

Pressure to consolidate employment programs in the 1970s resulted in the Comprehensive Employment and Training Program (CETA). CETA decategorized federal and state "single issue" employment programs, placing all programs for special populations under the control of prime sponsors that could be city or county governments. It required these entities to develop a comprehensive policy for manpower development in their local areas. This transfer of responsibility to the local level marked the decentralization of employment training. The amount of direct employment training also declined during this period. The Work Incentive Program, the Job Corps, and On-the-Job Training, which involved a subsidy paid to employers for hiring and training workers, were the only programs remaining that provided job training (Janoski, 1990).

In 1982, the Job Training and Partnership Act (JTPA) replaced CETA, decreasing program expenditures and placing local business at the center of employment policy decision making through Private Industry Councils (Guttman, 1983). The Act eliminated on-the-job training and limited the amount of wages that trainees could receive (Janoski, 1990). JTPA provided resources to poor, uneducated adults and youth through public and private training institutions. Program regulations were enforced by the Department of Labor and overseen by private industry councils, state job-training coordinating councils, or, in some states, workforce development departments (Levitan, Mangum, & Mangum, 1998).

The JTPA legislation targeted a variety of different groups. It provided employment training for impoverished and undereducated adults and year-round and summer employment and training programs for youth. Migrant and seasonal farm workers were provided with skill enhancement and job placement services, and funds were allocated for grants to Native American tribes to offer basic skills training, occupational skills training, work experience, and on-the-job training to their members. Also, the Job Corps program targeted impoverished youth with severe educational deficits and other employment barriers. This intensive, long-term job training and remedial education program included health care, counseling, and job placement assistance in a residential setting (General Accounting Office [GAO], 1995b).

A key issue regarding employment programs is their overabundance and disconnectedness and the resulting inefficiency. A 1995 Government Accounting Office report (GAO, 1995a) indicated that 163 programs targeting different populations were funded by 15 federal agencies. The large number of programs was due to the targeting of different populations by different legislation. This includes youth, people with disabilities, welfare recipients, displaced workers, the elderly, farm workers, Native Americans, and veterans (Shapiro et al., 1998). In reference to individuals with disabilities, a 1996 GAO report identified 26 programs that provided skill training and job search assistance to individuals with disabilities. Welfare recipients are targeted by the Temporary Assistance for Needy Families (TANF) program, which replaced the AFDC program and its training component, Job Opportunities for Basic Skills program (JOBS) in 1996. The JOBS program required states to implement programs to increase the self-sufficiency of AFDC recipients; these included assessment, basic skills training, job skills training, job development, and job placement (Bane & Ellwood, 1994). Instead of the basic education strategy promoted in the JOBS program, TANF regulations provide 2 years of cash assistance and then require participants to work. TANF only allows training to be counted as a work activity for those who have not finished high school and for a limited amount of vocational training (U.S. Congress Committee on Ways and Means, 1998b). ·

After many years of debate in Congress, a bill attempting to consolidate the abundance of programs was enacted. The Workforce Investment Act of 1998 (PL 105-220) was signed into law by President Clinton in August (Social Legislation Information Service, 1998). The new legislation uses block grants for employment, training, and literacy to coordinate activities of over 60 federal employment programs. Although the final compromise does not achieve the level of consolidation proposed in some versions of the bill, it repeals JTPA and aims to coordinate multiple federal programs through locally controlled workforce development systems. One key component of the legislation is the one-stop service delivery system. This requires that each workforce investment area have at least one location where the public can gain access to different levels of services. Second, the work-first focus gives priority to core services that link individuals immediately to employment, such as job readiness, placement, and retention services. Intensive services, such as assessment and counseling, and training services, such as on-the-job and classroom training, are reserved for those who are unable to obtain employment. Priority for allocation of these services is given to public assistance recipients and other low-income individuals. A third component of the legislation is the Individual Training Account. Eligible participants are given these accounts to purchase training services from eligible providers. A fourth component is the development of state and local workforce investment boards, which are responsible for developing strategic plans for workforce investment and performance evaluation.

Whereas employment training focuses on improving the labor supply, job placement focuses on labor supply management. Although both have often been offered by the same agencies and in the same programs, this has not always been the case. The history of job placement services actually began in the private sector. Labor shortages accompanying early American settlement during the early 19th century led to the emergence of private employment agencies, which recruited workers from Europe and Africa (Janoski, 1990; Martinez, 1976). Public labor exchanges began at the state level in Ohio in the 1890s, and soon after, employment offices were opened in 20 other states (Guzda, 1983; Janoski, 1990). Another 24 states began to regulate private labor exchanges but were discouraged by numerous Supreme Court actions. These judicial decisions reflected the typical laissez-faire view that government should limit its interference in the economy. In spite of this, job placement became a political issue prior to World War II, with demands for labor exchanges coming from both labor organizations and state unemployment offices (Janoski, 1990).

In response to this political pressure, President Woodrow Wilson created the U.S. Employment Service (USES) with an executive order in 1918. It took the place of the Division of Information, which had relocated immigrants throughout the country earlier in the century. The USES opened employment offices in 40 states and relied on state advisory boards for advice regarding the operation of these offices. High union-employer tensions present at this time weakened support for this agency and led to its deterioration during the Hoover administration and subsequent sidelining as the National Reemployment Agency assumed its duties during the Roosevelt administration (Leschohier, 1919, in Janoski, 1990).

In 1933, the Wagner-Peyser Act reestablished the USES. Its duties were undertaken through a voluntary confederation of state employment offices governed loosely by federal regulations. The USES recruited labor for the New Deal work relief programs in states without employment services. However, because the USES was also responsible for processing the large number of claims made for unemployment insurance during this time, its placement duties were much more limited than intended (Mucciaroni, 1990).

The importance of labor-supply management again increased during the Second World War, as workers were in scarce supply. At this time, the federal government took over the USES, highlighting the importance of government employment programs to national interests (Janoski, 1990). Employment programs were finally viewed as important to society at large, because they helped maintain a productive economy in a world of increasing education levels and changing organizational structures and management (Mucciaroni, 1990).

The USES continued to operate during the 1950s but listed only a small number of actual vacancies and focused only on the white lower-middle and working classes. Its decline during this time was due to a lack of organization; increasing competition from private employment agencies, union hiring halls, and civil service offices; and decreased funding due to the discontinuation of the local match requirement and the diversion of USES funds into the unemployment trust fund (Janoski, 1990). Although President Kennedy expanded the USES in 1961, the program did not have a large impact later in the decade because alternative programs were created during the War on Poverty; civil rights activists viewed USES as incapable of handling disadvantaged individuals (Janoski, 1990).

During the 1970s and early 1980s, placement services, in addition to training services, were under the control of CETA. During this period, the USES began computerizing job listings and making this information available. The 1976 CETA amendments provided incentives for prime sponsors to use the USES to place workers, but it was usually not the agency of choice, and this incentive was not continued in other legislation (Janoski, 1990).

Under JTPA, the Job Service was the entity that assisted individuals in finding jobs, through a nationwide network of over 1,800 offices. In recent years, the service experienced budget cuts, decreased the amount of counseling services, and relied on a self-help approach to job placement. This included America's Job Bank, which listed available jobs nationwide, and America's Talent Bank, which provided resumes for employers. The Workforce Investment Act of 1998 incorporates placement and information dissemination functions of Job Services into the one-stop delivery system. Job search and placement assistance are a core service prioritized in the Act. Other core services include career counseling, skills assessment, and job retention services.

LABOR DEMAND STRATEGIES

Whereas labor supply strategies focus on individuals, labor demand strategies focus on the availability of employment. Government policies can attempt to stimulate labor demand through the private market, by creating jobs directly or by increasing demand for disadvantaged workers.

Private Market Approaches

Economic policy addressing labor demand through the private market is rooted in Keynesian economics, which has two branches. Secular stagnationists believe that as the economy becomes unable to generate growth, policies that stimulate the economy are needed. Related interventions include increasing public investments and budgetary deficits. Commercial (or American) Keynesians have a more optimistic view of the market. Where secular stagnationists see stagnation, commercial Keynesians see a simple downturn in an economic cycle. Policy prescriptions for shortening the duration of these downturns include tax cuts, which quickly increase the amount of money available for consumer spending during recessionary periods (Mucciaroni, 1990).

Federal policy during the Great Depression used spending on public works projects and direct job creation to curb the human effects of the economic downturn. Even though the ideological foundations of commercial Keynesianism were laid during the late 1940s, the tax cut was completely absent as an economic recovery policy during the 1950s and emerged as an option in 1962 as recovery from the 1960-1961 recession slowed. When President Kennedy recognized the level of support in the business community, he and his Council of Economic Advisors embraced the idea. The tax cut remains a popular economic stimulation policy offered by conservatives (Mucciaroni, 1990).

Other policies attempt to stimulate labor demand at the local level. Local economic development projects focus on areas that have unusually low levels of business activity and high levels of unemployment. Beginning in the 1930s, the federal government in the New Deal enacted legislation aimed at creating jobs in poor areas. These programs were expanded during the War on Poverty and again during the Carter administration. Community Development Block Grant funding emerged through the Department of Housing and Urban Development to support housing, public works, and economic development projects in these areas. Although the program continues today, funding was drastically cut during President Reagan's tenure in the 1980s (Levitan et al., 1998).

Focusing specifically on businesses, the Reagan administration's Enterprise Zones provided businesses that relocated in poor areas incentives in the form of tax relief and loosening of regulations. The Clinton administration has continued the Reagan concept but changed the name of the program. Empowerment Zones and Enterprise Communities now receive federal funding to attract businesses that will create jobs in impoverished areas. Critics claim that such programs do not actually create jobs. Rather, they move businesses from one location to another and actually hurt existing businesses in these and adjacent areas. Also, incentives offered are often not sufficient to overcome barriers to business relocation in these areas, such as an unskilled workforce, poor infrastructure, and lack of amenities (Levitan et al., 1998).

In addition to these programs, the U.S. Department of Commerce's Economic Development Administration has a goal of increasing business investment and creating jobs in labor-surplus areas that are experiencing many business failures and high levels of foreclosures. The Economic Development Administration provides grants, loan guarantees, technical assistance for public works, and business development assistance. Also, the Farmer's Home Administration (FmHA) funds grants, loans, loan guarantees, and technical assistance to develop business activities in low-income rural areas (GAO, 1997; FmHA, 1980; Levitan et al., 1998; USDA, 1997).

Beyond influencing overall job creation at the national and local levels, government can attempt to increase jobs available to disadvantaged groups by making these individuals more desirable to employers. One mechanism for doing this is offering monetary incentives to employers. In the United States, the Targeted Job Tax Credit program was enacted in 1978 to entice employers to hire members of hard-to-employ target groups in exchange for federal tax credits. Findings of an evaluation done by the U.S. Department of Labor (1994), however, showed that the program failed to induce employers to hire target group members, projecting employers would have hired 92% of the individuals in question without the tax incentive. In addition, the program was not cost-effective, returning 37 cents to the dollar. Finally, it provided participants only with entry-level, low-paying, low-skilled, part-time jobs without benefits (U.S. Department of Labor, 1994). The program expired in 1994 and, at the recommendation of the Secretary of the Department of Labor, was not reauthorized.

Public Job Creation

Government policy has also focused on direct public job creation to increase labor demand during times of large surpluses in labor. During the Depression, for instance, mass unemployment of one quarter of all workers created a crisis in the United States (Mucciaroni, 1990). It was then that job creation programs emerged for the first time since before the Civil War. President Hoover's 1932 Emergency Relief and Construction Act loaned money to states and cities to create jobs. Franklin D. Roosevelt's New Deal included numerous programs that created jobs. The Civilian Conservation Corps, targeting single men between 18 and 25 years of age from needy families. The Public Works Administration dispensed loans and grants to federal, state, and local government units to undertake construction projects aimed at stimulating industrial growth. The Federal Emergency Relief Administration (FERA) provided direct unemployment relief and work programs (Janoski, 1990). The Civil Works Administration created a massive temporary public works project paying minimal benefits to over 16 million people (Jansson, 1997). The Works Progress Administration, although initiated to create self-liquidating capital-intensive projects, became the largest New Deal work program, focusing primarily on providing public employment through labor intensive projects. This New Deal approach to employment problems was ended by the Second World War, when labor was again in demand (Janoski, 1990).

Except for a minor effort by President Truman to target defense contract procurement to high unemployment areas in his 1952 Defense Manpower Policy Executive Order, public job creation was absent in the United States from the beginning of World War II until its reemergence in the 1970s. Then, high levels of unemployment led to a series of laws authorizing public job creation programs. Constructors of the Emergency Employment Act of 1971 saw the market failing to create enough jobs and viewed guaranteed public sector employment as a temporary solution to the temporary unemployment problem. The Act created 140,000 jobs. In addition, Title II of CETA provided public employment to counter the predicted effects of the imminent oil embargo (Mucciaroni, 1990).

The simultaneous existence of high rates of inflation and unemployment during the 1974-1975 recession, known as stagflation, was a new condition in the modern economy, which made increasing spending to stimulate the economy an unpopular position. This led policy makers to seek a new route to decrease unemployment. At the time, public sector employment was viewed positively, and with the support of Congress, President Ford increased the number of public sector jobs to 170,000 (Janoski, 1990).

While the 1974 Emergency Unemployment Assistance Act was a countercyclical measure that provided public service employment for all unemployed people during periods of economic downturns, this endorsement of public service employment was short-lived. The 1976 Emergency Jobs Program Extension Act limited program eligibility to the disadvantaged and enrollment to 1 year. In addition, the Full Employment and Balanced Growth Act of 1978 set specific goals for reducing unemployment and inflation and noted that policies intending to reduce inflation should not increase unemployment. Again demonstrating the anti-intervention preference of the bill's supporters, the Act stressed that jobs should come only from the private sector, with public jobs being a last resort and paying low wages so as not to interfere with wages in the private sector (Mucciaroni, 1990).

The 1978 CETA Reauthorization Act tightened eligibility for public employment even further, focusing on the severely disadvantaged. The result of this intense focus was to decrease the participation of local government in CETA programs. Consequently, community-based organizations with limited technical program knowledge or administrative capacity were left as the sole implementers of the programs (Janoski, 1990).

Just after the second oil shock hit the nation in 1979, Ronald Reagan entered the White House. His opposition to direct government intervention in the labor market led to severe cuts in the budgets of labor market programs during the early part of his administration. Job creation projects enacted by CETA, for instance, were slashed by over 75% (Janoski, 1990).

Since the Reagan Administration, public employment programs have not regained wide political support. One remnant of government job creation programs, however, is in the Senior Community Service Program, which provides 150,000 part-time jobs to individuals over 55, with an income 125% of the poverty line (Levitan et al., 1998).

Equal Employment Opportunity

Another way to increase demand for certain categories of workers is to increase the cost of employer discrimination against these groups. Anti-discrimination legislation attempts to prevent wage or hiring discrimination on the basis of race, gender, ethnicity, religion, or disability status. Thus, it increases the demand for the labor of groups that are often not preferred in the labor market.

Laws attempting to prevent discrimination in the workplace began with legislation at the state level. For example, in 1884, the state of Massachusetts passed a law protecting those seeking employment from discrimination on the basis of religion. By 1945, 22 states had laws against religious discrimination pertaining to civil service employees, and 11 states had provisions against discrimination on the basis of race (Skrentny, 1996, p. 28).

At the federal level, equal employment opportunity policy is relatively new. The 1963 Equal Pay Act was the first major federal equal employment opportunity legislation enacted by Congress. It requires that employers pay equal wages to men and women undertaking equal work (Levitan et al., 1998). The next year, the Civil Rights Act of 1964 was passed. This Act, among other things, mandates nondiscrimination in employment on the basis of race, creed, or color (Rose, 1994). Unfortunately, the effectiveness of the legislation was limited by a lack of enforcement authority in the Equal Employment Opportunity Commission (EEOC). Initially, the only way to implement the Act was through lawsuits filed by the Attorney General or private citizens. Thus, the success of the Act depended on the willingness of the Attorney General to file lawsuits and on the opinions of the courts. Substantive decisions did not emerge from the law until 1969, when the Supreme Court prohibited practices that were discriminatory in effect, not just intent. This included instituting employment tests for positions that did not previously require them. To broaden the scope of the Act, President Johnson's 1965 Executive Order 11246 required businesses acquiring federal contracts over $10,000 to abide by the law and also to act affirmatively in ensuring the employment and fair treatment of individuals of all races (Harvey, 1973).

Other categories of workers have been added to those protected by the original legislation. Employment discrimination on the basis of age was made illegal by the 1967 Age Discrimination in Employment Act. The 1973 Vocational Rehabilitation Act added individuals with disabilities to the list by prohibiting discrimination against them in promotion and hiring decisions in businesses and programs receiving federal money. The 1990 Americans With Disabilities Act made employment discrimination on the basis of disability illegal in general and called for reasonable accommodations to allow such individuals to work (EEOC, 1998a; Levitan et al., 1998).

The Equal Employment Act of 1972 amended Title VII of the Civil Rights Act to include state, local, and federal governments, and it granted the EEOC the authority to file discrimination lawsuits, strengthening the power of the law considerably. Between 1972 and 1975, numerous court decisions against large companies such as American Telephone and Telegraph (AT&T), Albermarle, and others "captured the attention of business across the country" (Rose, 1994, p. 47), encouraging them to promote equal opportunity in employment. Court decisions supported past wage remuneration for discrimination and prohibited the use of employment screening devices that led to discriminatory outcomes (Levitan et al., 1998).

Whereas most of the laws implemented during the 1960s focused on making the hiring and promotion practices of employers fair, two Supreme Court decisions in 1979 targeted the outcome of these practices. *Griggs et al. v. Duke Power Company* (1971) found seemingly neutral employment practices to be illegal if their result negatively affected targeted groups and the criteria involved were not job-related. Thus, education requirements and tests not related to the job in question could not be used in hiring and promotion decisions if target groups were disadvantaged as a result. In *United Steelworkers of America v. Weber et al.* (1979), the Supreme Court supported affirmative action plans as long as these plans were designed to overcome an existing imbalance, they were temporary, and they did not infringe on the rights of majority workers (Levitan et al., 1998).

The tide turned against race-conscious hiring and promotion goals in the 1980s. This change was led by decisions of the Justice Department, the Reagan administration's requirement that intent to discriminate be demonstrated before laws were enforced, and substantial cuts in the budget of the EEOC (Levitan et al., 1998). As a result, the EEOC failed to bring forward any suits regarding testing or adverse impact between 1983 and January 1989 (Rose, 1994).

Recent changes in equal employment laws have been mixed. In 1989, the Supreme Court overturned *Griggs,* weakening EEOC's power to enforce legislation. Congress responded with the 1991 Civil Rights Amendment, which increased penalties for violation of equal employment opportunity law. Since the mid 1990s, increased criticism of affirmative action has emerged, in particular with opponents arguing that women and minorities no longer need legal protection (Levitan et al., 1998).

REGULATORY LAWS PROTECTING WORKERS

In addition to laws that attempt to prepare workers for jobs or make jobs available to workers, several types of laws have been enacted to protect workers from a variety of difficult circumstances. These include job loss, dangerous working conditions, unfair wages, and benefits mismanagement.

Job Loss Protections

Before the Depression, the United States had neither a system of unemployment insurance nor a system of labor exchange. The Unemployment Compensation Program was created by the Social Security act of 1935 (PL 74-271). The goal of the program, which is still in effect, is "to provide temporary and partial wage replacement to involuntarily unemployed workers who were recently employed . . . and . . . to help stabilize the economy during recessions" (U.S. Congress, 1998d, p. 327). The basis of the system is outlined in the Federal Unemployment Tax Act of 1938 and Titles II, IX, and XII of the Social Security Act. Unemployment insurance is funded by taxes paid by employers on the first $7,000 paid to each worker. Although eligibility varies by state, the amount of recent employment, earnings of the workers, and ability and willingness to look for work are key factors in all states. Individuals are usually disqualified if they left their previous job without good cause, were terminated for misconduct, or left due to a labor dispute. Benefits are a fraction of the individual's income and limited to a 26-week state benefit that can be extended to 39 weeks with the Federal-State Extended Benefits Program. An additional 7 weeks are also available under a rarely used trigger option in times of high unemployment (U.S. Congress, 1998d).

In addition to unemployment insurance, other job-loss protection programs target specific types of workers. To protect workers from layoffs due to foreign trade, several programs have been implemented since the 1970s. The Trade Adjustment Assistance Program, legislated under section 221-50 of the Trade Act of 1974, provides a trade adjustment allowance, employment service, training, job search assistance, and a relocation allowance to certified workers. This program is administered by the Employment and Training Administration of the Department of Labor in each state. Eligible individuals include those in firms or portions of firms in which a significant proportion of the workers are in danger of layoff or have already been laid off due to a decline in the firm's sales and/or production resulting from increased imports of like or competitive items produced abroad (U.S. Congress, 1998c).

The NAFTA Worker Security Act, or subchapter D of Title II of the Trade Act of 1974, established the North American Free Trade Agreement (NAFTA) Transitional Adjustment Assistance Program for workers adversely affected by NAFTA. Providing the same benefits as the Trade Adjustment Assistance Program, this program targets individuals faced with layoffs due to a decline in the firm's sales or production in the face of Mexican or Canadian imports or a shift in the firm's production to a company subsidiary in Canada or Mexico (U.S. Congress, 1998a). Also, Title III of the Job Training Partnership Act provides employment and training for dislocated workers who lost their jobs due to large-scale dislocation. Services include training, job search assistance, and a relocation allowance (Levitan et. al., 1998).

In addition, the 1988 Worker Adjustment and Retraining Notification Act requires businesses with over 100 employees to give 2 months notice to employees who will lose their jobs due to layoffs or plant closings (Levitan et al., 1998). Also, the Veterans Employment Rights Act ensures that people who have served in active duty in the armed forces have a right to be rehired by their employer once they return from service (U.S. Congress, 1986). The Workforce Investment Act of 1998 continues these programs but encourages linkages between them and other programs at the local level.

Work Conditions

Beyond dislocation subsidies and retraining programs, government policy places limits on the environment in which individuals work to protect their health and physical well-being. The Occupational Safety and Health Administration (OSHA) or OSHA-approved state systems administer the Occupational Safety and Health Act, which regulates safety and health conditions in most industries in the private sector. The regulations require employers to maintain healthful and safe work environments and workers to adhere to workplace conduct guidelines (Hartnett, 1996; Mintz, 1984). The Occupational Safety and Health Act was passed into law in 1970 and amended in 1990. It supersedes original safety legislation enacted under the Walsh-Healy Act, Services Contract Act, Contract Work Hours and Safety Standards Act, the Arts and Humanities Act, and the Longshore and Harbor Workers Compensation Act (Hartnett, 1996).

Benefit and Wage Protection

Other policies aim to ensure fair treatment of workers by employers regarding their benefits and wages. To protect retirement or pension benefits, the Employee Retirement and Income Security Act (ERISA) requires employers to ensure certain types of benefits and regulates pension administration, disclosure, and reporting (Bureau of National Affairs, 1986).

To protect workers' jobs in times of family illness, the Wage and Hour Division of the Employment Standards Administration of the Department of Labor administers the Family and Medical Leave Act of 1993. This Act requires employers with 50 or more employees to allow up to 12 weeks of unpaid leave to eligible employees for the serious illness of a family member or the birth or adoption of a child (EEOC, 1998b).

Because many Americans remain poor despite working full-time, some policies have been enacted to increase the monetary returns of work. The Fair Labor Standards Act, enacted in 1938, requires that employers pay the minimum wage to covered employees and overtime of one-and-one-half times the regular wage for hours worked over 40 in 1 week. It also restricts the amount of hours worked and type of jobs worked by children under 16. The federal minimum wage began at $.25 per hour in 1938 (Norlund, 1997) and reached $5.15 per hour in 1997. Bernstein and Schmidt (1997) evaluated the impact of the 1996-1997 increases in the minimum wage and found that the wages of 10 million workers were increased. About 46% of workers who benefitted worked full-time, gains were realized disproportionately by low-income working householders, and no significant job losses resulted.

Unfortunately, for individuals attempting to raise a family, the minimum wage is often insufficient to bring their income above the poverty line (Levitan et al., 1998), and many workers are not covered by the law (Bernstein & Schmidt, 1997). Thus, Congress created the Earned Income Tax Credit in 1975 (Karger & Stoesz, 1994) to bring the incomes of low-wage workers supporting families above the poverty threshold (Levitan et al., 1998).

ISSUES AND CONTROVERSIES

In the midst of the wide range of employment policies enacted in the United States, numerous issues and controversies remain. Some are timely and address the structure of current policy, whereas others address more basic philosophical concerns. The most fundamental question is whether or not the government should mediate disparities in the labor market. Many economists would argue that any intervention by the government in these economic issues is harmful because it impedes the operation of the market. The market is seen as a natural system that will work out irregularities. Others, like the secular stagnationist Keynesians and commercial Keynesians, pose that government can effectively enact policy to stimulate labor demand (Mucciaroni, 1990).

Once the reality of government intervention in the labor market is accepted, the goal of employment policy determines appropriate policy action. Some argue that the proper goal is full employment, whereas others argue that the only appropriate goal is to protect workers from harm or severe market fluctuations or to raise individuals out of poverty. Clearly, throughout history, policy makers in the United States have responded to a multitude of goals, and these disparate goals are reflected in the complex conglomeration of employment policies that exist. According to Mucciaroni (1990), confused and conflicting objectives are one of the key reasons for the political failure of employment policies.

Providing employment for all who are willing and able to work is a goal of some employment policies. However, government must decide which strategy to use to increase employment. The structure of this chapter actually reflects this debate: Policy can target either labor supply or labor demand. The decision to focus on either of these depends on the perceived cause of unemployment. Labor supply policies are enacted when unemployment is seen as a product of an unskilled, unmotivated workforce with few social supports or of a breakdown in informal systems that connect individuals to jobs. Many of the 163 employment programs noted in the 1995 GAO report address the lack of skills of potential workers. The education and training components aim to invest in the human capital of workers. Job readiness programs assume that individuals are not working because they are unmotivated or lack the soft skills necessary to find a job. These programs aim to motivate individuals to enter the labor force. Job placement and job information services such as Job Services' America's Job Bank assume that individuals are not working because they lack information about available jobs. Such programs provide employment information to individuals and assist them in applying for jobs.

In contrast, labor demand policy views the undersupply of jobs as the primary cause of unemployment. Job creation is intended to remedy this. However, the best way to create these needed jobs is another point of contention. Traditional Keynesians advocate increasing government expenditures to stimulate the economy, whereas commercial Keynesians favor tax relief to businesses. Some see employment generation as a private sector activity in which government has only a small facilitating role, whereas others see the role of government as including job creation. Although such activity was not popular in the 1990s, the federal government has directly provided jobs for workers during different periods of high labor supply, including the New Deal era and during the high unemployment of the 1970s.

Those in favor of protecting workers from harm as a main goal of employment policy support regulatory policies such as those advanced by the Occupational Safety and Health Act. When protection from unforseen job loss induced by market forces is the goal, policies such as Unemployment Insurance and the Trade Adjustment Assistance program are supported. Those who think policy should protect workers' benefits from employer negligence support policies such as ERISA and the Family Medical Leave Act. If the goal of employment policy is to reduce poverty, policies such as the minimum wage and the earned income tax credit are supported.

Additional issues arise once the desired type of policy is chosen. One is the target population of the policy. Many policies are categorical, targeting the poor, minorities, and women. Proponents of this approach argue that spending scarce resources on the most needy is the best tactic. Opponents note that the political ramifications of this is to alienate constituencies that would support universal programs. Mucciaroni (1990) argues that the failure of the employment policy of the 1960s was due in part to the poverty focus of programs, which alienated potential supporters.

One of the most consistent criticisms of employment policy beginning in the 1960s was the chaotic administrative design. Programs teetered between being overly centralized and overly decentralized. During times of overcentralization, the federal government funneled grant money from numerous programs directly to local areas, bypassing state administrative structures and maintaining federal oversight of each contract. The subsequent overdecentralization was characterized by regional Department of Labor offices overseeing local programs. The ineffectiveness of this strategy was primarily due to a lack of knowledge at the local level about how to run employment and training programs (Mucciaroni, 1990). The new Workforce Investment Act attempts to achieve a balance by giving control to both local and state entities and by allocating funds for technical assistance and program evaluation.

Another commonly cited problem is program duplication. Past duplication of administrative structures and a few cases of blatant corruption have led to a public perception of employment training programs as being inefficient, ineffective, and suffering from gross mismanagement (Mucciaroni, 1990). Recent changes seek to consolidate federal programs and devolve authority to local entities through the one-stop delivery system.

Regarding program goals, the current policy focus is increasing labor supply immediately, with worker-quality improvements as a secondary concern. Given the current economic climate, characterized by high labor demand, this is understandable and may be effective in the short term. However, it is important to remember that the economy is cyclical, and a downturn will occur. Thus, policy makers must ask what effect current policy will have on the adjustment of workers to these downturns and whether the need to fill the immediate demand for labor outweighs the need to prepare workers for their position in the changing global marketplace.

REFERENCES

Bane, M. J., & Ellwood, D. T. (1994). *Welfare realities: From rhetoric to reform.* Cambridge, MA: Harvard University Press.

Bernstein, J., & Schmitt, J. (1997). *Making work pay: The impact of the 1997-98 minimum wage increase.* Economic Policy Institute: http://epinet.org/mwsum.html

Bureau of National Affairs. (1986). Joint explanatory statement of the committee of conference on ERISA. In *ERISA: Selected legislative history, 1974-1985.* Washington, DC: Author.

Equal Employment Opportunity Commission. (1998a). *Disability discrimination: Employment discrimination prohibited by the Americans with Disability Act.* Washington, DC: Author.

Equal Employment Opportunity Commission, Office of Legal Counsel. (1998b). *The Family Medical Leave Act, the Americans with Disabilities Act, and Title VII of the Civil Rights Act of 1964.* Washington, DC: Author.

Farmers Home Administration (FmHA) (1980). *A brief history of FmHA.* Washington, DC: Author.

General Accounting Office. (1995a). *Multiple employment and training programs: Major overhaul needed to reduce costs, streamline the bureaucracy, and improve results.* Testimony of Clarence Crawford before Committee on Labor and Human Resources. Washington, DC: Author.

General Accounting Office. (1995b). *Welfare to work: AFDC training program spends billions, but not well focused on employment.* Testimony of Jane L. Ross before the Committee on Labor and Human Resources, United States Senate. Washington, DC: Author.

General Accounting Office. (1996). *Job Training and Partnership Act: Long-term earnings and employment outcomes* (GAO/HEHS-96-40). Washington DC: Author.

General Accounting Office. (1997). *Rural development: Availability of capital for agriculture, business, & infrastructure.* Washington, DC: Author.

Griggs et al. v. Duke Power Co., certiorari to the U.S. Court of Appeals for the Fourth Circuit, No. 124. Argued December 13, 1970. Decided March 8, 1971.

Guttman, R. (1983). Job Training Partnership Act: New help for the unemployed. *Monthly Labor Review, 106*(3), 3-10.

Guzda, H. (1983). The U.S. employment service at 50. *Monthly Labor Review, 106*(6), 12-19.

Hartnett, J. (1996). A political history of workplace safety. In *OSHA in the real world.* Santa Monica, CA: Merritt.

Harvey, J. C. (1973). *Black civil rights during the Johnson administration.* Jackson: University and College Press of Mississippi.

Janoski, T. (1990). *The political economy of unemployment: Active labor market policy in West Germany and the United States.* Berkeley: University of California Press.

Jansson, B. S. (1997). The early states of the New Deal. In *The reluctant welfare state: A history of American social welfare policies.* Pacific Grove, CA: Brooks/Cole.

Karger, H. J., & Stoesz, D. (1994). *American social welfare policy: A pluralistic approach* (2nd ed.). White Plains, NY: Longman.

Levitan, S. A., Mangum, G. L., & Mangum S. L. (1998). *Programs in aid of the poor* (7th ed.). Baltimore, MD: Johns Hopkins University Press.

Martinez, T. (1976). *The human market place.* New Brunswick, NJ: Transaction Books.

Mintz, B. W. (1984). *OSHA: History, law, and policy.* Washington, DC: Bureau of National Affairs.

Mucciaroni, G. (1990). *The political failure of employment policy: 1945-1982.* Pittsburg, PA: University of Pittsburgh Press.

Norlund, W. J. (1997). *The quest for a living wage: The history of the federal minimum wage program.* Westport, CT: Greenwood.

Rose, D. (1994). Twenty-five years later: Where do we stand on equal employment opportunity law enforcement? In P. Burstein (Ed.), *Equal employment opportunity: Labor market discrimination and public policy.* New York: Aldine De Gruyter.

Skrentny, J. D. (1996). *The ironies of affirmative action: Politics, culture, and justice in America.* London: University of Chicago Press.

Social Legislation Information Service. (1998). *Washington Social Legislation Bulletin, 35*(40), 157-158.

United Steelworkers of America, AFL-CIO-CLC v. Weber et al., certiorari to the U.S. Court of Appeals for the Fifth Circuit, No. 78-432. Argued March 28, 1979. Decided June 27, 1979.

U.S. Congress, Committee on Ways and Means. (1998a). NAFTA Workers Security Act. In *Green Book,* 105th Congress. Washington, DC: Government Printing Office.

U.S. Congress, Committee on Ways and Means. (1998b). Temporary Assistance for Needy Families. In *Green Book,* 105th Congress. Washington, DC: Government Printing Office.

U.S. Congress, Committee on Ways and Means. (1998c). Trade Adjustment Assistance. In *Green Book,* 105th Congress. Washington, DC: Government Printing Office.

U.S. Congress, Committee on Ways and Means. (1998d). Unemployment compensation. In *Green Book,* 105th Congress. Washington, DC: Government Printing Office.

U.S. Congress. (1986). *Veterans readjustment appointment authority extension and improvements report* (Report 99-627 to House of Representatives, 99th Congress, 2nd session). Washington, DC: Author.

U.S. Congress. (1986). *Veterans rights report* (Report 99-626 to House of Representatives, 99th Congress, 2nd session). Washington, DC: Author.

U.S. Department of Agriculture. (1997). *Business and industry guaranteed loan program.* Washington, DC: Author.

U.S. Department of Labor. (1994). *Targeted jobs tax credit program: Employment inducement or employer windfall?* Washington, DC: Author.

CHAPTER TWENTY-TWO

Education and Social Welfare Policy

MARTIN B. TRACY

PATSY DILLS TRACY

This chapter explores the interdependency between public education and social welfare policies for poor, minority, and marginalized populations in the United States as related to civil society and democracy. Although both education and welfare policies are controversial and highly visible public policy issues, relatively little attention is paid to the influence that policies in one have on the other, or on society as a whole. Currently, both public social welfare and public education programs are encountering pressure for extensive reforms that involve increasing program accountability and strengthening capacities of communities and families through a systematic devolution of programs and services (Staeheli, Kodras, & Flint, 1997; Whitty, Power, & Halpin, 1998). It is beneficial to consider the shift in educational and social welfare policy decision-making processes under devolution by examining the historical and current conditions that are helping to shape the interdependency between these two powerful instruments of democracy.

Much of the public discussion on education policy, when linked with social welfare policy, is limited to the role of educational and training programs targeted to welfare recipients. This gives a very narrow focus to public education as a component of welfare policy to improve the employability of people on welfare in the hope of getting—and keeping—them off welfare through education. But educational policies and resources aimed at poor and minority welfare recipients in the United States are peripheral in the extreme. The overarching goal of public education is much more comprehensive and significant than the reduction of welfare rolls. Its most fundamental purpose is to sustain a democratic society.

Stated somewhat differently, most public discourse on educational policies within the context of welfare policies is extremely limited in scope and nature. This limitation has serious implications for current national and state reforms in both policy areas. One major implication is the lack of attention given to the role of public education as an instrument in welfare and educational reforms for strengthening civil society and democracy, especially as policies relate to achieving greater social, political, and economic inclusiveness of poor, minority, and marginalized populations.

This chapter will address the issue of public education and social welfare policies as mechanisms for civil society through three related sections. The first section will provide an overview of policy evolution of public education in relationship to social welfare. This discussion will accentuate the theories of the American philosopher and educator, John Dewey, who regarded education as a public good and an essential component of civil society (Carr & Hartnett, 1997). The second section will examine the primary issues in current debates on policies related to educational reform as it pertains to welfare reform. This will include a focus on the "devolution evolution," which is altering the balance of shared responsibility for education and social welfare among local, state, and federal governments, especially as it relates to the poor, minorities, and vulnerable women. The third section will provide some specific examples of the trend toward redirecting decision-making authority and responsibility for social programs to the local community.

OVERVIEW OF EDUCATION POLICY EVOLUTION FOR THE POOR

Public education that included the poor and minorities was very difficult to establish throughout the early history of the United States (Schneider, 1938). Schools that evolved in the late 1800s, prompted by the labor needs of industrialization, were greatly influenced by concepts imbedded in Jacksonian democracy, which began in 1828. During this period, democracy centered around reform that was particularly designed to create a more egalitarian society through reforms that focused on individual behavior. This included efforts to extend suffrage, temperance, poor relief, humane treatment of the insane, rehabilitation of criminals, and child welfare. Significantly, free public education was the reform effort best designed for the development of egalitarianism and democracy inclusive of the poor (Axinn & Levin, 1982). The value of public education in this regard was given credence by Horace Mann's dictum that public education is "the great equalizer of the condition of men—the balance-wheel of the social machinery" (quoted in Axinn & Levin, 1982, p. 46). This view gave strength to the idea that only through public education can the rich and poor be brought together. Axinn and Levin note,

> There was widespread agreement that "universal and complete" education "would do more than all things to obliterate factitious distinctions in society." Democracy could be real, if the poor could be made the equal of the rich. Education could instill the means and will to make it so. (p. 46)

The development of egalitarianism through education, however, was left to the domain of the states and localities, not the federal government. The concept of public education spread quickly in the East, followed by the West and mid-Atlantic states by the middle of the 19th century. The South lagged behind and had no statewide systems of public education until after the Civil War (Axinn & Levin, 1982).

During the period of Confederate Reconstruction following the Civil War, education policy was a central focus of the Bureau of Refugees, Freedman, and Abandoned Land, commonly referred to as the Freedman's Bureau, which was designed to provide war relief to all races. This program's greatest success was in education, establishing day, night, Sunday, and industrial schools, including colleges and universities (Franklin, 1970) that were primarily attended by blacks because whites preferred not to go to school with the freedmen. In collaboration with philanthropic organizations and religious institutions, the Freedman's Bureau helped found such predominantly African American educational institutions as Howard University, Hampton Institute, Atlanta University, Fisk University, and Talladega College.

Education and other relief measures during Reconstruction were intended to pave the way for a more egalitarian society based on increased opportunities of the poor and minorities in decision-making processes and in providing benefits and services that would promote the general welfare (Franklin, 1970). This was an attempt to promote the fundamental principles of democracy, based on the belief that a combination of education and social welfare programs contributes to the growth of all members of society.

Despite the post-Civil War efforts to enhance society by combining education and social welfare policies, the pressures of a rapidly industrializing nation diminished the emphasis on egalitarianism. Thus, from the turn of the 20th century until World War II, public educational policy that directly affected the poor was focused on a response to the workforce needs of expanding industrial development in urban areas. Heavily reliant on impoverished male and female immigrants and poor minority laborers, public education was aimed not only at training a workforce for industry, but at socializing foreign laborers in American Protestant work ethics and social and political values. There were at least five major features of public education that served to define education for low-income populations related to overt efforts at socialization (Oakes, 1993).

The first such feature is that of the relationship between school and work, when secondary education became the primary mechanism for training workers for industrial jobs. The second is referred to as differentiated education. This meant that the intellectual and skill capacities of poor immigrants and minorities were largely seen as genetically limited to learning basic labor skills in industrial work. This view contributed to the development of an educational system that differentiated between vocational and academic training.

A third feature was Anglo-conformity and Americanization, whereby educational policy was aimed at mainstreaming the poor and immigrants into American Protestant social and political value systems. A fourth was scientific management. Under this approach, educational focus was on skills and knowledge that could be easily identified and measured, leading to specializations and standardized outcome measures of skills and intelligence.

Finally, there was meritocracy, by which educational opportunity was determined by merit, based on standardized tests that placed poor immigrants with English as a second language in noncompetitive positions for quality education and employment. Thus, public educational policies in the early part of this century reinforced many stereotypes regarding immigrants and minorities and set the stage for a sustained focus on the poor as a class that required socialization to work ethics and social values. It is important to note, moreover, that there were serious reservations about whether any amount of education could overcome the ingrained or biological inferiority of the poor. This predominant perspective led to an emphasis on vocational education for the poor and special needs students, which was considered to be the most successful approach to training immigrants and minorities in individual achievement and merit. Education for these groups emphasized training for life skills rather than developing conceptual or rational thought, enhancing aesthetic understanding, or nurturing critical or creative faculties (Shapiro, 1990). This dichotomy in education and human potentials of the time was identified as rooted in the class nature of society by John Dewey (Shapiro, 1990).

The Influence of Dewey

By the turn of the century, John Dewey had begun extolling the virtues of education, including scientific approaches, for all members of society as a fundamental prerequisite for a more democratic and egalitarian society (Dewey, 1916, 1927; Geiger, 1951; Seigfried, 1996). He argued that what people lacked, including the poor and minorities, was not intelligence, but the sharing of information through education and active participation of the public (Carr & Hartnett, 1997). This belief was also a basic tenet of the various educational initiatives of mutual aid or mutual improvement societies, which sponsored charitable schools or shared learning in working-class homes (Davies, 1997). Whereas the dominant theories of education and egalitarianism in Jacksonian democracy had promoted reforms for individuals, Dewey contended that it was impossible to distinguish individuals from society in that they are both elements of a single process of dialectical and dynamic growth and social change (Carr & Hartnett, 1997). Therefore, any successful educational or social welfare reforms must be considerate of their interdependence within the context of a social system at a national or community level.

A concrete example of this concept is reflected in the early settlement house movement, which emphasized the interdependence of education, social services, and interaction at the community level for poor foreign-born immigrants (White, 1959). It is no coincidence that John Dewey was an active participant in various projects and programs of Hull House in Chicago (Campbell, 1995), as well as a close colleague of Hull House founder Jane Addams, who shared his views of education as a primary mechanism to reduce poverty and social exclusion (Addams, 1929; Greenstone, 1979). Dewey influenced many aspects of education, and his ideas on the interrelationship of education, democracy, and civil society were incorporated into federal social welfare programs following the Great Depression of the 1930s.

Dewey (1916, 1927) also laid much of the foundation for connecting education to civil society, as reflected in current welfare reforms that promote community-based programs. He argued that democracy places a high responsibility on individuals to be aware of community issues, community needs, and the consequences of actions taken collectively (Campbell, 1995). He stressed that decisions based on the needs of the community should not be passed on to some higher authority or outside agent. The public must take responsibility for solving its problems (Parsons, 1997).

Post-World War II

The role of the federal government in influencing public education and social welfare greatly accelerated following the end of the World War II. The first major federal legislation after the war was the Servicemen's Readjustment Act of 1944 (the GI Bill). It received support from both populist conservatives and New Deal liberals, not only to reward returning soldiers, but also to ward off postwar unemployment (Skocpol, 1997). Getting men in college and training programs would not only reduce immediate pressure on the labor market, it would also provide the education needed to prepare a workforce that would better enable the United States to keep pace with the demand for technology and consumerism. Beyond this, however, few federal programs were targeted for the poor, minorities, and women until the 1960s.

The discovery of the breadth and depth of poverty in the United States in the late 1950s and early 1960s, accompanied by a declining pool of laborers due to demographic shifts, led to a series of federal actions aimed at improving education, economic opportunities, and welfare benefits for the poor, many of which were constructed around civil rights and the War on Poverty (Segal & Brzuzy, 1998). The Supreme Court's decision on *Brown et al. v. Board of Education* (1954), which overruled the "separate but equal" doctrine and prepared the way for subsequent civil rights actions, had profound impact on both education and welfare policies related to racial inequality.

It was not until the mid-1960s, however, that the Economic Opportunity Act of 1964 created a series of programs aimed at reducing inequities and poverty through a combination of education and welfare programs, including the Job Corps, the Upward Bound program to prevent school dropout and encourage dropouts to return to school, VISTA (Volunteers in Service to America), and community action programs. The Head Start program for poor preschool children was also started under the Economic Opportunity Act. Head Start exemplified a comprehensive and systemic policy perspective on the interdependency of education, medical care, nutrition, and parental involvement, which prepared children not only for school but for society. Several limitations on the program in terms of funding, availability, and time-limited restrictions, however, have reduced its potential in addressing the educational and welfare needs of poor children and their families.

In many respects, the constraints on Head Start reflect the characteristics of many of the anti-poverty programs of the 1960s, which may be described as "add-on" programs for the poor to enhance educational opportunities in a time of economic prosperity. Significantly, this did not include structural change in the decision-making process, policy formulation, or implementation (Oakes, 1993).

An additional attempt to use education as a mechanism to address the inequities of poverty in the 1960s was focused on increasing opportunities for higher education under the Higher Education Act of 1965. Along with student loans and institutional aid, the Act was part of a comprehensive approach to facilitate the transition to a Great Society based on the Deweyan principle of the power of education to reform society (Parsons, 1997).

In the 1970s, education and welfare policies were influenced by social and political reactions to dramatic changes in the economy marked by inflation, recession, unemployment, and a shift in political orientation to a renewed emphasis on individualism and a market economy that "trickles down" economic benefits to those willing to work for them. As the realities of the need to compete in a global economy became apparent to business and government, school systems became both the scapegoat for the poor economy and the hope for the future (Oakes, 1993). This led to a concerted effort in the early 1980s to develop policies that would address what was perceived to be a growing crisis in educational mediocrity, accompanied by an increasing public and government annoyance with an untrained and apparently unmotivated welfare-dependent population that had lost its work ethic.

Programs for the Poor and Minorities

Federal policies for the at-risk welfare population over the past three decades have been targeted at employment training through multiple add-on programs. A recent tabulation identified 154 federal programs involved in employment training, administered through 14 different federal departments (Segal & Brzuzy, 1998). Some selected programs for disadvantaged populations under the Department of Education have included School Dropout Demonstration, Migrant Education, Adult Education for the Homeless, Vocational Education, English Literacy Program, and the Student Literacy Corps. Programs in the Department of Health and Human Services consist of Job Opportunities and Basic Skills programs, Community Service Block Grant, Refugee and Entrant Assistance, and the Health Career Opportunity Program. In the Department of Labor, there have been the Job Training Partnership Act (JTPA), Veterans Employment Program, Apprenticeship Training, Targeted Jobs Tax Credit, and the Homeless Veterans Reintegration Project (Segal & Brzuzy, 1998) and, most recently, the Workforce Investment Act of 1998.

The Comprehensive Education and Training Act (CETA) was created in 1973 to provide entry-level jobs in the private sector for young urban minority people and the chronically unemployed. CETA was replaced in the early 1980s by JTPA, to shift the emphasis to the private sector through subsidies to retrain unemployed workers and to train disadvantaged youth. Unfortunately, JTPA received less funding, did not create new jobs, and provided fewer social support services for participants (Levitan & Shapiro, 1987, cited in Segal and Brzuzy, 1998). Without adequate social support systems, it is not surprising that studies have shown that the effectiveness of JTPA has been marginal in terms of long-term and sustainable gains (Berlin & Sum, 1988; Segal & Brzuzy, 1998).

Federal education and welfare legislation in the past few decades that has recognized the interdependence of providing social protection, support, and education for the poor includes the Family Education Rights and Privacy Act of 1974, the Child Abuse and Prevention Act of 1974, the Child Welfare Act of 1980, the Mental Health Act of 1983, the School Improvement Act of 1988, and the Family Support Act of 1988 (Freeman, 1995).

The value of interdependence and coordinated programs is also reflected in the new Workforce Investment Act (1998), which replaces federal statutes governing programs related to job training, adult education and literacy, and vocational rehabilitation with streamlined and more flexible components of workforce development systems. The Act consolidates programs operated under JTPA, and the primary intent was to strengthen the linkage between the programs through newly instituted state and local area workforce boards, one-stop systems, and a variety of integrated state plans based on unified approaches and performance standards.

Federal legislation for students with disabilities also reflects tacit acknowledgment of multiple education and social welfare needs related to training and employment: Section 504 of the Rehabilitation Act of 1973 (handicapped people's rights), the Education for All Handicapped Children Act of 1975, the Education for the Handicapped Amendments of 1986, the Americans With Disabilities Act of 1990, and the Education of the Handicapped Act Amendment of 1990 (Freeman, 1995).

CURRENT ISSUES

Devolution

Dominating much of current social welfare and education policy in the United States, as well as most of the industrialized world, is a "devolution revolution" aimed at changing decision-making processes and funding streams through the reallocation of power and authority from federal to local jurisdictions. Public support for reducing the influence of the federal government has been growing for the past several decades in various policy arenas. With regard to education and social welfare policies, devolution has been fueled by social and economic concerns at the community level that are linked to a publicly perceived erosion of local control and responsibility. Dominant federal policy influence, accompanied by submissive local policy-making authority, is often identified as the source of a wide range of societal ills reflected in increases in violence, drug abuse, and school dropout rates, along with rises in teen pregnancies and welfare dependency (Cope, 1997; Shelley, 1997; Whitty et al., 1998). The causes of these unsettling social indicators are frequently associated with a weakening social fabric among families and communities (McKnight, 1995). They are also intertwined among a variety of observed educational and social welfare program deficiencies.

A recent intensification of the devolution response has been made possible by a politically conservative environment that has restructured the scale and scope of government operations, shifting administrative and fiscal responsibility to states and localities (Cope, 1997). Devolution is aimed at generating a better balance among a mix of public/private, formal/informal, state/local, and community/family interactions in developing and delivering education and social welfare programs. It is also anticipated that devolution will lead to improved program effectiveness and efficiency under a concept of "new public management" based on market-type mechanisms and autonomy in decision making (Leeuw, 1997; Organization for Economic Cooperation and Development, 1995).

Education Policies

The educational crisis of the 1980s was brought to public attention with the publication of *A Nation at Risk* (Gardner, 1983), supplemented by similar reports that cited the demise of the education of the American workforce, including *Action for Excellence* and *Making the Grade*. Significant to this discussion is that the focus of these reform reports is on education that is limited to jobs, security, stability, defense, and prosperity. Equality or egalitarianism is given little attention except as a peripheral spinoff (Oakes, 1993).

A decade and a half after the warnings of a major report on the status of education in the United States in *A Nation at Risk,* there are indications that the subsequent changes in educational programs have had little impact. A recent conference sponsored by the Heritage Foundation produced a reform manifesto entitled *A Nation Still at Risk* (1998), which contends that the nation is still awash in a sea of intellectual and moral mediocrity. With respect to poor and minority children, the report notes that they tend to go to the worst schools, have less expected of them, are taught by less knowledgeable teachers, and have the least power to alter bad situations.

There are also serious concerns that failures in U.S. education are adversely affecting the economy and threatening the nation's competitiveness in a global market. Students are often viewed not only as technologically unprepared, but as lacking in the ability to think critically, respond with flexibility to new situations, or demonstrate concern for their community (Cuban, 1992).

Somewhat reminiscent of the features of public education at the turn of the 20th century, which were designed to train immigrant workers in skills for specific industrial tasks, various aspects of contemporary education and welfare policy reforms reflect solutions aimed at unidimensional problems. This has led to a categorical problem-solving approach to deal with problems that are conducive to simplified definition, identification, and measurement. This approach fits well with efforts to ensure that policies and programs are accountable through quantifiable outcome measures such as test scores, graduation rates, employment rates, and salaries.

A focus on performance indicators, however, transforms education from a process of learning and socialization into a product (Whitty et al., 1998). One drawback to an easily measured product approach is that it tends to neglect the fact that student performance is more typically determined by multiple dimensions, including a wide range of complex socioeconomic and familial factors (Mintrom & Vergari, 1997) that are difficult to define, identify, or measure and are particularly elusive of unidimensional treatment methods. This is especially true in lower-income families, where normal functioning is complicated by a shortage of economic and social resources, often compounded by housing, transportation, and health- and mental health-related problems. Nevertheless, specific goals and outcome measures continue to play a dominant role in public education policy, just as they do in public welfare policy.

The use of specific measurable goals in education were given a boost in 1989, when President Bush worked with state governors to launch America 2000. This program called for national standards in core subjects and the promotion of increased school quality. It was followed in 1994 by the Clinton administration's Goals 2000: The Educate America Act, which emphasized the development of standards by states and local school districts. A major difference between the 1989 and 1994 federal education policy initiatives is that the former was unfunded whereas Goals 2000 provided block grant funding. However, the funding was not without federal regulations, although they were opposed by most state officials reflecting a desire for more, rather than less, independence from Washington. In keeping with the intent of Goals 2000, while protesting federal influence, the 1996 National Education Summit supported improving state and local academic standards, but not those that are federally prescribed (Mintrom & Vergari, 1997).

Public Funding

Another current issue is that of public funding for education. As noted earlier, a major factor behind public education is that all of society benefits from a well-educated, well-informed, and skilled population, which is critical to a sustainable democracy. Public funds, of course, help to ensure that all children will have an opportunity to obtain a K through 12 education. In recent years, public funding has shifted from local school districts to state and federal governments, although local and state funds still account for over 90% of all financing (Mintrom & Vergari, 1997). There has also been a greater centralization of responsibility for public school finance, including more efforts in many states to increase accountability to state officials through evidence of school performance.

Charter Schools, Open Enrollment, and Voucher Programs

Three recent education initiatives—charter schools, open enrollment, and voucher programs—constitute efforts to circumvent perceived limitations in the public school systems. By 1997, 26 states had established charter school laws that are intended to (a) introduce greater choice in public education, (b) increase public school competition and accountability, and (c) provide greater opportunities for innovation in school management and pedagogy (Mintrom & Vergari, 1997). The charter school circumvents most of the bureaucratic obstacles found in traditional public schools and is given more freedom in decisions regarding personnel, curriculum, and contracts for services. This is granted in exchange for a higher level of accountability.

Open enrollment gives parents more choice in where they may send their children to school. It is also seen as an instrument to create healthy competition between schools to attract the best students, leading to improved performance and accountability. Studies have substantiated that open enrollment has led to increased parental and teacher involvement in planning, leading to curriculum changes and improved support systems (Mintrom & Vergari, 1997).

A third approach to improving performance and accountability within the context of devolution are voucher programs. Vouchers deviate from support for traditional public education in that they use funds from private foundations to subsidize attendance at private schools. In Milwaukee and Cleveland, publicly funded vouchers have been specifically targeted to assist low-income families. An important critique of these options is that there is little evidence to suggest that they have brought about sustained improvement in educational opportunities for low-income and marginalized people (Whitty et al., 1998).

Partnerships and Community

As the brief discussion on current issues suggests, the two dominant objectives of reform influencing education and social welfare policies are (a) improving program performance and accountability (including outcome measures) and (b) placing more of the burden of responsibility for efficient and effective education and welfare programs on communities through devolution policy. These efforts have not been limited to merely shifting power from federal to state governments. Rather, they have involved redirecting decision-making power to localities through the development of community partnerships.

The federal government itself has taken an active role in promoting devolution through partnerships at the state and community levels. The intent of important recent social and economic federal legislation is to promote collaboration between employers, employees, civic leaders, educators, and consumers in assuming more responsibility for improved education and welfare programs in their communities. Four overlapping examples serve to illustrate the growing emphasis on education, welfare, and societal interdependency through community partnering. The first example is taken from education reform (School-to-Work Opportunities Act of 1994). The second is from welfare reform (Personal Responsibility and Work Opportunities Reconciliation Act of 1996). The third example is from a multidimensional initiative for economic and social development (Empowerment Zone and Enterprise Community program). The last example is the federal school-based learning center program.

School-to-Work

The School-to-Work Opportunities Act of 1994 provides states with federal assistance to develop and implement statewide systems that respond to regional economic conditions and labor requirements. It is important to note that the goals of this Act are not limited to implementing new curriculum or training that will make students more employable and more competitive in the labor market. A critical aspect of the Act is to help facilitate systemic change in which education, employment, and communities interact to create a supportive environment that normalizes work as an integral part of life and fosters a seamless transition from education to employment.

Significantly, the primary strategy to achieve this interaction is the mandated collaboration among employers, labor, community groups, educators, professionals, civic leaders, parents, and students at the local level. Following strict guidelines to safeguard a wide range of representation in the community, including business, the prescribed format for receiving federal funds forces the development of community partnerships. Thereby, it lays the groundwork for increased interaction and interdependency among diverse components of the community.

Personal Responsibility and Work Opportunity Reconciliation Act

The major federal legislation for welfare reform is the Personal Responsibility and Work Opportunity Reconciliation Act of 1996. The Act is best known for its attempts to reduce the number of recipients under the Temporary Assistance to Needy Families, which replaced the Aid to Families with Dependent Children program. Although this is a major objective, in many states, welfare reform has been more concerned with a comprehensive restructuring of social services. Typically, this has involved efforts to change the balance between public/private, state/local government, and community/family responsibility for social welfare. In these instances, welfare reform reflects a systemic response to the process of the devolution of social welfare policies and programs, a process that minimizes government and maximizes community involvement (Cope, 1997). Indeed, this is characteristic of welfare reforms associated with devolution throughout the industrialized world (Chassard, 1997; Michaelis, Miller, & Stevens, 1997).

A primary feature of many welfare reform programs in the United States and other nations is to broaden the role of human service delivery systems to bring families together with a team of professional service providers. This opens up opportunities for families to be more active participants in making decisions and planning strategies that will help lead to self-sufficiency. Such efforts are closely linked to civil society approaches to coping with social exclusion and poverty by building on "social capital" through increased participation of those marginalized groups who are most affected by welfare policy reforms (White, 1997). Increased involvement of families and communities is also reflected in a vast array of successful local initiatives in neighborhoods around the nation (Schorr, 1997; Tam, 1998), often assisted by private foundations such as the Annie E. Casey Foundation (1995).

Empowerment Zones/Enterprise Communities

The third example of federal legislation that promotes welfare and education interdependency through community partnering is the Empowerment Zone and Enterprise Community program, part of the Omnibus Budget Reconciliation Act of 1993. The primary focus of this program, which authorized the special use of Social Service Block Grant Funds, is local economic development. However, the program also includes a mandate for the development of community social service programs. As in the case of the school-to-work initiatives and welfare reform, the legislation acknowledges that social support systems are critical to the success of job acquisition and retention, as well as business development.

Eligibility for these programs is based not only on economic criteria but on the community's ability to demonstrate a high level of cooperation and solidarity among all sectors. The programs are also models of "complementarity between top-down and bottom-up strategies" (Organization for Economic Cooperation and Development, 1997b, p. 91). Again, the ability to obtain external funding support from the federal government is dependent on community responsiveness in restructuring its approach to commerce, education, training, and human services through new models of partnering.

21st-Century Community Learning Centers

A final example of the federal emphasis on interaction between community organizations, which also links education with social services, is Title X, Part I, of the Elementary and Secondary Education Act. This Act authorizes funds to provide expanded learning opportunities for participating children in a safe, drug-free, and supervised environment. Awards for a community learning center are determined in large part by programs that demonstrate a collaborative effort to be undertaken by public schools with community-based organizations, related public agencies, and businesses. The intent is to provide a program within a school that provides educational, recreational, health, and social service programs. In 1999, new awards under this Act will approximate $100 million for an estimated 300 new grants, on top of the 600 or so grants already awarded.

Clearly, the formulae for new mixes of private-public, state-local government, and community-family programs that contribute to civil society, social cohesion, and democracy through education, income, social service, and labor policies are complex and varied. Although most of the emerging configurations are too new to allow accurate evaluation, the experiments that are under way will eventually provide a better understanding of what works or, at minimum, what is the "best practice" possible under a given set of social, political and economic circumstances.

Role of Private Foundations

It is also important to note the emerging role of private foundations in providing funds to stimulate community action through partnerships in higher education. One primary example is the Kellogg Foundation's (1999) Food Systems Profession Education initiative started in 1994 in selected land-grant universities. The initiative is aimed at developing partnerships among universities and between universities and communities that will facilitate community building through shared visions and processes. It is another effort that increases community participation, including the most needy members of the community, in decisions on the role and function of higher education that directly affect local social and economic conditions.

SUMMARY

In 1990, the various governments of the Organization for Economic Cooperation and Development (OECD) met to endorse the development of high-quality and universally accessible education and training. The emphasis at the most recent meeting of this group in 1996 was lifelong learning for all. To a large extent, the meetings have been prompted by the growing isolation or social exclusion of the most vulnerable and disadvantaged populations. With support from the U.S. Department of Education and the College Board, a series of documents, articles, and other written materials addressing this concern over the 6 interim years was recently published under the title *Education and Equity in OECD Countries* (OECD, 1997). Two brief overlapping quotations from the report are particularly relevant for summarizing the main points of this chapter:

> Educational disadvantage is neither a single nor simple phenomenon nor does it have one main cause; it is the result of complex interactions of home, socio-economic and community, and educational factors. (p. 106)

> Education should not be considered exclusively in terms of meeting other ends (better employment prospects, income chances, greater security), but as promoting social and cultural participation, and thereby contributing to the reduction of marginality and exclusion. (p. 103)

The idea that multiple causes exclude the poor and minorities from social participation and economic wealth, contained in these quotes, is critical to understanding the role of interdependent public education and social welfare support systems that exist to promote the development of civil society and democracy that serves everyone.

Education and social welfare policies share a common goal of increasing opportunities for the poor by promoting egalitarianism through democratic principles of interaction, participation, communication, and open dialogue, as expounded by John Dewey, Horace Mann, and Jane Addams, among numerous others. This is consistent with the current efforts of policy devolution, which is designed to rebuild communities by placing more of the burden of responsibility for education and welfare on partnerships between the federal, state, and local governments, public and private sectors, families and social service agencies, commerce and consumers, and educators and parents. The difficulty is in finding the appropriate mechanisms to achieve a sustainable and effective balance between the complex systems involved in maintaining a democratic society. Reweaving the social fabric to more fully engage and include the poor and vulnerable in their quest for increased self-sufficiency will require close collaboration between education and social welfare policies and programs.

REFERENCES

A nation still at risk. (1998, July-August, 1998). *Policy Review*, pp. 23-29.

Addams, J. (1929, November 15). A toast to John Dewey. *The Survey*, pp. 03-204.

Annie E. Casey Foundation. (1995). *The path of most resistence: Reflections on lessons learned from new futures.* Baltimore, MD: Author.

Axinn, J., & Levin, H. (1982). *Social welfare: A history of the American response to need* (2nd ed.). New York: Harper & Row.

Berlin, G., & Sum, A. (1988). *Toward a more perfect union: Basic skills, poor families, and our economic future* (Occasional Paper No. 3). New York: Ford Foundation.

Brown et al. v. Board of Education of Topeka et al., appeal from the U.S. District Court for the District of Kansas, No. 1. Argued December 9, 1952. Reargued December 8, 1953. Decided May 17, 1954.

Campbell, J. (1995). *Understanding John Dewey: Nature and cooperative intelligence.* Chicago: Open Court.

Carr, W., & Hartnett, A. (1997). *Education and the struggle for democracy: The politics of educational ideas.* Philadelphia: Open University Press.

Chassard, Y. (1997). Social protection in the European Union: Recent trends and prospects. In *Adapting to new economic and social realities: What challenges, opportunities, and new tasks for social security* (pp. 161-167). Geneva: International Social Security Association.

Cope, M. (1997). Responsibility, regulation, and retrenchment: The end of welfare? In L. A. Staeheli, J. E. Kodras, & C. Flint (Eds.), *State devolution in America: Implications for a diverse society* (pp. 206-220). Thousand Oaks, CA: Sage.

Cuban, L. (1992). Policies for public schooling in the 1990s. In J. A. Pechman (Ed.), *Fulfilling America's promise* (pp. 25-49). Ithaca, NY: Cornell University Press.

Davies, S. (1997). Two conceptions of welfare: Voluntarism and incorporationism. In E. F. Paul, F. D. Miller, Jr., & J. Paul (Eds.), *The welfare state* (pp. 39-68). New York: Cambridge University Press.

Dewey, J. (1916). *Democracy and education.* New York: Free Press.

Dewey, J. (1927). *The public and its problems.* Athens, OH: Swallow Press.

Education Commission of the States, Task Force on Education for Economic Growth. *Action for excellence: A comprehensive plan to improve our nation's schools:* Denver, CO: Author.

Franklin, J. H. (1970, December). Public welfare in the South during the Reconstruction era, 1865-80. *Social Service Review, 44,* 379-392.

Freeman, E. M. (1995). School social work overview. In R. I. Edwards (Ed.), *Encyclopedia of social work* (19th ed., pp. 2087-2099). Washington, DC: National Association of Social Workers.

Gardner, D. P. (1983). *A nation at risk: The imperative for educational reform. An open letter to the American people. A report to the nation and the Secretary of Education.* Washington, DC: Government Printing Office.

Geiger, G. R. (1951). Dewey's social and political philosophy. In P. Schilpp (Ed.), *The philosophy of John Dewey* (pp. 335-368). New York: Tudor.

Greenstone, J. D. (1979). Dorothea Dix and Jane Addams: From transcendentalism to pragmatism in American social reform. *Social Service Review, 53,* 547-555.

Kellogg Foundation. (1999). *Visions of change in higher education.* http://www.wkkf.org/Publications/VisionsBk/Default.htm

Leeuw, F. L. (1997). Solidarity between public sector organizations: The problem of social cohesion in the asymmetric society. *Rationality and Society, 9*(4), 469-488.

Levitan, S. A., & Shapiro, I. (1987). *Working but poor.* Baltimore, MD: Johns Hopkins University Press.

McKnight, J. (1995). *The careless society: Community and its counterfeits.* New York: Basic Books.

Michaelis, W., Miller, R., & Stevens, B. (1997). Economic flexibility and social cohesion in the twenty-first century: An overview of the issues and key points of discussion. In *Societal cohesion and the globalising economy: What does the future hold?* (pp. 7-25). Paris: Organization for Economic Cooperation and Development.

Mintrom, M., & Vergari, S. (1997). Education reform and accountability issues in an intergovernmental context. *Publius: The Journal of Federalism, 27*(2), 143-166.

Oakes, J. (1993). Tracking, inequality, and the rhetoric of reform: Why schools don't change. In H. S. Shapiro & D. E. Purpel (Eds.) *Critical social issues in American education: Toward the 21st Century* (pp. 85-102). New York: Longman.

Organization for Economic Cooperation and Development. (1995). *Governance in transition: Public management reforms in Organization for Economic Cooperation and Development countries.* Paris: Author.

Organization for Economic Cooperation and Development. (1997a). *Education and equality in OECD countries.* Paris: Author.

Organization for Economic Cooperation and Development. (1997b). *Partnership in the United States.* Paris: Author.

Parsons, M. D. (1997). *Power and politics: Federal higher education policy making in the 1990s.* Albany: State University of New York Press.

Schneider, D. M. (1938, September). The patchwork of relief in provincial New York, 1664-1775. *Social Service Review, 12,* 464-494.

Schorr, L. B. (1997). *Common purpose: Strengthening families and neighborhoods to rebuild America.* New York: Anchor.

Segal, E. A., & Brzuzy, S. (1998). *Social welfare policy, programs, and best practices.* Itasca, IL: F. E. Peacock.

Seigfried, C. H. (1996). *Pragmatism and feminism: Reweaving the social fabric.* Chicago: University of Chicago Press.

Shapiro, S. (1990). *Between capitalism and democracy: Educational policy and the crisis of the welfare state.* New York: Bergin & Garvey.

Shelley, F. M. (1997). Education policy and the 104th Congress. In L. A. Staeheli, J. E. Kodras, & C. Flint (Eds.), *State devolution in America: Implications for a diverse society* (pp. 221-232). Thousand Oaks, CA: Sage.

Skocpol, T. (1997). The G.I. Bill and U.S. social policy, past and future. In E. F. Paul, F. D. Miller, Jr., & J. Paul (Eds.), *The welfare state* (pp. 95-115). New York: Cambridge University Press.

Staeheli, L. A., Kodras, J. E., & Flint, C. (Eds.). (1997). *State devolution in America: Implications for a diverse society.* Thousand Oaks, CA: Sage.

Tam, H. (1998). *Communitarianism: A new agenda for politics and citizenship.* New York: New York University Press.

Twentieth Century Fund, Task Force on Federal Elementary and Secondary Policy. (1983). *Making the grade.* New York: Author.

White, G. (1997). Civil society, social exclusion, and poverty alleviation. In C. Gore & J. B. Figueiredo (Eds.), *Social exclusion and anti-poverty policy: A debate* (pp. 82-91). Geneva: International Institute for Labour Studies.

White, G. C. (1959, March). Social settlements and immigrant neighbors, 1886-1914. *Social Service Review, 33,* 55-66.

Whitty, G., Power, S., & Halpin, D. (1998). *Devolution & choice in education: The school, the state, and the market.* Philadelphia: Open University Press.

Workforce Investment Act of 1998 (H.R.1385): Summary and description of Final Compromise. Http:// .region10.doleta.gov/wia_nga.htm

CHAPTER TWENTY-THREE

Urban Development Policy

ROBERT J. WASTE

Former Atlanta mayor Maynard Jackson put the case for the primacy of urban development policy starkly when he noted,

> Japan spends 5 percent of its gross national product on urban infrastructure needs, the U.S. spends less than .05 percent. . . . We are a nation of cities. Eighty percent of Americans live on 2 percent of America's land surface. If we don't save America's cities, we won't save America's children. (Jackson, interview on *Morning Edition,* National Public Radio, July 15, 1992, cited in Waste, 1998, p. 113)

This chapter describes the historical evolution and contemporary ramifications of place-based social policy, policies designed to address the concerns of the vast majority of Americans, the more than 80% of us crowded into the urbanized 2% of our collective landscape—urban areas that we have historically referred to as *cities*. More recently, the Census Bureau has referred to these places as *metropolitan statistical areas,* and, in scholarly terms, they have been called *multinucleated metropolitan regions* (Gottdiener, 1985), *technoburbs* (Fishman, 1987, p. 184), *edge cities* (Garreau, 1991), *post-suburban regions* (Kling, Olin, & Poster, 1991), *polycentric metropolitan forms* (Blakely & Ames, 1992, p. 436), *citistate* regions (Peirce, 1995; Peirce, Johnson, & Hall, 1993; Hill, Wolman, & Ford, 1995; Savitch, Collins, Sanders, & Markham, 1993; Voith, 1992), and interdependent *regional economic commons* (Barnes & Ledebur, 1997). As the foregoing list of academic terms for describing the urban arena of social policy illustrates, the study of cities—and the development of American social policy to address the challenges facing urban residents—has undergone a gradual evolution from policies (and academic concepts) that focus primarily on center cities and center-city residents to the shared policies and concerns, the "interwoven destinies" (Cisneros, 1993, p. 24), of both the central city and suburban residents of America's sprawling metropolitan regions.

Both America's center cities and the suburban fringe are facing tremendous challenges. As a recent study has indicated (Waste, 1998), 44 of the largest metropolitan areas in the United States, containing over 40% of the nation's residents, have, since the early 1980s, been seemingly locked into a permanent urban crisis, a crisis of hunger, crime, poverty, and infrastructure decay. About 30 million Americans suffer from hunger on a daily basis. Every 15 minutes a child in an American city is killed by gunfire. About 20% of the bridges, highways, and basic infrastructure of American cities are obsolete. America has responded to these more recent placed-based urban problems, and to urban problems in general, with a series of policies and programs dating back to the Great Depression and the post-World War II era.

THE HISTORICAL EVOLUTION OF URBAN DEVELOPMENT SERVICES AND POLICIES

Although America's city residents benefitted from the universal social welfare entitlement policies such as the Social Security Act (1935) and the "alphabet soup" employment programs (e.g., the Works Progress Administration/WPA, the Civilian Conservation Corps/CCC, etc.) that accompanied the Great Depression and the New Deal era, American social policy to aid urban development was quite limited. A small set of national grants-in-aid programs to local governments during the early 1930s, funded at an annual level of $30 million, grew by the 1960s to annual federal-local transfer levels averaging $7 billion—about 8% of all federal spending—in the 1960s, and a historic high of $91 billion or 16% of all national government spending by 1980 (Ross & Levine, 1996; Ross, Levine, & Stedman, 1991). Federal expenditures on behalf of urban areas declined dramatically in the Reagan and Bush years, falling to $88 billion or 11% of all federal spending. Federal urban spending increased slightly in the Clinton years, averaging $200 billion annually, a figure equal to 14% of all federal spending.

1940s and 1950s Urban Aid Programs and Suburban Growth

The initial grants-in-aid programs grew modestly at first. Congress enacted the National Housing Act in 1934. The Housing Act created the Federal Housing Administration to create government-insured home mortgages to prop up the failing home building industry and the Federal Saving and Loan Insurance Corporation to insure

the savings of individual depositers who had lost their confidence after the bank failures and savings crises of the Great Depression. These early federal urban aid service
strategies signaled a trend that was to remain constant in federal policies toward cities
for several decades; assistance was directed toward industries such as home building,
banking, and savings and loans and only indirectly to places such as center cities. In
fact, these early policies and later urban development policies proved to aid suburban
growth as much or more than urban or center growth and development.

The social policies aimed at urban aid in the 1940s and 1950s exacerbated this urban fringe or suburban bias in urban aid programs. The federal Housing Act of 1949
created the Urban Renewal Agency and signaled the beginning of a decade of urban
renewal in center cities. This renewal effort was called "Negro removal" or the "federal bulldozer" (Anderson, 1964, pp. 6-8; Lemann, 1994, p. 3) by its detractors. From
1950 to 1960, urban renewal funds were spent to raze over 120,000 substandard
center-city housing units, which were replaced with fewer than 30,000 housing units.
Many of the newer units were consolidated in low-income public housing complexes,
which eventually became a source of controversy and, in the late 1990s, were being
renovated, sold to tenants, or demolished by the federal government.

The eradication of low-quality but affordable center-city housing stock via the Urban Renewal Agency program indirectly promoted suburban growth at the expense of
the center city, as did two other post-World War II programs, the GI Bill of Rights and
the Veteran's Administration (VA) Home Loan Program. These latter two programs
provided low-cost loans to World War II vets requiring no down payments on new
homes, most of which were to be found in the suburban housing market of post-World
War II America. The outer fringe areas of cities and the newly created suburban housing markets—the post-war Levittown phenomenon—were made all the more accessible by an unparalleled era of freeway construction promoted by the federal government in the Highway Act of 1956.

Urban development services created in the 1940s and 1950s, ironically, created a
boom market for suburban housing, a decline in affordable center-city housing stock,
and a federally subsidized freeway system and home loan purchase program that increasingly left center-city residents isolated from their more affluent suburban/metro-
politan neighbors. During the War on Poverty of the 1960s, the federal government
attempted to frame urban development programs that would assist the increasingly
isolated inner-city poor.

Urban Services and the 1960s War on Poverty

The 1960s saw the enactment of several key universal social welfare measures that
indirectly assisted the urban poor, including the Food Stamp program (1964), the
Civil Rights Act (1964), the Voting Rights Act (1965), and Medicare (1965). The im-

pact that enactment of these programs had on poorer Americans in general as well as Americans in urban areas can hardly be exaggerated. Although the specific causal relationship between these programs and the dramatic reduction in American poverty levels during the 1960s is still the cause of lively debate in some quarters (Lockhart, 1986; Murray, 1984; Schwarz & Volgy, 1992), the dramatic results of these federal programs seem factually indisputable. Urban and rural poverty levels were cut in half in the Lyndon Johnson years, from a high of 22% in 1960 to a low of 12% by the time that Johnson left office in January 1969. As I have observed elsewhere (Waste, 1998, p. 54), this is noteworthy, given that no president since Johnson has reduced the federal poverty level by more than 1.5%. Poverty nationally declined 0.7% under Richard Nixon, increased 0.2% under Gerald Ford, increased 2.4% under Jimmy Carter, decreased 1.2% under Ronald Reagan, increased 2.3% under George Bush, and decreased less than 2% during the Clinton administration years.

The Rise of the Community Action Program and Model Cities

Each of these 1960s-era civil rights or anti-poverty programs had positive if indirect impacts on cities, as did the key War on Poverty legislation, the Economic Opportunity Act of 1964, which created the food stamp and the low-income school lunch programs, Head Start, Upward Bound, Volunteers in Service to America, and the Legal Services program. To this anti-poverty package, the Johnson administration added a Community Action Program. Unlike the earlier universal civil rights or anti-poverty War on Poverty approaches of the Johnson years, the Community Action Program was place-based funding services and programs in poor neighborhoods, provided directly by creating local community action agencies designed to operate without the assistance or interference of elected or appointed state or local officials. Unpopular with mayors, governors, and local officials, the Community Action Program gave way in 1966 to a second targeted urban aid approach, the Model Cities program. Originally created to target only a few cities with extremely poor neighborhoods, the 1966 Model Cities legislation eventually covered 60 cities, was funded with $1 billion in grants, and required clear coordination with local, state, and even regional elected and appointed officials. Originally designed to aid targeted high-poverty neighborhoods in a small number of cities, Model Cities grew to include far more targets than those originally designated, and Model Cities funds were used by many cities for citywide services including schools, sewers, sanitation, and police (Herson & Bolland, 1991).

General Revenue Sharing, Special Revenue Sharing, and Cities

With the election of a new and more conservative president in 1968 and the general unpopularity of targeted programs with many urban local and elected officials

(Caputo, 1976), Congress adopted General Revenue Sharing in the State and Local Government Assistance Act of 1972, allocating more than $30 billion over a 5-year period to state and local governments, based not on need per se but on the population of the political unit in question. Supported later by both Presidents Gerald Ford and Jimmy Carter, revenue sharing was eventually eliminated in 1986 under President Ronald Reagan.

Soon after the creation of General Revenue Sharing, Congress enacted a follow-up Special Revenue Sharing urban service package. These two block-grant programs, the 1974 Housing and Community Development Block Grant program (CDBG) and the 1977 Urban Development Action Grant programs, were slightly more targeted than the earlier population-based General Revenue Sharing program. The 1974 CDBG program "blocked" seven earlier grant-in-aid programs for cities for such spending projects as sewers and urban renewal and allowed any city over 50,000 in population—that applied—to receive CDBG funding automatically. Extremely controversial with academic urban policy scholars (DeLeon & LeGates, 1976; Lovell & Korey, 1975; Marshall & Waste, 1977; Nathan & Domel, 1978; Nenno, 1974) because of the loose federal oversight of local spending and the automatic nature of the grants to all applying jurisdictions, CDBG continues to be popular in both city and national political circles and continues to be funded to the current day.

Urban Policy and Services in the Carter, Reagan, and Bush Years

The Carter administration attempted to move away from the loose oversight General Revenue Sharing/block-grant urban aid approach with the Urban Development Action Grant program enacted in 1977. Under this program, federal funding to cities would be provided only if cities could demonstrate that the money would be spent in designated distressed areas and create a local partnership to leverage the funds provided by the federal government. The "high strings" highly targeted Urban Development Action Grant approach was terminated by the Reagan administration, which dramatically reduced funding and services aimed at American cities. The Reagan administration reduced annual federal spending to urban areas by 57%, reduced the budget of the U.S. Department of Housing and Urban Development from 7% of the federal budget to 1% by 1989, reduced the authorization for assisted housing funding from annual levels of $27 billion in 1980 to $7.5 billion annually in the later Reagan years, and reduced the number of public units of housing from 129,000 to 19,000 between 1980 and 1989—a level of reductions so sharp that one prominent critic charged the Reagan and Bush administrations with "abandoning cities" (Ross & Levine, 1996, pp. 426-429).

The Bush administration years, 1989-1992, saw few federal urban service initiatives, despite a dramatic urban riot in South Central Los Angeles in 1992. Tax incentive areas created in distressed urban areas, known as *urban enterprise zones*, were discussed by Jack Kemp, the Bush administration HUD Secretary, but were not actually implemented during this time. Rather, they were implemented as Empowerment Zones by the subsequent Bill Clinton administration. The Bush administration is notable in the urban policy arena primarily for the passage of the "Ice Tea Act"—the Intermodal Surface Transportation Efficiency Act (ISTEA) in 1991. ISTEA mandates that urban regions create a Metropolitan Planning Organization to ensure regional coordination on transportation issues to make cities eligible to receive millions of dollars in federal highway and transportation funds. Renewed and expanded in 1998, ISTEA has significant potential to encourage region-wide cooperation on transportation issues in American urban regions.

The Clinton Urban Aid/Service Policy Package

The Clinton administration urban service policy package is notable for three accomplishments: (a) the creation of Empowerment Zones in six cities (Atlanta, Baltimore, Chicago, Detroit, New York City, and Philadelphia), two supplemental zones (Cleveland and Los Angeles), three rural zones, and 65 enterprise communities; (b) the passage of the 1994 Crime Bill, which attempted to place 100,000 police on city streets; and (c) an October 1998 budget compromise with Congress in which the Clinton administration extracted a $1.1 billion funding authorization for 100,000 teachers aimed at reducing class sizes in K-3 public schools from a national average of 22 students to an average of 18 students per classroom.

The Evolution of Federal Urban Social Policies Services: A Summary

From World War II to the present, federal assistance to urban areas has evolved from early grants-in-aid to broad needs-based entitlement programs for disadvantaged city residents in such programs as Head Start and food stamps. Early needs-based programs to aid needy cities and urban regions, such as Model Cities and Urban Development Action Grants, were eventually replaced by population (versus needs-based) formula grant programs such as revenue sharing and CDBG. After the demise of revenue sharing, the population-based formulaic CDBG program and the more decentralized ISTEA program remain the key urban federal programs of the late 1990s. Against the backdrop of these programs, the limited use of empowerment zones in the Clinton administration represents a small step back into targeted needs-based urban aid strategies in the late 1990s.

Thus, from World War II to the present, federal urban aid strategies have swung from small specific grants to broad universal entitlements, to more targeted grants again, to dramatically lower levels of federal urban aid, back again to a steady increase in population-based entitlements, and, more recently, a combination of broad or universal benefits (e.g., CDBG, ISTEA, and increased police and teachers for all urban and suburban jurisdictions) and more narrowly targeted needs-based interventions (i.e., empowerment, supplemental or rural zones, and enterprise communities).

SERVICE DELIVERY: CURRENT LEGISLATION AND ADMINISTRATION ARRANGEMENTS

The primary urban service program at the federal level is the continuing CDBG program, administered centrally by HUD. The key decentralized program, as noted earlier, is ISTEA, which was re-authorized by Congress in 1998. ISTEA, administered nationally by the Department of Transportation, is administered within each urban region by the regional Metropolitan Planning Organization authorized under the ISTEA Act. HUD also administers the limited-scale urban Empowerment Zone program described above, a Section 8 low-income housing assistance and voucher program, a small number of "Move to Opportunity" programs modeled after the Chicago Gautreaux urban core to suburban rim residential dispersion program, and the "Continuum of Care" homeless assistance programs developed by HUD to respond to spending and programs authorized by Congress in the McKinney Homeless Assistance Act of 1987 and subsequent congressional reauthorizations.

To remain eligible for CDBG funding, cities and counties are required to file annual Comprehensive Housing and Affordability Survey reports to HUD. Cities compete for McKinney Act funding by submitting Continuum of Care applications to HUD, and they also have competed in the past for designation as Empowerment Zones or Enterprise Communities. Cities and counties also apply to the Department of Justice for funding for additional police officers under the mechanism established by the 1994 Crime Bill. Funding for and administration of the Clinton administration's 100,000-teacher initiative, presumably administered nationally by the U.S. Department of Education, is, as of this writing, not yet clear.

Since the United States federal government administration was divided up into 10 regional offices under the New Federalism approach pioneered by President Richard Nixon in 1969, cities and counties have typically developed close working relations with one or more HUD and Department of Justice offices and officials centered in 1 of the 10 regional offices nearest the city or county in question.

Larger cities also regularly maintain liaison and information-seeking activities with the Washington, D.C.-based national headquarters of HUD and the Department of Justice. The latter task has not been made easier for cities in the Clinton administration due to a downsizing of the Washington, D.C., HUD office staff, budget, and mission. Threatened with the elimination of HUD after the congressional elections of 1994, then-Secretary Henry Cisneros began a program of reinventing HUD that continues to the present day. The reinvented HUD administrative structure has a decidedly reorganized look. Over 60 categorical grants were combined into three broad, flexible, performance-based grant programs. Local managers were given more authority to dismantle, sell, or rehabilitate federally funded housing projects. Many of these sites were turned over to residents in experimental resident/manager programs, whereas other residents were given vouchers in Move to Opportunity demonstration projects.

SOCIAL, POLITICAL, AND ECONOMIC
FACTORS INFLUENCING POLICIES

The social conditions of cities and the challenges faced by American cities have changed very little over the past decade. As we noted at the outset of this chapter, cities are experiencing significant challenges on several fronts: violent crime, hunger, poverty, and infrastructure decay. These challenges have remained so fixed in American urban life over the past decade that one observer has labeled it a "permanent crisis" for American cities (Waste, 1998, pp. 1-9). If the scope of the permanent crisis in American cities has remained relatively stable over the past decade, the shape of that crisis has changed, if only slightly. Although it is still more prevalent than in the period between World War II and the early 1960s, violent crime has decreased slightly, and urban poverty, which earlier characterized impoverished urban core areas, is to be found increasingly in suburban areas and inner-ring suburban neighborhoods. Beginning in 1990, 42% of all metropolitan poor people lived not in the center city but in suburban or inner-ring neighborhoods.

Urban crime abated in 1997 to an average of 6.9 homicides per 1,000 people, the lowest rate in three decades. This decline was due to (a) innovations in community policing in large cities with populations exceeding 1 million, (b) a drop in gun-related violence among juveniles, (c) changing demographics in youth and adults earlier involved in gun-related crime and crack cocaine trafficking, (d) the limited success of "three strikes" incarceration laws enacted by state legislatures.

In the late 1990s, cities and urban problems and policy proposals lacked political clout in American national politics and policy making. Urban issues lacked clout because suburban voters were widely perceived as more important to presidential and congressional elections than center-city voters (Barnes, 1995; Phillips, 1994). Urban areas also lacked political clout because of the structural rural bias of the U.S. Senate, which as Robert Dahl (1980) and others (Waste, 1998) have pointed out, has an absolute voting majority drawn from the 26 smallest states, a figure equivalent to only 17% of the 1990 U.S. population. In this sense, the Senate serves as an anti-urban anchor functionally preventing the emergence of urban issues and policies in American national politics.

Finally, even when social welfare or urban policy proposals are advanced in the presidential or congressional national policy arena, serious differences separate both politicians and social welfare scholars over the best approach to delivering such services and benefits. Advocates such as Harvard's Wilson (1988, 1989, 1990, 1992, 1996a, 1996b) and Skocpol (1985, 1990a, 1990b, 1994, 1996) have argued that social welfare reforms require broad universalistic benefits and political alliances such as those on which Social Security (1935) and Medicare (1965) were premised. Other scholars, such as Massey and Denton (1987, 1988, 1989, 1994) and Massey and Eggers (1990, 1994), have argued that social conditions vary significantly from ethnic group to ethnic group and between and within regions. Following that logic, social programs ought not to be national or universal in scope but specifically targeted to aid a given region, ethnicity, gender, or economic class. Other commentators have supported the Massey, Denton, and Eggers targeting position, arguing that the political and economic climate of the late 1990s and early 21st century requires either a more place-based or targeted approach. Further compounding this argument is an argument within the argument, with Wilson favoring "universalism within targeting" and Skocpol favoring a far more expensive "targeting within universalism" approach, suggesting 1930s and 1960s-era wide-scale, national assistance to impoverished groups in urban areas and elsewhere.

This controversy in the scholarly and policy-making community is mirrored in the urban policies and programs enacted in Congress during the Clinton administration, which enacted both place-based targeted programs such as Empowerment Zones and more universalistic—if still somewhat limited in scope and scale—programs such as the 100,000-police or 100,000-teacher initiatives. It is significant that the Clinton administration failed to secure passage of the largest universal social welfare program proposed, the national health insurance proposal, a program directly relevant to urban policy because, as one observer noted, the "vast majority of the 37 millions without health-care insurance are urban residents" (Peirce et al., 1993, p. 7).

ISSUES ARISING FROM THE DESCRIPTIVE ACCOUNT: "THINK NATIONALLY, ACT LOCALLY"

Ironically, one result of the policy-making gridlock that resulted from the impact of the structural suburban/anti-urban bias in American national politics and the disagreement among politicians and the scholarly community over targeted or place-based versus universal or entitlement approaches to social policy in general, and urban policy in specific, has been the emergence of a number of local initiatives to aid local metropolitan regions. Urban areas have constructed several local or regional alternatives to nationally advanced or nationally funded urban social welfare policies. Several cities, with local and philanthropic foundation funding, have used Community Development Corporations (CDCs) to allow neighborhood residents to fund and direct limited neighborhood redevelopment projects. Urban areas have used CDCs in a limited fashion since the 1960s, but more recently, several cities—including, notably, New York City, Newark, and Baltimore—have used CDCs to aid low-income neighborhood revitalization efforts and to provide increased access to and increased housing units for low-income residents.

Second, aided by a national Council on Sustainable Development appointed by President Clinton and a Brookings Institution Urban and Metropolitan Center sustainable cities project, several urban areas are exploring "livable cities" or "sustainable cities" considerations. These include cleaning up urban brown fields and regional cooperation in job creating and addressing the "spatial mismatch" between the residences of the urban poor and the location of employment opportunities within their given urban areas. Although the sustainable cities dialogue has just begun, these local/regional efforts to coordinate and provide leadership in addressing problems within given American urban regions is likely to constitute a key focus of emerging urban policy in the early 21st century. Following the aphorism, "thinking globally and acting locally," urban areas in the next century may well think nationally, but, given the constraints of American national politics and policy making, act locally. As in the past, the U.S. Conference of Mayors will continue to lobby for large-scale Marshall Plan-style urban aid programs—as they did following the South Central Los Angeles riots of 1992, when they sought—unsuccessfully—a $35 billion urban aid program. But in the foreseeable future, such cities and their mayors will have to settle for a composite mix of local/regional and limited federal efforts to alleviate the problems of cities.

CURRENT CONTROVERSIES: WHO POLICES THE POLICE BILL?

The current major national social welfare policies affecting cities are the recent Police Bill, the Teacher Corps, and the Empowerment Zone program. Let us consider the Police Bill and the Teacher Corps proposal first. The 100,000 police and teachers initiatives are neither strictly needs-based (targeting) nor strictly population-based (universalistic) formulas. Indeed, one early study of police allocations indicates that of the first 40,000 officers authorized by the 1994 Crime Bill, more than half went to cities with below average crime rates or jurisdictions so small that they are not required by the federal government to report crime data to the Uniform Crime Reporting Program (Meckler, 1996; Waste, 1998). In short, the Police Bill needs considerable policing before it adequately addresses the problems of violent crime and endangerment in American urban neighborhoods.

Although it is too early to predict the outcome of the 100,000 teachers initiative, unless it is administered with a formula avoiding the allocation problems inherent in the Police Bill, it too may prove ineffective in addressing urban social welfare needs. The structural problems of American urban public education, including relatively low salaries, infrastructure decay, increasing demand, and ambiguous education expectations from the state, national, and local school districts, is not subject to amelioration by a $12 billion, 7-year, 100,000-teacher program aimed at reducing class sizes nationally for the first through third grade. The $1.1 billion first-year appropriation in 1999 is, however, a start. Had that appropriation been successfully combined with the $112 billion that the General Accounting Office (GAO) estimates is necessary to put urban schools in good condition, observers might have reason to be more sanguine about the prognosis for city schools. At the turn of the century, as America prepares to head across the celebrated "bridge to the 21st century," it seems almost certain that the nation will carry both its dangerous and impoverished urban neighborhoods and its dilapidated urban school system across that bridge.

Empowerment Zones and Urban Areas

There are three reasons to surmise that any gains from the Empowerment Zone program will be extremely limited. First, the $3 billion level of funding is insufficient to finance large-scale change in urban America. Remember, as we noted earlier, that U.S. mayors requested a $35 billion urban aid package following the 1992 urban unrest in South Central Los Angeles. Second, the Urban Empowerment Zones, which create tax incentives for firms relocating to low income urban areas, are premised on a tax abatement policy previously extended by several of the states and which tried and found wanting in Great Britain (Erickson & Friedman, 1991; Green & Brintnall, 1991). Third, as one observer has noted, architects of the Urban Empowerment Zone program at the national level have low expectations for the program, expecting that of the six key sites, perhaps one will "produce visible economic success, while the rest can only hope to be somewhat safer and less deteriorated looking" (Lemann, 1994, p. 54). In the words of urban scholar Dennis Keating (1994), even success at all six key sites would, in terms of the overall national urban condition, amount to a "demonstration of the ability of the federal government to gild the ghetto (at least six) so as to make a demonstrable impact on social problems" (p. 4).

CONCLUSION: URBAN POLICY—HISTORY, CURRENT POLICIES, AND FUTURE PROSPECTS

As this chapter has illustrated, in the post-World War II period, America has embraced an evolving and deepening policy of responsibility for the growth, decline, and social conditions of America's urban areas. The present decade, and the decades of the 1970s and 1980s, represents a retreat from the national activism in urban problem solving and urban policies and programs advanced in the 1960s. The 1990s have been characterized by a long-term "permanent crisis" in America's cities, featuring high levels of poverty, hunger, crime, infrastructure decay, eroding public schools, and low-income neighborhoods. Recent efforts by Congress, the Clinton administration, and a reinvented HUD to address urban social conditions have resulted in three urban programs—the 100,000 Teacher and Police initiatives, and the Urban Empowerment Zone programs—coupled with earlier funding under the CDBG program and ISTEA. Whether these limited federal urban policy efforts, coupled with CDCs and other local/regional efforts at producing sustainable urban regions, will suffice to address the seemingly intractable presence of a permanent crisis in America's urban areas is the central question facing urban policy analysts for the both the short- and long-term future.

REFERENCES

Anderson, M. (1964). *The federal bulldozer: A critical analysis of urban renewal, 1949-1962.* Cambridge: MIT Press.

Barnes, W. (1995). Urban policies and urban impacts after Reagan. In R. W. Caves (Ed.), *Exploring urban America* (pp. 110-118). Thousand Oaks, CA: Sage. (Reprinted from *Urban Affairs Quarterly, 25,* 562-573, 1990)

Barnes, W., & Ledebur, L. (1997). *The new regional economics.* Thousand Oaks, CA: Sage.

Blakely, E. J., & Ames, D. L. (1992). Changing places: American planning policy for the 1990s. *Journal of Urban Affairs, 14,* 423-446.

Caputo, D. A. (1976). *Urban America: The policy alternatives.* San Francisco: W. H. Freeman.

Cisneros, H. (Ed.). (1993). *Interwoven destinies: Cities and the nation.* New York: Norton.

Dahl, R. A. (1980). *Democracy in the United States: Promise and performance* (3rd ed.) Chicago: Rand McNally.

DeLeon, R., & LeGates, R. (1976). *A redistribution effects of special revenue sharing for community development* (Working Paper No. 17). Berkeley: University of California, Institute of Governmental Studies.

Erickson, R. E., & Friedman, S. W. (1991). *Comparative dimensions of state enterprise zones: New directions in economic development.* Newbury Park, CA: Sage.

Fishman, R. (1987). *Bourgeois utopias.* New York: Basic Books.

Garreau, J. (1991). *Edge cities: Life on the frontier.* New York: Doubleday.

Gottdiener, M. (1985). *The social production of urban space.* Austin: University of Texas Press.

Green, R. E., & Brintnall, M. (1991). Conclusions and lessons learned. In R. E. Green (Ed.), *Enterprise zones: New directions in economic development* (pp. 241-257). Newbury Park, CA: Sage.

Herson, L. J. R., & Bolland, J. M. (1991). *The urban web: Politics, policy, and theory.* Chicago: Nelson-Hall.

Hill, E. W. N., Wolman, H. L., & Ford, C. C., III. (1995). Can suburbs succeed without their central cities? Examining the suburban dependance hypothesis, *Urban Affairs Review, 31,* 147-174.

Keating, D. (1994, November 5). *Guilding the ghetto: The debate revisited.* Paper presented at the American Collegiate Schools of Planning Annual Meeting, Tempe, Arizona.

Kling, R., Olin, S., & Poster, M. (Eds.). (1991). *Post-suburban California: The transformation of Orange County since World War II.* Berkeley: University of California Press.

Lemann, N. (1994, January 9). The myth of community development. *New York Times Magazine,* pp. 26-31, 53-60.

Lockhart, C. (1986). *Gaining ground.* Berkeley: University of California Press.

Lovell, C., & Korey, J. (1975). The effects of general revenue sharing on ninety-seven cities in Southern California. In *General revenue sharing utilization project: Vol. 2.* Washington DC: National Science Foundation, Research Applied to National Needs.

Marshall, D. R., & Waste, R. J. (1977). *Large cities responses to the Community Development Act.* Davis: University of California, Davis, Institute of Governmental Affairs.

Massey, D., & Denton, N. A. (1987). Trends in the residential segregation of blacks, Hispanics, and Asians. *American Sociological Review, 52,* 802-825.

Massey, D., & Denton, N. A. (1988). Suburbanization and segregation in U.S. metropolitan areas. *American Journal of Sociology, 94,* 592-626.

Massey, D., & Denton, N. A. (1989). Hypersegregation in U.S. metropolitan areas. *Demography, 26,* 373-391.

Massey, D., & Denton, N. A. (1994). *American apartheid: Segregation and the making of the underclass.* Cambridge, MA: Harvard University Press.

Massey, D. S., & Eggers, M. L. (1990). The ecology of inequality: Minorities and the concentration of poverty, 1970-1980. *American Journal of Sociology, 95,* 1153-1188.

Massey, D. S., & Eggers, M. L. (1994). The spatial concentration of affluence and poverty during the 1970s. *Urban Affairs Quarterly, 29,* 299-315.

Meckler, L. (1996, November 6). Crime bill doesn't always put more cops on the street. *Sacramento Bee,* p. A6.

Murray, C. (1984). *Losing ground: American social policy, 1950-1980.* New York: Basic Books.

Nathan, R. P., & Domel, P. R. (1978). Federal-local relations under block grants. *Political Science Quarterly, 93,* 421-442.

Nenno, M. (1974). Housing and Community Development Act of 1974. *Journal of Housing, 31,* 345-362.

Peirce, N. (1995, November 21). In Indianapolis, a mayor and unions work together to streamline government. *Sacramento Bee,* p. B7.

Peirce, N., Johnson, C. W., & Hall, J. S. (1993). *Citistates: Does the American city have a future? How urban America can prosper in a competitive world.* Washington, DC: Seven Locks Press.

Phillips, K. (1994). *Boiling point.* New York: Harper Perennial.

Ross, B. H., & Levine, M. A. (1996). *Urban politics: Power in metropolitan America* (5th ed.). Itasca, NY: F. E. Peacock.

Ross, B. H., Levine, M. A., & Stedman, M. S. (1991). *Urban politics: Power in metropolitan America* (4th ed.). Itasca, NY: F. E. Peacock.

Savitch, H. V., Collins, D., Sanders, D., & Markham, J. P. (1993). Ties that bind: Central cities, suburbs, and the new metropolitan region. *Economic Development Quarterly, 7,* 341-357.

Schwarz, J. E., & Volgy, T. J. (1992). *The forgotten Americans.* New York: Norton.

Skocpol, T. (1985, August 17). *Brother can you spare a job? Work and welfare in the United States.* Paper presented at the annual meeting of the American Sociological Association, Washington, DC.

Skocpol, T. (1990a, Spring). Sustainable social policy: Fighting poverty without poverty programs. *The American Prospect,* pp. 58-70.

Skocpol, T. (1990b, August 30-September 2). *Targeting within universalism: Politically viable policies to combat poverty in the U.S.* Paper presented at the Annual Meeting of the American Political Science Association, San Francisco.

Skocpol, T. (1994). *Protecting soldiers and mothers: The political origins of social policy in the United States.* Cambridge, MA: Harvard University Press.

Skocpol, T. (1996). Delivering for young families: The resonance of the GI Bill. *The American Prospect, 28,* 66-72.

Voith, R. (1992). City and suburban growth: Substitutes or complements? Federal Reserve Bank of Philadelphia. *Business Review,* pp. 21-31.

Waste, R. J. (1998). *Independent cities: Rethinking U.S. urban policy.* New York: Oxford University Press.

Wilson, W. J. (1988). American social policy and the ghetto underclass. *Dissent, 35*(1), 57-64.

Wilson, W. J. (Ed.). (1989). The ghetto underclass: Social science perspectives. *Annals of the American Academy of Political and Social Science, 501,* 26-47.

Wilson, W. J. (1990). Race and the democratic coalition. *The American Prospect, 1*(1), 1-17.

Wilson, W. J. (1992, March 17). The right message. *New York Times,* p. A15.

Wilson, W. J. (1996a, August 18). When work disappears. *New York Times Sunday Magazine,* pp. 26-33, 48-53.

Wilson, W. J. (1996b). *When work disappears: The world of the new urban poor.* New York: Knopf.

PART FOUR

The Political Economy of Social Policy

This part of the book contains an overview of the major theoretical and ideological orientations in social policy thinking today. These different orientations provide very different insights into social policy. They reveal that social policy is not a technical or politically neutral activity but, rather, draws on wider ideological, economic and political ideas. These ideas comprise a rich and complex political economy which frames discussions about social policy.

The first chapter in Part IV discusses the institutional approach to social policy that dominated the field for many years. Systematically formulated by scholars at the London School of Economics in England, institutionalism also had considerable appeal in the United States and provided a conceptual basis for much thinking about social policy in the decades following the World War II.

The institutional approach was challenged by conservative thinkers whose ideas about social policy became ascendant in the 1980s. As shown in

Chapter 25, the conservative approach gives expression to diverse themes that are generally, although not exclusively, opposed to government intervention in social welfare.

Chapter 26 discusses the critical approach to social policy. This approach is rooted in Marxist thought. Although Marxist accounts of social policy do not have much support today, newer versions of critical social policy continue to influence the field. These include social policy ideas that are linked to radical populist movements, feminist and anti-racist analysis, and postmodernist thinking.

The pluralist approach, which is discussed in the next chapter, advocates a mix of government, nonprofit, and commercial interventions designed to maximize people's welfare. Pluralism opposes the emphasis on government exclusivity that characterizes institutional thought. It rejects the institutionalist's claim that government is the best agent for promoting the well-being of all.

Drawing on the insights of critical theory, Chapter 28 offers a feminist perspective on social policy. It shows that the gender dimension has, until recently, been seriously neglected in social policy analysis. It demonstrates that gender issues are central to the field. This is equally true of race and cultural diversity. Even though social policy has historically been influenced by race and ethnic considerations, few accounts of the evolution of social policy have paid attention to these realities. As the authors of Chapter 30 show, a proper analysis of social policy in the United States must examine the ever present reality of race.

As discussed in Chapter 29, social development offers a relatively new perspective on social policy. It is based on the argument that people's welfare is inextricably linked to the economy and that social policies and economic policies need to be harmonized. Economic development policies that raise standards of living for all should be actively fostered, and these should be linked to social welfare programs that contribute positively to economic development.

The relationship between social policy and the environment is examined in Chapter 31, the final chapter of Part IV. The authors argue for ecologically sensitive social policies that not only enhance people's welfare but do so in conjunction with policies that relate social policy to wider environmental concerns.

CHAPTER TWENTY-FOUR

The Institutional
Approach to Social Policy

JAMES MIDGLEY

The institutional approach to social policy comprises a set of normative prescriptions for enhancing people's welfare. The most fundamental of these is that social welfare is best enhanced through the agency of government. Inspired by progressive liberalism and social democratic ideology, proponents of the institutionalist approach believe that social needs should be addressed through a range of statutory interventions, including fiscal measures, legal regulations, and the provision of a comprehensive system of social services. They contend that these interventions "institutionalize" social programs, embedding them in the very fabric of society.

Institutional ideas have been widely applied in policy making and implementation during this century and have shaped the expansion of government intervention in social welfare. Institutional social policies and programs are characterized by their statutory authority, public funding, bureaucratic direction, and universality of coverage. One of the most frequently cited examples of an institutional social program is the British national health service, which provides a range of tax-funded medical and health services to all citizens, without regard for their ability to pay. Tax-funded child benefits and universal social insurance programs are also typical of institutional social welfare.

Although most industrial nations have programs of this kind, those in Western Europe, and particularly Scandinavia, are usually extolled for exemplifying institutional ideals. Because these nations have introduced extensive social service programs that cater to the population as a whole, they are often described as *welfare states*. It is claimed that the welfare states have most successfully modified the economic market to combine the wealth-generating potential of capitalism with social goals and have found a viable middle way between unfettered capitalism and authoritarian communism.

This chapter describes the institutional approach. It traces its historical origins in the progressive reforms of social democratic and liberal governments that have sought to expand statutory social welfare since the end of the 19th century. The writings of academic thinkers who advocated institutional ideas are also discussed. After summarizing the salient features of the institutional approach, the chapter concludes with a brief appraisal of its contribution, as well as an assessment of its role in shaping social policy making in the future.

HISTORY OF THE INSTITUTIONAL APPROACH

The evolution of the institutional approach was propelled both by ideas and by developments taking place in the world of policy making and administration. Academic scholars played a critical role in formulating institutional ideas, drawing on religious teachings, progressive social thought, utopianism, and socialism. Their writings melded with the activism of working people, the campaigns of social reformers, and the political programs of progressive governments committed to the institutionalist agenda.

As was noted earlier, the institutionalist agenda is motivated by a desire to use the agency of the state to promote social welfare. Historically, the state played a very limited role in social welfare. People's welfare was seen to be the product of their own efforts, the support of their families and kin, and, in the case of those who could not meet their own needs, of the church and other charities. It was during the reign of Elizabeth I that the state first began to assume a significant role in social welfare. The Elizabethan Poor Law of 1601 is regarded as a milestone in the evolution of public welfare, laying the foundation for the expansion of state involvement both in Britain and the United States.

The idea that governments should alleviate social distress and enhance the welfare of their citizens gained momentum during the late 19th century. Reform-minded politicians, intellectuals, trade union members, religious leaders, and middle-class activists believed that governments could ameliorate social wrongs and improve social conditions. They drew extensively on the findings of social surveys and statistical studies to expose social injustice and social neglect, campaigning for the regulation of working conditions, the prohibition of child labor, the end of economic exploitation, and the introduction of social services. Because of these activities, the end of the 19th century is known as the Progressive Era. As was shown in Chapter 8 of this book, the efforts of progressive reformers resulted in the creation of new social programs such as mother's pensions and workmen's compensation. However, efforts to introduce health or unemployment insurance, as well as comprehensive contributory retirement pensions, were not successful.

Social insurance originated in Germany in the 1880s and was soon adopted in other European countries. In the United States, the campaign to introduce social insurance evolved more slowly, and it was only in 1935 that the Social Security Act was passed. The Social Security Act is regarded by many social policy writers as the crowning achievement of the New Deal and the nation's single most important social program. Social Security is also one of a few social programs in the United States that is based on institutional ideas.

Many scholars believe that the New Deal institutionalized the principle of government responsibility for social welfare and shaped the American welfare state (Dolgoff & Feldstein, 1980; Handel, 1982). Others do not think that the American people have ever fully accepted the principle of government welfare responsibility and contend that the United States remains a "reluctant welfare state" (Jansson, 1993). Nevertheless, the New Deal did lay the foundations for the subsequent expansion of social policy during the 1960s, when President Johnson's War on Poverty and Great Society programs were established. Together with the Progressive Era, periods of social policy expansion such as the New Deal and War on Poverty were significant not only because government involvement in social welfare increased, but because this popularized the idea that social welfare is the legitimate responsibility of the state.

Theoretical Ideas

By the 1960s, academic writers began to formulate theories about the role of the state in social welfare. Some scholars, such as Harold Wilensky and Charles Lebeaux (1965), provided explanations of the growth of government involvement in social welfare. They expounded the thesis that the expansion of government responsibility was an inevitable by-product of industrialization. Because industrialization undermined traditional welfare institutions (such as the extended family) and created new social problems that demanded concerted action, governments were compelled to intervene. Marxist writers (Ginsberg, 1979; Gough, 1979; Offe, 1984) rejected this interpretation, arguing instead that the state became involved in social welfare to prevent social unrest and preserve the interests of capitalism. Social democratic scholars (Korpi, 1983; Stephens, 1979) took a different position, claiming that the expansion of government involvement in social welfare was the result of the struggle of working-class movements and their allies to use the state for progressive social purposes.

These theoretical explanations were augmented by normative accounts that were less concerned with explaining the causes of the expansion of government involvement in social welfare than with legitimizing it. The most important of these normative accounts were formulated by T. H. Marshall and Richard Titmuss of the London School of Economics in England. Both had a profound influence on social policy thinking and helped popularize the institutional approach in social policy circles in the United States.

Marshall (1950) argued that government social welfare provision is the culmination of the historical evolution of citizenship rights. Historically, the rights of citizenship were not accorded to all human beings. Slaves, peasant farmers, laborers, and workers were not regarded as citizens and were not permitted to share the rights enjoyed by the aristocracy. However, as citizenship was gradually extended, civil and then political rights were granted. Marshall contends that the development of citizenship also requires the extension of social rights. People who live in poverty, and who are badly housed and poorly educated, cannot be regarded as citizens in the proper sense of the term. For this reason, the state must ensure that they have rights to an adequate income, housing, and education. The state must establish these rights in law and guarantee that they will be fulfilled. Marshall's ideas provided an appealing normative basis for state intervention in social welfare. Social rights are as sacred as civil and political rights and are to be fulfilled by the state.

Although he did not develop Marshall's thesis to any significant extent, Titmuss (1958, 1968, 1972, 1974) offered a compatible set of ideas that provided additional normative justifications for state welfare. He injected a strong ethical element into the debate arguing that social welfare should be the collective moral responsibility of citizens. Because the state represents its citizens, it is the proper agency through which citizens discharge their collective responsibility and give expression to their altruistic intentions. State provision is the most efficient way of expressing altruism. The use of the market is not only inefficient but morally repugnant. Institutionalized altruism through the state increases reciprocity and promotes social solidarity. Also, because the social services initiate redistributive fiscal processes, society becomes more equal. Altruism, solidarity, and equality all promote the ideals of the Good Society.

Diverse influences permeate Titmuss's writings. He was an active member of the British Fabian society and committed to its brand of democratic socialism. He was also a great admirer of Richard Tawney, the British Christian socialist, and it is clear that Christian and utopian elements characterize Titmuss's work. He was also influenced by earlier institutionalist writers, such as the 19th-century economist, Thorstein Veblen, who railed against the excesses of affluence in American society. Veblen inspired Titmuss's own brand of social criticism, which was fiercely directed at the proponents of individualism and the free market.

Titmuss drew a sharp distinction between economic and social goods. The former should, appropriately, be bought and sold on the economic market. The latter should only be delivered through collective means of provision. He was particularly critical of commercial social services in the United States, which he believed undermined the altruistic and moral imperatives of social welfare. Nevertheless, his ideas were well-received in the United States and his influence, although indirect, was significant in supporting the expansion of government social programs and promoting the idea of social welfare as a social right.

By enhancing the scholarly agenda of the Department of Social Science and Administration at the London School of Economics, Titmuss played in major role in promoting the study of social policy. The department had been founded in 1911 as a social work training program, but after his appointment as its first full professor in 1950, Titmuss expanded its scope by recruiting an interdisciplinary faculty who soon increased its reputation and influence in government circles. Most British universities followed the example of the London School of Economics and established similar academic units that promoted scholarly inquiry into social policy. These developments also helped strengthen social policy teaching and research at schools of social work and public policy in the United States.

The electoral successes of the radical Right in the 1980s posed a serious challenge for proponents of the institutional approach to social policy. Budgetary retrenchment, privatization, contracting out, decentralization, and other innovations have facilitated the emergence of a far more pluralistic social welfare system than institutionalists such as Titmuss would have approved, or even envisaged. Many commentators now believe that the institutional approach has run its course and that economic, electoral, and attitudinal changes will further undermine state involvement in social welfare. Apart from a small group of American writers who are known as neo-institutionalists (Evans, Rueschemeyer, & Skocpol, 1985), there appears to be limited support for the institutional approach in social policy circles. This is not the case in most Western European nations, but even there, government responsibility for social welfare has been curtailed, and the hope that the state's involvement in social welfare will expand further has been abandoned.

THE NATURE OF THE INSTITUTIONAL APPROACH

The term *institutional social welfare* was coined by Wilensky and Lebeaux (1965). They contrasted the narrow role government historically played in providing social services to the most conspicuously needy with an approach that created comprehensive social programs for all citizens. The former approach they called *residual welfare*.

The latter they described as institutional social welfare. They claimed that a gradual historic shift from residual to institutional welfare was taking place and that this was resulting in the acceptance of social welfare as a normal, first-line function of society. Social welfare, they argued, was being institutionalized.

Wilensky and Lebeaux's (1965) account made a significant and durable contribution to the articulation of the institutional approach. However, they did not fully encompass all its dimensions. At the time their book was published, Titmuss had not articulated his own theory of collective altruism, which provided a moral legitimation for state social welfare. Nor did they discuss Marshall's ideas on social rights. Although the following account draws on their definition, it extends it by examining these and other contributions.

State Collectivism and Institutionalism

Collectivist ideology accords prime importance to collective forms of association in which people share resources and decision making. Cooperatives, trade unions, communes, and ultimately the state are examples of collectives. Collectivists believe that the state is jointly owned by its citizens and that shared decision making is a function of representative democracy. They also believe that the state is the most effective agent for meeting social needs.

Institutionalists are essentially collectivists even though they differ in the extent to which they advocate state responsibility for social welfare. Most believe that government should not merely augment but transcend the traditional role of the extended family, the community, and philanthropic endeavor, assuming a fundamental responsibility for social welfare. Although many institutionalists support a pluralistic conception that includes public support for nonprofit agencies, most reject commercial services, accepting Titmuss's view that the market is an inappropriate mechanism for meeting social needs. Marxists are collectivists, but most contend that the provision of statutory social services in capitalist society does little to promote social welfare. For this reason, institutional collectivism is usually associated with social democracy and progressive liberalism.

Although the Marxist critique of the institutional approach exerted some influence in academic circles in the 1970s, it was eclipsed by the radical Right. As was noted earlier, the radical Right mounted an effective attack on institutional ideas and began to dominate social policy thinking in the 1980s. Critiques offered by Milton Friedman (1962), Martin Feldstein (1974), and other economists claimed that government social programs had weakened the economy and were responsible for the high unemployment and inflation that characterized the 1970s. Social policy writers such as George Gilder (1981) and Charles Murray (1984) argued that government social programs had failed miserably to eradicate poverty and instead had created an impoverished underclass of people who became dependent on government aid. Murray was applauded by many Republican politicians for his insistence that state welfare had done more harm than good. His writings, and those of other critics of state welfare, contributed significantly to the retrenchment of government social programs and the weakened influence of institutionalist thinking in social policy circles in the 1980s.

Universality and Selectivity

Institutionalists believe that government intervention should be comprehensive and universal in scope. Although governments have been involved in social welfare on an organized basis since Elizabethan times, their involvement has historically been targeted at the most needy through means-tested programs. The institutional approach requires that government social programs embrace all citizens, without regard to income, and ensure that they are protected against the contingencies of modern life. Titmuss (1968) was a severe critic of selective, means-tested social services. These services were not only meager but stigmatized recipients and were often punitive. Although he campaigned for their replacement with universal social services, they continued to dominate social provisions even during the most generous years of the welfare state. In the United States, means-tested programs such as Aid to Families with Dependent Children, which has been replaced by the Temporary Assistance to Needy Families program, have long been criticized for their stigmatizing and punitive implications.

It is for this reason that institutionalists favor the adoption of universal social services such as Social Security, health insurance, and child allowances. An added dimension to universalism is the idea that government social services should be culturally accepted and embedded in society. Together with fiscal measures and statutory regulation, the social services should subsidize incomes, redistribute resources, prevent need, and raise standards of living for all. This means that social welfare must transcend its traditional safety net function and become an essential component of modern social life.

Critics of universalism reject these arguments and claim that there is no point in spending public revenues on those who do not need assistance. By targeting the social services, the government is better able to focus scarce resources on the poor. Their ideas have recently been used to criticize Social Security, which is one of the nation's few universal social programs. Critics contend that it would be more cost-effective if Social Security were replaced with a means-tested program suppporting the elderly poor. Those who have adequate savings or private pensions would then be spared the expense of paying onerous Social Security taxes. Although Social Security remains intact, it continues to be condemned by writers on the political Right for being wasteful, harmful to economic growth, and unnecessary (Feldstein, 1998; Ferrara, 1982; World Bank, 1994).

Institutionalism and Social Rights

Reference was made earlier to Marshall's (1950) theory of social rights, which provides an appealing normative rationale for the institutional perspective. As noted earlier, Marshall argued that the ideal of citizenship requires that civil and political rights be accompanied by social rights. By ensuring social rights, governments foster social justice and meet the ideals of the welfare state.

Although Marshall's ideas were widely adopted and formed the basis for the legal welfare rights campaigns fought by welfare recipients in the 1960 and 1970s, they have come under attack. Critics such as Lawrence Mead (1986, 1997) and Maurice Roche (1992) argue that the notion of social rights has been abused. Both authors insist that rights are not unconditional but involve reciprocal obligations. Many of those claiming social benefits do not discharge their obligations to society.

Mead's writing inspired the Republican Party's approach to welfare reform and resulted in the enactment of the Personal Responsibility and Work Opportunity Reconciliation Act in 1996. This legislation rejects the payment of benefits to needy people on the basis that they have a right to an adequate income. Instead, workfare and many other requirements now accompany the payment of these benefits. Proponents of the legislation believe these requirements will have a desirable impact on the lifestyles of the poor. Others are less sanguine about the future well-being of those who have been adversely affected by this legislation.

Institutionalism, Pragmatism, and the Middle Way

Although the institutional approach is inspired by progressive liberalism and social democratic ideas, it lacks the ideological fervor that characterizes much of the social policy literature of the radical Right and Marxist Left. It is not that institutionalists have no ideological commitment but rather that their ideological proclivities are tempered by a historical preference for empiricism and pragmatism.

The historical development of the institutional approach was significantly influenced by the use of empirical research for social reform purposes. Studies of poverty, child labor, and other social ills were effectively used by social reformers to expose social ills and promote social change. Institutionalism has also been influenced by the philosophical methodology of pragmatism. Pragmatism stresses the need to test the veracity of knowledge through experience. It rejects a priori theories, requiring that intellectual claims be verified before being accepted. Pragmatism contributed to a distrust in institutional circles of grand theories such as Marxism that offered appealing but a priori explanations and prescriptions.

This preference for pragmatic thinking has prompted the criticism that institutionalism is both atheoretical and ideologically limited. Robert Pinker (1971) lamented the lack of theoretical sophistication in institutionalist thinking, whereas Karl Popper (1961) characterized institutionalists as engaging in "piecemeal social engineering." However, as Ramesh Mishra (1977) observed, pragmatism is consistent with the institutionalist's reform agenda. Unlike Marxism and other grand theories that are committed to the radical transformation of society, the reform espoused by institutionalists is much more likely to be concerned with practical matters.

Although the reform of the institutionalist approach has been ridiculed by radicals on both the political Right and Left, institutionalists claim that their middle way between unfettered capitalism and authoritarian communism has fostered significant social improvements and high standards of living in those nations that have implemented institutional ideas. The Western European welfare states have made significant social gains by combining social welfare with economic growth. The wealth-generating vigor of capitalism has been successfully harmonized with social welfare. In addition, this has been achieved without coercion or intrusive authoritarian statism.

Several commentators have speculated on whether the welfare state is a manifestation of socialism or capitalism. Some writers believe that the welfare state gives expression to democratic socialist ideas, whereas others contend that it is essentially capitalist in nature (Ginsberg, 1979; Gough, 1979; Marshall, 1972; Offe, 1984). On the other hand, Pinker (1979) argued that the welfare state should not be regarded as a variant of either capitalism or socialism but as a new and distinctive social formation with its own unique features.

As was noted earlier, the institutionalists belief that the welfare state represents the best form of social organization has been challenged by both the political Left and Right. Marxists claim that the welfare state legitimizes capitalism and fails to address fundamental social needs and injustices. Those on the political right argue that it has sapped the vitality of enterprise, impeded economic growth, created a dependent and unproductive underclass, and undermined cherished moral values. These latter ideas have gained support and have seriously undermined the institutionalist position.

Altruism and the Moral Imperatives of Social Policy

Reference was previously made to the work of Richard Titmuss, whose ideas exerted a powerful influence on institutional thinking. Titmuss formulated a conception of social policy that emphasized the moral aspects of institutionalizing social welfare. His analysis went beyond an account of the advantages of engaging the state in social policy. Not only does the state have the authority and resources to effectively address social needs, its involvement has the desirable moral consequence of facilitating the expression of altruism, enhancing solidarity, promoting social inclusion, and fostering compassion. If people recognize that they "own" the state and that it represents their collective interests, they will be willing to pay their taxes to fund social service programs, not only to help the needy but to enhance the welfare of all. In this way, social policy serves fundamental moral purposes.

The moral elements in Titmuss's writings are most systematically developed in his best selling book, *The Gift Relationship* (1971). Using blood procurement and distribution as a case study, he argued, on the basis of a wealth of empirical data, that voluntary donation is the most effective way of meeting the need for blood. He was appalled by the use of the commercial market to supply blood in the United States, contending that the use of the market for this purpose is both inefficient and morally repugnant. He also insisted that social policy is not primarily about scientific theories or technical issues but about values and ideals. A system of social welfare based on desirable social values is infinitely superior to one based on technical arguments about the advantages of collective versus market provision.

Although Titmuss claimed the high moral ground in his advocacy of state welfare, writers on the political Right, such as Murray (1984), have responded with a value position of their own. As was noted earlier, Murray contends that government involvement in social welfare has had a negative moral impact, undermining marriage and the family, promoting profligacy, weakening the value of self-reliance, and creating widespread dependency. As Murray's contrasting position suggests, moral imperatives in social welfare are not absolutes but dependent on ideological persuasion.

THE FUTURE OF INSTITUTIONALISM

It was noted earlier that the institutional approach has been undermined by economic realities, ideological opposition, attitudinal changes, and other factors. The policy changes introduced by radical Right governments during the 1980s have significantly weakened the institutionalist position. Although many institutionalists hoped that the election of a Democratic President in 1992 would restore their influence, it was clear by the time of the 1996 election that the political Right continued to take the initiative and frame debates on social policy. Neo-institutionalist ideas have not exerted much influence in government policy-making circles, and supporters of institutional social programs continued to be on the defensive. For example, by the late 1990s, the campaign to privatize Social Security had gained momentum.

Although institutionalism continues to exert considerable influence in Europe, many believe that its impact on social policy thinking in the United States is now depleted. On the other hand, some writers believe that its basic premises remain valid and that a reformulation of some of its tenets could ensure its long-term vitality. Some writers (Gilbert & Gilbert, 1989) recommend that institutionalists adopt a more tolerant pluralistic stance, recognizing the inadequacies of state-managed social services and the need for contracting these services out on a more substantial scale to other providers. Others (Etzioni, 1993) believe that institutional ideas should be united with communitarian beliefs and that the state should actively encourage community participation in social policy formulation and implementation. Still others (Midgley, 1995, 1999; Sherraden, 1991) suggest that institutional beliefs about state responsibility for social welfare should place less emphasis on social rights and unconditional giving and instead stress the role of the state in promoting social investments that enhance the capacity of people to participate in the productive economy and meet their own social needs. However, although these different proposals may offer new directions for the institutional approach, it remains to be seen whether they will reinvigorate a set of ideas that previously exerted such a profound influence on social policy.

REFERENCES

Dolgoff, R., & Feldstein, D. (1980). *Understanding social welfare*. New York: Longman.

Etzioni, A. (1993). *The spirit of community: Rights, responsibilities, and the communitarian agenda*. New York: Crown.

Evans, P., Rueschemeyer, D., & Skocpol, T. (Eds.). (1985). *Bringing the state back in*. New York: Cambridge University Press.

Feldstein, M. (1974). Social security, induced retirement, and aggregate capital accumulation. *Journal of Political Economy, 83*(4), 447-475.

Feldstein, M. (Ed.). (1998). *Privatizing social security*. Chicago: University of Chicago Press.

Ferrara, P. J. (1982). *Social security: Averting the crisis*. Washington, DC: Cato Institute.

Friedman, M. (1962). *Capitalism and freedom*. Chicago: University of Chicago Press.

Gilbert, N., & Gilbert, B. (1989). *The enabling state: Modern welfare capitalism in America*. New York: Oxford University Press.

Gilder, G. (1981). *Wealth and poverty*. London: Buchan & Enright.

Ginsberg, N. (1979). *Class, capital, and social policy*. London: Macmillan.

Gough, I. (1979). *The political economy of the welfare state*. London: Macmillan.

Handel, G. (1982). *Social welfare in Western society*. New York: Random House.

Jansson, B. (1993). *The reluctant welfare state: A history of American social welfare policies*. Pacific Grove, CA: Brooks/Cole.

Korpi, W. (1983). *The social democratic class struggle*. London: Routledge & Kegan Paul.

Marshall, T. H. (1950). *Citizenship and social class and other essays*. Cambridge, UK: Cambridge University Press.

Marshall, T. H. (1972). Value problems of welfare capitalism. *Journal of Social Policy, 1*(1), 15-32.

Mead, L. (1986). *Beyond entitlement: The social obligations of citizenship*. New York: Basic Books.

Mead, L. (Ed.). (1997). *The new paternalism: Supervisory approaches to poverty*. Washington, DC: Brookings Institution.

Midgley, J. (1995). *Social development: The developmental perspective in social welfare*. Thousand Oaks, CA: Sage.

Midgley, J. (1999). Growth, redistribution, and welfare: Toward social investment. *Social Service Review,* 77(1), 3-21.

Mishra, R. (1977). *Society and social policy: Theories and practice of welfare.* London: Macmillan.

Murray, C. (1984). *Losing ground: American social policy, 1950-1980.* New York: Basic Books.

Offe, C. (1984). *Contradictions of the welfare state.* Cambridge: MIT Press.

Pinker, R. (1971). *Social theory and social policy.* London: Heinemann.

Pinker, R. (1979). *The idea of welfare.* London: Heinemann.

Popper, K. (1961). *The poverty of historicism.* London: Routledge & Kegan Paul.

Roche, M. (1992). *Rethinking citizenship: Welfare, ideology, and change in modern society.* Cambridge, MA: Polity.

Sherraden, M. (1991) *Assets and the poor: A new American welfare policy.* Armonk, NY: M. E. Sharpe.

Stephens, J. (1979). *The transition from capitalism to socialism.* London: Macmillan.

Titmuss, R. M. (1974). *Social policy: An introduction.* London: Allen & Unwin.

Titmuss, R. M. (1958). *Essays on the welfare state.* London: Allen & Unwin.

Titmuss, R. M. (1968). *Commitment to welfare.* London: Allen & Unwin.

Titmuss, R. M. (1971). *The gift relationship.* London: Allen & Unwin.

Wilensky, H., & Lebeaux, C. (1965). *Industrial society and social welfare.* New York: Free Press.

World Bank. (1994). *Averting the old age crisis: Policies to protect the old and promote growth.* New York: Oxford University Press.

CHAPTER TWENTY-FIVE

Conservative Approaches to Social Policy

LEON GINSBERG

During the past two decades, conservative ideas about social welfare grew to prominence, partly reflecting the 1980 election of Ronald Reagan (Ginsberg, 1987) and the election and re-election of Bill Clinton as president. Clinton called for fundamental changes in American social welfare policy in 1992 and was one of the most conservative post-World War II Democratic presidential candidates. Since 1935, when the Social Security Act was passed, political figures have supported and often expanded social welfare programs, a trend that Reagan, Clinton, and the U.S. Congress reversed.

The election in 1994 of Republican majorities in both houses of Congress, promising to implement the conservative Contract with America (Gillespie & Schellhas, 1994), also influenced shifts in U.S. social welfare policy. The election of Newt Gingrich, who led the development of the Contract and wrote about social reform (Gingrich, 1995), as Speaker of the House was another step toward major changes, which were popularly called welfare reform. In 1996, Congress passed and President Clinton signed the most far-reaching conservative social policy legislation in modern U.S. history, which is discussed later in this chapter.

BASIC CONCEPTS OF CONSERVATISM

Conservatism, as it is understood and practiced in the United States, is a blend of a variety of economic, political, and philosophical concepts. With origins in the 18th century, primarily in England, it has had a variety of adherents and points of view.

Conservatism began with several early economic thinkers, especially Adam Smith (1789). Smith propounded the notion of laissez-faire economics and was an early advocate of free enterprise. Essentially, *laissez-faire,* a French term, means that governments should leave economies alone. Smith believed that an invisible hand governed financial interactions and that free economic pursuits built economies and created wealth. In fact, he called his major work *The Wealth of Nations.*

His fundamental ideas remain widely accepted and popular today. They are fundamental to American economic activity and law, which attempt to guarantee competition, the pursuit of free economic development, the avoidance of monopolies, and relatively little government interference.

One of the criticisms of free enterprise economics is that after periods of growth and prosperity, such economies invariably collapse and require rebuilding. The economies of the largely free-enterprise economies of Asia, such as Indonesia, Japan, and Korea, which had significant growth for decades, declined dramatically in 1997 and 1998. This led to an Asian economic crisis. With help from international loans and stringent new economic controls, these economies are recovering. Social welfare programs, their advocates believe, mitigate against fractured economies. Otherwise, the human consequences of unbridled economic activity are severe, as they were in the United States during the Great Depression.

Basic to the development of conservative political ideas was England's Edmund Burke, a member of the House of Commons, who was one of the earliest writers and thinkers on the subject (Rathbone & Stephenson, 1985.) He believed in the virtue of conserving tradition and respecting government. Burke's writings were a reaction to the French Revolution, which he considered excessive. The assassinations of political leaders, the dramatic and violent break with earlier traditions, and the general chaos associated with the French Revolution disturbed him. He developed from his observations the theory of conservatism (although he did not use that term himself) and the need for conservative policies. Loyalty to the government, strong ties between government and the church, and limited suffrage were among his beliefs.

Parenthetically, although some consider conservatism to be the opposite of liberalism, others view these as similar. In fact, when this writer discussed the worldwide movement toward less government involvement in social welfare and called it conservative, the president of the International Federation of Social Workers (E. Envall, personal communication, May 22, 1998) said his organization launched a study group on neo-liberalism to explore the same issues. The classic definitions of liberalism are similar to the current American definitions of conservatism. In the U.S. context, those identified as liberals are usually thought to support government involvement in human affairs such as social welfare. American conservatives consider themselves equally interested in human betterment. However, they also tend to believe that government help usually causes more harm than good.

In the United States, conservatism generally describes those who oppose any government involvement in human affairs. Conservative thinkers are often especially negative toward government programs of social welfare, especially those of the federal government.

American conservative ideas about human welfare have a number of basic elements. Conservatives believe that individuals are responsible for themselves and their families. Each person must take care of him- or herself through employment or other sources of financial support and must provide for the family, which today means one's spouse and children. In earlier times, family responsibility laws often extended to siblings, parents, grandparents, and even nieces and nephews. Conservative thinkers also value order. Disorder, crime, and delinquency are condemned.

Conservatives also believe in a limited role for government. Government should be involved only in maintaining international relations through diplomacy, operating a money system, and maintaining a defense force. Conservatives believe that people have no responsibility to each other. One's only responsibility is to oneself. Therefore, concepts such as social welfare "entitlements" are contrary to the beliefs of conservative thinkers. Help for individuals ought to come from family and voluntary or religious charities, not through government. If government programs are desired, they ought to be organized and provided at the lowest levels, such as the state or city. Also, the worthy or "truly needy" poor are distinguished from the unworthy poor, a classic distinction in social welfare history. Worthy poor are children, older adults, and those with physical and some mental disabilities. The unworthy are the unemployed and those who are disabled by substance abuse. Thus, help should be means-tested rather than universal. People who seek help should prove their need and account for other assets or earnings before being helped. Liberal advocates are likely to prefer universal programs such as Social Security, which are provided regardless of wealth or lack of it.

Conservatives also emphasize religion, law, and patriotic loyalty. Citizens should be raised and continuously encouraged to be supportive and loyal to their basic institutions, such as the church and the government. Conservatives (and most other Americans, as well) have a strong belief in private property because this is seen as fundamental to a just society. Finally, conservatives are more skeptical than others about the perfectability of human beings, especially through governmental efforts.

HISTORY OF MODERN AMERICAN CONSERVATIVE THOUGHT

For much of American history, conservative political thought dominated national law and social policy. Ideas of human services and social responsibilities, such as that which essentially became encoded in the Social Security Act of 1935, were practically unheard of in American government until the 20th century. The agrarian, spacious America of the 18th and 19th centuries had little room for grand schemes of social welfare. Families were supposed to take care of themselves; farm families could provide themselves with sufficient food and housing through subsistence economic activity.

Of course, as Day (1997) and others suggest, social welfare institutions have a long history in the United States. Private and local government programs, such as orphanages and charitable organizations that operated in England, were imported to the United States. Social reformers such as Jane Addams and her colleagues at Hull House in Chicago (Davis & McCree, 1969) worked to change the environment for the urban poor. They and others who agreed with them pressed for social reforms and government involvement through many avenues, including the White House conferences on children, which began in 1909 (Coll, 1977). Institutions such as the Children's Bureau were established in the federal government, but these efforts were primarily advisory to state governments rather than serving to administer federal social welfare programs.

Dorothea Dix, the reformer and advocate of services for people with mental disabilities, helped persuade Congress to pass a bill to provide federal funds for the construction and operation of asylums. However, the legislation was vetoed by President Franklin Pierce in 1854 (Axinn & Levin, 1996) because he thought the Constitution prohibited the federal government from giving aid to people with problems. As a result, presidents and Congress stayed away from national social welfare programs, which were assumed to be the responsibilities of the states.

Therefore, many modern American conservative pronouncements date from the 1930s, when Franklin Delano Roosevelt's New Deal brought federal social welfare programs to the United States for the first time. The Social Security Act of 1935, which is still the basic social welfare law of the United States although it has been modified through amendments extensively and regularly, provided programs to overcome the poverty that arose from the Great Depression. Roosevelt's administration also tried food stamps as a means to provide surplus food to low-income people, a program that became national, after a gap of several years, during President Johnson's Great Society programs (Johnson, 1998).

Herbert Hoover, who served as president during the Depression and was defeated by Roosevelt in 1932, partly because of the angry public response to the economic difficulties, wrote frequently about his opposition to the New Deal and its programs (e.g., Hoover, 1956). He was one of the earliest conservative critics, and many of his charges against government social welfare are echoed by later and contemporary conservative thinkers, writers, and politicians.

The major human services efforts of the New Deal, as they evolved, included paid work for unemployed people through programs such as the Works Progress Administration and the Civilian Conservation Corps; prevention of poverty for older adults, survivors, and people with disabilities through the Social Security program, and welfare help such as Supplemental Security Income and Aid to Families with Dependent Children (AFDC).

Social welfare assistance was augmented by most presidents between Roosevelt and Reagan. Richard M. Nixon, who is usually considered a conservative, proposed the most generous public assistance program in U.S. history, the Family Assistance Plan, which was not passed by Congress (Moynihan, 1969).

Among the most important efforts were those made through programs such as the Economic Opportunity Act of 1965, Head Start, work-study, job training, and the addition of medical assistance through Medicare for the elderly and Medicaid for low-income people under President Lyndon B. Johnson.

Perhaps the most important political influence on modern American conservative thinking was Barry Goldwater, who was the 1964 candidate for president on the Republican ticket. Goldwater, who died in 1998, was a long-time U.S. senator from Arizona. Senator Goldwater was one of the first in modern times to take a strongly conservative posture on social programs, including Social Security and public welfare (Goldwater, 1990). He was defeated handily by Lyndon B. Johnson, whose administration was second only to Roosevelt, Johnson's mentor, in proposing and securing passage of social welfare programs. Johnson also sponsored civil and voting rights legislation, which Goldwater, although not racially prejudiced, opposed on the grounds that those were not federal government issues. He was an articulate opponent of almost all of the federal initiatives for solving human problems such as civil rights deprivations and poverty. He remained strongly opposed to any efforts to impose regulations and special help for disadvantaged groups by the federal government, strictly on the basis of his conservative ideology, which he explained in *The Conscience of a Conservative* (Goldwater, 1990).

Among the most influential conservative social welfare thinkers and policy makers was President Ronald Reagan, who served from 1981 to 1989. Reagan's position, which he developed as governor of California and brought to the U.S. federal government, was that government had no business engaging in other than the traditional government functions of operating a money system, maintaining international relations, and providing a national defense. His presidential objectives included reducing the size of the federal government and removing the federal government, to whatever extent was possible, from the fields of human services and social welfare. He worked to achieve those goals by reducing large portions of the federal bureaucracy and giving the states block grants to operate programs formerly defined as federal. Reagan also proposed, and Congress accepted, reductions in the funds the federal government would provide to the states for social services. Increasingly, under the Reagan administration, the states became the operators of the social welfare programs with significantly reduced federal involvement and supervision. However, in his last year in office, Reagan signed into law the Family Support Act of 1988, which liberalized AFDC, the nation's primary public assistance program for low-income families with children.

It is important to note that conservative Republicans were not the only ones to call for major changes in social welfare—so did President Bill Clinton. Clinton made political campaign promises in 1992 of ending welfare as we know it, as mentioned earlier. He spoke favorably of time limits on receipt of public assistance, for example, which became part of the 1996 Act.

When Congress passed the Personal Responsibility and Work Opportunity Reconciliation Act of 1996, Clinton signed it. Although many of Clinton's supporters doubted that he wanted to reform welfare as radically as the 1996 Act did, he clearly had supported similar kinds of action in his own political campaigns. Some of his closest colleagues and supporters (Edelman, 1997) said President Clinton did not need to support such a bill to win reelection and that he could have achieved similar objectives while supporting and more fully implementing the Family Support Act of 1988, which was already the law. However, the changes contained in the new law were popular not only with conservative politicians but also with the larger public.

CURRENT CONSERVATIVE POLITICAL THOUGHT

In the current era, as mentioned above, social welfare changed dramatically under the leadership of the Republican U.S. Congress, which was elected in 1994. For the first time since the 1950s, both the U.S. Senate and the U.S. House of Representatives had majority Republican membership. Both Newt Gingrich, the Speaker of the House, and Congressman Dick Armey (1996), who became second in command to Gingrich, wrote and spoke often about changing the federal approach to social welfare (Gillespie & Schellhas, 1994; Gingrich, 1995). Both were influential in formulating the aforementioned Contract With America. Armey (1996) wrote about eliminating the income tax and replacing it with a flat tax. By 1996, with the passage of the welfare reform legislation discussed earlier and explicated later in this chapter, they had succeeded in implementing many of the reforms long sought by conservative social thinkers, such as placing time limits on the receipt of federally financed welfare assistance, requiring teenage mothers to live with their parents or other responsible adults to receive help, and insisting on work as a condition for receiving aid.

Of course, there are many other political figures in both major political parties who support conservative approaches to social welfare. Altogether, it appears they constitute a majority of U.S. policy makers in the late 20th century. Southern members of the U.S. Senate and Congress from both parties tend toward conservative positions. So do many governors throughout the nation, who have implemented welfare-tightening policies that go beyond the provisions of the federal requirements.

Among the best-known conservative thinkers in recent U.S. history have been Milton Friedman, Barry Goldwater, Charles Murray, and Irving Kristol. In addition, a few minority group thinkers and writers have questioned some of the premises of the modern social welfare programs of the United States.

Milton Friedman is a Nobel prize-winning economist from the University of Chicago whose reputation and contribution to economic thinking is in monetarism. However, his basic concepts about social welfare are grounded in his belief that the Social Security system and other social welfare programs are ill-advised and inappropriate under American law and tradition (Friedman & Friedman, 1980).

Writing with his wife, Rose, in 1980, Friedman said that the Social Security retirement program or Old Age, Survivors, and Dependents' Insurance ought to be eliminated. The Friedmans say the trust fund approaches of Social Security are propagandistic, and the benefits are really paid out of current collections from younger workers to retirees. The Friedmans question whether Social Security is a reliable insurance program. Instead, he and his wife call it a "tax combined with transfer payments." They also find that the Social Security tax is regressive, in that lower income people pay a greater percentage of their earnings than do the wealthiest people. Ideally, they suggest, people would buy their own retirement and life insurance on the private market. Friedman generally believes that government engagement in large-scale insurance schemes is an improper and inefficient arrangement. He and his wife may be correct in believing the burden of Social Security payments falls most heavily on the lowest-paid workers in terms of percentages of income paid. The rate is the same for all workers, but there is a ceiling on the amount on which the tax is paid. Workers who exceed that maximum, therefore, pay a lower rate. However, Social Security advocates view Social Security not as a tax-supported government program but as an insurance program in which premiums earn benefits. The higher the wages earned, the higher the premiums. And there is a maximum benefit, just as there is a ceiling on the amount on which the premiums are paid. Some of these ideas are reflected in current doubts among younger workers that they will ever receive Social Security benefits. That is true even though the Social Security program is considered sound through 2032 and could, with minor adjustments in the benefit ages and other elements, be made solvent for all of the foreseeable future.

The Friedmans are also noteworthy for proposing a negative income tax to replace existing programs of poverty assistance, such as AFDC. They suggested that poverty could be overcome through the income tax system. Low wage earners with families would receive more than they paid in taxes in the form of refunds. In fact, the United States established such an arrangement many years ago and called it the Earned Income Tax Credit, in which low-income people receive a rebate on their income taxes, frequently more than they paid in taxes if they are among the working poor and have families. The tax credit and the negative income tax are similar in concept.

One of the more articulate conservative thinkers and writers of the modern era is Charles Murray, a sociologist. His 1984 book *Losing Ground* made the compelling case that public assistance programs and social welfare services of all kinds cause the problems they are supposed to resolve. He thinks that assistance programs for low-income families give assistance to women with children and reduce the importance of men in low-income families, which, in turn, causes social problems and economic decline in low-income communities. Murray believes he is correct, not only about public assistance and Social Security but also about such programs as unemployment compensation and virtually anything else directly for the benefit of people. Murray describes himself as a libertarian with strong anti-government program convictions. He proposes doing away with all government assistance programs.

Perhaps his best-known work was written with the late R. J. Hernnstein. *The Bell Curve* (Hernnstein & Murray, 1994) attempts to demonstrate that significant differences in IQ reflect significant differences among groups of people. That book caused an uproar, partly because it made the case that group IQ differences left some groups disadvantaged whereas others fared better. Minority groups, especially African Americans, as well as many statisticians and scientists, believed *The Bell Curve*'s conclusions were in error.

Many advocates of human services and equity for disadvantaged people missed the book's lengthy discussion of the need for a more humane society that would simplify work, participation in government, and other elements of everyday life. The authors believe that many of the problems of disadvantage result from a society that is too complicated as much as from more traditional economic difficulties.

On the opposite side of the argument, Hernnstein and Murray (1994) suggested that the United States was becoming a custodial state, caring for and supervising the lives of large numbers of citizens who are incapable of taking care of themselves. They suggested that such a state of affairs could create even greater problems: a growing underclass isolated in public housing, the resurgence of virulent racism, and growth of social welfare programs resulting from government's even more adamant insistence on changing the behavior of disadvantaged people.

George Gilder is a leading U.S. economist, and he, too, is one of the most important welfare reform theorists of the modern era. He questions the correctness of ideas such as entitlements and was a major proponent of the elimination of federally supported welfare programs (Gilder, 1981, 1995). In his writings, Gilder has supported family allowances. He also thought that AFDC was incorrect in its permanence as a support for clients. He prefers shorter-term, crisis-based assistance and would probably be more supportive of the new Temporary Assistance for Needy Families (TANF) program.

Gilder suggests that welfare assistance programs such as AFDC kept people poor because being poor was a condition for receiving help. In essence, people were paid to forgo work. He especially thinks that, prior to the 1996 reforms, the program made men irresponsible because it was usually women who were eligible for and who received aid. Married men work harder than bachelors, he notes, and without AFDC, men would have to be the supporters of many women and children. The deterioration of American communities, Gilder suggests, is a result of welfare assistance, an idea he shares with Murray.

David Frum (1996) is another prominent conservative writer. He suggests that current laws make it difficult for society to enforce morality. For example, landlords may find that anti-discrimination laws make it difficult to require their tenants to be married. Communities cannot discriminate against people born out of wedlock, which also does little to discourage nonmarried unions. Similarly, restaurants and other public facilities cannot reject customers whose appearances or behavior might be unacceptable to the proprietors. Therefore, social legislation may conflict with efforts to promote morality.

Much of Irving Kristol's early writing was liberal, but his current work is considered conservative or neo-conservative. He supports the kinds of changes made in social welfare policy, although he doubted such ideas would prevail (Kristol, 1996).

One of the principal concerns of many conservative thinkers is affirmative action, although few oppose equal opportunity for all people without regard to their ethnicity or gender. Their concern is that affirmative action is reverse discrimination or an effort to give special preferences to selected groups. Although that is not the intention of affirmative action programs, this belief has caused some states to reduce or eliminate affirmative action efforts.

Although most organized minority groups such as those involving African Americans, Hispanics, Asian Americans, Latinos, and Native Americans support affirmative action efforts, there are some writers who represent conservative points of few and who are also members of minority groups.

One of the most prominent is Robert Woodson, director of the National Center for Neighborhood Enterprise and formerly an employee of the American Enterprise Institute and the Urban League. Woodson, who was educated as a professional social worker, doubts the virtues of affirmative action and even the motives and performance of some elected African American officials. He has expressed concern about some African American politicians, who, he believes, have used their political successes and their positions to better their own condition, without being equally concerned about the most disadvantaged among their own ethnic group.

Woodson (1981) is a supporter of the mediating structures approach, which is discussed in more detail later, for venting youth crime, among other things. Essentially, that approach suggests that social problems be solved through structures that exist between individuals and government. The large bureaucracies that dispense assistance and services to disadvantaged people can often be more oppressive than supportive and may also create dependency rather than fostering independence, Woodson suggests.

Another minority person who has questioned much of what has occurred in some elements of the Civil Rights Movement is Thomas Sowell (1983), of the Hoover Institution in Palo Alto, California. Sowell has written often about the inadequacies of affirmative action and the necessity for equal treatment and self-help. In some ways, his writings, which appear in books, professional journals, and in a regular column in *Forbes* magazine, are similar to the writings of Murray and Gilder, although he differs with Murray about some of the conclusions in *The Bell Curve*. Sowell favors self-help and believes that minority group members who are disadvantaged can, through their own efforts, resolve their social and economic problems as other groups of Americans have done in the past. Sowell also believes that affirmative action, which he equates with preferences for selected groups, is a source of conflict in the United States as well as other nations that make such efforts.

Another conservative African American writer is Glenn Loury (1987), a noted social scientist who raises questions about some of the policy activities designed to bring equality to minority group people.

Although most of the prominent writers on conservative social welfare issues are men, some women advocate similar approaches. Phyllis Schlafly (1977) is one of the best-known conservative writers. She presents her views in a newspaper column, in her books, and in lectures. She calls her organized efforts "The Eagle Forum."

Of course, the late Ayn Rand (1984, 1989), the author of several novels and other books on economic freedom, is a major figure in conservative writing and in conservative circles. Peg Luksik (1996) of Pennsylvania has headed an organization called the National Parents Commission, which takes conservative social policy positions.

Conservative Think Tanks and Media

Several organizations study conservative ideas and provide support for conservative thinkers and writers. The Heritage Foundation, with headquarters in Washington, D.C., is one of the primary sources of conservative literature and information.

The American Enterprise Institute takes a generally conservative posture and has been the organizational affiliation of Charles Murray and, for a time, Robert Woodson. Thomas Sowell is affiliated with the Hoover Institution in California. In addition, several magazines are conservatively oriented. For example, *Forbes,* an influential business periodical, is edited by Steve Forbes, who was a candidate for the Republican presidential nomination in 1996. He writes a column for each issue. Casper Weinberger, Secretary of Health, Education, and Welfare under President Richard Nixon, also writes regularly for *Forbes.* Thomas Sowell is another *Forbes* columnist.

The *National Review* is William F. Buckley's magazine. Beginning in the 1950s and 1960s, Buckley, of course, was one of the earliest spokespersons for conservative viewpoints. Other magazines, such as *The American Spectator,* take decidedly conservative positions. *The Washington Times* newspaper is probably the leading consistently conservative newspaper in the nation, although many others take generally conservative editorial positions.

Conservative media are also critical of foundations that appear to pursue liberal objectives. For example, in 1996, *Forbes* published an article (McMenamin, 1996) that criticized the Annie E. Casey Foundation and the Robert Wood Johnson Foundation for their pursuit of public policies that helped achieve their objectives. The two foundations are among those most involved in human services. The *Forbes* article charges that foundations spend $100 million annually to influence state and local social welfare policy.

Among the most influential of popular conservative voices are several radio and television talk show personalities. Among the best-known is Rush Limbaugh (1992, 1993), who conducts a 3-hour daily conversation with listeners and callers and who has also written books on his ideas. Some observers credit him with helping influence the Republican successes in the 1994 congressional elections. G. Gordon Liddy (1991, 1997), one of the convicted perpetrators of the Watergate political crimes under President Richard M. Nixon (Johnson, 1998), hosts a daily radio talk show and is a writer. Liddy was also a U.S. Marine and for a time served with the Federal Bureau of Investigation.

Oliver North, who was initially found guilty of crimes in the Iran-Contra scandals under President Ronald Reagan and whose conviction was reversed on appeal, is also a media host. North, like Liddy, is a former Marine and was involved in national defense programs under President Reagan. He has published a book (North & Roth, 1994) and videotapes.

In addition, Tony Brown (1995), an African American television personality with a regular show called *Tony Brown's Journal,* has also raised questions about some efforts to improve the quality of life of minority group members and especially about welfare programs.

CONSERVATIVE THOUGHT AND SOCIAL POLICY

One manifestation of conservative thought in the area of social policy is mediating structures. The idea of mediating structures is propounded by a variety of conservative writers, particularly sociologist Peter Berger (1986, 1990) and others who have suggested that local, community-based, community-run organizations have the best chance of overcoming the kinds of problems social welfare programs are designed to reduce. Such structures mediate between those in need and governments to solve problems with local solutions and without the massive structures associated with federal programs. Robert Woodson (1981), who was discussed earlier, is another advocate of the mediating structures solution to human welfare problems.

Mediating structures are, very simply, nongovernmental organizations that provide human services. The concern of some of their advocates is that governments, as they grow more rapidly into welfare states, require more and more resources to meet more and more perceived human needs. As government grows, albeit for humanitarian purposes, capitalism and free enterprise are undermined, they insist. Advocates would argue that leaving the solutions to human problems in the hands of mediating structures provides mechanisms for dealing with human problems without having such negative effects on government.

Economics and Public Social Policy

Much of the conflict over social welfare policy from an economic perspective has reflected differences between those who support theories of a market economy and those who advocate the kind of planned, government-run economy contemplated by Marx and more contemporary followers of some of his theories, such as the late Michael Harrington (1962, 1976). Harrington argued that capitalism was inherently unjust and that social welfare made capitalism work by tempering its worst effects.

The theories of John Maynard Keynes (1965, 1971), which propose a system of balancing the economy through government policy, provide another economic antidote to uncontrolled capitalism. Keynes's ideas are regularly used by American government and by presidents of both parties.

Whether or not a nation prospers has a great deal to do with a number of factors of geography, climate, and basic social systems, even more than the nation's use of market or planning mechanisms, according to some writers (Landes, 1998). For example, communism never seemed to work well in Russia, despite decades of enforced central planning and control. Nearby Scandinavia, on the other hand, has practiced a kind of democratic socialism for equally long periods of time and prospers while meeting the social welfare needs of its citizens.

Religion and Conservatism

Some religious groups also tend to associate themselves with capitalism and, therefore, with conservatism. John D. Rockefeller, the founder of one of America's wealthiest families, acknowledged the close connection between his Protestant faith and practice (Baptist) and capitalism (Chernow, 1998). He said he was trained always to work and save. One writer says that Rockefeller demonstrates the accuracy of Max Weber's (1980) thesis that there is a close link between Protestantism and capitalism.

Opposition to social welfare programs may also be found in the writings and speeches of some religious conservatives, both Protestant and Roman Catholic. Religious fundamentalist leaders such as the Rev. Jerry Falwell generally take a position against the social welfare programs of the federal and sometimes the state governments, arguing that they contribute to immorality and lack of economic enterprise and self-sufficiency. Programs such as family assistance encourage people to have children whether or not they are married, fundamentalists say, which also conflicts with the basic values of most Protestant religious organizations.

The former head of the Christian Coalition, Ralph Reed (1996a, 1996b) also takes negative positions on social welfare programs. For example, he has proposed chastity education programs in the schools to discourage teen pregnancy and supported abstinence as the birth control approach to be taught in schools. He also supported reducing welfare payments and making divorce more difficult. Reed is now a political consultant (Bandy, 1998).

Some Roman Catholic philosophers also oppose social welfare programs as reducing or eliminating the individual initiative and responsibility for behavior. Michael Novak (1993) believes that the Catholic ethic and capitalism are entwined. He also quotes Pope John Paul II as suggesting that government involvement in dealing with community problems destroys the initiative of those communities to deal with their own problems. Like Murray and others, Novak makes the case that social welfare programs not only fail to resolve problems such as the underclass and urban crime but actually contribute to their growth.

Business Interests and Conservative Thought

Business has traditionally supported conservative ideas toward social welfare in some respects. However, business has also traditionally been the largest supporter, besides government, of social welfare programs, especially the voluntary agencies. Many boards of social services agencies include business men and women, and many such individuals chair those boards. United Way organizations, nonprofit foundations, and corporations are all allies of human services. However, if there is conflict between business needs and social welfare needs, the assumption has been that the business and economic development needs should prevail. The fundamental idea is that a strong economy and business activity are the best antidotes to social need and that poverty can be overcome by a strong economy. There is no substitute for a strong economy, according to economic development advocates. Government intervention may be harmful, as Adam Smith suggested, and it certainly lacks the growth opportunities provided by free enterprise economics.

Nonmarket, or economically planned, socialist governments have taken positions against the market economy ideas of Smith and other free enterprise economic theorists. But some (Elliott, 1998; Yergin & Stanislaw, 1998) say that business and the state are no longer in conflict and that almost all governments, including India, the former Soviet bloc, and Western Europe, follow free market ideas and programs. Margaret Thatcher, who was Prime Minister of Great Britain in the 1970s and 1980s, and Ronald Reagan are given credit for the changes. As one writer put it, nations have learned "there never was nor ever will be a bureaucracy so omniscient that it can rival the market's subtlety" (Elliott, 1998, p. 37).

In any case, the United States is not alone in rejecting welfare growth and focusing on economic development, work programs for people who are disadvantaged, and personal responsibility for one's own well-being. Many other nations that might once have worked toward centrally planned economies are adopting, to some degree, the U.S. and United Kingdom strategies that have been effective in improving and building their economies.

Current Social Welfare Programs

In several ways, current social welfare programs are in pursuit of current conservative policies. Some specifics are mentioned in this section.

One of Ronald Reagan's goals for social welfare policy was to disentangle the federal government from social programs. Although he and his supporters did not suggest total abandonment of social programs, they transferred the operation of many programs from the federal government to the states, with only minimal federal involvement and supervision. Blocks of funds, in smaller amounts than the programs had once commanded, were given to the states to use as they saw fit in solving or treating their own social problems. Block grants were developed in 1981 for many former categorical federal programs. They are a critical part of the new financial assistance program for disadvantaged people.

The Personal Responsibility and Work Opportunity Reconciliation Act of 1996 (PL 104-193) made the most important changes in American social welfare since those programs began in 1935. Essentially, the 1996 Act did away with the standardized, federal program of support for AFDC. It was replaced with block grants to the states, which have great latitude in designing and operating public assistance.

The new legislation, which was implemented in 1997, allows for states to limit assistance to families to as few as 2 years. Under the federal legislation, states may not provide assistance using federal funds for more than 5 years of the client's whole lifetime. States have the option of providing assistance to up to 20% of their clients for more than 5 years, if they deem it necessary to do so. And, of course, states, so long as they use no federal funds, can continue assistance to families with no limits.

There are also rigid requirements for work or training for those who are eligible for the Temporary Assistance for Needy Families (TANF) program, which replaced AFDC in the new legislation. In addition, there are many other features such as requirements that teenage mothers live with their parents or other responsible adults if they are to receive benefits. Incentives are given to states that show a reduction in out-of-wedlock births without an increase in the abortion rate. Strict limits on assistance for immigrants and for unmarried food stamp recipients were incorporated into the legislation but later softened. Thus far, the assistance rolls have been dramatically reduced in the United States. How much that is a function of the new law and how much it is a function of a very strong economy in the 1990s is uncertain.

Clearly, conservative positions have a renewed and significant influence on American welfare policy, which is likely to continue for the foreseeable future. This chapter has traced the origins of those positions, described some of the more important theories and theorists of recent decades, and outlined the practical consequences of the influence of conservative social welfare policy.

REFERENCES

Armey, D. (1996). *The flat tax*. New York: Fawcett Columbine.

Axinn, J., & Levin, H. (1996). *Social welfare: A history of the American response to need* (4th ed.). New York: Longman.

Bandy, L. (1998, June 28). Fair set up own defeat. *The Columbia, South Carolina State*, p. D1.

Berger, P. (Ed.) (1990). *The capitalist spirit: Toward a religious ethic of wealth creation*. San Francisco: ICS Press.

Berger, P. L. (1986). *The capitalist revolution: Fifty propositions about prosperity, equality, and liberty*. New York: Basic Books.

Brown, T. (1995). *Black lies, white lies: The truth according to Tony Brown*. New York: William Morrow.

Chernow, R. (1998). *Titan: The life of John D. Rockefeller, Sr*. New York: Random House.

Coll, B. D. (1977). Social welfare: History. In J. B. Turner (Ed. in Chief), *The encyclopedia of social work* (16th ed., pp. 1503-1512). New York: National Association of Social Workers.

Davis, A. F., & McCree, M. L. (1969). *Eighty years at Hull House*. Chicago: Quadrangle Books.

Day, P. J. (1997). *A new history of social welfare*. Boston: Allyn & Bacon.

Edelman, P. (1997, March). The worst thing Bill Clinton has done. *The Atlantic Monthly*, pp. 43-58.

Elliott, M. (1998, May 4). The romance of the marketplace. *Newsweek*, p. 37.

Friedman, M., & Friedman, R. (1980). *Free to choose: A personal statement*. New York: Avon.

Frum, D. (1996). *What's right*. New York: Basic Books.

Gilder, G. (1981). *Wealth and poverty*. New York: Basic Books.

Gilder, G. (1995, June). End welfare reform as we know it. *The American Spectator*. pp. 24-27.

Gillespie, E., & Schellhas, B. (1994). *Contract With America: The bold plan by Representative Newt Gingrich, Representative Dick Armey, and the House Republicans to change the nation.* New York: Random House.

Gingrich, N. (1995). *To renew America.* New York: Harper-Collins.

Ginsberg, L. (1987). Economic, political, and social context. In A. Minahan (Ed. in Chief), *Encyclopedia of social work* (18th ed.). Silver Springs, MD: NASW Press.

Goldwater, B. (1990). *The conscience of a conservative* (with a new introduction by Patrick Buchanan). Washington, DC: Regnery Gateway.

Harrington, M. (1962). *The other America.* New York: Penguin.

Harrington, M. (1976). *The twilight of capitalism.* New York: Simon & Schuster.

Hernnstein, R. J., & Murray, C. (1994). *The bell curve: Intelligence and class structure in American life.* New York: Free Press.

Hoover, H. (1956). The welfare state: Road to collectivism. In A. Ebenstein (Ed.), *Great political thinkers: Plato to the present* (2nd ed.). New York: Rinehart.

Johnson, P. (1998). *A history of the American people.* New York: Harper Collins.

Keynes, J. M. (1965). *The general theory of employment, interest, and money.* New York: Harcourt, Brace & World.

Keynes, J. M. (1971). *The collected writings of John Maynard Keynes* (Vols. 1-30). Cambridge, UK: Macmillan.

Kristol, I. (1996). A conservative welfare state. In M. Gerson (Ed.), *The essential neoconservative reader* (pp. 283-287). New York: Addison-Wesley.

Landes, D. S. (1998). *The wealth and poverty of nations.* New York: Norton.

Liddy, G. G. (1991). *The monkey handlers.* New York: St. Martin's.

Liddy, G. G. (1997). *Will: The autobiography of G. Gordon Liddy.* New York: St. Martin's.

Limbaugh, R. H., III. (1992). *The way things ought to be.* New York: Pocket Books.

Limbaugh, R. H., III. (1993). *See, I told you so.* New York: Pocket Books.

Loury, G. C. (1987). Why should we care about inequality? In E. F. Paul, F. D. Miller, J. Paul, & J. Aherns (Eds.), *Equal opportunity* (pp. 249-271). New York: Basil Blackwell.

Luksik, P. (1996, Winter). *National parents commission: Up close* (Special Ed. 1). Johnstown, PA: National Parents Commission.

McMenamin, B. (1996, December 16). Trojan horse money. *Forbes,* pp. 123-126.

Moynihan, D. P. (1969). *Maximum feasible misunderstanding.* New York: Free Press.

Murray, C. (1980). *Losing ground: American social policy, 1950-1980.* New York: Broadway Books.

North, O. L., & Roth, D. (1994). *One more mission: Oliver North returns to Vietnam.* New York: Harper Prism.

Novak, M. (1993). *The Catholic ethic and the spirit of capitalism.* New York: Free Press.

Rand, A. (1984). *Capitalism, the unknown ideal.* New York: New American Library.

Rand, A. (1989). *The virtue of selfishness: A new concept of egoism.* New York: New American Library.

Rathbone, C., & Stephenson, M. (1985). *Longman pocket companions guide to political quotations.* Essex, UK: Longman.

Reed, R. (1996a). *Active faith: How Christians are changing the soul of American politics.* New York: Free Press.

Reed, R. (1996b). *After the revolution: How the Christian coalition is impacting America.* Dallas, TX: Word Publishing.

Schlafly, P. (1977). *The power of the positive woman.* New Rochelle, NY: Arlington House.

Smith, A. (1789). *The wealth of nations.* New York: Knopf, Everyman's Library.

Sowell, T. (1983). *The economics and politics of race: An international perspective.* New York: William Morrow.

Weber, M. (1980). *The Protestant ethic and the spirit of capitalism.* Englewood Cliffs, NJ: Prentice Hall.

Woodson, R. L. (1981). *A summons to life: Mediating structures and the prevention of youth crime.* Cambridge, MA: Ballinger.

Yergin, D., & Stanislaw, J. (1998). *The commanding heights: The battle between government and the marketplace that is remaking the modern world.* New York: Simon & Schuster.

CHAPTER TWENTY-SIX

Critical Social Policy

DEMETRIUS S. IATRIDIS

The term *critical* is used in philosophy and social science literature to denote the analysis of capitalist change and the mutating forms of domination that accompanies this change. It is also associated with New Left, feminist, neo-Marxist, and anti-discriminatory policy analysis in the context of contradictions between progressive rhetoric of egalitarianism and the reality of racial and class discrimination. Critical theory traditions have drawn inspiration from many theorists, including Marx, Kant, Hegel, Weber, the Frankfurt School, Foucault, Habermas, Derrida, Freire, and Giroux (Kincheloe & McLaren, 1994).

Critical theory perspectives in social policy are fundamentally based on postmodern social science inquiries and arguments about social structures and the state in advanced capitalist societies. Included in this perspective is the notion that capitalist societies and their dominant statist, corporatist, and neo-liberal institutions serve primarily the profit interests of an oppressive class (rich white males), which legislates for and controls racial and ethnic groups, the poor, women, the powerless, and cultural minorities.

In this sense, critical theory has traditionally focused on post-positivist critiques of institutional policies and programs in advanced capitalism, including state welfare. The latter they consider to represent typically ruling class, race, and gender interests (Forester, 1993; Foucault, 1972; Ginsberg, 1992; Gough, 1979; Gough & Steinberg, 1981; Gough & Thomas, 1993; Leonard, 1994, 1996, 1997; Piven & Cloward, 1971, 1996). Critical perpsectives, especially the liberating work of Marcuse, previously provided the philosophical voice of the New Left regarding political emancipation (Gibson, 1986; Marcuse, 1996; Wexler, 1991). Advocacy for liberation, emancipation, and empowerment of underrepresented people in the advanced capitalism of Western countries is a central ideological theme and principle of critical social policy (Popkewitz, 1990; Roberts, 1990).

In the United States, Britain, and Western Europe, critical social policy is associated with social reformist movements against socioeconomic oppression, in the context of social justice to restructure the social economy. It is associated with public policy discourse, including social reformist community approaches to social reconstruction, civil rights, social care, community activism and radicalism, racial and gender equality, and cultural diversity. Inherent contradictions and oppressive elements in statist, administrative welfare—associated with Fabian and Titmussian policies—are typical focuses of critical analysis.

RECENT EVOLUTION OF CRITICAL SOCIAL POLICY

Critical social policy did not evolve suddenly and does not operate in a vacuum. Rather, it developed in three related contextual frames related to public policy controversies. First, critical theory in social inquiry; second, social policy planning as a discipline and practice in its own right; and third, the transformation of social economy after World War II. The combination of all three together provided the context of public policy controversies and discourse. The controversies include the unprecedented expansion and transformation of capitalist modes following World War II, the globalization of the economy, the support for free market ideology, and the inextricable link between economic logic and social policy goals in advanced capitalist countries. The discourse has accelerated the role of critical social policy and enhanced its practice.

A Mode of Critical Theory

Critical theory typically refers to the theoretical traditions developed some 70 years ago by the Frankfurt Institute of Social Research at the University of Frankurt in Germany (called the Frankfurt School). Its leaders, including Theodor Adorno, Erich Fromm, Max Horkheimer, Leo Lowenthal, and Herbert Marcuse, believing that injustice and subjugation shaped the world, focused their attention on reinterpreting the forms of domination associated with Nazism, fascism, and the changing nature of capitalism (Glaser & Strauss, 1967; Morris, 1994).

The theory's unified dialectical critique of society and discourse for human emancipation associated with post-positivism and postmodernism emerged later as a result of multiple historical developments. They included the frustration of some of the movement's leaders with the American social science establishment and its a priori, traditional belief that empiricism and positivism could describe and accurately measure any dimension of human behavior (Kellner, 1990). Frustration was also fueled by the forms of domination emerging from a post-Enlightenment culture nurtured by advanced capitalism (Billings, 1992).

Frustration with positivism opened the road to dialectical inquiries on the social construction of experience, post-positivist, and postmodern critical approaches. The disillusionment with capitalist culture helped to identify critical theory with concerns about power relations, the state in a free market, and class structures. Combined, they led to the conviction that a reconstruction of social sciences, and the understanding of power relations in society, could eventually lead to a more egalitarian and democratic social order.

In this context, critical theory downgrades positivist, technicist, value-neutral, and rational views of reality as an "old" view of knowledge: dated, raw empiricism, mindless quantification, anti-humanism, legitimation of the status quo, and pretentiousness (Turner, 1985). Notably, critical theory rejects the positivist notion that science and scientific methods can acquire knowledge of human social reality by empirical knowledge alone (i.e., only by sensory experience). It also rejects the idea that objective reality is separate from the observer and can be understood through objective observation independent of the observer (Ammasari, 1992; Gibbs, 1983; Greenwood, 1995; Tyson, 1992). It denies that social science, including policy science, can be scientific in the same way as physics or mathematics (Adler, 1964; Kolb, 1964). It does not accept that ethical concerns are meaningless in the context of scientific inquiry or that setting goals is nonrational and arbitrary because goals concern only ethics and philosophy (Turner, 1992); nor does it agree that social science inquiry can only select means to an end, not goals.

Under strong criticism by several social science schools of thought (Kuhn, 1962), positivism dissolved in a plurality of approaches, while new, post-positivist perspectives (Nagel, 1961), including critical social science and critical social policy, emerged.

Post-positivism favors new perspectives based on the notion that all knowledge is constructed (constructivism) and consists of what individuals create and express. Notably, post-positivists argue that in the real world, the choice of goals is more important than the choice of rational technical means to achieve them. They claim that scientific methodology is not and cannot be value-free and objective because opting for scientism, rationalism, and empiricism at the exclusion of other perspectives, is itself a value orientation and an oxymoron (Eckstein, 1967; Lerner & Lasswell, 1951; Raymond, 1968). They believe that empiricism and rational technical models cannot resolve social issues of choice among conflicting but desirable social goals, offering no direction to interventions for social change; people create knowledge from the interaction between their existing knowledge or beliefs and the new ideas or situations they encounter.

Critical theory relies heavily on several post-positive, postmodern schools of thought. For example, critical theorists are inspired by phenomenology in that they link knowledge to action and to subjective meanings of the problem to the actors, suggesting that knowledge is constructed in a community rather than having an independent existence. The notion that a given whole is problematic (not given) and that people create knowledge from the interaction between their existing knowledge or beliefs and the new ideas they encounter is inspired by constructivism. The assumption that there is a set of social structures that are unobservable but that generate observable social phenomena reflects structuralism (Habermas, 1970, 1973, 1974, 1991; White, 1988).

Social Policy Planning

Critical social policy, as an advocacy mode of social policy planning, is associated with developments regarding the nature and role of social planning in contemporary capitalist societies. In advanced capitalism, there are different contexts of social policy discourse. Two contexts are, however, crucial. These are economic rationality and advocacy for ill-represented groups. That is, social policy planning includes two fundamental strategic modes of interventions for social change or for maintaining the status quo. One is its economic-rational mode (technical rationality), and the other is its social justice-political mode. In its economic-rational mode, social policy planning seeks to identify issues of policy choice, to construct a search of options, to gather data relevant to the choice among options, to set up criteria for choice, and to recommend choices. Technical rationality is based mainly on asocial, ahistorical, and value-neutral technicist and empirical approaches.

In its social justice-political mode, social policy planning seeks to identify the issue frames in the policy discourse and to specify the forum in which the discourse occurs. That is, it seeks to identify and analyze the political power game of interests and domination that is at stake in any given policy issue or controversy and to explore the social justice, ethical, and value structures that underlie the controversy. The justice-political mode is based mainly on advocacy, distributive social justice, racial and gender equality, and democratic self-determination for individuals, groups, and communities. Empowerment, emancipation, and liberation are central themes of these modes.

Between the two poles (technical rationality and social justice) are several other modes of social policy planning that constitute combinations of technological logic and social justice-political goals.

Critical social policy is best understood, and more accurately represented, in the context of the social justice-political mode of social policy planning. In this mode, it is concerned with both the social justice that underlies public policy controversies in capitalism and the historical, social transformation of the social economy. Planners enter into the policy arena as value-committed and value-critical actors, seeking strategically to advocate for social change of a kind that empowers underrepresented classes and social groups.

A Mode Emerging From Post-Second World War Developments

Critical social policy is not a newcomer in public policy discourse. The ancient origins of social policy planning reflect striking similarities with contemporary concerns regarding rationality, social justice, and equality. For example, ancient Mesopotamia established the legal Code of Hammurabi, and ancient Greeks debated female roles and equality in Plato's *Republic* and in Aristotle's *Politics and Ethics* (Lasswell, 1971). Social policy planning's nature and approaches, however, differ considerably in the contemporary scene.

Four seminal socioeconomic developments in the post-Second World War era have shaped recent modes of critical social policy and its discourse. The first is war technology, which includes operations research, as well as behavioral and management scientific investigations. These developments provided policy makers with ahistorical, asocial, and value-free technical frameworks and tools to guide their action in finding solutions to major problems (Lerner & Lasswell, 1951). In this sense, technological developments influenced the emergence of technical modes of social policy planning. They also contributed to the emergence of the technical aspects of social policy planning as a macrolevel, positivist process of objective reality and rational choice in interventions for action by groups and communities (Dear, Briar, & Van Ry, 1986; Einbinder, 1995; Figueira-McDonough, 1993; Frey, 1987; Haynes & Mickelson, 1986; Iatridis, 1995; Jansson, 1984, 1994; Mayer, 1985; Nulman, 1983; Pierson, 1994; Tropman, 1987; Vining & Weimer, 1992; Wyers, 1991). The policy science movement is also seen as one outcome of this development. Perceived as a structured rationality and organized creativity to improve policy making, the movement is concerned with efficiency and the technical allocation of resources. Dror (1971), however, suggests that the movement is also concerned with relations between knowledge and power and the social significance of science.

The second development concerns the social consensus of dominant classes about worldwide reconstruction and ways to meet human needs within advanced capitalism, notably at the end of the Second World War in the 1940s, 1950s, and 1960s. The social consensus of major political groups in the postwar period supported the state as provider of social programs and services within the capitalist framework. The democracies of the West, chastened by the brutalities of pure capitalism, the two World Wars, and the Great Depression, accepted the necessity of a mixed economy for socio-economic reconstruction. They concluded that a market economy needed to be tamed and domesticated to coexist with ever-expanding capitalist state welfare systems and to become decent, stable, and just. Inherent in this was the notion that states have responsibilities to improve well-being and social structures while, at the same time, maintaining strong capitalist economies. In this context, Western societies, including the United States, Britain, and Scandinavian countries, expanded social reforms on the wave of worldwide reconstruction and a long economic boom. This development is associated with shifts of social policy planning approaches toward the social justice-political pole of the continuum.

The third development, occurring in the middle 1970s, concerns the disintegration of the postwar social consensus and the end of the expansion of labor demand, labor movements, and the welfare state. The economic stagnation and declining rates of economic growth of the 1970s, massive restructuring of capital and labor, new forces of production, mass communication, technology, globalization, and the resurgence of organized business as a political force undermined the social coalition of elite political forces.

Fourth, the revived credulity in pure markets, and a shift to radical Right ideologies in the 1980s, brought about by radical socioeconomic developments, moved social policy planning away from the state to local governments and to residual, low-cost social programs. In this context, Keynesianism was attacked because it favored increased central government spending and social welfare programs in economic crises. At the same time, political forces of the Left and the Right intensified their assault against social policy planning's ideological orientations, notably state welfare provision of programs and services for well-being. The fragmenting of the social coalition and the shift to the Right moved the trend away from collective frames of social policy planning toward individualistic technological approaches of unfettered markets, which is the technicist mode of the social policy planning continuum.

CRITICAL SOCIAL POLICY NOTIONS REVISITED

Critical social policy's canons for social change focus on community radicalism, democratic social liberation, empowerment, and emancipation. In the process, the canons challenge capitalist institutional structures dominating society. In this context, critical social policy practice is associated with social reform struggles, community radicalism, and anti-discriminatory movements for just and equal social relations. Typically, such practice is characterized by radical analyses of community structures and institutions (Blaug, 1995; Code, 1991; Fenby, 1991; Forester, 1993; Ginsberg,

1979, 1992; Leonard, 1994, 1997; Piven & Cloward, 1996; Rossiter, 1996; Taylor, 1996; Tyson, 1992). Advocating distributive socioeconomic justice goals, equality, human emancipation, and community radical action, critical social policy is committed to social liberation goals rather than to empirical, value-neutral, apolitical, or asocial technical interventions and research.

Power and Social Structure

Critical social policy assumes that contemporary advanced capitalist societies and their state institutions are oppressive in that they systematically encourage the development of certain societal groups at the expense of others. Explicit in analyses of socioeconomic issues are concerns with oppression, exploitation, and social injustice involving power, race, gender, income, wealth, poverty, and education.

Critical perspectives contend that capitalist societies and their dominant institutions serve primarily the interests of an oppressive class of rich white males who legislate for and control the poor, women, and the powerless, as well as cultural ethnic minorities. Using principles and ideas that serve their own interests, elitist classes and government pretend instead that their policies and programs protect the poor, women, the powerless, and the disadvantaged (Abramovitz, 1994; Ginsberg, 1992; Gough, 1979; Piven & Cloward, 1971, 1977).

Critical perspectives have also helped to analyze state welfare and its crisis, critiquing liberal, Fabian, social democratic, and democratic centralist approaches to social services that emerged in the post-Second World War era. The critical social policy critique included the policies of Beveridge and the Labor Party in Britain, as well as New Deal and Great Society programs in the United States. Welfare states of democratic centralism in the former Soviet Union were also challenged as top to bottom domination, devoid of citizen participation in social policy making.

Critical perspectives were also used to respond to the radical Right's attacks on state welfare (Ackerman, 1982; Ginsberg, 1992; Iatridis, 1983, 1988, 1994; Lekachman, 1982; Rousseas, 1982). Reaganomics and Thatcherism inspired policies in favor of the ruling, elite, corporate class and against the poor. Critical approaches, using class and power analyses and emphasizing empowerment, emancipation, caring, human needs, and Keynesian perspectives, critiqued the ideology and power interests of the radical Right. Under the pretense of protecting the poor, while in fact favoring the rich, Reaganomic policies and programs drastically reduced taxation on corporations and high-income groups, increasing their profits, and they cut deeply state social expenditures. The shift to the Right revived residual, workfare, and lower cost forms of social programs by delegating responsibility for state social care to local authority and control.

Critical social policy advocacy has also focused on society's gender oppression and inequality. Dubois and Duellik-Klein (1983) claim that critical approaches illuminate the ways in which dominant members of society have perpetuated hierarchical social structure assumptions in all aspects of institutional norms. Critical analysis has provided insights that transcend patriarchal and traditional societal gender roles. It refocused the way women and female welfare recipients perceive themselves and interpret their tasks (Bernstein, 1978; Code, 1991; Fenby, 1991). This encourages action based on what people actually do (transcending rationalism) and what their knowledge is (transcending positivism) and considers a dialectic interplay between actors's values and rationalizations. From this perspective, the attention to values and the use of the self provides a different understanding of power relations in gender and feminist analyses and illuminates more accurately the woman's situation and problems (Abramovitz, 1996; Davis, 1985; Ehrenreich & Piven, 1984; Pascal, 1991).

Critical social policy has been applied in several other domains, including housing and the bureaucratization of professional practice. In the field of housing and homelessness, its analysis indicates that mainstream social policy approaches are inadequate, simplistic, and atheoretical, failing to explain the relation between social structure or key institutions and the problem. Nor do mainstream approaches directly explain the lack of effective social policy and provision for low-cost housing and homeless people (Evans, 1991; Haar & Iatridis, 1974; Johnson, 1991; Neal, 1997). Critical social policy uses alternative theoretical perspectives, which focus on subjectivity, power, powerlessness, and postmodernism (Neal, 1997; Somerville, 1992).

Habermas's (1971) analysis of the crucial transformation of liberal capitalism to advanced monopolistic capitalism is associated with the changing role of the state in the economy. This change gave rise to the administrative state and to the decreased role of the public in decision making, notably, in the state welfare discourse (Kaivisto & Valiverronen, 1996; Kellner, 1989; Leonard, 1997). Habermas's theory of communicative action has been used to analyze the bureaucratization and quality of some forms of critical analysis. Critical analyses highlighted dissatisfaction about solutions being offered to professions by mainstream social policy and management. Critical social policy considers such solutions overly mechanical, instrumental conceptions of human reason, or face-to-face interaction; therefore, such solutions are adjudged inappropriate for designing human care (Blaug, 1995).

Habermas's work to improve communicative methods has implications for social work practice in the areas of supervision, agency policy, training, assessments and monitoring, staff support groups, action learning and empowerment groups, user involvement, and social work research (Forester, 1987; Lucas, 1993; Lukacs, 1971; Masson, 1990; Mullender & Ward, 1991).

Intervention for Social Change

Advocacy and empowerment interventions for social change call for attainment of strong emancipatory, democratic, anti-discriminatory, social liberation goals. Status quo frames and socioeconomic inequalities constitute social injustice.

Critical social policy encourages oppressed individuals, groups, and communities to examine societal structures as well as their own values and beliefs. The advocacy-empowerment approach exposes the ways in which social and cultural realities may be hindering the human potential of all people (Lather, 1991).

Implicit in this perspective is the notion that individuals, groups, and communities do not need didactic experts to lead them, because they are capable of becoming enlightened about hidden influences in their own situations of social economy. Emancipatory action and praxis leading to social change will occur once people, groups, and communities are enlightened, empowered, and organized. Responding to the experience and needs of communities and groups can inspire and guide the process of sociocultural transformation and liberation.

By explaining the links between society's institutions and the everyday behavior of individuals, groups, and communities, the poor and powerless can see how poorly their ideology serves their interests and development. Power, as a property of relationships, is transactional and dynamic. When power as force and dominance is the reality, the social systems that evolve become stratified. Power is viewed as a limited commodity that must be acquired (Marcuse, 1996). In most societies, hierarchical relationships are considered normal, and typically, society's institutions (families, schools, community agencies, the media, government bodies, and churches) enforce the dominant values.

Dynamic and Eclectic Inquiry

Critical inquiry is dynamic, open-ended, qualitative, and constantly evolving to integrate empirical, interpretive, phenomenological, ethical, and other critical social science perspectives.

Implicit is the notion that critical inquiry—which includes observing, asking, acting, and reflecting—expands reflective practice (Comstock, 1982; Freire, 1986; Lather, 1991; Morgain, 1994; Schon, 1983; Tremmel, 1993). In this sense, it seeks to integrate styles of policy analysis and research in innovative ways. Rather than providing distinct explanations or hypotheses to test, critical inquiry encourages emancipatory challenges in diverse domains, including social policy planning, public administration, housing, and urban planning (Adorno, 1973; Bernstein, 1988; Fay, 1975, 1977; Forester, 1993; Fromm, 1941; Giddens, 1984).

CRITICAL SOCIAL POLICY IN WELFARE STATE DISCOURSE

Critical social policy discourse is reflected in critical explanations of the nature, outcomes, and future of welfare states in advanced capitalist countries. These explanations have facilitated a major appraisal of government social welfare programs in these countries.

The Critical Social Policy Critique

The four socioeconomic developments in the post-second world war era, which were described earlier, explain fluctuations in the trend toward greater or lesser state interventions in the social welfare field. In the 1940s, 1950s, and 1960s, the social coalition of elitist forces regarding worldwide reconstruction and ways to meet human needs supported expansions of the welfare state within advanced capitalist countries, including the United States, Britain, Sweden, and Denmark. Social welfare reform and the capitalist market seemed to coexist.

The disintegration of the social coalition in the 1970s and 1980s, the shift to the Right, and economic globalization supported radical constructions in welfare states and social expenditures. Understandably, this raised serious questions about the potential of market-state welfare coexistence, notably as advocated by Fabian and Titmussian assumptions.

Further analyses based on critical approaches and especially class, race, and gender power issues, provide insightful and persuasive explanations of the nature and future of welfare states in advanced capitalism. The central focus of such analyses relates to the key social divisions of class, race, and gender (Ginsberg, 1992; Iatridis, 1994; Leonard, 1997; Olofsson, 1988; Taylor, 1996; Williams, 1989).

Critical accounts of the welfare state in a post-Enlightenment culture include five conclusions. First, welfare states operate in the context of a patriarchal and racially structured capitalism. Having institutionalized class, race, and gender divisions and inequalities, these structures are dominated by common elements shared by wealthy capitalist states, notably patriarchal and racially structured capitalism.

Second, the function of state welfare in advanced capitalism is the interpretation and application of the political consensus (ruling class) to contain or restructure class relations. Third, the leading class (the advantaged) favors residual, paternalistic, and sexist social welfare policies, whereas the working class (the disadvantaged) and social movements favor socially just, democratic approaches and adequate standards.

Fourth, welfare states are products of a combination of working-class struggle and capital's requirements for the reproduction of labor power. Capital is engaged in struggles for profits and fair competition, whereas the working class is involved in struggles for a decent standard of living and more egalitarian sharing of society's output. Welfare states are structured by requirements necessary to the continued survival of modern capitalism. This contrasts sharply with functionalist analyses that state welfare fulfills functions (functionalism) essential for the maintenance of the political consensus, social integration, and economic equilibrium and growth. It also contrasts with the notion (Fabian-Titmussian in nature) that social welfare represents the rights of citizenship and promotes social solidarity.

Finally, social welfare expands or contracts as a response of governments to pressures from class conflicts, including organized labor, corporatist coalitions, and social movements. In brief, governments respond to pressures from the prerequisites of capitalist markets for profit; thus, they are pushed into (or away from) expansion of social welfare policies and programs. In this context, state welfare in the United States developed because of two peaks of popular pressure and social reform: the New Deal of the 1930s and the rapid expansion of social programs in the Great Society era of the 1960s.

Figure 26.1 depicts the advocacy and reformist context of critical social policy analysis as a challenge to inequitable institutions to change, adapt, and evolve to empower the powerless and increase their well-being.

Guidelines for Reconstructing Social Welfare

Critical social policy has typically focused most of its attention on comprehensive critiques of current welfare states in advanced capitalism. As a brief analysis of critical social policy literature indicates, the future of state welfare and articulations of specific proposals for its future have received less attention.

Notably, the conclusion that welfare states epitomize the requirements of capitalism for profit and survival at the expense of the poor and powerless does not suggest a bright future for reforms of current residual social welfare systems. Is it perhaps an oxymoron to perpetuate an inherently flawed system by cosmetic changes? The path from critique to solution is typically far more unpredictable, and most authors are understandably reluctant to predict future events. This includes providing solutions to complex and evolving issues that depend on rather uncertain socioeconomic parameters. Nevertheless, writers of critical social policy have suggested some guidelines for restructuring social welfare.

The main thrust of these suggestions about the future of social welfare is organized around the issue of postmodernism, state power, and capitalist requirements (Ginsberg, 1992; Leonard, 1997). There are five overarching notions of this thrust.

First, the old welfare state, once the epitome of moral progress in democratic societies, is no longer the ideal. Some of the basic ideological foundations of current welfare states have disintegrated as a result of challenges to modernism by profound social and cultural changes. This includes social democratic assumptions (Fabian and Titmussian in origin) of an ever-expanding, universalistic welfare state based on altru-

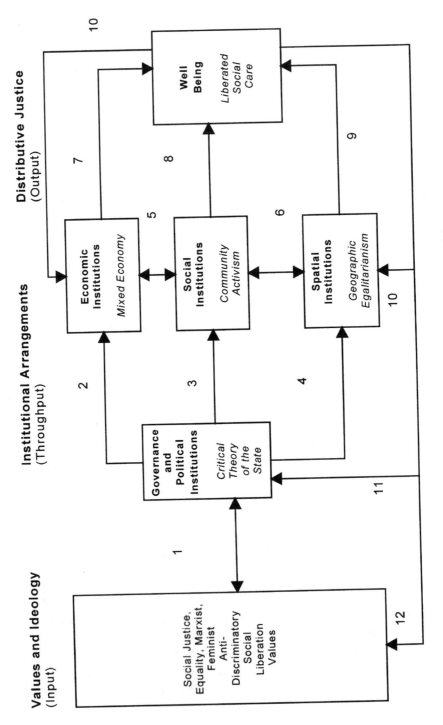

Figure 26.1. A Critical Social Policy Model

ism to improve standards of living of all citizens, notably the working class (Leonard, 1997).

Second, the goals of reconstruction reflect the tenets of critical social policy critiques of welfare states. They aim to achieve an emancipatory social welfare that would be built from the ground up, rather than from a centralist plan dictated by those in positions of power. This contrasts sharply with typical cosmetic social reform efforts based on and implemented by administrative and professional expertise. This new social welfare has community participation as a prerequisite.

Third, Marxist and feminist perspectives can provide adequate ethical guidelines for reconstructing an emancipatory postmodern welfare state. postmodernism, in the context of Marxism and feminism, can provide the theoretical framework of action and political struggle in the field of social welfare (Leonard, 1997).

Fourth, in the proposed emancipatory concept, social welfare is visualized as a process (rather than a plan) that is not exclusionary, respects diversity and diverse ways of meeting human needs, is not subordinated to old or new kinds of domination, or expert power, and calls for the participation of people to determine their own welfare.

Finally, recognizing the central importance of political struggles and pressures, and considering the critique of state and political parties in the social welfare field as instruments of domination, critical thinkers suggest that the proposed emancipatory social welfare system requires the construction of a political party as a "confederation of diversities." This is viewed as an organized political alliance of a wide range of social movements, each pursuing its own vision, but representing a united front of solidarity committed to a struggle of mass politics to meet common human needs and interests (Leonard, 1997). In brief, social justice and liberal equality cannot be rejected. If they are, society is left with two bleak alternatives: rely on the logic and institutions of the economic market or on public provisions delivered by professionals and bureaucrats.

CONCLUSION

Critical analysis in social policy constitutes a philosophical and social science platform for egalitarian, insightful, and convincing explanations of the nature, the development, and the consequences of social policies and programs in advanced capitalist societies. Despite current swings to the radical Right, and policies of drastic reductions in state social expenditures in most advanced capitalist countries (or maybe because of them), critical theory and social policy have maintained and increased their ability to challenge the status quo for reforming the social economy. In the last seven decades, critical writers have made several innovative ontological and epistemological contributions in social science inquiry. Their commitment to social liberation movements and their compelling analyses of the changing nature of advanced capitalism have contributed to the understanding of the inherent socioeconomic domination reflected in current societal institutions. The social issues associated with current analyses in critical social policy have long standing in social science literature, but critical theoretical frames for inquiry transcend the traditional approaches of the past.

Because these approaches clearly transcend traditional limits of mainstream social policy planning, critical theory approaches have evoked loyalty from proponents and hostility from opponents. Whether for or against critical social policy, it is problematic to ignore it. The fact that critical theory is still vibrant for almost seven decades after its development in Frankfurt, Germany, testifies to its utility.

Certain methodological and conceptual questions in emerging critical approaches require attention. Even those who support critical analysis argue for more methodological and theoretical clarity. Opponents argue that, in practice, critical social policy is less of a methodology than a commitment or vision. Its actual applications, in this view, are vague and unclear about distinct methodology and tools to guide specific operations. Opponents also argue that critical social policy's commitment to advocacy for the oppressed and powerless can be dysfunctional in a pluralistic society where many power conflicts prevail. By necessity, they argue, critical analysis ignores ideologies and interests of other social classes and population groups.

Critical social policy literature reflects arguments both for and against welfare states. Is this an antithesis and oxymoron, or rather a harmonious symbiotic coexistence? While viewing the welfare state as fundamentally oppressive (notably for poor people, blacks, women, and ethnic minorities), supporters also argue that welfare states can generate positive gains in social justice and equality (notably as a result of pressure from low-income groups and the bottom of the social stratification pyramid) in the sense that without welfare states, racial and gender inequalities would be greater.

From a critical perspective, the welfare state embodies and reflects capitalist patriarchal and racist domination. Having institutionalized ruling-class interests, welfare state policies and programs represent capitalist power structures. This raises an issue about the future of welfare states in capitalism. Can the welfare state be radically transformed within capitalist structures? Does egalitarian social welfare reform necessitate a different environment of social economy as a prerequisite for substantive change? Critical writers do not believe that the state or the economic market can be the principle around which to organize future social welfare. This leaves the community as the fundamental alternative for building radical social welfare reform. If so, what community-oriented approaches are both feasible and effective, given the trend toward globalization? Community coalitions, partnerships, and federated action have yet to produce new directions for general reform. Are new political community or party organizations a realistic possibility in the immediate future? Only time will tell.

REFERENCES

Abramovitz, M. (1994). Challenging the myths of welfare reform from a women's perspective. *Social Justice, 21*(1), 17-21.

Abramovitz, M. (1996, Summer). Under attack, fighting back: Women and welfare in the United States. *New York Monthly,* p. 25.

Ackerman, F. (1982). *Reaganomics: Rhetoric vs. reality.* Boston: South End Press.

Adler, F. (1964). Positivism. In J. Gould & W. L. Kolb (Eds.), *Dictionary of the social sciences* (pp. 520-522). New York: Free Press.

Adorno, T. (1973). *Negative dialectics.* New York: Seabury Press.

Ammasari, P. (1992). Epistemology. In E. F. Borgatta (Ed.), *Encyclopedia of sociology* (Vol. 1, pp. 550-554). New York: Macmillan.

Bernstein, R. J. (1978). *The restructuring of social and political theory.* Philadelphia: University of Pennsylvania Press.

Bernstein, R. J. (1988). *Beyond objectivism and relativism.* Philadelphia: University of Pennsylvania Press.

Billings, D. (1992). Critical theory. In E. F. Borgatta (Ed.), *Encyclopedia of sociology* (Vol. 1, pp. 384-390). New York: Macmillan.

Blaug, R. (1995). Distortion of the face to face: Communicative reasons and social work practice. *British Journal of Social Work, 25,* 423-439.

Code, L. (1991). *What can she know? Feminist theory and the construction of knowledge.* Ithaca, NY: Cornell University Press.

Comstock, D. E. (1982). A method for critical research. In E. Bredo & W. Feinberg (Eds.), *Knowledge and values in social and educational research* (pp. 370-390). Philadelphia: Temple University Press.

Davis, L. (1985). Female and male voices in social work. *Social Work, 30*(2), 106-113.

Dear, R. B., Briar, K. H., & Van Ry, A. (1986, March). *Policy practice: A "new" method coming of age.* Paper presented at the Annual Program Meeting, Council on Social Work Education, Miami, FL.

Dror, Y. (1971). *Design for policy sciences.* New York: Elsevier.

Dubois, B., & Duellik-Klein, R. (1983). Passionate scholarship: Notes on values, knowing, and method. In G. Bowles & R. Duelli-Klein (Eds.) *Theories in women's studies* (pp. 105-116). Boston: Routledge & Kegan.

Eckstein, J. (1967). Political science and public policy. In I. Pool (Ed.), *Contemporary political science: Toward empirical theory* (p. 143). New York: McGraw-Hill.

Ehrenreich, B., & Piven, F. F. (1984). *The feminization of poverty.* Washington, DC: Institute for Policy Studies.

Einbinder, S. D. (1995). Policy analysis. In *Encyclopedia of social work* (19th ed., pp. 1849-1855). Washington, DC: National Association of Social Workers.

Evans, A. (1991). *Alternatives to bed and breakfast: Temporary housing solutions for homeless people.* London: National Housing and Town Planning Council.

Fay, B. (1975). *Social theory and political practice.* London: Unwin Hyman.

Fay, B. (1977). How people change themselves: The relationship between critical theory and its audience. In T. Ball (Ed.), *Political theory and praxis: New perspectives* (pp. 200-233). Minneapolis: University of Minnesota press.

Fenby, B. L. (1991, Spring). Feminist theory, critical theory, and management's romance with the technical. *Affilia, 1,* 20-37.

Figueira-McDonough, J. (1993). Policy practice: The neglected side of social work intervention. *Social Work, 38,* 179-188.

Forester, J. (Ed.). (1987). *Critical theory and public life.* Cambridge: MIT Press.

Forester, J. (Ed.). (1993). *Critical theory, public policy, and planning practice: Toward a critical pragmatism.* Albany: State University of New York Press.

Foucault, M. (1972). *The archeology of knowledge.* London: Tavistock.

Freire, P. (1986). *Pedagogy of the oppressed.* (M. B. Ramos, Trans.) New York: Continuum.

Frey, G. A. (1987, March). *Toward a conceptual framework for policy-related social work practice*. Paper presented at the Community Organization and Social Administration Symposium, Council on Social Work Education, St. Louis, MO.

Fromm, E. (1941). *Escape from freedom*. New York: Avon.

Gibbs, L. E. (1983). Evaluation research: Scientist or advocate? *Journal of Social Science Research, 7*, 81-92.

Gibson, R. (1986). *Critical theory and education*. London: Hodder & Stroughton.

Giddens, A. (1984). *The constitution of society: Outline of the theory of structuration*. Cambridge, MA: Polity.

Ginsberg, N. (1979). *Class, capital, and social policy*. London: Macmillan.

Ginsberg, N. (1992). *Divisions of welfare: A critical introduction to comparative social policy*. Newbury Park, CA: Sage.

Glaser, B. G., & Strauss, A. L. (1967). *The discovery of grounded theory: Strategies for qualitative research*. Chicago: Aldine.

Gough, I. (1979). *The political economy of the welfare state*. Basingstoke, UK: Macmillan.

Gough, I., & Steinberg, A. (1981). The welfare state, capitalism, and crisis. *Journal of Political Power and Social Theory, 2*, 141-171.

Gough, I., & Thomas, T. (1993). *Cross-national variation in need satisfaction*. Manchester, UK: Manchester Papers in Social Policy.

Greenwood, E. (1995). Social science and social work: A theory of their relationship. *Social Service Review, 29*, 20-33.

Haar, C., & Iatridis, D. (1974). *Housing and the poor in suburbia: Public policy at the grass roots*. Boston: Ballinger.

Habermas, J. (1970). Towards a theory of communicative competence. *Inquiry, 13*, 360-375.

Habermas, J. (1971). *Knowledge and human interests* (J. Shapiro, Trans.). Boston: Beacon.

Habermas, J. (1973). *Theory and practice* (J. Viestel, Trans.) Boston: Beacon.

Habermas, J. (1974). *Theory and practice*. London: Heinemann.

Habermas, J. (1991). *Communication and the evolution of society*. Cambridge, MA: Polity.

Haynes, K. S., & Mickelson, J. S. (1986). *Affecting change: Social workers in the political arena*. New York: Longman.

Iatridis, D. (1983). Neoconservatism revisited. *Social Work, 28*, 101-103.

Iatridis, D. (1988). The new social deficit: Neoconservatism's policy of social underdevelopment. *Social Work Journal, 33*, 11-15.

Iatridis, D. (1994). *Social policy: Institutional context of social development and human services*. Monterey, CA: Brooks/Cole.

Iatridis, D. (1995). Policy practice. *Encyclopedia of social work* (19th ed., pp. 1855-1866). Washington, DC: National Association of Social Workers.

Jansson, B. S. (1984). *Theory and practice of social welfare policy: Analysis, processes, and current issues*. Belmont, CA: Wadsworth.

Jansson, B. S. (1994). *Social policy: From theory to practice* (2nd ed.). Monterey, CA: Brooks/Cole.

Johnson, B. (1991). *A typology of homelessness* (Final report for Scottish Homes). Edinborough, UK: Scottish Homes.

Kaivisto, J., & Valiverronen, E. (1996). The resurgence of critical theories in public sphere. *Journal of Communication Inquiry, 20*(2), 18-35.

Kellner, D. (1989). *Critical theory, Marxism, and modernity*. Baltimore: Johns Hopkins University Press.

Kellner, D. (1990). Critical theory and the crisis of social theory. *Sociological Perspectives, 33*, 11-33.

Kincheloe, J. L., & McLaren, P. L. (1994). Rethinking critical theory and qualitative research. In K. H. Denzin & Y. S. Lincoln (Eds.), *Handbook of qualitative research*. Thousand Oaks, CA: Sage.

Kolb, W. L. (1964). Science. In J. Gould & W. L. Kolb (Eds.), *Dictionary of the social sciences* (pp. 620-622). New York: Free Press.

Kuhn, T. S. (1962). *The structure of scientific revolutions*. Chicago: University of Chicago Press.

Lasswell, H. D. (1971). *A preview of policy sciences*. New York: American Elsevier.

Lather, P. (1991). *Getting smart: Feminist research and pedagogy within the postmodern*. New York: Routledge.

Lekachman, R. (1982). *Greed is not enough: Reaganomics*. New York: Pantheon.

Leonard, P. (1994). Knowledge, power, and postmodernism: Implications for the practice of a critical social work education. *Canadian Social Work Review, 44,* 11-26.

Leonard, P. (1996). New approaches to welfare theory. *Canadian Social Work Review, 13*(2), 246-247.

Leonard, P. (1997). *Postmodern welfare*. Thousand Oaks, CA: Sage.

Lerner, D., & Lasswell, H. D. (1951). *The policy sciences in the United States*. Paris: A. Colin.

Lucas, J. (1993). Searching for answers. *Open Mind 63*, p. 17.

Lukacs, G. (1971). *History of class consciousness*. Cambridge: MIT Press. (Original work published 1923)

Marcuse, H. (1996). *Eros and civilization*. Boston: Beacon.

Masson, H. (1990). Training for competence in child protection work. *Social Work Education, 9,* 35-43.

Mayer, R. R. (1985). *Policy and program planning: A developmental perspective*. Englewood Cliffs, NJ: Prentice Hall.

Morgain, C. A. (1994). Enlightenment for emancipation: A critical theory of self-formation. *Family Relations, 43,* 325-335.

Morris, T. (1994). Alternative paradigms: A source of social work practive research. *Arete, 18,* 31-34.

Mullender, A., & Ward, D. (1991). *Self-directed group work: Users take action for empowerment*. London: Whiting & Bird.

Nagel, E. (1961). *The structure of science: Problems in the logic of scientific explanations*. New York: Harcourt, Brace & World.

Neal, J. (1997). Homelessness and theory reconstructed: *Housing Studies, 12,* 47-61.

Nulman, E. (1983). Family therapy and advocacy: Directions for the future. *Social Work, 28,* 19-22.

Olofsson, G. (1988). After the working-class movement: The new social movements. *Acta Sociologica, 31,* 1.

Pascal, G. (1991). *Social policy: A feminist analysis*. London: Routledge.

Pierson, P. (1994). *Dismantling the welfare state? Reagan, Thatcher, and the politics of retrenchment*. Cambridge, UK: Cambridge University Press.

Piven, F., & Cloward, R. (1971). *Regulating the poor*. New York: Vintage.

Piven, F., & Cloward, R. (1977). *Poor people's movements*. New York: Vintage.

Piven, F., & Cloward, R. (1996). Welfare reform and the new class war. In M. B. Lykes (Ed.), *Myths about the powerlessness: Contesting social inequalities* (pp. 72-86). Philadelphia: Temple University Press.

Popkewitz, T. A. (1990). Whose future? Whose past: Notes on critical theory and methodology. In E. G. Cuba (Ed.) *The paradigm dialog*. Newbury Park, CA: Sage.

Raymond, H. (1968, December 15). Sociologist sees intellectual peril. *New York Times*, p. 11.

Roberts, H. (1990). *Doing feminist research*. London: Routledge.

Rossiter, A. B. (1996). A perspective in critical social work. *Journal of Progressive Human Services, 7*(2), 23-41.

Rousseas, S. (1982). *The political economy of Reaganomics: A critique*. New York: Armonk.

Schon, D. A. (1983). *The reflective practitioner: How professionals think in action*. New York: Basic Books.

Somerville, P. (1992). Homelessness and the meaning of home: Rooflessness or rootlessness? *International Journal of Urban and Regional Research, 16,* 529-539.

Taylor, D. (Ed.) (1996). *Critical social policy: A reader*. London: Sage.

Tremmel, R. (1993). Zen and the art of reflective practice in teacher education. *Harvard Educational Review, 63,* 434-458.

Tropman, J. E. (1987). Policy analysis. *Encyclopedia of social work* (Vol. 1). Silver Springs, MD: National Association of Social Workers.

Turner, J. H. (1985). In defense of positivism. *Sociological Theory, 3,* 24-30.

Turner, J. H. (1992). Positivism. In E. F. Borgatta (Ed.), *Encyclopedia of sociology* (Vol. 1, pp. 1509-1512). New York: Macmillan.

Tyson, K. B. (1992). A new approach to relevant scientific research for practitioners: The heuristic paradigm. *Social Work, 37,* 541.

Vining, S., & Weimer, D. (1992, Spring). Welfare economics as the foundation for public policy analysis: Incomplete and flawed but nevertheless desirable. *Journal of Socioeconomics, 21*(1), 25-37.

Wexler, P. (1991). *Critical theory now.* Philadelphia: Falmer.

White, S. K. (1988). *The recent work of Jurgen Habermas.* Cambridge, UK: Cambridge University Press.

Williams, F. (1989). *Social policy: A critical introduction.* Cambridge, MA: Polity.

Wyers, N. L. (1991). Policy practice in social work: Models and issues. *Journal of Social Work Education, 27,* 241-250.

CHAPTER TWENTY-SEVEN

Welfare Pluralism and Social Policy

NEIL GILBERT

Welfare pluralism, sometimes referred to as the *mixed economy of welfare,* has played an increasingly prominent role in social policy discourse since the late 1970s. According to Johnson (1987), heightened interest in this idea began to build in Britain after publication of the 1978 Wolfenden Report on *The Future of Voluntary Organisations,* which specifically referred to welfare pluralism in developing the notion that the voluntary sector was one of four sectors that could provide social welfare benefits. The Wolfenden Report sought to expand the role of the voluntary sector as part of pluralistic arrangements for the provision of social welfare, although not necessarily at the expense of state-sponsored provisions. As the idea of welfare pluralism gained currency, efforts were made to analyze the design of the mixed economy of social welfare and how it operates.

STRUCTURE AND FUNCTION

At one level, the structure of welfare pluralism can be seen as composed of four sectors—government, voluntary, informal, and commercial—through which social provisions can be delivered to assist citizens in need. At another level, these four sectors can be seen as imbedded in the public and private domains of the social market of the welfare state, which is separate but overlapping with the economic market of capitalist society. From this perspective, welfare pluralism is analyzed not only as using various modes to meet needs through the four sectors, but as a system for the finance and delivery of social provisions that functions outside the market economy. This view draws on Marshall's (1972) observation:

> In contrast to the economic process, it is a fundamental principle of the Welfare State that the market value of an individual cannot be the measure of his right to welfare. The central function of welfare, in fact, is to supersede the market by taking goods and services out of it, or in some way to control and modify its operations so as to produce a result which it would not have produced itself. (p. 19)

Figure 27.1 illustrates the structure of welfare pluralism in the context of social and economic markets. The distinction between social and economic markets rests on the principles and motives that guide the allocation of provisions. The social market of the welfare state allocates goods and services primarily in response to human need, dependency, altruistic sentiments, social obligations, charitable motives, and desire for communal security. In contrast, goods and services in a capitalist society are produced and distributed through the economic market, ideally on the basis of entrepreneurial initiative, productivity, consumer choice, ability to pay, and a desire for profit (Gilbert, 1983).

As shown in Figure 27.1, the social market contains both a public and a private domain. The public domain encompasses the government sector, which consists of federal, state, and local agencies and accounts for the largest portion of goods and services distributed in the welfare state. There are three methods of allocating social welfare transfers through the public domain: first, direct expenditures via government grants; second, indirect spending through special tax subsidies, such as deductions, exemptions, and credit subsidies; and third, transfers achieved through the regulatory powers of government, for example, rent controls.

The private domain includes the informal sector, made up of networks of family and friends that provide mutual aid and social support; the voluntary sector, composed of nonprofit social welfare agencies; and the commercial sector of profit-oriented firms. The latter overlaps with the activities of the economic market, which to some extent blurs the boundary between the private domain of the social market and the economic market. The activities of profit-oriented firms in the social market are usually devoted more to the delivery than to the financing of social provisions. But there are cases in which profit-making firms subsidize social transfers; for example, when housing developers set aside a number of units for rent or sale below market value to low-income households. However, these cases are often a response to regulatory measures attached to government loans for housing development. Hence, they

Social Market			Economic Market	
Public Domain	*Private Domain*			
Direct provision of transfers by federal, state, and local government; indirect transfers through tax expenditures; regulatory transfers	Informal supports by family and friends	Services by voluntary (nonprofit) groups	Services by for-profit agencies	Goods and services produced by profit-making enterprise

Figure 27.1. Welfare Pluralism in the Social Market

represent more of a regulatory transfer promoted by the government sector than private acts of charity.

The example of how regulatory transfers are generated through the interaction of the government and commercial sectors reveals not only the permeable character of the different sectors, but also some of the functional complexity of pluralism as it operates in the social market. Not only are there different sectors, but each sector can exercise either partial or full responsibility for the financing and the delivery of various social provisions. A government agency, for example, can hire its own staff to provide day care services for low-income mothers, or, through purchase-of-service arrangements, it may pay to have the service provided by a voluntary agency, a profit-making enterprise, or members of the client's family. In this manner, the roles of government, voluntary, profit-oriented, and informal sectors are variously combined in the pluralistic or mixed economy of welfare. The extent to which these different sectors contribute to the mixed economy has changed over time. As the balance among these sectors shifts, new configurations emerge, altering the distinctive nature of the social market and the character of the welfare state.

TRENDS: DECENTRALIZATION AND THE CHANGING BALANCE OF PUBLIC-PRIVATE RESPONSIBILITY

An examination of the development of social welfare programs in the United States reveals three broad patterns of responsibility among the four sectors of welfare pluralism during the 20th century. From the turn of the century through 1935, welfare transfers were largely community-based. Under these arrangements local government, voluntary charitable institutions, family, and neighbors provided the major sources of aid for those unable to meet their needs through the market economy. Although the federal government occasionally funded private welfare services as far back as 1819, when it provided support for the Hartford Asylum for the Deaf and Dumb, the federal role in social welfare did not take on the character of a large-scale systematic effort until the mid-1930s. Previously, allocations through the social market were a distinctly local affair, which relied heavily on voluntary charity organizations and informal sources to finance and deliver welfare transfers (Leiby, 1978).

Under the New Deal in the mid-1930s, the federal government assumed major responsibility for social welfare provisions financed and delivered mainly through public agencies. This was the start of the North American version of the welfare state. Direct federal and state government expenditures for social welfare climbed from 4% of the gross national product in 1929 to 9% in 1940 and 19.5% in 1976, after which they declined slightly, leveling off at about 18.5%. The structure of the welfare state that emerged between 1935 and the 1970s included a public domain, which financed and delivered welfare transfers through federal, state, and local units of government, and a private domain in which transfers flowed through voluntary nonprofit agencies and informal networks of families and friends. These government, voluntary, and informal sectors operated in separate spheres that only occasionally joined together, while profit-making enterprises were, for the most part, excluded from the main line of activity in the social market.

Compared to most European welfare states at that time, the role of the government sector was somewhat less vigorous, and voluntary nonprofit agencies performed more actively in the United States. Overall, through the early 1970s, the general pattern in the United States involved a system of welfare pluralism in which government directly financed and publicly delivered social welfare provisions that were supplemented by private activities of voluntary nonprofit agencies and informal networks.

Since the early 1970s, the balance between activities in the public and private domains has undergone notable changes, with responsibilities for the delivery of social provisions increasingly transferred to agencies in the private domain.

This trend toward privatization of social welfare was spurred by the 1974 Title XX amendments to the Social Security Act, which permitted purchase-of-service arrangements: Government agencies could contract for welfare services to be produced and delivered by private organizations, whose donations qualified for part of the state's required local matching share of social services grants (Gilbert, 1983).

By 1980, as purchase of service arrangements multiplied, federal agencies provided over 50% of the financial support received by private nonprofit social service and community development organizations (Salamon & Abramson, 1982). The widely documented movement toward privatization not only enlarged the range of benefits provided under government contract with nonprofit welfare agencies, it also

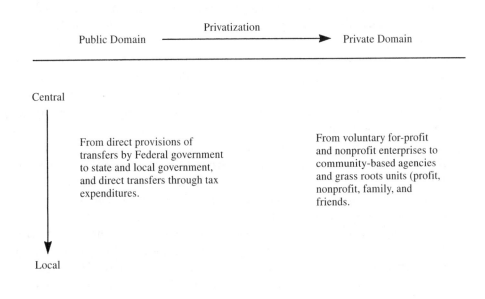

Public Domain — Privatization → Private Domain

Central

From direct provisions of
transfers by Federal government
to state and local government,
and direct transfers through tax
expenditures.

From voluntary for-profit
and nonprofit enterprises to
community-based agencies
and grass roots units (profit,
nonprofit, family, and
friends.

Local

Figure 27.2. Trends in Welfare Pluralism: Privatization and Decentralization

created an opportunity for the production and delivery of welfare services by profit-making organizations (Gilbert & Terrell, 1998; Johnson, 1995; Kamerman & Kahn, 1989). Indeed, by the mid-1990s, proprietary agencies were prominently represented among the service providers in the areas of nursing home care, homemaker aides, day care, child welfare, health care, and housing (Gilbert & Tang, 1995, p. 170).

As illustrated in Figure 27.2, the shift toward privatization of the mixed economy of welfare has been accompanied by a related movement toward decentralization. In the public domain, this development is reflected in the devolution of authority from central government to local units. Devolution was initially promoted in the early 1970s under the Nixon administration's New Federalism, which sought, in Nixon's (1971) words, "to set states and localities free—free to set new priorities, free to meet unmet needs, free to make their own mistakes, yes, but also free to score splendid successes which otherwise would never be realized" (p. 170). The devolution of authority was achieved through a change in federal methods of financing social welfare that involved issuing block grants, which afford states wide discretion to set policies in response to local needs, rather than categorical grants, which set federal guidelines to limit local decision making.

The move toward decentralization was advanced under the Reagan administration in the 1980s and continues apace with the Clinton administration in the late 1990s, as seen in passage of the Personal Responsibility and Work Opportunity Reconciliation Act of 1996, under which categorical grants for the Aid to Families With Dependent Children program were replaced by block grant allocations—the Temporary Assistance to Needy Families program.

Another approach to decentralization involves the increasing use of tax expenditures, vouchers for housing, and credit subsidies (Gilbert & Gilbert, 1989). Although the distribution of these benefits is administered by the federal government, the locus of decision making on how the cash benefits are actually consumed is highly decentralized, resting in the hands of individual recipients. From this perspective, social welfare policies that provide cash/voucher benefits represent a market model of decentralization; as Alice Rivlin (1971) explains, this is "the most extreme form of decentralization" (p. 122). This form of decentralization (which focuses on the authority to decide what is consumed) is tightly linked to privatization of social welfare delivery, as the individual recipients of cash, tax expenditures, vouchers, and credit subsidies are free to purchase the goods and services they require in the private sector.

More generally, in recent years, the movement toward decentralization and privatization under welfare pluralism has gained impetus from the collapse of command economies in Russia and Eastern Europe and the immense fiscal pressures coming to bear on the industrialized welfare states, which have diminished public faith in the capacity of central governments to ensure social well-being (and raised the stock of capitalism in public acceptance).

In the private domain, the move toward decentralization is driven, in part, by a growing interest in the revitalization of civil society (Berger & Neuhaus, 1996; Krauthammer, 1995; Osborne & Kaposvari, 1997). Community-based agencies and grassroots organizations are seen as mediating institutions that provide a cushion of civil society between the individual and the state. The value of such structural arrangements is not a new idea. Almost a century ago, the French sociologist Emile Durkheim (1893/1933) observed,

> Where the State is the only environment in which people can live communal lives, they inevitably lose contact, become detached, and society disintegrates. A nation can be maintained only if between the State and the individual there are intercalated a whole series of secondary groups near enough to the individuals to attract them strongly in their sphere of action and drag them in this way into the general torrent of social life. (p. 28)

Today, both liberals and conservatives trumpet the virtues of civil society. "When civil society is strong," according to Senator Dan Coats (1996), "it infuses a community with its warmth, trains its people to be good citizens, and transmits values between generations. When it is weak, no amount of police or politics can provide a substitute" (p. 25). In a similar vein, Putnam (1993) observes, that "focusing on the indirect effects of civic norms and networks is a much-needed corrective to an exclusive emphasis on the formal institutions of government as an explanation for our collective discontents" (p. 35). This interest in strengthening the mediating structures of local networks has stimulated efforts to contract with grassroots and community-based agencies for the delivery of social welfare provisions through the private domain.

ISSUES OF WELFARE PLURALISM

As a theoretical perspective on the welfare state, the pluralistic approach conveys a model of descriptive neutrality. The discourse of "welfare mix" recognizes that the finance and delivery of social welfare are conducted through both public and private domains and draws attention to the challenge of finding the most efficient and effective combination of public/private efforts. There appears to be something here for everyone. Conservatives can advocate the merits of private efforts, and liberals can emphasize the virtues of public measures, while allowing that in the end there will always be some mix.

However, as Kvist and Torfing (1996) point out, implicit "in the academic and political endorsement of welfare mix/welfare pluralism is a belief that the state cannot adequately solve the social problems. Sometimes, the state is even seen as contributing to or augmenting social problems" (p. 13). Thus, they note that "state failures" are often discussed as reasons for the welfare mix. These concerns are more a criticism of the trends toward privatization and decentralization in welfare pluralism than a compelling case against the pluralistic model per se. It could also be said that pluralists still recognize a basic role for the state (and that those favoring a statist model implicitly argue that only the state can adequately solve social problems).

The trends toward privatization and decentralization in welfare pluralism are supported by several popular assumptions that raise a number of issues. These assumptions are, first, that privatization offers the most efficient approach to the production and delivery of social services; and second, that local units of government are better able to serve the social welfare needs of citizens than central government because they are constituted closer to the people being served and bypass the impediments of massive federal bureaucracies. A third assumption is that grassroots and community-based organizations are still more effective than local public agencies because they are less bureaucratic, reside even closer to the people being served, and strengthen the mediating structures of civil society.

Regarding the first assumption, the case for the efficiency of privatization is based on both the presumed advantages of competition and the failings of public bureaucracies that operate outside the cost constraints and incentives to innovate spurred by competitive markets. Those who question this assumption should note that the market metaphor does not apply to social welfare transactions, which involve services subsidized by public funds. When public funds are used to purchase services from private providers, market discipline does not operate because these third-party arrangements undermine the forces of competition responsive to consumer choice. The entire transaction is perceived by neither the individual consumer, who receives private services that are publicly subsidized, nor the purchasing body (public agency), which does not receive the service. Moreover, social service consumer populations are often vulnerable—children, elderly, and poor—and not well-informed consumers; in the absence of the market discipline imposed by well-informed consumers who pay for what they get, third-party purchase of services can have a difficult time ensuring the quality of services being delivered. The question of ensuring quality leads into another potential problem of privatization; namely, that the transaction costs of contracting are quite high, requiring complicated measurement to determine the price of units of service being purchased and expensive procedures to then monitor the quality of what is delivered.

Still, the issue remains, are private agencies more efficient and effective vehicles for the delivery of social welfare benefits than their public counterparts? And if private agencies are more efficient, is there a difference between those that are voluntary and those that operate for-profit. On these formidable questions, the research findings are inconclusive, muddled by intervening factors such as agency size and geographic location, along with the difficulty of equating the substantive quality and effectiveness of social welfare services (Kantor & Summers, 1987). For example, research on day care finds that for-profit centers charge a lower hourly fee than nonprofit centers under religious and independent sponsorship. But the for-profit centers have a higher child-staff ratio, a lower percentage of teachers with college degrees, a higher rate of staff turnover, and fewer physical and cognitive examinations (Kisker, 1991).

Regarding the second assumption, it is often true that local governments are more knowledgeable than large centralized units about problems in their areas and more responsive to the special needs of their constituencies. Also, small units can more easily experiment, and if they fail, all is not lost. However, there are also limits to what local units can accomplish and advantages that reside in working through larger units of national government. Localism can be parochial and oppressive. In small local units of government, it is easier to weld a cohesive majority that may disregard the interests of others. For example, through the late 1960s, claims of states' rights were used to protect the power and privileges of whites in the South. Also, national units command greater resources than local governments, which amplifies their technical and administrative capacity. State and local units, by their very nature, can do little to affect problems of national scope.

The third assumption concerns the virtues of contracting with grassroots community-based organizations to deliver publicly financed social welfare provisions. These organizations are thought to be effective in meeting local needs and accountable to people in their communities. Moreover, by shrinking the role of government in the delivery of social services and shifting responsibility to community organizations, Krauthammer (1995) suggests that these "mediating institutions will once again have the space to flower, reclaiming their rightful place at the center of a revitalized civil society" (p. 17). But these attributes bear closer examination than is usually afforded by those who support the movement toward privatization and decentralization.

Whether community-based organizations are more effective in delivering social services than public bureaucracies is an empirical question. The facts that they reside closer to the people being served, are less bureaucratic, and are more responsive to local influences, may suggest that services will be more personal and, perhaps, intrusive, but it does not guarantee greater effectiveness in service delivery. McConnell (1966) offers a classic statement of some of the problematic aspects of localism:

> Impersonality is the guarantee of individual freedom characteristic of the large unit. Impersonality means an avoidance of arbitrary official action, the following of prescribed procedure, conformance to established rules, and escape from bias whether for or against any individual. Impersonality, and the privacy and freedom it confers, may be despised, and the human warmth and community concern for the personal affairs of individuals characteristic of the small community preferred. Nevertheless, the values involved are different, and are to a considerable degree antagonistic. (p. 107)

There is another consequence of shifting service delivery from the public domain to community-based organizations, which has not been fully articulated. Public bureaucracies represent the last stronghold of the union movement in the United States. From 1970 to 1991, union membership declined from 28% to 16% of the labor force. While union membership in the private sector was declining, the number of union members in government employment increased. In 1970, government workers accounted for 10% of union membership; by 1991, they accounted for 40% of unionized labor. One of the reasons, of course, is that organized labor in government is largely in the service sector; unlike industrial production, these service jobs could not be shipped overseas to be performed at lower costs. Instead, they are now being contracted out to local community organizations, which are relatively small, voluntary, nonprofit units that have few ties to organized labor. The lower costs and flexibility of community organizations may be desirable. But in analyzing the direction of welfare pluralism, the trade-offs should be made explicit, particularly the implications for the future of organized labor in the social services.

Finally, at a more general level, the changing balance between both public and private and central and local responsibility for the delivery of social provisions in the mixed economy of welfare raises a fundamental question as to whether the emerging character of welfare pluralism in the late 1990s represents a new paradigm for social protection (Gilbert, 1998).

REFERENCES

Berger, P., & Neuhaus, J. (1996). *To empower people: From state to civil society* (M. Novak, Ed.). Washington, DC: AEI Press.

Coats, D. (1996, January/February). Can Congress revive civil society? *Policy Review,* No. 75, p. 25.

Durkheim, E. (1933). *The division of labor in society* (G. Simpson, Trans.). New York: Free Press. (English translation first published in 1893)

Gilbert, N. (1983). *Capitalism and the welfare state; Dilemmas of social benevolence.* New Haven, CT: Yale University Press.

Gilbert, N. (1998). Remodeling social welfare. *Society, 35*(5), 8-13.

Gilbert, N., & Gilbert, B. (1989). *The enabling state.* New York: Oxford University Press.

Gilbert, N., & Tang, K. L. (1995). The United States. In N. Johnson (Ed.), *Private markets in health and welfare.* Oxford, UK: Berg.

Gilbert, N., & Terrell, P. (1998). *Dimensions of social welfare policy* (4th ed.). Boston: Allyn & Bacon.

Johnson, N. (1987). *The welfare state in transition: The theory and practice of welfare pluralism.* Amherst: University Massachusetts Press.

Johnson, N. (Ed.). (1995). *Private markets in health and welfare.* Oxford, UK: Berg.

Kamerman, S., & Kahn, A. (Eds.). (1989). *Privatization and the welfare state.* Princeton, NJ: Princeton University Press.

Kantor, R., & Summers, D. (1987). Doing well while doing good: Dilemmas of performance measurement in nonprofit organizations and the need for multiple-constituency approach. In W. Powell (Ed.), *The non-profit sector: A research handbook.* New Haven, CT: Yale University Press.

Kisker, E. (1991). *A profile of child care settings: Early education and care in 1990–Executive summary.* Washington, DC: U.S. Department of Education.

Krauthammer, C. (1995, Fall). A social conservative credo. *The Public Interest, 121,* 15-22.

Kvist, J., & Torfing, J. (1996). *Changing welfare state models* (Working Paper No. 5). Copenhagen, Denmark: Center for Welfare State Research.

Leiby, J. (1978). *A history of social welfare and social work in the United States.* New York: Columbia University Press.

Marshall, T. H. (1972). Value problems of welfare capitalism. *Journal of Social Policy, 1*(1), 19-20.

McConnell, G. (1966). *Private power and American democracy.* New York: Knopf.

Nixon, R. (1971, February 8). Message to Congress on general revenue sharing. *Weekly Compilation of Presidential Documents, 7,* 170.

Osborne, S., & Kaposvari, A. (1997). Towards a civil society? Exploring its meaning in the context of post-communist Hungary. *European Journal of Social Policy, 7,* 3.

Putnam, R. (1993, Spring). The prosperous community: Social capital and public life. *The American Prospect, 13,* 31-35.

Rivlin, A. (1971) *Systematic thinking for social action.* Washington, DC: Brookings Institution.

Salamon, L., & Abramson, A. (1982). The nonprofit sector. In J. Palmer & I. Sawhill (Eds.), *The Reagan experiment.* Washington, DC: Urban Institute.

CHAPTER TWENTY-EIGHT

Feminist Approaches
to Social Policy

CHERYL HYDE

Feminist approaches to social policy are broadly concerned with issues relevant to the social, economic, and political well-being of women and their families and to the structural apparatuses and collective processes that either empower or subordinate women. Such analyses are necessary correctives to gender-blind and androcentric perspectives, which dominate discussions of social policy. There has been an explosion of multidisciplinary feminist scholarship on social policy. Scholars in fields such as law, political science, history, sociology, and social work have all contributed. Central themes in these efforts are the reclamation of women's experiences and the illumination of the gendered dynamics of social welfare.

Myriad social policies and programs touch the lives of women—child care, reproductive rights, workplace equity, income maintenance, divorce, educational access, sexual violence, and so forth (Blankenship, 1993; Gelb & Palley, 1996; Hill & Tigges, 1995; Lewis, 1986; Miller, 1990; Petchesky, 1990; Sapiro, 1990; Schneider, 1990). In this chapter, primary emphasis is on feminist understandings of welfare policies in the United States. A focus on welfare brings into sharpest relief the gendered biases within policy theories and practices. Women make up most of the recipients and providers of what is generally termed *welfare*, and at the core of the controversial welfare debates is one on sexual politics and gender roles (Abramovitz, 1988; Fraser & Gordon, 1994; Gordon, 1988, 1990; Hill & Tigges, 1995; Kamerman, 1995; Koven &

Michel, 1993; Lewis, 1986; Miller, 1990; Mink, 1990, 1995, 1998; Orloff, 1993, 1996, 1998; Sainsbury, 1996a, 1996b, 1996c; Sapiro, 1990). Although there are important feminist studies of social policy development in other countries, space limitations prevent more than cursory attention to these works (Estes, 1998; Hill & Tigges, 1995; Hobson, 1993; Kamerman, 1995; Koven & Michel, 1993; Orloff, 1993, 1996; Sainsbury, 1996a, 1996b).

The chapter begins with a brief summary of two predominant approaches to the understanding of social policy. This is followed by an overview of feminist responses to these arguments, as well as theoretical innovations by feminist scholars. The chapter concludes with consideration of the next steps within this body of feminist knowledge and action.

DOMINANT SOCIAL POLICY PARADIGMS

Feminist approaches to social policy are, to a large extent, remedies to prevailing understandings of what policy is and ought to be. At present, much of social policy practice in the United States is influenced by a conservative, often right-wing agenda. At the core of this agenda are patriarchal views of male and female roles and responsibilities. For the conservative movement, social policy has become an important vehicle to achieve a more traditional society (Conover & Gray, 1983; Hyde, 1995; Marshall, 1995; Sidel, 1996).

A patriarchal family structure, with husband as breadwinner and wife as homemaker, is the bedrock of the conservative social agenda. Conservative groups oppose policies and programs that suggest the possibility of women's independence. For example, anti-abortion rhetoric, in part, focuses on women going against "their true nature" as mothers. Opposition to domestic violence legislation was premised on the belief that shelters for battered women were unnecessary rest and relaxation homes where women were turned against the family (Hyde, 1995; Marshall, 1995). "Family friendly" corporate policies, such as child care, are viewed as threats to family life by allowing women the option of employment.

No policy issue captures conservative views on women and family better than welfare. Welfare discourse has always distinguished between deserving and undeserving women, the former having performed society's role of wife and mother, whereas the latter did not (typically, they were unwed mothers) (Abramovitz, 1988; Gordon, 1995; Kunzel, 1993). Currently, conservative activists and policy makers (unfortunately joined by some liberals) invoke an outright misogynistic portrayal of women who are welfare recipients.

For example, culture of poverty arguments condemned the "welfare culture" as pathological. By extension, women on welfare were deemed lazy, promiscuous, and deceitful. In his 1973 book, *The Politics of Guaranteed Income,* Senator Daniel P. Moynihan foreshadowed current debates by arguing that welfare programs create an unnatural state of dependency that is antithetical to being a healthy, normal adult. This notion of welfare dependency is at the center of current welfare debates. Politicians and opinion makers rail against welfare recipients, likening their need for state assistance to a drug habit (Fraser & Gordon, 1994). Ruth Sidel (1996) notes that "the rhetoric has escalated to previously unimagined levels of hyperbole and vitriol" (p. 5), which serve only to scapegoat and stigmatize poor women. Other scholars have reached the same conclusion (Abramovitz, 1988, 1996; Mink, 1998).

This derogatory rhetoric, which now invokes the term *culture of illegitimacy* to describe welfare recipients and blame them for their circumstances, continues unabated. It is reflected in both popular opinion and in welfare policy changes of the Reagan, Bush, and Clinton administrations (Abramovitz, 1996; Albelda & Tilly, 1996; Mink, 1998). Such an approach explicitly focuses on gender. Economic (and moral) salvation for women is through the patriarchal family structure that entails marriage and traditional gender roles, all measures supported by conservative social policy (Abramovitz, 1996; Mink, 1995, 1998; Sainsbury, 1996c; Sidel, 1996).

There is another, seemingly more benign approach to the understanding of social policy. Well-represented in mainstream policy texts and readers, these are so-called gender-blind (or neutral) accounts. Discussions emphasize the issues, programs, and structures relevant to the design and implementation of social policy. Women, as a group, might be referred to as primary recipients of certain policy initiatives—but this is more a demographic than an analytical point. Little attention is paid to the ways in which policies differentially reward and punish men and women, or to the distinctly gendered realities of the labor market and family (Gordon, 1990; Nelson, 1990; Sapiro, 1990). Gender, as it shapes and is shaped by social policy, is invisible as an analytical construct.

Even rigorous liberal and progressive accounts of social policy are blind to gendered realities (Gordon, 1988, 1990; Hobson, 1993; Orloff, 1993; Sainsbury, 1996a, 1996c). Michael Harrington, in his classic *The Other America* (1962), did not systematically discuss the distinct worlds of poor men and women. His concern was "the poor." Neo-Marxist analyses of the welfare state (O'Connor, 1973; Offe, 1984; Piven & Cloward, 1993) do little to illuminate the gendered dynamics of the state. Consideration of gender differences is also largely absent in mainstream examinations of social rights, citizenship, and claims to state provisions (Esping-Anderson, 1990; Esping-Anderson & Korpi, 1987; Marshall, 1950). Yet, as will be discussed later, men and women do not share common experiences as the poor, the welfare recipient, or the citizen.

Neither conservative nor gender-blind approaches capture the historical or current economic, political, or cultural situations of women. Feminist theory and practice focus on remedying these distortions and omissions. Feminist scholarship on social policy directly challenges these approaches by capturing the realities of women's lives and revealing the gendered dynamics of policy practice.

FEMINIST VIEWPOINTS

Despite a shared goal of correcting misconceptions and inaccuracies of these prevailing views on social policy, there is no singular feminist response to these accounts or one feminist analysis of the state and its policies. There are many feminist perspectives—liberal, Marxist, psychoanalytic, radical, and cultural, each with its own assumptions and points of debate (Delmar, 1986; Miller, 1990; Pateman, 1986). Yet, fundamentally, feminist scholarship is a commitment to "address women's lives and experience in their own terms, to create theory grounded in the actual experience and language of women" (DuBois, 1983, p. 108). Feminism is concerned with enlarging the choices that women have in their lives (Pateman, 1986).

Feminist understandings of social policy reflect these differences. Perspectives vary in emphasis regarding the regulatory role of the state, the state as a potential ally in the empowerment of women, the agency of women, the effectiveness of legislative versus protest strategies, and so forth. Yet, there is consensus that the state, through its policies and programs, reinforces traditional assumptions about gender roles and thus supports a gender regime that privileges men (Abramovitz, 1988, 1996; Connell, 1987; Fraser, 1989; Fraser & Gordon, 1994; Gordon, 1990; Lewis, 1986; Miller, 1990; Orloff, 1996; Sainsbury, 1996a, 1996b; Sapiro, 1990; Schneider, 1990; Sidel, 1996).

Women's Realities

Perhaps the most direct response to gender-blind and especially conservative accounts is to document the economic, social, and political conditions of women. In the last 30 years, feminists have engaged in extensive efforts to reveal the private troubles of women and reframe them as public issues. This documentation has occurred despite opposition or lack of interest by the state and its functionary institutions, such as police, courts, and hospitals.

Efforts have spanned every possible issue or cause. New understandings of sexual violence shift attention from blaming the victim to holding institutions accountable for retraumatizing the victim. Concern over the seriousness of women's illnesses has led to growing demand for better medical research on and care of, for example, breast cancer patients. Careful examination of the unique developmental needs of adolescent girls gives credence to calls for more anti-sexist educational measures. Extensive economic research continues to underscore the inequitable job situations with which women contend, despite important policies such as the Equal Pay Act and Title VII. There is, however, a constant tension between claiming small policy victories and remaining vigilant about the realities for women and their families (Gelb & Palley, 1996; Spalter-Roth & Schreiber, 1995).

Given the current welfare debates, feminist scholars have been prodigious in research on the plight of poor women. Pearce's (1978) germinal article, "The Feminization of Poverty," is a touchstone for much of this research. She argued, quite simply, that more women than men were impoverished and that this trend would increase at an alarming rate. It has continued—the majority of the poor remain women and their children (Goldberg, 1990; Goldberg & Kremen, 1990; Sidel, 1996). In 1997, the overall poverty rate was 13.3%. For women, it was 14.9%, and for children, 19.9%. However, for households headed by women, the rate was 31.6%, and for children in these households, 49% (Dalaker & Naifeh, 1998). It is important to understand that poverty is also racialized. People of color make up a disproportionate number of those in poverty. The poverty rate for blacks is 26.5% and for Hispanics, 27.1%; in all racial categories, the female poverty rate is higher than that for males (Dalaker & Naifeh, 1998; see also Amott, 1990).

Feminist scholars delve into the reasons for these disturbing poverty trends. Much of this work has focused on women's relationship to the workforce. Even with increased labor force participation, women's work is still marked by pay inequity, job segregation, and devalued occupations. Part-time and contingency work, framed as flexible job options, does not come with sufficient pay or benefits. Jobs for which poor women qualify do not provide adequate wages or benefits to lift them and their families out of poverty. The absence of comprehensive child care compounds women's employment difficulties (Albelda & Tilly, 1997; Blankenship, 1993; Edin & Lein, 1997; Goldberg, 1990; Goldberg & Kremen, 1990; Mink, 1998; Sidel, 1996). The lack of work equity heightens women's dependency on male wages.

Others examine the relationship between labor expectations and family structure, specifically, the ways in which domestic responsibilities undercut earning potential (Abramovitz, 1988; Blankenship, 1993; Goldberg & Kremen, 1990; Gordon, 1988; Kamerman, 1995; Lewis, 1986). Regardless of their particular economic situation, mothers are overwhelming responsible for child rearing; wives and daughters are the primary caregivers for elderly family members (Hooyman & Gonyea, 1995). Yet, women receive little economic compensation for this unpaid domestic and maternal labor, which further ties them to men's incomes (Fraser & Gordon, 1994; Gordon, 1988; Pearce, 1990).

Labor force participation and family roles influence the economic health not only of young and middle-aged adults, but also of the elderly. Women's labor force participation is often marked by periods of detachment (for child rearing or lack of jobs). This, coupled with lower wages, has a negative cumulative effect on retirement income. Women, who were homemakers throughout their lives, depend on their spouses' earnings for income in old age. Because of these trends, older women are at higher risk of poverty. Compared to men, almost twice as many women over age 65 are in poverty (13.1% vs. 7.0%). For women over age 75, the chances of impoverishment are more than double those for men (15.2% vs. 7.5%) (Dalaker & Naifeh, 1998). Estes (1998) notes that these economic trends and social expectations, coupled with inadequate or short-sighted policies, constitute "a war on women."

Because women experience higher rates of poverty than do men, whether they work or engage in "appropriate" roles such as wife and mother, feminist scholars also concentrate on documenting the conditions of women in poverty (Abramovitz, 1988, 1996; Albelda & Tilly, 1996, 1997; Amott, 1990; Goldberg, 1990; Goldberg & Kremen, 1990; Mink, 1998; Pearce, 1990). They seek to refute the stereotypes of women on welfare and underscore the societal measures that "stack the deck" against them. For example, Edin and Lein (1997) detailed the work ethic, rational choices, and futile job searches of poor and near-poor women. Neither welfare nor work are sufficient to support a family, and consequently, women are often forced to engage in (technically) fraudulent behavior to secure needed resources. Other feminist scholars have focused on challenges of single motherhood (Mink, 1998; Mulroy, 1988; Polakow, 1993), homelessness (Arrighi, 1997; Mulroy, 1988, 1995), paternity and child support (Josephson, 1997; Mink, 1998), and domestic violence as reasons for needing welfare assistance (Albelda, Colten, & Cosenza, 1997; Davis & Kraham, 1995). Feminist scholarship paints a much different portrait of the economic and political status of women than do either the conservative or gender-blind theorists.

Women's Actions and Resistance

Women are not, however, passive recipients of economic, political, or social subordination. Feminist accounts of historical and contemporary policy development are replete with portrayals of women as policy advocates and activists. Feminist scholarship has examined and informed collective action. Although tensions exist between researchers and activists, important steps have been made. Historically, women assumed important roles in developing policies that benefitted other women and their children. Feminist historians situated these efforts in the larger feminist struggles of the particular era, rather than adopting the more masculinist style of focusing on "the influential person." For example, Kunzel's (1993) analysis of the emergence of social work as a profession is a tale of competing interest groups of women. Sarvasy (1992) details the debates between equality and difference feminists and how they informed welfare state development. Gordon's (1995) account of the events leading up to the New Deal is an examination of varying feminist ideologies and political strategies of that time. White (1993), Giddings (1984), and Hine (1986) reveal the extensive nature of black female activism, especially in the post-slavery period. Both Boris (1993) and Gordon (1991, 1995) illuminate the differences between white and black activists during the Progressive and New Deal eras. This research conveys the activism and leadership of women, particularly during the first decades of the 20th century. Other studies support this analysis (Brenner & Laslett, 1991; Mink, 1995; Nelson, 1990; Sapiro, 1990; Sklar, 1993; Skocpol & Ritler, 1995).

The contemporary feminist movement has engaged in numerous activities to expand women's economic, political, and social rights and to halt the severe measures designed to undercut the progress of women. Legislative reforms have allowed for greater access to education, employment, credit, and pensions (Gelb & Palley, 1996; Spalter-Roth & Schreiber, 1995). Demands have been made on the state to fiscally support feminist initiatives, such as anti-violence organizations (Hyde, 1992, 1995; Lewis, 1986; Matthews, 1995; Reinelt, 1995). Feminist policy networks continue working for greater equity for women.

Actions by the feminist movement also extend to establishing alternatives to the welfare state (Brenner & Laslett, 1991; Hyde, 1992; Lewis, 1986; Sarvasy, 1992). Feminist self-help efforts of the late 1960s and 1970s were, in effect, rejections of the state's treatment of women. Establishing a health center or battered women's shelter sent a message that women, not the state, would provide for the well-being of others. Since the late 1970s, a major source of contention within the movement has been the relationship between feminist service organizations and state funding. Although they receive resources, the likelihood of co-optation makes these organizations vulnerable to state control (Hyde, 1992, 1995; Matthews, 1995; Reinelt, 1995).

Specific to welfare policies and programs, women have engaged in protest politics through the National Welfare Rights Organization and other welfare rights activities (Abramovitz, 1996; Dujon & Withorn, 1996; Gordon, 1988; Piven & Cloward, 1979; West, 1981). This female-based protest movement advocates for a living wage, expansion of welfare benefits, and the rights of women to receive adequate assistance to be mothers. Welfare rights activists are situated in a tenuous position. They simultaneously critique the current system for its draconian measures while defending the rights of poor women to secure benefits from it.

Gendered Analyses of the State

By documenting the experiences, actions, and treatment of women, feminists have developed a comprehensive body of knowledge on the gendered dynamics of the state (Orloff, 1996). Gendered analyses deconstruct assumptions and actions and expose the differential treatment of men and women. These examinations indicate how prevailing approaches serve the patriarchal structure of the state. Social policies aid in the reproduction of gender norms and roles and thus support male privilege within a gendered regime (Connell, 1987; Gordon, 1988, 1990; Miller, 1990; Nelson, 1990; Petchesky, 1990; Sainsbury, 1996c).

Consider the gender-blind approaches toward social policy presented earlier. Feminist analysis suggests that these accounts are not neutral but mask deeply embedded patriarchal assumptions. Within a gender-blind framework, terms such as *breadwinner, dependents,* and *the family* are discussed as if they were not associated with particular gender roles of men/husband, wife, and children or with a nuclear unit headed by a male breadwinner (Fraser, 1989; Lewis, 1986). The structure of benefit provision through public insurance, private employers, and means-tested programs reflects these assumptions. This design clearly privileges workers with attachments to the primary labor market because they have greater access to social insurance and private employer plans. These workers are overwhelmingly men, usually white and skilled. This structure serves to reinforce a male breadwinner/female homemaker family model and sets a double standard for welfare provision (Abramovitz, 1988; Fraser & Gordon, 1994; Gordon, 1988, 1990; Nelson, 1990; Orloff, 1993, 1996).

There are two related themes in gendered analyses of the state, specifically the welfare state. The first centers on its gendered origins, particularly during the Progressive and New Deal eras. Feminist social histories mentioned earlier focus on the women's movements of these time periods, with emphasis on the maternalist reform measures designed to protect women as workers and especially as mothers, while providing for the care of children (Gordon, 1995; Hobson, 1993; Koven & Michel, 1993; Nelson, 1990; Sklar, 1993). The espousal of the sanctity of motherhood, although useful at that time in gaining some benefits for widows and deserted wives, essentially reified women's place in the domestic or private sphere. A two-track gender system emerged in which women were viewed as charity recipients whereas men, as worker-citizens in the public sphere, were entitled to state compensation. This division remains largely in place today.

By the 1920s, the maternalist movements waned, falling victim to a male-dominated political arena, a resurgence of fundamentalist religious groups, the business boom, and a post-war backlash against social justice campaigns. These developments attenuated the reformers' abilities to obtain full entitlements for women. By the New Deal, it was virtually impossible to secure benefits for working mothers. Women were consigned to the home, whereas men were viewed as worker-citizens in the public arena. Nonetheless, early maternalist reforms provided the foundation for the welfare state (Gordon, 1995; Hobson, 1993; Koven & Michel, 1993; Nelson, 1990; Sklar, 1993; Skocpol & Ritler, 1995).

The other theme focuses on the ways in which the state regulates gender, which makes explicit the consequences of Progressive Era and New Deal developments. Through legislation, court decisions, and administrative mandates, the state shapes the options available for women and, of course, for men, too. Consider reproductive rights, specifically abortion. In 1973, the court legalized abortion (*Roe v. Wade*), yet, through subsequent state measures, that choice has been limited. Through such procedures, there is a regulation of motherhood and sexuality (Petchesky, 1990). Efforts to restrict the availability of birth control reflect similar regulatory impulses (Mink, 1998; Schneider, 1990).

This regulatory function is quite pronounced in the provision of welfare. Feminist analysis suggests ways in which political, cultural, and economic elites (and often the general public) blame society's ills on women on welfare—making poor women "the enemy" (Sidel, 1996). In stigmatizing welfare recipients, the policy process reinforces an avoidance of state assistance and reliance on traditional family roles and structures (Abramovitz, 1988, 1996; Miller, 1990; Mink, 1990, 1998).

The gendered messages of the current state are paradoxical, however, and intersect with race and class. Poor women are now expected to work and to marry; that is, to be dependent on both a boss and husband for economic security. A core component of welfare reform is workfare, which has altered the gendered division of labor for poor women (Orloff, 1998). As welfare rights advocates have discovered, arguing in favor of single poor women receiving "mothering" wages has met with considerable backlash. This is a paradoxical contrast to the Progressive Era. Public sentiment and political will has little sympathy for the "stay at home" mom if she needs state assistance to do this. That option is only open to married women with a husband who earns a sufficient wage. In this way, the state regulates motherhood (Abramovitz, 1988; Mink, 1995, 1998).

The state, through welfare policies and procedures, also regulates the lives of women as workers. Although some progress has been made in ending employment discrimination, women still lack wage equity (Albelda & Tilly, 1997; Blankenship, 1993; Goldberg, 1990; Miller, 1990). Under new workfare programs, women's labor is substantially devalued. Child care and health benefits remain unavailable to many women workers, furthering their dependence on a male wage.

Finally, the state regulates women's lives through its reliance on women as unpaid caregivers to meet societal health and social needs (Hooyman & Gonyea, 1995; Sapiro, 1990). This unpaid caregiving labor occurs in family units that are expected to be self-sufficient. Thus, male wages play an increasingly significant role in family security. This bolsters the male breadwinner/female homemaker family model. Economic and political forces collude to enforce a *family ethic* or *family wage ideology* in which the male gains dominance because of his wage-earning capacity (Abramovitz, 1988; Gerson, 1993; Gordon, 1988).

The labor market makes few allowances for these caregiving demands, and many employers benefit from the economic devaluation of women's labor at home and on the job. Women are economically trapped (Abramovitz, 1996; Gordon, 1988; Sapiro, 1990). Thus, the state and the labor market assume, depend on, and reinforce a family structure that in actuality is only reflected in 12% of American families. Gendered analyses of social policy clearly reveal how women's lives are regulated in ways that limit their options but uphold patriarchal values.

NEXT STEPS: MELDING GENDER, RACE, AND CLASS

Feminist understandings of social policy have illuminated the experiences of women and the ways in which policy theory and practice regulate gender. These are important and needed contributions to larger understandings of state functioning, social rights, and citizenship. Yet, feminist scholarship still has steps to take before a fully gendered analysis is accomplished.

Using feminist insights regarding the breadwinner model and its subordination of women, some researchers have begun to examine the lives of marginalized men, who also do not benefit from the dominant policy structure (Connell, 1995; Edin, 1998; Lerman & Ooms, 1993; Murphy, 1998a, 1998b; Stier & Tienda, 1993). Although popularized accounts of these men often refer to them as "deadbeats," the more comprehensive studies argue that anyone who fails to live up to the designated roles of the breadwinner model will not gain assistance. For men, this comes in the form of public degradation and a lack of targeted services. The current welfare system is constructed in a way that keeps these men marginalized. This research, taken with existing feminist scholarship, suggests a more complex gendered analysis.

Feminist research also continues to grapple with the infusion of race, class, and other social categories into gendered accounts (Amott, 1990; Blankenship, 1993; Boris, 1993; Hill & Tigges, 1995; Hobson, 1993; Orloff, 1998; Quadagno, 1994). Feminist scholarship risks reifying gender, without paying careful attention to other social contexts. Yet, to fully understand gender means that attention must be paid to the ways in which all cultural attributes shape, and are shaped by, one another.

These themes are likely to be prominent in feminist social policy in the future. The core of feminist scholarship, however, is likely to remain focused on revealing the life choices of women and how these choices are enhanced or constrained by social policy. As the devolution of the public sector continues, and conservatives continue to mount policy initiatives designed to limit gender options for men and women, the insights of feminist theory and practice become all the more important.

REFERENCES

Abramovitz, M. (1988). *Regulating the lives of women: Social welfare policy from colonial times to the present.* Boston: South End Press.

Abramovitz, M. (1996). *Under attack, fighting back: Women and welfare in the United States.* New York: Monthly Review Press.

Albelda, R., Colten, M. E., & Cosenza, C. (1997). *In harm's way? Domestic violence, AFDC receipt, and welfare reform in Massachusetts.* Boston: Center for Social Policy Research and the McCormack Institute.

Albelda, R., & Tilly, C. (1996). It's a family affair: Women, poverty, and welfare. In D. Dujon & A. Withorn (Eds.), *For crying out loud: Women's poverty in the United States* (pp. 79-86). Boston: South End Press.

Albelda, R., & Tilly, C. (1997). *Glass ceilings and bottomless pits: Women's work, women's poverty.* Boston: South End Press.

Amott, T. (1990). Black women and AFDC: Making entitlement out of necessity. In L. Gordon (Ed.), *Women, the state, and welfare* (pp. 280-300). Madison: The University of Wisconsin Press.

Arrighi, B. (1997). *America's shame: Women and children in shelter and the degradation of family roles.* Westport, CT: Praeger.

Blankenship, K. (1993). Bringing gender and race in: U.S. employment discrimination policy. *Gender & Society, 7*(2), 204-226.

Boris, E. (1993). The power of motherhood: Black and white activist women redefine the political. In S. Koven & S. Michel (Eds.), *Mothers of a new world: Maternalist politics and the origins of welfare states* (pp. 213-246). New York: Routledge.

Brenner, J., & Laslett, B.(1991). Gender, social reproduction, and women's self-organization: Considering the U.S. welfare state. *Gender & Society, 5*(3), 311-333.

Connell, R. W. (1987). *Gender & power: Society, the person, and sexual politics.* Stanford, CA: Stanford University Press.

Connell, R. W. (1995). *Masculinities.* Los Angeles: University of California Press.

Conover, P., & Gray, V. (1983). *Feminism and the new right: Conflict over the American family.* New York: Praeger.

Dalaker, J., & Naifeh, M. (1998). *Poverty in the United States: 1997* (Current Population Reports P60-201). Washington, DC: Bureau of the Census.

Davis, M., & Kraham, S. (1995, Summer). Protecting women's welfare in the face of violence. *Fordham Urban Law Journal, 22,* 1141-1157.

Delmar, R. (1986). What is feminism? In J. Mitchell & A. Oakley (Eds.), *What is feminism?* (pp. 8-33). Oxford, UK: Basil Blackwell.

DuBois, B. (1983). Passionate scholarship: Notes on values, knowing, and method in feminist social science. In G. Bowles & R. Duelli-Klein (Eds.), *Theories of women's studies* (pp. 105-113). London: Rouledge & Kegan Paul.

Dujon, D., & Withorn, A. (Eds.). (1996). *For crying out loud: Women's poverty in the United States.* Boston: South End Press.

Edin, K. (1998). *"Single" mothers and "absent" fathers: Real-life families, work, and social welfare categories.* Paper presented at the Annual Meeting of American Sociological Association, San Francisco.

Edin, K., & Lein, L. (1997). *Making ends meet: How single mothers survive welfare and low-wage work.* New York: Russell Sage Foundation.

Esping-Anderson, G. (1990). *The three worlds of welfare capitalism.* Princeton, NJ: Princeton University Press.

Esping-Anderson, G., & Korpi, W. (1987). From poor relief to institutional welfare states: The development of Scandinavian social policy. In R. Erikson, E. J. Hanso, S. Ringen, & H. Uusitalo (Eds.), *The Scandinavian model: Welfare states and welfare research* (pp. 39-74). New York: M. E. Sharpe.

Estes, C. (1998). *Crisis, the welfare state, and aging: Capitalism and the post-industrial state.* Paper presented at the Annual Meeting of the American Sociological Association, San Francisco.

Fraser, N. (1989). *Unruly practices: Power, discourse, and gender in contemporary social theory.* Minneapolis: University of Minnesota Press.

Fraser, N., & Gordon, L. (1994). A genealogy of dependency: Tracing a keyword of the U.S. welfare state. *Signs, 19*(2), 309-336.

Gelb, J., & Palley, M. (1996). *Women and public policies: Reassessing gender politics.* Charlottesville: University Press of Virginia.

Gerson, K. (1993). *No man's land: Men's changing commitments to family and work*. New York: Basic Books.

Giddings, P. (1984). *When and where I enter: The impact of black women on race and sex in America*. Toronto: Bantam Books.

Goldberg, G. (1990). The United States: Feminization of poverty amidst plenty. In G. Goldberg & E. Kremen (Eds.), *The feminization of poverty: Only in America?* (pp. 17-58). New York: Greenwood.

Goldberg, G., & Kremen, E. (1990). The feminization of poverty: Discovered in America. In G. Goldberg & E. Kremen (Eds.), *The feminization of poverty: Only in America?* (pp. 1-16). New York: Greenwood.

Gordon, L. (1988). What does welfare regulate? *Social Research, 55*(4), 609-630.

Gordon, L. (1990). The new feminist scholarship on the welfare state. In L. Gordon (Ed.), *Women, the state, and welfare* (pp. 9-35). Madison: The University of Wisconsin Press.

Gordon, L. (1991, September). Black and white visions of welfare: Women's welfare activism, 1890-1945. *Journal of American History, 788,* 559-590.

Gordon, L. (1995). *Pitied but not entitled: Single mothers and the history of welfare*. New York: Free Press.

Harrington, M. (1962). *The other America: Poverty in the United States*. New York: Penguin.

Hill, D., & Tigges, L. (1995). Gendering welfare state theory: A cross-national study of women's public pension quality. *Gender & Society, 9*(1), 99-119.

Hine, D. (1986). Lifting the veil, shattering the silence: Black women's history in slavery and freedom. In D. C. Hine (Ed.), *The state of Afro-American history, past, present, and future* (pp. 223-252). Baton Rouge: Louisiana State University Press.

Hobson, B. (1993). Feminist strategies and gendered discourses in welfare states: Married women's right to work in the United States and Sweden. In S. Koven & S. Michel (Eds.), *Mothers of a new world: Maternalist politics and the origins of welfare states* (pp. 398-422). New York: Routledge.

Hooyman, N., & Gonyea, J. (1995). *Feminist perspectives on family care: Policies for gender justice*. Thousand Oaks, Ca: Sage.

Hyde, C. (1992). The ideational system of social movement agencies: An examination of feminist health centers. In Y. Hasenfeld (Ed.), *Human services as complex organizations* (pp. 121-144). Newbury Park, CA: Sage.

Hyde, C. (1995). Feminist social movement organizations survive the new right. In M. Ferree & P. Martin (Eds.), *Feminist organizations: Harvest of the new women's movement* (pp. 306-322). Philadelphia: Temple University Press.

Josephson, J. (1997). *Gender, families, and state: Child support policy in the United States*. Lanham, MD: Rowman & Littlefield.

Kammerman, S. (1995). Gender role and family structure changes in the advanced industrialized west: Implications for social policy. In K. McFate, R. Lawson, & W. J. Wilson (Eds.), *Poverty, inequality, and the future of social policy* (pp. 231-256). New York: Russell Sage Foundation.

Koven, S., & Michel, S. (1993). Introduction: "Mother worlds." In S. Koven & S. Michel (Eds.), *Mothers of a new world: Maternalist politics and the origins of welfare states* (pp. 1-33). New York: Routledge.

Kunzel, R. (1993). *Fallen women, problem girls: Unmarried mothers and the professionalization of social work, 1890-1945*. New Haven, CT: Yale University Press.

Lerman, R., & Ooms, T. (Eds.). (1993). *Young unwed fathers: Changing roles and emerging policies*. Philadelphia: Temple University Press.

Lewis, J. (1986). Feminism and welfare. In J. Mitchell & A. Oakley (Eds.), *What is feminism?* (pp. 85-100). Oxford, UK: Basil Blackwell.

Marshall, S. (1995). Confrontation and co-optation in antifeminist organizations. In M. Ferree & P. Martin (Eds.), *Feminist organizations: Harvest of the new women's movement* (pp. 323-337). Philadelphia: Temple University Press.

Marshall, T. H. (1950). *Citizenship and social class and other essays*. Cambridge, UK: Cambridge University Press.

Matthews, N. (1995). Feminist clashes with the state: Tactical choices by state-funded rape crisis centers. In M. Ferree & P. Martin (Eds.), *Feminist organizations: Harvest of the new women's movement* (pp. 291-305). Philadelphia: Temple University Press.

Miller, D. (1990). *Women and social welfare: A feminist analysis.* New York: Praeger.

Mink, G. (1990). The lady and the tramp: Gender, race, and the origins of the American welfare state. In L. Gordon (Ed.), *Women, the state, and welfare* (pp. 92-122). Madison: The University of Wisconsin Press.

Mink, G. (1995). *Wages of motherhood: Inequality in the welfare state.* Ithaca, NY: Cornell University Press.

Mink, G. (1998). *Welfare's end.* Ithaca, NY: Cornell University Press.

Mulroy, E. (Ed.). (1988). *Women as single parents: Confronting institutional barriers in the courts, the workplace, and the housing market.* Dover, MA: Auburn House.

Mulroy, E. (1995). *The newly uprooted: Single mothers in urban life.* Westport, CT: Auburn House.

Murphy, E. (1998a). *A hole in the safety net: Low income young men and social welfare.* Paper presented at the Annual Meeting of the American Sociological Association, San Francisco.

Murphy, E. (1998b). *Survival strategies for low-income young men: Implications for policy and practice.* Paper presented at the Annual Meeting of the Council on Social Work Education, Orlando, FL.

Nelson, B. (1990). The origins of the two-channel welfare state: Workmen's compensation and mothers' aid. In L. Gordon (Ed.), *Women, the state, and welfare* (pp. 123-151). Madison: The University of Wisconsin Press.

O'Connor, J. (1973). *The fiscal crisis of the state.* New York: St. Martin's.

Offe, C. (1984). *The contradictions of the welfare state.* Cambridge: MIT Press.

Orloff, A. (1993). Gender and the social rights of citizenship: The comparative analysis of gender relations and welfare states. *American Sociological Review, 58,* 303-328.

Orloff, A. (1996). *Gender and the welfare state* (Working paper 1996/79). Madrid: Centre for Advanced Study in the Social Sciences.

Orloff, A. (1998). *Ending the entitlement of poor mothers, expanding the claims of poor employed parents: Gender, race, class in contemporary U.S. social policy.* Paper presented at the Annual Meeting of the American Sociological Association, San Francisco.

Pateman, C. (1986). Introduction: The theoretical subversiveness of feminism. In C. Pateman & E. Gross (Eds.), *Feminist challenges: Social and political theory* (pp. 1-10). Boston: Northeastern University Press.

Pearce, D. (1978, Winter/Spring). The feminization of poverty: Women, work, and welfare. *Urban & Social Change Review,* pp. 28-36.

Pearce, D. (1990). Welfare is not for women: Why the war on poverty cannot conquer the feminization of poverty. In L. Gordon (Ed.), *Women, the state, and welfare* (pp. 265-279). Madison: The University of Wisconsin Press.

Petchesky, R. (1990). *Abortion and woman's choice: The state, sexuality, and reproductive freedom* (2nd ed.). Boston: Northeastern University Press.

Piven, F., & Cloward, R. (1979). *Poor people's movements: Why they succeed, how they fail.* New York: Vintage.

Piven, F., & Cloward, R. (1993). *Regulating the poor: The functions of public welfare* (2nd ed). New York: Vintage.

Polakow, V. (1993). *Lives on the edge: Single mothers and their children in the other America.* Chicago: University of Chicago Press.

Quadagno, J. (1994). *The color of welfare.* New York: Oxford University Press.

Reinelt, C. (1995). Moving onto the terrain of the state: The battered women's movement and the politics of engagement. In M. Ferree & P. Martin (Eds.), *Feminist organizations: Harvest of the new women's movement* (pp. 84-104). Philadelphia: Temple University Press.

Sainsbury, D. (1996a). *Gender, equality, and welfare states.* New York: Cambridge University Press.

Sainsbury, D. (Ed.). (1996b). *Gendering welfare states.* Thousand Oaks, CA: Sage.

Sainsbury, D. (1996c). Women's and men's social rights: Gendering dimensions of welfare states. In D. Sainsbury (Ed.), *Gendering welfare states* (pp. 150-169). Thousand Oaks, CA: Sage.

Sapiro, V. (1990). The gender basis of American social policy. In L. Gordon (Ed.), *Women, the state, and welfare* (pp. 36-54). Madison: The University of Wisconsin Press.

Sarvasy, W. (1992). Beyond the difference versus equality policy debates: Postsuffrage feminism, citizenship, and the quest for a feminist welfare state. *Signs, 17*(2), 329-360.

Schneider, E. (1990). The dialectic of rights and politics: Perspectives from the women's movement. In L. Gordon (Ed.), *Women, the state, and welfare* (pp. 226-249). Madison: The University of Wisconsin Press.

Sidel, R. (1996). *Keeping women and children last: America's war on the poor.* New York: Penguin.

Sklar, K. (1993). The historical foundations of women's power in the creation of the American welfare state, 1830-1930. In S. Koven & S. Michel (Eds.), *Mothers of a new world: Maternalist politics and the origins of welfare states* (pp. 43-83). New York: Routledge.

Skocpol, T., & Ritler, G. (1995). Gender and the origins of modern social policies in Britain and the United States. In T. Skocpol (Ed.), *Social policy in the United States: Future possibilities in historical perspective* (pp. 72-135). Princeton, NJ: Princeton University Press.

Spalter-Roth, R., & Schreiber, R. (1995). Outsider issues and insider tactics: Strategic tensions in the women's policy network during the 1980s. In M. Ferree & P. Martin (Eds.), *Feminist organizations: Harvest of the new women's movement* (pp. 105-127). Philadelphia: Temple University Press.

Stier, H., & Tienda, M. (1993). Are men marginal to the family? Insights from Chicago's inner city. In J. Hood (Ed.), *Men, work, and family* (pp. 23-44). Newbury Park, CA: Sage.

West, G. (1981). *The national welfare rights movement: The social protest of poor women.* New York: Praeger.

White, D. (1993). The cost of club work, the price of black feminism. In N. Hewitt & S. Lebsock (Eds.), *Visible women: New essays on American activism* (pp. 247-269). Urbana: University of Illinois Press.

CHAPTER TWENTY-NINE

The Social Development Perspective in Social Policy

JAMES MIDGLEY

MICHAEL SHERRADEN

The social development perspective has attracted increasing attention in social policy circles in recent years. Although not widely implemented, it is finding expression in programs such as welfare to work, supported employment for people with disabilities, asset accounts, and community economic development programs. As this approach is being more clearly articulated, it may have wider appeal, challenging those who advocate social expenditure reductions, social service privatization, and even the abolition of all government involvement in social welfare.

The social development perspective has been primarily associated with social policy in the developing countries (an example of early work is United Nations, 1969) and with the efforts of international agencies such as the United Nations, UNICEF, and the International Labor Organization to promote social programs that are compatible with the need for economic development. Although a developmental approach has been adopted in some industrial countries, such as Sweden, much of the literature on the subject has been produced by the international agencies, and much of it remains unfamiliar to Western scholars.

It is only in recent years that social policy writers in the Western industrial nations have been exposed to the social development approach. Some have recognized its potential to transcend outmoded debates about the merits of the institutional and re-sidual models, which have characterized ideological differences between New Deal liberals and conservatives for many years. Some also believe that social development's concern with economic progress provides a useful basis for social policy in a post-industrial economy faced with the challenges of globalization and rapid economic change.

This chapter describes the social development perspective in social policy, paying particular attention to the various strategies that are being used to implement this ap-proach. Its key premises are also discussed. The chapter concludes with a brief discus-sion of some of the issues and controversies arising out of the adoption of this ap-proach.

THE SOCIAL DEVELOPMENT PERSPECTIVE

The social development perspective can best be understood when contrasted with the income support and social service approach that has dominated social policy for most of this century. Social policy has historically been based on the premise that govern-ments should enhance the welfare of their citizens through social services, legal regu-lations, and fiscal measures. However, there have been sharp disagreements about the extent to which government should play this role. Liberals have traditionally favored the institutional model, which advocates extensive state involvement and universal social service provision. On the other hand, conservatives have preferred the residual model, which prescribes a minimal role for government and restricted income sup-ports and social services that are targeted to the needy. Despite these differences, both recognize the need for government involvement. Although some conservatives advo-cate the abolition of all state responsibility for social welfare, most believe that some government intervention will be required. Many conservatives contend that the state should contract with nonprofit and commercial organizations to provide these serv-ices on its behalf.

The conservative approach now exerts a powerful influence on social policy think-ing (Ginsberg, 1998). Conservatives claim that the welfare state, which has character-ized social policy since the New Deal, has fostered massive welfare dependency, cre-ated an intolerable tax burden and hindered economic development. They argue that shifting resources out of the productive economy to unproductive social expenditures has stifled economic growth. In addition, they claim that the transfer of social benefits to large numbers of needy people encourages indolence, dependency, and deviance. These arguments have resonated with the electorate, and, in recent years, support for the conservative position has increased. In the current climate of budgetary retrench-ment, privatization, and neglect, advocates of the institutional approach have been put on the defensive and have been unable to articulate a politically successful rationale for social welfare.

It was suggested earlier that the social development perspective offers an alternative view of social policy that transcends debates about residual and institutional welfare (Midgley, 1996). It transcends these debates by encouraging the adoption of social programs that are primarily concerned not with providing social services but with enhancing the capacities of needy people to participate in the productive economy. Social development proponents believe that participation in the productive economy is the primary means by which most people meet their social needs. They claim that many of those who are currently receiving social benefits can enhance their welfare through economic participation. Although there are some who will always require social supports, they are in the minority. Unlike the traditional social service approach, the social development perspective thus seeks to shift the emphasis from consumption-based and maintenance-oriented services to social programs that contribute directly to economic development. Instead of detracting from economic growth, these programs enhance economic participation and contribute to development. For this reason, the social development approach is also known as the *social investment* or, more technically, as the *productivist* approach to social policy (Midgley, 1999). Work by Gilbert (1983), Esping-Anderson (1990), and others on the integration of social policy and market economies helps to lay the groundwork for thinking about productivist approaches in Western welfare states.

However, it must be stressed that social development does require state involvement and public expenditures. It does not merely urge social welfare clients to become economically productive but insists that adequate investments are made to ensure that these clients have the skills, knowledge, resources, opportunities, incentives, and subsidies to participate effectively in the productive economy. Although social investments are often initiated and facilitated by the state, most social development advocates believe that government action should be combined with individual and community efforts to enhance economic participation. Although some social development writers place more emphasis on the role of the state than others, they recognize that social development is essentially pluralist in its approach (Midgley, 1995).

Social development is concerned not only with transforming the consumption-based social service approach of the traditional welfare system, but also with ensuring that economic development brings tangible benefits to ordinary people. It focuses not only on the recipients of the social services but on economic policies that enhance the welfare of the whole population. Its advocates are critical of economic ideas claiming that the free-market will, of itself, create wealth and prosperity for all. They contend that governments have a key role to play in ensuring that ordinary people have the skills and knowledge to participate effectively in the economy, that employment and self-employment opportunities are maximized, and that the benefits of economic growth are equitably distributed. They also believe that governments should protect the vulnerable from economic exploitation and encourage the payment of wages that support a decent standard of living. Although few social development advocates believe in extensive state regulation of the economy, they urge the creation of a wider economic climate in which the government promotes development strategies that are income maximizing, asset building, inclusive, and equitable (Midgley, 1995; Sherraden, 1991).

Another feature of the social development approach is its emphasis on the integration of economic and social policy. This requires the creation of formal arrangements that will effectively link economic and social policies. In many countries, governmental organizations concerned with social welfare have few ties to those that are engaged in economic development. The social development perspective seeks to end the bifurcation of economic and social policy and to ensure that social policy is not subsidiary to the economy. Instead, it advocates an integrative approach that regards economic and social development as two aspects of the same process.

Unlike the traditional social service approach, social development is not static, relying on the transfer of resources from the productive economy to those in need; instead, it is based on the idea that people's welfare can be enhanced through continued material progress. Social development thus gives formal expression to the belief that progressive social change is both desirable and possible. In keeping with this tradition, social development is essentially optimistic, believing that steady improvements in human welfare are possible through judicious government intervention in combination with individual enterprise and community effort. Social development also stresses the importance of material welfare, which requires that social policy be primarily concerned with fostering improvements in income, wealth, health, housing, and the other elements that compose an acceptable standard of living and the ability to plan and invest for the future. As will be shown, these ideas are controversial. The ability of the proponents of the social development perspective to make them appealing will ultimately determine its viability in the arena of competing ideas about human well-being.

IMPLEMENTING THE SOCIAL DEVELOPMENT PERSPECTIVE

The ideas attending the social development approach find expression in a number of policies, programs, and projects that are productivist, investment-oriented, and committed to enhancing economic participation among those individuals, groups, and communities that have traditionally been served by government social programs. Social development seeks to enhance capacities to participate and function effectively in the productive economy. Social development advocates believe that those who are currently maintained on social benefits would prefer to be productive members of society and enjoy the incomes, investments, career opportunities, and lifestyles that many middle-class people take for granted. The prospect of being maintained in dependence, stigmatized, and demeaned is hardly desirable.

The following are some of the social development strategies that have been adopted. Although evidence to support their viability is being collected, more research is needed to refine these approaches and ensure that their implementation will, in fact, promote economic participation and enhance the well-being of those who have traditionally been served by the welfare system. Although the following strategies are enumerated separately, they can be combined to promote social development goals. They can also be combined with traditional social services approaches so that clients can simultaneously be provided with social service supports while becoming economically active.

Human Development and Human Capital Investments

Human development refers to increasing the capacities and functioning of individuals, an activity likely to have multiple positive outcomes (Sen, 1985). Attention to human development as a central theme can be credited in part to Mahbub ul Haq (1995), who pioneered the human development reports of the United Nations. According to the 1990 Human Development Report:

> Human development is a process of enlarging people's choices. The most critical of these wide-ranging choices are to live a long and healthy life, to be educated, and to have access to resources needed for a decent standard of living. . . . The process of development should at least create a conducive environment for people, individually and collectively, to develop their full potential and to have a reasonable chance of leading productive and creative lives in accord with their needs and interests. (United Nations Development Program, 1990, p. 1)

Key human development factors are represented by the basic needs of nutrition, primary health care, literacy, and basic housing (Streeten, with Burki, Haq, Hicks, & Stewart, 1981). There is considerable empirical evidence that investments in nutrition, primary health care, education, and basic housing yield positive social returns in increased participation, connectedness, and social stability, with positive economic returns in increased productivity, higher economic growth, and reduced income and asset inequality (Beverly & Sherraden, 1997).

Human capital refers to the store of knowledge and skills that individuals possess, although this term can also include other individual characteristics such as health, creativity, energy, and so on. Human capital is most often measured by level of education and skill training. A solid body of evidence indicates that human capital investments yield high returns in economic performance (Becker, 1993). Indeed, estimates of human capital as a proportion of the total wealth of modern economies range to 75% and higher. In other words, most of the value in modern economies resides inside of people, rather than in land, buildings, machines, and other forms of tangible assets. Moreover, the importance of human capital increases with technological development. In addition, there is evidence that human capital investments enhance human development in improved nutrition and health. Given its overwhelming role in development of individuals, families, communities, and societies, investments in human capital should be in the forefront of social policy and should be a focus of social work and other applied social professions. This idea was suggested several decades ago by Schultz (1959).

Investments That Promote Employment and Self-Employment

Employment policy has been a central feature of the welfare states of Western Europe during the last half of the 20th century. In these nations, labor markets have been regulated to protect the incomes and job security of workers. The United States, in contrast, has not embraced strong labor market policies; employment-related policies make up no more than 2% of total federal spending, and regulation of incomes and job security is almost nonexistent. An important exception is the federal minimum wage law. With globalization of the world economy and with economic integration of the European Community at the end of the 20th century, the dynamism of European economies has been hampered by national labor protections and, in general, these policies are becoming weaker. The likely trend in most nations will be toward labor markets with only limited regulation by public policy. This will very likely promote employment but at high costs to workers, who will bear the brunt of global wage competition and economic dislocations. Moreover, there are disturbing trends in the United States of increasing wage inequality over the past two decades, which may be due in part to higher skill demands in the Information Age economy and lack of educational preparation on the part of many workers (Levy, 1999).

In this environment, there has been increasing emphasis on self-employment, often called microenterprise, as an economic strategy for disadvantaged workers and communities. Community economic development specialists in the United States and other economically advanced nations have looked to international examples, most notably the Grameen Bank of Bangladesh, as models for adaptation. Some aspects of these models have been oversold, especially the extreme emphasis on credit and peer lending. Many people in this movement refer to their work as *microcredit,* implying that loans are all that is needed for self-employment, which is unfortunately misleading. Also, peer lending has by and large not been successful in the United States. Nonetheless, there is an important role for microenterprise in development strategies for the small proportion of social welfare clients and poor people who are interested in pursuing this option. Although income effects are typically modest, entrepreneurs report very positive impacts regarding satisfaction with the business, sense of control over their life, learning, ability to take care of their families, and other social development factors (Sherraden, Sanders, & Sherraden, 1998).

Social Capital Investments

Programs that promote social capital formation are suited to the needs of deprived low-income communities that are often the location of crime, poverty, deprivation, and neglect. Investments in social capital are intended to strengthen social networks, foster civic engagement, and promote community solidarity not only because these are desirable goals in their own right but because they have positive implications for economic development. Research indicates that enhanced community integration can promote local economic development. In an important book, Robert Putnam and his coworkers (Putnam, with Leonardi & Nanetti, 1993) found that regions in Italy with well-developed civic traditions have higher rates of economic development than those regions where social integration is low. Their research suggests that social programs that promote civic engagement contribute positively to economic development.

Social programs directed at poor communities have tended to focus on providing and coordinating social services or mobilizing local residents for political purposes. Community organization, as this approach is known, has been infused with the notion of empowerment. Empowerment facilitates local political activism designed to secure resources to improve local conditions. Although community organization has not totally ignored the need for local economic development, the field has been dominated by the empowerment and social service approaches.

In more recent years, more attention has focused on the need for community economic development (Sherraden & Ninacs, 1998). Local enterprises, credit opportunities, employment generation, and asset building have been emphasized to a greater extent than before. In this context, community organizers are being urged to focus on projects that have direct relevance to economic development. This involves both the creation of social capital and the direction of social capital toward productive activities (Midgley & Livermore, 1998). Community workers should collaborate closely with planners and local economic development specialists to create new enterprises (particularly among women and low-income clients), encourage communities to support local enterprises, assist in the creation of local community development agencies, help to create networks for employment referral, and attract external investment for local economic development.

Investments in Individual and Community Assets

In the policies of modern states, *welfare* or well-being has been defined primarily in terms of income. Income is assumed to represent consumption (although the empirical relationship is not always strong), and consumption equals welfare, by definition in welfare economics. On this narrow intellectual base, the welfare state was constructed in the 20th century, and for many decades, the assumption that consumption equals well-being went largely unchallenged. However, in the 1990s, questions have arisen about whether income-and-consumption by itself is a sufficient policy definition for well-being. Sherraden (1991) has pointed out that income approaches are designed for maintenance rather than development. He has suggested that impoverished individuals and communities should build financial and tangible assets if they are to make investments in education, home ownership, businesses, and other strategies that will enable them to develop economically.

As an instrument for asset-based policy, Sherraden has proposed individual development accounts (IDAs), which are matched savings accounts for the poor. The rationale behind IDAs is that saving is due in large part to structures and incentives rather than personal preferences (Beverly & Sherraden, in press) and that assets have multiple positive effects in addition to deferred consumption. These effects may include stronger orientation toward the future, greater effort to enhance the value of assets, stronger social connectedness and community involvement, and improved well-being of offspring (Sherraden, 1991). Overall, research indicates that assets do have many such positive effects (Boshara, Scanlon, & Page-Adams, 1998; Page-Adams & Sherraden, 1997).

IDAs have a growing presence in public policy and community development. IDAs were included as a state option in the 1996 welfare reform law in the United States, and 25 or more states have included IDAs in their state plans. In addition, almost all states have now raised asset limits in welfare policies, allowing the welfare poor to accumulate somewhat more assets without losing eligibility for the program. In 1998, the Assets for Independence Act was passed, creating $125 million in federal funding for IDAs over 5 years. In addition to federal resources, funding for IDA projects is coming from foundations, corporations, and state and local governments. This eclectic mix of private and public partnerships may signal a new form of social development policy, in which government and private sector combine efforts in creative, almost entrepreneurial fashion, responding to particular issues.

Investments That Remove Barriers to Economic Participation

If the participation of social welfare clients in the productive economy is to be enhanced, steps must be taken to remove the barriers that impede economic participation. Those who currently receive social benefits face serious barriers to economic participation. However, the removal of these barriers presents a formidable challenge. It is a matter not only of providing clients with the knowledge and skills they need to be employable, or of assisting them to find employment, but of overcoming obstacles that impede economic participation. It is now widely recognized that those on income support face serious difficulties in securing transportation to work, access to affordable day care, and other resources that are available to many middle-class people. The barriers facing those with physical and mental disabilities who seek to become economically active are even more formidable and, as is widely recognized, many will require supports if they are to participate effectively in the productive economy. Barriers to asset accumulation, which have long characterized means-tested social welfare programs, are also a major impediment to the development of households and communities. Such asset limits should be liberalized and, where possible, eliminated altogether.

It is equally important that entrenched, institutionalized obstacles to economic participation be addressed. These include the problems of prejudice and discrimination based on race and ethnicity, gender, nationality, disability, age, and other factors that impede people's careers and life chances. Unless these challenges are met, the effectiveness of skills development, job placement and employment programs, and asset building will continue to be impeded.

Compared with many other countries, the United States has made much progress in addressing these concerns. Well-defined anti-discriminatory and affirmative action programs have been adopted, and, in certain fields, such as employment for people with disabilities and racial discrimination in mortgage lending, the achievements have been considerable. The Americans With Disabilities Act is widely regarded as a major step toward removing the barriers that limit economic participation among people with disabilities. The Community Reinvestment Act has broadened opportunities for home ownership. Nevertheless, much more needs to be done to ensure that those who seek to be economically active attain this goal. The rise of anti-affirmative action sentiment, and the popular notion that welfare clients are given unfair advantage through education, job training, and other investments that are not available to all, are disturbing. If these attitudes become entrenched, many of those who strive to function in the productive economy will face increasing hardship.

Investments in Cost-Effective Programs

The social development approach also requires that social programs be carefully evaluated to determine their cost effectiveness. The social services have often been accused of being wasteful, inefficient, and excessively bureaucratic. Critics have claimed that these programs are seldom subjected to careful, independent scrutiny. Indeed, it is often argued that they are perpetuated for political and other extraneous reasons.

They may favor a particular constituency of clients, who have a vested interest in their perpetuation. Politicians and bureaucrats may for similar reasons connive to maintain these programs irrespective of their effectiveness. The result is that resources are transferred out of the productive economy to maintain wasteful social services that harm economic development.

Although these claims are often exaggerated, efficiency is not always given as much priority as it deserves, and programs are not always rigorously evaluated to determine whether they do, in fact, meet their stated goals. Although sophisticated techniques of program evaluation are now available, they are not always properly implemented to determine the effectiveness of programs, and sometimes, their findings are disregarded. This is often the case when political considerations play a major role in the development of particular programs.

Efficiency is a major consideration in social development. Because social development is primarily concerned with investments, it is obviously desirable to assess the effectiveness of these investments. Greater use should be made of technologies that calculate social investment returns. The future success of the social development model will, to a large extent, depend on whether it can be demonstrated that social investments do in fact bring positive returns of this kind.

CONTROVERSIES IN SOCIAL DEVELOPMENT

Despite growing interest in the social development perspective, it has not been widely adopted or even accepted in social policy circles. Many aspects of the social development approach remain controversial, and different views about its usefulness have been expressed. Indeed, advocates of the social development approach have been criticized on several grounds.

For example, the political implications of their ideas have been challenged. Some critics have claimed that social development is little more than an expedient effort to secure electoral support for social programs without addressing the fundamental challenges of poverty and inequality in society. Whereas these critics come from the political Left, others from the Right claim that social development is a back-door attempt to perpetuate government involvement in social welfare at a time when voters have rejected the failed welfare statism of the past. Still others are concerned that the social development approach will be exploited by those who advocate social service retrenchments and will result in little more than exhortations to the needy to find work and become self-sufficient. These critics are concerned that the emphasis on economic participation will overlook the real hardships that many welfare recipients face in securing employment, resulting in further deprivation and neglect.

Another controversy deals with some of the philosophical ideas attending the social development approach. For example, the emphasis placed on progress and particularly material progress by social development writers has been challenged by those who claim that a continued emphasis on economic development will result in greater environmental damage, more mindless consumerism, and a weakening of traditional cultural values. Economic development should not, they believe, be confused with progress. Indeed, they argue that economic development has often caused more harm than good. Other writers are skeptical of the very notion of social progress embodied in social development. They accuse social development writers of being naively utopian. Social progress is an illusion at a time when violence, ethnic conflict, inequality, and racism characterize the human condition. Until these fundamental issues are addressed, talk of social progress through social development is unrealistic. A similar argument is made by post-modernist writers, who contend that social transformation is no longer possible in an increasingly fragmented world characterized by individualism, localism, and ethnocentrism. The prescriptions for large-scale planning contained in social development thinking are simply unworkable in the postmodern era, they say.

Although other criticisms of social development have also been made, those listed above are perhaps the most challenging to those who believe that social development is a viable, innovative perspective in social policy. Despite evidence showing that the social development approach offers promising directions for the future, these and other criticisms will have to be addressed if social development is to be adopted as a viable alternative to conventional social welfare policy.

REFERENCES

Becker, G. (1993). *Human capital: A theoretical and empirical analysis, with special reference to education* (3rd ed.). Chicago: University of Chicago Press.

Beverly, S., & Sherraden, M. (1997). Human investment as a social development strategy. *Social Development Issues, 19*(1), 1-18.

Beverly, S., & Sherraden, M. (in press). Institutional determinants of savings: Implications for low-income households. *Journal of Socio-Economics.*

Boshara, R., Scanlon, E., & Page-Adams, D. (1998). *Building assets.* Washington, DC: Corporation for Enterprise Development.

Esping-Anderson, G. (1990). *The three worlds of welfare capitalism.* Princeton, NJ: Princeton University Press.

Gilbert, N. (1983). *Capitalism and the welfare state.* New Haven, CT: Yale University Press.

Ginsberg, L. (1998). *Conservative social welfare policy: A description and analysis.* Chicago: Nelson Hall.

Haq, M. U. (1995). *Reflections on human development.* New York: Oxford University Press.

Levy, F. (1999). *The new dollars and dreams: American incomes and economic change.* New York: Russell Sage Foundation.

Midgley. J. (1995). *Social development: The developmental perspective in social welfare.* Thousand Oaks, CA: Sage.

Midgley, J. (1996). Toward a developmental model of social policy: Relevance of the Third World experience. *Journal of Sociology and Social Welfare, 23*(1), 59-74.

Midgley, J. (1999). Growth, redistribution and welfare: Toward social investment. *Social Service Review, 77*(1), 3-21.

Midgley, J., & Livermore, M. (1998). Social capital and local economic development: Implications for community social work practice. *Journal of Community Practice, 5*(1/2), 29-40.

Page-Adams, D., & Sherraden, M. (1997). Asset building as a community revitalization strategy. *Social Work, 42*(5), 423-434.

Putnam, R. D., with Leonardi, R., & Nanetti, R. Y. (1993). *Making democracy work: Civic traditions in modern Italy.* Princeton, NJ: Princeton University Press.

Schultz, T. W. (1959). Investment in man: An economist's view. *Social Service Review, 33,* 109-117.

Sen, A. (1985). *Commodities and capabilities.* New York: Elsevier.

Sherraden, M. (1991). *Assets and the poor: A new American welfare policy.* Armonk, NY: M. E. Sharpe.

Sherraden, M. S., & Ninacs, W. (Eds.). (1998). *Community economic development and social work.* New York: Haworth.

Sherraden, M. S., Sanders, C., & Sherraden, M. (1998). *Through the eyes of the entrepreneurs: Microenterprise as an antipoverty strategy, research report.* St. Louis, MO: Washington University, Center for Social Development.

Streeten, P., with Burki, S. J., Haq, M. U., Hicks, N., & Stewart, F. (1981). *First things first: Meeting basic human needs in developing countries.* New York: Oxford University Press.

United Nations. (1969). *The role of social factors in development, expert group meeting on social policy and planning* (Background paper no. 2). Stockholm: Author.

United Nations Development Program (1990). *Human development report 1990.* New York: Oxford University Press.

CHAPTER THIRTY

Race, Politics, and Social Policy

LORI PARHAM

JILL QUADAGNO

Political theorists who attempt to trace the grand panorama of American politics have often failed to recognize the way racial inequality has reshaped America's social, economic, and political institutions (Burham, 1970; Morone, 1990; Phillips, 1990). Yet, a central component of American political development has been conflict over racial equality. The racial dynamics of American society are embedded in the historical development of its social policies, and all social policies organize and enforce the racial politics of everyday life (Omi & Winant, 1994). This chapter examines current policy trends in the context of the continuing political struggle to reshape social institutions that have been organized around racial conflict.

In recent decades, there has been an increase in politically conservative ideologies. Race, along with arguments over individual versus universal rights, has been fundamental to this expansion. The result has been what Edsall and Edsall (1990) describe as a "polarization of the electorate built on mutually reinforcing divisions of the electorate and of policies protecting or advancing the interests of specific groups; and finally whites against blacks" (p. 254). We argue that race has become an ambiguous moral force in contemporary American politics, which influences the strategies and tactics of politics and also the way individuals define the function and responsibility of government.

THE LEGACY OF THE NEW DEAL

Racial inequality became embedded in major American social programs during the New Deal. At the core of the New Deal was the Social Security Act of 1935, which created two programs of social insurance, Old Age Insurance and unemployment insurance, and two means-tested programs for the poor, Old Age Assistance and Aid to Dependent Children. Because the legislation could not win a majority vote in Congress without the support of southern Democrats, a compromise was reached. Southerners would support the Social Security Act as long as labor arrangements in the South were left undisturbed. The compromise meant that agricultural and domestic work, jobs held by three fifths of all black workers, were excluded from the social insurance programs. Instead, they were relegated to the means-tested welfare programs where local welfare authorities could determine benefit levels and set eligibility rules (Quadagno, 1994). Because of local discretion, black women and children were largely excluded from Aid to Dependent Children, especially in the South (Amott, 1993).

Other New Deal programs also reproduced racial inequality in their rules and structure. The National Labor Relations Act, or Wagner Act of 1935, granted workers the right to organize unions and bargain collectively (Domhoff, 1990). It also permitted labor organizations to exclude African Americans and to establish separate, racially segregated unions. From 1936 to 1955, when the AFL merged with the CIO, the skilled trade unions maintained policies of racial exclusion and segregation with the tacit approval of the federal government (King, 1995).

The New Deal also preserved and reinforced patterns of racial segregation through housing policy. The Federal Housing Authority encouraged redlining: A red line was literally drawn around areas of cities considered too risky for loans for economic *or* racial reasons. Not surprisingly, most redlined areas were largely minority neighborhoods. Until 1949, the Authority also encouraged the use of restrictive covenants that banned African Americans from given neighborhoods, and it refused to insure mortgages in integrated neighborhoods. Finally, public housing also extended racial segregation, as authorities located new projects in racially segregated neighborhoods and intentionally selected tenants by race (Quadagno, 1994).

Although the New Deal provided income security against job loss, injury, and old age to white working men and their families, it also reproduced the racial divisions that were embedded in the political and social institutions of the nation.

THE LEGACY OF THE GREAT SOCIETY

Following World War II, thousands of African Americans migrated from the rural South to urban areas, particularly in the Northeast and Midwest. In 1940, 77% of African Americans lived in the South; by 1970, only 53% did. The presence of black migrants in northern cities moved the American dilemma from the periphery to the center of national politics and created the preconditions for the black struggle for civil rights in the 1950s and 1960s. Arriving in America's industrial cities after earlier waves of ethnic immigrants, the black migrants found their opportunities for employment limited to unskilled industrial jobs with little room for upward mobility. This created high levels of unemployment or marginal employment for blacks, which, in turn, forced many to look for support in welfare programs, especially Aid to Families With Dependent Children, to survive economically (Skocpol, 1998).

As the Civil Rights Movement swept across the nation, it demanded the dismantling of segregated institutions in the South; the creation of opportunities for employment, education, and housing; and the expansion of social benefits to address the specific needs of the black population (Skocpol, 1998). Instead of adding a new tier of social protection, however, President Lyndon Johnson embarked on a War on Poverty. Johnson began preparing his anti-poverty programs just months after the 1963 March on Washington, where African Americans proclaimed the need for freedom (the vote) and jobs. The Economic Opportunity Act of 1964 provided federal funds for job training, community improvement, education, and health. As resources poured into local communities, they became absorbed into the struggle for racial equality, creating a backlash by whites against the welfare state.

Community Action

The core anti-poverty program was community action, which was under the jurisdiction of the new Office of Economic Opportunity. The Office, in turn, delegated responsibility to community action agencies. These agencies established neighborhood health centers, emergency food and medical services, job and literacy training, alcoholic counseling, drug rehabilitation, and migrant workers' assistance. Community action also fed resources into local civil rights organizations, which used these resources to pursue the struggle for political equality.

In Mississippi, for example, federal funds were used to circumvent local politicians, local educational institutions, and local welfare authorities. One program, Operation Star, established 18 centers—primarily in remote rural areas—to train the poor in literacy, arithmetic, and social skills. Star also integrated its programs. Statewide, 13% of Star trainees were white, whereas 55% of the staff was black. Community action thus undermined the patronage-based system of party politics, empowered racially integrated community organizations, and created new distributive networks. It also introduced a profusion of resources into the ghettos and established a network of affiliated agencies that became the first patronage source of jobs open to black Americans.

Community action provided opportunities for black men and women to enter politics. When Johnson declared the War on Poverty, there were no black mayors and only 70 elected black officials at any level of government. Five years later, there were 1,500 elected black officials; by 1981, 5,014 blacks held elective office, including 170 mayors. Many of the new leaders gained their experience and visibility from community action programs, where they campaigned for the poverty boards, chaired meetings, lobbied, litigated, and delivered speeches (Morone, 1990).

Although community action programs proved positive for African Americans fighting for political equality, they met with disapproval from many local residents. After a riot in 1967 that was linked indirectly to the local community action agency in Newark, New Jersey, the Office of Economic Opportunity shut down that program. Public antagonism and local resentment extended beyond Newark, however, and the Office was rapidly taken apart as its core programs went to other agencies. Then, in 1973, President Nixon unceremoniously abolished the agency, wiping the inner cities off the legislative agenda for the next 20 years.

Job Training and the Origins of Affirmative Action

Since the New Deal, the federal government had tacitly allowed the skilled trades unions to exclude African Americans. A shift in federal policy began after a riot erupted in Watts, a poor black neighborhood in Los Angeles, highlighting the need to increase employment opportunities in urban ghettos.

Immediately after the riot, existing job training programs were expanded, and new programs were added. Because trainees were recruited from urban ghettos, by 1968, African Americans constituted 47% of the Neighborhood Youth Corps, 81% of the Concentrated Employment Programs, and 59% of the Job Corps. As poor black men and women moved out of federal job training programs and into the labor market, their inability to obtain employment made visible the barriers to equal opportunity erected by the unions. Racial targeting of job training programs put the federal government on a collision course with the skilled trade unions as job training programs became involved in the pursuit of civil rights (Quadagno, 1994).

Title VII of the Civil Rights Act of 1964 banned discrimination in employment on the basis of race and prohibited discrimination in the admission of members (Omi & Winant, 1994). Then, in 1968, the U.S. Department of Labor ruled that contractors could not receive federal contracts unless they took "affirmative action." Taking affirmative action meant proving that minorities would be represented in all trades on the job and in all phases of the work.

Under the new regulations, the Equal Employment Opportunity Commission could now require all unions to report on whether they were complying with affirmative action and then decide if the union was discriminating. If it was, the Commission could turn the case over to the Attorney General to bring a civil suit against the offenders. In practice, the right to sue had little significance, because few people with employment grievances could afford a lawsuit, and such grievances were difficult to prove (Quadagno, 1994).

In the long run, the conflict over union discrimination triggered a backlash by white laborers against the Democratic Party. Their resentment was translated into political support for independent candidate George Wallace in the 1968 presidential election. The backlash undermined the party's power base and created a constituency of Reagan Democrats in the 1980s.

Housing Policy

From the New Deal to the 1960s, federal housing policy encouraged private home ownership on a racially discriminatory basis. Not until 1968, following a week of rioting across the nation, did Congress passed a fair housing bill. Title VIII of the Civil Rights Act of 1968 banned discrimination in the sale, rental, or financing of most housing units and brought millions of single-family homes owned by private individuals under federal fair housing law. The Act charged the Secretary of Housing and Urban Development (HUD) not merely with dealing with specific cases of housing discrimination but also with creating a broad range of affirmative action activities. The Act also mandated that the Department use its own programs to achieve open occupancy and to reorient programs that had previously been used to improve housing for whites while only providing limited housing for African Americans in inner cities.

Initially, HUD attempted to use its authority to pressure suburban communities to integrate by withholding federal funds. The response of the suburbs to this "open communities" policy was widespread opposition, and Nixon backed away from enforcement. In the inner cities, subsidized housing remained racially segregated, and during the 1970s, the supply of federally subsidized housing declined, as federal funds for these programs were slashed (Slessarev, 1988).

Welfare for Poor Mothers

No program better exemplifies the racially divisive character of social welfare programs in the United States than Aid to Families with Dependent Children (AFDC), which evolved out of Aid to Dependent Children. During the 1960s, African American women entered the program in record numbers, in part due to rising need in inner cities but also because of assistance provided by legal advocates funded by Great Society programs (Amott, 1993). By 1974, 45% of all AFDC recipients were black, reversing the historical pattern of excluding African American women and children.

As state budgets rose in concert with the expanding welfare rolls, reducing spending became a major political issue. The result was a plan to replace AFDC with a guaranteed annual income for all the working and nonworking poor. Proposed during the administration of Richard Nixon, the Family Assistance Plan would have provided a basic income to all families on welfare and would also have allowed low-income workers to receive some benefits, with the amount of the benefit declining as earnings rose (Quadagno, 1994).

The Family Assistance Plan was passed in the House and initially had strong support in the Senate. Yet, the bill was never reported out of the Senate Finance Committee, and 2 years later, a substantially altered bill was defeated. Southern congressmen opposed the plan because they feared a guaranteed income would reduce the supply of low-wage labor in the South. Welfare beneficiaries in northern states also opposed the plan because their current benefits were higher than what the Family Assistance Plan would have provided. Ironically, after the bill's defeat, most states embarked on substantial cuts in welfare benefits and removed many people from the rolls.

In retrospect, the War on Poverty was a key turning point in social provision in the United States. The community action programs that might have provided a precedent for extensive intervention in the inner cities, and prevented the spiral of decline so painfully visible to observers on all sides of the political spectrum, became instead embroiled in the task of extending political rights to African Americans. As a result, the nation turned its back on the cities. The job training programs that might have initiated a commitment to full employment and established a partnership between the federal government and the trade unions instead became the source of internecine warfare within the trade union movement. The funds for housing that briefly poured into the inner cities might have improved the quality and expanded the quantity of the nation's housing supply. However, the racial backlash that ensued when integration became linked to housing undermined public support for a national housing agenda. Since Nixon's presidency, federal housing production has not come close to the early 1970s levels, and no President since then has advocated suburban housing integration (Orfield, 1988).

THE RISE OF THE NEW RIGHT

The implementation of social policies in the 1960s redefined liberalism, with racial equality as the central priority. Equal opportunity for civil rights through government intervention was the promise of this new racial liberalism. In response, a New Right conservativism emerged during the 1970s that played on the vulnerability of the targeted policies of the 1960s. The New Right replaced straightforward race appeals with negative racial symbols and code words to create a "new politics of race" (Williams, 1998, p. 422). These code words helped mobilize conservative opinion and provided the justification for repealing redistributive social programs. When, in 1980, the Republican Party took a conservative civil rights stance, Republicans made gains at every level of electoral competition, from state legislative seats to the White House. Racial conservatism had once again become a political asset. Under the presidency of Ronald Reagan, the policies and programs that were created in the 1960s, those whose primary beneficiaries were African Americans, Latinos, and the working poor, experienced the deepest cutbacks (Williams, 1998). Targets of the New Right agenda include affirmative action, welfare, and housing programs.

The Dismantling of Affirmative Action

Affirmative action remains one of the most polarizing of civil rights issues. A strong majority of African Americans favor preferences to correct for past discrimination, whereas the overwhelming majority of whites oppose such programs. In fact, polls show that white respondents believe they are at greater risk of discrimination at work than African Americans are, by a margin of two to one (Steeh & Krysan, 1996, p. 140).

During the Carter presidency, opponents of affirmative action fought to undermine affirmative action policy. One important court decision, *Regents of the University of California vs. Bakke* (1978), helped to change the parameters of affirmative action policy. In 1978, the Supreme Court heard the case of Allan Bakke, who challenged the University of California, Davis's medical school policy for setting aside 16 out of 100 openings for "disadvantaged" students. The Supreme Court ruled in favor of Bakke, who was a white man. Another important opinion came from Supreme Court Justice Powell, who found that race could be used as a "plus" determinant in admissions by universities to pursue a diverse student body (Edsall & Edsall, 1992, p. 126).

Under the Reagan administration, opposition to race-based affirmative action became a matter of policy and partisan strategy. Republicans outlined two distinct and contradictory visions of America: a Republican vision of individual ambition and equal opportunity and a Democratic vision of welfare dependence and anti-democratic special preference (Edsall & Edsall, 1992, p. 187). The federal government actively participated, providing resources, leadership, and legitimacy for opponents of affirmative action. One Republican effort focused on white fears of affirmative action and claimed that color-blind, merit-based policies were needed instead. For conservatives, racial inequity no longer existed—past injustices were not to be remedied by government action (Williams, 1998).

The assault on affirmative action affected policies and budgets, as well. Between 1981 and 1983, the budgets of the Equal Employment Opportunity Commission and the Office of Federal Contract Compliance Programs were reduced by 10% and 24%, respectively. Both agencies had been important sources of pressure on the private sector in implementing affirmative action programs in employment (Edsall & Edsall, 1992, p. 187).

By the early 1990s, opponents of affirmative action had obtained a number of high-level government offices, while, to prevent erosion of existing programs, supporters of affirmative action were forced to abandon advocacy of the preferences and set-aside orders that had become so unpopular. When Republicans won control of both houses of Congress in the mid-term elections of 1994, the GOP put the Clinton administration on the defensive in regard to civil rights issues. Clinton's response to the GOP was a White House review of affirmative action. With the help of close advisers, Clinton issued a report on affirmative action in July 1995 that said, "mend it, but don't end it" (Edley, 1996, p. 39). Although Clinton asserted that affirmative action was not at the root of the nation's economic and social problems, he was unclear as to how the mending of affirmative action policies would be accomplished (Edley, 1996).

Several court decisions further undermined affirmative action in employment and education. In 1995, the U.S. Supreme Court limited the scope of affirmative action programs under *Adarand Constructors, Inc. v. Peña*, although the programs were not ruled unconstitutional so long as they were presented as remedies for demonstrated prior discrimination (Parikh, 1997). Then, in 1996, the courts made two decisions that confirmed that supporters of affirmative action could not depend on the courts to uphold policies in the future and would instead be forced to fight more electoral battles. In the first, *Hopwood v. State of Texas* (1996), a white woman, Cheryl Hopwood, who was denied admission to the University of Texas Law School, sued the university. A federal appeals court affirmed Hopwood's suit and barred race preferences in the University of Texas admissions process. In the second, the Supreme Court refused to hear appeals from opponents of California's Proposition 209, an amendment to the state constitution that bars California state and local governments from using race- and gender-based "preferences" in education, contracting, and hiring. The effect was to end most public affirmative action programs, from contracting and set-asides to minority recruitment and tutoring. This refusal by the Court suggests its willingness to relegate such decisions to state discretion. The results of this action can already been seen in the number of states that are working on similar measures.

A number of bills designed to dismantle affirmative action have also been introduced into Congress. Republican Senator Jesse Helms of North Carolina introduced a bill to amend the Civil Rights Act of 1964 to make preferential treatment an unlawful employment practice. In the 105th Congress, however, efforts by the New Right to repeal affirmative action programs all but ceased. Opponents are currently putting more effort into state and local initiatives to repeal or scale back affirmative action programs. The first success came in California. On November 5, 1996, the California Civil Rights Initiative undid three decades of court-led and executive-ordered affirmative action (Parham, 1998). The California case represented the start of a focused and well-financed movement, attacking affirmative action on three fronts: statewide ballot initiatives, lawsuits, and federal legislation. As debates about affirmative action continue, voters remain divided over its meaning, its effectiveness, and its constitutionality.

Racial Concentration in Housing

The fight for fair housing that emerged from the Civil Rights Movement became much more complex as whites fled the central cities, and these areas began to decay. The passage of the Civil Rights Act in 1964 and the Fair Housing Act in 1968 were intended to remedy the inequalities resulting from segregation and discrimination. Many people thought these policies would significantly narrow the socioeconomic gap between blacks and whites. Thirty years later, rigid housing segregation remains firmly entrenched in most American cities (Coulibaly, Green, & James, 1998).

In the past three decades, the demography of cities has changed dramatically. Suburbanization decreased the white population of the cities and intensified the degree of racial concentration. In 1960, the population was evenly divided between cities, suburbs, and rural areas, but by 1990, suburbs contained almost half of the nation's population (Wilson, 1996, p. 184). By 1970, urban areas were characterized by a predominantly black central city surrounded by mostly white suburbs (Massey & Denton, 1993). In 1980, suburbs were 71% white and 23% black in the North, and 65% white and 34% black in the South. Even within the suburbs, racial segregation persisted.

Minority families, whose choice of residence is often constrained by racial segregation and housing discrimination, are overrepresented in central cities, while the proportion of white Americans continues to decrease. To reverse this intense racial concentration, at least 70% of black residents in the 30 metropolitan areas with the largest black populations would need to move to the suburbs.

Racial concentration is accompanied by declining quality of life in urban ghettos. Deteriorating conditions are due in part to declining federal support for basic urban programs since the 1980s. In turn, lessened federal support is linked to the diminishing influence of cities in national politics, a factor that provided the foundation for the New Federalism, the transfer of responsibility for social programs from the federal government to the states. This increased the significance of race in metropolitan areas.

The Reagan administration and the National Association of Realtors worked together to weaken HUD's already limited authority to enforce fair housing policy. When Reagan took office, his cabinet appointees took an aggressive anti-civil rights position, reversing policies that HUD had adopted under the Fair Housing Act. Under

Reagan, the number of cases prosecuted for defying the legislation dropped dramatically. Between 1968 and 1978, an average of 32 cases per year were prosecuted. However, during Reagan's first year in office, not one case was initiated (Massey & Denton, 1993).

During the Reagan era, subsidized housing was also criticized for being too costly and inefficient. The Section 8 Housing Assistance Program was authorized in 1974. It was the largest source of low-income housing in the United States in which the federal government provided housing assistance payments for construction, rehabilitation, and existing homes to eligible low-and moderate-income families. Although 782,000 families were on waiting lists for housing in 1986, with an overall average wait of 1 year, the Reagan administration still proposed cuts (Coulibaly et al., 1998, p. 34). Whereas the Carter administration had requested funding for 260,000 subsidized housing units, Reagan requested funding for only 175,000 and also proposed an increase in the percentage of income paid by public housing tenants from 25% to 30% over 5 years. The cutbacks continued in 1982 when the Reagan administration cut funds for the construction of new subsidized housing units except housing for the elderly and handicapped. As a result of these cuts, federal spending on housing for the poor fell from $26.1 billion in 1981 to $2.8 billion in 1985 (Slessarev, 1988).

Racial discrimination by private lenders has also contributed to the deterioration of inner cities. Congress made an effort to confront the discriminatory practices of the lending industry in the 1970s. The Home Mortgage Disclosure Act of 1975 mandated that banks report which neighborhoods received home improvement and mortgage loans, and the Community Reinvestment Act of 1977 required that banks prove they were providing credit to low-income areas, which had a history of being unable to secure assets. Because these policies lacked direction for implementation and follow-up by the responsible agencies, discrimination continued (Massey & Denton, 1993).

When Democrats regained control of the Senate in 1986, efforts to amend the Fair Housing Act of 1968 were initiated. In 1988, Congress passed amendments to the Fair Housing Act, measures that were supported by the National Association of Realtors and Vice President George Bush. The amendments extended the time required to file a housing discrimination complaint, increased the penalties of those who discriminated, gave HUD Secretaries the authority to investigate discrimination without waiting for private complaints, and expanded the role of the Justice Department in enforcing fair housing (Massey & Denton, 1993).

When Clinton took office in 1992, the picture of America's cities was bleak. The cumulative effects of economic decline, poverty, crime, and fiscal distress, which began in the late 1970s, along with the 1989 to 1992 recession, could not be ignored. However, Democrats could not agree on urban policy proposals. Aware of the opposition that would come from linking the urban poor to the suburban middle class through metropolitan approaches to urban problems, Democrats rejected traditional urban programs. Instead, they sought to promote community and economic development by building on the off-budget and regulatory urban policies initiated in the 1980s. These included creating empowerment zones and community credit financial institutions and strengthening the Community Reinvestment Act (Mollenkopf, 1998). These programs have been relatively unsuccessful, however, "getting bogged down in the local political marshes" (Mollenkopf, 1998, p. 495).

Republicans, on the other hand, believed the urban programs were fundamentally flawed and aimed to reverse or sharply reduce them. After Republicans gained control of the House in the 1994 elections, they threatened to dismantle HUD. In response, HUD Secretary Henry Cisneros proposed changes to the Department that would drastically reduce government regulation of urban programs and federal control over local housing authorities. The changes were not implemented but did receive strong support from Congress (Mollenkopf, 1998).

In September 1996, President Clinton signed legislation that would deny any new Section 8 vouchers. This put nonprofit housing production at risk. Nonprofit community development corporations typically account for most housing construction in poor neighborhoods. Their resources are derived from many sources, public and private, national and local, and they require some tenants to have Section 8 vouchers to guarantee long-term rent, which makes the project equitable (Mollenkopf, 1998).

Currently, plans are under way to privatize public housing and demolish 100,000 public housing units over the next 5 years, without any guarantee of replacement (Gotham, 1998). The result of this new system of federal housing decentralization and privatization has been to decrease inner-city investment by both the private and public sectors and reinforce residential segregation. According to a 1996 report from the Mayor's Task Force on Race Relations, "the low rate of black loans is the result of continuing racial discrimination in the local lending and housing market and reflects a universal abandonment of inner-city communities" (Gotham, 1998, p. 18).

Welfare Reform

In the 1980s, the racial nature of the welfare state was reflected in increasing public opposition to social programs that targeted the poor and in rhetoric that equated the use of AFDC and food stamps with laziness and moral incompetence (Baca Zinn, 1989). Between 1978 and 1983, AFDC spending fell more than 10%, eligibility requirements were tightened, and nominal benefits failed to keep pace with the inflation rate (Burtless, 1994). Attacks on the program increased throughout the decade as New Right critics argued that redistributive programs caused more harm than good by creating a disincentive to work and that most social programs only worsened the conditions of people whose lives they were intended to improve (Joffe, 1998). Using a racially coded discourse, these critics described AFDC as a program that created "pathological dependency" and a "welfare culture;" its beneficiaries became "unwed mothers" and "welfare queens" (Schram, 1995).

Conservatives also linked AFDC and other social programs to negative images of big government and advocated giving states more discretion and authority over programs. The Omnibus Budget Reconciliation Act of 1981 gave states the opportunity to develop programs aimed at mobilizing AFDC mothers to work. Some programs supplemented work, whereas others involved community work experience (Ozawa, 1994). This legislation was followed by the Family Support Act of 1988, which contained reforms designed to increase the potential earnings of welfare recipients. This Act mandated that states provide more employment and training alternatives to adults receiving AFDC and encourage them to look for work. The law also required that states establish a Job Opportunities and Basic Skills Program (Handler & Hasenfeld, 1991).

The Family Support Act was ineffective in achieving its goals for several reasons. One problem was that most AFDC beneficiaries received no economic benefit from working unless they also received health care and subsidized child care (McFate, 1995). Another problem was that the Act had been implemented during an economic downturn. As job growth stagnated in the early 1990s, and state budgets and antipoverty efforts tightened further, enrollment in AFDC increased from 3.8 million families in late 1989 to 4.7 million families by the end of 1992 (Heclo, 1994).

Although the percentage of AFDC beneficiaries who were African American had declined from 45% in 1973 to 36% by 1994, the public still viewed the program as one dominated by blacks. The campaign against welfare beneficiaries created a political climate conducive to abolishing the program. The Personal Responsibility and Work Opportunity Reconciliation Act was passed by Congress and signed into law by President Clinton in August 1996. It marked the beginning of a historic experiment in welfare reform, ending the program's status as a federal entitlement and transforming the welfare system into one that requires work in exchange for time-limited assistance. The legislation includes mandatory work requirements, a performance bonus to reward states for moving welfare recipients into jobs, comprehensive child support enforcement, and support for moving families from welfare to work—including increased funding for child care and guaranteed medical coverage. However, it gives considerable autonomy to the states in how they respond to federal requirements.

The consequences of the legislation are not completely known, partly because information must be collected from the states. However, in the year from August 1996 to September 1997, 2.4 million beneficiaries were removed from the welfare rolls (U.S. Department of Health and Human Services, 1998). The success of welfare reform will depend greatly on whether former welfare recipients are able to find employment above subsistence wages. The first studies show that just over half of those who have left the welfare rolls have found jobs. Those who have found work are mainly employed in the service and retail industries at wages between $5.50 and $7 an hour, higher than minimum wage but not sufficient to raise family income above the poverty level. Child care and transportation continue to pose impediments for many poor mothers, and most families continue to receive some form of public help, most commonly, food stamps, child care, and Medicaid. About one fifth of the families that leave welfare return within several months (National Conference of State Legislators, 1998).

CONCLUSION

Before President Clinton was elected in 1992, it was unclear if the Republican racial agenda would fade or if the policies implemented under Reagan and Bush were part of an agenda that would continue to affect social policy decisions (Schwartz, 1998). Now, it is clear that race continues to be a central factor in policy making. The New Right's racial project denies the significance of race, advocates a "color-blind" racial politics, and opposes government intervention in the private sector (Omi & Winant, 1994). The Clinton administration's response to the New Right agenda has been to "rearticulate the neo-conservative and New Right racial projects of the Reagan-Bush years in a centrist framework of moderate redistribution and cultural universalism" (Omi & Winant, 1994, p. 147). Both strategies subsequently deny the significance of race in influencing social policy decisions. The polarization that has developed between the conservative and democratic agendas hinders our ability to confront the true racial inequality that is undermining the American creed. Failing to recognize the way that racial inequality has reshaped America's social, economic, and political institutions denies an important part of American history.

REFERENCES

Adarand Constructors, Inc., v. Peña, 515 U.S. 200 (1995).

Amott, T. (1993). *Caught in the crisis.* New York: Monthly Review Press.

Baca Zinn, M. (1989). Family, race, and poverty in the eighties. *Signs, 14*(4), 856-875.

Burham, W. D. (1970). *Critical elections and the mainsprings of American politics.* New York: Norton.

Burtless, G. (1994). Public spending on the poor: Historical trends and economic limits. In S. Danziger, G. D. Sandefur, & D. Weinberg (Eds.), *Confronting poverty prescriptions for change.* New York: Russell Sage Foundation.

Cheryl J. Hopwood v. State of Texas, 78 F.3d 932 (5th Cir., 1996).

Coulibaly, M., Green, R. D., & James, D. M. (1998). *Segregation in federally subsidized low-income housing in the United States.* London: Praeger.

Domhoff, G. W. (1990). *The power elite and the state.* New York: Aldine de Gruyter.

Edley, C., Jr. (1996). *Not all black and white: Affirmative action and American values.* New York: Hill & Wang.

Edsall, T. B., & Edsall, M. D. (1990). Race. *Atlantic Monthly, 267*(5), 253-276.

Edsall, T. B., & Edsall, M. D. (1992). *Chain reaction: The impact of race, rights, and taxes on American politics.* New York: Norton.

Gotham, K. F. (1998). Blind faith in the free market: Urban poverty, residential segregation, and federal housing retrenchment, 1970-1995. *Sociological Inquiry, 68*(1), 1-31.

Handler, J., & Hasenfeld, Y. (1991). *The moral construction of poverty: Welfare reform in America.* London: Sage.

Heclo, H. (1994). Poverty politics. In S. Danziger, G. D. Sandefur, & D. Weinberg (Eds.), *Confronting poverty prescriptions for change.* New York: Russell Sage Foundation.

Joffe, C. (1998). Welfare reform and reproductive politics on a collision course: Contradictions in the conservative agenda. In Y. H. Lo Clarence & M. Schwartz (Eds.), (1998). *Social policy and the conservative agenda.* New York: Blackwell.

King, D. (1995). *Actively seeking work?* Chicago: University of Chicago Press.

Massey, D. S., & Denton, N. A. (1993). *American apartheid: Segregation and the making of the underclass.* Cambridge, MA: Harvard University Press.

McFate, K. (1995). Trampolines, safety nets, or free fall? Labor market policies and social assistance in the 1980s. In K. McFate, R. Lawson, & W. J. Wilson (Eds.), *Poverty, inequality, and the future of social policy.* New York: Russell Sage Foundation.

Mollenkopf, J. (1998). Urban policy at the crossroads. In M. Weir (Ed.), *The social divide.* New York: Russell Sage Foundation.

Morone, J. (1990). *The democratic wish.* New York: Basic Books.

National Conference of State Legislatures. (1998, March 24). *Tracking recipients after they leave welfare: Summaries of state follow-up studies.* http://www.ncsl.org/statefed/welfare/followup.htm.

Omi, M., & Winant, H. (1994). *Racial formation in the United States.* New York: Routledge.

Orfield, G. (1988). Race and the liberal agenda: The loss of the integrationist dream, 1965-1974. In M. Weir, A. Orloff, & T. Skocpol (Eds.), *The politics of social policy in the United States.* Princeton, NJ: Princeton University Press.

Ozawa, M. N. (1994). Women, children, and welfare reform. *Affilia, 9*(4), 338-359.

Parham, L. (1998). *Race and the politics of affirmative action.* Paper presented at Annual Meeting of American Sociological Association, San Francisco.

Parikh, S. (1997). *The politics of preference.* Ann Arbor: University of Michigan Press.

Phillips, K. (1990). *The politics of rich and poor.* New York: Random House.

Quadagno, J. (1994). *The color of welfare.* New York: Oxford University Press.

Regents of the University of California v. Bakke, 438 U.S. 265 (1978).

Schram, S. (1995). *Words of welfare: The poverty of social science and the social science of poverty.* Minneapolis: University of Minnesota Press.

Schwartz, M. (1998). Introduction: What went right? Why the Clinton Administration did not alter the conservative trajectory in federal policy. In Y. H. Lo Clarence & M. Schwartz (Eds.), *Social policy and the conservative agenda.* New York: Blackwell.

Skocpol, T. (1998). The limits of the New Deal system and the roots of contemporary welfare dilemmas. In M. Weir, A. Orloff, & T. Skocpol (Eds.), *The politics of social policy in the United States.* Princeton, NJ: Princeton University Press.

Slessarev, H. (1988). Racial tensions and institutional support: Social programs during a period of retrenchment. In M. Weir, A. Orloff, & T. Skocpol (Eds.), *The politics of social policy in the United States* (pp. 342-351). Princeton, NJ: Princeton University Press.

Steeh, C., & Krysan, M. (1996). The polls-trends: Affirmative action and the public, 1970-1995. *Public Opinion Quarterly, 60,* 128-158.

U.S. Department of Health and Human Services, Administration for Children and Families. (1998, August 20). *Program evaluation and policy research.* http://aspe.os.dhhs.gov/96gb/08tanf.txt

Williams, L. F. (1998). Race and the politics of social policy. In M. Weir (Ed.), *The social divide.* New York: Russell Sage Foundation.

Wilson, W. J. (1996). *When work disappears.* New York: Knopf.

CHAPTER THIRTY-ONE

Social Policy and the Physical Environment

MARIE D. HOFF

JOHN G. MCNUTT

This chapter describes how environmental problems affect social welfare and establishes the environmental components of a range of social policy issues. The discussion concludes with proposals for approaches to move beyond industrial social welfare to a social policy model grounded in the principles and practices of sustainable social development.

In this discussion, we argue that traditional models of social welfare, based on models of the economy that do not take into account the key role of the resource base, have outlived their usefulness for guiding social policy making. Despite their significant theoretical and ideological differences, all these models fail to account for the physical environment as the necessary foundation of social well-being (McNutt, 1994). As environmental resources are increasingly depleted and degraded, we need a new paradigm to guide progress toward building caring, functional human societies. Sustainable social development, as the new model for social policy, is characterized by a simultaneous, integrated strategy to pursue environmental protection, economic development, and sociocultural well-being as one set of goals (Daly & Cobb, 1994; Hoff & McNutt, 1994; Olson, 1995).

LOSS AND DEGRADATION OF ENVIRONMENTAL RESOURCES

The most fundamental social problem in any society is lack of ready access to the basic necessities of life: clean air and water; a safe, adequate food supply; secure housing; and energy supplies for cooking and heating—all of which come directly from a sustaining natural environment. Yet, in every country in the world, the sources of life's basic necessities are being depleted or polluted at alarming and possibly irreversible rates.

A toxic mix of various chemicals causes constantly rising levels of air pollution. Most dangerous is the rising rate of carbon emissions—6.25 billion tons in 1996 constitutes a fourfold increase since 1950 (Flavin & Dunn, 1998). In 1995, the Intergovernmental Panel on Climate Change (2,500 scientists sponsored by the United Nations) voiced overwhelming agreement that global warming and climate change due to carbon emissions "poses substantial risks to the natural world and human society" (Flavin & Dunn, 1998, p. 113; Vig & Kraft, 1997, pp. 369-370). The most serious consequence of climate change is the threat to the continued viability of food production.

The National Environmental Protection Agency estimates that it would cost $13 billion *per year* over the next 20 years to clean up and rebuild the nation's infrastructure for delivering safe, adequate water supplies (U.S. House of Representatives, 1997). Clean, safe drinking water is a threatened commodity. As many as 1,000 deaths and 400,000 illnesses per year may be due to unsafe drinking water (Kraft & Vig, 1997). Groundwater, the source of drinking water for about 50% of the nation, is being used up at rates far exceeding the rate of replenishment. Depletion of groundwater and underground aquifers is occurring most rapidly in some of the nation's major food-producing areas, such as California and the high plains (Postel, 1996; Reisner, 1993). Reduced quality of the water supply is due to inadequate treatment of industrial, agricultural, and municipal waste water, whereas reduced supply is attributable to wasteful irrigation methods and increasing industrial and urban demand. Worldwide, poor sanitation and waste treatment procedures leave perhaps 2 billion people without clean water. Pollution and depletion of water supplies are also destroying world fisheries, which are a major source of protein for a billion people in Asia (Weber, 1993). In the United States, two major threatened species in fisheries are Atlantic cod and Pacific salmon (McGinn, 1998).

The United Nations estimates that between 1945 and 1990, soil degradation, due to unsustainable agricultural practices, affected 26% of agricultural land in North America and 74% in Central America (Gardner, 1996). Highways, dams, industrial expansion, and residential sprawl also remove rich agricultural land from production. The Santa Clara Valley of California—once a rich fruit-growing region—is now renamed Silicon Valley, a center for the electronics industry. Grains are the staple of the human diet. Soil loss, along with growing population and slowing growth in crop yields, is contributing to a sharply declining world grain supply. Crop loss in another country, such as China, can drive up the cost of food significantly (Brown, 1995; Gardner, 1996, p. 10).

Renewable resources, such as food and timber, come from interactive dynamic ecological systems. To understand the full magnitude of the impact of environmental losses, it is necessary to appreciate how loss or disequilibrium in one element of the ecosystem affects all others. Most pervasive are the threats from global warming and climate change: coastal lands lost to rising oceans, habitat loss, extinction or migration of species, and, perhaps, major collapses in agricultural productivity. "Mean annual temperatures for three of the past eight years are warmer than any other year since (at least) 1400" (Mann, Bradley, & Hughes, 1998, p. 779).

Depletion of renewable and nonrenewable resources, including species extinction, is one major pole of environmental loss. The other is the massive poisoning of the globe from the thousands of chemicals in use today in every facet of modern life: household and building construction, agriculture, industry (including electronics), transportation, health care, military, recreation, media, and entertainment. Of the thousands of chemical compounds on the market, only a few have been identified and tested for safety by the National Environmental Protection Agency (Rogge, 1994). "The inadequate progress is especially worrisome in light of new evidence that some of those chemicals may disrupt human immune and reproductive systems and cause neurotoxic disorders" (Kraft & Vig, 1997, p. 22).

RELATIONSHIPS BETWEEN SOCIAL POLICY AND ENVIRONMENTAL PROBLEMS

Environmental conditions and social problems and needs have an oscillating, spiralling interaction: Deficiencies, losses, and toxification of the physical environment lead to serious social problems; and social and economic policies and practices lead to serious threats to the viability of the physical environment. Figure 31.1 illustrates the critical role of the resource base in decisions for social welfare. Not only does the resource base provide the critical foundation for the economic system, but it has an independent effect on well-being. The industrial and agricultural sectors of the economy (and even the information sector) are clearly dependent on extractive processes (mining, logging, farming, etc.) for both raw materials and productive energy. The despoliation and depletion of natural resources are critical problems for most of the economic system. In addition, the degradation of the natural environment leads to physical and psychological illnesses, community destruction, and the devastation of

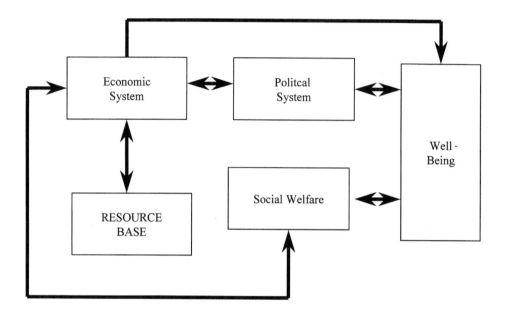

Figure 31.1. Relationship Between Social Welfare and the Resource Base

aesthetic values that also directly affect individual and community welfare (Hoff &
McNutt, 1994; Wachtel, 1989). Social welfare policy is concerned with well-being
(Iatridis, 1994), and environmental conditions have a direct effect on human well-
being, in addition to their role in the economy. Many contemporary models of social
welfare include the environment as part of the economy (Iatridis, 1994; Titmuss,
1974; Wilensky & Lebeaux, 1965). On balance, this view ignores the direct impact of
the environment and fails to acknowledge that prevailing economic theories give little
attention to the role of the environment in the fuctioning of the economy (Daly, 1996;
Daly & Cobb, 1994; Hawken, 1993; Lutz & Lux, 1988).

   The social policy enterprise must begin to explicitly address the integration of social, economic, and environmental goals. This involves restoration and preservation
of the natural environment—development of industrial, agricultural, and consumer
practices that do not damage or deplete the environment beyond sustainable levels. It
also requires measurable improvements in indicators of human welfare and development, such as health, morbidity, and mortality statistics, literacy and educational levels, reduced crime and violence rates, improved housing quality and availability, full
employment and reduction in poverty rates, and increased civic participation and lei-

sure (measures of social capital).[1] Effects of environmental problems on social well-being and social policy measures to address these concerns are addressed in the following paragraphs.

Health Policy

Threats from various toxic chemicals constitute the most observable health effects of environmental practices (Rogge, 1994). Air pollution is considered to be the major environmental contributor to the 40% rise in asthma between 1981 and 1991 in the United States ("Asthma–United States," 1995). Poor children in urban areas are at special risk from respiratory problems related to air quality. Widespread radiation poisoning, which causes thyroid disease, from nuclear bomb tests in the 1950s is now acknowledged to be more pervasive than the government had previously acknowledged (Ortmeyer & Makhijani, 1997). Navajo and white workers continue to suffer numerous forms of cancer from mining radioactive minerals (Dawson, 1994; Dawson, Madsen, & Spykerman, 1997), and numerous communities around the country are concerned about leakage of radioactive materials into their groundwater.

Precise cause-effect relationships between exposure to specific toxic materials and cancer or other health problems are difficult to establish. Various scientific investigations continue to explore the etiology of various diseases and the effects of chemicals on fetal and child development. What is certain is that most forms of cancer are rising (Misch, 1994). Therefore, national health policy—still largely devoted to funding secondary and tertiary medical care—needs to be reoriented toward a public health and education approach to disease prevention, including reduction in the heavy reliance on chemicals for both industrial and household uses.

Poverty and Inequality

Social policy concerns include values of equity and fairness in the distribution of social costs and benefits across classes and groups (Titmuss, 1974). Significant environmental injustices exist within and between nations. Children face special risks of damage from environmental threats. Depletion of resources or extinction of species can be viewed as a form of theft—an ethical violation of the rights of future generations (Garbarino, 1992). Governmental research (General Accounting Office, 1983) and other studies (Bryant & Mohai, 1992; Commission for Racial Justice, 1987; Rogge, 1994) have established that ethnic minority and low-income communities, urban and rural, bear highly disproportionate burdens of environmental threats of all kinds: dangerous industries and waste disposal sites; polluted soil, water, and air; poor housing, with problems such as lead paint poisoning and inefficient, costly energy systems. Globally, environmental injustice takes two major forms: shipment of waste products from wealthier nations to financially strapped poor nations around the globe and the disproportionate consumption of the world's natural resources by the wealthy nations of the world. The United States has 5% of the world's population yet uses 30% of world fossil fuel supplies.

Violence

Environmentally and socially ravaged urban areas are afflicted with extraordinary levels of violence and other symptoms of social dysfunction, such as high rates of suicide, mental hospitalization, and juvenile crime (Wilson, 1996). During the past decade, much broad-based research has been developed to demonstrate the nature of linkages among environmental exploitation, low levels of social spending, impoverishment of people, and high levels of social violence within and between nations (Alvares, 1994; Athanasiou, 1996; George, 1988, 1992; Korten, 1995; Shiva, 1991; Thomas, 1995; Wolpin, 1986).

The rise of paramilitary, white supremacist groups in the western United States is closely associated with economic and social struggles over natural resources, such as fish, minerals, timber, water use, wildlife management, grazing rights, and a host of other local issues (Reisner, 1993; Wilkinson, 1992; Zakin, 1993).[2] Numerous communities are experiencing conflict over issues such as disposal sites for waste, siting of military bombing ranges, and cleanup of past environmental damage from industry and the military. The American tendency toward litigation has prolonged these disputes and has made them extremely costly. Some communities are experimenting with voluntary community-level decision making to resolve environmental disputes (Johnson, 1998), but legislation could help legitimitize and fund these nonlitigious conflict resolution methods.

Agriculture and Food Policy

Federal policies pertaining to food supply (hunger issues), food safety (food-borne disease concerns), and agricultural policy (economic concerns of producers) are regulated by an uncoordinated maze of government agencies. National policy making should begin to develop explicit objectives that integrate and redirect strategies to achieve all three. The majority of federal and state research money and agricultural subsidies goes toward large, primarily corporate producers for agricultural methods that are highly dependent on irrigation and heavy infusions of chemical fertilizers and pesticides. Family farming is in sharp decline over the past two decades, and food safety concerns are increasing among consumers. New integrated approaches would begin with support for organic agriculture and restoration of diversified family farming in the United States. Such a redirection of national agricultural policy would promote a number of goals: soil renewal through increased recycling of organic materials; decreased reliance on imported food and petroleum; decreased health risks to farm workers and consumers from toxic substances; increased employment, as such methods are more labor-intensive; and rural community revitalization through population maintenance. Redirection of national agricultural policy away from dependence on imported food and petroleum products would constitute a new political conception of national security.

Urban gardening is a burgeoning community movement in many cities across the country. It is becoming a favored strategy for youth development and rehabilitation. It provides nutritional benefits from fresh local produce; reduces food costs and pollution by lessening dependence on produce trucked at great expense; encourages entrepreneurship, healthy exercise, and neighborhood socialization; contributes to ecological education; and aids the revitalization of often seriously damaged urban soils. Finally, urban gardening fosters aesthetic values, which support emotional well-being. Some local governments provide support in the form of land, site preparation and maintenance, materials, and gardening instruction. Local and state legislation could provide increased funds for this promising social and environmental trend (Lawrence & Milstein, 1997; Nelson, 1996).

Housing and Community Development Policy

National housing and community development policy ignores environmental considerations. Because housing is primarily viewed as a profit-generating commodity, most planning decisions are made without a commitment to preserve the environment or minimize the use of resources, especially nonrenewables, such as minerals or fossil fuels. Housing development patterns in the United States are profligate in their use of environmental resources: The trend is toward larger houses, which use more land space and require more materials and energy to build and maintain. Urban and rural sprawl is a major contributor to loss of agricultural land in the United States. Public policy places few restrictions on these private preferences. In addition, housing for the poor has been a declining national priority for the past two decades (Moroney & Krysik, 1998).

Redirection of national housing and community development policy toward environmental sustainability would potentially support the goals of decency and affordability for the poor and near-poor. And, like urban gardening, a shift in housing policy would have the potential to contribute to community revitalization. Municipalities and other levels of government need to strengthen housing policy instruments including zoning, planning, and taxation to encourage more density; experimentation with renewable, low-cost building materials;[3] and greater energy efficiency and recycling of household waste. Density reduces transportation costs and increases social contact, whereas energy and materials efficiencies decrease costs. Community design can facilitate environmental goals and the building of social capital, which, in turn, fosters strong communities and economies (Midgley & Livermore, 1998; Putnam, with Leonardi & Nanetti, 1993).

Energy and Transportation Policy

Since the oil embargo of 1973, policy makers and social welfare professionals are more aware of the high costs of heating and transportation, especially for the poor. Nevertheless, U.S. energy policy has continued to increase our dependence on imported oil and has neglected conservation and alternative energy development (Romm, 1991). As global warming and climate change have come to be recognized as serious environmental threats, there is more general awareness of the negative impact of worldwide dependence on fossil fuels, which are the major source of air pollution. Nuclear power, once promised as a low-cost alternative, is coming to be recognized as a costly and dangerous alternative.

National investment in wind and solar energy is very limited, although it is increasing in some parts of the country. Development of public transit lags far behind the marked American preference for private automobiles, which consume enormous quantities of fuel, materials, and land space. Public policy redirection toward development of soft-path energy, efficiency, conservation, and public transit would promote environmental protection goals, while supporting social policy goals of providing low-cost transportation and home heating for working-class and poor population groups.

Waste Disposal

Many U.S. communities are struggling with problems related to the disposal of waste generated by industrial, agricultural, and consumer activities. The issue has numerous facets. Older cities are faced with brownfields—urban areas severely poisoned by industrial waste. Rural areas face severe threats of groundwater pollution from intense concentrations of corporate-produced animals, such as hogs and dairy cows. Numerous rural communities, including Native American communities on reservations, are fighting the siting of solid waste (municipal garbage) disposal facilities in their communities. The nuclear weapons and energy industry has created waste disposal and toxic threats that may persist for literally tens of thousands of years. American consumer habits—the "throw-away" mentality—contribute, as does the excessive packaging of consumer products.

Waste disposal policy has numerous social policy dimensions: social justice issues in the siting of facilities, health and safety threats, and waste disposal battles that divide community members, creating intense conflict and consuming personal energy. Democratic decision making, open government, and fairness in burden- and risk-bearing are some of the social values at stake in the current management of waste disposal (Kauffman, 1994). Public policy redirection of waste disposal should be guided by three goals: reduction of the quantity and toxicity of waste generated by both consumers and producers of agricultural and industrial products, increase in research and experimentation in the reuse (recycling) of materials that are wasted in production processes, and fairness in the siting of necessary waste facilities. Waste disposal policy provides a sharp illustration of how social policy requires both value changes and serious research foundations for success. Wasteful consumer values and habits must be redirected, but research is essential to provide the technological means to reduce waste in the production process.

Population Policy

The world's population is currently 5.8 billion people, and it is estimated to grow to 7.7 billion or more in the next 50 years. The current U.S. population of 267 million is projected to grow to 333 million by the year 2025 (Tobin, 1997, p. 323). Population issues are one of the most complex and controversial components of both environmental and social policy. Poor nations resent the accusation that their population growth is the cause of global environmental depletion, pointing out that the affluent, industrialized nations of the North consume the largest share of natural resources of the Earth (Tobin, 1997). However, substantial international consensus has gradually developed that population stabilization is necessary to save the physical integrity of the planet and improve the quality of life for humanity (Independent Commission on Population and Quality of Life, 1996). At the 1994 U.N. conference on population, held in Cairo, Egypt, national representatives reached substantial agreement that increased education, social, and economic development opportunities for girls and women is the essential policy approach to population control (Independent Commission, 1996; United Nations, 1995).

In the United States, population policy is intertwined with political and religious division over abortion and with concern over the extent of government intrusion into family and personal privacy. It also overlaps with immigration policy, a perennial but growing public policy issue. The United States has the highest teen pregnancy and single parenthood rates in the industrialized world (Bronfenbrenner, McClelland, Wethington, & Ceci, 1996). Religious and cultural values must be acknowledged and respected in family planning policy and services. However, the principle agreed to at the Cairo conference also applies domestically: Social policy must address more specifically the developmental needs of girls and women, particularly teenagers from disadvantaged socioeconomic backgrounds, as essential factors in population stabilization in the United States (Furstenberg & Brooks-Gunn, 1989; Wilson, 1996).

SOCIAL POLICY MEASURES FOR SUSTAINABLE SOCIETIES

In the United States, social welfare policy arose to respond to the most egregrious side effects of modern industrial capitalism, namely, unemployment and income loss for those unable to work for reasons of disability or old age. Social policy measures that promote individual and social development are largely separated from public policy measures that maintain the economic apparatus. Social costs of industrial capitalism, such as sickness and disease resulting from workplace pollution and toxins, have not been adequately accounted for; nor has the need to promote excessive consumerism and new perceptions of needs to maintain the complex system of production and continuous growth.

Neither have environmental costs been factored into the pricing equation. Environmental resources have been, until very recently, largely treated as public goods or "externalities;" that is, not as a properly priced and discounted variable in the computation of the actual cost of a product (Repetto, 1992).

Although it would be impossible to internalize every degree of social and environmental cost of economic production, public policy should begin to move toward that broad goal. Moreover, the environmental and social benefits of new economic methods and patterns of production should be assessed. A number of countries in Europe, as well as Canada and Japan, are developing national accounting systems to measure net progress toward environmental, economic, and social goals (Stead & Stead, 1992). Known as Quality of Life Indicators, or an Index of Sustainable Social Welfare (Daly & Cobb, 1994), such systems identify and subtract environmental losses as costs, in addition to costs associated with social problems such as crime or health problems due to environmental or employment practices.

These types of indicators provide a foundation of information to support the integration of social and environmental policy with economic policy measures: Social and environmental costs would be minimized by efficient firms, and they in turn would competitively drive out firms that deplete or pollute the environment or that cause severe social disruptions and human stress. In summary, social policy should move from a model in which it serves as a handmaid to deal with the unfortunate aftereffects of industrial capitalism to a positive model for environmentally sustainable social policy. Redirected national priorities to support this agenda include the following:

Significantly expanded government funding for research to develop sustainable techniques of production of food, energy, low-impact housing, and transportation. Previously, the term frequently used was *appropriate* technology. A better term to define the goal is *sustainable* technology: methods of material production that neither destroy the renewable capacities of the environmental base nor destroy or diminish the human person and the community (Daly, 1996; Hawken, 1993; Stead & Stead, 1992). Unfortunately, the mood in Congress is to reduce funding for research on new environmental technologies, from $139 million in 1995 to $46 million in 1996 (Vig & Kraft, 1997, p. 383). This was done in spite of studies suggesting that energy transition alone could save the economy $1.8 trillion and generate 1 million jobs by 2010 (Vig & Kraft, 1997).

Integrated urban and rural development policy: planning for techniques to encourage greater urban density while also promoting the economic and social viability of rural areas. Little concerted policy or funding muscle is directed toward promotion of this goal of regional planning (Roberts, 1994). The environmental goals of regional planning are to preserve open space, resource quality (soil, water, and air), and habitat of native biological species, whereas the social goals are to preserve and enhance human community through social networking and improved supports for quality of life. Regional planning also includes international diplomatic challenges, as the United States must cooperate with Canada, to restore and jointly manage the Great Lakes region, and with Mexico to develop social and environmental protections in the burgeoning manufacturing activity along the border.

Redirection of tax policy to penalize and or reward appropriately the use, pollution, depletion, or restoration of environmental resources. The fundamental principle is to stop subsidies for and penalize resource waste or depletion and to shift tax policy toward incentives and rewards for environmental protection on the part of both consumers and producers (Roodman, 1997; Roseland, 1998). Examples include pollution and packaging taxes or tax incentives for use of recycled or more energy-efficient materials. Such changes are often cost-efficient, as well.

Strengthening of regulatory agencies. It is critical that enforcement of environmental safety standards be augmented. Although this is difficult in an era of regulatory reform and devolution, it is a crucial social need (Freeman, 1997).

Strengthened public participation mechanisms for social, economic, and environmental decision making to support and enhance citizenship behavior. Public participation enhances the quality of public decision making. Modern technology such as television and the Internet can be used creatively to structure and increase public participation (Schuler, 1996). Community-based, voluntaristic decision-making structures to solve environmental problems and conflicts may also increase participation. A new term, *civic environmentalism* (John, 1994), describes these types of voluntary efforts, and case examples have been developed to evaluate their effectiveness for strengthening or decreasing democratic representation (Hoff, 1998; John, 1994; Johnson, 1998).

Public policy to enhance community building as an antidote to consumerism. Through increased public policy supports for the arts, amateur athletics, and voluntarism, public policy can enhance individual and social capital (skills and abilities) and provide low-impact recreational outlets as alternatives to environmentally destructive consumerism as a way of life.[4] A growing body of social research suggests that strong communities with engaged, active citizens also are more likely to achieve economic development (Midgley & Livermore, 1998).

U.S. social policy cannot be developed in isolation in an increasingly interdependent world. "Emerging environmental threats on the national and international agenda are even more formidable than the first generation of problems addressed by government in the 1970s" (Kraft & Vig, 1997, p. 26). The United States takes an aggressive role in influencing several key international policy issues in which social and environmental considerations are inextricably interrelated. As discussed earlier, increased support is needed for education and economic supports for girls and women and family planning technology; for development of universal social security systems in every country to diminish reliance on an increasing population to fund old-age insurance; and for increased health services in poor communities to improve child survival rates. Another factor is the reduction of Third World debt. International lending institutions frequently require countries to reduce social and health spending and to sell off natural resources to service their external debts.[5] These harmful policies will require political pressure to reverse. American social policy development should also support movement toward democratization of global economic structures, implementation of international standards for environmental protection, and universal enforcement of human rights standards. Social welfare and the guarantee of a viable physical environment in any one country have become interdependent issues requiring acute redirection in local, national, and international policy making.

NOTES

1. See Putnam et al.'s (1993) study of civic traditions in Italy, which developed historical, empirical evidence that regions and cities with strong civic participation have long been more economically prosperous. Such studies of social capital, or the density of social relationships, are burgeoning in the United States (Midgley & Livermore, 1998). See also Livermore and Midgley's (1998) case study of how

an intervention in one impoverished neighborhood in Baton Rouge, Louisiana, focused on strengthening human and social capital.

2. See the newspaper, *High Country News,* for regular coverage of the interaction between environmental issues and economic survival concerns of communities in the American West.

3. In several parts of the country, such as the city of Tucson, Arizona, small-scale experiments in use of alternative building materials, such as straw bales and cobb, are taking place.

4. See Paul L. Wachtel (1989), *The Poverty of Affluence,* for a book-length treatment of the negative psychological impacts of affluence and consumption-oriented lifestyles.

5. George (1992) analyzes how Third World debt also harms citizens of wealthier nations. Issues include: environmental effects, drugs, taxpayer subsidies for lending banks, lost jobs and markets, immigration, and conflict and war. See also Bruce Rich (1994), *Mortgaging the Earth,* for a comprehensive study of relationships among international lending, environmental depletion, and failed social development.

REFERENCES

Alvares, C. (1994). *Science, development, and violence.* Delhi: Oxford University Press.

Asthma–United States, 1982-1992. (1995). *Morbidity and Mortality Weekly Report, 43*(51 & 52), 952-955.

Athanasiou, T. (1996). *Divided planet: The ecology of rich and poor.* Boston: Little, Brown.

Bronfenbrenner, U., McClelland, P., Wethington, W., & Ceci, S. J. (Eds.). (1996). *The state of Americans: This generation and the next.* New York: Free Press.

Brown, L. R. (1995). *Who will feed China? Wake-up call for a small planet.* New York: Norton.

Bryant, B., & Mohai, P. (1992). *Race and the incidence of environmental hazards.* Boulder, CO: Westview.

Commission for Racial Justice: United Church of Christ. (1987). *Toxic wastes and race in the United States.* New York: Author.

Daly, H. E. (1996). *Beyond growth: The economics of sustainable development.* Boston: Beacon.

Daly, H. E., & Cobb, J. B., Jr. (1994). *For the common good: Redirecting the economy toward community, the environment, and a sustainable future* (2nd ed.). Boston: Beacon.

Dawson, S. E. (1994). Navajo uranium workers and the environment: Technological disaster survival strategies. In M. D. Hoff & J. G. McNutt (Eds.), *The global environmental crisis: Implications for social welfare and social work* (pp. 150-169). Aldershot, UK: Avebury Books.

Dawson, S. E., Madsen, G., & Spykerman, B. R. (1997). Public health issues concerning American Indian and non-Indian uranium millworkers. *Journal of Health and Social Policy, 8*(3), 41-56.

Flavin, C., & Dunn, S. (1998) Responding to the threat of climate change. In L. R. Brown (Ed.), *State of world report 1998* (pp. 113-130). New York: Norton.

Freeman, A. M., III. (1997). Economics, incentives, and environmental regulation. In N. J. Vig & M. E. Kraft (Eds.), *Environmental policy in the 1990s* (pp. 187-207). Washington, DC: Congressional Quarterly Press.

Furstenberg, F. F., Jr., & Brooks-Gunn, J. (1989). Causes and consequences of teenage pregnancy and childbearing. In M. N. Ozawa (Ed.), *Women's life cycle and economic insecurity* (pp. 69-100). New York: Praeger.

Garbarino, J. (1992). *Toward a sustainable society: An economic, social, and environmental agenda for our children's future.* Chicago: Noble Press.

Gardner, G. (1996, July). *Shrinking fields: Cropland loss in a world of eight billion* (Worldwatch Paper No. 131). Washington, DC: World Watch Institute.

General Accounting Office. (1983, June). *Siting of hazardous waste landfills and their correlation with the racial and socio-economic status of surrounding communities* (Report NO. GAO/RCED-83-168). Washington, DC: Government Printing Office.

George, S. (1988). *A fate worse than debt.* New York: Grove.

George, S. (1992). *The debt boomerang*. London: Pluto.

Hawken, P. (1993). *The ecology of commerce: A declaration of sustainability*. New York: Harper Business.

Hoff, M. D. (1998). The Willapa alliance: The role of a voluntary organization in fostering regional action for sustainability. In M. D. Hoff (Ed.), *Sustainable community development: Studies in economic, environmental, and cultural revitalization* (pp. 177-192). Boca Raton, FL: Lewis.

Hoff, M. D., & McNutt, J. G. (Eds.). (1994). *The global environmental crisis: Implications for social welfare and social work*. Aldershot, UK: Avebury Books.

Iatridis, D. (1994). *Social welfare policy*. Belmont, CA: Wadsworth.

Independent Commission on Population and Quality of Life. (1996). *Caring for the future*. Oxford, UK: Oxford University Press.

John, D. (1994). *Civic environmentalism: Alternatives to regulation in states and communities*. Washington, DC: Congressional Quarterly Press.

Johnson, K. (1998). The Henry's Fork Watershed Council: Community-based participation in regional environmental management. In M. D. Hoff (Ed.), *Sustainable community development: Studies in economic, environmental, and cultural revitalization* (pp. 165-176). Boca Raton, FL: Lewis.

Kauffman, S. E. (1994). Citizen participation in environmental decisions: Policy, reality, and considerations for community organizing. In M. D. Hoff & J. G. McNutt (Eds.), *The global environmental crisis: Implications for social welfare and social work* (pp. 219-239). Aldershot, UK: Avebury Books.

Korten, D. C. (1995). *When corporations rule the world*. West Hartford, CT: Kumarian Press.

Kraft, M. E., & Vig, N. J. (1997). Environmental policy from the 1970s to the 1990s. In N. J. Vig & M. E. Kraft (Eds.), *Environmental policy in the 1990s* (3rd ed., pp. 1-30). Washington, DC: Congressional Quarterly Press.

Lawrence, K., & Milstein, S. (1997). City farms: The Big Apple's city-wide network of urban food producers. *GEO Grassroots Economic Organizing*, No. 28, 1, 3-4.

Livermore, M., & Midgley, J. (1998). The contribution of universities to building sustainable communities: The community university partnership. In M. D. Hoff (Ed.), *Sustainable community development: Studies in economic, environmental, and cultural revitalization* (pp. 123-138). Boca Raton, FL: Lewis.

Lutz, M. E., & Lux, K. (1988). *Humanistic economics: The new challenge*. New York: Bootstrap Press.

Mann, M. E., Bradley, R. S., & Hughes, M. K. (1998). Global-scale temperature climate patterns and forcing over the past six centuries. *Nature, 392*(6678), 779-787.

McGinn, A. P. (1998). Promoting sustainable fisheries. In L. R. Brown et al. (Eds.) *State of the world report 1998* (pp. 59-78). New York: Norton.

McNutt, J. G. (1994). Social welfare policy and the environmental crisis: It's time to rethink our traditional models. In M. D. Hoff & J. G. McNutt (Eds.), *The global environmental crisis: Implications for social welfare and social work* (pp. 36-52). Aldershot, UK: Avebury Books.

Midgley, J., & Livermore, M. (1998). Social capital and local economic development: Implications for community social work practice. *Journal of Community Practice, 5*(1/2), 29-40.

Misch, A. (1994). Assessing environmental health risk. In L. Brown et al. (Eds.), *State of the world report 1994* (pp. 117-136). New York: Norton.

Moroney, R. M., & Krysik, J. (1998). *Social policy and social work: Critical essays on the welfare state* (2nd ed.). New York: Aldine de Gruyter.

Nelson, T. (1996). Urban agriculture. *World Watch, 9*(6), 10-17.

Olson, R. L. (1995). Sustainability as a social vision. *Journal of Social Issues, 51*(4), 15-35.

Ortmeyer, P., & Makhijani, A. (1997). Worse than we knew. *The Bulletin of the Atomic Scientists, 53*(6), 46-50.

Postel, S. (1996). Forging a sustainable water strategy. In L. R. Brown et al. (Eds.), *State of the world report 1996* (pp. 40-59). New York: Norton.

Putnam, R. D., with Leonardi, R., & Nanetti, R. Y. (1993). *Making democracy work: Civic traditions in modern Italy*. Princeton, NJ: Princeton University Press.

Reisner, M. (1993). *Cadillac desert: The American West and its disappearing water*. New York: Penguin.

Repetto, R. (1992). Accounting for environmental assets. *Scientific American, 266*(6), 94-100.

Rich, B. (1994). *Mortgaging the Earth: The World Bank, environmental impoverishment, and the crisis of development.* Boston: Beacon.

Roberts, P. (1994). Sustainable regional planning. *Regional Studies, 28*(8), 781-787.

Rogge, M. E. (1994). Environmental injustice: Social welfare and toxic waste. In M. D. Hoff & J. G. McNutt (Eds.), *The global environmental crisis: Implications for social welfare and social work* (pp. 53-74). Aldershot, UK: Avebury Books.

Romm, J. (1991). Needed—A no-regrets energy policy. *Bulletin of the Atomic Scientists, 47*(6), 31-36.

Roodman, D. M. (1997). *Getting the signals right: Tax reform to protect the environment and the economy* (Worldwatch Paper No. 134). Washington, DC: World Watch Institute.

Roseland, M. (1998). *Toward sustainable communities* (rev). Gabriola Island, BC: New Society Publishers.

Schuler, D. (1996). *New community networks: Wired for change.* Reading, MA: Addison-Wesley.

Shiva, V. (1991). *The violence of the green revolution.* London: Zed Books.

Stead, W. E., & Stead, J. G. (1992). *Management for a small planet: Strategic decision making and the environment.* Newbury Park, CA: Sage.

Thomas, W. (1995). *Scorched Earth: The military's assault on the environment.* Philadelphia: New Society Publishers.

Titmuss, R. (1974). *Social policy: An introduction.* London: Allen & Unwin.

Tobin, R. J. (1997). Environment, population, and the developing world. In N. J. Vig & M. E. Kraft (Eds.), *Environmental policy in the 1990s* (3rd ed., pp.321-344). Washington, DC: Congressional Quarterly Press.

United Nations. (1995). *Population consensus at Cairo, Mexico City, and Bucharest: An analytical comparison.* New York: Author.

U.S. House of Representatives. (1997, April 23). *Meeting clean water and drinking water infrastructure needs.* Testimony of R. Persiasepe, Assistant Administrator, Office of Water, U.S. Environmental Protection Agency, before the Subcommittee on Water Resources and the Environment; 105th Congress, 2nd Session (No. 1024-A-01 1024-B-01). Washington, DC: Government Printing Office.

Vig, N. J., & Kraft, M. E. (1997). The new environmental agenda. In N. J. Vig & M. E. Kraft (Eds.), *Environmental policy in the 1990s* (3rd ed., pp. 365-389). Washington, DC: Congressional Quarterly Press.

Wachtel, P. L. (1989). *The poverty of affluence: A psychological portrait of the American way of life.* Philadelphia: New Society Publishers.

Weber, P. (1993, November). *Abandoned seas: Reversing the decline of the oceans* (Worldwatch Paper No. 116). Washington, DC: World Watch Institute.

Wilensky, H. L., & Lebeaux, C. N. (1965). *Industrial society and social welfare.* New York: Free Press.

Wilkinson, C. F. (1992). *Crossing the next meridian: Land, water, and the future of the West.* Washington, DC: Island Press.

Wilson, W. J. (1996). *When work disappears.* New York: Knopf.

Wolpin, M. D. (1986). *Militarization, internal repression, and social welfare in the Third World.* London: Croom Helm.

Zakin, S. 1993). *Coyotes and town dogs: Earth First and the environmental movement.* New York: Viking/Penguin.

PART FIVE

Conclusion: International and Future Perspectives on Social Policy

The final part of the book deals with two issues, namely the broader international context in which social policy operates and the future of social policy.

Although discussions about social policy in the United States are seldom related to international trends, the first chapter in Part V shows that domestic social policy has long been affected by international events. In many cases, the international context has directly influenced social policy development. For example, the government of the United States is a signator to many international conventions and treaties and, because of these concords, agrees to comply with minimum standards of service delivery and entitlement. Social policy in the United States is also influenced by the informal flow of information about policy developments elsewhere. This chapter urges social policy makers to be more cognizant of innovations in other parts of the world and, where appropriate, to learn from these experiences.

Chapter 33, the final chapter of the book, speculates on the future of social policy. It draws on many of the book's other chapters to offer different scenarios for social policy development and for the well-being of the nation's people. It suggests that social policy will in the future be characterized by greater pluralism and that the role of the federal government will not be as significant as it was in the past. It considers whether these trends will be harmful or beneficial to people's welfare.

CHAPTER THIRTY-TWO

International Aspects
of Social Policy

ALFRED J. KAHN

SHEILA B. KAMERMAN

This chapter will focus on the ways in which international developments and institutions impinge on social policy developments within the United States. In an era of economic and social globalization, can social policy be purely national? The chapter will argue that social policy was never purely national, is not in the present, and is likely to be even less so in the future. Social policy can no longer be thought of in solely national terms in an economically and politically globalized economy.

Why the need to make the case? In the post-World War I euphoria about American economic and political leadership, and in reaction to the cynicism of Versailles as contrasted with the idealism of Wilson, strong isolationist themes appeared in the United States and were overcome only by the imperatives of World War II. The nation's economic and military achievements during and after the war supported doctrines about a unique American character. That, and an underlying belief in the "specialness" of the history of this "first new nation" and in an American "exceptionalism," tended to define the country as set apart (and to some, as morally superior). We might export goods, technology, knowledge, and our experience with government, as we might import goods, styles, cultural materials, and even workers, scholars, and performers.

But large numbers of Americans doubted and still doubt that we have policy lessons to learn.

Let us look at the record.

THE EARLIER RECORD

Pre-Revolutionary War America was settled overwhelmingly by the English and, unsurprisingly, England's Poor Law set the main public pattern in the 17th and 18th centuries in the colonies and, later, in the states. Subsequently, during the 19th century, the country continued to be influenced by English and occasionally German and other continental influences through visitors and reports, as it experienced the transition to a wage economy, required by the Industrial Revolution, and shared with Victorian England the problem of taming the exploding cities and their poor populations (Boyer, 1978). Americans were much influenced by England as they developed public workhouses and private (church and nonsectarian) Associations for the Improvement of the Conditions of the Poor and Provident Societies, YMCAs and YWCAs, Boys' and Girls' Clubs, and child protection agencies, as well as Charity Organization Societies, settlement houses, and kindergartens. Le Play's studies of expenditures and budgets in Belgium in mid-19th century, Booth's studies of the life and labor of the people of London between 1886 and 1907, and the later work of Rountree in York inspired and guided late 19th-century studies of social problems and poverty, including the 1905 poverty report of Hunter in Chicago and the famous Pittsburgh Survey (Polansky, 1975). When American states began social insurance and labor legislation in the Progressive Era, they had reports of European developments in hand (Skocpol, 1992).

After World War I, when the United States became a more powerful nation, some social policy borrowing began to occur from west to east, in particular, with regard to social work education and casework practice. Nonetheless, east-west borrowing continued to be dominant. Thus, for example, the Social Security Act of 1935 was clearly influenced by what had been developed in Europe, again with special attention to Germany and England, and with American adaptations required by our federal system and the political strategies of President Franklin D. Roosevelt.

POST-WORLD WAR II TO THE 1980s: THE SHARED
EXPERIENCES OF MODERN INDUSTRIALIZED SOCIETIES

Following World War II, social policy learning and borrowing became increasingly active in both directions across the Atlantic. Although the experience of World War II

was felt far more directly in Europe than in the United States, leading to major new social policy initiatives in many countries that set standards yet to be achieved, subsequent experiences were far more likely to be shared.

Common demographic, economic, and technological trends have confronted all
the advanced industrialized societies with similar challenges. For example, more than
half of all births in the Scandinavian countries are now out of wedlock, as are about
one third in Finland, France, and Britain. American rates are slightly lower. Marriage
rates in Europe are about half those in the United States; but so are divorce rates, although they are rising. Traditional families continue to decline in significance in
Europe as in America. Two-earner husband/wife families, reconstituted families, and
families headed by cohabiting but not legally married couples now dominate the family environments in which children are reared. Yes, there are differences in female labor force participation rates, swings in fertility, differences in teen pregnancy rates,
and different definitions of what some things (long-term stable cohabitation without
marriage) signify. But the important thing even so is similarity of directions and challenges and the possibility of learning from differences. And some important differences (teen childbearing) occasion special interest and exploration. The advanced industrialized countries are a single demographic universe, and thus, most must face
similar issues.

The two most visible current illustrations are, first, the aging of the population
while birth rates fall and, second, the rising rates of labor force participation among
women with very young children. The industrial world is facing the shared issue of
pension costs and pension financing while at the other end of the age spectrum, because most mothers of infants, toddlers, and preschoolers are now in the paid labor
force, there is the issue of what kind of early childhood care and education to provide,
under what auspices to provide such care, how to finance this, how to staff such a program, and what curricular and program concepts to use.

On another front, all relatively rich and stable countries among the pluralistic democracies are the obvious destinations of people seeking asylum, refugees, and immigrants from the poor, conflict-torn, authoritarian, underdeveloped, or transitional
lands everywhere. Policies and programs in response are a high priority everywhere,
even though the scale of the challenge, whether measured in sheer numbers or as a
percentage of native population, varies considerably.

To move to another part of the policy spectrum, we refer to post-secondary education. Technological advance, explosion of knowledge, and economic factors face
countries with the issue of the normative levels of the education of its youth. Whether
out of concern for the quality of human capital with which it responds to economic
challenges, out of a perspective on justice and equal opportunity, or a view of
the country's cultural and civil traditions, all of the advanced industrialized world

has been "churning" in this area: access, financial support to students and to higher education institutions, opportunities for advanced study and research, transitions into employment, the nature of the core curriculum and whether there should be one.

There is no need to belabor the point. Whatever the needs and differences of the developing and transitional worlds, there is considerable sharing of experiences in the advanced industrialized world, and therefore considerable sharing of problems, issues, and tasks. And given the shared levels of education, research, sophistication (despite historical, religious, and cultural differences), and the value systems of pluralistic democracies, it is hardly surprising that countries know about, consider, and sometimes adopt or adapt one another's solutions and innovations. In this context, the United States, for all of its economic and political power and the many areas of technology, science, and popular culture in which it is seen in a leadership role, is also a learner, a cooperator, a borrower, and a participant. For example, as we began to design child support legislation in the 1970s and to discuss family policy, we learned much from Europe. At one point relatively recently, German apprenticeship programs were intensively examined in this country. Our thesis is that this is a growing and increasing, yet inevitable process. Some of the mechanisms, vehicles, and pathways of the process merit attention.

THE MECHANISMS OF INTERNATIONALIZATION

Demonstration of Effects

We visit one another's countries as tourists, professionals, business people, scholars, exchange students, or members of delegations of one sort of another, or perhaps to retrace ancestral roots. Americans, who did most of the international visiting until relatively recently, discovered that their friends and colleagues were entitled to paid and job-protected leaves following childbirth, one-month and longer paid vacations from work, healthy and happy children in universal preschool programs, and health care that is readily available to all. None of this is formal or systematic, but it introduces a different world of experiences and options, raising new issues for policy discussion.

The media, too, have facilitated more shared experiences. Television, in particular, has brought war, famine, floods, and earthquakes into the living rooms of Americans, Europeans, Asians, and others—and stimulated widespread concern with natural and man-made disasters. Societal responses, we hope, are far more immediate and personal issues than ever before.

Competitiveness

As professionals, scholars, or citizen consumers of the media, we are exposed to international rankings with regard to infant mortality, low birth weight, child inoculation rates, child poverty, literacy, reading-math-science scores, and rates of high school completion, revealed in annual reports such as UNICEF's *The Progress of Nations and State of the Child,* The United Nation's *Human Development Report,* and the World Bank's *World Development Report.* Some of these numbers instigate professional exploration, political action, and interest group advocacy. We are not proud to rank 19th in infant mortality rates, when all of our European counterparts and a mix of transitional economies and newly industrializing Asian countries rank ahead of us with significantly lower rates.

Mandates

The International Labor Organization, headquartered in Geneva, Switzerland, has a long history of setting norms, targets, and labor and industry standards that have affected the United States, along with the rest of the world. Conventions, agreements, and covenants adopted by the United Nations have had even more significant impacts. *The Economist* magazine recently noted, in connection with the 50th anniversary of the Universal Declaration of Human Rights, that the "world's central legal institution, the United Nations, was the brainchild of Franklin D. Roosevelt who began planning for it soon after the United States entered the war. His wife, Eleanor, was one of the prime movers behind the adoption of the Universal Declaration of Human Rights" ("A Bad Time," 1998, p. 16).

But the U.S. public in some instances, and its Congress in others, does not readily accept and adopt international mandates, even when our citizens contribute substantially to their formulation. Traditionally there has been suspicion of foreign involvement, and it can reach paranoid intensity under some circumstances. Moreover, unlike the many unitary parliamentary systems that find ratification of covenants relatively easier, U.S. federalism and our separation of powers offer a major obstacle course for all major covenants. For example, can the Senate provide all the assurances called for in the 1989 Convention on the Rights of the Child, given the pre-eminence of state law in most areas of family law, child welfare, and education?

Yet, the failure to ratify, often after signing, is not the whole story. What is also relevant is that these various internationally adopted instruments create international norms. Even where we are well in advance of world practice, as we are in many of these fields, such as the status of women, the covenants nonetheless are useful in some instances. Where we do not conform, reformers and advocates have a point of departure. The subject gets into public discussion. Sometimes, it goes further. Commenting on the Universal Declaration of Human Rights, Wronka (1995) observes that "this document, which was originally meant to be hortatory, is increasingly referred to, at least in the United States, as 'customary international law' " (p. 1407). He buttresses his argument with a series of U.S. court decisions, including a finding against a military commander for torturing and murdering a Paraguan high school student. In short, without "authoritative legal status in the United States" the Declaration "is beginning to substantively affect U.S. legal jurisprudence" (p. 1407).

The United States also participates in many other U.N. activities and projects, often initiatives of the General Assembly or the Economic and Social Council. The special "years" and "decades" dedicated to spotlighting the elderly, the handicapped, or children highlight policy and program issues, often in the context of elaborate factual reporting and trend analysis, as well as international comparisons. Although the developing world is often in focus, the rich countries are not ignored—whether in the World Summit on Social Development (Denmark), the Beijing conference on women, or other initiatives—or in the annual U.N. reports on Human Development. Mandates and commitments aside, all of this keeps some U.S. issues visible and offers challenges—and rallying points for leaders and advocates.

Collaboration

The United States plays a leading role in the Organization for Economic Cooperation and Development (OECD), which has expanded to include 29 advanced, industrialized, pluralistic democracies. Although formally focused on economic policy, this organization has, over the years, carried out projects, convened expert groups, and conducted ministerial level intergovernmental meetings with regard to female labor force participation, child care, aging, lone-mother families, income transfers, work training, youth policy, education at all levels, tax policy, urban policy—and various interrelationships among these. The rationales have stressed the relationships of various of these arenas, and others, to a conception of active labor market policy, or equal opportunity, or technological progress, or human capital investment—and even to pension finance.

In fact, in the past several years, concerned about pension financing under almost universally experienced population aging, OECD has promoted, among other things, facilitating female labor force participation through adequate child care policy, thus improving the ratio of currently employed workers to retirees.

OECD's regular data series (including expenditure and tax data and various social indicators), their annual national accounts reports, the analyses of the tax situations of average worker families in different countries—as well as the conferences and project reports—play an important role in disseminating valuable information to public officials in all countries. Although the organization is not as visible to the media as is the United Nations, and although public officials and civil servants in all countries—especially in the executive branch—are exposed to it rather than the public at large, the OECD is extraordinarily successful in creating an ongoing international conversation about critical issues in economic and social policy. See, for example, *Family, Market, and Community: Equity and Efficiency in Social Policy* (OCED, 1997). One could wish for more congressional exposure, as well. We do not mean to ignore the neo-liberal slant of OECD, or the considerable American and British influence, especially during the restructuring of the 1980s and 1990s, but in the spirit of balanced debate, eclectic policy making, and appreciation of international exchange, one must value this organization, which exposes the United States to world developments, thinking, and viewpoints about opportunities. Indeed, in some sense, each of the sources of information and exchange is controversial for some Americans, but the sum total of interactions means that we are hardly alone in thinking about our social policies.

Cross-National Research and Societal Learning

We here offer a personal illustration of learning from other countries. Although in our own professional careers, we have been involved with all of the above from time to time and in varied capacities, our own efforts at systematic contributions to the domestic social policy debate from the broader international experience have taken the form of a cross-national research program that parallels and feeds into our U.S. policy research and activity. We realized long ago that one can no more develop a full perspective on policy systems and policy substance by studying policy in one country than the clinician can conceive and elaborate a personality theory on the basis of one case. The political science answer is the comparative study. The world is an arena of natural experiments.

For over 25 years, we have conducted studies of social policy issues, many in child and family policy, encompassing income transfers (cash and tax benefits), employment-related policies (maternity and parental leaves), and personal social services—all with a view toward enriching the policy debate in the United States. Because of the objective of immediate relevance, most of this work has been in the advanced industrialized world, much of it in Europe. We have been concerned more with understanding consequences of policies for families, children, and sometimes the community and the work environment than with accounting for countries' choices, but that, too, has sometimes been the question. We understand that policies must fit into the cultural, societal, and political context and therefore are often not directly transferable, but we see the value of enriching and elaborating the option menus in fields in which the United States "needs to act" (Kamerman & Kahn, 1994).

At one time, we were pioneers and among the few with such preoccupations. More recently, as Europe has organized itself more formally and, then, as what are called the "countries in transition" entered the picture, such work became more popular and has been systematized and expanded, as we note below.

First, to clarify, here are some personal illustrations. Our studies in the industrial world, from the 1970s to those currently under way, have been concerned with various topics. We have asked what types of policies and programs have been developed in western and northern Europe on behalf of typical families, "not for the poor alone" (Kahn & Kamerman, 1975). We have also examined the issue of whether governments deliberately or implicitly undertake to develop family policy and, if so, in what domains and how (Kamerman & Kahn, 1978). Another issue has been concerned with how personal social services are organized and delivered in industrial societies. This included a look at socialist Europe, which had labeled social work a capitalist instrument (Kamerman & Kahn, 1980). We have also examined the experiences with child care and family benefits as alternatives or possibly complementary strategies for coping with family needs when both parents (or a single parent) work (Kamerman & Kahn, 1981). Our research has also focused on how public (social) assistance fits into a full income maintenance and tax package in helping families at different earnings levels (or without earnings) and how generous income transfers are elsewhere as compared with those in the United States (Kahn & Kamerman, 1983). We have questioned how countries cope with the child support question when parents separate and divorce and whether "advance maintenance" (government support guarantees or child support assurance) is a successful program when the noncustodial parent does not contribute (Kahn & Kamerman, 1988). Another issue is extended parental leaves and how such leaves affect child care policies, labor force participation, and income transfer packages (Kamerman & Kahn, 1991). We asked what the policy options are for responding to the needs and problems of lone mothers and their children, as seen in the European experience (Kamerman & Kahn, 1988). Finally, we have speculated on what the United States can learn about "starting right" in the rearing of its youngest children, from countries with exemplar programs and policies relating to income, time, and services (Kamerman & Kahn, 1995).

Of course, the study and report writing are only a beginning. The contributions to domestic programs and policy require dissemination, education, and advocacy. Impact, if any, can be limited and slow.

Major Current Vehicles

Interchange, cross-national contacts, and collaboration are at all-time highs, and data about other parts of the world, particularly the industrial world, are more available in more systematic form than ever. This is inevitable given the technology of the Information Age and the great values recently placed on national and international transparency with regard to the economy, the polity, health, and human rights.

In our brief sketch, we note, first, that where once there was little European interest in cross-national policy research and data collection, the European Community, now the European Union, began, as it grew, to attend to child care and family policy. Although not formally in the Union's competence, such social policy issues as parental leave and child care are relevant to its concerns with regard to the labor force and the status of women. A European Child Care Observatory with country reporters and, later, a European Observatory on Poverty and a European Family Observatory, similarly structured, have provided annual updates on developments in member countries, as well as special reports on topics of general interest. (The Child Care Observatory has been discontinued, and the Poverty Observatory has been replaced by a European Observatory on Social Exclusion.) A growing system of statistics and social indicators out of Eurostat enriches the picture of demography, programs, expenditures, and various aspects of policy. What is more, the growth of the European Union and the fall of the East-West wall have stimulated a rich array of cross-national research by European scholars, where once interest was limited. We might mention studies of poverty, child support, social assistance, lone mothers, and the workforce.

In brief, there is now a significant body of information and evaluated experience for cross-national learning and stimulation. On a smaller scale, but with much interest in family policy, there is also relevant output from the Council of Europe.

By now, the two-way flow is extensive. There are visiting scholars at universities and think tanks, often at work on cross-national issues and always available to clarify developments in their own countries. The major learned societies and professional groups are an active arena of shared and joint learning. We might cite the long-term deliberations and projects related to poverty of the International Sociological Association; the family policy, divorce, child support, and other deliberations of the International Society of Family Law; and the range of topical themes at the International Council on Social Welfare.

Associated with international and learned societies and associations, but also independent of them, is an extraordinary roster of international journals covering the fields under discussion. Indeed, the proliferation poses both a cost problem for libraries and a time-challenge for interested policy scholars and officials.

A major international collaboration with a very strong American presence, the Luxembourg Income Study, has built up an extensive micro database over the past two decades that includes 25 modern industrialized states, has perfected the adaptations to ensure comparability, and has supplied the associated institutional and program information that permits the most extensive comparative studies of poverty, family income packages by family type, and specific income-related policy questions. Researchers all over the world are supplied with disks of constantly updated data and codes. Summer conferences and workshops provide the occasion for exchange and for training young scholars. A parallel program, the Luxembourg Employment Study, is now being implemented as well. All now have rich web sites, which provide current information about important policy-relevant developments.

Knowing about other countries is no longer a monopoly enjoyed by scholars, specialists, public officials, or travelers. The media have discovered aspects of social policy on which they can report to interested audiences, whether in the daily press, general magazines, or on television and radio. The casual reader or audience member learns about welfare, social security, health systems, child care, or parental leaves, sometimes in sophisticated coverage and at other times in oversimplified and brief presentations.

GLOBALIZATION AND THE IMPACT ON SOCIAL POLICY

Globalization is the current buzzword used to describe the growing internationalization of the production of goods and services and the flow of capital. Economists, political scientists, sociologists, area specialists, and policy analysts are discussing the world economy and the implications of global economic developments for the future of social policy (Clayton & Pontusson, 1997; Cohen, 1998; Daly, 1998; Garrett, 1997; Pierson, 1994, 1997). There is a debate regarding whether globalization applies only to the changes occurring to the world economy as national economies are internationalized, or whether it also applies to current changes in political, social, and cultural institutions. Despite widespread agreement that worldwide competition means that economies with high wage costs will lose jobs to those with cheaper labor, there continues to be debate as well about whether such job loss is limited to unskilled work; whether, ultimately, it is good or bad for national economies; whether it will affect the composition of the wage package, or just the overall size; and whether a "race to the bottom" among welfare states will follow, reducing wages and cutting social expenditures. Most important, there is a debate regarding the overall process of globalization, whether it is the cause of welfare state retrenchment, and whether it will lead to high rates of dependency, either on unemployment benefits or social assistance or both, thereby raising social expenditures, reducing social security contributions, and leading to cuts in benefits and services. The ultimate concern for many is how will these developments affect social policy.

Many believe that globalization is ultimately a positive process, even though they see the difficulties it creates. For example, jobs can migrate from high-wage and high-benefit countries to low-wage and low-benefit labor markets, country budgets and economic policies can be undercut by currency speculation and developments in world equity and bond markets, precious aspects of national identity may be eroded. Others are much concerned about the impacts on population. As the president of the Washington-based Economic Policy Institute recently observed,

The mobility of private capital has now outstripped the capacity of governments and inter-national agencies to keep markets from self-destructing or to shield their people from the brutal consequences. One result . . . is a rising hostility to globalization. A precondition to any solution is the building of institutions and policies that serve the interests of the world's workers. (Faux, 1998, p. 1)

Even *The Economist* magazine, a proponent of the free market, commented re-cently, as it noted the unexpected problems generated in the East Asian economies by the recklessness of hedge funds. "The idea of globalization as irreversible," *The Economist* said, "inevitably will face stiff challenges" ("Special Report," 1998a, p. 16).

Whichever the correct assessment of globalization, there is no denying that the ad-vanced industrialized societies now share policy agendas, with answers to be discov-ered by joint learning, learning from one another, exchange, consensus, and experi-ence. We can debate about contours and likely governance, but—to shift the metaphor—we are in the same boat. A potentially helpful process is under way but will be a hesitant one because countries are not sure whether to trust it and how far. But they need to understand it together.

Societal learning is no longer a question of East/West learning or trans-Atlantic two-way learning. Instead, it is an issue of shared experiences and problems and the need to work together to participate in the development of policy and program re-sponses. Social policy can no longer be purely national; it requires international or re-gional or multinational initiatives. It involves countries working together to respond to the same or similar challenges.

To illustrate: A June 1998 Stockholm meeting on pension policy, jointly sponsored by the Swedish government and the International Social Security Association, one in a series, capped a consultative process and drew on a specially commissioned study (Thompson, 1998). The sessions probed a series of social security/public pension/pri-vate pension models for the future developing in Europe, North America, Central and South America, and East Asia, in the light of economic and demographic develop-ments. In a context of sophisticated understanding of the consequences of free inter-national markets, it was possible to examine the known advantages and caveats for systems based on advance funding, individual accounts, and public management, with special attention to what can be said about pension impacts on the economy. The meeting's purpose was described by the organizers in these terms: "to assist policy makers and social security organizations throughout the world to understand the is-sues, to widen the debate on the future of social security, and to choose alternatives best suited to their circumstances" (International Social Security Association, 1998).

Similar, parallel undertakings are under way in many fields of policy concern, such as early child care and education, youth training and education, and shared work on needed technologies and data systems such as childhood social indicators and poverty measures. Therefore, in conclusion, the answer to our original question is that early on, the United States learned and borrowed from others. Later on, it continued to learn and borrow but also provided opportunities for others to learn from us and promoted initiatives that others borrowed from, too. Now, we all learn and borrow, sometimes from one another, more often as part of the same global pool of knowledge, experience, and ongoing exploration. Social policy is a shared arena.

REFERENCES

A bad time to be an ostrich. (1998, December 19). *The Economist,* p. 15.

Boyer, P. (1978). *Urban masses and moral order in America, 1820-1920.* Cambridge, MA: Harvard University Press.

Clayton, R., & Pontusson, J. (1997). *Welfare retrenchment and public sector restructuring in advanced capitalist societies.* Ithaca, NY: Cornell University, Department of Government.

Cohen, D. (1998). *The wealth of the world and the poverty of nations.* Cambridge: MIT Press.

Daly, M. (1998, July). *Globalization and Bismarkian welfare states.* Paper presented at the Conference on Globalization and Social Policy, Lincoln, England.

Faux, J. (1998, Fall). Fools rush in: Unfettered global finance threatens prosperity at home and abroad. *Economic Policy Institute Journal,* p. 1.

Garrett, G. (1997). *Partisan politics in a global economy.* New York: Cambridge University Press.

International Social Security Association. (1998). *The future of social security, June 29-July 1, 1998.* Meeting announcement.

Kahn, A. J., & Kamerman, S. B. (1975). *Not for the poor alone: Social services in Europe.* Philadelphia: Temple University Press.

Kahn, A. J., & Kamerman, S. B. (1983). *Income transfers for families with children: An eight-country study.* Philadelphia, PA: Temple University Press.

Kahn, A. J., & Kamerman, S. B. (Eds.). (1988) *Child support: From debt collection to social policy.* Newbury Park, CA: Sage.

Kamerman, S. B., & Kahn, A. J. (Eds.). (1978). *Family policy: Government and families in fourteen countries.* New York: Columbia University Press.

Kamerman, S. B., & Kahn, A. J. (1980). *Social services in international perspective.* Rutgers, NJ: Transaction Books. (Reprint of 1977 report published by U.S. Government Printing Office)

Kamerman, S. B., & Kahn, A. J. (1981). *Child care, family benefits, and working parents: A study in comparative family policy analysis.* New York: Columbia University Press.

Kamerman, S. B., & Kahn, A. J. (1988). *Mothers alone: Strategies for a time of change.* Dover, MA: Auburn House.

Kamerman. S. B., & Kahn, A. J. (Eds.). (1991). *Child care, parental leave, and the under 3s: Policy innovation in Europe.* Westport, CT: Greenwood.

Kamerman, S. B., & Kahn, A. J. (1994). Methodological cautions for comparative research in social protection. In International Social Security Association (Ed.), *The international comparisons of social security policies and systems* (pp. 281-287). Geneva: International Social Security Association.

Kamerman, S. B., & Kahn, A. J. (1995). *Starting right: How America neglects its youngest children and what we can do about it.* New York: Oxford University Press.

Organization for Economic Cooperation and Development. (1997). *Family, market, and community: Equity and efficiency in social policy.* Paris: OECD.

Pierson, P. (1994). *Dismantling the welfare state.* New York: Cambridge University Press.

Pierson, P. (1997). *The new politics of the welfare state* (Working Paper No. 3/95). Bremen, Germany: University of Bremen, Center for Social Policy Research.

Polansky, N. (Ed.). (1975). *Social work research.* Chicago: University of Chicago Press.

Polanyi, K. (1959). *The great transformation.* Boston: Beacon.

Skocpol, T. (1992). *Protecting soldiers and mothers: The political origins of social policy in the United States.* Cambridge, MA: Harvard University Press.

Special report: A survey of human rights law. (1998, December 5), *The Economist,* p. 16.

Thompson, L. (1998). *Older and wiser: The economics of public pensions.* Washington, DC: Urban Institute Press.

Wronka, J. (1995). Human rights. In *Encyclopedia of social work* (19th ed., Vol. 2, pp. 1405-1418). Washington, DC: NASW Press.

CHAPTER THIRTY-THREE

The Future of Social Policy

JAMES MIDGLEY

MARTIN B. TRACY

MICHELLE LIVERMORE

This book has sought to provide a comprehensive overview of American social policy. Its authors have dealt with many diverse aspects of the field, including the nature of social policy making, the history of social policy, social policy for the social services, and the political economy of social policy. By covering a wide field, the book has sought to provide a state of the art account of American social policy at the end of the 20th century.

As social policy faces the challenges of a new century, an attempt to speculate on its future character and direction is appropriate. Social policy is subject to many complex influences and unpredictable events, and it is extremely difficult to predict future trends in the field. Nevertheless, it may be possible to identify the major factors that will shape social policy development. By understanding these factors, it may be possible to glimpse the future of social policy.

Social policy is not simply a technical process governed by efficiency criteria; it is subject to the impersonal forces of economics, demography, and sociocultural change, as well as ideologies that offer very different perspectives on how human welfare can be enhanced. Both sets of factors exert an indirect but powerful influence on social policy makers. Although policy makers may seek to focus narrowly on program outcomes and the most efficient way of meeting them, they are invariably influenced by these wider forces.

An understanding of the role of ideology and of wider economic, demographic, and social forces is highly relevant to any attempt to speculate on the future direction of social policy. By examining these factors, it may be possible to gain insights into how social policy will evolve. As this chapter will endeavor to show, such factors combine in complex ways to shape and determine the future of social policy.

FORCES FOR CHANGE AND SOCIAL POLICY

Social policy makers are affected by the wider social, economic, political, and cultural context in which they work and make decisions. By understanding this environment and seeking to assess its impact on decision making, it may be possible to speculate meaningfully on the way social policy will evolve as it accommodates and responds to these forces.

Economic factors are obviously very influential in determining current and future social policy events. As shown in Chapter 9, the Great Depression created enormous social needs that exerted pressures on government to respond. Similarly, the economic difficulties of the 1970s, which were associated with high inflation and unemployment, contributed to the redirection of social policy thinking in the 1980s. By blaming economic difficulties on social expenditures, conservative thinkers legitimated the retrenchment of social programs.

The economic boom of the late 1990s has created a very different climate for social policy. With prosperity and a balanced budget, the alarmist claims of conservative thinkers have been undermined, and few citizens today appear to support further retrenchments in social welfare on the ground that additional budget cuts will stimulate economic growth. However, there is concern that the prosperity of recent years will not be sustained. If the economy experiences a downturn, as many believe is likely, social policy will again be faced with fiscal pressures that will restrict government intervention in social welfare.

A major influence on the future of American social policy will be the pressures of economic globalization. With its relatively open economy, the United States is particularly exposed to these forces. Although the country's currency remains strong, recession in East Asia and other world regions is already harming American exports, and it is probable that financial speculators will begin to invest in other currencies to the detriment of the American economy. Further deindustrialization, particularly in traditional industries, is also likely. Unemployment may again become a major problem. In addition, job security will be undermined. As a result of economic globalization, employment will become more transient, and many more workers will cycle between jobs over their lifetimes.

Demographic factors will continue to play an important role in social policy. Of these, the aging of the population will perhaps be the most significant. As the population ages, pressure for enhanced services will increase. Immigration will also affect the nature of social policy in the future. Although immigrants do not place major demands on the social services, it is likely that social policy making will need to respond to the increased cultural diversity of American society. The influence of increased diversity is already being felt in many social service fields, especially in education and health care.

The emergence of a postmodern culture will also influence the future of social policy. Many social scientists are convinced that the values and ideals of Enlightenment modernism—as exemplified by a belief in rationalism and progress, the acceptance of encompassing ideologies, and strong, centralized government—is giving way to decentralization, fragmentation, and localism. Ethnicity, religious belief, and traditionalism are becoming more important than the grand ideologies of modernist thought, and mass consumerism has become a dominant cultural and economic preoccupation. Today, people are increasingly cynical about the possibility of progress, and fewer participate in the political process than ever before.

In this sociocultural climate, traditional ideological beliefs are being reshaped by identity politics. As shown in Chapter 2 of this book, social policy debates have increasingly focused on gender, race, ethnicity, and sexual orientation. The declining influence of the labor movement has also contributed to the weakening of class-based modernist social welfare ideologies. In addition, with greater decentralization, social policy may be increasingly determined at the state and local level, undermining centralism and promoting further social fragmentation. With the enactment of welfare reform, decentralization is now well established, and its effects will be felt even more strongly as federal funding for state and local social services is likely to decline.

A post-modern culture is also characterized by a tendency toward depoliticization and a lack of interest in major ideological controversies. Postmodern scholars contend that people today are more concerned with consumption and with popular culture than with issues of ideology and political struggle. They are also increasingly focused on local rather than national or international events. In addition, electoral turnout in recent times has been small, and political campaigns are increasingly focused on the relatively small proportion of the population that actually votes. Generally, those who vote are disproportionately white, middle-class, suburban, and conservative. The changing nature of electoral politics now influences political decision making to a significant extent. These realities were most evident in the congressional election of 1994, when the Republican Party secured a substantial majority in Congress. Majorities of this kind are obviously extremely important in determining the future of social policy. However, the role of political factors can be overstated. As the congressional election of 1998 revealed, electoral politics are mercurial. In addition, the political process is not only governed by the voting strength of parties but by popular opinion, the influence of the media, and, of course, by wider economic and social forces.

Changing electoral realities, wider public opinion, and the media now play a major role in shaping social policy. Media messages that oversimplify complex social issues but appeal to middle-class people can have a powerful effect on policy makers. For example, media images about welfare and crime have been effectively used in national elections and have pressured policy makers to adopt increasing punitive positions. Few politicians will openly oppose the death penalty, mandatory imprisonment for minor drug offenses, and other stringent penal measures, which are having such a major impact on social policy.

The future direction of social policy will be significantly influenced by these electoral realities. Just as social policy making previously depended on the labor movement for support, middle-class preferences now increasingly determine the nature of social policy. This trend has fostered increased privatization and retrenchment, which liberal politicians and the liberal labor movement have not been able to halt. It is clear that future innovations in social policy will have to be based on ideas that appeal to this constituency. If they are to be successful, new social policy approaches will also have to be attuned to the wider economic, demographic, and cultural environment.

IDEAS, IDEOLOGIES, AND THE FUTURE OF SOCIAL POLICY

Ideas and ideologies play a major role in social policy. As was shown in the section of this book dealing with the history of social policy, ideologies exerted a powerful influence on the way social policies evolved over the years. In conjunction with economic, social, and other forces, ideologies offered plausible solutions to current problems. The social policy of the New Deal drew extensively on collectivist ideology, whereas the social policy changes of the Reagan era gave expression to the values and ideals of individualism. These ideologies formed the basis for different normative prescriptions that guide social policy making.

Today, the ideological struggle appears to be more muted. Nevertheless, there is no shortage of normative recommendations about how social policy should evolve. These normative proposals are the product of intellectual endeavors, and they compete with each other in seeking to exert influence on policy makers. They are, therefore, very important in determining the future direction of social policy.

For many years, social policy debates were dominated by the advocacy of institutionalism versus residualism. The New Deal legitimated institutionalist thinking but, as most social policy writers recognize, institutionalism never directed social policy in the United States to the extent that it did in Europe. Although many policy makers hoped that the country would gradually implement institutional ideas, the Reagan era challenged this vision and instead advocated a radical return to the residualism of the 19th century.

If fully implemented, the shift toward residualism would have resulted in a massive curtailment of government involvement in social welfare and reduced the role of the state to one of providing limited assistance to the most desperately needy. However, this goal was never realized. Although the social services were retrenched, a more fragmented, pluralist system of provision, rather than a truly residualist "Poor Law State," emerged. As shown in Chapter 27 on welfare pluralism, privatization did not significantly reduce government involvement but instead resulted in widespread contracting with private providers. Contrary to the residualist tenet of reducing social expenditures to a bare minimum, the state continued to meet the costs of social provision. The new pluralism not only sustained the nonprofit sector but created a new commercial welfare industry that has reaped significant profits in fields as diverse as elder care, corrections, and child welfare.

Today, pluralism dominates social policy. Indeed, it may be argued that it creates a viable equilibrium between institutionalism and residualism and that this equilibrium benefits both welfare recipients and taxpayers, who are assured that efficiency will be optimized. Many policy makers favor welfare pluralism and believe that it offers the most efficient and humane approach for meeting social needs. It is likely that pluralism will continue to dominate social policy thinking for the foreseeable future. It is also likely that its influence will expand further. For example, it is probable that Social Security, which embodies institutional ideas, will be partially privatized, giving further expression to pluralist thinking.

The institutionalization of pluralism has been a primary feature of social policy during the Clinton era. Although New Democrat thinkers at the Progressive Policy Institute and elsewhere sought to formulate a coherent approach to social policy that could inform the Clinton administration's agenda, David Stoesz (1996) has shown that a new paradigm did not emerge. Instead, social policy under the Clinton administration has primarily been a reaction to the more systematic agenda of the Right and an attempt to respond to its electoral challenge.

Although the Clinton administration vaguely suggested that its approach to social policy was influenced by communitarian ideas, it did not formulate a coherent communitarian approach to social welfare. Nevertheless, it has been suggested that communitarian ideas offer a viable basis for social policy at the end of the 20th century (McNutt, 1997). Indeed, communitarian leaders (Etzioni, 1993) have made the same claim and have offered social policy proposals for social welfare within a wider attempt to reinvigorate the populist tradition in American culture. However, communitarianism has not gained a mass following. Nor has it produced a coherent social policy agenda that gives expression to populist impulses to an extent that approaches the achievements of the Johnson administration in the 1960s. Instead, communitarianism's centrism appears to be more compatible with the institutionalized pluralism of the Clinton presidency. As such, it is hardly innovative or electorally alluring.

The Clinton administration found these ideas congenial, and communitarian themes often accompanied its policy pronouncements. However, it never fully embraced communitarianism, and toward the end of its term, a more coherent formulation of its pluralist position began to emerge. After the failure of the Republicans to impeach the president, the administration began to promote what it called the Third Way. This approach drew extensively on the efforts of European socialist parties to repackage their ideology. At a meeting with European socialist leaders organized by the Democratic Leadership Council in Spring 1999, the various dimensions of a Third Way approach were discussed, and its social policy implications were articulated. However, it is unlikely that these efforts will result in a coherent conceptualization of a new approach to social welfare that will transcend Clintonian pluralism.

Despite the institutionalization of welfare pluralism under the Clinton administration, some writers on the radical Right continue to argue for the total abolition of government social programs. Although the advocates of abolition began to organize during the Reagan era, their hopes were not realized and, as noted earlier, government remains the primary funder and provider of social services today. Nevertheless, the abolitionist view continues to be expressed, most effectively perhaps in the writing of Marvin Olasky (1992), who argues that government involvement in social welfare has stifled philanthropic giving and suppressed the capacity for religious and other charities to respond effectively to social need. Although abolitionism has considerable support among religious fundamentalists, it is not popular with most of the nonprofit community, which is dependent on public subsidies and not so sanguine about its ability to function effectively without government aid.

Another normative approach that is exerting some influence on social policy thinking is the "new paternalism" or supervisory approach of Lawrence Mead (1986, 1997) and his colleagues. As was shown in Chapter 24 of this book, Mead believes that the notion of social rights, which has exerted a strong influence on social policy, should be replaced by the notion of reciprocal obligation. This idea requires that those who receive social benefits change their lifestyles, engage in productive employment, educate their children, and meet various other obligations to society. This approach has been adopted in the so-called welfare reform legislation of 1996 and imposes a number of requirements on those receiving income support. It is likely that these ideas will continue to exert a strong influence on social policy thinking in the future.

Chapter 29 described the social development or social investment approach to social policy. This approach transcends the institutional-residual debate by advocating social programs that are primarily concerned not with providing social services but with enhancing the capacities of needy people to participate in the productive economy. Its proponents believe that participation in the productive economy is the primary means by which most people meet their social needs. They contend that many of those who receive social benefits can also meet their needs through economic participation. Although not widely implemented, this approach is finding expression in programs such as welfare to work, supported employment for people with disabilities, asset accounts, and community economic development programs.

SOCIAL POLICY IN THE FUTURE

It has already been suggested that the future direction of American social policy will depend on two major sets of factors. First, the impersonal forces of economics, demographics, and sociocultural change will create pressures on policy makers to respond in ways that transcend simple ideological beliefs or the immediate gains of political advantage. Second, normative prescriptions based on ideological preferences will also continue to influence policy makers. These two sets of factors will interact in complex ways to differentially influence the future of social policy.

Of these factors, it is likely that the economic forces of globalization, demographics, and sociocultural change will play a more important role than the unconditional commitment to ideology that characterized much social policy thinking in the past. Although ideological factors will continue to exert a strong influence and should not be underestimated, the ideological resolve that characterized the culture wars of the 1980s appears to have lost intensity. The policy-making process now appears to be more pragmatic, and greater compromises between different camps have been forged. This is not to deny the fact that social policy thinking has shifted, particularly in academic circles, from a commitment to institutionalism toward greater pluralism, privatization, and decentralization. Although many social policy commentators regard this as a move to the Right, others believe that it represents a viable compromise between the Left-leaning statism of the past and the radical advocacy of abolitionism. Although abolitionism, paternalism, and developmentalism offer new normative approaches for social policy, it is likely that pluralism will continue to characterize social policy for the foreseeable future.

The acceptance of a pluralist position is likely to be nurtured by wider social and economic forces. Although the economic situation in the United States at the end of the 1990s is extremely positive and hardly conducive to pessimism, it is very likely that the economy will experience a downturn as it has in the past. Further deindustri-alization and the increasingly competitive demands of globalization are likely to re-sult in higher unemployment and social need. These economic trends may result in re-newed fiscal pressures that will limit the ability of government to respond. In addition, the competitive demands of the global economy are likely to continue to re-strain social welfare expenditures.

It is also likely that the aging of the population will create greater demands for serv-ices. However, with economic uncertainty, the fiscal resources to meet these needs may be increasingly strained. As public revenues decline with the end of the boom cycle, and government maintains its commitment to pluralism, middle-class people will rely increasingly on their own resources to meet their needs. It is likely that serv-ices to the poor will continue to be badly funded, haphazardly implemented, and in-creasingly fragmented.

The social services will, in all likelihood, also be characterized by greater decen-tralization and localism. As noted earlier, federalism is gradually being replaced by lo-calism, and federal funding for the social services is likely to decline. With the passing of welfare reform legislation in 1996, means-tested income support is now firmly in the hands of states, and it is likely that other federal responsibilities will also be de-volved. In keeping with this trend, it is likely that the social services will be marked by greater cultural diversity. More services catering to particular ethnic groups are likely to emerge. Another important factor that has not been adequately addressed by social policy writers is the likely impact of information technology on social welfare, not only through the adoption of new technologies for service delivery, but through the changes which the information revolution will make in society as a whole.

These trends can be interpreted either in optimistic or pessimistic terms. Pessimists believe that increased devolution and localization will result in further fragmentation and unevenness in social service provision. They also believe that retrenchment and privatization will result in the increasing disengagement of the middle class from the public social services. Although the social services may become more responsive to the cultural needs of ethnic minorities, their identification with low-income minority groups will result in less support from the white suburban middle class and limit their willingness to pay the taxes needed to fund these services. These factors are likely to result in a perpetuation of pluralism and residualism for the foreseeable future. It is highly unlikely, as some social policy advocates hope, that there will be a return to the Golden Age of welfare statism, as personified by the New Deal and the social policy innovations of the Johnson administration. Pluralism, fragmentation, decentraliza-tion, and inadequate funding will probably characterize the social services for the foreseeable future.

Optimists do not believe that these trends will necessarily result in greater neglect and hardship for the poor and needy. They view the shift toward greater pluralism as a welcome attempt to balance the excessive statism of the past with the pressures for privatization and retrenchment. Pluralism will not encourage middle-class disengagement but instead provide middle-class people with new opportunities to use the social services in ways that are compatible with current social and economic realities. For example, the possible introduction of individual savings accounts as a part of social security reform will, they contend, promote greater middle-class participation. Nor will increased localism result in fragmentation and unevenness in services. Instead, it will foster greater democratic participation and involvement in social policy making and implementation. Pluralism is also consistent with the realization that the welfare of the population is not only affected by public social services but by interdependent factors including education, labor markets, community participation, and economic development. The overlapping and interdependent nature of these activities is compatible with the institutionalization of a pluralist position and a more effective means of addressing the needs of individuals, children, families, and communities than the provision of statutory social services.

Both scenarios are plausible. It may also be the case that unforeseen factors may govern the future direction of social policy. Similarly, despite the rhetoric of retrenchment, the status quo may be preserved. It is also possible that social policy may again emerge as a central preoccupation of American political and social life. But, if this is to be the case, it will require new, visionary ideas that are responsive to current realities, as well as the leadership and resolve to ensure their implementation.

REFERENCES

Etzioni, A. (1993). *The spirit of community: Rights, responsibilities, and the communitarian agenda.* New York: Crown.

McNutt, J. (1997). New communitarian thought and the future of social policy. *Journal of Sociology and Social Welfare, 24*(4), 45-56.

Mead, L. (1986). *Beyond entitlement: The social obligations of citizenship.* New York: Basic Books.

Mead, L. (Ed.). (1997). *The new paternalism: Supervisory approaches to poverty.* Washington, DC: Brookings Institution.

Olasky, M. (1992). *The tragedy of American compassion.* Washington, DC: Regnery Gateway.

Stoesz, D. (1996). *Small change: Domestic policy under the Clinton presidency.* White Plains, NY: Longman.

Index

About the Editors

James Midgley is Harry and Riva Specht Professor and Dean of the School of Social Welfare at the University of California at Berkeley. He was previously at Louisiana State University, where he served as Dean of the School of Social Work from 1986 to 1993 and as Associate Vice Chancellor from 1993 to 1996. Prior to serving at LSU, he taught at the London School of Economics and the University of Cape Town. He has published 17 books, more than 50 chapters in edited collections, and about 75 articles in leading social policy, social work and development journals. He serves on the editorial boards of several leading journals. In 1996, he received the *International Rhoda Sarnat Prize* from the National Association of Social Workers for his efforts to enhance public recognition of social work. His work focuses on social policy, international social welfare, and social development.

Martin B. Tracy is Professor and Director of the School of Social Work, College of Education, Southern Illinois University at Carbondale. He has published policy analyses on a variety of issues related to social security and income support systems for the elderly, especially women, in Europe and economically developing countries in Asia. His books include *Social Policies for the Elderly in Third World Nations, International Handbook on Old-Age Insurance* (with Fred Pampel) and *Challenges to Social Security* (with James Midgley). His current work focuses on social exclusion and social cohesion in Europe, Australia and the United States. He is a consultant to the International Social Security Association in Geneva, Switzerland.

Michelle Livermore is Instructor in the Department of Sociology at Louisiana State University. She was previously a Research Associate in the Office of Research and Graduate Studies at Louisiana State University where she directed the University's Community-University Partnership. She has published in the *Journal of Social Work Education*, the *Journal of Community Practice* and the *Journal of Applied Social Sciences,* as well as several book chapters on poverty and social development. Her work focuses on the social development approach to social policy and community practice.

About the Contributors

Jill Duerr Berrick is Director of the Center for Social Service Research and Associate Adjunct Professor at the School of Social Welfare, University of California, Berkeley. She teaches courses on social policy, social sciences research, and social work administration. She is currently involved in studies that examine the association of child welfare and changes in welfare policy. She is also an authority on kinship foster care. Her most recent book is *The Tender Years: Toward Developmentally Sensitive Child Welfare Services for Young Children.*

Katherine Briar-Lawson is Professor and Associate Dean for Research and Doctoral Studies at the University of Utah Graduate School of Social Work. She is the co-principal investigator on several regional child welfare grants. She has served as a consultant to over 40 states and was assistant secretary for CYF in Washington State.

James W. Callicutt is Professor and Associate Dean in the School of Social Work at the University of Texas at Arlington, where he has also served as interim dean and professor. He has held social work positions in mental health settings in Tennessee and Massachusetts. As a consultant for community mental health centers in eastern Maine and in Texas, he obtained federal funds to operate mental health and substance abuse programs, directed planning projects, and conducted research. He coedited *Mental Health Policy and Practice Today* (with Ted Watkins) and *Social Work and Mental Health* (with Pedro Lecca).

Pranab Chatterjee is Professor of Social Work at the Mandel School of Applied Social Sciences at Case Western Reserve University. He is author of *Approaches to the Wel-*

fare State (1996) and *Repackaging the Welfare State* (1999). He served as Editor-in-Chief of *The Journal of Applied Social Sciences.*

Phyllis J. Day is a retired professor of social policy. She is author of *A New History of Social Welfare* and editor of *Social Working: Exercises in Generalist Practice* (with Sandra Shelley).

Diana M. DiNitto is Cullen Trust Centennial Professor of Alcohol Studies and Education and Distinguished Teaching Professor at the School of Social Work, University of Texas at Austin. She has published *Social Work: Issues and Opportunities in a Changing Profession, Chemical Dependency: A Systems Approach,* and *Social Welfare: Politics and Public Policy.*

Jeanette Drews is Associate Professor at the University of Utah Graduate School of Social Work. Her work has focused on the promotion of complex issues such as inclusion and choice as cutting-edge priorities for service provision for people with developmental disabilities. She was the key author of the 1990 Report of Congress that evaluated the state of state services. She was also commissioned by the state agency for Services for People with Disabilities to develop a model for choice making for people with mental retardation; this model is the foundation for the development of a statewide system of services driven by choice.

Neil Gilbert is Chernin Professor of Social Welfare at the University of California at Berkeley, and director of the Center for Comparative Study of Family Welfare and Poverty. His recent books include *Welfare Justice: Restoring Social Equity* and *Combating Child Abuse.*

Leon Ginsberg is Carolina Distinguished Professor at the College of Social Work, University of South Carolina. He previously served as chancellor of the Board of Regents for Higher Education and commissioner for human services in West Virginia. He is the author of many books on social work and social welfare. His recent books include *Understanding Social Problems, Policies, and Programs* and *Conservative Social Welfare Policy.*

Kevin Fox Gotham is Assistant Professor of Sociology at Tulane University. His current research focus is on urban planning and housing policy, with particular interests in federal home mortgage programs and public housing. He has published a variety of articles on the impact of race on mortgage-lending patterns, the rise of the modern U.S. real estate and housing industry, and the racially segregating effects of urban planning and revitalization initiatives.

Mary F. Hayden is Research Director at the Research and Training Center on Community Integration at the University of Minnesota. She has conducted research and published extensively in the fields of developmental disabilities and social policy. With Brian Abery, she is coeditor of *Challenges for a Service System in Transition: Ensuring Quality Community Experiences for Persons with Developmental Disabilities.* She has also published in the areas of self-advocacy, criminal justice and people with mental retardation, and families with mental retardation. She has been an adviser for Self-Advocates Becoming Empowered since 1990.

John M. Herrick is Associate Director and Professor of Social Work at the School of Social Work, Michigan State University. He is president of the Social Welfare History Group and has published on welfare reform and the roles of social workers in ameliorating ethnic conflict. He is coeditor of *Cultural Diversity in Michigan: Providing Culturally Competent Mental Health Services.*

Marie D. Hoff is Professor of Social Policy and Macro-Practice at the School of Social Work, Boise State University. Her publications include *The Global Environmental Crisis: Implications for Social Welfare and Social Work* (with John G. McNutt) and *Sustainable Community Development: Studies in Economic, Environmental, and Cultural Revitalization.*

Cheryl Hyde is Associate Professor at the School of Social Work, University of Maryland, Baltimore. Her scholarship focuses on organizational change in human service organizations and on gender issues and welfare policies. She is the former editor of the *Journal of Progressive Human Services.*

Demetrius S. Iatridis is Professor of Social Policy and Planning and Chair of the Social Planning Program at the Graduate School of Social Work at Boston College. His recent books include *Social Policy and Privatization in Central and Eastern Europe* (with June G. Hopps).

Bruce Jansson is Professor of Social Work at the University of Southern California. He is author of *Becoming an Effective Policy Advocate: From Policy Practice to Social Justice, The Reluctant Welfare State: American Social Welfare Policies, Past, Present, and Future,* and *Failed National Priorities from FDR to Clinton: The $9 Trillion Mistake.*

Alfred J. Kahn is Professor Emeritus of Social Work at Columbia University. He also serves as codirector of the Cross National Studies Research program at the school. He is author, coauthor, or editor of more than 30 books and 250 journal articles and book chapters. He has consulted widely in the United States and abroad for state and local governments, international organizations, private agencies, the State Department and U.N. agencies.

Sheila B. Kamerman is the Compton Foundation Centennial Professor for the Prevention of Children and Youth Problems at the School of Social Work at Columbia University. She is the author, coauthor, or editor of more than 30 books and almost 250 journal articles and book chapters. Her most recent books are *Starting Right: How America Neglects Its Youngest Children and What Can We Do About It* (1995) (with Alfred J. Kahn) and *Family Change and Family Policies in Great Britain, Canada, New Zealand, and the United States* (with Alfred J. Kahn).

Jennie Jacobs Kronenfeld is Professor in the Department of Sociology, Arizona State University. She has published over 90 articles and book chapters in medical sociology, public health, medicine, and health services research. She has written on the social and economic impact of coronary artery-bypass surgery, the federal role in health policy, public versus private models of service delivery in several different human services areas, and controversial issues in health care policy. Her current interests include health policy issues, especially access to health care and child health care issues, and research on preventive aspects of health care.

Leslie Leighninger is Professor of Social Work and Associate Dean at the School of Social Work, Louisiana State University. She is author of *Social Work: Search for Identity* and *Social Work: The Policy-Based Profession* (with Phillip R. Popple).

Robert Leighninger is editor of the *Journal of Sociology and Social Welfare*. He is based at the School of Social Work, Louisiana State University. His research currently focuses on New Deal public works programs, and he is completing a book on the Works Progress Administration in Louisiana.

John G. McNutt is Assistant Professor of Social Policy and Planning at the Graduate School of Social Work at Boston College. He is coeditor of *The Global Environmental Crisis: Implications for Social Welfare and Social Work* (with Marie Hoff).

Martha N. Ozawa is Bettie Bofinger Brown Professor of Social Policy at the George Warren Brown School of Social Work, Washington University, in St. Louis. She is the author of *Income Maintenance and Work Incentives: Toward a Synthesis* and the editor of *Women's Life Cycle and Economic Insecurity: Problems and Proposals*. She was a member of the editorial board for the 17th and 19th issues of *Encyclopedia of Social Work*. Her current research involves Social Security, retirement patterns, and distributive effects of transfer programs. She is a member of the Membership Committee of the National Academy of Social Insurance.

Lori Parham is a doctoral student in sociology at Florida State University. Her research interests include race and ethnicity, social movements, and social policy.

Dean Pierce is Professor of Social Work and Director of the School of Social Work at the University of Nevada at Reno. He is an active member of the Council on Social Work Education and serves on the Council's Commission of Accreditation. He also serves on Nevada's Licensing Board. He is author of *Policy for the Social Work Practitioner* and *Social Work and Society,* as well as numerous articles and papers on social policy practice and gay and lesbian issues.

Jill Quadagno is Professor of Sociology at Florida State University, where she holds the Mildred and Claude Pepper Eminent Scholar Chair in Social Gerontology. She is the author or editor of 10 books on aging or social policy. Her recent books include *The Color of Welfare: How Racism Undermined the War on Poverty* and *Ending a Career in the Auto Industry: 30 and Out.* She is a past president of the American Sociological Association.

Michael Reisch is Professor of Social Work at the University of Pennsylvania. His books include *From Charity to Enterprise: The Development of American Social Work in a Market Economy* (with Stanley Wenocur) and *Social Work in the 21st Century* (with Eileen Gambrill).

Margaret Severson is Assistant Professor of Social Work at the School of Social Welfare, University of Kansas. She has conducted research and published extensively in the area of correctional social work practice. She has served in a variety of capacities as the federal court-appointed expert in the long-standing Louisiana prison and jail litigation. She also provides technical assistance for the National Institute of Corrections, helping jails and prisons develop and enhance their mental health and suicide prevention programs.

Michael Sherraden is Benjamin E. Youngdahl Professor of Social Development and director of the Center for Social Development at the George Warren Brown School of Social Work at Washington University, St. Louis. He is author of *Assets and the Poor: A New American Welfare Policy* and coeditor of *Alternatives to Social Security: An International Inquiry.*

John Sinclair is a doctoral student at the Mandel School of Applied Social Sciences at Case Western Reserve University. He teaches at Case Western Reserve University and at Cleveland State University.

David Stoesz is Samuel S. Wurtzel Chair of Social Work at Virginia Commonwealth University. His recent books include *Small Change: Domestic Policy Under the Clinton Presidency, American Social Welfare Policy* (with Howard Karger), and *International Development* (with Charles Guzetta and Mark Lusk).

Fernando M. Torres-Gil is Associate Dean for Academic Affairs at the School of Public Policy and Social Research, University of California, Los Angeles. He is a professor of social welfare and policy studies and director of the UCLA Center for Policy Research on Aging. His publications include over 60 articles and four books, including *The*

New Aging: Politics and Change in America. He has extensive government and public policy experience having served as the first U.S. Assistant Secretary on Aging, a staff director of the U.S. House Select Committee on Aging, and a White House Fellow. He received his Ph.D. and M.S.W. from Brandeis University.

Patsy Dills Tracy is Clinical Associate Professor, School of Social Work, College of Education, Southern Illinois University at Carbondale. She has written on child welfare, social cohesion, civic society, and devolution in a cross-national context. Her current research focus is on child welfare and education policy reforms in industrial nations as they reflect the influence of John Dewey and Jane Addams. Her current studies are based on international trends and developments, as well as on experiences in rural settings in the lower Mississippi River delta region.

Valentine Villa is Adjunct Assistant Professor in the Department of Social Welfare and associate director of the Center for Policy Research on Aging for the School of Public Policy and Social Research at the University of California, Los Angeles. She has research interests in aging social policy and minority aging. Her specific focus is on assessing the effects that public policies have on the health and economic status of the elderly population. Her research in minority aging is investigating health status differentials across minority elderly populations, including comparative analyses of the Latino, Korean, African American, and non-Hispanic White populations.

Jane Waldfogel is Assistant Professor at the School of Social Work and Public Affairs at Columbia University. She is the author of *The Future of Child Protection* and numerous articles and book chapters on women's earnings, family leave, child care, and child welfare.

Robert J. Waste is Professor and Chair of the Department of Public Policy and Administration at California State University, Sacramento. His principal research areas are urban public policy, homelessness, concentrated urban poverty, state policy, and program evaluation. His published books include *The Ecology of City Policymaking* and *Independent Cities: Rethinking U.S. Urban Policy.* He serves on the editorial board of the *Journal of Urban Affairs* and on the Governing Board and as secretary-treasurer of the Urban Affairs Association, and he has served on the Advisory Council of the Urban Politics Section of the American Political Science Association and as the Albert A. Levin Chair of Urban Studies and Public Service at Cleveland State University.

James D. Wright is an author, educator, and the Charles and Leo Favrot Professor of Human Relations in the Department of Sociology at Tulane University. He has published 16 books on topics ranging from guns to poverty, drugs, and American politics, and he has written more than 250 journal articles, book chapters, essays, reviews, and polemics. He is also editor in chief of *Social Science Research.*